ULTRASOUND

A PATTERN APPROACH

ULTRASOUND

A PATTERN
APPROACH

Patricia Lipford Abbitt, M.D.

Associate Professor of Radiology
Department of Radiology
University of Florida College of Medicine
Gainesville, Florida

McGraw-Hill, Inc.
HEALTH PROFESSIONS DIVISION

New York   St. Louis   San Francisco   Auckland   Bogotá
Caracas   Lisbon   London   Madrid   Mexico City   Milan   Montreal
New Delhi   San Juan   Singapore   Sydney   Tokyo   Toronto

1234567890   KGPKGP   987654

ISBN 0-07-000031-X

This book was set in Times Roman by Compset, Inc.
The editors were Jane Pennington and Mariapaz Englis;
the production supervisor was Clare Stanley; the project
was managed by Printers Representatives, Inc.;
Quebecor Printing/Kingsport was printer and binder.
The cover and text designer was Marsha Cohen/Parallelogram.

This book is printed on acid-free paper.

Library of Congress Cataloging-in-Publication Data

Abbitt, Patricia L.
    Ultrasound : a pattern approach / Patricia L. Abbitt.
        p.   cm.
    Includes bibliographical references and index.
    ISBN 0-07-000031-X (alk. paper)
    1. Diagnosis, Ultrasonic.   2. Diagnosis, Ultrasonic—
Atlases.
    I. Title.
    [DNLM: 1. Ultrasonography.   2. Pattern Recognition,
Visual.   WB 289 A124a   1994]
RC78.7.U4A23 1994
616.07′543—dc20
DNLM/DLC
for Library of Congress   94-31372

*To my husband, John,
our sons, Sam and Hank,
and to my parents, Lelia and Andy Lipford.*

CONTENTS

Color Plates

CHAPTER 7

ADRENALS 281

CHAPTER 8

RETROPERITONEUM 297

CHAPTER 9

BLADDER 313

CHAPTER 10

UTERUS, CERVIX, AND VAGINA 331

CHAPTER 11

OVARY AND ADNEXA   347

CHAPTER 12

SCROTUM   391

CHAPTER 13

SOFT TISSUES   411

CHAPTER 14

RENAL TRANSPLANTS   425

PREFACE

During residency, we are taught a three-pronged approach to the analysis of an unknown case. This same system serves me well in my everyday practice of radiology.

1. *Describe the abnormality.* Give a description that would allow someone with his eyes closed to picture the abnormality. This requires generous use of adjectives, measurements, and other appropriate descriptors. Any pertinent negative findings should also be given. This description should be succinct, not a lengthy discourse. Obviously, if you are in a private practice setting, you may want to work out the description in your head rather than waxing eloquently at the viewbox. The description given, or pattern, is the essence of this book.

2. *Consider a list of pertinent differential diagnostic considerations based on the description.* This too should be to the point, not including every esoteric diagnosis possible. An organized way to consider the differential listing is by categories (e.g., neoplasms, infections, congenital abnormalities), putting the most likely category or most deadly diagnosis first and ranking the possibilities. As each differential diagnosis is put forth, the entity, its clinical manifestations and management, as well as associated imaging features, should be considered to help narrow down to the definitive diagnosis. The most favored two or three possible diagnoses should be put forth if a definite diagnosis cannot be made.

3. *Make some conclusions about what action or further imaging study may be appropriate to clarify or treat the abnormality.* Sometimes, nothing is necessary, and that observation is important to make when it is appropriate.

This technique emphasizes the description of the abnormality and is therefore considered a *pattern approach* to diagnosis. It is the basis of almost every radiologist's work, I am sure, but clearly some use the technique better than others. Many of us get stuck in the descriptive phase, providing only a description of the abnormality we see. Many ultrasound reports, for example, give an impression: "complex pelvic mass." This sort of description does not advance things a great deal for the gynecologist who referred the patient after palpating a mass!

Others get stuck in the differential listing, generating longer and longer lists, not knowing when to quit. Such a style renders a radiologist of little help to his clinician colleagues.

Finally, many of us find it hard to take that extra brave step in involving ourselves in the clinical arena by suggesting the next step, unless it is another imaging test. The idea of suggesting to the gynecologist that watching an adnexal mass for resolution might be useful or recommending transhepatic drainage of the biliary tree instead of ERCP to the gastroenterologist might seem quite bold to many.

This book reflects seven years of experience teaching residents and fellows the art of diagnostic ultrasound and the use of the pattern approach. This book's goal is to illustrate the pattern approach to ultrasound diagnosis using pathologically proven cases gained from clinical experience. Many of the patterns may seem similar or redundant, but they are presented because conditions may be described in different ways. Obviously, the same disease entity will appear in different patterns, since a certain condition can have different presentations. I have attempted to make pertinent differential lists, not including every diagnosis possible.

Commonly encountered misinterpretations and recurrent errors that I have either witnessed or *made* are emphasized so that the reader can benefit from previous mistakes.

ACKNOWLEDGMENTS

Without the technical genius of Linda Waters-Funk, this manuscript would never have happened. Jane Pennington and Mariapaz Ramos Englis at McGraw-Hill were most supportive and helpful during the evolutionary process. I appreciate the helpful proofreading of Carol Chowdhry. My appreciation also goes to Jeanette Ninas Johnson of Printers Representatives, who efficiently guided the book through the editorial production process.

To the numerous residents and fellows I have known at the University of Virginia and the University of Florida, I am forever in your debt, for as I saw you learn, I learned. I am grateful to the very talented technologists with whom I have worked, including Thelma Sims, Nancy Carter, Laurence Watson, Nancy Raynor, Chris Langford, Sarah Lewellyn, Michele Slack, and Laurie Stephens. Tremendously skilled, these individuals have taught me much.

I appreciate my congenial colleagues at the University of Florida, especially Gladys Torres, Sharon Burton, and Pablo Ros.

There will always be a very special place in my heart for the fine radiologists who taught me the subject matter and love of radiology. They include Theodore Keats, Peter Armstrong, Paul Dee, Hugh Shaffer, Norman Brenbridge, and Ellen Shaw de Paredes. I hope these individuals realize my gratitude to them.

ULTRASOUND

A PATTERN APPROACH

LIVER

PATTERNS

Hyperechoic Liver Mass(es)
Hypoechoic Liver Mass(es)
Cystic Lesions in the Liver
Highly Echogenic Liver Lesions
  Containing Calcification or Air
Target (Bull's-Eye) Lesions in the Liver
  or Spleen
Lesions in Liver and Spleen
Diffuse Echotexture Abnormality of the
  Liver

Lesions that Scallop the Liver
Biliary Ductal Dilatation
Material Within the Bile Ducts
Bile Duct Wall Thickening
Too Many Tubes in the Liver
Abnormalities of the Portal Vein
Brightly Echogenic Portal Triads
Periportal Masses

HYPERECHOIC LIVER MASS(ES)

Hemangioma*
Metastatic Disease*
Focal Fatty Change*
Hepatic Adenoma*
Hepatocellular Carcinoma*
Focal Nodular Hyperplasia (FNH)
Intrahepatic Cholangiocarcinoma
Angiosarcoma
Lipoma/Angiomyolipoma

VARIANTS

Fat in the Falciform Ligament
Diaphragmatic Insertion*

CHILDHOOD

Infantile Hemangioendothelioma*
Hepatoblastoma*

*May be multiple.

The normal liver is homogeneous and of medium echogenicity. Focal hyperechoic masses can be seen easily on the background of the normal liver.

Hemangioma (Figures 1.1–1.4)

The hemangioma is the most common benign liver tumor. The only tumor more common in the liver is a metastasis. Occurring more often in women, the hemangioma has an incidence with a reported range of 0.4 to 20 percent, usually cited at 1 to 2 percent.

The tumor is made up of vascular channels lined with endothelium and separated by fibrous stroma. Hemangiomas are believed to be congenital hamartomas with a honeycomb appearance microscopically. Usually solitary, they range in size from 1.5 to 20 cm. Hemangiomas are often located in the peripheral, subcapsular region of the liver. Sonographically, they are often uniformly hyperechoic, with well-defined borders and posterior acous-

1

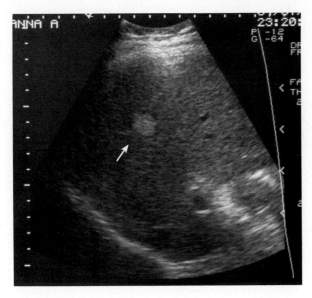

Figure 1.1
Hemangioma: A 15-mm well-defined hyperechoic mass was identified in the right lobe of the liver as an incidental finding in a patient being evaluated for gallstones. The patient had no history of primary malignancy.

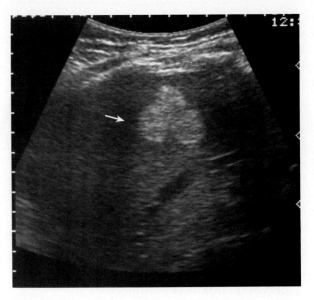

Figure 1.3
Hemangioma: A homogeneous hyperechoic heart-shaped mass was discovered in an elderly woman with breast carcinoma. Aspiration of the mass yielded bloody fluid and no malignant cells. Tagged red blood cell imaging confirmed the mass to be a hemangioma.

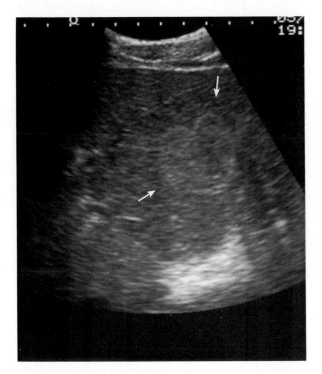

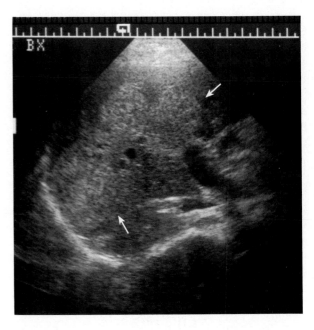

Figure 1.2
Hemangioma: A hyperechoic heart-shaped mass (*arrows*) was discovered in the left lobe of the liver during sonographic evaluation after kidney transplantation. Nuclear medicine tagged red blood cell imaging confirmed that it was a cavernous hemangioma of the liver.

Figure 1.4
Hemangioma: A large hemangioma of the liver diffusely infiltrated much of the right lobe of the liver. Notice the heterogeneous hyperechogenicity. Because the mass was symptomatic, hepatic resection was performed.

tic enhancement. The multiple interfaces of the endothelial channels result in the highly echogenic sonographic appearance of a typical hemangioma. Larger lesions may have more inhomogeneity of echogenicity, with irregular borders and diminished central echogenicity.

Since most hemangiomas are incidental findings on imaging studies and are clinically silent, their significance is secondary to confusion with more ominous causes of hepatic masses, such as metastases or hepatocellular carcinoma.

If the sonographic features are typical for hemangioma in a patient with no history of malignancy in whom the lesion is identified incidentally, follow-up sonography will confirm the stability of the lesion. If, on the other hand, the patient has a history of a primary tumor that could produce a hyperechoic metastasis (e.g., mucin-producing colon cancer or carcinoid tumor) or is at risk for hepatocellular carcinoma, the hemangioma may be indistinguishable sonographically. Further testing may be necessary to exclude malignancy and to diagnose hemangioma. Radionuclide tagged red blood cell scans are usually diagnostic of hemangioma with a deficit on early images and pooling of tagged red cells on delayed imaging. Magnetic resonance (MR) and dynamic contrast-enhanced computed tomography (CT) scans are often confirmatory of hemangioma. At MR, hemangiomas are usually of low signal on T_1-weighted images, becoming increasingly bright and of very high signal intensity on T_2-weighted sequences. Dynamic contrast-enhanced CT will show large peripheral vessels and enhancement of the low density lesion from the periphery. Biopsy of hemangioma is usually unnecessary when radionuclide-tagged red blood cell studies or MR imaging is available. Fine-needle aspiration of hemangioma is often unsuccessful for diagnosis, since bloody, nonmalignant fluid is usually obtained.

Metastatic Disease (Figures 1.5–1.8)

Often multiple, metastatic disease to the liver may present as a solitary mass. Metastatic disease to the liver is hyperechoic relative to the unaffected hepatic parenchyma in approximately one-third of cases. Well-circumscribed hyperechoic metastases can be indistinguishable sonographically from hemangiomas of the liver and are the most frequent mass to be differentiated. Metastatic disease from a number of primaries may yield hyperechoic lesions in the liver. Metastases from colonic, pancreatic, gastric, and other mucin-producing primaries frequently produce hyperechoic secondaries. Hypervascular metastases such as from islet cell tumors, carcinoid and choriocarcinoma are also likely to be

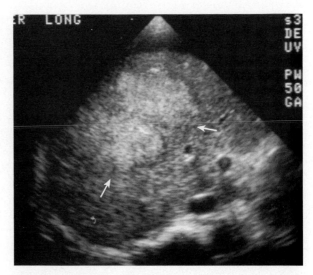

Figure 1.5
Metastatic colon carcinoma: An extensive area of hyperechogenicity was noted in the right lobe of the liver in this 54-year-old woman with metastatic colon carcinoma. Fine-needle aspiration confirmed the impression of metastatic disease.

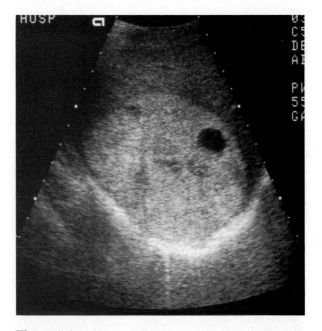

Figure 1.6
Metastatic carcinoid: A 60-year-old woman presented with a large, well-defined hyperechoic mass in the right lobe of the liver. The patient had no history of prior malignancy, and tagged red blood cell imaging suggested that the mass was not a hemangioma. Intraoperative fine-needle aspiration of the mass led to profound hypotension, suggesting the diagnosis of metastatic carcinoid. The primary tumor was located in the terminal ileum, and the patient underwent resection of both the primary tumor and the metastasis in the liver.

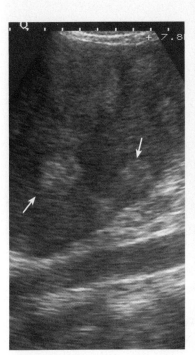

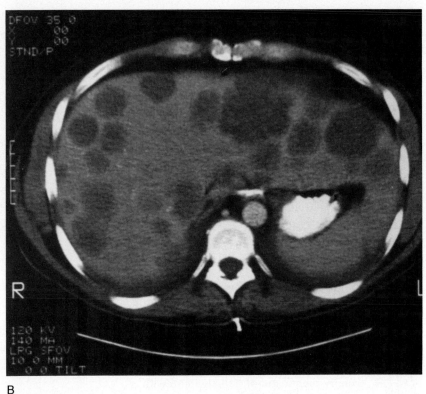

A   B

Figure 1.7

Metastatic colon carcinoma: (A) Multiple hyperechoic metastases (*arrows*) were obvious in this patient with abnormal liver functions and anorexia. Fine-needle aspiration yielded adenocarcinoma; follow-up barium enema located the primary. (B) CT confirmed the numerous metastases.

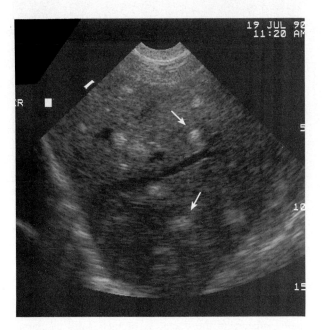

Figure 1.8

Metastatic colon carcinoma: Multiple metastases are present in this patient with known colon cancer.

echogenic. The hyperechogenicity of the masses is believed secondary to the mucin present or the multiple interfaces of the hypervascular masses. Metastatic breast carcinoma can be hyperechoic after treatment. Metastatic disease from the same primary may, however, have a variable sonographic appearance within the same patient with a mixture of hyperechoic, hypoechoic, and isoechoic lesions identifiable relative to more normal liver.

Percutaneous fine needle aspiration under ultrasound or CT guidance can confirm an impression of metastatic disease.

Focal Fatty Change (Figures 1.9–1.11)

Focal fatty change of the liver is an accumulation of triglycerides within hepatocytes. Associated etiologies of fatty change of the liver include obesity, alcoholism, pregnancy, medications such as steroids, starvation, diabetes, and hepatic toxins. Usually fatty change is diffuse, resulting in a generalized increase in echogenicity of the entire liver. In situations of focal fatty change, the appearance may mimic a focal echogenic hepatic lesion. Sonographic features that suggest focal fatty change rather than a liver mass include (1) no mass effect on hepatic vessels with vessels dissecting through areas of fatty change; (2) geographic borders of the

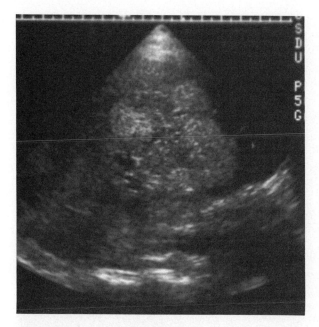

Figure 1.9

Fatty change: This 24-year-old pregnant woman underwent routine obstetric sonographic evaluation. Serendipitous visualization of the liver led to the observation of multiple hyperechoic masslike areas. The most likely diagnostic possibilities were felt to be metastatic disease or focal fatty change. Fatty liver was confirmed by CT and biopsy.

"mass," although well-circumscribed areas and irregular borders may also be seen; and (3) changing appearance of areas of fatty change on serial scans. Periportal fatty change and involvement adjacent to the falciform ligament are commonly affected areas of focal fat. Knowledge of the pattern of distribution, geographic margins, and lack of mass effect on vessels should allow focal fatty change to be differentiated from a mass lesion and make biopsy unnecessary. Use of CT, MR, or nuclear medicine imaging to prove there is no focal lesion may also assist in avoiding biopsy.

Hepatic Adenoma (Figure 1.12)

Hepatic adenomas, which are rare, benign epithelial tumors, have been clearly linked to the use of oral contraceptives. In recent decades adenomas have increased in incidence. Hepatic adenomas also are associated with certain metabolic diseases. For example, as many as 40 percent of patients with glycogen storage disease may have hepatic adenomas. In men, use of anabolic steroids may result in the development of an adenoma.

Although the adenoma may be asymptomatic, it may be discovered when the patient presents with an acute abdomen secondary to adenoma rupture and hemoperitoneum. In young women with he-

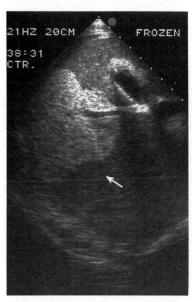
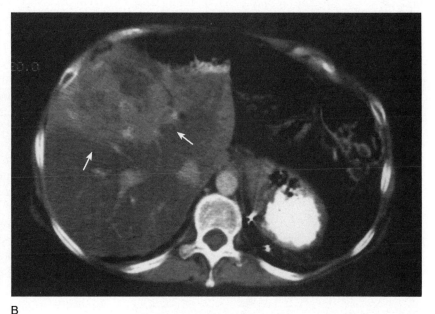

A   B

Figure 1.10

Fatty change: (A) This alcoholic patient was noted to have large geographic areas of hyperechogenicity in the liver. Note the lack of mass effect on the vasculature of the liver consistent with focal fatty change. (B) CT in another patient with fatty liver and focal sparing (*arrows*).

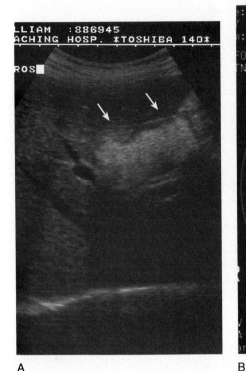
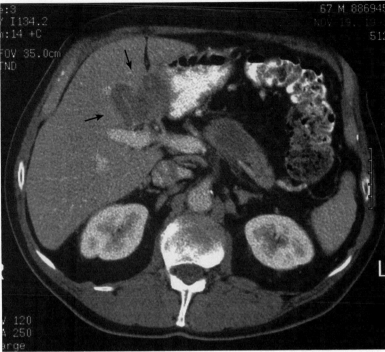

A   B

Figure 1.11

Fatty change: (A) A large area of fatty liver (*arrows*) is noted anterior to the portal vein in this patient with adenocarcinoma of the pancreas. Note the profound attenuation of the beam posterior to the fatty liver. Also, note the lack of mass effect on the portal vein. (B) CT on same patient showed large hypodense region anterior to portal vein.

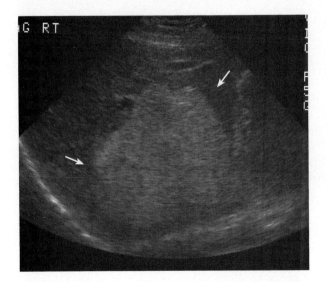

Figure 1.12

Hepatic adenoma: A large, lobulated hyperechoic mass (*arrows*) was discovered and resected in this young woman with a long history of oral contraceptive use.

moperitoneum, rupture of a hepatic adenoma is the second most likely etiology, ruptured ectopic pregnancy is the most common. The propensity of the hepatic adenoma to rupture and bleed makes it a surgical lesion. Degeneration into hepatocellular carcinoma occurs in some cases. This is another reason why surgery is recommended.

Usually, adenomas are solitary, often large (8–15 cm) masses that are well encapsulated. Multiple adenomas are sometimes seen. Generally, adenomas are hyperechoic relative to the liver due to the presence of fat in the mass. There may be central areas of hypoechogenicity related to central necrosis or hemorrhage. Large peripheral vessels may be present.

Adenomas imaged with radionuclide ^{99m}Tc sulfur colloid often show a defect or markedly diminished nuclide uptake secondary to the absence of Kupffer cells. Imaging with biliary agents will show little excretion in the typical adenoma. Exceptions to this pattern exist, but nuclear medicine can often suggest the correct diagnosis. MR imaging in which the typical adenoma is of high signal on T_1-weighted images because of intratumoral fat often suggests the diagnosis.

Differentiation from cavernous hemangioma or focal nodular hyperplasia (FNH) should be attempted, since neither hemangioma nor FNH is usually treated surgically.

Hepatocellular Carcinoma (Figure 1.13)

In the United States, most hepatocellular carcinomas arise within cirrhotic livers. Stigmata of liver disease that can be seen sonographically include a small, irregular liver, ascites, splenomegaly, and evidence of portosystemic collaterals.

Hepatocellular carcinoma is often hyperechoic and may be very similar in appearance to metastatic disease, fatty change within the liver, or cavernous hemangioma. With increasing size, hepatocellular carcinoma becomes inhomogeneous with central necrosis and fibrosis within the mass. Portal vein invasion may be an indication that the mass is hepatocellular carcinoma. Alpha-fetoprotein levels may be dramatically elevated.

Fibrolamellar carcinoma, which is a subtype of hepatocellular carcinoma, occurs in younger patients who may not have preexisting liver disease. Fibrolamellar carcinoma has a better prognosis than most typical hepatocellular carcinomas. Fibrolamellar carcinoma is typically a hyperechoic,

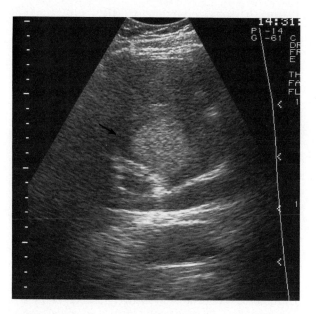

Figure 1.13
Hepatocellular carcinoma: This elderly patient with cirrhosis underwent wedge resection of a biopsy-proven hepatocellular carcinoma 18 months previously. This study demonstrated recurrent hepatocellular carcinoma anterior to the porta hepatis. Note the well-circumscribed hyperechoic mass (*arrow*). Alpha-fetoprotein levels were markedly elevated. The patient was treated with embolization therapy.

homogeneous mass with areas of calcification. Alpha-fetoprotein levels may be normal. Sonographically, fibrolamellar carcinoma needs differentiation from focal nodular hyperplasia most often.

Focal Nodular Hyperplasia (FNH)

Focal nodular hyperplasia (FNH) is usually a homogeneous hypoechoic or isoechoic, well-defined lesion with no calcification and a central scar. Sometimes FNH may be hyperechoic relative to surrounding normal liver.

Intrahepatic Cholangiocarcinoma

Cholangiocarcinoma is a neoplasm of the bile ductule that gives rise to a large intrahepatic mass only 10 percent of the time. A mucin-rich tumor with areas of dense fibrosis and foci of calcification, intrahepatic cholangiocarcinoma encases vessels rather than invading them. Sonographically, the mass may have a variable appearance, being either hypoechoic or hyperechoic. Cholangiocarcinoma is generally a homogeneous mass with rare areas of necrosis or hemorrhage. Cirrhosis is present in approximately 20 percent of cases.

Angiosarcoma Hepatic angiosarcoma is a rare malignancy of endothelial cells that line the vascular channels of the liver. It has been associated with exposure to hepatic toxins, such as Thorotrast, vinyl chloride, and arsenic.

Sonographically, hepatic angiosarcoma is seen as one or more hyperechoic masses with heterogeneity related to central hemorrhage.

Lipoma/Angiomyolipoma (Figure 1.14) Hepatic lipomas are well-circumscribed fatty tumors that are echogenic on ultrasound. A rare lesion, the hepatic lipoma may be indistinguishable from an angiomyolipoma, hemangioma, or metastasis of the liver.

VARIANTS

Fat in the Falciform Ligament (Figure 1.15)

Fatty deposition around the falciform ligament can mimic an intrahepatic mass and should not be mistaken as such. Recognition of the site and the typical triangular appearance will prevent misinterpretation.

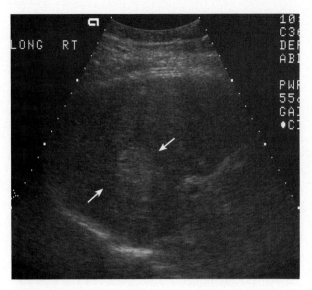

Figure 1.14
Angiomyolipoma of the liver: A very unusual mass (*arrows*) in the liver in this woman with tuberous sclerosis was identified. She had angiomyolipomas of both kidneys and in both lobes of the liver.

Diaphragmatic Insertion

Another normal variant that can mimic a hyperechoic liver lesion is a prominent diaphragmatic insertion usually seen in patients with emphysematous lung disease. Its peripheral location and multiplicity often allow it to be recognized.

CHILDHOOD

Infantile Hemangioendothelioma

Infantile hemangioendothelioma is a tumor of early childhood; 90 percent are discovered in the first 6 months of life. Clinically, infants have hepatomegaly, congestive heart failure in up to 25 percent, and thrombocytopenia secondary to sequestration of platelets. Up to 40 percent of patients may have cutaneous hemangiomas.

Sonographically, the lesions are similar to hemangiomas. Although frequently quite large, cystic areas and calcifications may be present. Over time the lesion becomes more echogenic, perhaps related to fibrosis. Large draining veins may be identified at presentation. The lesions are usually multiple but involute spontaneously over time.

Hepatoblastoma (Figure 1.16)

Hepatoblastoma develops in the first 3 years of life and is the most common primary hepatic malignancy in childhood. The clinical presentation is often abdominal swelling with anorexia or weight loss. Alpha-fetoprotein levels are often markedly elevated. Metastatic disease may be present at the time of tumor discovery.

Sonographically, the mass is a large, heterogeneous, hyperechoic solid mass that is lobulated and often multifocal. Calcification is frequently present.

Emphasis Points

When a solitary hyperechoic liver lesion is identified, the two most common differential possibilities are usually hemangioma or metastatic disease. If the patient has no history of malignancy sometimes followup scanning to prove lesion stability is sufficient. Rather than assuming the lesion is a metastatic deposit and initiating a costly work-up to find the primary (i.e., colonoscopy, barium enema, or CT scans), a hemangioma should be excluded by performing a tagged red blood cell study (my personal preference), MR, or dynamic CT. If the lesion is determined to be a hemangioma, the work-up can end. If the lesion is not a hemangioma, biopsy of the lesion is often an expeditious next step. If the lesion is metastatic, often the primary site can be suggested by examination of the histologic specimen from the liver.

Hepatocellular carcinoma usually develops in a cirrhotic liver. Recognition of portal vein thrombosis and a mass in the liver will be strong evidence that the mass is a hepatocellular carcinoma. Sometimes hepatocellular carcinoma is hard to recognize sonographically because the underlying cirrhotic liver is so irregular.

In an adult patient presenting with multiple hyperechoic lesions in the liver and no known primary, a likely diagnosis is metastatic disease from the gastrointestinal (GI) tract. Exceptions such as multiple hemangiomas and multiple adenomas can occur. Sometimes excluding multiple hemangiomas is helpful, followed by percutaneous biopsy if the exclusionary study is negative.

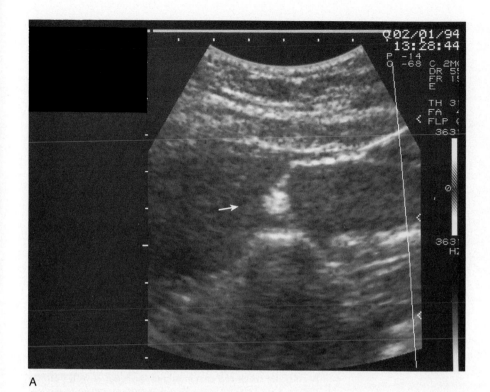

A

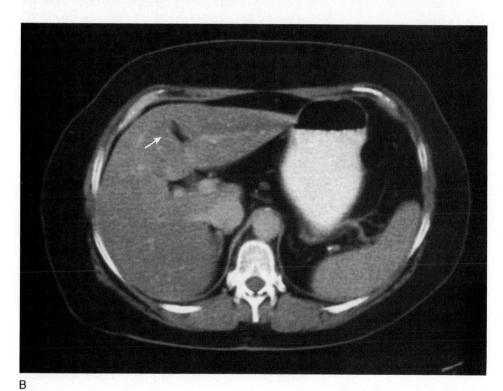

B

Figure 1.15

Fat in the falciform ligament: (A) A brightly echogenic tri-angular mass, easily mistaken for a metastatic deposit, was obvious in this patient. (B) CT on the same patient showed fat in the falciform ligament region.

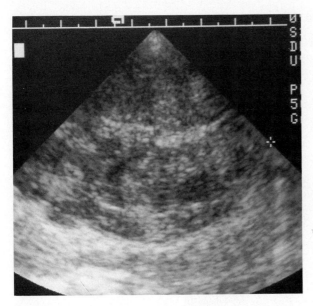

Figure 1.16
Hepatoblastoma: A large, heterogeneously echogenic mass was discovered in this infant with elevated alpha-fetoprotein levels.

HYPOECHOIC LIVER MASS(ES)

Metastatic Disease*
Lymphoma *
Abscesses*
   Pyogenic Abscesses
   Fungal Abscesses
Atypical Hemangioma*
Hepatocellular Carcinoma*
Focal Nodular Hyperplasia (FNH)*
Hepatic Adenoma*
Regenerating Nodules in Cirrhosis*
Focal Sparing in a Fatty Liver*
Hepatic Infarction*
Complicated Cyst

*May be multiple.

Metastatic Disease (Figures 1.17–1.20)

The most common cause of malignant hepatic masses, metastases outnumber primary malignant hepatic tumors nearly 18 : 1. The most common primary sites for metastases to the liver parenchyma are the colon, stomach, pancreas, breast, and lung. The liver is second only to lymph nodes as a site of metastatic disease.

   Liver function tests are unreliable for detecting metastases. Findings commonly encountered in patients with liver metastases include hepatomegaly, ascites, and jaundice.

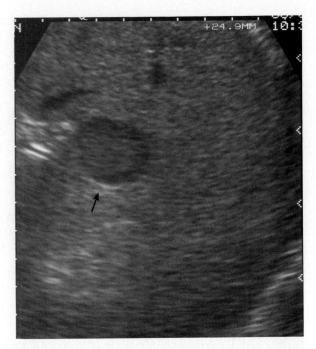

Figure 1.17
Metastatic small cell carcinoma of the lung: A well-defined 2.5-cm hypoechoic mass in the right lobe of the liver was proven by fine-needle aspiration to be a metastatic deposit of small cell carcinoma.

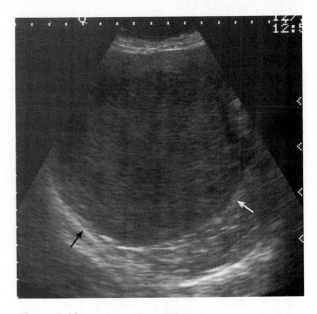

Figure 1.18
Metastatic colon carcinoma: A large hypoechoic mass (*arrows*) replaced much of the right lobe of the liver in a patient with a recently discovered cecal carcinoma. Although often hyperechoic, metastatic colon carcinoma may be hypoechoic relative to normal hepatic parenchyma.

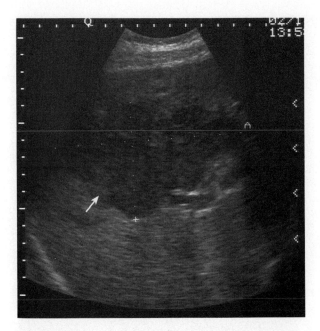

Figure 1.19
Metastatic renal cell carcinoma: A hypoechoic lesion anterior to the portal vein was identified in young man with renal cell carcinoma.

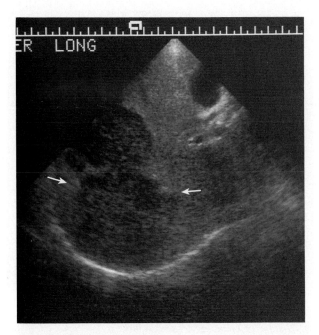

Figure 1.20
Metastatic squamous cell carcinoma of the cervix: Extensive metastatic disease to the liver from cervical carcinoma presented as large, multilobulated hypoechoic mass (*arrows*).

The sonographic appearance of metastatic disease will vary, depending upon the primary tumor type, and metastases from the same primary may have a variable appearance in the same patient. Some generalities about metastatic disease to the liver can be made. Colon, stomach, and pancreas primaries frequently yield hyperechoic metastases. Hypoechoic metastases are often from hypovascular and highly cellular primaries. Tumors that may have hypoechoic secondaries in the liver include lung carcinoma, cervical carcinoma, tumors of the head and neck, and melanoma.

Lymphoma (Figures 1.21–1.22)

Lymphoma is the prototypical example of a tumor causing very homogeneous, hypoechoic lesions in the liver. Lymphoma does not, however, usually cause focal hepatic masses; instead it usually diffusely infiltrates the liver. In AIDS patients with non-Hodgkin lymphoma, multiple rapidly changing hypoechoic masses may be present. Percutaneous biopsy can confirm the diagnosis.

Abscesses

Pyogenic Abscesses (Figures 1.23–1.24) Pyogenic liver abscesses are an uncommon diagnosis in Western society; they occur in only 1 percent of autopsy series. Liver abscesses may develop in a variety of ways. Most liver abscesses develop secondary to cholangitis related to biliary obstruction. In such a situation, the abscesses are multiple, involving both lobes of the liver. Before the use of antibiotics, portal vein pylephlebitis was responsible for most pyogenic hepatic abscesses. Pylephlebitis of the portal vein developed secondary to appendicitis, diverticulitis, inflammatory bowel disease, or necrotic gastrointestinal (GI) tumors. Liver abscess developing in this setting is usually solitary. Other modes of development of liver abscess include septicemia with transport of pyogenic material via the hepatic artery to both lobes of the liver, direct extension of abscess from adjacent organs, blunt or penetrating trauma, and superinfection of necrotic metastases.

Most liver abscesses are caused by anaerobic or mixed anaerobic and aerobic organisms. *E. coli* is most often cultured from adult patients and staphylococcal organisms are most often found in children.

Clinically, patients with pyogenic liver abscesses have fever, right upper quadrant pain, malaise, nausea, and vomiting. Usually, leukocytosis and abnormal liver function studies are present.

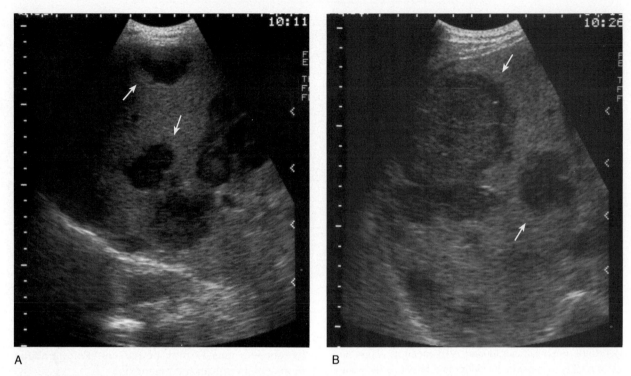

A

B

Figure 1.21
Non-Hodgkin lymphoma in AIDS patient: (A and B) This AIDS patient presented with abdominal pain and acute decompensation. Multiple hypoechoic masses of varying sizes were identified in the liver and later proved to be aggressive non-Hodgkin lymphoma.

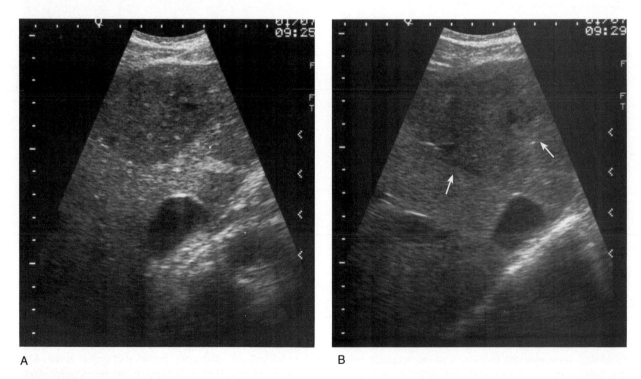

A

B

Figure 1.22
Non-Hodgkin lymphoma: (A and B) This focal lymphoma of the liver resolved with chemotherapy.

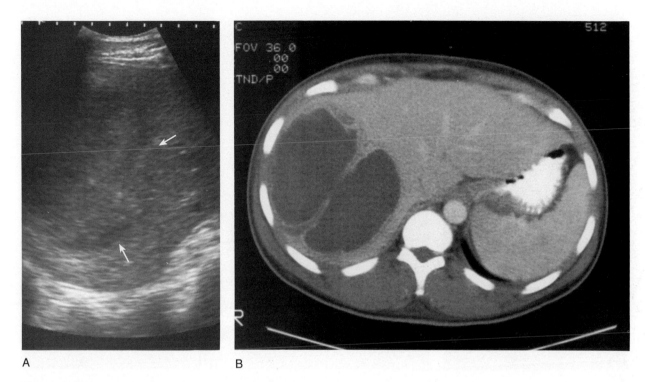

A   B

Figure 1.23

Pyogenic abscess: (A) A large hypoechoic region in the right lobe of the liver (*arrows*) was identified in this patient with spiking fevers, malaise, right upper quadrant pain, and septicemia. Percutaneous catheter drainage was used to decompress the abscess. (B) Note how cystic the collection appeared at CT.

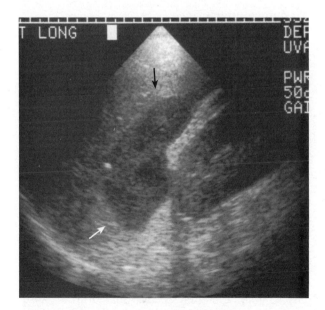

Figure 1.24

Pyogenic hepatic abscess: This elderly farmer noted flulike symptoms and persistent fevers. Sonographic evaluation demonstrated a lenticular collection in the right lobe of the liver that proved to be a pyogenic abscess treated with catheter drainage.

Sonographically, the appearance of liver abscesses will depend upon the age of the abscess. The sonographic appearance will change as the abscess evolves with therapy and time. Initially poorly defined and inhomogeneous, liver abscesses become hypoechoic and will evolve into cystic, complicated, well-defined lesions as suppuration increases. Air within an abscess may result in brightly echogenic foci with reverberation artifact.

Fungal Abscesses Candidiasis affecting the liver may result in small hypoechoic lesions in both lobes.

Atypical Hemangioma (Figure 1.25)

A common presentation of an "atypical hemangioma" is a solid lesion with at least a partially hypoechoic internal echo pattern. Many hemangiomas with an atypical sonographic appearance had an echogenic outer border and often a scalloped outline. Presence of fatty change in the liver can obscure the echogenic outer border of the mass. The hypoechogenicity seen centrally may be related to fibrosis, necrosis, and thrombosis within larger hemangiomas. As many as 40 percent of hemangiomas may be atypical in appearance with hypoechoic centers. Recognition that hemangiomas may have an atypical appearance should prompt additional imaging with nuclear medicine, MR, or CT to clar-

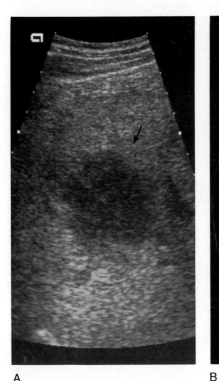

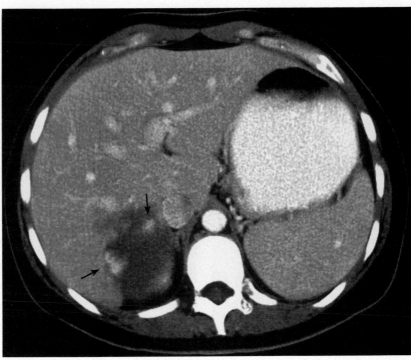

A   B

Figure 1.25

Atypical hemangioma: (A) In this patient with prostate cancer, three masses in the liver were detected. Prior to biopsy to exclude metastatic disease, nuclear medicine tagged red blood cell scanning showed the masses to be cavernous hemangiomas. Note the hypoechoic mass in a fatty liver. The mass has posterior enhancement. (B) CT showed peripheral enhancement, suggesting the correct diagnosis.

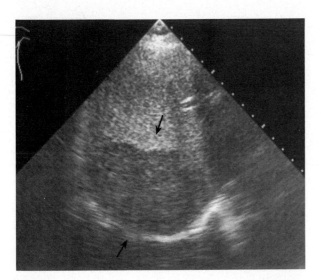

Figure 1.26

Hepatocellular carcinoma: Hepatocellular carcinoma presented as a large hypoechoic lesion in the right lobe of the liver in this elderly woman.

ify the diagnosis rather than attempting biopsy or alarming the patient by suggesting ominous neoplastic disease.

Hepatocellular Carcinoma (Figures 1.26–1.27)

Histologic variations in hepatocellular carcinoma can result in hypoechoic primary hepatic malignancies. Evidence of cirrhosis, portal vein involvement, and elevated levels of alpha-fetoprotein can suggest hepatocellular carcinoma, although biopsy would be necessary for definite clarification.

Focal Nodular Hyperplasia (Figure 1.28)

Focal nodular hyperplasia (FNH), the second most common benign hepatic neoplasm, represents 8 percent of primary hepatic masses. More common in women, FNH is often an incidental finding with few symptoms.

Sonographically, FNH is a well-defined, usually solitary, sometimes pedunculated mass. Associated hemorrhage or necrosis is rare, although a central scar may be identifiable. Most often FNH is 5 cm or smaller in maximum diameter, although it may replace an entire lobe of the liver. Usually the mass is homogeneous and hypoechoic or isoechoic relative to the rest of the liver.

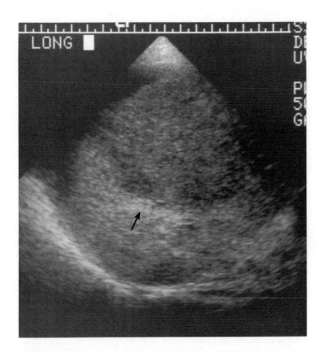

Figure 1.27
Hepatocellular carcinoma: Hepatocellular carcinoma was discovered in this patient with cirrhosis. A large mass and clinical deterioration of liver function were present. Portal vein invasion was identified by imaging.

Multiple FNH have been associated with vascular malformations and are thought to represent a hyperplastic response to an arterial malformation.

Hepatic Adenoma (Figure 1.29)

Usually hyperechoic, a hepatic adenoma may be hypoechoic, especially when compared with a diffusely fatty echogenic liver.

Regenerating Nodules in Cirrhosis (Figure 1.30)

Regenerating nodules occur in the severely cirrhotic liver. They may vary in size from 1 to 6 cm, although usually regenerating nodules are small and are responsible for the irregular contour of the cirrhotic liver. Uncommonly, a regenerating nodule can present as a larger, dominant hypoechoic mass within a cirrhotic liver. Such a mass requires evaluation, usually with biopsy to exclude more ominous diagnoses.

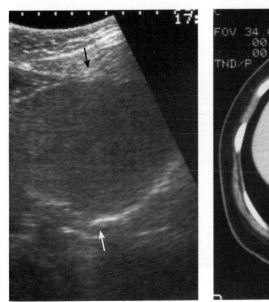

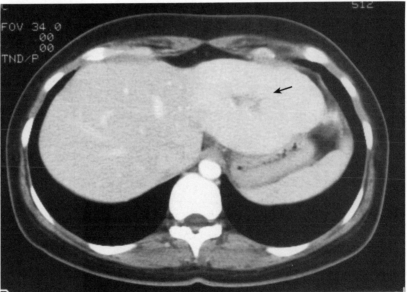

A   B

Figure 1.28
Focal nodular hyperplasia: (A) This isoechoic mass was identified within the liver by its mass effect. The mass could easily be overlooked, since there is little difference in echogenicity with normal liver. (B) Note central scar on CT (*arrow*). The contrast enhancement of focal nodular hyperplasia makes it nearly isodense to liver.

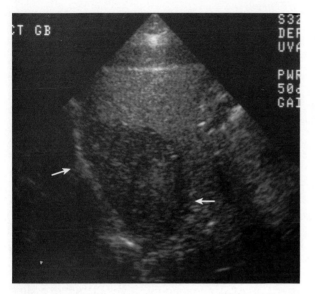

Figure 1.29
Hepatic adenoma: In this young woman on high-dose steroids for adrenal insufficiency, several hypoechoic lesions were visualized within an otherwise fatty liver. Biopsy of the masses confirmed that they were hepatic adenomas.

Focal Sparing in a Fatty Liver (Figure 1.31)

Patients with fatty change in the liver related to obesity, drugs, alcohol, starvation, or other causes may have focal sparing of the liver that can be misinterpreted as a focal hypoechoic lesion of the liver. Recognition of typical sites for focal sparing immediately anterior to the portal vein, medial to the falciform ligament, and adjacent to the gallbladder and recognition that the hepatic vessels course through the hypoechoic regions without distortion will allow the diagnosis to be made. Usually biopsy is not necessary; MR, CT, and nuclear medicine imaging can be used to confirm the diagnosis of focal sparing in a fatty liver. Follow-up scanning can also show rapid change in the appearance of the liver, favoring the diagnosis of fatty change with sparing.

Hepatic Infarction (Figures 1.32–1.33)

Infarction of the liver is not a usual occurrence, happening iatrogenically when embolization or liga-

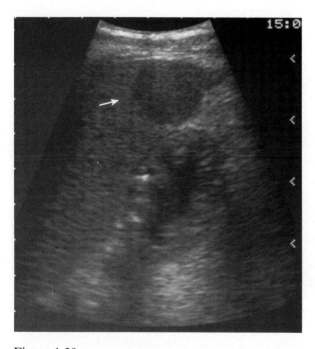

Figure 1.30
Regenerating nodule: Usually small, regenerating nodules may be responsible for the irregular contour of a cirrhotic liver. This 3-cm hypoechoic mass was identified in a patient with cirrhosis. Because of the concern for hepatocellular carcinoma, core biopsies of the lesion were performed. The histology of the lesion was that of a regenerating nodule.

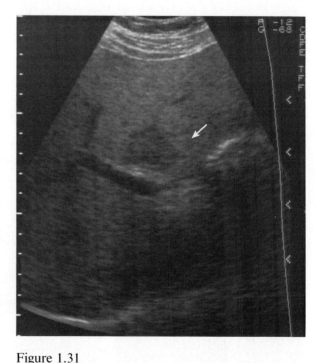

Figure 1.31
Focal sparing in a fatty liver: Fatty change in the liver makes the liver extremely echogenic. Focal sparing in a fatty liver frequently occurs anterior to the portal vein, medial to the falciform ligament, or adjacent to the gallbladder fossa. Knowledge of focal sparing and its common sites will allow it to be recognized. Focal sparing was seen here as an area of hypoechogenicity anterior to the portal vein.

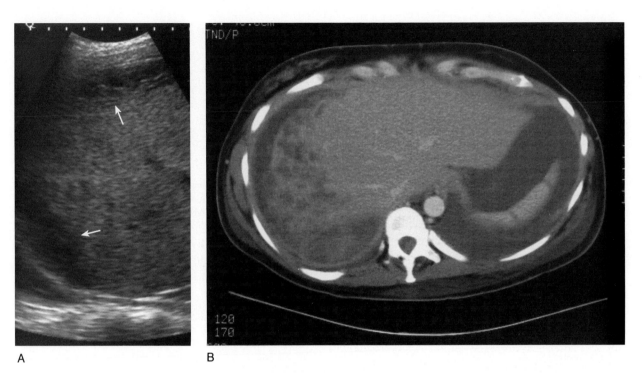

A   B

Figure 1.32
Hepatic infarction: (A) Extensive peripheral hypoechogenicity of hepatic infarction occurred in this patient after
embolization of the right hepatic artery. (B) CT confirmed
the hepatic infarction.

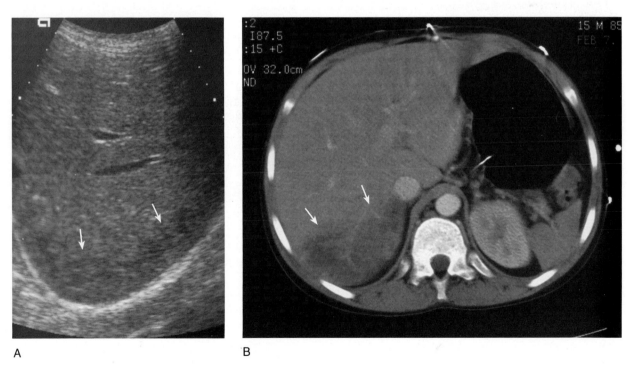

A   B

Figure 1.33
Hepatic infarction: (A) Peripheral hypoechogenicity developed in this liver transplant recipient in vaso-occlusive
crisis. (B) CT confirmed the peripheral infarction.

tion of the hepatic artery is done therapeutically. Liver transplant recipients may experience hepatic infarction if there is thrombosis of the operated vessels.

Complicated Cyst (Figure 1.34)

Bleeding into or infection of a preexisting hepatic cyst may result in a hypoechoic mass that is difficult to differentiate from other hypoechoic hepatic masses. Aspiration of the mass may be necessary to determine its etiology if previous studies showing an uncomplicated cyst are not available.

CYSTIC LESIONS IN THE LIVER

Simple Hepatic Cysts
Autosomal Dominant Polycystic Kidney
    Disease with Hepatic Involvement
Abscesses
    Pyogenic Abscesses
    Parasitic Abscesses
Posttraumatic Biloma or Hematoma
Caroli's Disease
Focally Dilated Biliary Tree
Biliary Cystadenoma/Cystadenocarcinoma
Necrotic Metastatic Disease
Intrahepatic Pancreatic Pseudocysts
Pseudoaneurysm/Arteriovenous
    Malformations
Adenoma/Hepatocellular Carcinoma with
    Hemorrhage

VARIANTS

Lymphoma

CHILDHOOD

Mesenchymal Hamartoma
Choledochal Cyst
Infantile Hemangioendothelioma

The recognition of a cystic mass in the liver should result in the consideration of specific etiologies outlined here.

Simple Hepatic Cysts (Figure 1.35)

Simple cysts of the liver, not related to parasitic disease, are believed to be congenital defects and are usually incidentally noted at sonography. These

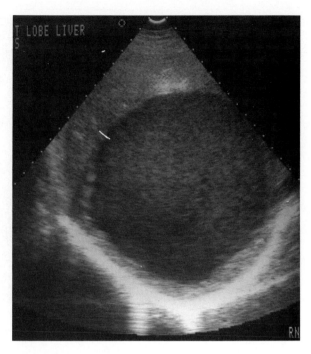

Figure 1.34
Complicated cyst: A well-defined hypoechoic mass in the right lobe of the liver proved to be a cyst filled with old blood. Other noncomplicated cysts were seen elsewhere in the liver. Aspiration was necessary to confirm the diagnosis.

congenital bile duct cysts are generally noted on imaging studies in the fifth through seventh decades of life. Hepatic cysts may be solitary or multiple.

Generally, simple hepatic cysts are asymptomatic unless they are complicated by hemorrhage or infection. Rarely, a simple liver cyst may cause obstruction of a biliary radicle by mass effect.

Sonographically, simple hepatic cysts are anechoic with a well-defined wall and posterior enhancement. Septations and soft tissue nodularity are uncommon but may be seen after internal hemorrhage. Calcification of the wall is unusual but may occur.

Alcohol ablation of hepatic cyst may be performed in the patient with symptoms referable to the cyst who does not desire surgical intervention. Catheter drainage of the cyst fluid and alcohol instillation to destroy the lining cells will eradicate the cyst.

Autosomal Dominant Polycystic Kidney Disease (Figure 1.36)

There is hepatic involvement by cysts in at least 40 percent of patients with autosomal dominant poly-

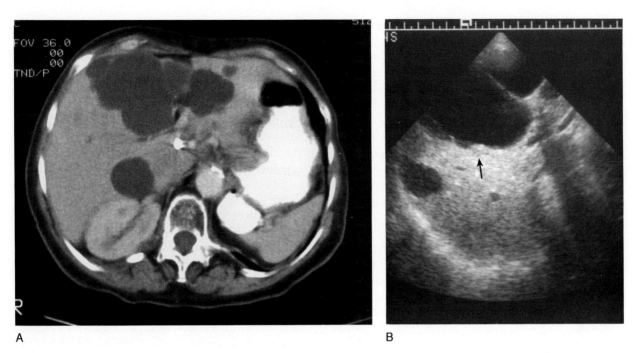

A   B

Figure 1.35
Simple cysts: (A) Multiple low-density lesions in the liver were discovered by CT in this elderly patient with breast carcinoma. (B) Ultrasound demonstrated all the masses to be simple cysts.

cystic kidney disease. Hepatic cysts may be seem as well as bilateral involvement of the kidneys, which are enlarged with cysts of varying sizes and shapes. Patients may have hepatomegaly with multiple hepatic cysts or multiple small cysts and no significant increase in hepatic volume. Most of the time hepatic function is normal.

These cysts are sonographically similar to simple hepatic cysts in that they have smooth walls and lack septations or mural nodules. With clot and fibrosis secondary to repeated bouts of internal cyst hemorrhage, the masses may look nearly solid. After repeated hemorrhage, the cysts may be diagnostically problematic.

Abscesses

Pyogenic Abscesses   Pyogenic abscesses may be isoechoic to liver in the early stages, and may become more cystic with increasing suppuration. Debris, wall irregularities, internal echoes, or septations may complicate these cystic masses. Gas, which is seen as highly echogenic foci with dirty shadowing, is seen in about 20 percent of pyogenic abscesses. Solitary liver abscesses are often multilocular. Percutaneous aspiration and drainage are

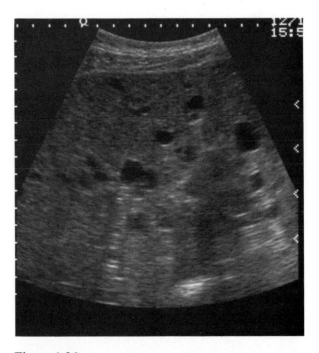

Figure 1.36
Autosomal dominant polycystic kidney disease with hepatic cysts: Multiple small cysts were present in the liver in this patient with autosomal dominant polycystic kidney disease.

often therapeutic, coupled with appropriate anti-biotic therapy. Before percutaneous drainage is undertaken, serologic studies should be performed to exclude parasitic causes of hepatic abscess. Spillage of the contents of an echinococcal cyst during percutaneous drainage may result in anaphylaxis. Care must be taken to avoid entering the pleural space when placing a catheter into a liver abscess and thereby extending the infection into the chest. Multilocular collections will often drain via one drainage catheter, but multiple catheters can be placed if additional loculations remain undrained after initial catheter placement.

Parasitic Abscesses (Figures 1.37–1.38) Parasitic abscesses include amebic and echinococcal lesions. Amebic infection is caused by contamination of food or water with *Entamoeba histolytica*. Ten to twenty percent of the world's population is thought to be infected with this protozoan, which spreads from the colon to the liver via the portal vein and initiates a hepatic abscess. Contaminated water is a frequent source of infection. Many patients have Mexican ancestry or have traveled to an infested area.

An amebic abscess is usually solitary, can be large, and is within the right lobe of the liver. Its

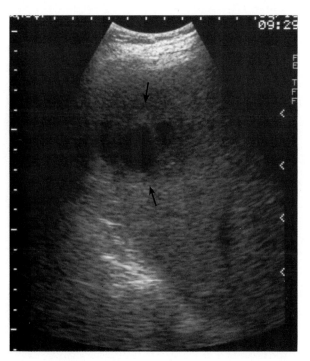

Figure 1.37
Amebic abscess: Serologic titers for ameba were positive and quite elevated in this patient with amebic abscess of the liver.

sonographic appearance is indistinguishable from pyogenic abscess.

Although percutaneous aspiration and drainage of amebic abscess are possible, medical therapy is often effective with such lesions. The diagnosis may be made by correlation with serum serology. The masses have necrotic "anchovy paste" material within them.

A common cause of liver cysts worldwide is echinococcal parasitic disease. Hydatid disease or infection with echinococcus granulosus is common in areas with sheep, since the sheep serve as the intermediate hosts for the organism. Involvement of the liver, which occurs in 75 percent of patients, includes unilocular cyst formation. These cysts may have a double lining and fine internal echoes representing the small solices. Daughter cysts may be demonstrable 70 percent of the time as secondary cysts or septated regions within a large cyst. Over time, echinococcal abscesses may fill with material, making them appear nearly solid, and they may eventually calcify (approximately 50 percent).

Generally, the diagnosis is suspected by the clinical history and imaging features. Aspiration with spillage of echinococcal abscesses may result in anaphylaxis and is generally avoided if possible. Patients are initially managed medically. If medical therapy fails, then surgical removal or destruction of the organisms with instillation of absolute alcohol or hypertonic saline can be performed in a controlled setting.

Posttraumatic Biloma or Hematoma (Figures 1.39–1.41)

Intrahepatic bilomas or hematomas occur after hepatic injury, which may be either iatrogenic or accidental.

Single or multiple collections may be seen after hepatic injury. Bilomas are fluid collections of varying sizes, sometimes with internal debris, that reflect injury to the biliary tree. Hematomas acutely may be seen sonographically only as echotexture abnormalities, which become more well defined and cystic with evolution. Internal septations are frequent in hematomas. With time, intrahepatic hematomas generally become smaller.

Caroli's Disease (Figure 1.42)

Caroli's disease is transmitted as an autosomal recessive disorder in which there is saccular dilatation of the intrahepatic biliary tree. Because of pools of static bile, there is a high incidence of calculus formation and cholangitis. The incidence of cholangio-

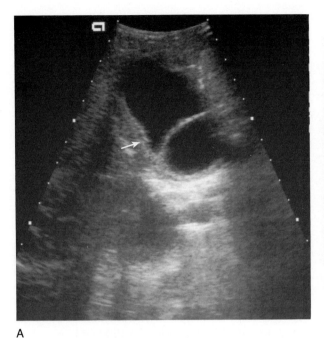

A

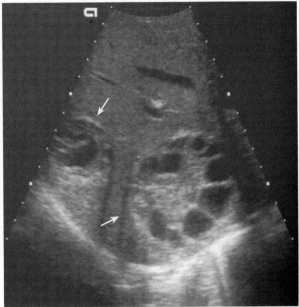

B

Figure 1.38
Echinococcal abscess: (A and B) After failure of medical therapy, multiple complicated cystic collections of echinococcal infection were treated with instillation of hypertonic saline of absolute alcohol. Note the multiloculated collection in the right lobe.

carcinoma is greater in patients with Caroli's disease than in the general population.

Sonographically, Caroli's disease is manifest by intrahepatic cystic spaces that communicate with the branching biliary tree. Debris and stones may be present within the saccular dilatations.

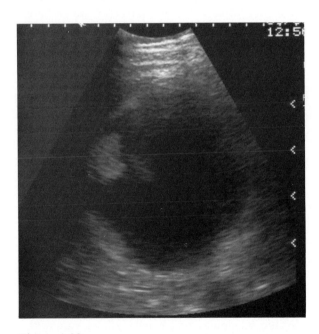

Figure 1.39
Posttraumatic biloma: This 28-year-old man suffered a major liver laceration in a motor vehicle accident. A large biloma developed in the central portion of the liver and required catheter drainage.

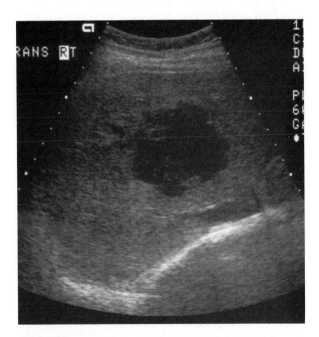

Figure 1.40
Hematoma: Four weeks after liver biopsy, a cystic collection in the right lobe of the liver persisted consistent with an evolving hematoma.

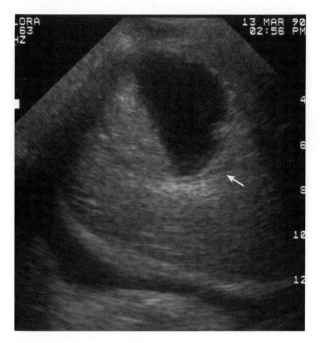

Figure 1.41
Infected biloma: A collection of infected bile developed near a drainage tube site in the right lobe of the liver. Percutaneous drainage eliminated the infected material.

Focally Dilated Biliary Duct (Figure 1.43)

A focally dilated biliary duct, usually obstructed by a benign or malignant lesion, can infrequently be misinterpreted as a focal cystic lesion of the liver.

Biliary Cystadenoma/Cystadenocarcinoma (Figure 1.44)

Biliary cystadenomas and cystadenocarcinomas constitute fewer than 5 percent of all intrahepatic cysts. These cystic masses are neoplasms arising from the biliary duct lining cells.

Generally, these masses arise in middle-aged women. The masses are most often intrahepatic, with only 15 percent located in an extrahepatic position. These cystic masses range in size from 3 to 25 cm and are often in the right lobe of the liver. Sonographically, the mass is cystic, with septations and wall irregularities.

A biliary cystadenoma may be indistinguishable sonographically from a congenital hepatic cyst. Reaccumulation of the cystic mass frequently occurs after drainage unless the entire wall has been removed. Histologic evaluation is usually necessary to differentiate the benign cystadenoma from the cystadenocarcinoma.

Necrotic Metastatic Disease (Figure 1.45)

Although the appearance of metastatic disease to the liver is variable, cystic metastases are relatively uncommon. Generally, cystic metastatic disease reflects rapid growth of the neoplasm rather than a cystic primary lesion. Thick-walled cavities with irregular margins and internal debris may be identified sonographically. Neoplasms that frequently become necrotic because of their rapid growth include choriocarcinoma, leiomyosarcoma, and small cell carcinoma. Ovarian carcinoma, a neoplasm that is often cystic, rarely causes intraparenchymal liver lesions; instead it studs the outer surface of the liver with cystic implants of tumor.

Intrahepatic Pancreatic Pseudocysts (Figure 1.46)

In patients with pancreatitis, exudation of fluid from the pancreas may occur and can track to nearby organs, such as the liver.

Pseudocysts will be encapsulated fluid collections within the liver, often with proteinaceous contents, which result in a fluid–debris level or diffuse low-level echoes within the mass. Associated inflammatory changes in the pancreas are to be expected.

Pseudoaneurysm/Arteriovenous Malformations (Figure 1.47)

Pseudoaneurysms of the hepatic artery can develop after liver biopsy or other injury to the liver. Gray-scale imaging will demonstrate a cystic mass; Doppler analysis will allow recognition of arterial inflow into the lesion.

Arteriovenous malformations will be cystic or tubular masses with high flow by Doppler. Embolization may be successful in lessening the high flow through the malformation.

Adenoma/Hepatocellular Carcinoma with Hemorrhage (Figure 1.48)

Hepatic adenomas and hepatocellular carcinomas are usually solid lesions, but both have a tendency to bleed, sometimes catastrophically. In situations of hepatic hemorrhage secondary to a preexisting lesion, a cystic component that is the hematoma can

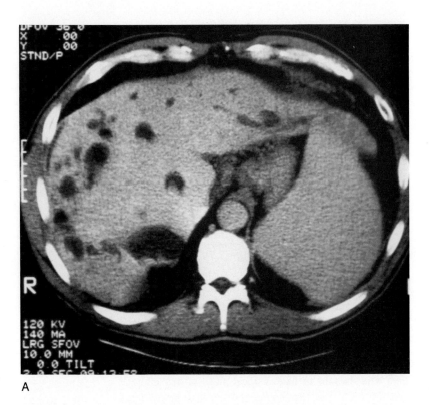

A

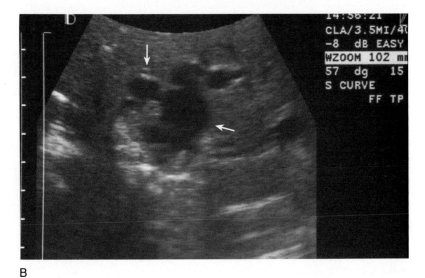

Figure 1.42
Caroli's disease: (A) Multiple saccular dilatations of the biliary tree characterize Caroli's disease. (B) US demonstrated the saccular dilatations.

B

usually be identified within or adjacent to the pathologic mass.

VARIANTS

Lymphoma

Lymphoma involving the liver does not usually give rise to focal masses, yet when focal masses are present, they are often quite low in echogenicity and appear nearly cystic. Careful sonographic scru-

tiny is necessary to confirm that the masses are, in fact, solid. Most often focal liver lesions in lymphoma are seen with non-Hodgkin lymphoma.

CHILDHOOD

Mesenchymal Hamartoma (Figure 1.49)

The mesenchymal hamartoma is a rare hepatic lesion, accounting for 8 percent of all childhood liver tumors and usually discovered in the first 3 years of

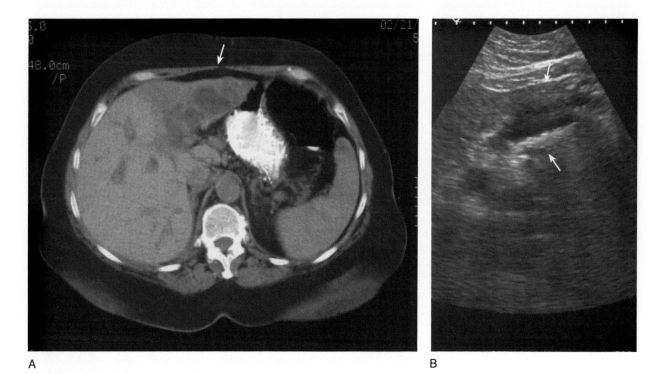

A   B

Figure 1.43
Focally dilated biliary duct filled with stones: (A) This patient was thought to have a focal mass in her left lobe
shown by CT. (B) Ultrasound showed it to be a dilated
biliary tree filled with stones proximal to a benign inflammatory stricture.

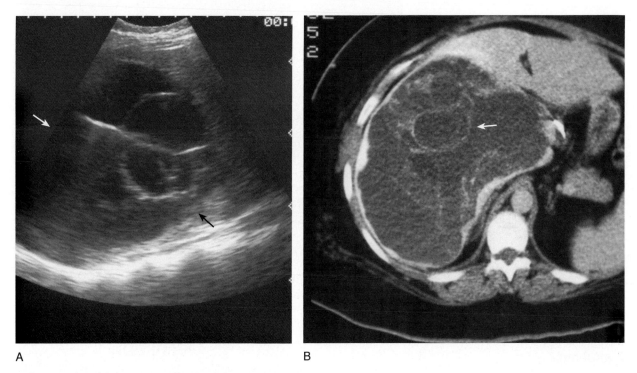

A   B

Figure 1.44
Biliary cystadenoma: (A) This multiseptate cystic mass in
the central liver recurred after surgical drainage 2 years
earlier. (B) CT images of a different patient showed the
enhancing septa of a biliary cystadenoma.

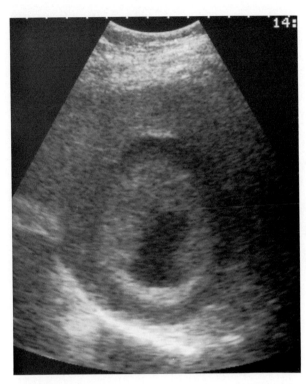

Figure 1.45
Necrotic metastases: A large mass with central necrosis developed in the liver in this patient with gastric leiomyosarcoma.

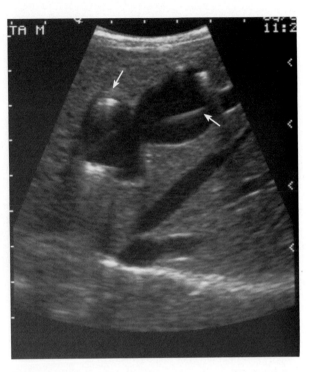

Figure 1.47
Arteriovenous malformation: Turbulent, high-velocity vascular flow was present within this cystic space in the liver. Note highly echogenic wires (*arrows*), placed to incite thrombosis within the arteriovenous malformation.

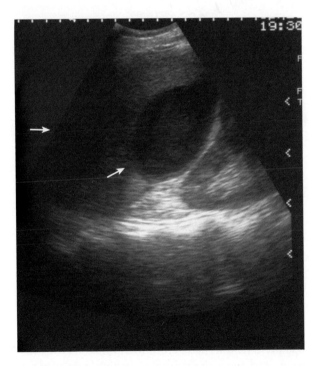

Figure 1.46
Intrahepatic pseudocyst: In this patient with severe pancreatitis and multiple fluid collections, a lenticular collection developed in the right lobe of the liver.

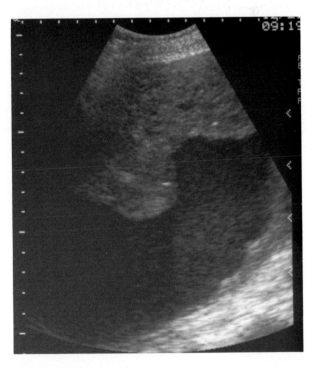

Figure 1.48
Hepatocellular carcinoma with hemorrhage: A large cystic area developed acutely in this patient with liver infiltrated with hepatocellular carcinoma.

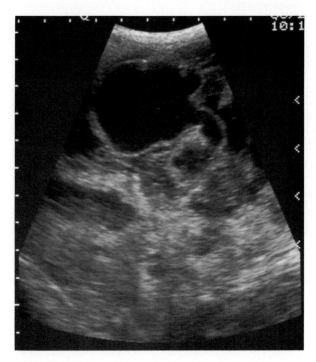

Figure 1.49

Mesenchymal hamartoma: This 1-year-old was noted clinically to have a large liver. Ultrasound evaluation demonstrated a large, multicompartmental mass that was surgically resected.

life. The hamartoma is not a true neoplasm but represents a benign developmental lesion.

The mass is often quite large, measuring 15 cm or more in diameter. Often well defined, encapsulated or pedunculated, the hepatic hamartoma is filled with gelatinous mesenchymal tissue, portal triads, and hepatocytes. Often the clinical history is of progressive abdominal enlargement, although rapid size changes may occur as the cyst fluid accumulates.

Sonographically, the mass is a cystic, multiseptate lesion that is well encapsulated.

Because the hamartoma is not a neoplasm, it does not require extensive surgery. Drainage, marsupialization, or simple excision may be sufficient.

This mass is differentiated from hepatoblastoma and infantile hemangioendothelioma by its prominent cystic constituency.

Choledochal Cyst (Figure 1.50)

A choledochal cyst may result in a cystic mass within the substance of the liver or closely associated with the hilum of the liver. Choledochal cysts are the most common congenital lesion of the bili-

ary tree; 80 percent are diagnosed in childhood. Clinically, patients have intermittent jaundice, recurrent right upper quadrant pain, and recurrent fevers. Sonographically, a large cyst may be identified in the right upper quadrant near the hilum of the liver. Communication with the biliary tree can be recognized.

Infantile Hemangioendothelioma

Cystic spaces within this mass may be present. Heterogeneous hyperechoic features with calcification may predominate.

HIGHLY ECHOGENIC LIVER LESIONS CONTAINING CALCIFICATION OR AIR

Calcified Liver Masses
Granulomatous Disease/Fungal Disease
Metastatic Disease
Parasitic Abscesses
Posttraumatic Hematomas
Air-Filled Liver Masses
Abscess
Postembolization Neoplasms

VARIANT

Gallbladder Contracted Around Stones/
Porcelain Gallbladder

Masses within the liver that contain either calcifications or air may have similar sonographic appearances with highly echogenic foci in the mass that shadow or have posterior ringdown. Often the clinical situation of the patient will allow the etiology of the mass to be determined, but correlative imaging with CT or plain films is often helpful.

Calcified Liver Masses

Granulomatous Disease/Fungal Disease (Figures 1.51–1.52) Evidence of granulomatous disease affecting the liver is common, with focally calcified granulomas frequently identified as highly echogenic foci scattered within the substance of the liver (or spleen) causing shadowing. Patients are usually asymptomatic from the granulomatous disease, and the calcified areas in the liver serve as stigmata that previous infection has occurred.

Patients with candidiasis may develop calcifications in their foci of disease.

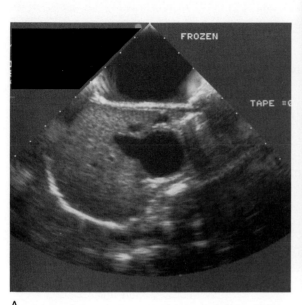

A

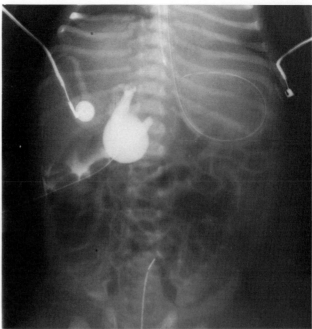

B

Figure 1.50

Choledochal cyst: (A) A large cyst in the porta hepatis was identified in this child with recurrent fever and right upper quadrant pain. (B) Operative cholangiogram demonstrated the cyst's relationship to the biliary radicles.

Figure 1.51

Granuloma: A dense calcification with shadowing served as stigmata of previous granulomatous infection with histoplasmosis.

In AIDS patients receiving aerosolized pentamidine for prophylaxis against *Pneumocystis carinii* pneumonia, extrapulmonary pneumocystis may develop. Blood levels of pentamidine may be insufficient to combat extrapulmonary infection, and sonographic evidence of infection may be identifiable. Initially multiple and hypoechoic, foci of *Pneumocystis carinii* infection in the liver may calcify, resulting in multiple, small calcified foci of abnormality.

Metastatic Disease (Figures 1.53–1.55) Metastatic involvement of the liver may have associated calcifications, especially in mucin-producing neoplasms such as colon, pancreas, and stomach primaries.

Sonographically, these lesions will be hyperechoic with shadowing if calcification is a predominant feature.

Parasitic Abscesses (Figure 1.56) Echinococcal abscesses may have calcified rims. Up to 50 percent of such lesions calcify. Multiloculated cystic masses with highly echogenic shadowing walls may be seen.

Posttraumatic Hematomas Rarely, patients with a history of substantial blunt trauma to the abdomen may have calcifications in a subcapsular hematoma or within the substance of the liver related to the distant trauma.

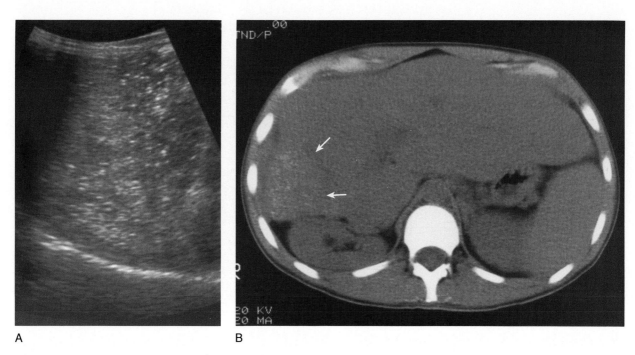

A   B

Figure 1.52

Candidiasis: (A) This immunocompromised patient developed calcifications in the liver secondary to treated candidiasis. (B) CT confirmed fine calcifications.

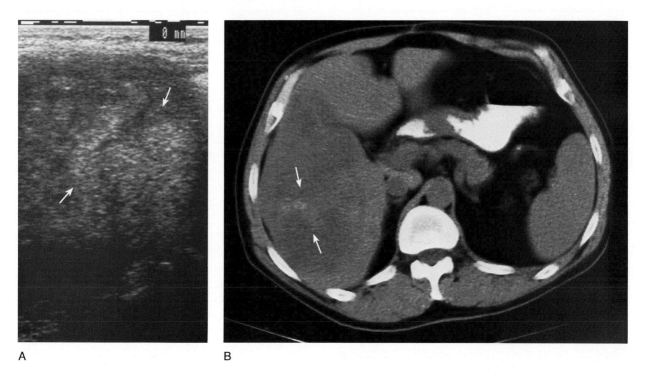

A   B

Figure 1.53

Calcified colon carcinoma metastases: (A) Highly echogenic foci within metastatic disease were present in this woman with colon carcinoma. (B) Unenhanced CT confirmed the extensive metastatic disease and the fine calcifications within the mass.

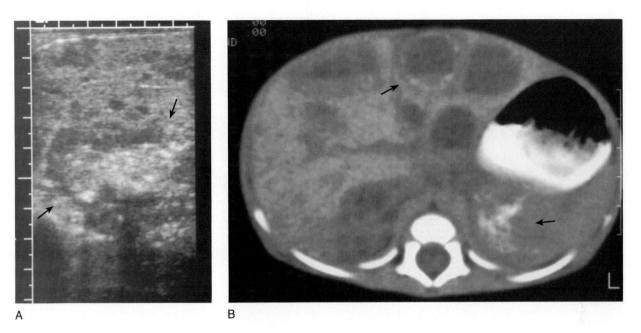

A   B

Figure 1.54
Metastatic neuroblastoma: (A) Calcified hepatic metastases were present in this newborn with congenital neuroblastoma. (B) CT of the same patient. Note the calcified primary tumor of the left adrenal.

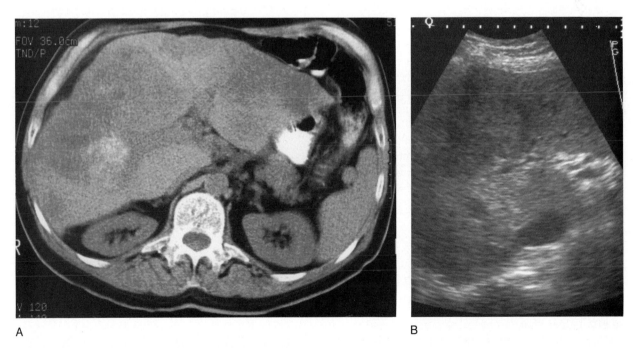

A   B

Figure 1.55
Metastatic colon carcinoma: (A) Calcifications within metastatic colon carcinoma deposits are present on unenhanced CT. (B) Same patient examined by sonography.

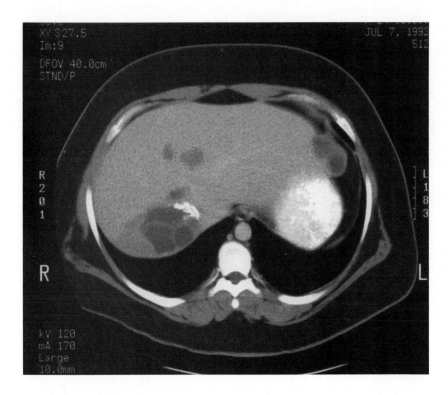

Figure 1.56
Echinococcal abscesses: CT showed rimlike calcifications in patient with parasitic abscess of liver.

Air-Filled Liver Masses

Abscess (Figures 1.57–1.58)   Hepatic abscess with gas-forming organisms may have highly echogenic foci with ringdown identifying the presence of air within the collection.

Postembolization Neoplasms (Figure 1.59)   Air can be identified in hepatic tumors after embolization procedures, not because air has been introduced but due, rather, to necrosis and infarction within the mass. Because patients suffer pain, fever, and leukocytosis after embolization procedures, the mass may be misinterpreted as an abscess. The presence of air within an embolized tumor may be expected and can persist for weeks after embolization.

VARIANT

Gallbladder Contracted Around Stones/ Porcelain Gallbladder (Figure 1.60)

A gallbladder that is chronically fibrotic and contracted around stones or diffusely calcified can be mistaken for a calcified intrahepatic mass. Knowledge of the location of the gallbladder fossa and relevant surgical history will allow the correct conclusions to be made. Correlative imaging with CT or plain films may be helpful.

Emphasis Point

If it is difficult sonographically to determine whether a mass has air or calcification within it, CT scanning is very helpful for differentiation.

TARGET (BULL'S-EYE) LESIONS IN THE LIVER OR SPLEEN

Metastatic Disease
Candidiasis
Atypical Hemangioma/Focal Nodular
    Hyperplasia

VARIANT

Fluid Around Fat in Falciform Ligament

A target lesion is the description given to a mass with a hypoechoic rim and echogenic center. Metastatic disease or infectious foci are the most common causes of target lesions.

Metastatic Disease (Figures 1.61–1.62)

Target lesions of the liver and spleen are most often secondary to metastatic disease from primaries such as melanoma or breast carcinoma. Other metastases can have the target lesion appearance.

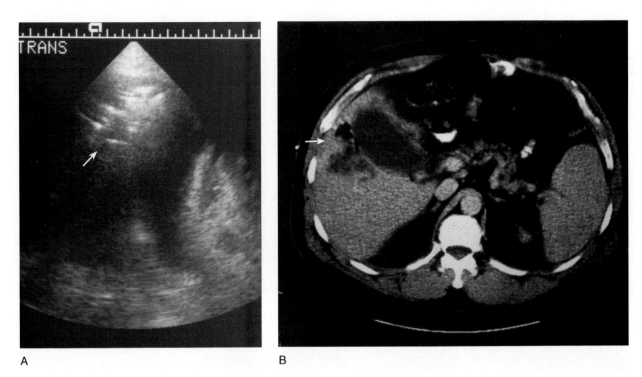

A   B

Figure 1.57

Liver abscess: (A) Perforation of the gallbladder resulted in
an abscess of the liver with air. Sonographically, the collection next to the fundus of the gallbladder was highly echogenic with ringdown artifact (*arrow*). (B) CT confirmed the
presence of air in the pericholecystic collection (*arrow*).

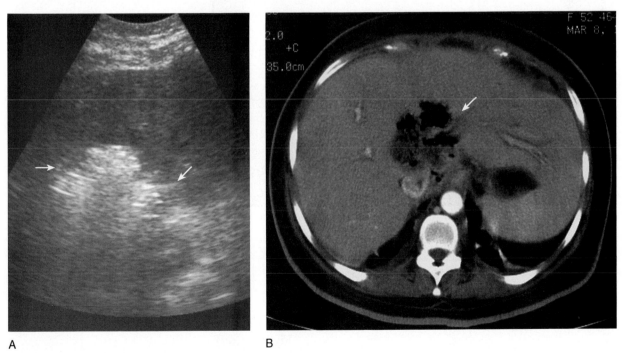

A   B

Figure 1.58

Abscess: (A) Highly echogenic mass in the liver caused
significant degradation posterior to it secondary to a large
quantity of air. (B) CT image confirmed the large air-containing collection.

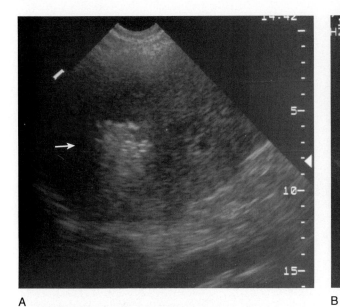

A

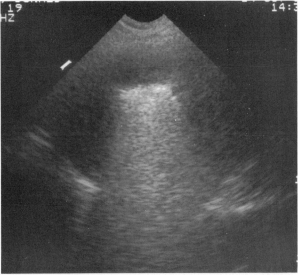

B

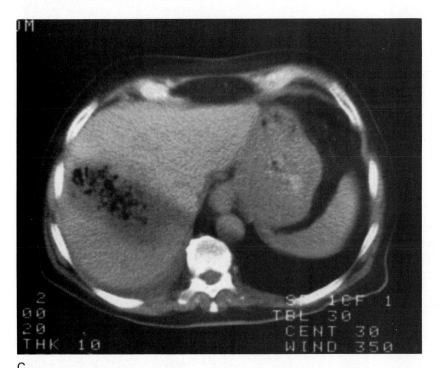

C

Figure 1.59
Embolized hepatocellular carcinoma: (A and B) A brightly echogenic mass with ringdown was seen in this patient after embolization for hepatocellular carcinoma. (C) CT showed the residual air-containing mass. The patient had no signs of infection.

Candidiasis (Figure 1.63)

The target appearance is not the only sonographic pattern for candidiasis, since hypoechoic lesions, hyperechoic lesions, and "wheel within a wheel" lesions may also be seen.

Hemangioma/Focal Nodular Hyperplasia

Focal benign masses of the liver, including hemangiomas and focal nodular hyperplasia, may result in the so-called target or bull's eye lesion. These masses will usually be solitary.

VARIANT

Fluid Around Fat in Falciform Ligament (Figure 1.64)

Fluid around the fat of the falciform ligament can in some cases have the appearance of a bull's-eye lesion. Recognition of ascites elsewhere in the abdomen may provide the tip necessary to make the diagnosis.

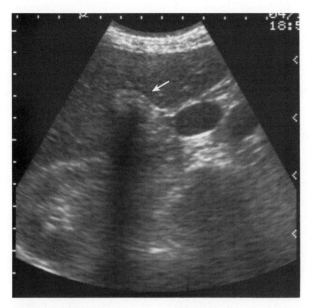

Figure 1.60
Contracted gallbladder: A gallbladder contracted around stones (*arrow*) mimicked a calcified liver lesion in this patient.

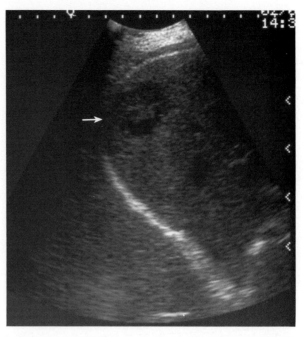

Figure 1.61
Metastatic melanoma: A 3 cm-target lesion developed in the right lobe of the liver in a patient with a distant history of malignant melanoma. Fine-needle aspiration confirmed metastatic melanoma at this site.

LESIONS IN LIVER *AND* SPLEEN

   Neoplastic Lesions
   Infectious Foci, Including Bacterial or Fungal
      Organisms
   Noninfectious, Nonneoplastic Causes

Focal lesions affecting *both* the liver and spleen generally occur in two major categories of disease: neoplastic or infectious.

Neoplastic Lesions (Figure 1.65)

Neoplastic lesions affecting both liver and the spleen are primarily carcinomas that metastasize via the systemic circulation, such as breast or lung primaries. This is in contrast to tumors that metastasize primarily via the portal circulation. Colon carcinoma usually affects the parenchyma of the liver and spleen only in the terminal stages of disease. Other neoplasms causing splenic and hepatic involvement are melanoma and lymphoproliferative disorders, such as lymphoma.

Infectious Foci, Including Bacterial or Fungal Organisms (Figure 1.66)

Infectious causes for lesions in the liver and spleen include subacute bacterial endocarditis, with showers

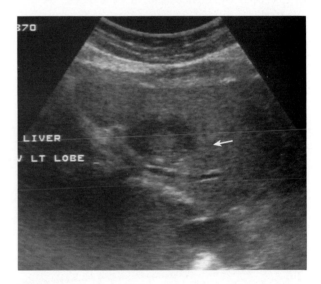

Figure 1.62
Metastatic breast carcinoma: A lesion with an echogenic center and hypoechoic rim was identified in the left lobe of the liver. Histology of the lesion matched the patient's previous breast primary.

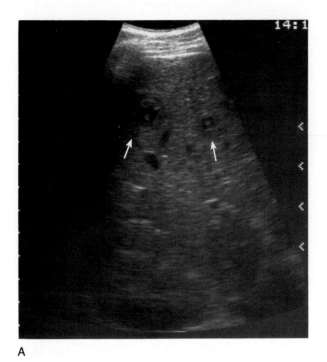

A

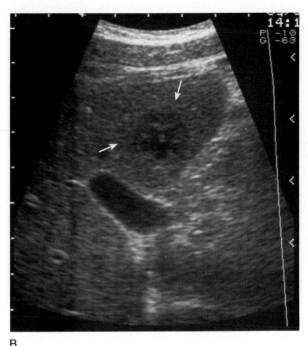

B

Figure 1.63

Candidiasis: (A) This immunocompromised 17-year-old developed disseminated candidiasis with target lesions in both the liver and spleen. With therapy the lesions gradually became less obvious and, in some cases, calcified. (B) Magnified view of one lesion.

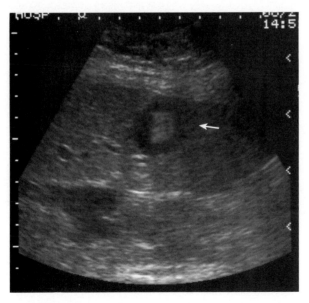

Figure 1.64

Fluid around the falciform ligament: This liver transplant recipient developed ascites that surrounded the fat in the falciform ligament, resulting in a bull's-eye or target lesion.

of septic emboli to both organs, and granulomatous conditions, such as tuberculosis or histoplasmosis or fungal organisms, usually in immunocompromised patients.

Noninfectious Nonneoplastic Causes

Noninfectious lesions may be present in both the liver and spleen in patients with conditions such as sarcoidosis.

Fine-needle aspiration and culture may be necessary to differentiate the various etiologic agents.

DIFFUSE ECHOTEXTURE ABNORMALITY OF THE LIVER

Hepatocellular Disease/Cirrhosis
Metastatic Disease/Hepatocellular Carcinoma
Posttraumatic Change
Fatty Change
Infiltrative, Nonneoplastic Lesions Involving
    the Liver
Vascular Insult (Arterial or Venous)

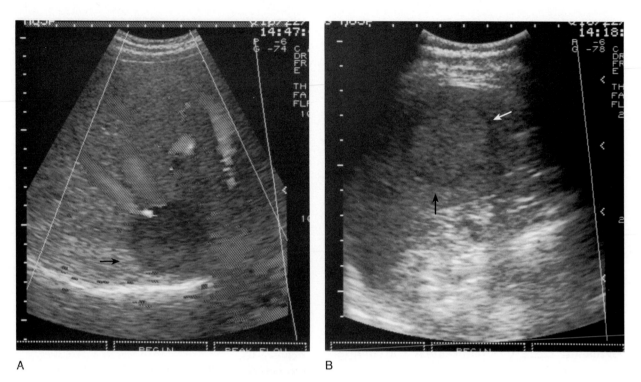

A   B

Figure 1.65
Metastatic melanoma: Lesions of both the liver and spleen were present in this patient with disseminated malignant melanoma (A). Note the lesion within the liver. (B) Note the splenic mass (*arrows*).

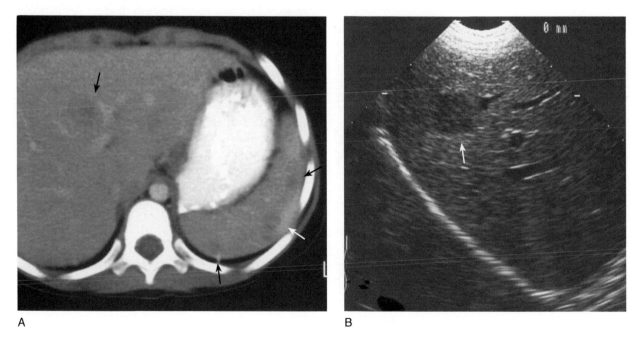

A   B

Figure 1.66
Cat scratch fever: (A) Focal hypoechoic lesions were present in both the liver and spleen in this child with cat scratch fever. (B) Hepatic lesions illustrated here.

Usually the healthy liver demonstrates a very homogeneous sonographic echotexture. In situations of generalized liver disease or diffuse infiltrative processes involving the liver, the sonographic echogenicity may be diffusely inhomogeneous and irregular.

Hepatocellular Disease/Cirrhosis (Figure 1.67)

In patients with severe hepatocellular disease and cirrhosis from whatever cause (e.g., alcohol abuse, chronic hepatitis, biliary cirrhosis) the sonographic echogenicity of the liver may be very irregular. A focal mass may not necessarily be identifiable, but the entire liver texture is heterogeneous. The echotexture abnormality reflects the distortion and irregularity at the histologic level with fibrosis and sinusoidal disease seen in the diseased cirrhotic liver.

Metastatic Disease/Hepatocellular Carcinoma (Figures 1.68–1.73)

Conditions that use the hepatic architecture as a scaffolding on which to infiltrate the liver may also cause a diffusely abnormal echotexture of the liver. Diffuse infiltration of the liver by metastatic disease, lymphoma, or hepatocellular carcinoma may result in a heterogeneous, diffusely abnormal echo-

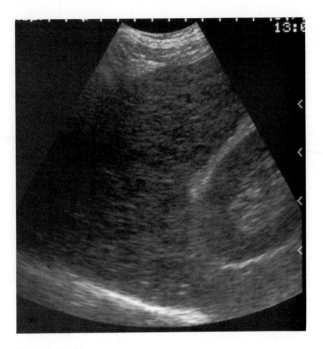

Figure 1.68

Cirrhosis/hepatocellular carcioma: This 54-year-old man with severe liver disease had markedly abnormal liver echogenicity and elevated alpha-fetoprotein. Biopsy of the right lobe yielded hepatocellular carcinoma although no discrete mass was seen.

genicity. In such cases, focal masses may be difficult to delineate but, by using higher-frequency transducers and magnification modes, clarification of whether the abnormal echogenicity is a reflection of many small masses in the liver can be made. A high level of suspicion is necessary to make the appropriate diagnosis.

Metastatic diseases that can diffusely infiltrate the liver include small cell lung carcinoma, melanoma, breast carcinoma, and carcinoid tumor.

In patients with cirrhosis and a preexisting irregular hepatic echogenicity, detection of hepatocellular carcinoma arising within the cirrhotic liver may be difficult sonographically. Both cirrhosis and multifocal or diffusely infiltrative hepatocellular carcinoma may give rise to an irregular, inhomogeneous sonographic echotexture. Correlative imaging with CT or MR may help distinguish a focal mass in the liver. Sudden clinical deterioration in a patient with known liver disease or marked elevation of serum alpha-fetoprotein levels may herald the development of hepatocellular carcinoma within a cirrhotic liver. New onset of portal vein thrombosis in the setting of a diffusely diseased liver may be secondary to bland thrombosis related to stasis and stagnation in the portal vein, but invasion of the portal vein by hepatocellular carcinoma must be re-

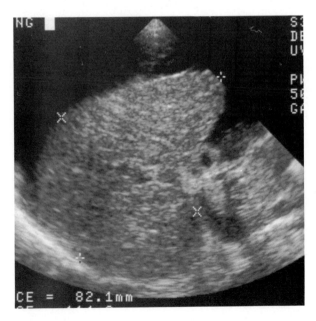

Figure 1.67

Cirrhosis: This 45-year-old woman with primary biliary cirrhosis being evaluated for orthotopic liver transplantation had a small, markedly irregular liver with abnormal echogenicity.

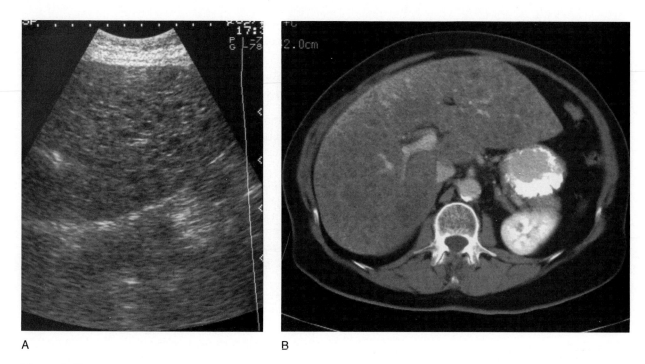

A   B

Figure 1.69
Diffuse metastatic melanoma: (A) Diffusely abnormal echogenicity in this patient was secondary to extensive metastatic disease. (B) CT confirms the subtle heterogeneity of liver texture.

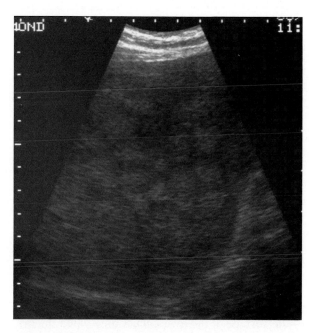

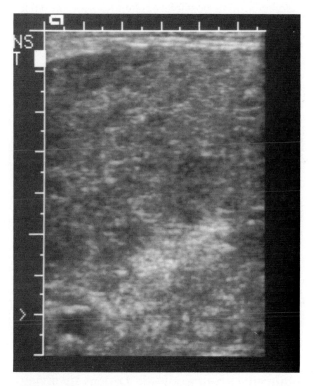

Figure 1.70
Metastatic lung carcinoma: Extensive metastatic involvement of the liver was identified in this patient with a markedly inhomogeneous liver texture.

Figure 1.71
Metastatic neuroblastoma: Extensive metastatic disease was present in this newborn with congenital neuroblastoma. Note the abnormal echogenicity of the right lobe of the liver.

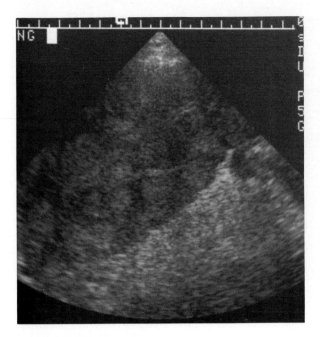

Figure 1.72
Metastatic breast carcinoma: Extensive echotexture abnormality was present in this woman with metastatic disease of the liver.

membered as a possible explanation for the sonographic findings of a diffusely abnormal liver echogenicity and portal vein thrombosis.

Posttraumatic Change (Figures 1.74–1.75)

Acute injury to the liver may result in a diffusely abnormal echogenicity seen sonographically. In some cases, severe injury to the liver may be difficult to assess with ultrasound. For this reason, in situations of acute trauma, CT scanning is usually the preferred method of screening for hepatic injury. Follow-up of patients with hepatic injury may be adequately done by using ultrasound to screen for fluid collections.

Fatty Change

Patients with irregular fatty change to the liver may have inhomogeneous echogenicity. Recognition of no mass effect on vessels and correlation with CT may confirm that no focal lesions are present.

Infiltrative, Nonneoplastic Lesions Involving the Liver

Infiltrative, nonneoplastic lesions may involve the liver and cause abnormal echotexture. Biopsy may be necessary to distinguish the etiology. Sarcoidosis

is an example of such a noninfectious, nonneoplastic condition.

Vascular Insult (Arterial or Venous) (Figure 1.76)

It is unusual for the liver to suffer significant vascular compromise, but in Budd–Chiari syndrome with hepatic vein thrombosis, the liver may become acutely inhomogeneous sonographically. Arterial infarction is usually limited to liver transplant patients with arterial thrombosis or patients receiving ligation or embolization of the hepatic artery secondary to uncontrolled hemorrhage. In such situations, the hepatic architecture may be sonographically irregular.

Emphasis Points

Diffuse metastatic disease of the liver may be so extensive and permeative as to make it difficult to recognize. Diffuse metastatic disease may not be correctly identified, being either overlooked or incorrectly diagnosed as biliary obstruction.

Recognition of a diffusely abnormal liver in a cirrhotic patient with portal vein thrombosis should raise the possibility of hepatocellular carcinoma.

CT or MR may be helpful in identifying discrete abnormalities when the liver echogenicity is diffusely abnormal.

LESIONS THAT SCALLOP THE LIVER

Subcapsular Hematoma
Subphrenic Abscess
Implants of Tumor
    Ovarian Carcinoma and Other Causes of
        Carcinomatosis
    Pseudomyxoma Peritonei

The recognition of a concave border of the surface of the liver suggests that material is either within the subcapsular space of the liver or outside the liver compressing its solid substance. Deformity of the surface of the liver occurs only when the material is under pressure because of loculation or other causes of high pressure. Free abdominal fluid will not deform the contour of the liver, but will instead surround the liver.

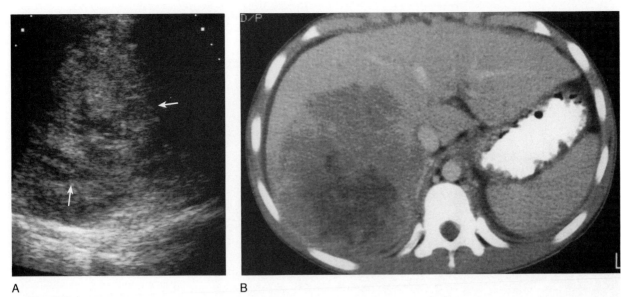

A   B

Figure 1.73
Hepatocellular carcinoma: (A) This 15-year-old with chronic active hepatitis presented with acute deterioration of liver function. Sonography showed a heterogeneously echogenic right lobe of the liver and obliteration of the right hepatic vein. No discrete mass was visualized. (B) CT showed a large low-density mass in the right lobe of the liver with portal vein invasion and numerous pulmonary metastases. Hepatocellular carcinoma was present at autopsy.

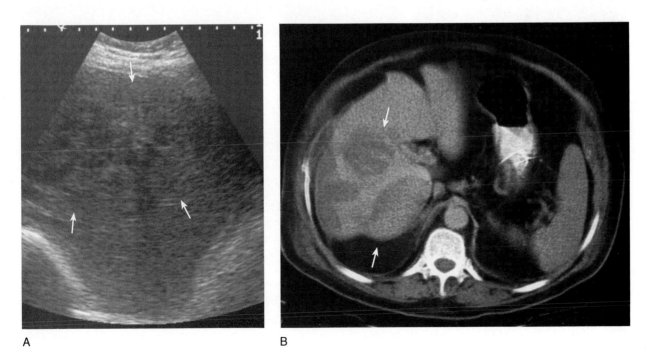

A   B

Figure 1.74
Posttraumatic liver: (A) Markedly heterogeneous liver echogenicity (*arrows*) was present in this patient after 24 attempts to enter his nondilated biliary tree percutaneously. (B) On subsequent scans, large hematomas had developed (*arrows*).

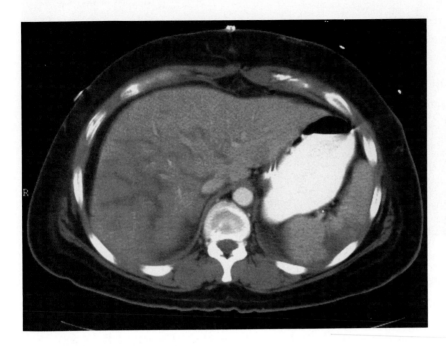

Figure 1.75
Posttraumatic liver: CT images of liver lacerations after an automobile accident demonstrated the advantage of using CT in acute hepatic injury. Sonographic images showed subtle echogenicity disturbance that could have been overlooked.

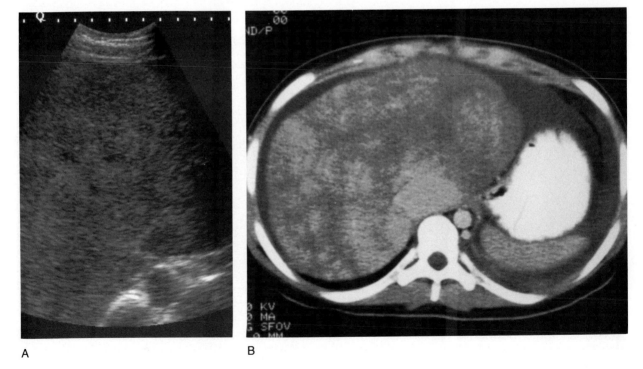

A   B

Figure 1.76
Budd–Chiari syndrome: (A) Diffuse hepatic enlargement and heterogeneity of echogenicity were present in this patient with acute hepatic vein thrombosis secondary to hypercoaguability related to oral contraceptives. (B) Correlation CT images showed patchy contrast enhancement.

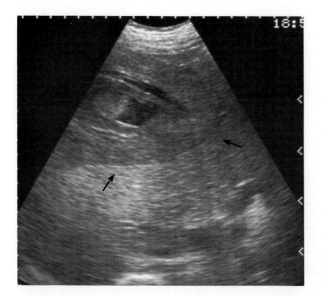

Figure 1.77
Subcapsular hematoma: This 38-year-old woman suffered spontaneous rupture of the liver during pregnancy. Note the extensive heterogeneous hematoma, causing significant mass effect upon the surface of the right lobe of the liver (*arrows*). Hepatic rupture was managed surgically.

Subcapsular Hematoma (Figures 1.77–1.79)

Subcapsular hematoma of the liver may occur after trauma, in patients on anticoagulation, and in patients with hepatic abnormalities predisposing to hemorrhage. Patients with hepatic adenomas, hepatocellular carcinoma, and diffuse hepatic abnormalities such as the HELLP syndrome in pregnant patients may have hepatic rupture with the development of subcapsular hematoma. Often the etiology of a subcapsular hematoma of the liver is obvious.

Acute subcapsular hematoma of the liver deforms the hepatic surface and appears sonographically solid with a heterogeneous echogenicity. Over time, cystic evolution of a subcapsular hematoma occurs. The hematoma retracts in size and becomes more cystic in appearance, often with multiple septations.

Subphrenic Abscess (Figures 1.80–1.82)

Loculated fluid collections such as a postoperative subphrenic abscess may deform the surface of the liver. Low-level echoes, debris, and even air may be identified sonographically. Abscesses in the subdiaphragmatic spaces may be amenable to percutaneous decompression.

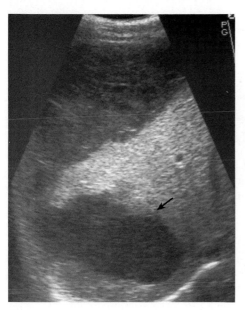

A

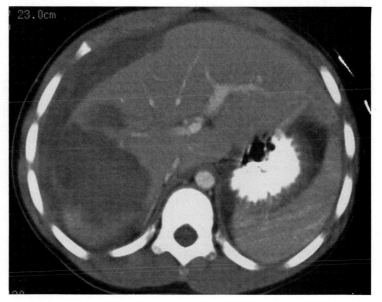

B

Figure 1.78
Subcapsular hematoma: (A) This 8-year-old girl suffered a liver laceration after a fall from a trampoline. Notice the intrahepatic hematoma (*arrow*), which extends into the subcapsular space, scalloping the liver edge. (B) Correlative CT images.

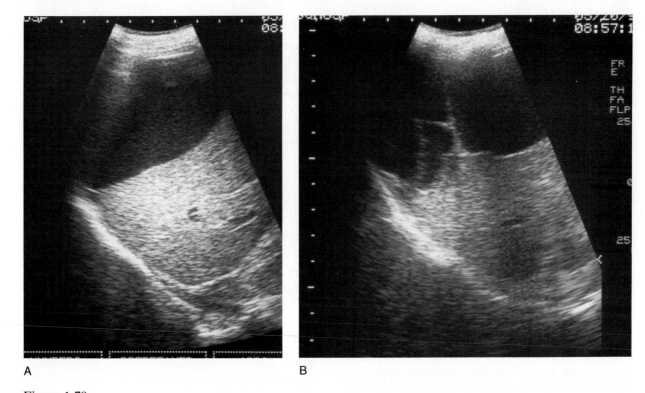

A   B

Figure 1.79

Subacute subcapsular hematoma: (A and B) This young woman had experienced a major fall several weeks prior to this examination and complained of right shoulder pain. The septated cystic lesion indenting the edge of the liver was aspirated and was found to be old blood, consistent with a resolving subcapsular hematoma.

Implants of Tumor

Ovarian Carcinoma and Other Causes of Carcinomatosis (Figure 1.83)   Implants of a tumor on the surface of the liver can result in deformity of the liver's normal contour. The prototypical neoplasm that implants on the liver is ovarian epithelial tumor, although any neoplasm resulting in abdominal carcinomatosis may grow in this manner.

Pseudomyxoma Peritonei (Figure 1.84)   Patients with pseudomyxoma peritonei have gelatinous material filling the abdomen, usually after rupture of a low-grade mucinous malignancy of either the ovary or appendix. This gelatinous material can deform the liver, causing concavity of its surface.

Emphasis Points

Lesions which scallop the liver need to be differentiated from intraparenchymal hepatic lesions. The border between the mass and the liver can be used to determine whether the mass is inside or outside the liver.

Recognition of scalloping of the outer contour of the liver allows a fairly short differential possibility list to be employed. Generally, the etiologic agent can be determined.

BILIARY DUCTAL DILATATION

Intrahepatic Dilatation: Focal Dilatation Only

Focal Liver Lesion
Benign Stricture of Bile Ducts
Cholangiocarcinoma

To recognize focal intrahepatic biliary dilatation requires a thorough, careful examination of the entire liver. The biliary radicles run through the substance of the liver accompanying portal vein branches. Nondilated intrahepatic biliary ducts measure less than 2 mm. The presence of ducts 2 mm or greater is consistent with biliary dilatation. Once biliary dilatation is recognized, the point of obstruction should be determined and the possible etiology elucidated. Recent studies have demonstrated ultrasound to be quite accurate in locating the level of obstruction and cause of biliary dilatation. Cer-

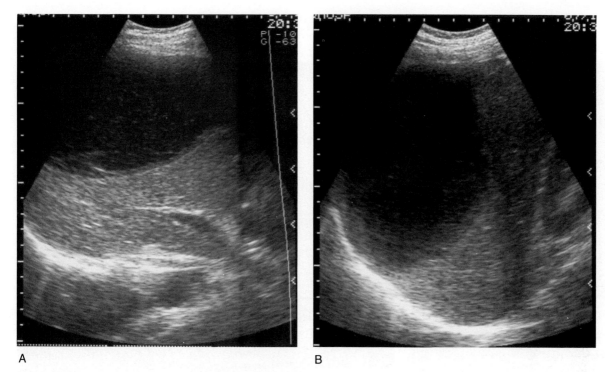

A

B

Figure 1.80

Subphrenic abscess: (A and B) This 62-year-old man, 10 days after gastrectomy for lymphoma, developed a tense collection in the right upper quadrant. Percutaneous drainage of the collection yielded grossly purulent material. Note how the collection scallops the liver edge.

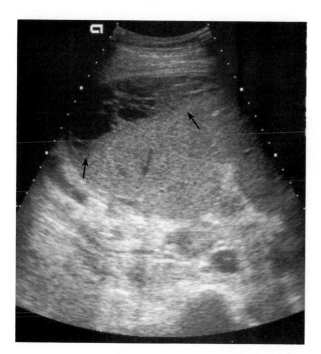

Figure 1.81

Subphrenic abscess: This elderly patient developed a loculated subphrenic collection indenting the liver (*arrows*) several days after colonic perforation related to diverticulitis. Note the multiple septations within the collections.

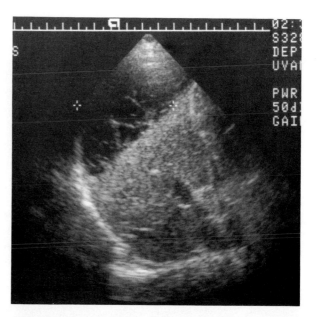

Figure 1.82

Subphrenic CSF collection: A septated collection of cerebrospinal fluid around the tip of the shunt developed in a young patient with meningomyelocele and shunt failure.

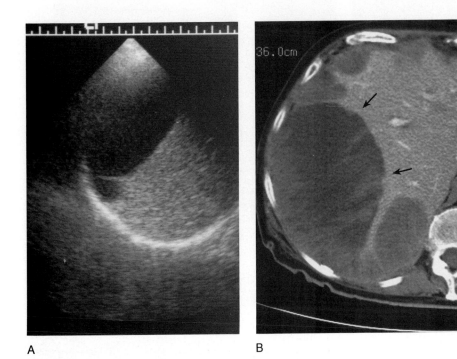

A   B

Figure 1.83

Tumor implant: (A) Scalloping cystic collections adjacent
to the liver heralded the return of metastatic disease in
this woman with ovarian carcinomatosis. Aspiration of
the collection yielded abundant malignant cells. (B) CT of
different patient with malignant implants scalloping the
liver surface.

tainly the quality of machine used, the technique for
scanning, and the experience of the operator influence the accuracy of the ultrasound evaluation.
Several current studies have shown ultrasound to
be accurate more than 90 percent of the time in determining the level of obstruction and less accurate
in determining the cause of obstruction.

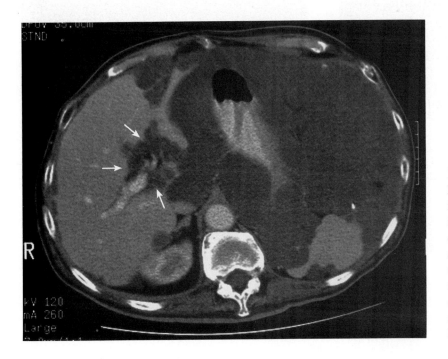

Figure 1.84

Pseudomyxoma peritonei: The gelatinous material that fills the abdomen
in pseudomyxoma peritonei indented the liver in the porta hepatis
and around the falciform ligament in
this patient with history of a mucocele of the appendix that ruptured at
surgery. Ultrasound showed cystic
and solid areas, with septations and
low level echoes.

Focal Liver Lesion (Figures 1.85–1.86) Focal intrahepatic biliary ductal dilatation without extrahepatic dilatation may be secondary to disease processes of the hepatic parenchyma that impinge on the biliary tree or processes intrinsic to the biliary tree itself. Conditions of the hepatocytes that obstruct the biliary tree, with focal dilatation of the more proximal biliary tree, include cirrhosis, hepatocellular carcinoma, and metastatic disease.

Cirrhosis from whatever cause distorts the normal hepatic architecture by the development of fibrosis within the sinusoidal bed. Such fibrosis and architectural distortion can result in proximal biliary dilatation related to biliary obstruction. Infiltrative hepatocellular carcinoma and metastatic disease in the liver can cause focal biliary dilatation as well. Focal masses or echotexture abnormality of the liver adjacent to focal biliary dilatation may be secondary to neoplastic involvement of the liver. Focal masses in the liver, such as a liver cyst or focal liver metastases, can obstruct a discrete bile ductule.

Benign Stricture of Bile Ducts (Figure 1.87) If there is a focally dilated segment of the biliary tree and no hepatic mass or stone is identified, stricture of the biliary tree, of either a benign or malignant etiology, may be responsible. Sonographically, it is usually difficult to distinguish the two. Benign, inflammatory stricture related to either sclerosing

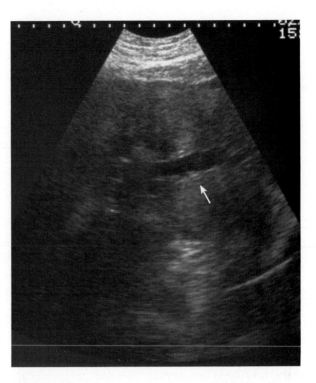

Figure 1.86
Metastatic disease of the liver: Focally dilated ducts (*arrows*) were secondary to metastatic involvement by lung carcinoma.

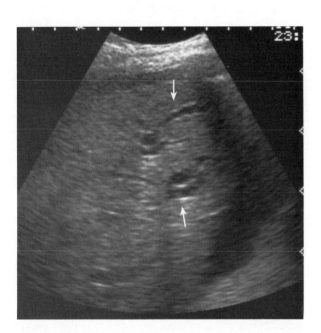

Figure 1.85
Hepatocellular carcinoma: Focally dilated ducts (*arrows*) were isolated to one lobe of the liver in this patient with extensive hepatocellular carcinoma.

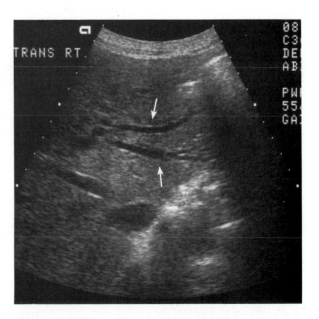

Figure 1.87
Sclerosing cholangitis: Focally dilated tubular biliary radicals were seen in this patient, who required constant biliary stenting.

cholangitis or previous surgery can cause focal biliary dilatation. A history of bile duct injury at the time of previous surgery would explain focal biliary dilatation.

Cholangiocarcinoma (Figure 1.88)   Without a history of previous surgery resulting in bile duct stricture and with sonographic findings of focal biliary dilatation, especially in the left lobe, cholangiocarcinoma arising within the bile ducts must be considered and is often the leading diagnostic consideration.

Cholangiocarcinoma arises from the epithelial cells of the biliary tree. Approximately one-half of cholangiocarcinomas arise at the bifurcation of the biliary ducts where they join to form the common hepatic duct. Ductal dilatation within both lobes of the liver or dilatation of the radicles in only one lobe may result, depending upon the growth pattern of the tumor. A tumor at the confluence of ducts is known as a Klatskin tumor. This tumor is infiltrative, and often no obvious lesion is seen on imaging, only the dilated intrahepatic radicles and the abrupt transition to a decompressed extrahepatic biliary tree. A polypoid tumor within the ducts is uncommon. Diagnosis of cholangiocarcinoma is supported by a cholangiographic contrast study of a malignant-appearing stricture of the biliary tree. Stenting and establishment of adequate drainage can relieve biliary obstruction and prevent sepsis. Biopsy of the stricture often yields the diagnosis of cholangiocarcinoma. In some cases, surgical bypass of the tumor is helpful.

Emphasis Point

It is unusual to be able to image a mass when cholangiocarcinoma is present. Recognition of localized biliary ductal dilatation without a stone, hepatic abnormality, or previous operative injury should suggest the diagnosis of cholangiocarcinoma. The cholangiocarcinoma may not be seen sonographically, but its strategic location leads to biliary dilatation, and its presence can be predicted.

Obstruction at the Hilum of the Liver

Cholangiocarcinoma
Inflammatory/Postoperative Stricture
Stones
Gallbladder Carcinoma/Portal Adenopathy
Mirizzi Syndrome
Parasites

Cholangiocarcinoma (Figure 1.89)   Cholangiocarcinoma at the confluence of ducts, called a Klatskin tumor, can cause intrahepatic biliary dilatation affecting both lobes, usually without an obvious mass. The extrahepatic biliary system usually is not dilated. In a patient with no previous history of surgery in the right upper quadrant, who has no gallstones and has dilated ducts in both hepatic lobes with a decompressed extrahepatic biliary tree, cholangiocarcinoma is likely.

Inflammatory/Postoperative Stricture (Figure 1.90–1.91)   Inflammatory stricture related to operative injury or cholangitis gives a sonographic image identical to that of cholangiocarcinoma. Stones or sludge may develop behind the obstructing stricture. Careful assessment of clinical history, with attention to episodes of cholangitis and periods of upper abdominal pain, fever, and jaundice, or known injury to the biliary tree, will be helpful in distinguishing the suspected benign stricture from the malignant one. Dilatation of the intrahepatic biliary ducts without extrahepatic biliary dilatation is the pattern seen in patients who suffer common bile duct injury at the time of laparoscopic cholecystectomy.

Stones   Common duct stones usually move into the distal duct unless they are too large or there is a stricture of the duct that prevents their egress into the distal duct. If multiple stones are present in the duct, the stones will pile up, filling the duct. Sonographically, the highest or more proximal stones may be the only ones seen. Stones lodged in the duct at the hilum of the liver are generally easy to see, since the acoustic window provided by the right lobe of the liver facilitates their visualization. Patients with previous surgery and resultant choledochoenterostomy may develop strictures just beyond the hilum of the liver that are related to fibrotic postsurgical stricture or recurrent tumor. Stones and sludge sometimes develop proximal to the obstruction.

Gallbladder Carcinoma/Portal Adenopathy (Figures 1.92–1.93)   Malignancies such as gallbladder carcinoma or metastatic adenopathy in the porta hepatis may obstruct the biliary tree at the hepatic hilum, resulting in dilatation of the biliary tree in both lobes of the liver and a decompressed extrahepatic biliary tree.

Mirizzi Syndrome (Figure 1.94)   Extrinsic compression of the common hepatic duct by a stone impacted in either the gallbladder neck or cystic duct can cause ductal dilatation of both lobes of the liver

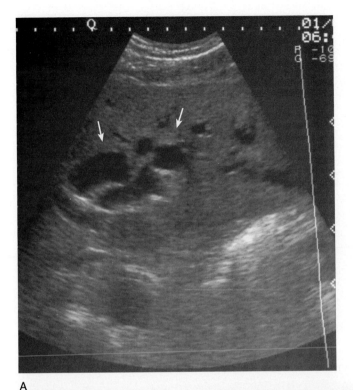

A

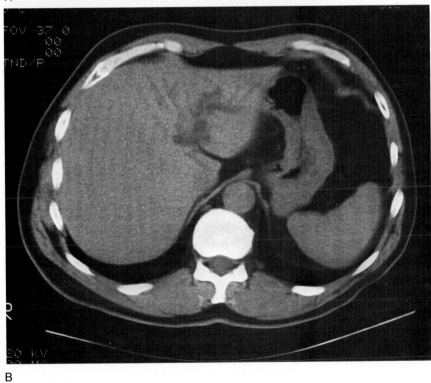

B

Figure 1.88
Cholangiocarcinoma: (A) Ductal dilatation (*arrows*) in the left lobe of the liver without dilated ducts in the right was present in this patient, who had no history of surgery and no gallstones on examination. (B) CT confirmed the ultrasound findings. Cholangiocarcinoma was confirmed after stenting by washings of the biliary tree.

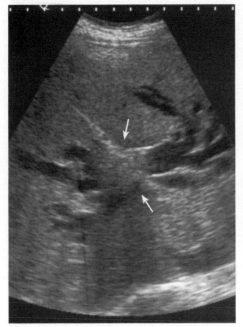
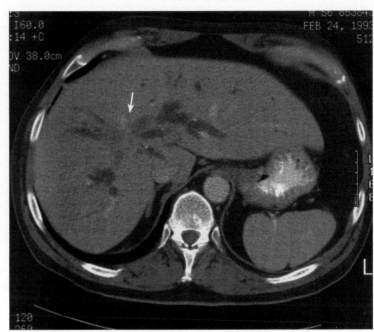

A   B

Figure 1.89

Cholangiocarcinoma (Klatskin tumor): (A) In this 60-year-old man with jaundice, moderately dilated biliary radicles were demonstrated in both lobes of the liver. An echogenic area (*arrows*) was identified at the level of obstruction in the hilum of the liver. Cholangiocarcinoma was suspected. (B) CT confirmed the obstructing, ill-defined density (*arrow*) in the hilum of the liver. The obstructing malignancy was treated with wallstents to relieve the biliary obstruction.

and a decompressed distal duct. Such extrinsic compression of the biliary tree with associated proximal ductal dilatation is known as the Mirizzi syndrome. The Mirizzi syndrome is a complication of chronic cholelithiasis, resulting in an inflammatory stricture caused by pressure from a stone and obstructive jaundice. This condition is sometimes difficult to recognize preoperatively, although it is important to recognize in order to avoid operative mishap to the ductal system.

Parasites   Clonorchiasis is caused by an infestation of adult liver flukes, which live in both small and medium intrahepatic bile ducts. This parasitic disease, acquired by the ingestion of raw freshwater fish, is prevalent in the Far East but has been seen with increasing frequency in the West.

Sonographically, patients with clonorchiasis have diffuse dilatation of the small intrahepatic ducts. The extrahepatic biliary tree may be unaf-

fected or only mildly dilated. Nonshadowing echogenic material within the ducts, representing aggregates of the worms, may be seen. Although the small and medium intrahepatic biliary ducts are the normal habitat for clonorchiasis and cholangitis develops secondary to the worms' presence, evidence of the worms may sometimes be identified in the gallbladder and extrahepatic biliary tree. There is an increased incidence of cholangiocarcinoma in patients with *Clonorchis* infestation.

Emphasis Points

Recognition that the level of obstruction of the biliary tree is at the hilum of the liver is important to derive the appropriate differential possibilities but is even more important to dictate subsequent therapy. Patients with obstruction of both lobes of the liver and decompressed extrahepatic biliary tree may need drainage tubes through the liver to obtain adequate decompression and prevent sepsis. Endo-

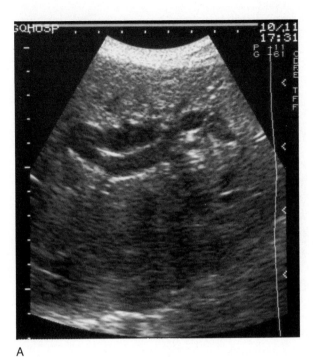

A

Figure 1.90

Postoperative stricture: (A) During laparoscopic cholecystectomy, an injury to the common duct occurred. Follow-up imaging showed ductal dilatation in both lobes of
the liver. (B) ERCP showed the distal common duct to
be normal, with obstruction at the hilum of the liver (*arrow*). (C) Transhepatic cholangiography demonstrated intrahepatic dilatation and ductal occlusion at the hilum of
the liver.

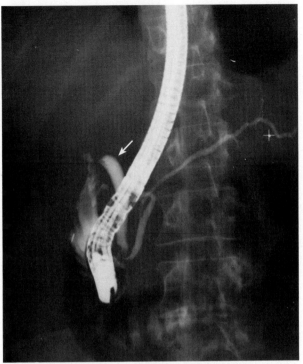

B

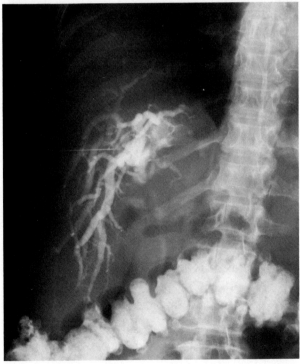

C

scopic retrograde pancreatography (ERCP),
cholecystostomy, or only one drainage tube
may be inadequate for satisfactory drainage
secondary to the site of obstruction.

The patient with a hilar cholangiocarcinoma
may present with fairly dramatic ductal dilatation without an obvious mass. The cholangiocarcinoma is strategically located, leading
to biliary dilatation even when a mass cannot
be seen. The inability to visualize the obstructing mass either sonographically or at
CT should not dissuade one from suggesting
the correct diagnosis of cholangiocarcinoma.
In only about 10 percent of cases is an intrahepatic cholangiocarcinoma recognized as a
mass in the liver.

It may be difficult to prove the diagnosis of
cholangiocarcinoma; multiple washings and
attempts to aspirate the area may be required
to get cytologic confirmation.

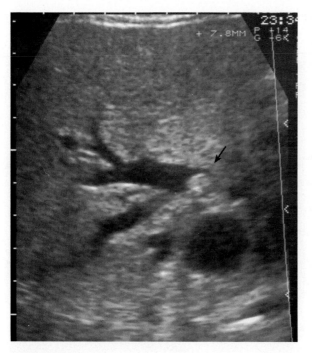

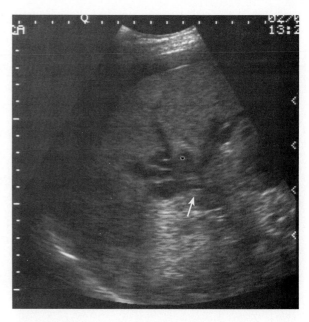

Figure 1.91
Postoperative stricture: This elderly man developed jaundice after resection of a cholangiocarcinoma of the distal common duct with formation of a choledochoenterostomy. Biliary dilatation was present with sludge proximal to the level of obstruction (*arrow*). Fibrosis, not recurrent tumor, was discovered at surgery for anastomosis reconstruction.

Figure 1.92
Portal adenopathy: This young man with disseminated rhabdomyosarcoma presented with biliary obstruction (*arrow*) secondary to portal adenopathy. The distal duct was not dilated.

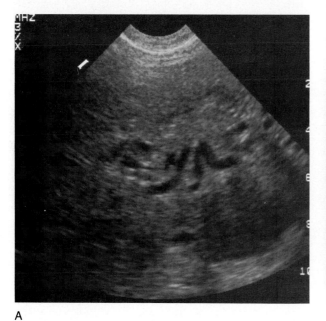

A

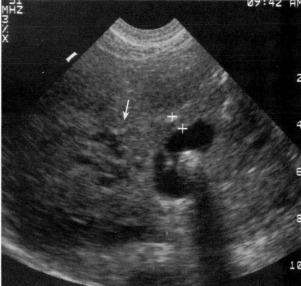

B

Figure 1.93
Gallbladder carcinoma: (A and B) Dilated ducts (*arrow*) in both lobes of the liver were caused by an obliterative mass filling the gallbladder lumen and growing into the liver. Note gallstones within the very thick-walled gallbladder. Bilateral transhepatic drainage tubes were necessary for decompression.

50

Figure 1.94

Mirizzi syndrome: (A) In this elderly patient with jaundice, a dilated biliary tree could be followed to the level of the gallbladder neck. A stone was impacted in the neck of the gallbladder (*arrow*). Mirizzi syndrome may be difficult to distinguish from cholangio-carcinoma preoperatively. (B) Cholangiographic study showed extrinsic narrowing of the biliary tree at the hilum of the liver (*arrows*).

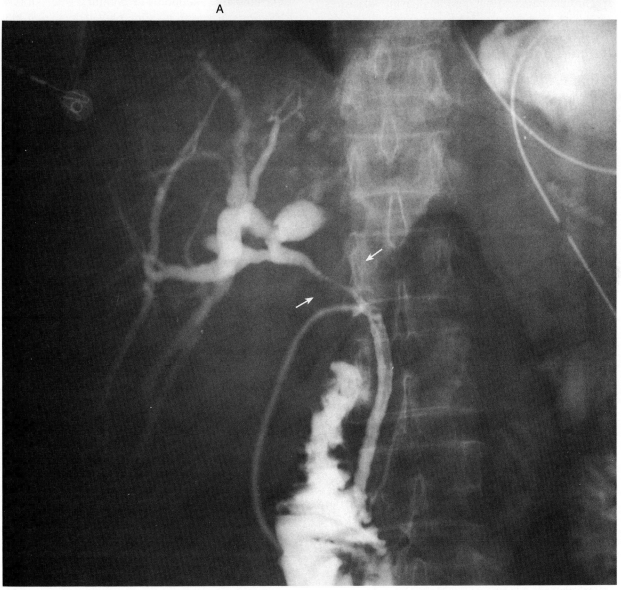

A

B

Distal Common Bile Duct Obstruction

Common Duct Stone
Benign Stricture
AIDS Cholangitis
Malignant Obstruction
Granular Cell Tumor

CHILDHOOD

Choledochocele

Dilatation of the intra- and extrahepatic biliary tree down to the level of the distal common bile duct may have a variety of causes, including distal common duct stone, benign strictures related to acute or chronic pancreatitis, and malignant strictures secondary to pancreatic carcinomas, ampullary carcinomas, or cholangiocarcinomas. Recognition that biliary dilatation extends to the distal common duct has diagnostic and therapeutic implications.

Common Duct Stone (Figure 1.95) Distal common duct stones may cause intra- and extrahepatic biliary dilatation but may be difficult to visualize secondary to the presence of gas in the nearby duodenum. Stones located near the hilum of the liver are easier to demonstrate sonographically, since the liver can be used as an acoustic window. Common duct stones are less frequently located at the liver's hilum and are more often in the distal duct. Positioning the patient in the supine left posterior oblique position as well as the erect and right posterior oblique position will facilitate recognition of the entire duct. Operator patience during the examination is imperative to demonstrate choledocholithiasis. Ductal dilatation makes recognition of common duct stones easier, although stones may be identified in nondilated systems. Common duct stones do not necessarily shadow, especially if they are within the substance of the pancreas or are small. Higher-frequency transducers (5–7 mHz) may allow stone shadowing to be recognized. Correlation with laboratory values can help the operator determine the likelihood of common duct stones. Elevations of serum alkaline phosphatase and bilirubin may be present in situations of biliary obstruction. Functional nuclear medicine biliary studies that show no excretion from the liver suggest common duct obstruction.

Benign Stricture (Figures 1.96–1.97) Benign narrowings of the distal common duct may be present in acute or chronic pancreatitis. The distal common duct travels through the pancreas on its way to the ampulla, and processes causing inflammation and edema or fibrosis of the pancreas may narrow

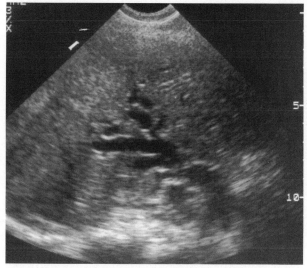

A

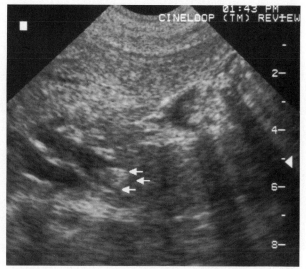

B

Figure 1.95

Choledocholithiasis—distal common duct: (A and B) Intra- and extrahepatic biliary ductal dilatation were obvious in this patient with a stone in the distal duct (*arrows*). The stone was successfully extracted by ERCP. Additional stones were present in the gallbladder.

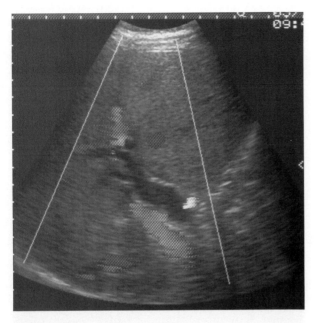

Figure 1.96

Common duct dilatation secondary to severe hemorrhagic pancreatitis: The dilated extrahepatic common duct was dilated in the porta hepatis. The portal vein is posteriorly located and the hepatic artery anterior. The patient had severe acute pancreatitis secondary to alcohol abuse.

the distal common duct. In such situations, intra- and extrahepatic biliary ductal dilatation will be present and can be followed down to the distal duct, where an abrupt caliber change will be recognized. Frequently, abnormalities in the pancreas can be recognized, allowing the etiology of common bile duct obstruction to be distinguished. Decreased echogenicity of the pancreatic tissue and pancreatic swelling are frequently seen with acute pancreatitis. Peripancreatic fluid in the lesser sac and left anterior pararenal spaces may also be noted. Changes in the pancreas suggesting chronic disease may include pancreatic calcifications, pancreatic duct dilatation, tortuosity, and pseudocysts. Sometimes focal pancreatitis cannot be distinguished from pancreatic neoplasm by imaging.

AIDS Cholangitis The biliary tree is frequently affected in AIDS patients with cytomegalovirus, cryptosporidium, and HIV itself. Multiple organisms may be detected in some patients. Dilatation of the intra- and extrahepatic biliary tree in a pattern of papillary stenosis with an echogenic nodule at the distal duct may be seen. Multiple levels of stricturing and biliary system wall thickening may

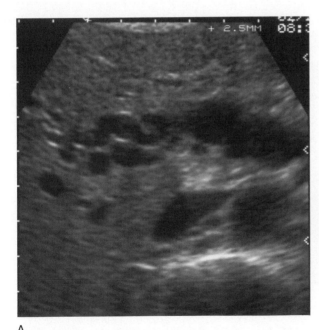

A

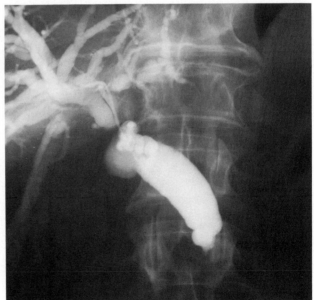

B

Figure 1.97

Stricture from chronic pancreatitis: (A) A tortuous, dilated biliary tree was obvious in this patient with presumed malignant obstruction of the distal duct. Surgery was performed to bypass the distal obstruction. (B) Cholangiographic study from the same patient showed high-grade obstruction at the level of the pancreas. At surgery, no malignancy was found.

also be identified. This entity needs to be differentiated from sclerosing cholangitis. An echogenic nodule is identifiable at the distal end of the common duct in two-thirds of patients with AIDS cholangitis. This nodule is an edematous papilla of Vater, often secondary to infection.

Malignant Obstruction (Figures 1.98–1.99)

Carcinoma of the pancreas is increasing in incidence and is a cause of distal common bile duct obstruction. A focal hypoechoic mass in the pancreas with atrophy of the pancreatic body and tail may be demonstrated sonographically in patients with pancreatic carcinoma. Carcinoma of the ampulla or duodenum may be difficult to differentiate sonographically from pancreatic carcinoma.

Recognition of the level of biliary ductal dilatation by ultrasound is useful not only to generate a differential diagnosis of the causes of biliary dilatation at that level, but to prescribe the appropriate therapeutic intervention based on the level of biliary obstruction. For distal duct obstruction either by stone or neoplasia, endoscopic visualization (ERCP) with papillotomy and stone extraction or biopsy and stent placement are possible. Percutaneous transhepatic cholangiography (PTC) with

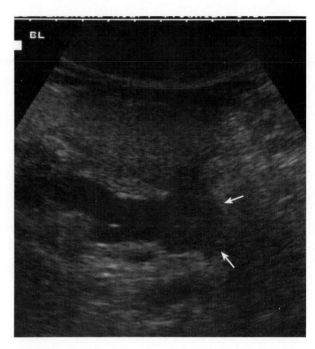

Figure 1.98
Pancreatic carcinoma: A focal hypoechoic mass (*arrows*) in the pancreatic head caused obstruction of the biliary tree. Metastatic disease of the liver was demonstrated as well.

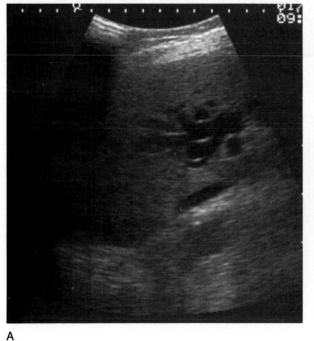

A

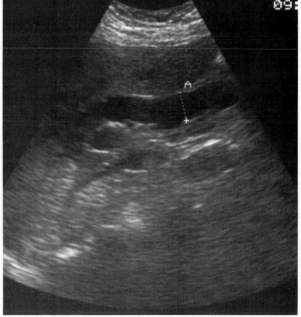

B

Figure 1.99
Cholangiocarcinoma: (A and B) Intra- and extrahepatic biliary ductal dilatation were present down to the distal duct. A cholangiocarcinoma of the distal duct was biopsied at ERCP.

stenting is more often efficacious in proximal ductal obstruction. If there is ductal dilatation involving both lobes of the liver, as in the case of a Klatskin tumor, percutaneous drainage tubes may be necessary in both lobes to decompress both systems satisfactorily. ERCP in the setting of a Klatskin tumor is often unsuccessful in obtaining adequate decompression of the dilated, obstructed biliary tree.

Granular Cell Tumor   Granular cell tumor is a rare, benign, polypoid tumor of the biliary tree that occurs most often in young black women and can cause intra- and extrahepatic biliary dilatation.

CHILDHOOD

Choledochocele (Figure 1.100)   One form of congenital biliary abnormality is extrahepatic biliary dilatation down to the head of the pancreas. Dilatation of the common duct into the intramural portion of the duodenum is seen. Surgical repair is often necessary.

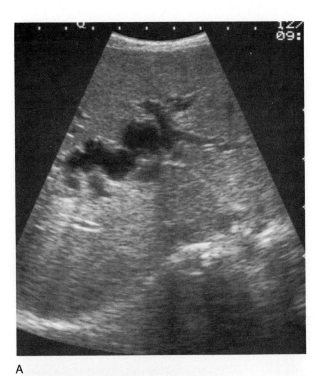

A

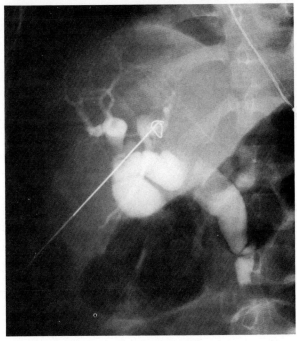

B

Figure 1.100
Choledochocele: (A and B) Dilatation of the intra- and extrahepatic biliary tree was seen by ultrasound and cholangiogram in this young child.

Emphasis Points

In patients with jaundice, the first question for the sonographer is whether or not there is biliary dilatation. Once biliary dilatation is recognized, the level of dilatation as determined by a caliber change in the biliary tree and the etiology for biliary dilatation should be investigated. A careful examination is required.

Recognition of the level of obstruction—distal duct versus hilum of the liver—not only will help determine the different etiologic agents, but will determine the next appropriate therapeutic intervention. Distal obstruction will be most often evaluated and treated by ERCP, where sphincterotomy, extraction of distal duct stones, and stenting can take place. Proximal obstruction at the hilum of the liver can be relieved via percutaneous tube placement through the liver.

Obstruction of the biliary system *without* dilatation is thought to occur in approximately 15 to 20 percent of patients. Dilatation may not be seen early in obstruction, with partially obstructing stones or lesions, and in patients with severe liver disease. In patients with cirrhosis, the ducts may not be able to dilate, despite being obstructed, because the liver is firm and fibrotic.

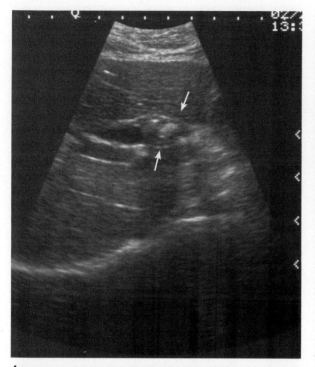

A

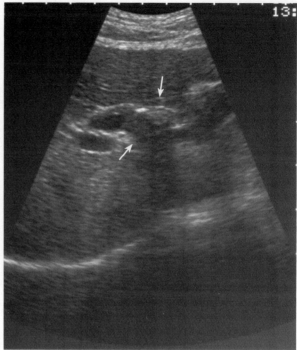

B

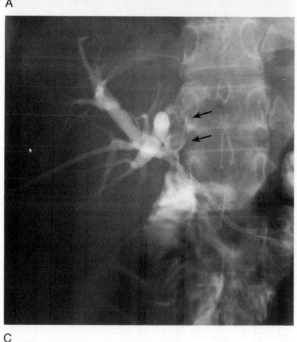

C

Figure 1.101
Stones in common bile duct: (A, B, C) Years after chole-dochoenterostomy, this patient had developed stones (*arrows*) in the common duct proximal to the surgical anastomosis, which was strictured. Transhepatic tube placement with stone extraction and stricture dilatation were performed.

MATERIAL WITHIN BILE DUCTS

Stones
Neoplasm
Sludge/Debris
Parasites
Fungus Balls
Hemorrhage
Stent/Drainage Tubes
Air

Material within the biliary tree is usually easiest to see if the system is dilated. Highly echogenic material, such as stones and air, can be readily seen. Soft tissue material that does not create a shadow may blend into the liver, making it difficult to recognize.

Stones (Figures 1.101–1.105)

Biliary tract stones usually develop within the gallbladder and may move into the biliary ductal

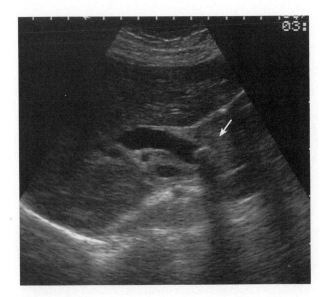

Figure 1.102
Common duct stones: Highly echogenic stones (*arrow*) with shadowing were seen near the hilum of the liver in this patient with multiple common duct stones.

system as they travel via the cystic duct into the extrahepatic biliary tree. In postcholecystectomy patients, stones may arise and reside within the intra- or extrahepatic biliary tree, especially if there are recurrent bouts of infectious cholangitis or if there is relative stasis of bile in the biliary tree (e.g., proximal to a stricture).

Recurrent pyogenic cholangitis or Oriental cholangiohepatitis is the prototypical example of stone formation in the biliary tree resulting from recurrent infection. Patients with Caroli's disease often have stones in their biliary tree, a result of the congenital saccular dilatations of the biliary tree and stasis.

In patients with stone passage from the gallbladder into the biliary tree, the ductal dilatation that accompanies obstruction facilitates visualization of the stones. Stones are more easily seen when they are large and close to the hilum of the liver, but most stones travel to the distal common bile duct, a site more difficult to visualize sonographically. Echogenic foci with or without shadowing constitute the sonographic appearance of biliary calculi.

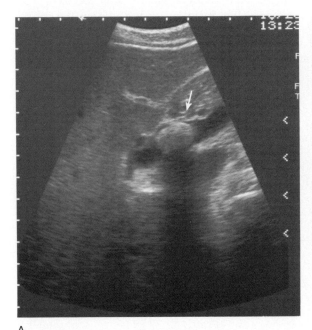

A

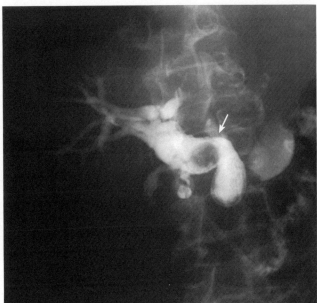

B

Figure 1.103
Large common duct stone: (A) An elderly man was admitted for a presumed myocardial infarction. Cardiac studies were unrevealing. Sonography demonstrated a large, obstructing stone (*arrow*) in the extrahepatic biliary tree. (B) The stone (*arrow*) was crushed and extracted through a transhepatic tube.

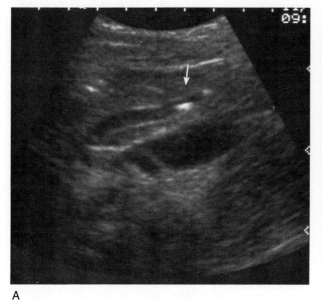

A

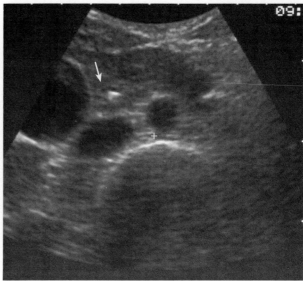

B

Figure 1.104

Choledocholithiasis—distal common duct: (A and B) Several stones were identifiable as highly echogenic foci within the biliary tree. The bile ducts were nondilated, although the patient's clinical laboratory results were consistent with obstruction.

Neoplasms

Neoplasms of the biliary tree—either primary lesions, such as cholangiocarcinoma and granular cell tumors, or metastatic disease—are rarely identified as soft tissue masses. More often their presence is indicated by the obstruction and biliary dilatation they cause.

Sludge/Debris (Figure 1.106)

Debris may accumulate behind an area of relative obstruction, such as a postoperative benign stricture or a malignant stricture. Sludge and infective debris do not usually cause shadowing and may be difficult to identify because, by filling up the biliary ductal system, they obscure the contrast provided by the dilated, fluid-filled biliary tree. Casts of mudlike material may be present in recurrent pyogenic cholangitis. The debris indicates that the system is obstructed.

Parasites

Liver flukes are rarely seen in this country, but they can be seen as wormlike intrabiliary structures in those patients affected.

Fungus Balls (Figure 1.107)

Conglomerates of fungal material may form balls of sludge within the biliary tree. Such material is indistinguishable sonographically from soft tissue material produced by other causes within the biliary

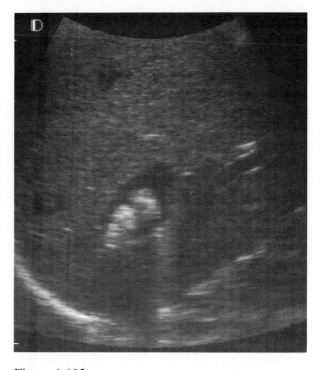

Figure 1.105

Caroli's disease with stones: Intrahepatic saccular dilatations of the biliary tree with large stones were identified in this patient, a young woman with Caroli's disease.

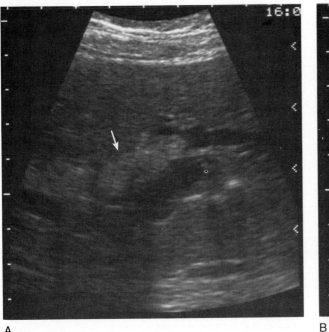

A   B

Figure 1.106
Sludge in dilated ducts: This patient suffered an injury to her common duct during laparoscopic cholecystectomy and developed a stricture. (A and B) Sludge and debris (*arrows*) built up within the obstructed ductal system prior to decompression. Because of the lack of shadowing and the echogenicity of the sludge, the level of obstruction was overlooked.

ducts. Usually in immunocompromised patients, fungal debris, often balls of hyphae, may fill the biliary tree. Systemic antifungal medications may need to be administered.

Hemorrhage

Bleeding into the biliary ducts may accompany blunt or surgical trauma. Usually the history is

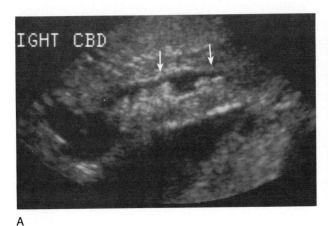

A

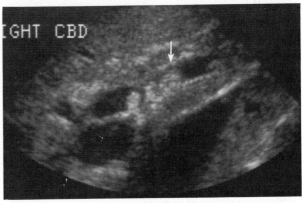

B

Figure 1.107
Fungus balls: (A and B) Balls of fungal hyphae (*arrows*) were extracted from the biliary tree in this patient with AIDS. Fungus balls were present in both the gallbladder and the biliary tree. Note the row of soft tissue balls in the common duct.

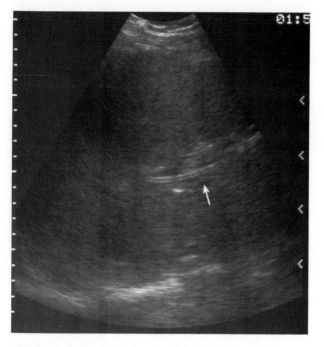

Figure 1.108
Stent: A nasobiliary tube had been placed at ERCP to establish biliary drainage. Note the parallel, highly echogenic walls of the stent (*arrow*).

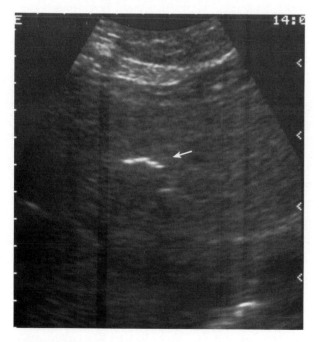

Figure 1.109
Pneumobilia: Brightly echogenic linear collections of air were seen in this patient after ERCP with papillotomy. No dilated ducts were visualized.

clear. Bleeding into the biliary system after a liver biopsy may be self-limited or may necessitate intervention. Blood in the biliary system may be indistinguishable from other sources of biliary ductal soft tissue echogenicity. The clinical history and presentation of the patient as well as possible resolution without intervention may allow the precise diagnosis to be made.

Stent/Drainage Tubes (Figure 1.108)

In most cases, the patient or the patient's referring physician is well aware of the presence of a biliary drainage tube or wall stent. The sonographic appearance of biliary drainage devices is characteristic. Wall stents are large-bore devices with two parallel walls, often highly echogenic, that traverse an obstruction of the biliary tree. Nasobiliary drainage tubes or percutaneous transhepatic drains are usually smaller-bore catheters with echogenic parallel walls that do not usually cause a shadow under ultrasonographic evaluation. If the drainage tube becomes encrusted with debris or is adjacent to stone material, prominent shadowing may be seen.

Air (Figure 1.109)

Air may be identified within the biliary tree as highly echogenic, shimmering foci with a "ring-down" artifact. Usually air is noted in the biliary tree in situations in which Oddi's sphincter is incompetent, such as after ERCP with sphincterotomy or after surgical creation of a choledochoenterostomy as a biliary diversionary procedure. Fistulization of the biliary tree to the bowel by stone passage or severe inflammatory processes may also result in air within the biliary ducts.

The left lobe of the liver should be screened for pneumobilia since in the supine position it is the most anterior portion of the liver. Small amounts of air may be visualized in the left lobe without evidence of pneumobilia on the right. The presence of pneumobilia may obscure recognition of stones in the biliary tree.

BILE DUCT WALL THICKENING

Sclerosing Cholangitis
Infectious Cholangitis
AIDS Cholangitis
Cholangiocarcinoma
Liver Fluke Infestation
Wall Thickening After Liver Transplantation

Sclerosing Cholangitis

Sclerosing cholangitis is a condition of unknown etiology in which there is noninfectious inflammation of the biliary tree. Inflammation of the biliary tree results in multiple bile duct strictures. The walls of the bile ducts may be smooth or irregularly thickened. The wall thickening may compromise the lumen of the bile duct, causing parameters that are clinically obstructive. Sclerosing cholangitis occurs more often in men than in women and is associated in one-third of the cases with inflammatory bowel disease, retroperitoneal fibrosis, or thyroiditis.

Infectious Cholangitis

Infectious cholangitis is often associated with biliary stone disease or manipulation of the common duct endoscopically or at surgery. Common duct stones result in biliary obstruction, and secondary pyogenic cholangitis ensues. Debris in the common duct, biliary ductal dilatation, and wall thickening of the bile ducts may be seen sonographically.

AIDS Cholangitis (Figure 1.110)

The biliary tree is commonly involved by opportunistic infection in patients with AIDS. Cytomegalovirus (CMV) and cryptosporidium are common pathogens affecting the biliary tree directly. Biliary dilatation with thickening of the distal common duct and obstruction may be identified with both organisms. Recent work has suggested that HIV itself may infest the biliary tract. Multiple levels of stricturing and bile duct wall thickening may be identified.

Cholangiocarcinoma (Figure 1.111)

A tumor arising from the epithelial cells of the biliary tree may manifest primarily as bile duct wall thickening. Cholangiocarcinoma is an adenocarcinoma that may develop in either the intra- or extrahepatic biliary tree, often arising at the confluence of the right and left hepatic ducts in the hilum of the liver.

Liver Fluke Infestation

The liver fluke, *Clonorchis sinensis,* infests small and medium-sized intrahepatic biliary ducts in many patients from the Far East. The chronic biliary infestation of the liver fluke causes increased echogenicity and wall thickening of the biliary tree

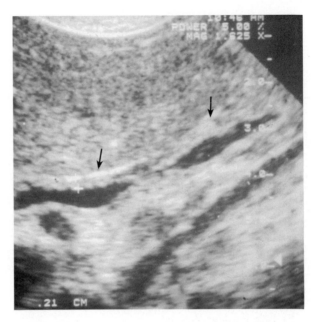

Figure 1.110
AIDS cholangitis: Thickening of the bile duct wall (*arrows*) was obvious in this patient with AIDS.

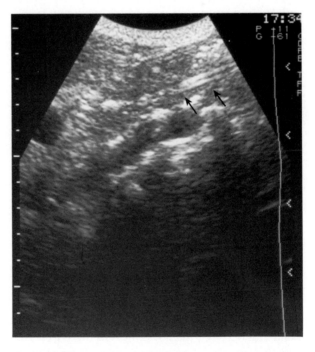

Figure 1.111
Cholangiocarcinoma: Malignant ductal wall thickening encompassed the biliary drainage stent (*arrows*) in this patient.

seen sonographically. Dilatation of the intrahepatic biliary tree without extrahepatic dilatation is common.

Wall Thickening After Liver Transplantation

Thickening of the bile ducts after liver transplantation may reflect edema of the bile ducts related to either rejection of the graft or arterial compromise, resulting in ischemia of the biliary tree. Recurrence of sclerosing cholangitis in the new organ could produce a similar sonographic appearance.

TOO MANY TUBES IN THE LIVER

    Dilated Biliary Ducts
    Intrahepatic Varices
    Recanalized Paraumbilical Vein
    Venous Anomalies
    Large Draining Vessels Around Masses
    Stents/Shunts

Dilated Biliary Ducts (Figure 1.112)

Dilatation of the intrahepatic biliary system will result in the sonographic picture of "too many tubes" in the liver. If the biliary tree is dilated, the sonographer must determine the level of obstruction and the cause (see "Biliary Ductal Dilatation").

Intrahepatic Varices (Figure 1.113)

Dilated, comma-shaped varices can course through the liver when there is portal hypertension and cirrhosis. Prominent intrahepatic varices are frequently seen in hepatic venous occlusion, as in Budd–Chiari syndrome.

Recanalized Paraumbilical Vein (Figure 1.114)

Sonographic recognition of a recanalized paraumbilical vein is evidence of portal hypertension. The recanalized paraumbilical vein is a portosystemic collateral between the left branch of the portal vein and the superficial epigastric veins of the anterior abdominal wall. The typical course from the left portal vein through the falciform ligament to the region of the umbilicus is an indication of this particular collateral pathway.

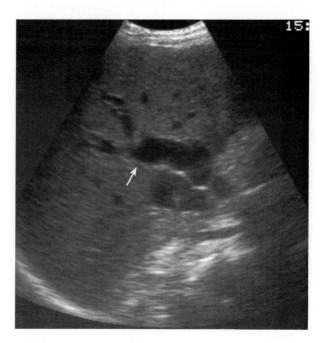

Figure 1.112
Dilated biliary ducts: Recognition of dilated biliary ducts must spark an investigation as to the cause and level of obstruction.

Venous Anomalies (Figure 1.115)

Vein-to-vein connections that are congenital abnormalities may sometimes be noted incidentally during sonographic evaluation.

Large Draining Vessels Around Masses (Figure 1.116)

Large peripheral draining vessels may be identified surrounding liver masses, such as adenomas, hepatocellular carcinoma, or focal nodular hyperplasia.

Stents/Shunts (Figure 1.117)

Percutaneously placed wallstents or vascular shunts are usually easy to see sonographically secondary to their brightly echogenic walls. In most cases, they are placed to relieve a biliary stricture, caused by either a malignant or benign mass, or to provide improved venous drainage through the liver (as with a TIPS catheter).

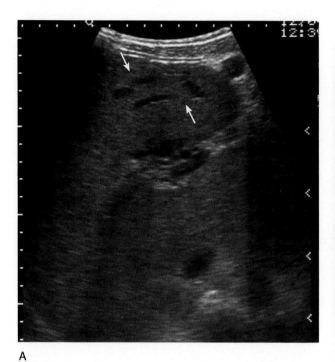

A

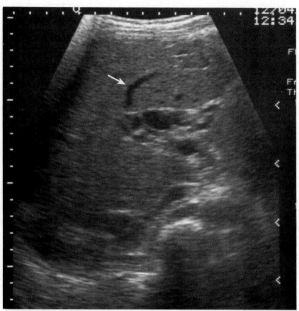

B

Figure 1.113
Intrahepatic varices: (A and B) In this young woman with Budd–Chiari syndrome, multiple comma-shaped varices (*arrows*) were visible in the liver parenchyma. (C [Plate 1]) Color Doppler image of a similar patient.

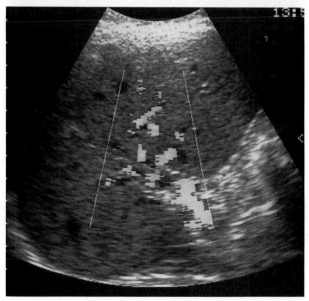

C

ABNORMALITIES OF THE PORTAL VEIN

Enlargement of the Portal Vein Secondary to Portal Hypertension
Engorgement of the Portal Vein Secondary to Thrombosis
Thrombosis of the Portal Vein
    Cirrhosis/Hepatocellular Disease
    Tumor Thrombus (Hepatocellular Carcinoma)
    Extrahepatic Portal Vein Thrombosis in Normal Liver
Chronic Changes of Portal Vein Thrombosis
    Thickened Portal Vein Walls
    Cavernous Transformation of the Portal Vein
Echogenic Foci in the Portal Vein: Calcification versus Air

The portal vein drains the gastrointestinal tract, including both the small and large intestines, and supplies the majority of the hepatic blood sup-

ply. Evaluation of the portal vein is integral to any examination of the abdomen, especially in a patient with liver disease, since evidence of portal hypertension and complications can frequently be identified.

Enlargement of the Portal Vein Secondary to Portal Hypertension (Figure 1.118)

The portal vein normally measures approximately 7 cm in length and 6.3 ± 2.3 mm in diameter. During

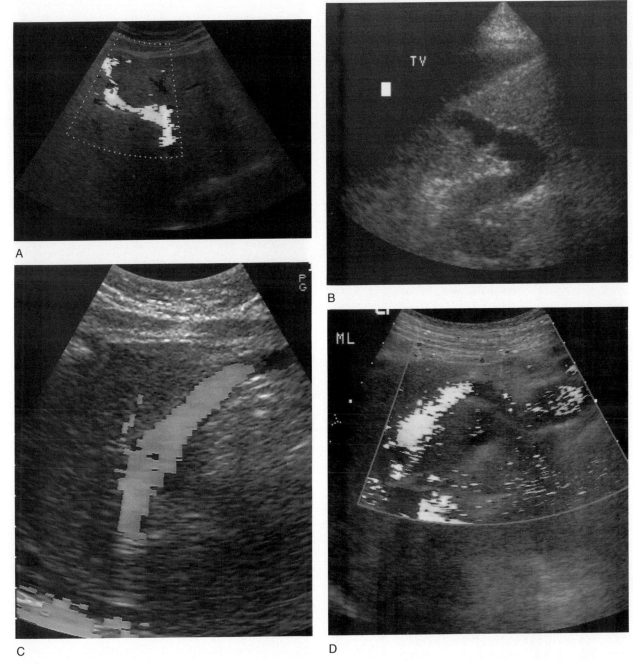

Figure 1.114
Recanalized paraumbilical vein: (A [Plate 2], B, C [Plate
3], D [Plate 4]) Recognition of a recanalized paraumbilical
vein coursing from the left portal vein, through the falciform ligament, to the anterior abdominal wall is firm evidence of portal hypertension. In most cases of a recanalized paraumbilical vein, the portal vein, at least the left
branch, is patent.

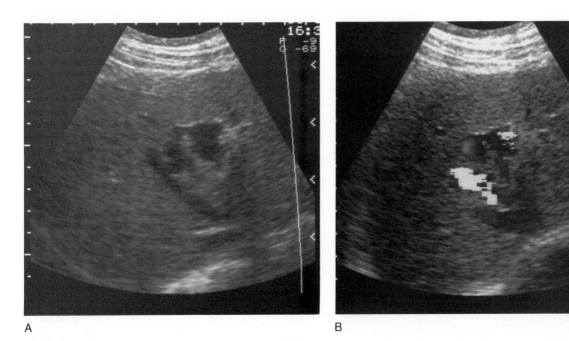

A   B

Figure 1.115

Congenital venous malformation: (A) A venous malformation was incidentally detected in this patient during routine abdominal imaging. (B [Plate 5]) Color Doppler confirmed its vascular origin.

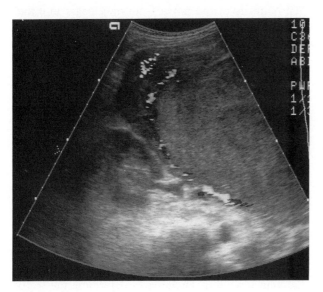

Figure 1.116

Large draining veins: Veins surround this large hepatic adenoma (Plate 6). MR confirmed the large draining vessels.

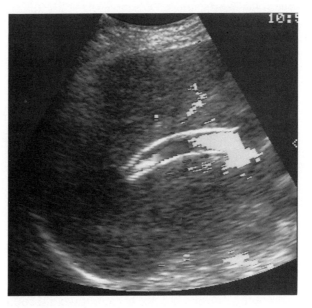

Figure 1.117

TIPS shunt (Plate 7): A percutaneously placed portal–caval stent diminished this patient's life-threatening episodes of GI hemorrhage. Note the highly echogenic parallel walls of the stent.

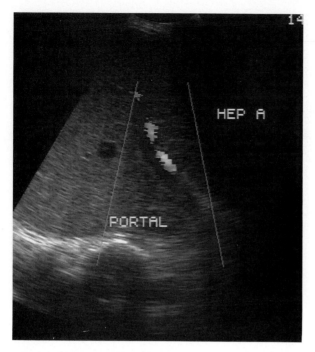

Figure 1.118
Reversal of flow direction in the portal vein (Plate 8): In this young woman with Budd–Chiari syndrome secondary to hypercoagulability, flow in the portal vein was discovered to be hepatofugal in the opposite direction from that in the hepatic artery. On subsequent scans, thrombosis of the portal vein was noted.

Valsalva maneuvers in normal patients, the portal vein may engorge, measuring up to 13 mm in diameter. In patients with liver disease and subsequent portal hypertension, the portal vein may be significantly larger. In the patient with portal hypertension, the velocity of the blood coming to the liver from the GI tract is slowed by the development of high vascular resistance within the sinusoidal bed of the cirrhotic liver. Enlargement of the portal vein allows the same volume of blood to arrive at the liver despite its lower velocity. As cirrhosis and fibrosis within the liver increase, alternate methods of drainage around the liver will develop, with flow into newly opened portosystemic collaterals. Flow in the portal vein may become hepatofugal in direction, away from the high vascular resistance within the liver.

Several collaterals can develop. The coronary vein is a collateral connecting the short gastric veins to the inferior vena cava. This collateral may be identified at the gastroesophageal junction, causing esophageal and gastric varices that may be seen as a "tangle" of vessels. Identification of a patent paraumbilical vein that unites the left portal vein branch to the superficial epigastric veins of the anterior abdominal wall is clear evidence of portal hypertension. In such a case, the left portal vein branch may be prominent and the collateral may be followed though the area of the ligamentum teres to the superficial abdominal wall and umbilicus. Other collateral pathways include splenorenal collaterals, gallbladder varices, and rectal varices.

Engorgement of the Portal Vein Secondary to Thrombosis

As collateral pathways increase and the velocity of blood in the portal vein diminishes, thrombosis of the portal vein may occur. The portal vein may be engorged when it is thrombosed, either with acute thrombosis or tumor thrombus. Acute thrombosis, similar to deep venous thrombosis of the lower extremities, distends the vein. An acute thrombus may fill the vein with solid heterogeneous clot or be hypoechoic, nearly cystic in appearance. Bland thrombosis can be verified by the lack of a Doppler signal from the vein. As the clot ages, it retracts, shrinking the portal vein lumen.

Thrombosis of the Portal Vein (Figure 1.119)

Thrombosis of the portal vein may begin in either the intra- or extrahepatic portions of the vessel.

Cirrhosis/Hepatocellular Disease Intrahepatic portal vein thrombosis frequently accompanies hepatocellular disease. Cirrhosis develops secondary to a variety of causes, including chronic viral hepatitis, toxins such as alcohol, and congenital disorders such as Wilson's disease or α_1-antitrypsin deficiency. In the cirrhotic liver, the sinusoidal bed, normally a site of low vascular resistance, becomes a distorted, fibrotic high-resistance bed. The portal vein branches within a cirrhotic liver are therefore susceptible to thrombosis. In fact, in a patient with liver failure who is being evaluated for possible intrahepatic portal–caval shunt placement (TIPS) or liver transplantation, the patency status of the portal vein is critical. Imaging to determine the status of the portal vein is imperative in such patients, who are at high risk for thrombosis.

Generally, in patients with cirrhosis resulting in portal vein thrombosis, the clinical and imaging features of liver disease predominate. Splenomegaly, ascites, a small and irregular liver, and portosystemic collaterals are seen.

Patients with Budd–Chiari syndrome or hepatic vein thrombosis develop portal vein thrombosis at

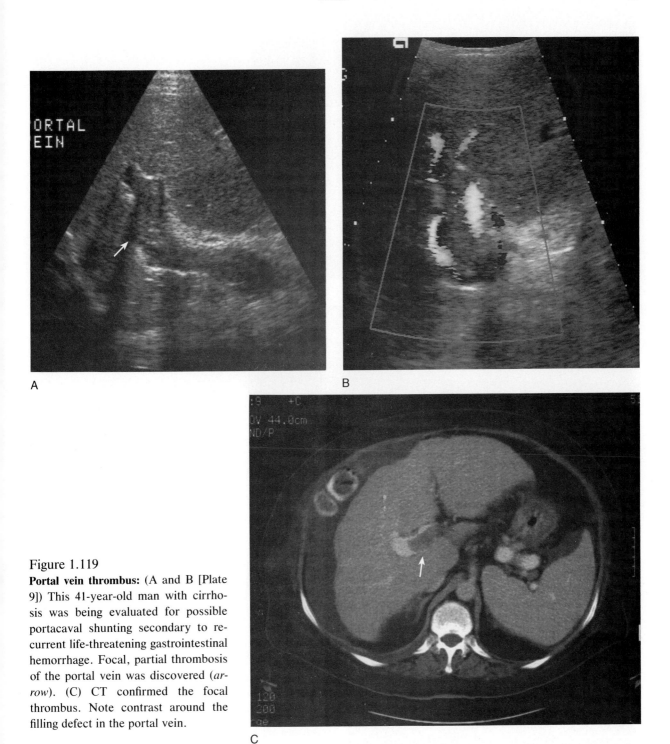

Figure 1.119
Portal vein thrombus: (A and B [Plate 9]) This 41-year-old man with cirrhosis was being evaluated for possible portacaval shunting secondary to recurrent life-threatening gastrointestinal hemorrhage. Focal, partial thrombosis of the portal vein was discovered (*arrow*). (C) CT confirmed the focal thrombus. Note contrast around the filling defect in the portal vein.

least 20 percent of the time. The liver is essentially a venous-to-venous anastomosis, and thrombosis of venous outflow from the liver can result in portal vein occlusion. Predisposing causes of hepatic vein thrombosis include oral contraceptive use, trauma, tumor, and hypercoagulable states. In many situations, the cause of hepatic vein thrombosis is un-

known but similar to causes of portal vein thrombosis.

In Budd–Chiari, stigmata of cirrhosis are not necessarily present at the time of acute thrombosis. Hepatomegaly, massive ascites, and nonvisualization of the hepatic veins may be present. In some situations, focal thrombi may be seen within the

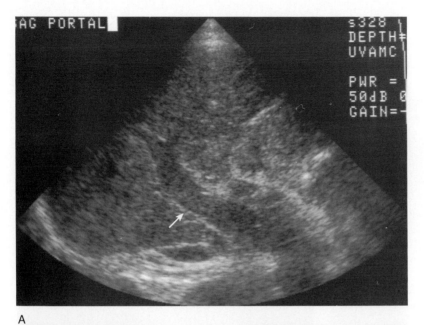

A

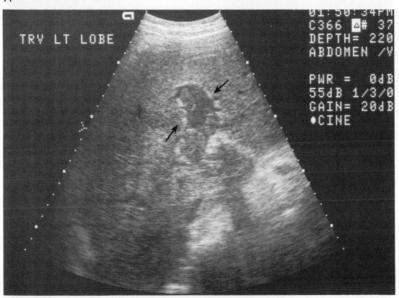

B

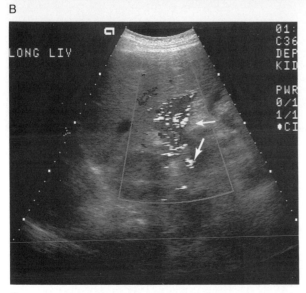

C

Figure 1.120

Tumor invasion of the portal vein: (A and B) This 38-year-old with chronic active hepatitis had an acute deterioration of liver function. Sonography demonstrated engorgement of a thrombus-filled right and main portal vein (*arrows*) with inhomogeneity of the right lobe of the liver, suggesting hepatocellular carcinoma. (C [Plate 10]) Arterial signal was present within the tumor thrombus consistent with neovascularity. Biopsy confirmed hepatocellular carcinoma.

vessels. Enlargement of the caudate lobe occurs, since the caudate drains independently into the inferior vena cava and in such a situation takes over more of the liver's drainage and function.

Tumor Thrombus (Hepatocellular Carcinoma) (Figures 1.120–1.121)

Not all thrombi in the portal vein are bland thrombi. Hepatocellular carcinoma usually develop in a diseased liver, and has a marked propensity to invade venous structures in the liver. In one pathologic study of hepatocellular carcinoma, 70 percent of the cases had portal vein thrombus and 13 percent had hepatic vein thrombus. Extension of hepatocellular carcinoma into the extrahepatic portal vein is thought to occur at least 32 percent of the time.

Hepatocellular carcinoma is one of the most common malignancies worldwide. It is very common in East Asia and in South Africa. Most patients have cirrhosis secondary to hepatitis B exposure. In Western society, many hepatocellular carcinomas arise within the liver, which is cirrhotic, often secondary to alcohol abuse. At least one-half of hepatocellular carcinomas in this country arise within livers with preexisting cirrhosis.

Hepatocellular carcinoma may be difficult to identify on imaging studies because the underlying liver is diseased. Sonographically, hepatocellular carcinoma may be a unifocal mass, multifocal masses, or a diffusely infiltrative irregular area of involvement. Since the echogenicity of a cirrhotic liver may already be irregular, recognition of new-onset portal vein thrombosis may suggest the development of hepatocellular carcinoma in the diseased liver. Identification of echogenic material within the lumen of the vein and lack of appropriate venous flow will confirm portal vein thrombosis. A tumor thrombus may have arterial flow within it and even arteriovenous shunting. Detection of arterial blood flow in a hepatofugal direction within the thrombosed portal vein will differentiate tumoral from bland thrombus. Bland thrombus will not have neovascularity or arterial signal within it. Tumor thrombus will have arterial flow with high diastolic flow. Aspiration of portal vein thrombus has been performed to differentiate bland from neoplastic thrombus. Other imaging studies, specifically CT and MR, may allow better definition of the neoplastic mass than sonography.

Since hepatocellular carcinoma tumor thrombus is identified by diagnostic testing approximately 30 to 36 percent of the time and is uncommon with liver metastases, recognition of a liver mass and portal vein thrombosis makes hepatocellular carcinoma the presumptive diagnosis. Patients with portal or hepatic vein invasion and hepatocellular car-

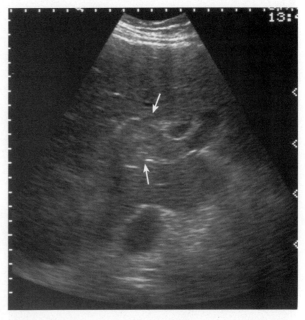

Figure 1.121

Tumoral thrombus: A cirrhotic patient with portal vein thrombosis (*arrows*) had extensive tumor by biopsy. Note hepatization of the portal vein or filling in of the vessel lumen by solid material. The left portal vein branch had sluggish flow.

cinoma have a poor prognosis and usually are not candidates for surgery.

Thrombosis of the portal vein occurs in 5 to 8 percent of patients with metastatic disease, as determined by autopsy studies. Portal vein thrombosis occurs in patients with extensive metastic disease, rather than in those with a small burden of disease. Portal vein thrombosis with metastatic disease is usually secondary to stasis and encasement of the vein by adenopathy and extensive parenchymal involvement rather than by tumor invasion of the vein.

Extrahepatic Portal Vein Thrombosis in Normal Liver

Thrombosis of the extrahepatic portion of the portal vein may occur in the patient with a normal liver. In such a circumstance, the extrahepatic portal vein is injured at surgery or by trauma, or is encased by portal adenopathy, by neoplasm, or as a result of pancreatitis. Hypercoagulable states, such as myeloproliferative disorders or neoplastic conditions, may cause extrahepatic portal venous occlusion. Septic thrombophlebitis of the portal vein occurs when the portal vein is a conduit for septic material from the GI tract, such as that resulting from an unrecognized ruptured appendix, Crohn's disease, diverticulitis, or a necrotic carci-

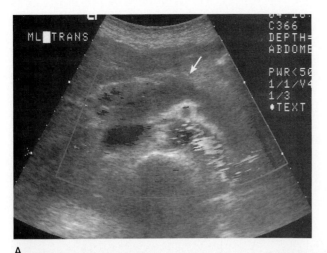

A

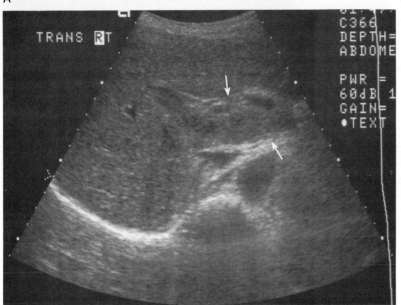

B

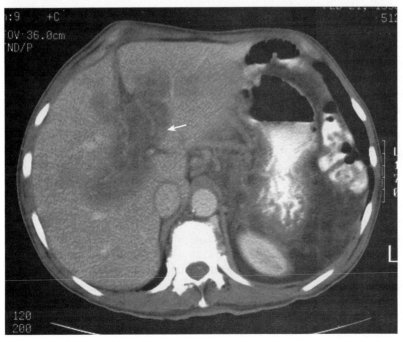

C

Figure 1.122
Thrombosis of the splenic and portal veins: (A [Plate 11] and B) Extensive splanchnic thrombosis occurred in this 56-year-old woman after splenectomy for a myeloproliferative disorder. Note distended thrombosed splenic and portal vein. (C) CT confirmed extensive thrombosis. Periportal edema was noted as well.

noma. Especially in children, thrombosis of the portal vein and inflammatory processes of the liver, such as liver abscess, may be associated with inflammatory GI processes.

In the patient with a normal liver and extrahepatic portal vein thrombosis, hepatopedal collaterals will develop to bypass the occluded segment of the portal vein. Such a tangle of vessels in the porta hepatis, bypassing the obstructed portal vein, is called cavernous transformation of the portal vein. During evaluations of patients with portal hypertension, the hepatopedal collaterals of cavernous transformation may be misinterpreted as a patent portal vein. Recognition that the normal course and size of the portal vein are not present and that, instead, there are numerous tortuous collateral vessels will lead to correct recognition that the portal vein has been replaced by the collateral vessels.

Hypercoagulable State (Figures 1.122–1.123)

Patients with myeloproliferative disorders frequently develop thrombotic complications. Since the portal venous system transports blood at a relatively low flow rate between two venous circulations, it is susceptible to thrombosis, especially in

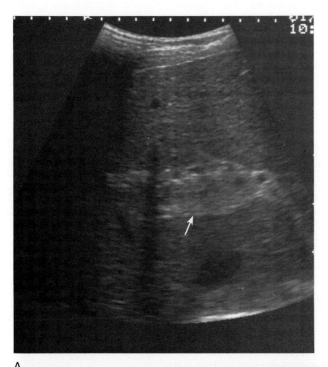

A

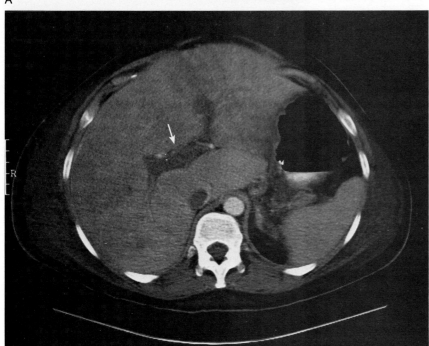

B

Figure 1.123

Portal vein thrombosis: (A) Hypercoagulability led to portal vein thrombosis (*arrow*) in this postpartum 38-year-old woman. (B) CT image of the same patient.

situations of hypercoagulability. After splenectomy, thrombocytosis results, which may cause thrombosis. Patients undergoing splenectomy for hematologic disorders have a disparate risk of portal or mesenteric vein thrombosis. Blood viscosity, platelet numbers, and platelet function abnormalities all contribute to thromboembolic complications, which may occur immediately postoperatively or weeks to months later.

Congenital enzymatic deficiencies—including protein C deficiency, protein S deficiency, and antithrombin III deficiency—can result in extrahepatic portal vein thrombosis with an otherwise normal liver.

After Liver Transplantation

The incidence of postoperative portal vein thrombosis after liver transplantation is reported at 1 to 2 percent. Predisposing causes for postoperative portal vein thrombosis in a liver transplant recipient include previous portosystemic shunt, previous splenectomy, or portal vein thrombosis that existed prior to surgery. Previous splenectomy, previous surgically placed portosystemic shunts, and large spontaneous splenorenal shunts all diminish the flow through the portal vein and thus predispose to thrombosis. Usually, portal vein thrombosis after liver transplantation occurs soon after the surgery. Early diagnosis is important for graft salvage.

Often surgical treatment is needed for posttransplantation portal vein thrombosis. Sometimes, however, nonoperative management is acceptable, especially if no significant compromise of the graft is present.

Pylephlebitis

In children and young adults, portal vein thrombosis in the absence of liver disease is uncommon. Inflammatory processes in the abdomen may lead to portal vein thrombosis when the liver is normal. Before the age of antibiotics, pylephlebitis was the most common cause of liver abscesses, as the portal vein could serve as a conduit for infected material from the GI tract.

In neonates, phlebitis of the umbilical vein, often initiated by umbilical catheterization, may occur.

Congenital stenosis of the portal vein and idiopathic causes of portal vein thrombosis may result in portal vein thrombosis as well.

Chronic Changes of Portal Vein Thrombosis

Thickened Portal Vein Walls (Figures 1.124–1.125)
Acute portal vein thrombosis distends the vessel lumen. If the patient with bland portal vein

thrombosis is serially imaged, recanalization of the portal vein may occur, which results in the reestablishment of blood flow through the lumen of the portal vein. Thickening and irregularity of the wall of the portal vein may be noted sonographically, and reestablished flow in the portal vein may be revealed by Doppler.

Calcifications in the thickened portal vein wall or in the thrombus itself may develop. The calcifications can be confirmed on plain films or at CT. Findings of old, recanalized portal vein thrombosis should be noted if the patient is being considered for shunting procedures such as TIPS or liver transplantation. Evidence of a thickened, partially calcified portal vein may exclude the patient from certain types of shunting or surgical consideration.

Cavernous Transformation of the Portal Vein (Figures 1.126–1.127)
Replacement of the thrombosed portal vein by a tangle of collaterals in the porta hepatis is evidence of previous portal vein thrombosis. Care must be taken not to mistake a large or dominant collateral for the portal vein. Hepatopedal collaterals in the porta hepatis may be present with an otherwise normal liver; the normal portal vein will be obliterated or quite diminutive.

Echogenic Foci in the Portal Vein: Calcification Versus Air (Figures 1.128–1.130)

Calcifications within the portal vein are seen sonographically as highly echogenic foci with shadowing. Usually, calcifications are within a thrombus or within a thickened vein wall. The calcification is the sequel to previous portal vein thrombosis. Calcifications of the portal vein have been described in neonates with congenital anomalies, including chromosomal abnormalities and physical defects, such as cardiac malformations and low-set ears. Calcification may be seen weeks or months after acute portal vein thrombosis from whatever cause. Confirmation of portal vein calcification is sometimes possible with plain film but is more reliably obtained by CT.

Air within the portal venous system is seen sonographically as small, highly reflective foci that move quickly in the flowing blood. Acoustic shadowing is not always present. These high-amplitude microbubbles of air are not to be confused with the multiple low-level echoes seen in blood vessels with slowly moving blood. Such low-level echoes are aggregates of red blood cells.

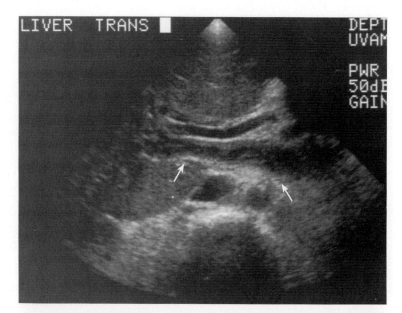

Figure 1.124
Thickened portal vein walls: Recanalization of a previously thrombosed portal vein was obvious on gray-scale sonography with irregularity and thickening of the vessel wall (*arrows*).

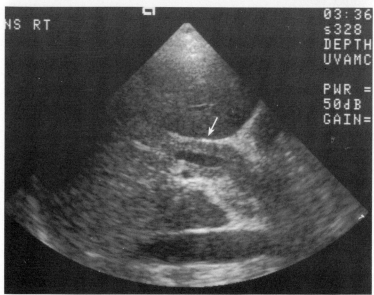

Figure 1.125
Recanalized portal vein: In this patient with recurrent bouts of pancreatitis and gastrointestinal hemorrhage, marked wall thickening and a small central lumen are identifiable (*arrow*), confirming the clinically suspected portal vein occlusion in the past.

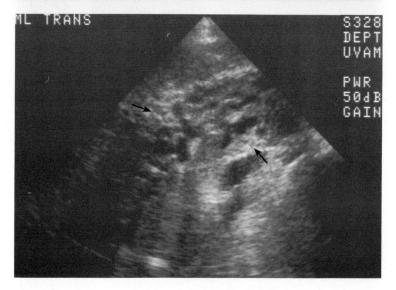

Figure 1.126
Cavernous transformation of the portal vein: A tangle of small, tortuous vessels (*arrows*) is present in the porta hepatis in this patient with a structurally normal liver and extrahepatic portal vein occlusion.

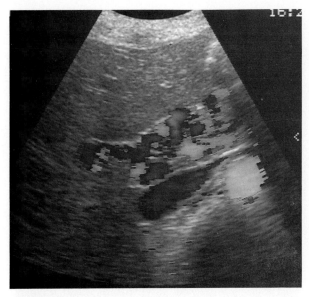

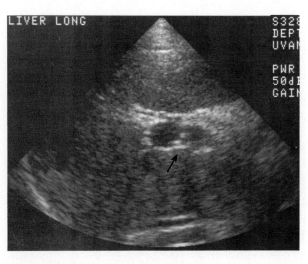

Figure 1.127
Cavernous transformation of the portal vein (Plate 12): Six weeks after well-documented portal vein thrombosis related to surgical injury of the portal vein, small hepatopedal collaterals fill the porta hepatis.

Figure 1.128
Calcifications of the portal vein: Calcifications (*arrow*) (confirmed by plain films) were present in this young woman 18 months after acute portal vein thrombosis. The main portal vein was recanalized by Doppler.

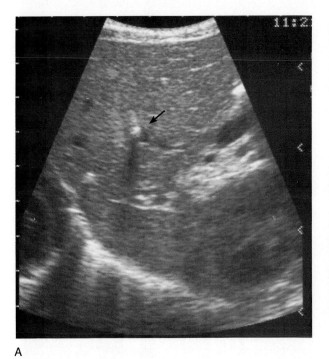

A

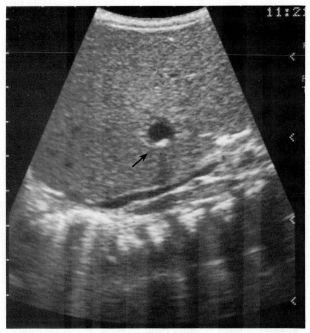

B

Figure 1.129
Calcifications of the portal vein: (A and B) Calcification in the portal vein was detected in this infant after a long stay in the intensive care nursery after delivery. The infant had had an umbilical venous catheter during his hospitalization. CT confirmed the sonographic findings.

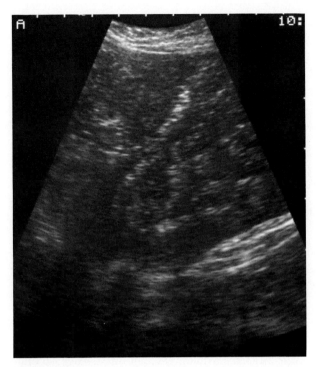

Figure 1.130
Microbubbles of air within the portal vein: At real time, swiftly flowing, brightly echogenic microbubbles of air were seen in the portal vein. Liver parenchymal echogenicity was abnormal, secondary to air trapped in the sinusoids. The patient underwent exploratory laparotomy. No obvious cause of portal venous air was found.

The flow of microbubbles of air within the portal vein may be intermittent and transient, lasting minutes to hours. The intermittent nature may be related to peristaltic activity of the bowel, which facilitates flow if the bowel mucosa is disrupted. Air within portal vein radicles gives the liver parenchyma a patchy, highly echogenic appearance.

Portal venous air usually is identified in situations of bowel ischemia, infarction, or fulminant infection with a gas-forming organism. Disruption of the integrity of the bowel mucosa may lead to the presence of air in the splanchnic and portal systems. Neonates with necrotizing enterocolitis may have sonographically detected air in their portal or splanchnic venous systems before it is identified radiographically. This allows aggressive treatment to be instituted before radiographic changes take place. It has been shown that radiographically detected air has an ominous prognosis for the patient perhaps related to the extent or volume of portal venous air. Sonography is a sensitive way to detect small amounts of venous air in either the portal vein or hepatic parenchyma, because gas is an excellent reflector of sound.

Emphasis Points

The actual thrombus in acute portal vein thrombosis may not necessarily be seen with gray-scale imaging. Lack of a Doppler signal by either color flow or spectral analysis will confirm the presence of thrombosis. Care to sample correctly with Doppler is necessary. Sampling at a 90° angle will suggest no flow even when flow may be present.

Hepatocellular carcinoma may be difficult to identify sonographically, since the only abnormality may be a diffuse echotexture abnormality of the liver. Recognition of portal vein thrombosis and abnormal liver texture may suggest the diagnosis of hepatocellular carcinoma. Arterial flow within portal vein thrombus is consistent with neovascularity. CT or MR may show a definitive mass. Correlation with α-fetoprotein results or biopsy may be diagnostic.

Cavernous transformation of the portal vein occurs when a tangle of hepatopedal collaterals replaces the obliterated portal vein. In evaluating the patient with portal hypertension prior to portacaval shunt placement or liver transplantation, recognition of cavernous transformation manifest by the tangle of vessels and absence of a normal portal vein is imperative for successful management of the patient. A large hepatopedal collateral may be misinterpreted as the portal vein. TIPS procedures and liver transplantation may be difficult in such a situation.

Cavernous transformation of the portal vein may be discovered when portal hypertension is evaluated and may be the only evidence of previous extrahepatic portal vein thrombosis. Often the etiology for portal vein occlusion will be unknown.

It is usually easy to differentiate portal venous gas from portal vein calcifications. Portal venous gas is rapidly moving and usually is found in an ill patient. Portal vein calcifications accompany other signs of portal hypertension with collaterals, splenomegaly, and sometimes ascites. Calcium or air in the portal vein can be easily differentiated by CT.

BRIGHTLY ECHOGENIC PORTAL TRIADS

Pneumobilia
Multiple Stones in Ducts/Oriental
    Cholangiohepatitis
Intrahepatic Arterial Calcifications
Calcifications in Portal Vein Thrombosis
Air in Portal Vein Radicles
Diminished Echogenicity of Hepatic
    Parenchyma

The portal triads of the liver are made up of a portal venous radicle accompanied by a branch of the hepatic artery and a branch of the biliary tree. A very brightly echogenic portal triad may be secondary to the presence of air or calcium in either of the structures of the portal triad or may be related to markedly diminished echogenicity of the surrounding hepatic parenchyma.

Pneumobilia (Figures 1.131–1.132)

Probably the most frequently encountered cause of brightly echogenic portal triads is pneumobilia. Air within the biliary tree is often seen secondary to a

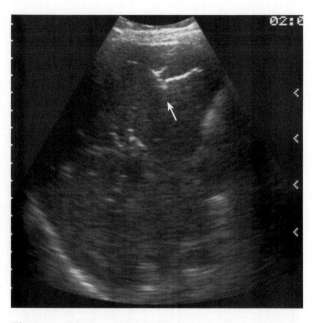

Figure 1.131
Pneumobilia: This liver transplant recipient underwent a choledochoenterostomy after an anastomotic stricture developed causing biliary obstruction. A follow-up scan showed extensive, highly echogenic linear collections of air in the biliary tree (*arrow*), confirming reflux of air into the liver via the patent choledochoenterostomy.

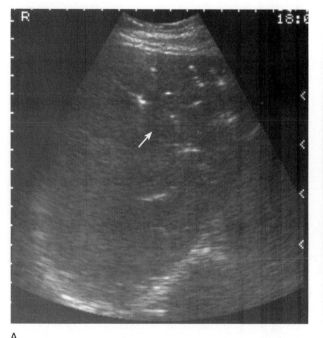

A

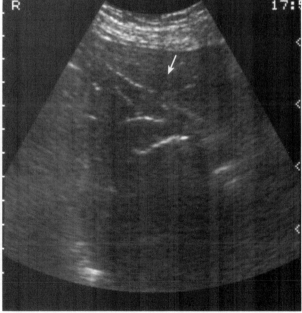

B

Figure 1.132
Pneumobilia: (A and B) After sphincterotomy for common duct stones, extensive pneumobilia is identified, especially in the left lobe of the liver.

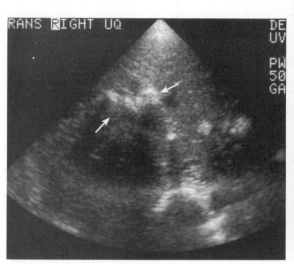

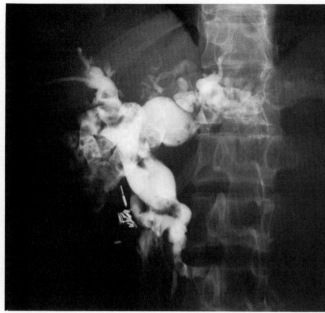

A B

Figure 1.133

Oriental cholangiohepatitis: (A) This young Asian woman with recurrent bouts of cholangitis has extensive, highly echogenic material with shadowing in the biliary ductal system. (B) Cholangiographic study of the same patient demonstrates innumerable biliary stones within the ducts. The patient had previously had choledochojejunostomy for improved drainage of the liver.

sphincterotomy, a choledochoenterostomy, or simply to incompetence of Oddi's sphincter. Air can freely reflux into the biliary tree in such situations. Often air is more prominent within the left lobe of the liver, since that is the most anterior portion of the liver when the patient is in the supine position. Usually, air can be differentiated from stones in the biliary tree, since air has a "ringdown" artifact and is sometimes said to have "dirty shadowing" rather than the clean, crisp shadow from a stone. The presence of air in the biliary tree may make it nearly impossible to identify stones sonographically, however.

Multiple Stones in Ducts/Oriental Cholangiohepatitis (Figure 1.133)

In the Western Hemisphere, it is unusual to have multiple cholesterol biliary stones filling the intra- and extrahepatic biliary tree. On the other hand, Oriental cholangiohepatitis, a condition with a variety of alternative names, such as recurrent pyogenic cholangitis and biliary obstruction syndrome of the Chinese, is very common in Asian immi-

grants to the United States. The patients have recurrent bouts of cholangitis with right upper quadrant pain, vomiting, and jaundice. The biliary tree is dilated and filled with extensive stone and calculus debris. The material may form a cast of the biliary tree. Primary infestation with the liver fluke may predispose to pyogenic cholangitis, and frequently the bile is infected with *Escherichia coli* or other enteric flora.

This condition has a variable sonographic appearance. Multiple brightly echogenic foci with extensive shadowing may be seen throughout the liver or may focally affect the left lobe preferentially. In other cases, castlike soft tissue material without shadowing may fill the biliary tree. The variable appearance is secondary to the variable makeup of the stone material and debris within the ducts. Pneumobilia accompanying the stone material may be related to previous surgery or stone passage.

Medical therapy is usually unsuccessful in recurrent pyogenic cholangitis, and surgery is necessary to improve drainage of the biliary tree. Often the left lobe of the liver is more severely affected and left lobectomy may be necessary. In other cases, choledochojejunostomy improves drainage of the biliary tree.

Intrahepatic Arterial Calcifications (Figure 1.134)

Extensive intrahepatic arterial calcifications may mimic pneumobilia or extensive stone material within the biliary tree. Extensive arterial calcifica-

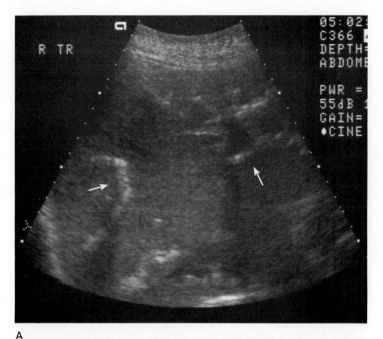

A

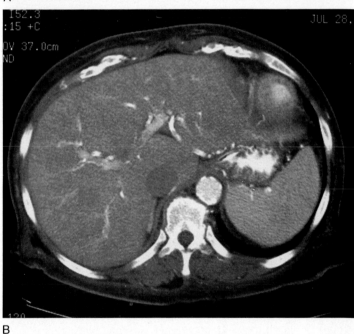

B

Figure 1.134

Intrahepatic arterial calcifications: (A) This elderly diabetic patient has dramatic calcification of the intrahepatic arterioles. (B) CT of the abdomen reveals calcification of numerous vessels in the abdomen.

tion is most often seen in patients with diabetes and renal insufficiency. Linear, tram-track calcifications may be identified on plain film or CT and allow the vascular calcifications to be differentiated from biliary stones or air.

Calcifications in Portal Vein Thrombosis (Figure 1.135)

Calcifications within portal vein radicles are usually fairly focal and not nearly as extensive as intra-arterial calcifications. Calcifications in the portal vein usually develop secondary to chronic portal vein thrombosis.

Air in Portal Vein Radicles (Figure 1.136)

Air within the portal venous radicles is often associated with mesenteric ischemia. Echogenic foci that are mobile in the portal vein radicles flow and are distributed out into the periphery of the liver. These microbubbles of air within the portal venous system may be associated with necrotizing enterocolitis in premature infants or with mesenteric ischemia or infarction in adults. Sonography is a more sensitive way to detect portal venous gas than plain radiography. Recognition of the mobile echogenic foci within the portal vein may be transient. Management of the patient will depend upon the cause of the portal venous air.

Diminished Echogenicity of Hepatic Parenchyma (Figure 1.137)

In situations in which the portal triads are surrounded by markedly hypoechoic hepatic parenchyma, the portal triads will appear more echogenic than normal. Acute fulminant hepatitis causes edema of hepatocytes and increases the echogenicity of the portal vein walls by causing inflammatory reaction and fibrosis. This leads to the so-called starry sky appearance. A similar "starry sky" appearance has been seen with hepatic infarction secondary to hepatic artery thrombosis after liver transplantation.

PERIPORTAL MASSES

Metastatic Lymphadenopathy
Lymphoma
Infectious Lymphadenopathy
Reactive Lymphadenopathy
Sarcoidosis
Splenosis
Varices
Mesenchymal Masses (Neuroma, Fibroma)

Periportal masses may be identified during routine sonographic studies of the abdomen. Enlarged lymph nodes, splenules, varices, and benign mesenchymal masses may explain their presence.

Metastatic Lymphadenopathy

Lymphadenopathy secondary to metastatic disease may be related to involvement from nearby primary malignancies, such as pancreatic carcinoma, gastric carcinoma, renal cell carcinoma, or cholangiocar-

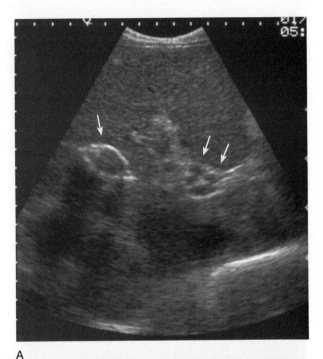

A

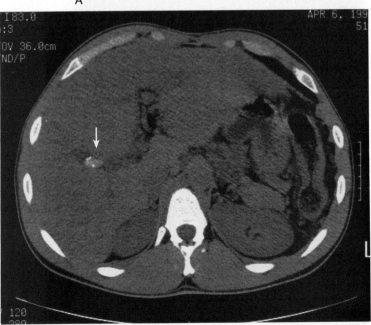

B

Figure 1.135
Portal vein calcifications: (A) Focal calcifications are seen as highly echogenic foci with shadowing in this patient with a distant history of portal vein occlusion. Note small collateral vessels at the porta hepatitis (*double arrows*). (B) Confirmatory CT shows calcification in portal vein.

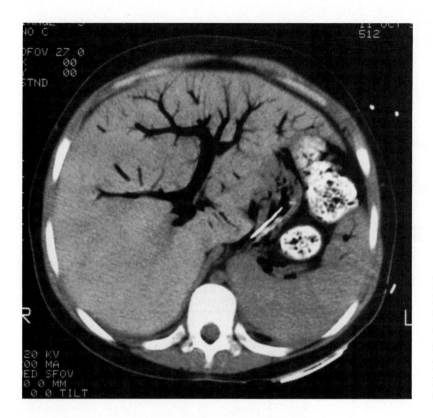

Figure 1.136

Portal venous air: Air is present within the portal venous system of a patient with mesenteric infarction. Sonographically, highly echogenic foci within the portal vein and its branches would be expected. These images were performed shortly before the patient's death.

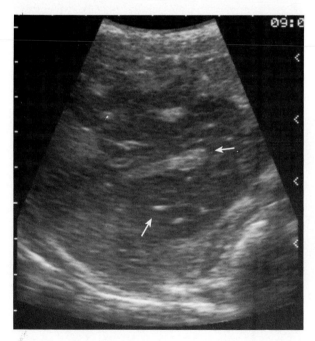

Figure 1.137

Hepatic infarction: The portal triads appear extremely echogenic (*arrows*) because the hepatic parenchyma is quite echo-poor. This liver transplant recipient suffered massive hepatic infarction secondary to vascular insufficiency to the allograft. Retransplantation was required.

cinoma. Involvement with metastatic disease from more distant primaries, such as lung and breast carcinoma and melanoma, may manifest by periportal lymphadenopathy. The primary site of malignancy may or may not be known.

Lymphoma (Figure 1.138)

Lymphadenopathy related to a generalized lymphoma may encase vessels in the pancreatic bed and liver hilum. The enlarged lymph nodes may be seen as a multilobulated mass of nodes or a sheet of tumor. Multiple individual masses may be seen. The masses are often homogeneous and hypoechoic, nearly cystic in appearance, although heterogeneity of echotexture is sometimes identified and related to histology, tumor necrosis, and internal nodal architecture. Generally, lymphadenopathy secondary to lymphoma is more hypoechoic than the often hyperechoic adenopathy of metastatic disease. Ultrasound will not recognize involvement in normal-sized nodes that occur in approximately 10 percent of patients with lymphoma. Patients with non-Hodgkin lymphoma more frequently have lymphadenopathy in this region than patients with Hodgkin lymphoma.

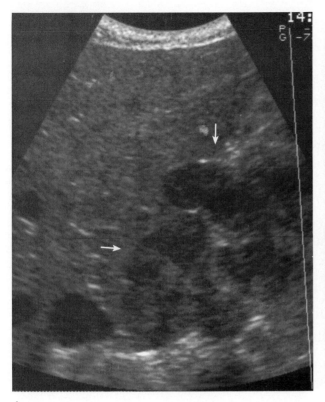

A

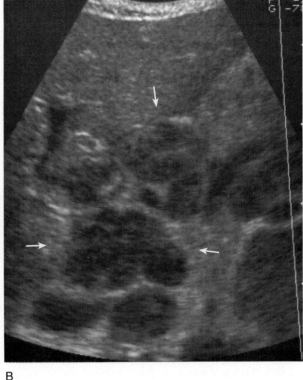

B

Figure 1.138

Periportal adenopathy: (A and B) Enlarged periportal lymph nodes were identified in this patient with lymphoma.

Infectious Lymphadenopathy (Figure 1.139)

Infectious lymphadenopathy is commonly seen in conditions of granulomatous infection with mycobacterium tuberculosis and atypical mycobacterium (MAI). Although it had previously been declining in incidence in the United States, in recent years tuberculosis has become more common.

The lymphadenopathy of tuberculosis can manifest as individually enlarged nodes or multilobulated masses of adenopathy. Central necrosis and cystic change are common as suppuration occurs. Omental caking and ascites may be identified as well.

Tuberculosis of the GI tract results from swallowing large doses of TB bacilli. The bacilli cause an inflammatory response that affects the mesenteric lymph nodes draining that portion of bowel. Hematogenous methods of spread are thought to be possible as well.

Other infectious etiologies may be associated with lymphadenopathy, such as hepatitis and cat scratch fever.

Reactive Lymphadenopathy

The reactive lymphadenopathy associated with HIV infection is usually not as bulky as lymph nodes infiltrated and replaced by neoplasm or infection. Patients with AIDS and lymphadenopathy may have reactive adenopathy as well as AIDS-related neoplasms, such as non-Hodgkin lymphoma or Kaposi sarcoma, or opportunistic infections, such as tuberculosis or atypical mycobacterium. Aspiration of the lymphadenopathy for cytologic and microbiologic evaluation may be necessary to plan a treatment strategy.

Sarcoidosis (Figure 1.140)

Sarcoidosis may have associated abdominal lymphadenopathy. There is nothing from an imaging perspective that makes the lymphadenopathy unique. In sarcoidosis, hepatosplenomegaly may be present as well. This is a noninfectious, nonneoplastic cause of lymphadenopathy. Whipple's disease may have associated lymphadenopathy, too.

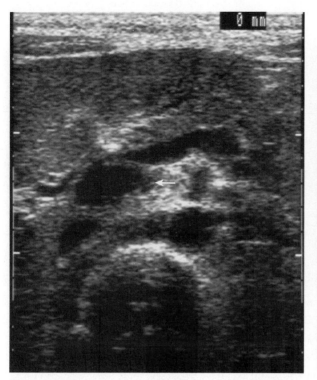

A

B

Figure 1.139
Infectious lymphadenopathy: (A and B) Hypoechoic masses in the periportal and epigastric regions proved to be necrotic tuberculous nodes when aspirated.

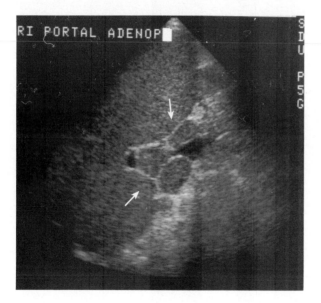

Figure 1.140
Sarcoidosis: Multiple enlarged lymph nodes in the periportal area were involved with sarcoidosis in this young male patient.

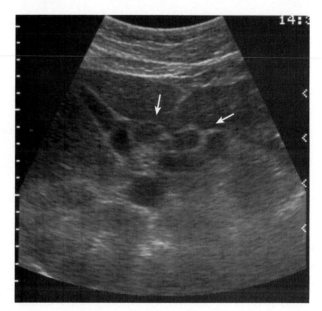

Figure 1.141
Splenosis: This young woman had suffered severe blunt trauma years before and had undergone splenectomy for a ruptured spleen. Ultrasound performed for abdominal pain showed multiple masses in the periportal region and down the right flank. The presumptive diagnosis was lymphoma. MR imaging with intravenous ferrite and sulfur-colloid-labeled radioisotopes allowed the recognition that the masses were multiple splenules.

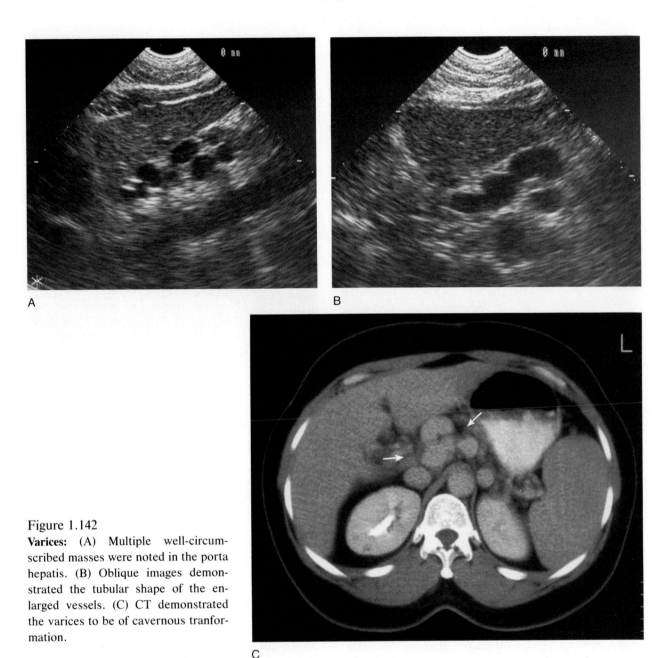

Figure 1.142
Varices: (A) Multiple well-circumscribed masses were noted in the porta hepatis. (B) Oblique images demonstrated the tubular shape of the enlarged vessels. (C) CT demonstrated the varices to be of cavernous tranformation.

Splenosis (Figure 1.141)

Multiple periportal masses that are indistinguishable from adenopathy have been described in splenosis. In patients who have trauma to the spleen necessitating surgical removal, small implants of splenic tissue may parasitize nearby peritoneal surfaces or the omentum and grow. These splenic implants may be interpreted as lymphadenopathy on imaging studies. Scanning with radionuclides of sulfur colloid or MR imaging with ferrite may make it possible to establish that the periportal masses are of reticuloendothelial origin. Biopsy of such masses may result in significant hemorrhage and should be avoided if possible.

Varices (Figure 1.142)

Multiple venous collaterals in the periportal regions may be present in patients with portal hypertension and cavernous transformation of the portal vein. Recognition of venous flow within the structure or the tubular shape of the vessel will allow its venous origin to be appreciated.

Mesenchymal Masses (Neuroma, Fibroma) (Figure 1.143)

Rarely, a benign mass may arise from the mesenchymal elements in the upper abdomen. Its appearance is nonspecific and it will probably need to be sampled to exclude more ominous etiologies.

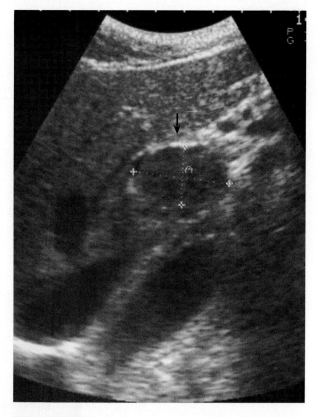

Figure 1.143

Hemangioma: This benign mesenchymal periportal mass was an incidental pickup during abdominal imaging. It measured 3 cm in its greatest dimension and impinged upon the portal vein. The mass was biopsied laparoscopically.

BIBLIOGRAPHY

Hyperechoic Liver Mass

Cottone M, Marceno MP, Maringhini A, et al.: Ultrasound in the diagnosis of hepatocellular carcinoma associated with cirrhosis. Radiology 147:517–519, 1983.

Curati WL, Halevy A, Gibson RN, Carr DH, Blumgart LH, Steiner RE: Ultrasound, CT and MRI comparison in primary and secondary tumors of the liver. Gastrointest Radiol 13:123–128, 1988.

Friedman AC, Lichtenstein JE, Goodman Z, et al.: Fibrolamellar hepatocellular carcinoma. Radiology 157:583–587, 1985.

Kaude JV, Felman AH, Hawkins IF Jr: Ultrasonography in primary hepatic tumors in early childhood. Pediatr Radiol 9:77–83, 1980.

Kudo M, Ikekubo K, Yamamoto K, et al.: Distinction between hemangioma of the liver and hepatocellular carcinoma: Value of labeled RBC–SPECT scanning. AJR 152:977–983, 1989.

Mungovan JA, Cronan JJ, Vacarro J: Hepatic cavernous hemangiomas: Lack of enlargement over time. Radiology 191:111–113, 1994.

Quinn SF, Gosink BB: Characteristic sonographic signs of hepatic fatty infiltration. AJR 145:753–755, 1985.

Ros PR: Focal liver masses other than metastases, in Gore RM (ed.): Syllabus for categorical course on gastrointestinal radiology. Reston, VA: American College of Radiology, 159–169, 1991.

Sheu JC, Chen DS, Sung JL, et al.: Hepatocellular carcinoma: US evaluation in the early stage. Radiology 155:463–467, 1985.

Smith WL, Franken EA, Mitros FA: Liver tumors in children. Semin Roentgenol 18:136–148, 1983.

Tanaka S, Kitamura T, Imaoka S, et al.: Hepatocellular carcinoma: Sonographic and histologic correlation. AJR 140:701–707, 1983.

Yates CK, Streight RA: Focal fatty infiltration of the liver simulating metastatic disease. Radiology 159:83–84, 1986.

Yoshikawa J, Matsui O, Takashima T, Sugiura H, Katayama K, Nishida Y, Tsuji M: Focal fatty change of the liver adjacent to the falciform ligament: CT and sonographic findings in five surgically confirmed cases. AJR 149:491–494, 1987.

Hypoechoic Liver Masses

Berland LL: Focal areas of decreased echogenicity in the liver at the porta hepatis. J Ultrasound Med 5:157–159, 1986.

Ginaldi S, Bernardino ME, Jing BS, Green B: Ultrasonographic patterns of hepatic lymphoma. Radiology 136:427–431, 1980.

Moody AR, Wilson SR: Atypical hepatic hemangioma: A suggestive sonographic morphology. Radiology 188:413–417, 1993.

Ros PR, Rasmussen JF, Li KCP: Radiology of malignant and benign liver tumors. Curr Probl Diagn Radiol 18:95–199, 1989.

Scott Jr WW, Sanders RC, Siegelman SS: Irregular fatty infiltration of the liver: Diagnostic dilemmas. AJR 135:67–71, 1980.

Viscomi GN, Gonzalez R, Taylor KJW: Histopathological correlation of ultrasound appearances of liver metastasis. J Clin Gastroenterol 3:395–400, 1981.

White EM, Simeone JF, Mueller PR, Grant EG, Choyke PL, Zeman RK: Focal periportal sparing in hepatic fatty infiltration: A cause of hepatic pseudomass on US. Radiology 162:57–59, 1987.

Cystic Lesions in the Liver

Barreda R, Ros PR: Diagnostic imaging of liver abscess. CRC Crit Rev Diagn Imaging 33:29–58, 1992.

Choi BI, Lim JH, Han MC, Lee DH, Kim SH, Kim YI, Kim C-W: Biliary cystadenoma and cystadenocarcinoma: CT and sonographic findings. Radiology 171:57–61, 1989.

Kaplan SB, Zajko AB, Koneru B: Hepatic bilomas due to hepatic artery thrombosis in liver transplant recipients: Percutaneous drainage and clinical outcome. Radiology 174:1031–1035, 1990.

Khuroo MS, Zargar SA, Mahejan R: Echinococcus granulosus cysts in the liver: Management with percutaneous drainage. Radiology 180:141–145, 1991.

Murphy BJ, Casillas J, Ros PR, Morillo G, Albores-Saavedra J, Rolfes DB: The CT appearance of cystic masses of the liver. RadioGraphics 9:307–322, 1989.

von Sinner WN: Ultrasound, CT and MRI of ruptured and disseminated hydatid cysts. Eur J Radiol 11:31–37, 1990.

vanSonnenberg E, Wroblicka JT, D'Agostino HB, Mathieson JRM, Casola G, O'Laoide R, Cooperberg PL: Symptomatic hepatic cysts: Percutaneous drainage and sclerosis. Radiology 190:387–392, 1994.

Highly Echogenic Liver Lesions Containing Calcification or Air

Bruneton JN, Ladree D, Caramella E, et al.: Ultrasonographic study of calcified hepatic metastases: A report of 13 cases. Gastrointest Radiol 7:61–63, 1982.

Darlak JJ, Moskowitz M, Kattan KR: Calcifications in the liver. Radiol Clin North Am 18:209–219, 1980.

Target (Bull's-Eye) Lesion in the Liver or Spleen

Pastakia B, Shawker TH, Thaler M, O'Leary T, Pizzo PA: Hepatosplenic candidiasis: Wheels within wheels. Radiology 166:417–421, 1988.

Biliary Ductal Dilatation

Garber SJ, Donald JJ, Lees WR: Cholangiocarcinoma: Ultrasound features and correlation of tumor position with survival. Abdomen Imaging 18:66–69, 1993.

Jackson VP, Lappas JC: Sonography of the Mirizzi syndrome. J Ultrasound Med 3:281–283, 1984.

Lim JH: Radiologic findings of clonorchiasis. AJR 155:1001–1008, 1990.

Lim JH, Ko YT, Lee DH, Kim SY: Clonorchiasis: Sonographic findings in 59 proved cases. AJR 152:761–764, 1989.

Machan L, Müller NL, Cooperberg PL: Sonographic diagnosis of Klatskin tumors. AJR 147:509–512, 1986.

Meyer DG, Weinstein B: Klatskin tumors of the bile ducts: Sonographic appearance. Radiology 148:803–804, 1983.

Spivey JR, Garrido JA, Reddy KR, Jeffers LJ, Schiff ER: ERCP documentation of obstructive jaundice caused by a solitary, centrally located benign hepatic cyst. Gastrointest Endoscopy 36:521–523, 1990.

Distal Common Bile Duct Obstruction

Da Silva F, Boudghene F, Lecomte I, Delage Y, Grange J-D, Bigot J-M: Sonography in AIDS-related cholangitis: Prevalence and cause of an echogenic nodule in the distal end of the common bile duct. AJR 160:1205–1207, 1993.

Dolmatch BL, Laing FC, Federle MP, Jeffrey RB, Cello J: AIDS-related cholangitis: Radiographic findings in nine patients. Radiology 163:313–316, 1987.

Gibson RN, Yeung E, Thompson JN, Carr DH, Hemingway AP, Bradpiece HA, et al: Bile duct obstruction: Radiologic evaluation of level, cause, and tumor resectability. Radiology 160:43–47, 1986.

Honickman SP, Mueller PR, Wittenberg J, et al: Ultrasound in obstructive jaundice: Prospective evaluation of site and cause. Radiology 147:511–515, 1983.

Koenigsberg M, Wiener SN, Walzer A: The accuracy of sonography in the differential diagnosis of obstructive jaundice: A comparison with cholangiography. Radiology 133:157–165, 1979.

Laing FC, Jeffrey RB, Wing VW: Improved visualization of choledocholithiasis by sonography. AJR 143:949–952, 1984.

Laing FC, Jeffrey RB Jr, Wing VW, Nyberg DA: Biliary dilatation: Defining the level and cause by real-time US. Radiology 160:39–42, 1986.

Rusin JA, Sivit CJ, Rakusan TA, Chandra RS: AIDS-related cholangitis in children: Sonographic findings. AJR 159:626–627, 1992.

Bile Duct Wall Thickening

Carroll BA, Oppenheimer DA: Sclerosing cholangitis: Sonographic demonstration of bile duct wall thickening. AJR 139:1016–1018, 1982.

Middleton WD, Surratt RS: Thickened bile duct wall simulating ductal dilatation on sonography. AJR 159:331–332, 1992.

Schulte SJ, Baron RL, Teefey SA, et al.: CT of the extrahepatic bile ducts: Wall thickness and contrast enhancement in normal and abnormal ducts. AJR 154:79–85, 1990.

Abnormalities of the Portal Vein

Albacete RA, Matthews MJ, Saini N: Portal vein thromboses in malignant hepatoma. Ann Intern Med 67:337–348, 1967.

Albertyn LE: Case report: Acute portal vein thrombosis. Clin Radiol 38:645–648, 1987.

Atri M, de Stempel J, Bret PM, et al: Incidence of portal vein thrombosis complicating liver metastasis as detected by duplex ultrasound. J Ultrasound Med 9:285–289, 1990.

Babcock DS: Ultrasound diagnosis of portal vein thrombosis as a complication of appendicitis. AJR 133:317–319, 1979.

Kowal-Vern A, Radhakrishnan J, Goldman J, et al: Mesenteric and portal vein thrombosis after splenectomy for autoimmune hemolytic anemia. J Clin Gastroenterol 10:108–110, 1988.

Langnas AN, Marujo W, Stratta RJ, et al: Vascular complications after orthotopic liver transplantation. Am J Surg 161:76–83, 1991.

Miller VE, Berland LL: Pulsed Doppler duplex sonography and CT of portal vein thrombosis. AJR 145:73–76, 1985.

Parvey HR, Raval B, Sandler CM: Portal vein thrombosis: Imaging findings. AJR 162:77–81, 1994.

Pozniak MA, Baus KM: Hepatofugal arterial signal in the main portal vein: An indicator of intravascular tumor spread. Radiology 180:663–666, 1991.

Slovis TL, Haller JO, Cohen HL, et al: Complicated appendiceal inflammatory disease in children: Pylephlebitis and liver abscess. Radiology 171:823–825, 1989.

Stieber AC, Zetti G, Todo S, et al: The spectrum of portal vein thrombosis in liver transplantation. Ann Surg 213:199–206, 1991.

Vilana R, Bru C, Bruix J, Castells A, Sole M, Rodes J: Fine-needle aspiration biopsy of portal vein thrombosis: Value in detecting malignant thrombosis. AJR 160:1285–1287, 1993.

Echogenic Foci in the Portal Vein: Calcification Versus Air

Ayuso C, Luburich P, Vilana R, Bru C, Bruix J: Calcifications in the portal venous system: Comparison of plain films, sonography and CT. AJR 159:321–323, 1992.

Baker SR, Broker MH, Charnsangavej C, et al: Calcification in the portal vein wall. Radiology 152:18, 1984.

Blanc WA, Berdon WE, Baker DH, et al: Calcified portal vein thromboemboli in newborn and stillborn infants. Radiology 88:287–292, 1967.

Dennis MA, Pretorius D, Manco-Johnson ML, Bangert-Burroughs K: CT detection of portal venous gas associated with suppurative cholangitis and cholecystitis. AJR 1017–1018, 1985.

Fisher JK: Computed tomography of colonic pneumatosis intestinalis with mesenteric and portal venous air. J Comput Assist Tomogr 8:573–574, 1984.

Friedman AP, Haller JO, Boyer B, et al: Calcified portal vein thromboemboli in infants: Radiography and ultrasonography. Radiology 140:381–382, 1981.

Kriegshauser JS, Reading CC, King BF, Welch TJ: Combined systemic and portal venous gas: Sonographic and CT detection in two cases. AJR 154:1219–1221, 1990.

Merritt CRB, Goldsmith JP, Sharp MJ: Sonographic detection of portal venous gas in infants with necrotizing enterocolitis. AJR 143:1059–1062, 1984.

Brightly Echogenic Portal Triads

Desai RK, Paushter DM, Armistead J: Intrahepatic arterial calcification mimicking pneumobilia. A potential pitfall in the ultrasound evaluation of biliary tract disease. J Ultrasound Med 8:333–335, 1989.

Federle MP, Cello JP, Laing FC, Jeffrey RB Jr: Recurrent pyogenic cholangitis in Asian immigrants. Use of ultrasonography, computed tomography, and cholangiography. Radiology 143:151–156, 1982.

Periportal Masses

Epstein BM, Mann JH: CT of abdominal tuberculosis. AJR 139:861–866, 1982.

Storm BL, Abbitt PL, Allen DA, Ros PR: Splenosis: Superparamagnetic iron oxide–enhanced MR imaging. AJR 159:333–335, 1992.

Toppet V, Souayah H, Delplace O, Alard S, Moreau J, Levy J, Spehl M: Lymph node enlargement as a sign of acute hepatitis A in children. Pediatr Radiol 20:249–252, 1990.

GALLBLADDER

```
┌─────────────────────────────────────────────┐
│                  PATTERNS                     │
│                                               │
│  Diffuse Gallbladder Wall Thickening          │
│  Focal Gallbladder Wall Thickening            │
│  Highly Echogenic Gallbladder Wall: Calcium   │
│      versus Air                               │
│  Soft Tissue Material Within the Gallbladder  │
│  Enlargement of the Gallbladder               │
│  Nonvisualization of the Gallbladder          │
│  Septations Within the Gallbladder            │
│  Pericholecystic Fluid                        │
└─────────────────────────────────────────────┘
```

DIFFUSE GALLBLADDER WALL THICKENING

Intrinsic Gallbladder Disease
    Cholecystitis
    Adenomyomatosis
    Gallbladder Carcinoma
Gallbladder Wall Thickening Unrelated to
    Gallbladder Disease
Varices

VARIANT

Contraction of the Gallbladder

The normal gallbladder wall is pencil-lead thin, measuring 2–3 mm or less in a fasting patient. When gallbladder wall thickness is measured, the wall adjacent to the liver should be measured in a plane perpendicular to the transducer so as not to overestimate the thickness. Many times, simple visualization of the gallbladder wall is sufficient to say whether wall thickness is normal or not. Diffuse gallbladder wall thickening may occur in conditions intrinsic to the gallbladder but is seen perhaps more commonly in situations unrelated to gallbladder disease.

Intrinsic Gallbladder Disease (Figures 2.1–2.6)

Cholecystitis   Thickening of the gallbladder wall may occur in conditions of intrinsic gallbladder disease, such as with acute or chronic cholecystitis, adenomyomatosis, or gallbladder carcinoma. Wall thickening in such situations is related to inflammation, fibrosis, glandular proliferation, or tumor infiltration. Two different patterns of gallbladder wall thickening have been described. One pattern, "three-layer thickening," consists of a hypoechoic band between hyperechoic bands. This pattern has been contrasted to gallbladder wall thickening, in which there are many alternating bands of echogenicity. This second pattern has been described as the "striated" pattern of gallbladder wall thickening.

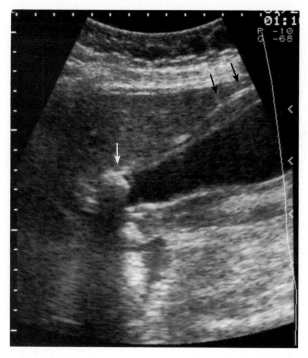

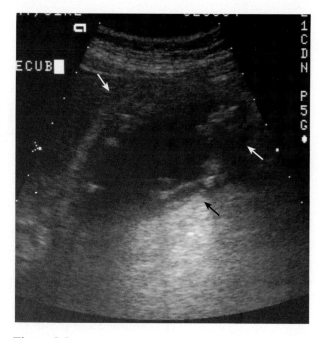

Figure 2.1
Acute cholecystitis: This young woman presented with severe right upper quadrant pain, fever, and leukocytosis. Sonography showed a 2.5-cm stone impacted in the neck of the gallbladder (*arrow*) and marked gallbladder wall thickening (*double arrows*). At surgery, a necrotic gallbladder was removed.

Figure 2.3
Chronic cholecystitis: Marked wall irregularities and thickening were noted in this elderly patient being evaluated for possible hydronephrosis. The patient had no acute complaints. Severe chronic sclerosing cholecystitis was found histologically at cholecystectomy.

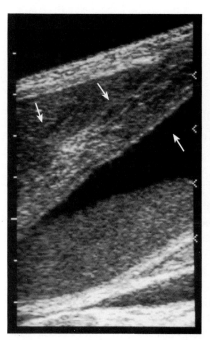

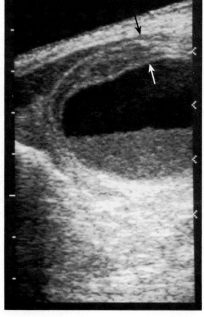

A   B

Figure 2.2
Acute acalculous cholecystitis: This elderly patient was hospitalized after fracturing her hip. During her prolonged hospitalization, right upper quadrant pain and leukocytosis developed. (A and B) Sonography showed sludge and dramatic gallbladder wall thickening (*arrows*). At surgery, acute acalculous cholecystitis was discovered.

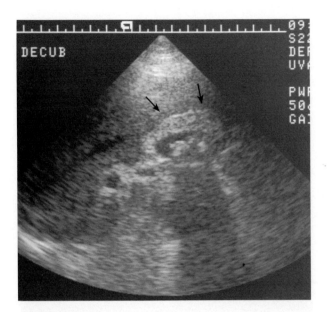

Figure 2.4

Chronic cholecystitis: A markedly thickened gallbladder wall was present in this gallbladder that was contracted down around stones.

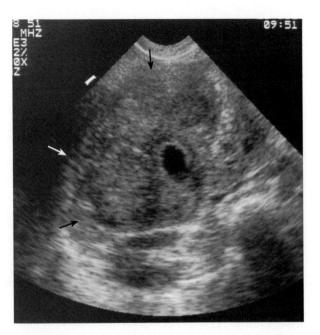

Figure 2.6

Gallbladder carcinoma: This elderly woman presented with jaundice. Ultrasound evaluation showed intrahepatic biliary ductal dilatation involving both lobes of the liver. The gallbladder was very abnormal. Marked gallbladder wall thickening merged with the substance of the liver (*arrows*). Numerous gallstones were present. Biopsy of the abnormal gallbladder wall proved adenocarcinoma of gallbladder origin.

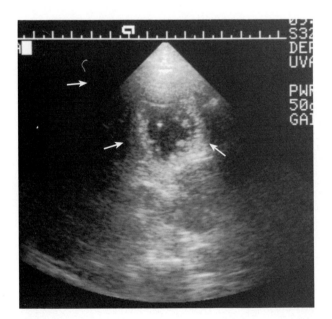

Figure 2.5

Multiple cholesterol polyps–cholesterolosis: This young pregnant woman complained of recurrent right upper quadrant pain. No stones were identified, but the gallbladder wall was studded with innumerable cholesterol polyps (*arrows*). The gallbladder was removed postpartum.

Some studies have reported marked irregularities of the gallbladder wall and intraluminal membranes in patients with gangrenous cholecystitis. Gangrene of the gallbladder may result in complications in 16 to 25 percent of patients and death in up to 22 percent of patients. Recognition of gangrenous change of the gallbladder can result in early operation, avoiding perforation and abscess formation. Color Doppler may show hyperemia about the thickened, inflamed gallbladder wall.

Other reports suggested that striated gallbladder wall thickening was no more specific for cholecystitis than gallbladder wall thickening itself. In the clinical setting of acute cholecystitis, however, striated gallbladder wall thickening was good evidence for gangrenous cholecystitis. Sometimes patients lose their sensation of pain once infarction or gangrene of the gallbladder has occurred, making the Murphy's sign unreliable.

Adenomyomatosis Adenomyomatosis of the gallbladder may result in diffuse thickening of the gallbladder wall. Multiple diverticuli of the wall and numerous cholesterol polyps contribute to the thickened, irregular, often echogenic gallbladder wall.

Gallbladder Carcinoma   Diffuse thickening of the gallbladder wall and gallstones can sometimes be secondary to gallbladder carcinoma. Patients with gallbladder carcinoma almost always have gallstones. Chronic irritation and inflammation of the gallbladder associated with stones are thought to constitute an etiologic factor in the development of gallbladder carcinoma. Patients with gallbladder carcinoma often have had chronic complaints of dyspepsia, right upper quadrant discomfort, and fatty food intolerance. Most often, their complaints are not new or acute.

Gallbladder Wall Thickening Unrelated to Gallbladder Disease (Figures 2.7–2.11)

Very often the gallbladder wall is thickened in conditions in which there is no intrinsic gallbladder abnormality. Such noninflammatory causes of gallbladder wall thickening include congestive heart failure; hypoalbuminemia; acute or chronic liver

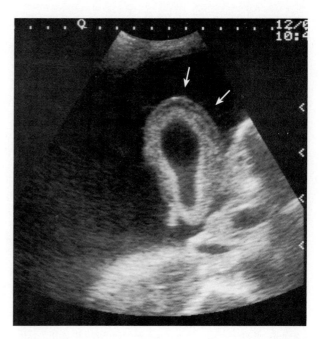

Figure 2.8
Gallbladder wall thickening related to liver disease and ascites: Pronounced gallbladder wall edema (*arrows*) was present in this patient prior to liver transplantation.

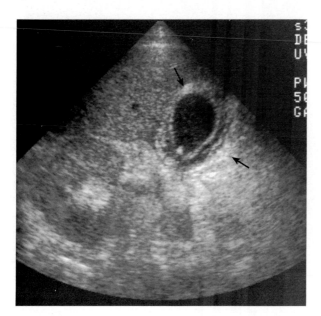

Figure 2.7
Acute fulminant hepatitis: Moderate gallbladder wall thickening (*arrows*) was present in this middle-aged woman with acute fulminant hepatitis. Ascites and diffusely diminished echogenicity of the liver were noted as well.

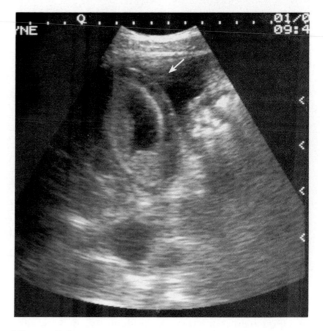

Figure 2.9
Gallbladder wall edema: Liver failure secondary to alcoholic liver disease was present in this patient with gallbladder wall thickening (*arrow*) and sludge.

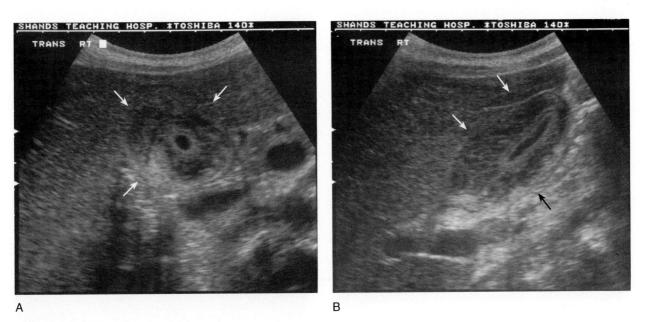

A   B

Figure 2.10

Gallbladder wall edema: Dramatic gallbladder wall thickening (*arrows*) was identified in this patient with renal failure secondary to renal transplant rejection.

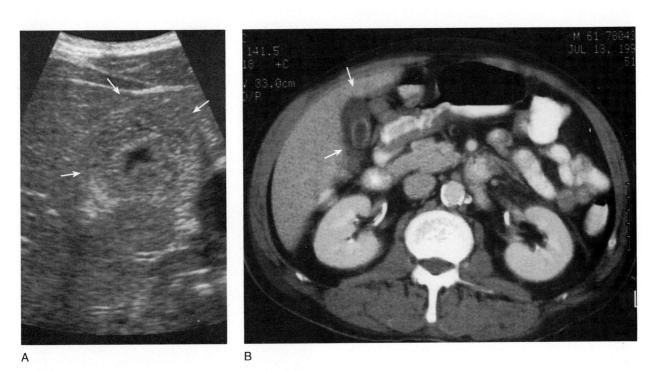

A   B

Figure 2.11

Gallbladder wall edema: (A) Wall thickening of the gallbladder (*arrows*) was present in this patient who required
aggressive fluid resuscitation for sepsis. A nuclear medicine biliary scan was normal without evidence of cystic
duct obstruction. (B) CT of the right upper quadrant
showed gallbladder wall thickening (*arrows*) that was misinterpreted as pericholecystic fluid.

disease, such as hepatitis or cirrhosis; renal failure; ascites; pancreatitis; and lymphatic obstruction related to portal adenopathy. Early investigations that suggested gallbladder wall thickening was specific for cholecystitis have been replaced by many observations that noninflammatory causes of striking wall edema are seen sonographically. Gallbladder wall thickening unrelated to gallbladder disease seems to be related to the same factors that lead to the formation of ascites—portal venous pressure and plasma oncotic pressure. Increased extravascular fluid in patients with liver, renal, and heart disease can result in striking gallbladder wall thickening. Gallbladder wall thickness can be a keen indicator of fluid overload states.

Gallbladder wall thickening seen in AIDS patients may be multifactorial in etiology, related to opportunistic infestation of the gallbladder by cryptosporidium, cytomegalovirus (CMV), or HIV itself. Other contributing etiologies include starvation, wasting and hypoproteinemia, and liver dysfunction accompanying the illness.

Studies have suggested that ultrasound can be used to differentiate malignant from benign causes of ascites by evaluating gallbladder wall thickness. Benign causes of ascites, including liver failure, congestive heart failure,and renal disease, lead to a markedly thickened gallbladder wall. A normal gallbladder wall thickness is often present with malignant ascites.

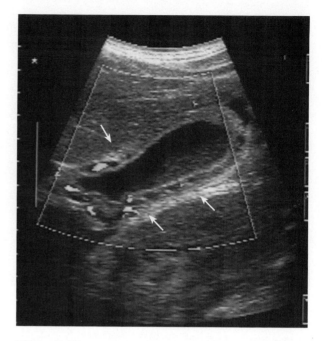

Figure 2.12
Varices of the gallbladder wall (Plate 13): Apparent wall thickening of the gallbladder was secondary to multiple varices of the gallbladder in this patient with portal vein thrombosis. (Case courtesy of Dr. Jennifer Hamrick-Turner, University of Mississippi.)

Varices (Figure 2.12)   Varices of the gallbladder wall can cause gallbladder wall thickening. Such varices occur in patients with portal hypertension, often with portal vein thrombosis. Color Doppler facilitates recognition of the varices in the gallbladder wall, allowing planning prior to surgery to prevent extensive blood loss.

VARIANT

Contraction of the Gallbladder (Figure 2.13)

One of the most frequently seen causes of relative gallbladder wall thickening is related to normal physiologic contraction of the gallbladder after eating. In patients with a mildly thickened gallbladder wall and contracted gallbladder lumen, inquiries regarding recent food ingestion are warranted, and a repeat study after fasting should be performed. A distended lumen and thin wall will be present if the gallbladder is functioning normally and the patient fasts prior to the evaluation.

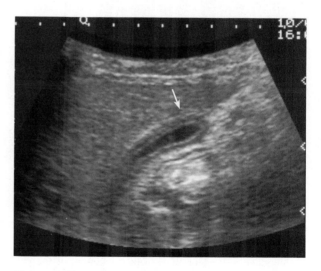

Figure 2.13
Normally contracted gallbladder: The gallbladder wall looked prominent in this patient with normal gallbladder function shortly after eating a meal. Note the small lumen of the gallbladder.

Emphasis Points

Gallbladder wall thickening is a very nonspecific sonographic sign. Although its presence may be related to acute inflammation of the gallbladder, gallbladder wall thickening is seen in a myriad of other conditions that have nothing to do with acute cholecystitis. Wall thickening without gallstones or tenderness is more likely secondary to cardiac, renal, or hepatic dysfunction than to inflammation of the gallbladder. Nuclear medicine functional studies of the biliary tree may be helpful in situations of gallbladder wall thickening without stones or pain to demonstrate patency of the cystic duct, making cholecystitis unlikely.

In my experience, the presence of gallstones and focal tenderness of the gallbladder (sonographic Murphy's sign) is a much more specific finding of acute cholecystitis than is gallbladder wall thickening. The sonographic Murphy's sign must be assessed correctly. Diffuse tenderness in the right upper quadrant from the liver, ribs, or duodenum is *not* a positive Murphy's sign. A positive sonographic Murphy's sign is pronounced tenderness when the transducer is applied directly to the gallbladder. It should be reproducible. With a demented or heavily sedated patient, the Murphy's sign may be unreliable.

Gallbladder wall thickening seen by CT is frequently misinterpreted as pericholecystic fluid, implying abscess formation or perforation of the gallbladder. The observation on CT of circumferential low density around the gallbladder should suggest wall thickening. Correlation of CT images with ultrasound will delineate wall thickening rather than pericholecystic fluid and allow the appropriate diagnostic considerations to be made.

FOCAL GALLBLADDER WALL THICKENING

Cholesterol Polyps/Adenomyomatosis
Cholecystitis (Acute, Chronic, or Gangrenous)
Gallbladder Carcinoma
Metastatic Disease of the Gallbladder
Wall Hematoma

Focal gallbladder wall thickening, in contrast to diffuse wall thickening, is almost always secondary to intrinsic gallbladder disease.

Cholesterol Polyp/Adenomyomatosis (Figure 2.14)

Frequently an incidental finding during an ultrasound examination, the cholesterol polyp of the gallbladder may be the most common cause of a focal (1–3 mm) gallbladder wall abnormality. The cholesterol polyp is differentiated from a small gallstone by its adherence to the gallbladder wall, its lack of mobility, and its failure to cast a shadow. Multiple cholesterol polyps are called cholesterolosis and result in the so-called strawberry gallbladder. Adenomyomatosis with Rokitansky–Aschoff sinuses or diverticuli of the gallbladder wall also may cause focal gallbladder wall thickening. Sometimes adenomyomatosis has associated "ringdown" artifact secondary to adherent or trapped cholesterol crystals.

Adenomatous polyps of the gallbladder, in contrast to cholesterol polyps, are unusual. These polyps may be centimeters in size, and a stalk can sometimes be identified as the polyp moves about in the gallbladder lumen.

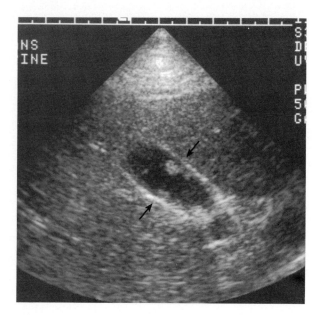

Figure 2.14

Cholesterol polyps: Several soft tissue nodules (*arrows*) that were adherent to the gallbladder wall and nonshadowing were identified in this patient with right upper quadrant pain.

Cholecystitis (Acute, Chronic, or Gangrenous) (Figures 2.15–2.16)

Focal wall irregularities of the gallbladder may be identified in the setting of inflammatory disease of the gallbladder. Fibrosis and inflammation are present with chronic cholecystitis. Hemorrhage, necrosis, and abscess formation are the histologic findings in acute or gangrenous disease. Patients with gangrene of the gallbladder are often quite ill with sepsis and need emergent surgery. Focal wall thickening in the relatively asymptomatic patient may be difficult to differentiate from gallbladder carcinoma.

Gallbladder Carcinoma (Figures 2.17–2.18)

Gallbladder carcinoma has three main ways of presenting: (1) diffuse wall thickening, (2) an obliterative mass that traps associated gallstones and invades the hepatic parenchyma, and (3) focal gallbladder wall thickening or mass.

Small focal tumors may be hard to diagnose because the focal wall thickening may be flat and difficult to discern if it is hidden beneath stones and sludge on the dependent wall of the gallbladder. Technical problems created by patient obesity and difficulties in visualizing the fundus of the gallbladder result in lower sensitivity in discovering early gallbladder carcinomas.

Metastatic Disease of the Gallbladder (Figure 2.19)

Focal wall thickening caused by metastatic disease of the gallbladder can be secondary to locally invasive tumors, such as pancreatic carcinoma, or to hematogenous spread from melanoma and lung or breast carcinomas.

Wall Hematoma (Figure 2.20)

Trauma to the gallbladder wall, especially iatrogenic trauma such as percutaneous tube placement or extracorporal shock wave lithotripsy (ESWL), may cause hemorrhage and focal thickening of the gallbladder wall. Such thickening should resolve with time.

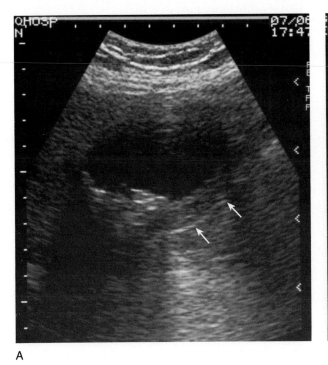

A

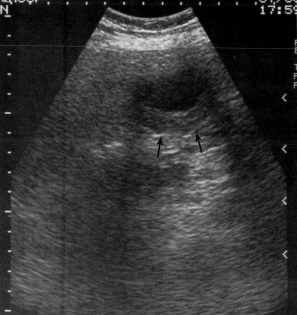

B

Figure 2.15

Focal chronic cholecystitis: (A and B) Focal wall thickening (*arrows*) nearly hidden by gallstones was secondary to chronic sclerosing cholecystitis. The preoperative diagnosis was gallbladder carcinoma.

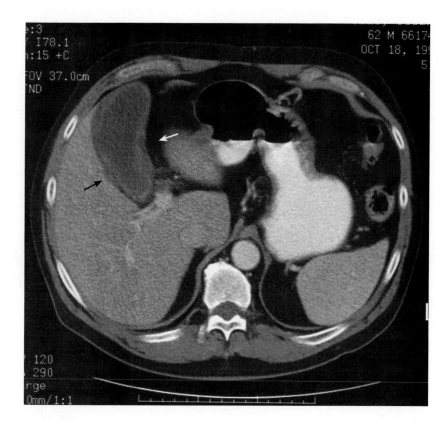

Figure 2.16
Acute cholecystitis: Focal gallbladder wall abnormalities were present in this patient with an acutely necrotic gallbladder. This immunocompromised patient was nontender.

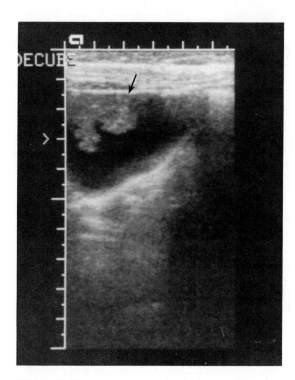

Figure 2.17
Gallbladder carcinoma: A polypoid mass in the fundus of the gallbladder was incidentally discovered in this elderly man with gallstones. Carcinoma was found histologically.

HIGHLY ECHOGENIC GALLBLADDER WALL: CALCIUM VERSUS AIR

Porcelain Gallbladder
Emphysematous Cholecystitis

VARIANTS

Contracted Gallbladder Around Stones/Air in Nearby Bowel
Air in the Lumen of the Gallbladder from Instrumentation

An abnormality of the gallbladder wall involving extremely echogenic foci in the wall that cause shadowing or reverberation reflects intrinsic gallbladder disease. This sonographic picture represents either a calcified gallbladder wall, as seen in patients with porcelain gallbladder, or air within the gallbladder wall in patients with emphysematous cholecystitis. Although the sonographic picture may look similar in these two situations, the clinical circumstances are usually quite different. The use of plain films or CT can readily differentiate the two conditions if there is confusion sonographically.

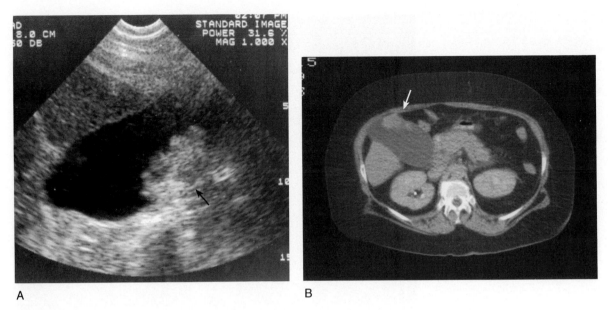

A   B

Figure 2.18
Gallbladder carcinoma: (A) A polypoid mass emanating
from the wall of the gallbladder was found to be malignant
at surgery. (B) Correlative CT images in the same patient.

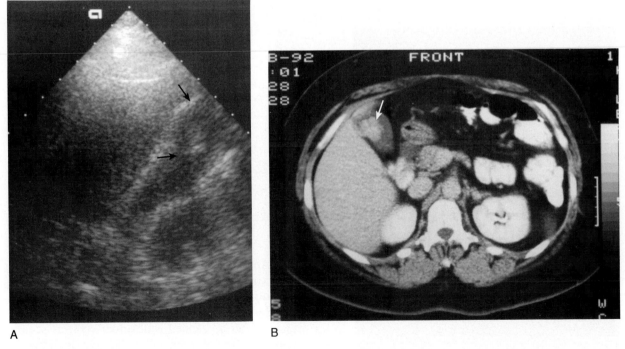

A   B

Figure 2.19
Melanoma metastatic to the gallbladder: (A) Focal fundal
thickening (*arrows*) was present in this patient with disseminated melanoma. (B) Note the mass in the gallbladder by CT. (Case courtesy of Dr. Jennifer Hamrick-
Turner, University of Mississippi.)

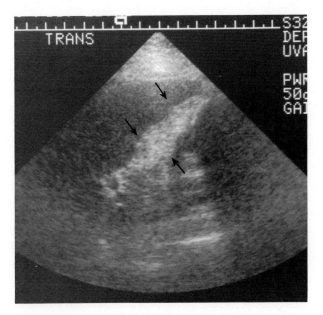

Figure 2.20
Gallbladder wall hematoma: Thickening of the gallbladder wall developed after gallbladder lithotripsy, taking weeks to resolve.

Porcelain Gallbladder (Figures 2.21–2.23)

A porcelain gallbladder occurs rarely, with an incidence of 0.06 to 0.8 percent in cholecystectomy specimens. Calcification of the gallbladder wall is associated with gallstones more than 95 percent of the time and occurs more often in women than in men, with a ratio of 5 : 1, much like the incidence of stones.

The pathogenesis of a porcelain gallbladder is unknown. Several hypotheses have been suggested, including dystrophic calcification from chronic infection and compromised blood flow, chronic irritation of the wall by stones, or chronic obstruction of the cystic duct with precipitation of calcium salts in the wall. Calcification of the gallbladder wall is associated with a higher incidence of gallbladder carcinoma, ranging from 11 percent to 33 percent, depending upon the series. The radiologist may be the first to recognize asymptomatic gallbladder wall calcification and must alert the referring physician to the high incidence of associated gallbladder carcinoma.

Clinically, the patient with a porcelain gallbladder does not usually present acutely but has chronic complaints of right upper quadrant pain, dyspepsia, bloating, and fatty food intolerance.

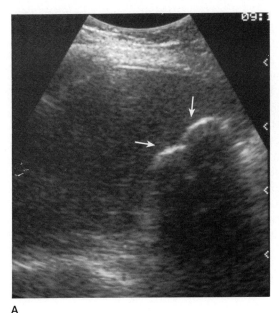

A

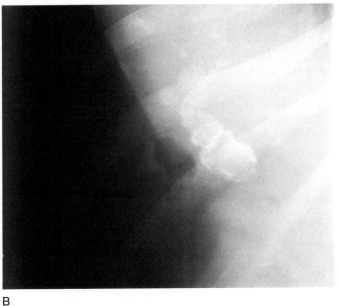

B

Figure 2.21
Porcelain gallbladder: (A) The gallbladder wall (*arrows*) was densely calcified and caused a large shadow, obscuring visualization of underlying structures. (B) Plain film confirmed the densely calcified gallbladder.

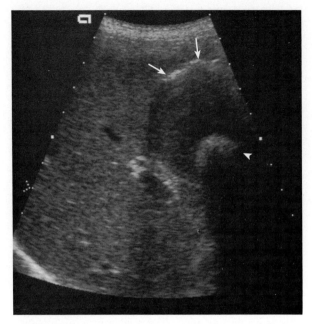

Figure 2.22
Porcelain gallbladder: Focal areas of wall calcification (*arrows*) were identified in this patient with a long history of gallstones (*arrowhead*).

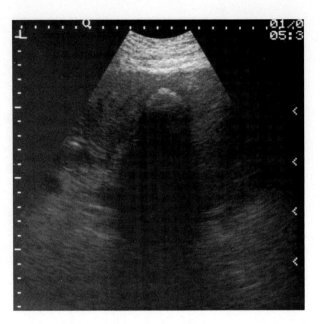

Figure 2.23
Porcelain gallbladder: Dense shadowing from the gallbladder fossa was noted in this patient.

Emphysematous Cholecystitis (Figures 2.24–2.25)

The sonographic image of emphysematous cholecystitis, in which there is air in the gallbladder wall and sometimes in the lumen of the gallbladder, may be difficult to differentiate from a porcelain gallbladder. In emphysematous cholecystitis, air is seen as highly echogenic foci in the gallbladder wall with shadowing or reverberations. Tiny microbubbles of air may rise from the dependent portions of the gallbladder lumen, much like rising bubbles in a champagne glass. The gas may shift in response to gravity as the patient changes position. Plain films or CT can confirm the presence of gallbladder wall air.

Nearly 40 percent of patients with emphysematous cholecystitis are diabetic. Ischemia of the gallbladder, sometimes with secondary infection by gas-forming organisms, is the underlying pathogenesis of the condition. Cholelithiasis is not the main pathogenetic factor in patients with emphysematous cholecystitis. Men are affected more often than women, with a ratio of 7 : 3, a remarkable difference when compared to the population that has stones. Gangrene and perforation of the gallbladder are much more common in emphysematous cholecystitis than in usual acute cholecystitis. Emphysematous cholecystitis is therefore considered a surgical emergency.

VARIANTS

Contracted Gallbladder Around Stones/Air in Nearby Bowel (Figure 2.26)

Other situations may be misinterpreted as calcification or air in the gallbladder wall. Sometimes patients with chronic cholecystitis in whom the gallbladder is contracted down around stones are difficult to differentiate from patients with porcelain gallbladder. When the gallbladder is contracted, it may be difficult to determine whether the wall is casting a shadow, as in porcelain gallbladder, or whether the shadow is emanating from the stones. In patients with a contracted or absent gallbladder, air in the nearby hepatic flexure or duodenum can be mistaken for an air-filled gallbladder. Cross-sectional imaging with CT makes it possible to differentiate these conditions. Repeat sonography when the patient has fasted can also facilitate gallbladder visualization.

Air in the Lumen of the Gallbladder from Instrumentation (Figure 2.27)

Air in the lumen of the gallbladder may get there in situations of emphysematous cholecystitis or may be related to instrumentation of the biliary tree, such as with ERCP. Air in the gallbladder lumen may change position with changes in patient positioning and cause posterior ringdown artifact.

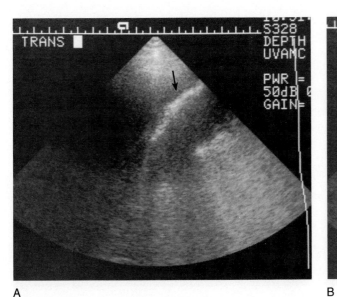

A

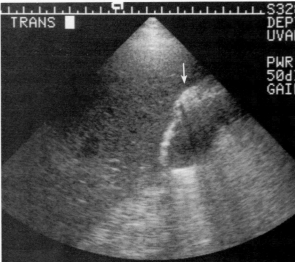

B

Figure 2.24
Emphysematous cholecystitis: (A and B) This elderly diabetic patient was confused at the time of the sonographic examination. Note the extremely echogenic gallbladder wall with little diagnostic information behind it. A necrotic gallbladder was surgically removed.

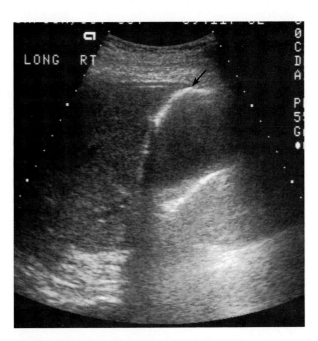

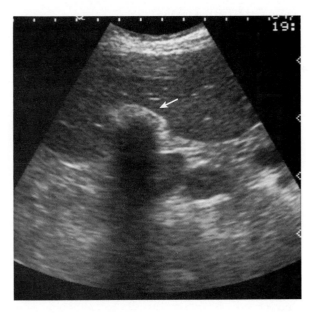

Figure 2.26
Chronic cholecystitis: The gallbladder wall was contracted down around stones. Even with patient fasting, the gallbladder did not distend. Sometimes it is difficult to differentiate a chronically contracted gallbladder with gallstones from a porcelain gallbladder. If the noncalcified wall can be seen anterior to the shadowing stone, then a contracted gallbladder is suggested.

Figure 2.25
Emphysematous cholecystitis: A brightly echogenic gallbladder wall (*arrow*) was present in this diabetic male after knee replacement. The condition proved fatal.

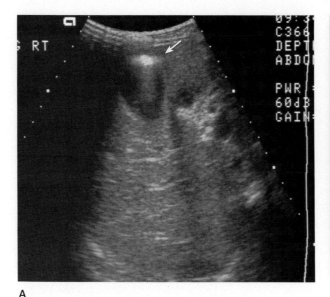

A   B

Figure 2.27

Air in gallbladder lumen after instrumentation: (A and B) The anterior portion of the gallbladder was brightly echogenic with ringdown artifact. The patient had just completed ERCP and had extensive biliary and gallbladder air.

SOFT TISSUE MATERIAL WITHIN THE GALLBLADDER

Chronic Fasting/Acalculous Cholecystitis
Obstruction of the Gallbladder or Biliary Tree
Gallbladder Hemorrhage/Infective Debris
Gallbladder Polyps
Gallbladder Carcinoma/Metastatic Disease
Extracorporeal Gallstone Lithotripsy
Artifacts

Chronic Fasting/Acalculous Cholecystitis (Figures 2.28–2.29)

Sludge of the gallbladder is the echogenic, particulate material and debris that accumulates in the gallbladder in patients who are fasting or obstructed. Sludge may fill the gallbladder lumen, may move about, and may become masslike (tumefactive sludge).

In the hospital setting, the most common situation in which sludge of the gallbladder is identified sonographically is in the critically ill, fasting patient. Typically, such patients are on parenteral nutrition and are not taking feedings by mouth. Patients in surgical intensive care units being treated for burns, or after trauma or surgery, often have a sludge-filled gallbladder, reflecting the absence of routine emptying of the gallbladder with eating.

Such chronically fasting patients may develop acalculous cholecystitis, manifest by a tender right upper quadrant, leukocytosis, and fever. In such patients, the inspissated, tarlike bile causes obstruction of the cystic duct even in the absence of gallstones. About 10 percent of patients with cholecystitis have acalculous cholecystitis and in these cases bile has usually been stagnant in the gallbladder.

Signs of inflammation with right upper quadrant tenderness and leukocytosis in the chronically hospitalized patient may suggest the diagnosis of acalculous cholecystitis. Nuclear medicine hepatobiliary scans can confirm cystic duct obstruction, although pharmaceuticals may need to be administered to facilitate gallbladder emptying and refilling, and thus prevent false-positive examinations. Even with administration of medications to facilitate gallbladder emptying, the cystic duct may not fill for quite some time, although no obstruction is present, resulting in a false-positive diagnosis. For this reason, nuclear medicine hepatobiliary scans may contribute little in this patient group.

Critically ill patients with prolonged hospitalization and signs of sepsis may benefit from percutaneous decompression of the gallbladder. Such a procedure may be performed portably at the patient's bedside in a relatively short time with little morbidity and may prove beneficial to the patient by eliminating or improving the septic parameters.

Obstruction of the Gallbladder or Biliary Tree (Figures 2.30–2.33)

Patients who are not chronically fasting and are found to have gallbladder sludge sonographically

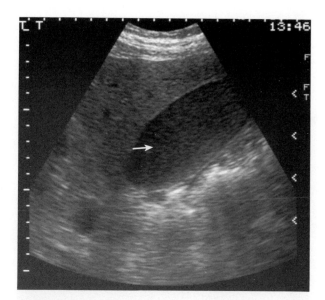

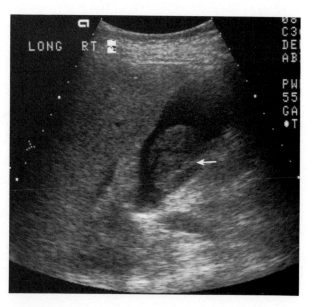

Figure 2.28
Gallbladder sludge: In this patient who had had a lengthy hospitalization related to severe burns, gallbladder sludge filled the gallbladder. Homogeneous low-level echoes were present.

Figure 2.29
Tumefactive sludge: A ball of sludge material (*arrow*) was visualized in this patient who had experienced a lengthy hospitalization for abdominal abscess.

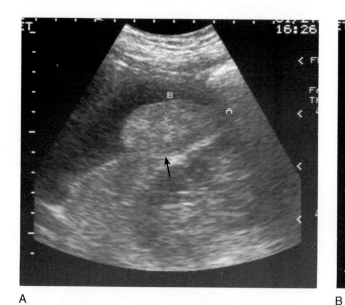

A

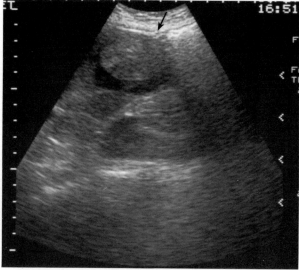

B

Figure 2.30
Tumefactive sludge: (A and B) This outpatient had a large ball-like mass of soft tissue material within the gallbladder, which moved about with changes in patient positioning. Because the patient had not been fasting, a site of biliary obstruction was sought and was found in the common bile duct.

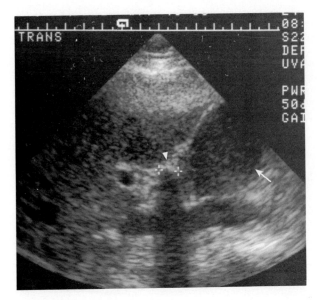

Figure 2.31
Sludge-filled gallbladder secondary to stone impacted in the neck: This patient had been eating normally, and sludge (*arrow*) was noted to distend the gallbladder. A large stone in the neck of the gallbladder (*arrowhead*) was felt responsible for the gallbladder sludge, suggesting that it caused chronic obstruction of the gallbladder.

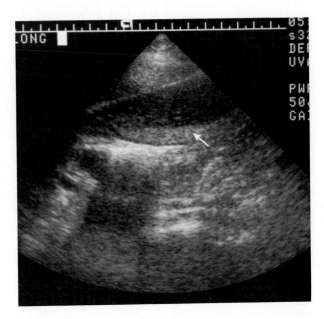

Figure 2.32
Layering sludge secondary to obstruction of the biliary tree by pancreatic carcinoma: The gallbladder was distended with sludge and had a debris level (*arrow*) in this elderly patient with biliary obstruction secondary to pancreatic head carcinoma.

must be evaluated for gallbladder or biliary obstruction. The presence of sludge in the patient who is eating normally suggests that the gallbladder cannot decompress itself even with the appropriate hormonal stimulation that accompanies eating. Ob-

struction to gallbladder emptying may result from a stone in the neck of the gallbladder, may be secondary to cystic duct obstruction by a stone, or may be related to obstruction of the extrahepatic biliary tree by benign postoperative strictures or malignant

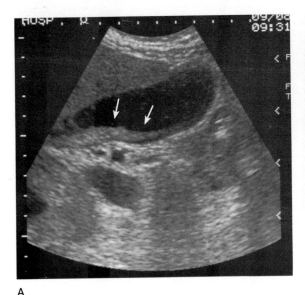

A

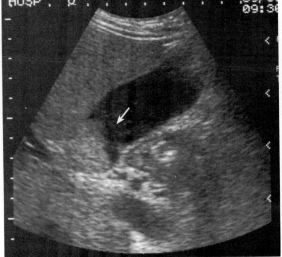

B

Figure 2.33
Sludge: The changing configuration of sludge (*arrows*) was obvious in this patient with pancreatitis.

masses. Observation of a sludge-filled gallbladder in a patient who has been eating normally prior to fasting for the sonogram must lead to a careful study that looks for the site of obstruction of gallbladder drainage.

Gallbladder Hemorrhage/Infective Debris (Figures 2.34–2.35)

Material that is sludgelike, in that it is particulate but does not shadow, may be seen in patients with hemorrhage or infective debris within the gallbladder. Patients may hemorrhage into the gallbladder lumen if they are receiving anticoagulants or have trauma to the liver, including liver biopsy. Those with infective material within the gallbladder will have symptoms of infection with leukocytosis and fever. Bacterial debris as well as fungal and parasitic organisms may accumulate within the gallbladder. Certain patients, especially those with HIV infection, may have multiple organism infection. Sometimes sludge, infective or not, becomes tumefactive or masslike in appearance. Changes in patient positioning may cause the sludge to move about.

Gallbladder Polyps

Soft tissue nodules adherent to the gallbladder wall are frequently cholesterol polyps, although rarely an adenomatous polyp may develop.

Gallbladder Carcinoma/Metastatic Disease (Figure 2.36)

One of the ways in which gallbladder carcinoma may manifest is a soft tissue mass that fills the gallbladder lumen. In such cases, stones are usually present, too. It has been suggested that stones reflect chronic inflammation and irritation of the gallbladder, which result in the eventual development of gallbladder carcinoma. Metastatic disease to the gallbladder may result in soft tissue material in the gallbladder. Usually such masses will not move with changes in patient position.

Extracorporeal Gallstone Lithotripsy (Figure 2.37)

Extracorporeal gallstone lithotripsy resulting in disintegration of gallstones may lead to a slurry of debris and sand within the gallbladder prior to passage into the extrahepatic biliary system. Time and administration of a fatty diet may facilitate passage

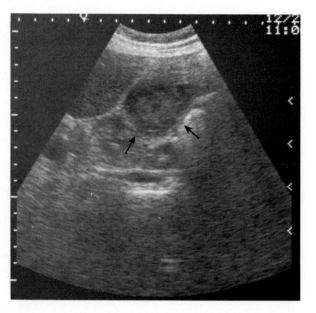

Figure 2.34
Gallbladder hemorrhage: This patient developed soft tissue material in the gallbladder (*arrows*) shortly after a percutaneous core biopsy of the liver that caused an intrahepatic hematoma. The soft tissue material was not present in the gallbladder on follow-up scans.

of the material from the gallbladder. Gallstone lithotripsy is only available in certain centers and is rarely performed now that there are improved methods of removing the gallbladder, such as laparoscopic cholecystectomy.

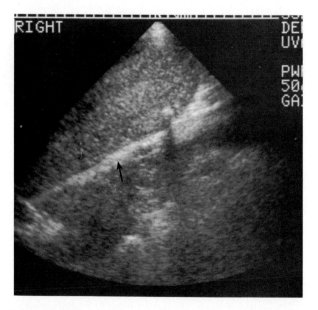

Figure 2.35
Infective debris: Purulent material (*arrow*) filled the gallbladder in this patient with acute cholecystitis.

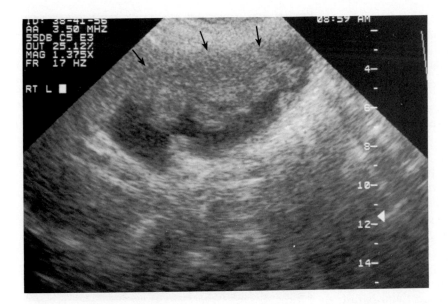

Figure 2.36
Gallbladder carcinoma: This elderly woman had gallstones and a polypoid mass of the gallbladder on sonographic evaluation.

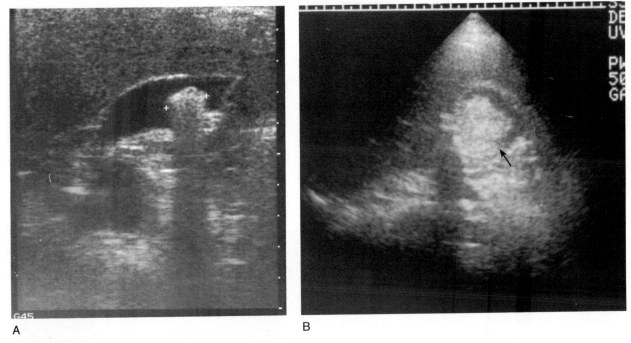

A

B

Figure 2.37
After ESWL: This 50-year-old man with gallstones had a slurry (*arrow*) of debris and stone material after extracorporeal lithotripsy of his stones. (A) Pre-ESWL. (B) Post-ESWL.

Artifacts

Artifacts may result in the apparent presence of sludge in the gallbladder. Careful attention to sonographic technique will lead to the realization that sludge is not present and that the finding is secondary to artifact. The "sludge" artifact will vary with changes in position of the transducer without changes in patient positioning.

Emphasis Points

While sludge is commonly seen in the chronically hospitalized, fasting patient, identification of sludge in an outpatient who has been eating normally should lead to a careful search for a point of obstruction, either of the gallbladder or of the biliary tree.

The chronically hospitalized septic patient with a sludge-filled, tender gallbladder without stones may benefit more from percutaneous drainage of the gallbladder than from further diagnostic imaging studies, such as nuclear medicine imaging, which may be falsely positive. A percutaneous drainage procedure that can be done at the bedside on such a critically ill, perhaps unstable patient, can be performed quickly, with little morbidity and potentially significant improvement.

ENLARGEMENT OF THE GALLBLADDER

Prolonged Fasting
Obstruction of the Gallbladder or Biliary Tree
Normal Gallbladder

CHILDHOOD

Hydrops (Kawasaki's Syndrome)

The size of the gallbladder is variable, but the organ usually measures 7–10 cm in length and 2–3 cm in width. The usual volume of the gallbladder is approximately 30–50 cm^3.

Prolonged Fasting (Figure 2.38)

The gallbladder becomes enlarged with prolonged fasting, especially in patients with diabetes or on anticholinergic medications. Bedridden patients on

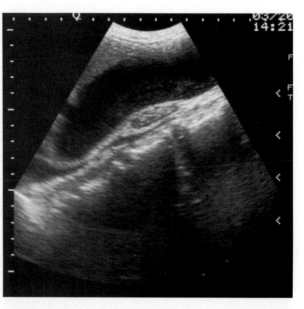

Figure 2.38
Prolonged fasting: Marked distention of the gallbladder was present in this patient after a prolonged intensive care hospitalization.

parenteral alimentation after trauma, pancreatitis, or other abdominal processes can be noted to have enlargement of the gallbladder.

Obstruction of the Gallbladder or Biliary Tree (Figures 2.39–2.40)

Obstruction of the gallbladder, cystic duct, or extrahepatic biliary tree may result in distention of the gallbladder. Stones or thick, inspissated bile most commonly obstruct the gallbladder or cystic duct, resulting in inability of the gallbladder to empty. Other processes, such as pancreatic carcinoma, pancreatitis, and strictures, may cause biliary tree obstruction and resultant gallbladder distention.

Normal Gallbladder

Sometimes the normal gallbladder can be quite large. Fatty foods can cause its decompression. A volume decrease of the gallbladder of 35 percent or more is expected after a fatty meal if the gallbladder is not obstructed.

CHILDHOOD

Hydrops (Kawasaki's Syndrome)

Hydrops of the gallbladder is massive distension of the gallbladder, usually seen in children. No stone

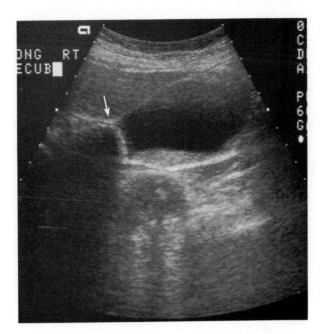

Figure 2.39
Obstruction of the gallbladder: A large stone (*arrow*) in the neck of the gallbladder obstructed normal gallbladder emptying. The gallbladder was distended.

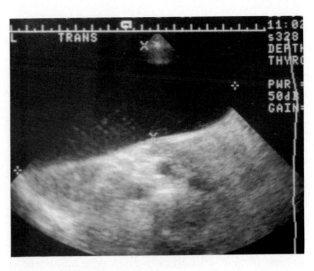

Figure 2.40
Obstruction of the gallbladder: A pancreatic head carcinoma causing biliary obstruction led to dramatic distention of the gallbladder. The gallbladder measured at least 14 cm in longitudinal dimension and could have been misinterpreted as a fluid collection if its origin had not been clarified.

is usually present. Hydrops of the gallbladder is probably secondary to a transient, self-limited obstruction of the cystic duct. Children with mucocutaneous lymph node syndrome or Kawasaki syndrome can develop dramatic distention of the gallbladder. Its pathogenesis is unknown, but it may result in the presentation of an acute abdomen. Functional studies of the biliary tree, such as nuclear medicine studies using Tc-99m IDA radionuclides, will demonstrate nonvisualization of the gallbladder in hydrops. Typhoid fever has also been reported to cause hydrops of the gallbladder.

The presence of a sonographic Murphy's sign and a massively distended gallbladder suggests superimposed infection of the distended, usually obstructed gallbladder. Prolonged distention and obstruction may lead to perforation of the ischemic fundus.

NONVISUALIZATION OF THE GALLBLADDER

Surgical Absence/Physiologically Contracted
　　Gallbladder
Abnormal Gallbladder
　　Contracted Gallbladder Around Stones/
　　Porcelain Gallbladder/Emphysematous
　　Cholecystitis

Liver Dysfunction
Hepatization of the Gallbladder
　　(Sludge-Filled)
Gallbladder Carcinoma
Ectopic Position of the Gallbladder

Surgical Absence/Physiologically Contracted Gallbladder (Figure 2.41)

Failure to identify the gallbladder sonographically is usually a result of either contraction of the gallbladder because the patient has recently eaten or prior surgical removal of the organ. Congenital absence is unusual.

The normal physiologically contracted gallbladder may be difficult to identify because it is small and can be masked by nearby duodenal gas. One possible remedy is to rescan the patient after appropriate fasting to allow bile to distend the gallbladder lumen.

Abnormal Gallbladder

Contracted Gallbladder Around Stones/Porcelain Gallbladder/Emphysematous Cholecystitis (Figure 2.42)　　Contraction of the gallbladder down around stones may result in failure to recognize the gallbladder. The chronically diseased and

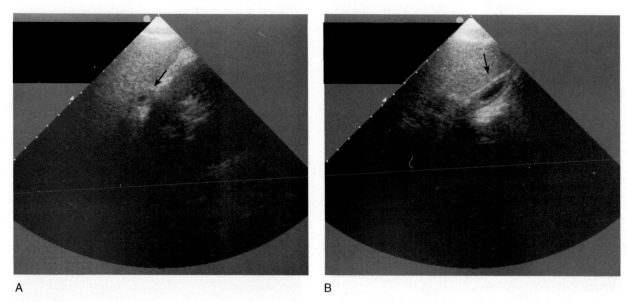

A   B

Figure 2.41
Physiologically contracted gallbladder: (A and B) A very
small, hard-to-see but normal gallbladder was present in
this patient after eating.

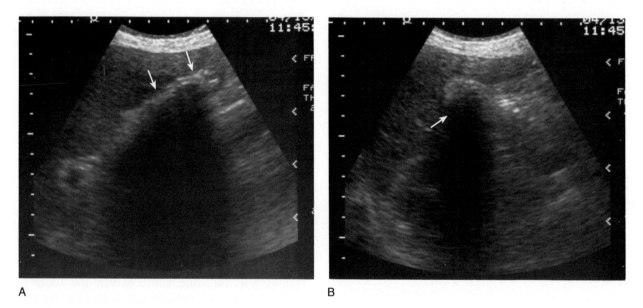

A   B

Figure 2.42
Contracted gallbladder around stones: (A and B) The contracted gallbladder was seen as an extremely echogenic
region with shadowing (*arrows*). When follow-up scanning after fasting showed no change, chronic cholecystitis
and stones were diagnosed.

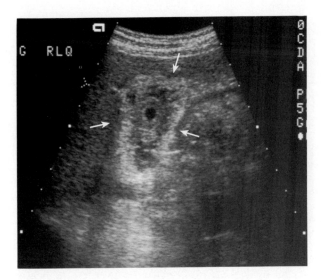

Figure 2.43
Contracted gallbladder secondary to liver dysfunction: Because liver function was poor, the gallbladder did not distend and was difficult to recognize secondary to marked wall thickening (*arrows*).

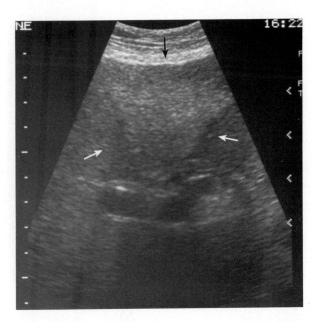

Figure 2.44
Hepatization of the gallbladder with sludge: In this chronically hospitalized patient, the gallbladder became filled with echogenic material (*arrows*), making its echogenicity similar to that of the liver. CT scan showed a distended, sludge-filled gallbladder of similar density to liver parenchyma on unenhanced images.

fibrotic gallbladder may not distend its lumen with bile even with fasting. The recognition of the gallbladder wall overlying the brightly echogenic shadowing stones will allow the correct diagnosis of a contracted gallbladder around stones to be differentiated from air in the duodenum. Real-time imaging while the patient drinks water will fill the duodenum with fluid and thus differentiate the duodenum from the gallbladder.

Calcification of the wall of the gallbladder itself, a porcelain gallbladder, may be difficult for the inexperienced to distinguish from gas-filled bowel. Similar sonographically to a gallbladder contracted around stones, a porcelain gallbladder will exhibit a very echogenic wall that will shadow. Plain films or tomographic cuts with CT may help verify the calcifications within the wall of the gallbladder.

Emphysematous cholecystitis may look sonographically similar to the porcelain gallbladder, although the clinical situation is usually very different.

Liver Dysfunction (Figure 2.43)

Liver dysfunction, such as that resulting from acute hepatitis, may cause nonfilling of the gallbladder related to relatively diminished bile production. This represents still another cause of gallbladder contraction that may lead to nonvisualization.

Hepatization of the Gallbladder (Sludge-Filled) (Figure 2.44)

Chronic fasting by a patient may result in echogenic sludge filling the gallbladder. The gallbladder of a chronically fasting patient may be so homogeneously filled with echoes as to make the gallbladder look "hepatized," or of similar echogenicity to nearby liver, thus making it difficult to differentiate from liver.

Gallbladder Carcinoma (Figure 2.45)

Gallbladder carcinoma can obliterate the lumen of the gallbladder by filling the gallbladder with tumor. In such a case, no recognizable normal gallbladder will be seen. Because most patients with gallbladder carcinoma have gallstones, trapped stones may be seen within the substance of the carcinomatous mass.

Ectopic Position of the Gallbladder (Figure 2.46)

Ectopic position of the gallbladder may result in its nonrecognition. Careful scanning in the upper ab-

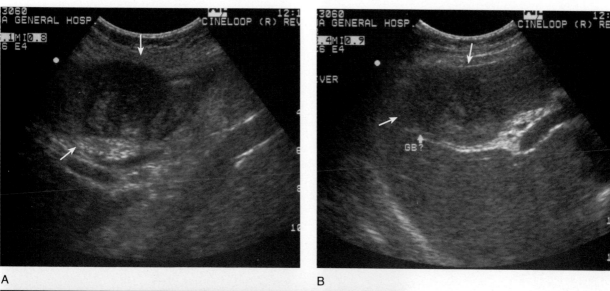

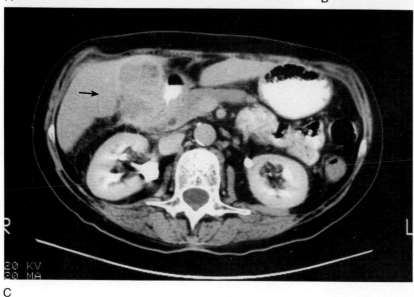

Figure 2.45
Gallbladder carcinoma: (A,B,C) Obliteration of the gallbladder lumen by tumor (*arrows*) made recognition of the gallbladder very difficult.

domen may reveal an unusual position of the gallbladder, which can be confirmed by functional studies of the gallbladder, such as a nuclear medicine hepatobiliary scan.

Emphasis Point

Congenital absence of the gallbladder is very rare. Nonvisualization or nonrecognition of the gallbladder is usually secondary to previous surgical removal or because the gallbladder is contracted or filled with stones, making it difficult to differentiate from bowel.

SEPTATIONS WITHIN THE GALLBLADDER

Normal Gallbladder Folds
Intraluminal Membranes in Acute Gangrenous
    Cholecystitis

Normal Gallbladder Folds (Figures 2.47–2.48)

Approximately 15 percent of patients have folds in the gallbladder that can be demonstrated sonographically. The so-called Phrygian cap is the description of a gallbladder fold that resembles the hat

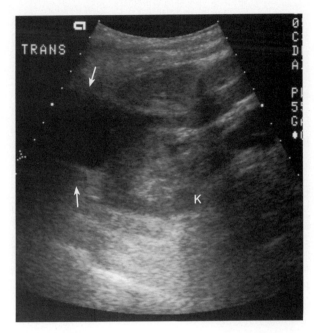

Figure 2.46
Ectopic location of gallbladder: The unusual position of the gallbladder (*arrows*) lateral to the right kidney (K) could make it difficult to recognize.

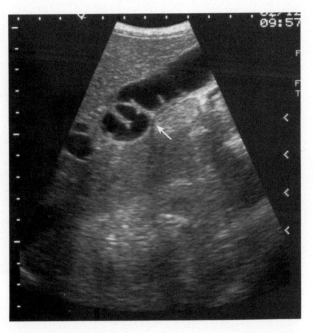

Figure 2.48
Gallbladder folds: Another example of normal but prominent folds of the gallbladder.

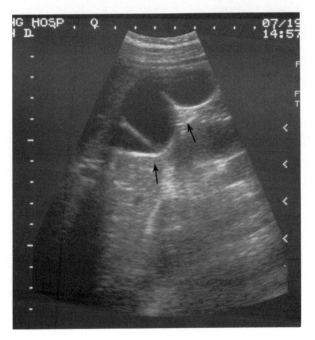

Figure 2.47
Junctional fold: Folds in the neck of the gallbladder were obvious in this patient.

worn by the slave Phrygians in ancient Egypt. The significance of folds is to recognize what they are and that they may compartmentalize the gallbladder somewhat, as there may be stones contained by a fold.

Intraluminal Membranes in Acute Gangrenous Cholecystitis (Figure 2.49)

In patients with severe acute inflammation of the gallbladder, intraluminal membranes connote the mucosal sloughing that accompanies the severe inflammatory reaction. Recognition of internal septations in the clinical setting of gallbladder inflammation suggests gangrenous cholecystitis and requires immediate surgery to prevent perforation.

PERICHOLECYSTIC FLUID

Generalized Ascites
Gallbladder Perforation
Nearby Organ Inflammation or Perforation

Fluid in the gallbladder fossa or pericholecystic region is often believed to originate from the gall-

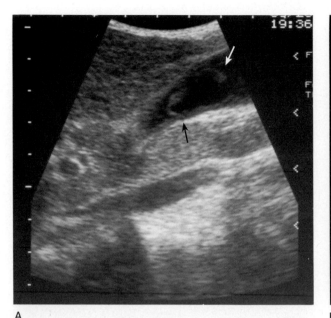

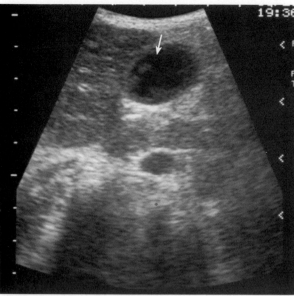

A   B

Figure 2.49

Gangrenous cholecystitis: Mucosal sloughing within the gallbladder lumen (*arrows*) was seen in this patient with severe gangrenous cholecystitis.

bladder. Other possibilities for the origin of the fluid must be considered.

Generalized Ascites (Figures 2.50–2.51)

The most common reason for fluid being present around the gallbladder is that the patient has generalized ascites. Ascites may be secondary to liver diseases, such as hepatitis or cirrhosis. Ascites may also be secondary to a number of other etiologies, including congestive heart failure, renal failure, malignancy, and carcinomatosis. Pelvic processes, such as pelvic inflammatory disease and ectopic pregnancy, can cause free abdominal fluid. Recognition that the pericholecystic fluid is part of a generalized process and is not just localized to the area around the gallbladder may remove the gallbladder as the etiologic agent of the ascites and the patient's complaints.

Gallbladder Perforation (Figure 2.52)

Pericholecystic fluid secondary to perforation of the gallbladder has been reported to occur in 2 to 19.5 percent of patients with acute cholecystitis and has a mortality of 19 to 24 percent. Perforation of the

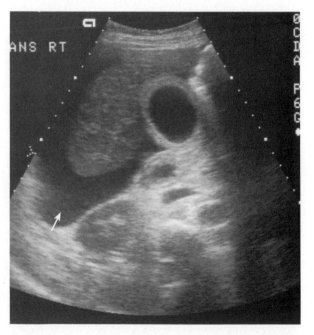

Figure 2.50

Generalized ascites: Fluid around the gallbladder was present also around the right lobe of the liver, down the flank, and in the pelvis in this patient with hepatitis.

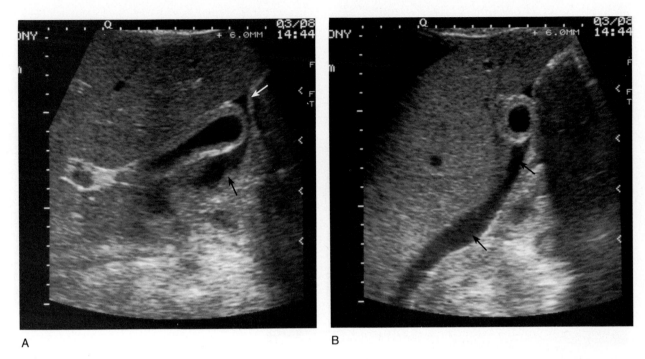

A
B

Figure 2.51
Generalized ascites: (A and B) Fluid surrounded the gall-bladder (*arrows*) as well as the liver in this patient with IVC thrombosis.

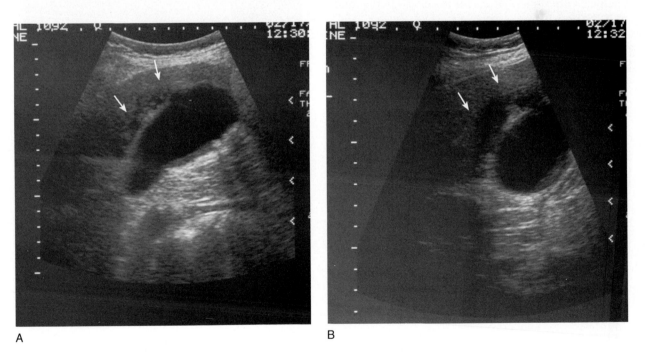

A
B

Figure 2.52
Gallbladder perforation: An irregular collection of peri-cholecystic fluid (*arrows*) was identified in this patient with sepsis, leukocytosis, and gallstones. At surgery, a perforated gallbladder was removed.

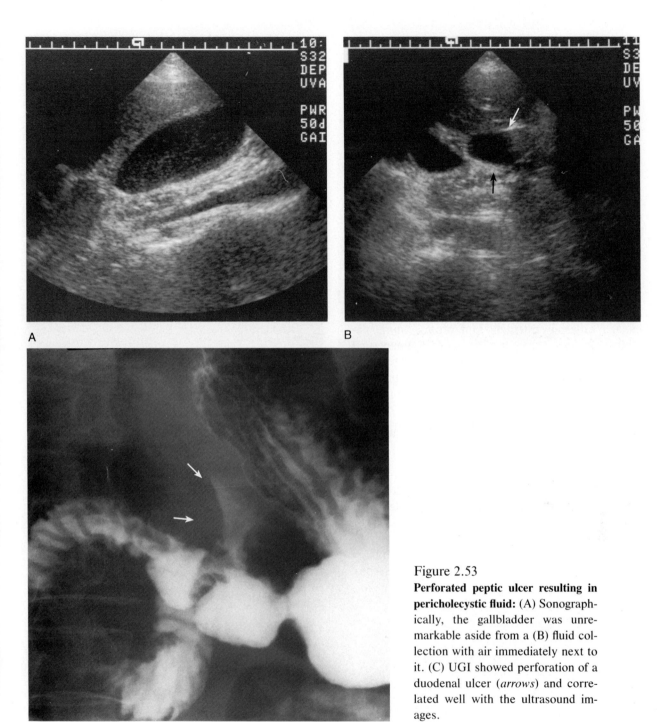

Figure 2.53

Perforated peptic ulcer resulting in pericholecystic fluid: (A) Sonographically, the gallbladder was unremarkable aside from a (B) fluid collection with air immediately next to it. (C) UGI showed perforation of a duodenal ulcer (*arrows*) and correlated well with the ultrasound images.

gallbladder generally occurs 3 to 7 days after the onset of symptoms of acute cholecystitis. The presumed mechanism of gallbladder perforation requires obstruction of the cystic duct by a stone or inspissated bile with distension of the gallbladder. The wall of the gallbladder becomes thin and ischemic, especially in the fundus, where the blood supply is the scantiest. This ischemia and necrosis eventually lead to perforation and pericholecystic fluid. The resultant abscess may have a variable ultrasound appearance. Cystic collections, complex collections with multiple septations, as well as highly echogenic foci (air) within pericholecystic collections may be identified. The abscess may dissect into the nearby hepatic parenchyma.

Increasingly, percutaneous drainage procedures of the gallbladder or pericholecystic fluid collections can be used to stabilize critically ill patients instead of using emergent laparotomy. Some patients can benefit from percutaneous drainage and some need emergent laparotomy. Cholecystectomy can then be performed on an elective basis in selected patients.

Nearby Organ Inflammation or Perforation (Figures 2.53–2.54)

Pericholecystic fluid can also result from problems originating from nearby organs, such as a perforated duodenal ulcer, pancreatitis, or problems related to the hepatic flexure, such as diverticulitis or perforation. Recognition of a relatively normal-appearing gallbladder and a possible source of epigastric fluid (e.g., a diffusely edematous pancreas) may explain localized pericholecystic fluid without implicating cholecystitis.

Emphasis Point

Frequently, fluid around the gallbladder is part of generalized abdominal ascites. Recognition that the fluid is a global peritoneal process rather than purely pericholecystic fluid results in different diagnostic considerations.

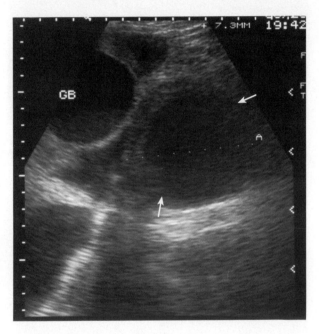

Figure 2.54

Pericholecystic fluid secondary to pancreatitis: Fluid around an inflamed pancreas (*arrows*) was seen in the pericholecystic region even without intrinsic gallbladder disease.

BIBLIOGRAPHY

Diffuse Gallbladder Wall Thickening

Cohan RH, Mahony BS, Bowie JD, Cooper C, Bakder ME, Illescas FF: Striated intramural gallbladder lucencies on US studies: Predictors of acute cholecystitis. Radiology 164:31–35, 1987.

Huang YS, Lee SD, Wu JC, et al: Utility of sonographic gallbladder wall patterns in differentiating malignant from cirrhotic ascites. J Clin Ultrasound 17:187–192, 1989.

Jeffrey RB, Laing FC, Wong W, Callen PW: Gangrenous cholecystitis: Diagnosis by ultrasound. Radiology 148:219–221, 1983.

Kaftori JK, Pery M, Green J, Gaitini D: Thickness of the gallbladder wall in patients with hypoalbuminemia: A sonographic study of patients on peritoneal dialysis. AJR 148:1117–1118, 1987.

Marti-Bonmati L, Andres JC, Aguado C: Sonographic relationship between gallbladder wall thickness and etiology of ascites. J Clin Ultrasound 17:497–501, 1989.

Ralls PW, Quinn MF, Juttner HU, Halls JM, Boswell WD: Gallbladder wall thickening: Patients without intrinsic gallbladder disease. AJR 137:65–68, 1981.

Shlaer WJ, Leopold GR, Scheible FW: Sonography of the thickened gallbladder wall: A nonspecific finding. AJR 136:337–339, 1981.

Simeone JF, Brink JA, Mueller PR, Compton C, Hahn PF, Saini S, Silverman SG, Tung G, Ferrucci JT: The sonographic diagnosis of acute gangrenous cholecystitis: Importance of the Murphy sign. AJR 152:289–290, 1989.

Teefey SA, Baron RL, Bigler SA: Sonography of the gallbladder: Significance of striated (layered) thickening of the gallbladder wall. AJR 156:945–947, 1991.

Tsujimoto F, Miyamoto Y, Tada S: Differentiation of benign from malignant ascites by sonographic evaluation of gallbladder wall. Radiology 157:503–504, 1985.

Wegener M, Borsch G, Schneider J, et al: Gallbladder wall thickening: A frequent finding in various nonbiliary disorders—a prospective ultrasonographic study. J Clin Ultrasound 15:307–312, 1987.

West MS, Garra BS, Horii SC, Hayes WS, Cooper C, Silverman PM, Zeman RK: Gallbladder varices: Imaging findings in patients with portal hypertension. Radiology 179:179–182, 1991.

Focal Gallbladder Wall Thickening

Kidney M, Goiney R, Cooperberg PL: Adenomyomatosis of the gallbladder: A pictorial exhibit. J Ultrasound Med 5:331–333, 1986.

Lane J, Buck J, Zeman RK: Primary carcinoma of the gallbladder: A pictorial essay. RadioGraphics 9:209–228, 1989.

Raghavendra BN, Subramanyam BR, Balthazar EJ, Horii SC, Megibow AJ, Hilton S: Sonography of adenomyomatosis of the gallbladder: Radiologic-pathologic correlation. Radiology 146:747–752, 1983.

Rice J, Sauerbrei EE, Semogas P, Cooperberg PL, Burhenne HJ: Sonographic appearance of adenomyomatosis of the gallbladder. J Clin Ultrasound 9:336–337, 1981.

Saigh J, Williams S, Cawley K, Anderson JC: Varices: A cause of focal gallbladder wall thickening. J Ultrasound Med 4:371–373, 1985.

Echogenic Gallbladder Wall with Shadowing Air Versus Calcium

Hunter ND, Macintosh PK: Acute emphysematous cholecystitis: An ultrasonic diagnosis. AJR 134:592–593, 1980.

Kane RA, Jacobs R, Katz J, Costello P: Porcelain gallbladder: Ultrasound and CT appearance. Radiology 152:137–141, 1984.

Nemcek AA Jr, Gore RM, Vogelzang RL, Grant M: The effervescent gallbladder: A sonographic sign of emphysematous cholecystitis. AJR 150:575–577, 1988.

Parulekar SG: Sonographic findings in acute emphysematous cholecystitis. Radiology 145:117–119, 1982.

Soft Tissue Material Within the Gallbladder

Fakhry J: Sonography of tumefactive biliary sludge. AJR 139:717–719, 1982.

Fiske CE, Filly RA: Pseudo-sludge. A spurious ultrasound appearance within the gallbladder. Radiology 144:631–632, 1982.

Grant EG, Smirniotopoulos JG: Intraluminal gallbladder hematoma: Sonographic evidence of hemobilia. J Clin Ultrasound 11:507–509, 1983.

Phillips G, Pochaczevsky R, Goodman J, et al.: Ultrasound patterns of metastatic tumors in the gallbladder. J Clin Ultrasound 10:379–383, 1982.

Enlargement of the Gallbladder

Barth RA, Brasch RC, Filly RA: Abdominal pseudotumor in childhood: Distended gallbladder with parenteral hyperalimentation. AJR 136:341–343, 1981.

Bradford BF, Reid BS, Weinstein BJ, Oh KS, Girdany BR: Ultrasonographic evaluation of the gallbladder in mucocutaneous lymph node syndrome. Radiology
142:381–384, 1982.

Chamberlain JW, Hight DW: Acute hydrops of the gallbladder in childhood. Surgery
68:899–905, 1970.

Cohen EK, Stringer DA, Smith CR, Daneman A: Hydrops of the gallbladder in typhoid
fever as demonstrated by sonography. J Clin Ultrasound 14:633, 1986.

Grisoni E, Fisher R, Izant R: Kawasaki syndrome: Report of four cases with acute
gallbladder hydrops. J Pediatr Surg 19:9–11, 1984.

Nonvisualization of the Gallbladder

Hammond DI: Unusual causes of sonographic nonvisualization or nonrecognition of
the gallbladder: A review. J Clin Ultrasound 16:77–85, 1988.

Laing FC, Gooding GAW, Herzog KA: Gallstones preventing ultrasonographic visualization of the gallbladder. Gastrointest Radiol 1:301–303, 1977.

MacDonald FR, Cooperberg PL, Cohen MM: The WES triad—a specific sonographic
sign of gallstones in the contracted gallbladder. Gastrointest Radiol 6:39–41, 1981.

Septations Within the Gallbladder

Jeffrey RB, Laing FC, Wong W, Callen PW: Gangrenous cholecystitis: Diagnosis by
ultrasound. Radiology 148:219–221, 1983.

Lev-Toaff AS, Friedman AC, Rindsberg SN, Caroline DF, Maurer AH, Radecki PD:
Multiseptate gallbladder: Incidental diagnosis on sonography. AJR 148:1119–1120,
1987.

Sukov RJ, Sample WF, Sarti DA, et al: Cholecystosonography: The junctional fold.
Radiology 133:435–436, 1979.

Pericholecystic Fluid

Fleischer AC, Muhletaler CA, Jones TB: Sonographic detection of gallbladder perforation. South Med J 75:606–607, 1982.

Madrazo BL, Francis I, Hricak H, et al.: Sonographic findings in perforation of the
gallbladder. AJR 139:491–496, 1982.

Takada T, Yasuda H, Uchiyama K, Hasegawa H, Asagoe T, Shikata J: Pericholecystic
abscess: Classification of US findings to determine the proper therapy. Radiology
172:693–697, 1989.

PANCREAS

PATTERNS

Pancreatic and Peripancreatic Cysts
Pancreatic Ductal Dilatation
Solid-Appearing Masses in the Pancreas

The normal pancreas in adults is usually hyperechoic relative to the liver and can be seen anterior to the splenic vein. In children, the pancreatic echogenicity is often equal to that of the liver. Differential possibilities causing cystic or solid masses or pancreatic ductal dilatation are considered here.

PANCREATIC AND PERIPANCREATIC CYSTS

Pancreatic Pseudocyst
Congenital Cysts
Cystic Neoplasms of the Pancreas
   Microcystic Adenoma
   Mucinous Cystic Neoplasms
   Other Cystic Neoplasms
Necrotic Lymphadenopathy
Pancreatic Abscess/Postoperative Abscess
Splenic Artery Aneurysm
Echinococcal Cyst

CHILDHOOD

Choledochal Cysts/Choledochocele
Duodenal Duplication Cysts

Pancreatic Pseudocyst (Figures 3.1–3.4)

A pseudocyst is the most common cause of a cystic mass of the pancreas. Pseudocysts are reported to complicate acute pancreatitis 3 to 10 percent of the time, especially when the pancreatitis is related to alcohol or is secondary to gallstone passage. These cystic masses mature over a period of approximately 4 weeks by developing a fibrous wall that does not have an epithelial lining. The lack of epithelial lining leads to the name *pseudocyst*. Within the cystic masses, there may be blood products, proteinaceous debris, and pancreatic fluid.

Sonographically, these cystic masses may be seen in the pancreatic bed, in the lesser sac, down the flanks, or into the pelvis or chest. The masses are usually well defined. Although a pseudocyst may be unilocular, multiple septations are often present. Low-level echoes and internal debris may be seen that result from hemorrhagic or proteinaceous material within the pseudocyst. Wall calcifications can sometimes be identified in old pseudocysts.

During an acute bout of pancreatitis, peripancreatic fluid collections may be seen sonographically. These collections often regress and lack a mature, well-defined wall. In acute, severe pancreatitis, the pancreas is often swollen and hypoechoic compared to normal. Small amounts of fluid may be identified in the lesser sac, pericholocystic region,

119

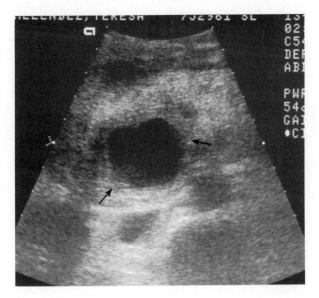

Figure 3.1
Pancreatic pseudocyst: Approximately 2 months after an episode of pancreatitis secondary to hyperlipidemia, a pseudocyst (*arrows*) in the head of the pancreas was decompressed surgically.

and left anterior pararenal space in patients with pancreatitis. Recognition of fluid in the left anterior pararenal space is good evidence for pancreatic inflamation. The term *pseudocyst* is used to describe the well-defined walled-off cystic structure that is present 4 to 6 weeks after an episode of pancreatitis.

Congenital Cysts (Figure 3.5)

True cysts of the pancreas are lined with epithelium and are thought to be anomalies of the pancreatic duct. Single, isolated pancreatic cysts are rare, but autosomal dominant polycystic kidney disease and von Hippel–Lindau syndrome are two clinical situations in which true pancreatic cysts may be present. In autosomal dominant polycystic kidney disease, approximately 10 percent of patients have pancreatic cysts. Usually, pancreatic involvement is less common than the cystic involvement of the kidneys and liver. The presence of cysts in all three organs helps to confirm the diagnosis of autosomal dominant polycystic kidney disease.

In von Hippel–Lindau syndrome, also an autosomal dominant condition, pancreatic cysts may be seen in up to 30 percent of patients on imaging studies. Autopsy studies show an even higher incidence of pancreatic cysts.

In cystic fibrosis, true pancreatic cysts may be identified, usually representing an obstructed dilated portion of the pancreatic duct. Cystic fibrosis is characterized by exocrine insufficiency related to inspissated, viscous secretions. Small cysts may be present pathologically with larger cysts identifiable on ultrasound examinations. Pancreatic atrophy and fibrosis develop in cystic fibrosis due to chronic obstruction by thick mucus.

Sonographically, true cysts may vary in size from microscopic to 5 cm. Cysts may be unilocular or multilocular and are generally, otherwise, anechoic, unless superimposed hemorrhage or infection has occurred. Foci of calcification may develop in the wall of these true cysts.

Cystic Neoplasms of the Pancreas

Cystic neoplasms represent 10–15 percent of all pancreatic cystic lesions and less than 5 percent of all pancreatic malignancies.

Microcystic Adenoma (Figure 3.6)   Microcystic adenomas make up 50 percent of primary pancreatic cystic neoplasms. They are benign neoplasms occurring in women older than 60 years of age. The masses are hypervascular and contain glycogen.

Sonographically, the mass is highly echogenic secondary to multiple septations and extensive honeycombing with small cysts (1mm–2cm) in the periphery of the mass. The presence of six or more small cysts within a mass suggests microcystic adenoma rather than mucinous cystic tumors. It is well established that microcystic adenomas are benign, and there have been no reported metastases or cases of malignant transformation. A central calcified scar may be identified in up to 20 percent of cases. If the microcystic adenoma can be recognized by imaging features and the patient is asymptomatic, surgery is unnecessary.

Mucinous Cystic Neoplasms (Figure 3.7)   Mucinous cystic tumors of the pancreas are malignant or potentially malignant mucinous tumors occurring most often in middle-aged women and commonly involving the body or tail of the pancreas. These slow-growing masses may invade nearby organs.

Sonographically, these tumors are unilocular or multiseptate cystic masses that may have wall calcifications and papillary nodules. The cystic cavities are often large (>2 cm) and contain mucoid material. It is often difficult to differentiate the benign from the malignant forms even at surgery. Even so, these tumors have a better prognosis generally than the more typical pancreatic adenocarcinoma. The localized tumor may be cured with complete resection.

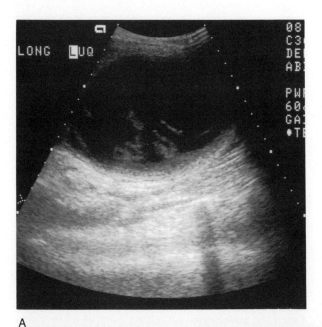

A

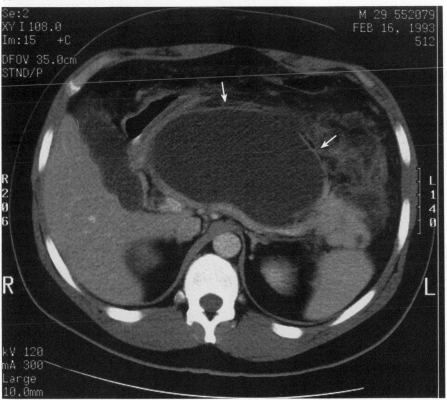

B

Figure 3.2

Pancreatic pseudocyst: (A) A large cystic mass of the pancreatic body and tail was present in this patient several months after a severe bout of pancreatitis. (B) CT images of a similar patient.

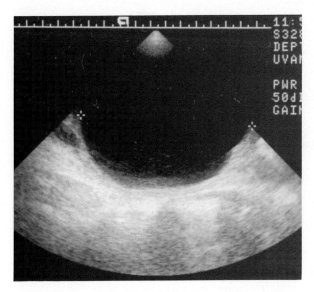

Figure 3.3
Pancreatic pseudocyst: Ultrasound of a large pseudocyst in the left flank; no internal echoes were present.

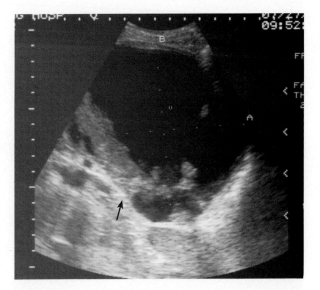

Figure 3.4
Pancreatic pseudocyst: Soft tissue material (*arrow*) was present in the pseudocyst of this 28-year-old woman.

Mucinous cystic neoplasms must be differentiated from a pancreatic pseudocyst. In a middle-aged or elderly woman with no history of or reason for pancreatitis, a malignant or potentially malignant mucinous mass of the pancreas must be considered. These tumors are frequently misinterpreted as pancreatic pseudocysts and are therefore treated inappropriately. Cytologic evaluation of the fluid obtained from a peripancreatic cystic collection may be necessary to exclude tumor.

Other Cystic Neoplasms (Figure 3.8) Most of the endocrine or islet cell tumors are small and solid, but occasionally a cystic tumor may be seen secondary to large size and central necrosis of the mass.

Anaplastic carcinoma of the pancreas grows rapidly and may undergo central necrosis. Usually large masses, these tumors have internal necrosis and hemorrhage.

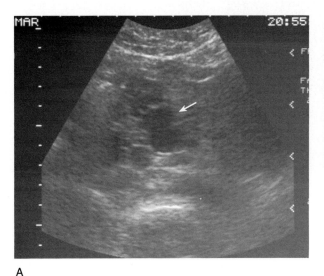

A

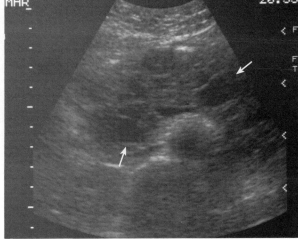

B

Figure 3.5
Congenital cysts of von Hippel–Lindau: Multiple cysts in the pancreas were present in this patient with bilateral renal masses and hemangioblastoma of the cerebellum.

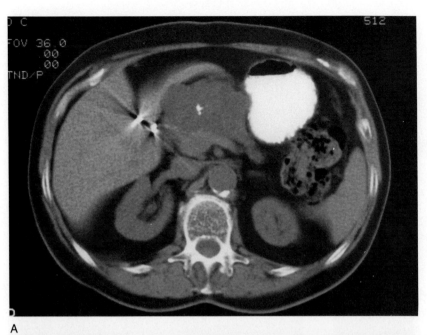

A

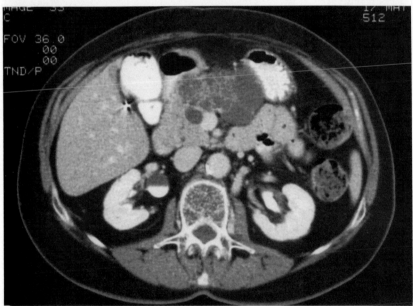

B

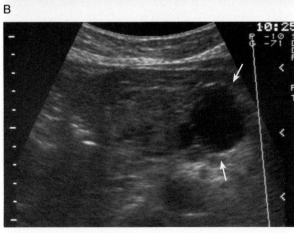

C

Figure 3.6

Microcystic adenoma of the pancreas: (A and B) This 62-year-old woman with abdominal pain underwent CT evaluation that gave a classic picture of microcystic adenoma. A central calcified scar was noted. Atrophy of the pancreatic tail was present. (C) Ultrasound showed an echogenic solid mass with multiple tiny peripheral cysts (*arrows*).

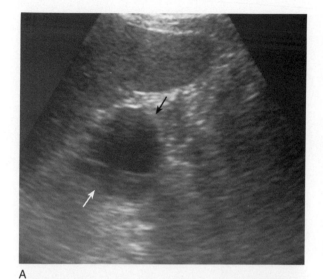

A

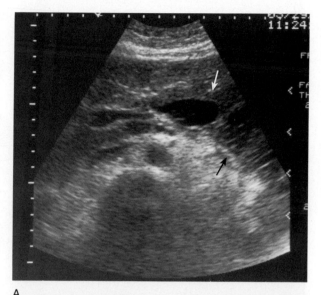

A

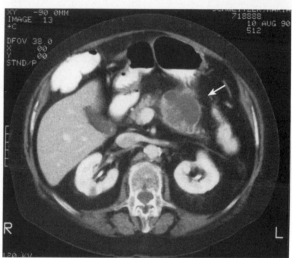

B

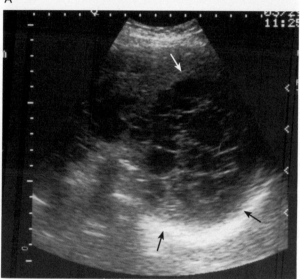

B

Figure 3.7

Mucinous cystic neoplasm of the pancreas: This 70-year-old woman was noted to have a 5-cm cystic mass in the tail of the pancreas. The presumptive diagnosis was of pancreatic pseudocyst, although the patient had no known predisposing condition. The patient underwent numerous aspiration and drainage procedures for the presumed pseudocyst, and the mass recurred on multiple occasions. Surgery was undertaken and a malignant mass was discovered.

Figure 3.8

Metastatic ovarian carcinoma: Recurrence of cystic, multiseptate ovarian carcinoma (*arrows*) was present in the lesser sac in this 65-year-old woman.

Papillary cystic tumor of the pancreas is a rare tumor occurring in young women, usually involving the tail of the pancreas.

Metastases to the pancreas from a variety of primary sites may grow rapidly and have central necrosis. Large lesions, especially from the ovary or secondary to melanoma, may have cystic components. Pancreatitis may be caused by the metastases' creating pancreatic duct obstruction or could be related to cell lysis when chemotherapy is given.

Necrotic Lymphadenopathy

Infectious or neoplastic lymphadenopathy in the peripancreatic region may undergo central necrosis, causing the nodes to appear cystic ultrasonographically. Aspiration of lymphadenopathy will allow differentiation of hyperplastic, infectious, or neoplastic etiologies.

Pancreatic Abscess/Postoperative Abscess (Figure 3.9)

Superimposed infection of necrotic pancreatic tissue and peripancreatic fluid is a serious complication of pancreatitis, as it leads to significant morbidity and greater mortality. Abscess of the pancreas is reported to occur in up to 20 percent of cases of severe pancreatitis. Some authors believe pancreatic abscess occurs more often when the pancreatitis is due to peptic ulcer disease or biliary disease rather than to other causes of pancreatitis.

Generally, pancreatic abscesses are ill-defined cystic masses with debris. Highly echogenic foci with shadowing can represent air.

Aspiration of peripancreatic fluid collections that complicate pancreatitis is frequently indicated to detect whether superimposed infection has occurred, especially when the patient has signs which suggest superimposed infection.

Debridement and drainage are most often performed surgically; yet some patients are successfully managed with percutaneous catheter drainage.

Subphrenic or postoperative abscesses may develop in close proximity to the pancreatic tail. Such abscesses may be related to a host of causes, including perforated peptic ulcers and collections in a splenectomy bed. The patient's clinical history can often allow the source to be defined.

Splenic Artery Aneurysm

Dilatation of the splenic artery may occur as a result of atherosclerotic disease of the vessel or secondary to inflammatory changes in a patient with pan-

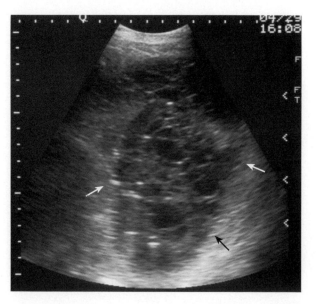

Figure 3.9
Left subphrenic abscess: A large, multiseptate mass with air filled the left upper quadrant and was in close association with the pancreas. A perforated gastric ulcer proved to be the cause.

creatitis. The splenic artery aneurysm will be a rounded cystic mass, often with peripheral calcification that may have turbulent arterial flow when Doppler investigation is performed.

Echinococcal Cyst

Hydatid disease of the pancreas is less common than liver involvement (which occurs 75 percent of the time) and lung involvement (occurring 15 percent of the time).

In patients with pancreatic involvement, ultrasound commonly shows multiple septations within the cysts, consistent with daughter cysts. Calcifications may develop in the walls of the cyst.

CHILDHOOD

Choledochal Cysts/Choledochocele (Figure 3.10)

Four types of choledochal cysts have been described:

1. A localized dilatation of the common bile duct beyond the cystic duct insertion.
2. A choledochocele of the intramural duodenal portion of the distal common duct.
3. A cystic diverticulum of the common duct.
4. Marked dilatation of the extrahepatic biliary system.

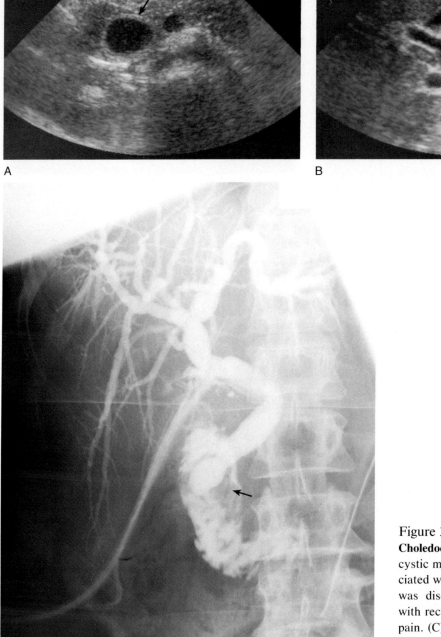

A

B

C

Figure 3.10
Choledochocele: (A and B) A small
cystic mass (*arrow*) intimately associated with the head of the pancreas
was discovered in this 8-year-old
with recurrent right upper quadrant
pain. (C) Surgical repair of the choledochocele was successful.

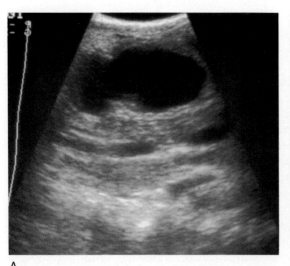

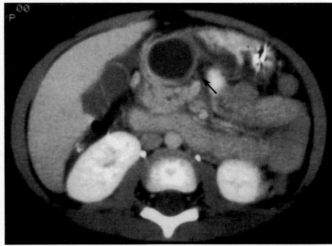

A   B

Figure 3.11
Duplication cyst: A well-defined cyst posterior to the stomach proved to be a duplication cyst in this child.

The choledochocele and diverticulum of the common duct might have the appearance of a cystic mass related to the pancreas.

Generally, two types of patients have this condition: the jaundiced neonate and the older child with recurrent bouts of pain, pancreatitis, and biliary stones. Cholangiography is often necessary preoperatively, but ultrasonography is the pivotal examination in these patients to suggest the diagnosis.

Duodenal Duplication Cysts (Figure 3.11)

Duodenal duplications are less common than duplications of the esophagus or distal small bowel. The patient may have vomiting and proximal bowel obstruction or may be noted incidentally to have an upper abdominal mass. Sonographically, duplication cysts have a well-defined wall, frequently with anechoic central portions.

Emphasis Point

Most cystic masses related to the pancreas are pseudocysts or peripancreatic fluid collections related to inflammation of the pancreas. In a middle-aged or elderly patient *without* any predisposing reason or history of pancreatitis, a potentially malignant mucinous cystic neoplasm of the pancreas must be considered.

PANCREATIC DUCTAL DILATATION

Obstruction of the Pancreatic Duct or Chronic Pancreatitis

VARIANTS

Splenic Vein Thrombosis
Posterior Wall of Stomach

The pancreatic duct may be seen normally at sonography in some patients and usually measures approximately 2–3 mm in luminal diameter. When the pancreatic duct is normal, the walls are parallel and approximately bisect the substance of the pancreas. As pancreatic ductal dilatation worsens, the duct walls lose their parallelity and become tortuous.

Obstruction of the Pancreatic Duct or Chronic Pancreatitis (Figures 3.12–3.16)

A dilated pancreatic duct may be misinterpreted as the splenic vein or splenic artery by the casual sonographer. Recognition of the vascular landmarks by color Doppler will allow the dilated pancreatic duct to be differentiated from vascular structures. A dilated, tortuous pancreatic duct may also be mistaken for a cystic mass unless its tubular nature is recognized.

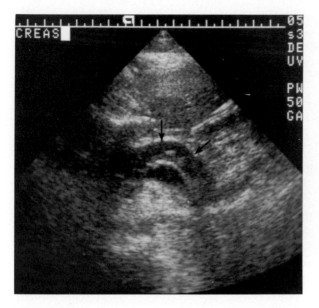

Figure 3.12
Adenocarcinoma of the pancreatic head: Atrophy of the pancreas with pancreatic ductal dilatation (*arrows*) was present in this patient with jaundice and pancreatic duct obstruction secondary to neoplasm in the head of the pancreas.

Pancreatic duct dilatation greater than 3 mm results from distal obstruction by a tumor or stone and more proximal dilatation or may be the sequel of chronic pancreatitis and pancreatic atrophy. Sometimes whether pancreatic ductal dilatation is secondary to chronic pancreatitis or pancreatic neoplasm can be difficult to determine. When pancreatic duct dilatation is recognized, clues to the etiology must be sought. Calcifications within the pancreas or within the pancreatic duct may suggest chronic pancreatitis as the cause of irregularity, beading, and dilatation of the pancreatic duct.

Focal masses in the head of the pancreas with atrophy of the body and tail and associated duct dilatation may be identified in neoplasia of the pancreas, such as adenocarcinoma. Focal masses and pancreatic duct dilatation may also result from pancreatitis and may be impossible to differentiate sonographically.

In children with familial pancreatitis, pancreatic ductal dilatation may be the only imaging finding of pancreatic abnormality and may predate clinical manifestations of abdominal pain and symptoms of pancreatitis.

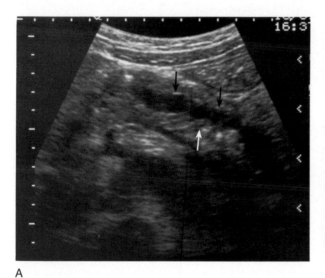

A

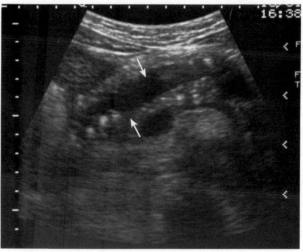

B

Figure 3.13
Pancreatic ductal dilatation secondary to chronic pancreatitis: (A and B) The pancreatic duct (*arrows*) measured 15 mm in this patient with chronic pancreatitis secondary to alcohol abuse. Multiple pancreatic calcifications are seen as highly echogenic foci within the pancreas.

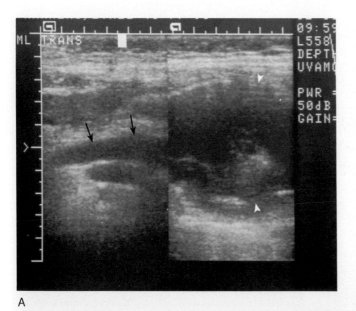

A

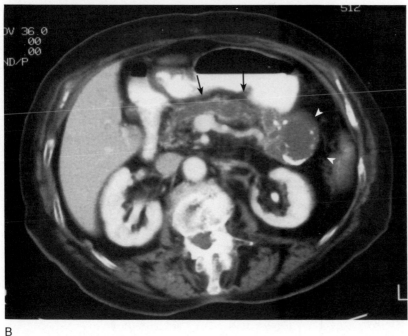

B

Figure 3.14
Pancreatic ductal dilatation and pseudocyst secondary to chronic pancreatitis: (A) A dilated pancreatic duct (*arrows*) that extends into a pseudocyst (*arrowheads*) in the tail of the pancreas was seen in this patient with recurrent pancreatitis. (B) CT confirmed the ultrasound findings.

VARIANTS

Splenic Vein Thrombosis (Figure 3.17)

An engorged, acutely thrombosed splenic vein may be mistaken sonographically for a dilated pancreatic duct. Recognition that the vein is not otherwise seen will allow the appropriate diagnosis to be made.

Posterior Wall of Stomach

Sometimes the posterior wall of the stomach can be mistaken for the pancreatic duct. Realization that the structure seen is part of the stomach can be facilitated by having the patient drink water to distend the stomach. The posterior wall of the stomach does not bisect the substance of the pancreas as the pancreatic duct should.

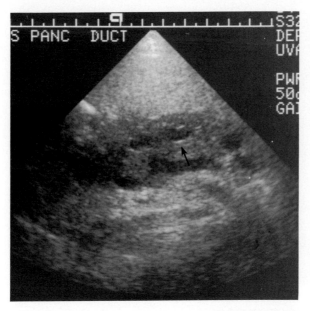

Figure 3.15
Acute pancreatitis superimposed upon chronic pancreatitis: A dilated pancreatic duct (*arrow*) was present in this patient with a swollen pancreas and previous episodes of pancreatitis.

Emphasis Points

Pancreatic ductal dilatation may be overlooked and confused with the splenic vein by the casual observer.

Whether pancreatic ductal dilatation is secondary to chronic pancreatitis or pancreatic neoplasm can sometimes be difficult to determine. Pancreatic calcifications, focal masses, and the clinical history may be helpful in differentiating the cause of ductal dilatation.

The posterior wall of the stomach may be mistaken for the pancreatic duct.

SOLID-APPEARING MASS IN THE PANCREAS

    Pancreatic Adenocarcinoma
    Pancreatitis
    Pancreatic Abscess
    Endocrine Neoplasms
    Metastatic Disease to the Pancreas
    Lymphomatous Involvement of the Pancreas
    Reactive/Infectious Lymphadenopathy

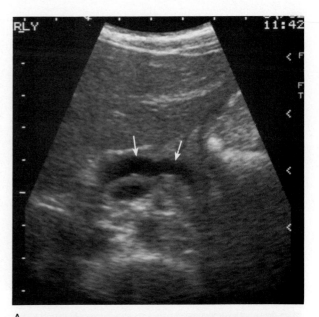

A

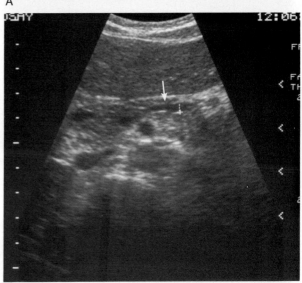

B

Figure 3.16
Familial pancreatitis: (A) Transmitted as an autosomal dominant trait, familial pancreatitis may be first illustrated by pancreatic ductal dilatation. This 10-year-old girl had had recurrent episodes of pancreatitis and had pancreatic ductal dilatation of approximately 1 cm. (B) A younger, asymptomatic sister was noted to have pancreatic ductal dilatation of a milder degree.

VARIANT

    Accessory Spleen

Most disease processes involving the pancreas, whether inflammatory or neoplastic, make it more hypoechoic than usual.

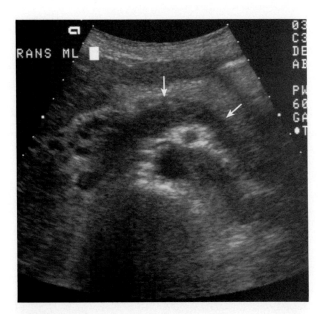

Figure 3.17
Splenic vein thrombosis: An engorged, thrombosed splenic vein could be misinterpreted as a dilated pancreatic duct by the casual observer. No flow was present by Doppler.

Pancreatic Adenocarcinoma (Figures 3.18–3.20)

Pancreatic adenocarcinoma arising from the ductal epithelium is the most common neoplasm of the pancreas. More common in men, blacks, and diabetics, pancreatic adenocarcinoma has a 5-year survival rate of 1 percent, and a mean survival time from diagnosis of 4 months. Pancreatic adenocarcinoma is the fourth leading cause of cancer death in the United States, after lung, colon, and breast cancer. The incidence of pancreatic carcinoma has increased in the past four decades.

A pancreatic carcinoma can become quite large before it is detected, especially if it is located in a relatively silent part of the gland, such as the body or tail. Tumors arising in the pancreatic head are usually detected earlier, since their growth results in biliary ductal obstruction and jaundice. Most tumors (70 percent) arise in the head of the gland, 15 to 20 percent arise in the body, and 5 percent are found in the tail. Some tumors are diffusely present throughout the gland.

Masses in the body and tail of the pancreas frequently show metastatic disease at the time of discovery. Metastases may be in the peripancreatic lymph nodes, liver, and lungs.

Sonographically, most pancreatic adenocarcinomas are hypoechoic solid masses. The mass is often poorly delimited, homogeneous, or inhomo-

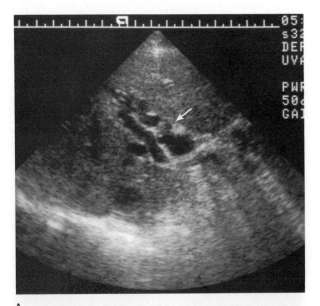

A

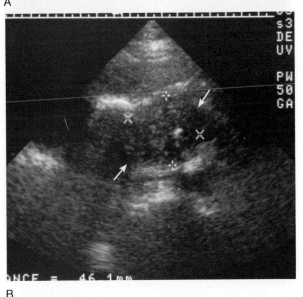

B

Figure 3.18
Pancreatic adenocarcinoma: This 66-year-old woman presented with painless jaundice. Sonography showed (A) biliary ductal dilatation (*arrow*) down to the head of the pancreas where (B) a 4.5-cm hypoechoic mass (*arrows*) was seen. There was atrophy of the body and tail of the pancreas.

geneous within the pancreatic bed. Besides the mass itself, other evidence of pancreatic neoplasm may be present, including an obstructed biliary tree, a dilated pancreatic duct, atrophy of the pancreas proximal to the obstruction, and vascular displacement or invasion. The double duct sign, with dilatation of the common bile duct and pancreatic duct, strongly suggests a pancreatic carcinoma causing obstruction of both systems.

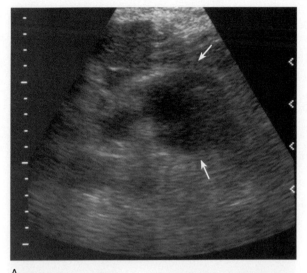

A

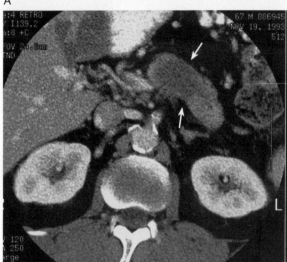

B

Figure 3.19
Pancreatic adenocarcinoma: (A) A focal hypoechoic mass in the mid-portion of the pancreas was demonstrated in this elderly man with back pain. No biliary ductal dilatation was present. (B) Correlative CT.

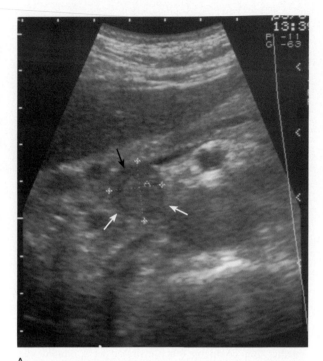

A

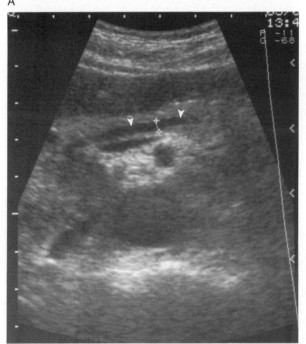

B

Figure 3.20
Pancreatic adenocarcinoma: A focal hypoechoic mass in the head of the pancreas was discovered in a 62-year-old woman with multiple liver metastases. (A and B) Ultrasound showed a hypoechoic mass (*arrows*) in the pancreatic head with mild pancreatic duct dilatation (*arrowheads*).

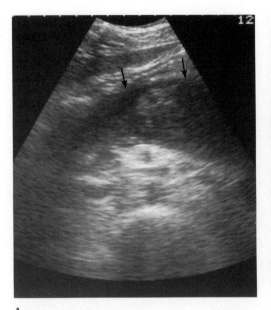
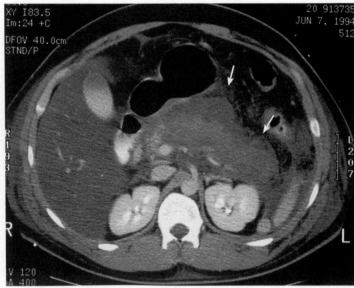

A   B

Figure 3.21

Severe pancreatitis: (A) Diffuse swelling of much of the body of the pancreas was seen in this 38-year-old man with acute pancreatitis secondary to alcohol abuse. (B) CT image of the same patient.

Ampullary carcinomas may have a better prognosis than many of the pancreatic carcinomas. Cholangiocarcinoma of the distal common bile duct may be difficult to distinguish by imaging features from a pancreatic head carcinoma.

Pancreatitis (Figure 3.21)

Focal pancreatitis is a commonly encountered hypoechoic mass in the pancreas that needs to be differentiated from pancreatic carcinoma. Other studies, such as CT, which can show peripancreatic stranding and inflammatory change, or ERCP, which will show changes of pancreatitis in the pancreatic duct, can suggest that the findings are related to benign disease rather than to carcinoma. Serial imaging or biopsy, with its risk of inciting or worsening pancreatitis, may be necessary to differentiate the two entities. Often, percutaneous biopsy is insufficient to exclude neoplasm. Usually differentiation of pancreatitis from neoplasm is an issue in patients with chronic pancreatitis and not acute pancreatitis, which is often clinically obvious.

Pancreatic Abscess (Figure 3.22)

A pancreatic abscess results from a superimposed infection of the inflamed pancreas, with resultant suppuration and liquefaction. Abscess formation represents a severe complication of pancreatitis; it significantly increases the risk of mortality and may prolong the hospitalization of the patient with pancreatitis.

Sonographically, the pancreatic abscess may appear to be nearly solid, with extensive internal debris. Aspiration of the solid-appearing region may be necessary to define its infected character. Generally, patients with a pancreatic abscess are toxic, with sepsis, elevated white count, tachycardia, and often fever. Surgical debridement or aggressive catheter drainage may be used for therapy.

Endocrine Neoplasm (Figures 3.23–3.24)

Endocrine neoplasms arise from the islet cells and may be hormonally active. Insulinomas, arising from the B cells, are the most common islet cell tumors and are most commonly located in the body or tail of the pancreas. These tumors are usually benign but cause hypoglycemic episodes. Most insulinomas are solitary and small, measuring less than 2 cm.

Gastrinomas are the second most common endocrine neoplasms, arising from the APUD (amine precursor uptake and decarboxylation) cells. Gastrinomas cause recurrent gastric and duodenal ulcers and elevated serum gastrin levels (Zollinger–Ellison syndrome). Although the gastric acid hypersecretion can be managed medically, surgical resection is usually performed for localized gastrinomas. Gastrinomas are malignant in the majority of cases.

Functioning endocrine tumors of the pancreas are very small in most cases, since their hormonal

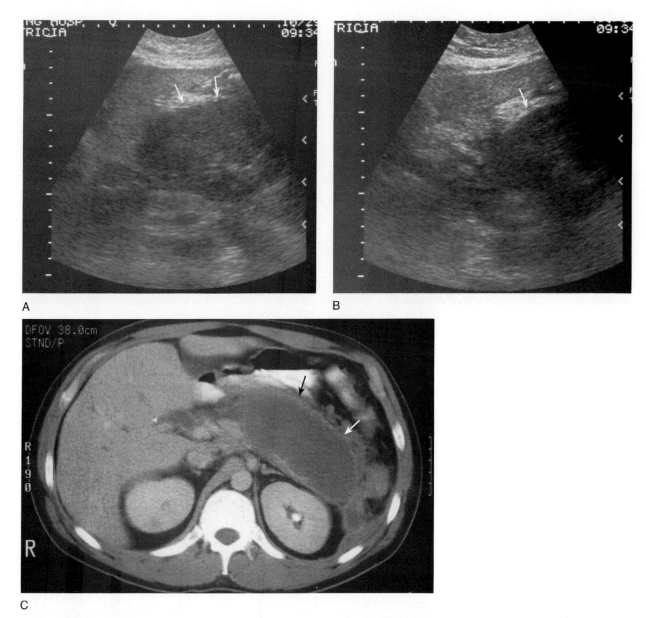

Figure 3.22

Pancreatic abscess: (A and B) This patient developed an abscess in necrotic pancreatic tissue after pancreatitis related to hyperlipidemia. Note the large, solid-appearing mass in the pancreatic bed by sonography. (C) Correlative CT. The abscess was surgically debrided.

activity leads to an investigation into their presence before they attain a large size. Intensive investigations, including CT and MR, may be unsuccessful. Surgical exploration and intraoperative ultrasound allow identification of some very small masses, some less than 1 cm in diameter.

Sonographically, the functioning endocrine tumors are usually small, solid, hypoechoic masses within the substance of the pancreas.

Nonfunctioning islet cell tumors are often large at discovery and have a high incidence of malignancy. These primary tumors of the pancreas are usually solid sonographically.

Lymphomatous Involvement of the Pancreas (Figure 3.25)

Non-Hodgkin lymphoma, especially Burkett's lymphoma, often involves peripancreatic nodes and sometimes intrapancreatic masses. These masses are hypoechoic, nearly cystic in appearance, and encase vessels, usually without invading them. Septations between enlarged lymph nodes and the multilobulated appearance of the nodal masses often suggest the diagnosis, which can be confirmed by percutaneous biopsy. Sometimes lymphomatous involvement of the pancreas may be difficult to differ-

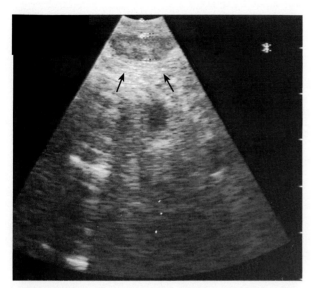

Figure 3.23

Insulinoma: Intraoperative sonography of the pancreas led to the discovery of a small, hypoechoic mass in the tail of the pancreas responsible for episodic hypoglycemia.

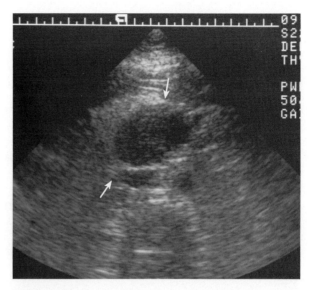

Figure 3.24

Gastrinoma: Transabdominal scanning located a large, hypoechoic solid mass in the head of the pancreas in this patient with severe, unrelenting peptic ulcer disease. The mass was removed, and the patient's condition improved.

entiate from primary pancreatic neoplasm by imaging studies.

Metastatic Disease of the Pancreas (Figure 3.26)

Metastatic involvement of the pancreas may result from contiguous spread to the pancreas from nearby neoplasms, such as those in the stomach, or from hematogenous spread from primary sites, such as lung, breast, ovary, and kidney. Often such patients have evidence of widespread metastatic disease.

Usually, pancreatic metastases are small and hypoechoic sonographically. Melanoma metastases to the pancreas are present at autopsy in 37.5 percent of patients and may be quite large.

Reactive/Infectious Lymphadenopathy

Reactive or infectious lymphadenopathy related to generalized abdominal processes, such as sarcoidosis or tuberculosis, may result in multilobulated solid masses in the pancreatic bed.

VARIANT

Accessory Spleen

The tail of the pancreas frequently has an intimate association with the splenic hilum. Splenules or an accessory spleen may be mistakenly identified as a

focal hypoechoic solid mass of the pancreatic tail. Close association with the spleen and, in some cases, a reason for expecting an accessory spleen (such as hypersplenism or previous resection of the spleen) make the correct diagnosis more likely.

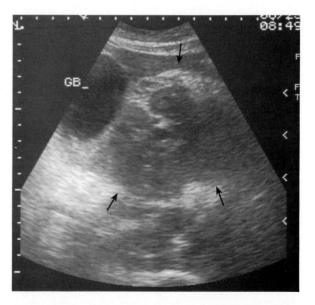

Figure 3.25

Non-Hodgkin lymphoma: The pancreatic bed was basically replaced by a large, multiobulated nodal mass in this 64-year-old man.

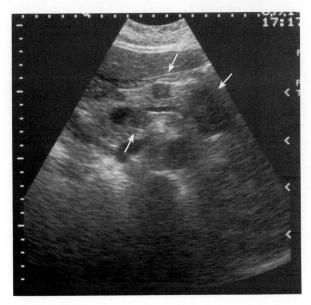

Figure 3.26
Metastatic renal cell carcinoma: Multiple hypoechoic solid masses in the pancreatic bed heralded the recurrence of renal cell carcinoma in this patient 4 years after radical nephrectomy.

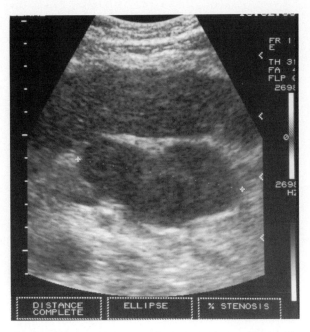

Figure 3.27
Metastatic adenocarcinoma of the colon: A solid mass developed in the pancreatic bed in this patient with a history of colon carcinoma.

Emphasis Points

Sometimes it is very difficult to establish the origin of the focal hypoechoic mass in the pancreas. Focal pancreatitis and neoplastic masses can be indistinguishable, both causing biliary dilatation, pancreatic ductal dilatation, pancreatic atrophy, and focal mass. Fine-needle aspiration can be helpful. Sometimes surgical exploration is required for diagnosis.

Pancreatic sonography can be difficult, requiring conscientious scanning. Overlying bowel gas may make visualization of the pancreas difficult. Filling the stomach with fluid by having the patient drink water and having the patient sit upright can aid in pancreatic imaging. Evidence of pancreatitis may be subtle, requiring careful examination for fluid in the left anterior pararenal space or lesser sac in conjunction with swelling and echotexture changes in the pancreas.

BIBLIOGRAPHY

Pancreatic and Peripancreatic Cysts

Friedman AC, Lichtenstein JE, Dachman AH: Cystic neoplasms of the pancreas: Radiological-pathological correlation. Radiology 149:45–50, 1983.

Fugazzola C, Procacci C, Bergamo Andreis IAB, et al.: Cystic tumors of the pancreas: Evaluation by ultrasonography and computed tomography. Gastrointest Radiol 16:53–61, 1991.

Hernaunz-Schulman M, Teele RL, Perez-Atayde A, Zollars L, Levine J, Black P, Kuligowska E: Pancreatic cystosis in cystic fibrosis. Radiology 158:629–631, 1986.

Johnson CD, Stephens DH, Charboneau JW, Carpenter HA, Welch TJ: Cystic pancreatic tumors: CT and sonographic assessment. AJR 151:1133–1138, 1988.

Kaplan JO, Isikoff MB, Barkin J, Livingstone AS: Necrotic carcinoma of the pancreas: "The pseudo-pseudocyst." J Comput Assist Tomogr 4(2):166–167, 1980.

Mathieu D, Guigui B, Valette PJ, Dao T-H, Bruneton JN, Bruel JM, Pringot J, Vasile N: Pancreatic cystic neoplasms. Radiol Clin North Am 27:163–176, 1989.

Ros PR, Hamrick-Turner JE, Chiechi MV, Ros LH, Gallego P, Burton SS: Cystic masses of the pancreas. RadioGraphics 12:673–686, 1992.

Sarti DA: Rapid development and spontaneous regression of pancreatic pseudocysts documented by ultrasound. Radiology 125:789–793, 1977.

Pancreatic Ductal Dilatation

Bryan PJ: Appearance of normal pancreatic duct: A study using real-time ultrasound. J Clin Ultrasound 10:63–66, 1982.

Didier D, Deschamps JP, Rohmer P, et al.: Evaluation of the pancreatic duct: A reappraisal based on a retrospective correlative study by sonography and pancreatography in 117 normal and pathologic subjects. Ultrasound Med Biol 9(5):509–518, 1983.

Hadidi A: Pancreatic duct diameter: Sonographic measurement in normal subjects. J Clin Ultrasound 11:17–22, 1983.

Weinstein DP, Weinstein BJ: Ultrasonic demonstration of the pancreatic duct: An analysis of 41 cases. Radiology 130:729–734, 1979.

Solid-Appearing Masses in the Pancreas

Buck JL, Hayes WS: Microcystic adenoma of the pancreas. RadioGraphics 10:313–322, 1990.

Campbell JP, Wilson SR: Pancreatic neoplasms: How useful is evaluation with US? Radiology 167:341–344, 1988.

Del Maschio A, Vanzulli A, Sironi S, et al.: Pancreatic cancer versus chronic pancreatitis: Diagnosis with CA 19-9 assessment, US, CT and CT-guided fine-needle biopsy. Radiology 178:95–99, 1991.

Galiber AK, Reading CC, Charboneau JW, et al.: Localization of pancreatic insulinoma: Comparison of pre- and intra-operative ultrasound with CT and angiography. Radiology 166:405–408, 1988.

Levine M, Danovitch S: Metastatic carcinoma to the pancreas: Another cause for acute pancreatitis. Am J Gastroenterol 60:290–294, 1973.

London JF, Shawker TH, Doppman JL, et al.: Zollinger–Ellison syndrome. Prospective assessment of abdominal ultrasound in the localization of gastrinomas. Radiology 178:763–767, 1991.

Neff CC, Simone JF, Wittenberg J, Mueller PR, Ferrucci JT Jr: Inflammatory pancreatic masses. Problems in differentiating focal pancreatitis from carcinoma. Radiology 150:35–38, 1984.

Rossi P, Allison DJ, Bezzi M, et al.: Endocrine tumors of the pancreas. Radiol Clin North Am 27(1):129–160, 1989.

C H A P T E R   4

SPLEEN

PATTERNS

Splenomegaly
Cystic Lesions of the Spleen
Focal, Solid-appearing Lesions of the Spleen
Calcifications in the Spleen
Perisplenic Collections

SPLENOMEGALY (Figures 4.1–4.2)

Leukemia/Lymphoma/Myeloproliferative
    Disorders
Portal Hypertension
Septicemia/Granulomatous Disease/Viral
    Illness
Venous Thrombosis
Hereditary Disorders
Extramedullary Hematopoiesis
Sarcoidosis/Collagen Vascular Diseases
Amyloidosis

The spleen is a lymphoid organ that acts as a filter for blood breakdown products.

Sonography is commonly used to assess for splenomegaly. Most often the determination of splenomegaly is a visual one, requiring experience. "If the spleen looks big, it is big." One study of nearly 800 normal adults found that 95 percent had a splenic length of less than 12 cm, a breadth of less than 7 cm, and a thickness of less than 5 cm. Such standards are helpful in judging splenic enlargement.

A variety of conditions can cause splenic enlargement.

Leukemia/Lymphoma/Myeloproliferative Disorders

The spleen may become enlarged in situations in which the hematopoietic elements are neoplastic, as with leukemia and lymphoma. Focal lesions may be seen, but diffuse enlargement is more commonly encountered. Lymphadenopathy may accompany splenomegaly. Some of the largest spleens are those of chronic leukemias and other indolent myeloproliferative disorders, such as polycythemia vera and myelofibrosis.

Portal Hypertension

Enlargement of the spleen secondary to vascular engorgement may be seen in patients with portal hypertension from a variety of causes. Portal hypertension is often secondary to liver disease related to alcohol abuse, chronic hepatitis, sclerosing cholangitis, primary biliary cirrhosis, and cryptogenic cirrhosis. Portal hypertension develops as fibrosis and distortion in the sinusoidal bed of the diseased liver cause vascular resistance to venous inflow from the GI tract.

Besides splenomegaly, stigmata of portal hypertension may be identified sonographically and

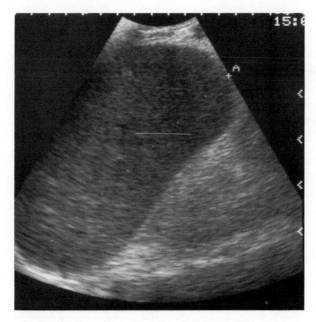

Figure 4.1
Splenomegaly secondary to portal hypertension: Moderate splenomegaly was observed in this young man with portal hypertension secondary to cirrhosis from chronic hepatitis.

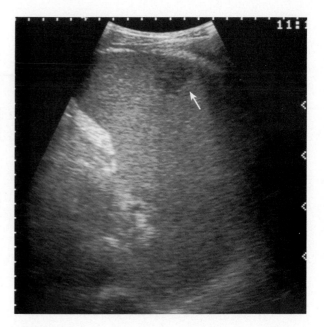

Figure 4.2
Splenomegaly of polycythemia vera: Massive splenomegaly was the stigma of a myeloproliferative disorder here. The spleen measured 20 cm longitudinally. Peripheral infarction was obvious (*arrow*).

may include a small, irregular cirrhotic liver, ascites, and portosystemic collaterals, such as varices in the splenic hilum or a recanalized paraumbilical vein. Portal hypertension that results from extrahepatic portal vein occlusion or obstruction may be seen with a structurally normal liver.

Septicemia/Granulomatous Disease/Viral Illness

The spleen may enlarge because of septicemia or in infectious conditions directly affecting the spleen, such as granulomatous diseases of tuberculosis, or histoplasmosis. Infectious mononucleosis is frequently associated with the development of splenomegaly of a moderate to marked degree. Malaria, typhus, and typhoid fever may result in splenomegaly. Splenomegaly is frequently seen in patients with AIDS. Enlargement of the spleen makes it more susceptible to injury and rupture.

Venous Thrombosis

Venous infarction of the spleen may result in gross splenic enlargement. Thrombosis of the splenic vein may be secondary to pancreatitis, pancreatic carcinoma, or hypercoagulable states or may be related to operative injury of the vein. Acute venous infarction may be associated with dramatic enlargement

of the spleen, with symptomatic left upper quadrant pain. Arterial infarction does not usually result in such massive splenic enlargement.

Hereditary Disorders

Hereditary conditions of hemolysis, such as hereditary spherocytosis and sickle cell anemia, may have associated splenomegaly. In hereditary spherocytosis, the spleen may need to be removed if hemolysis becomes excessive and the spleen becomes markedly enlarged. In sickle cell anemia, splenomegaly usually occurs early in the course of the condition, and autoinfarction of the spleen occurs over time. Usually, the teen-age patient with this condition has a small, infarcted spleen difficult to visualize sonographically.

Hereditary disorders that result in packing of the bone marrow may cause massive enlargement of the spleen, as the spleen becomes packed in a fashion similar to the bone marrow. Such packing disorders include Gaucher's and Wilson's diseases, in which lipid-laden macrophages fill the spleen.

Extramedullary Hematopoiesis

When the bone marrow is replaced by fibrosis in myelofibrosis or osteopetrosis, the spleen may take over hematopoietic function and thus enlarge.

Sarcoidosis/Collagen Vascular Diseases

Noninfectious inflammatory conditions, such as sarcoidosis, can affect the spleen, leading to splenic enlargement. Hepatic involvement and lymphadenopathy may be seen as well. Collagen vascular diseases, such as lupus or rheumatoid arthritis, may have associated splenomegaly. Symptomatic enlargement of the spleen in patients with rheumatoid arthritis is called Still's disease in children or Felty's syndrome.

Amyloidosis

Uncommonly, infiltration of the spleen with amyloid may result in diffuse enlargement.

Emphasis Point

Splenomegaly has many causes. Hematologic workup may be necessary to determine its cause. Percutaneous biopsy of the spleen to determine a cause for splenomegaly is rarely indicated.

CYSTIC LESIONS OF THE SPLEEN

Parasitic Disease
Posttraumatic Cyst
Epidermoid Cyst
Intrasplenic Pancreatic Pseudocyst
Splenic Infarction
Pyogenic Splenic Abscess
Metastatic Disease
Lymphangioma/Hemangioma

Parasitic Disease

The most common cause of splenic cysts worldwide is parasitic disease. Hydatid disease can be suspected if the patient has an appropriate travel history. Involvement of the spleen occurs in less than 2 percent of all patients infested with *Echinococcus*. Several serologic tests are available, and immunoelectrophoresis is a reliable laboratory screen for hydatid disease.

Sonographically, the cystic lesions of echinococcal infestation may be entirely anechoic. Daughter cysts may be seen as a small cyst within a larger cyst. Internal echoes may arise from debris, fibrinous material, and membranes within the cystic lesion. Calcification of the cyst wall frequently occurs and may mask the internal structure of the lesion. Percutaneous aspiration of the lesion can be performed to aid in diagnosis but should be done with care to prevent anaphylaxis. Usually, medical therapy is tried before percutaneous drainage is performed.

Posttraumatic Cyst

In the United States the most common cause of a splenic cyst is a posttraumatic cyst, more correctly called a pseudocyst because of its lack of an epithelial lining. Immediately after acute trauma to the spleen, intrasplenic hematomas may look nearly solid on ultrasound examinations, and it is only with time that intrasplenic hematomas may look cystic within the solid splenic tissue. Up to one-half of these patients will remember substantial trauma earlier in life.

Most posttraumatic cysts are solitary, unilocular, and large (up to 10 cm). These cystic lesions, representing evolving splenic hematomas, may have rimlike calcifications. Such cysts frequently have internal echoes related to hemorrhagic fluid within them.

Epidermoid Cyst (Figure 4.3)

Epidermoid cysts are congenital cysts that on histologic examination are lined with epithelial cells, differentiating them from posttraumatic pseudocysts. Bloody fluid and hemorrhagic debris may be present in these lesions and may cause these cystic lesions to appear nearly solid because of the diffuse homogeneous internal echoes of the proteinaceous fluid.

Intrasplenic Pancreatic Pseudocyst

A pancreatic pseudocyst can break into the substance of the spleen, and thus appear to be an intrasplenic lesion. Such pseudocysts are seen in patients with an appropriate history and other imaging features of pancreatitis, such as other peripancreatic fluid collections, and stigmata in the pancreas itself of inflammatory disease.

Splenic Infarction (Figure 4.4)

Large areas of infarction of the spleen may result in enlargement and liquefaction of the organ. Infarction may be related to embolic events or encasement of the splenic artery or vein by pancreatic processes, such as carcinoma or pancreatitis.

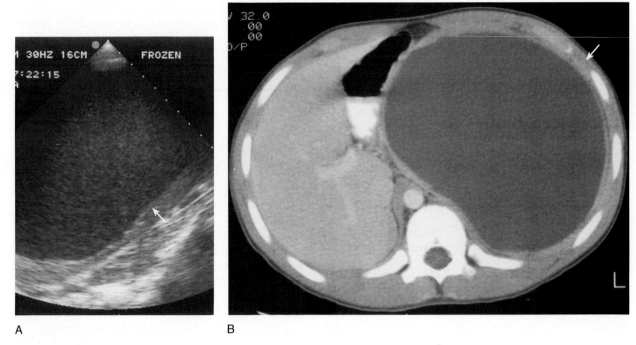

Figure 4.3
Epidermoid cyst: (A) This child with presumed splenomegaly clinically was found sonographically to have a
huge splenic cyst with homogeneous, low-level echoes.
(B) CT confirmed the large cyst and compression of the
normal spleen. The cyst was surgically decompressed.

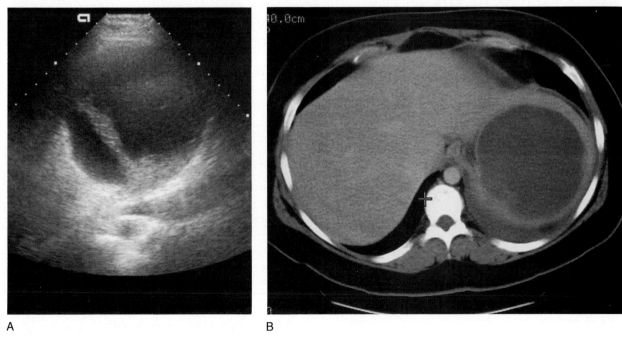

Figure 4.4
Splenic infarction: (A) Venous infarction caused the
spleen to develop a large cystic collection in the upper
portion. (B) Correlative CT. Aspiration yielded bloody
fluid. Splenectomy was performed.

Pyogenic Splenic Abscess (Figure 4.5)

Two primary mechanisms exist for the development of a splenic abscess: multiple splenic abscesses in an immunocompromised host with seeding via a hematogenous source and a large solitary abscess secondary to an infection of a preexisting splenic lesion, such as a hematoma. Direct inoculation of the spleen via trauma or surgery or nearby infectious processes may involve the spleen as well.

One or multiple cystic masses with internal echoes and septations may be imaged sonographically. Gas within the collection will suggest its infectious nature. Usually, the clinical course consists of fever, elevated white cell count, and sepsis. Per-

cutaneous catheter drainage may effectively control this abscess.

Metastatic Disease

Metastases from ovarian carcinoma may become implanted on the surface of the spleen. Other rapidly growing malignancies may undergo central necrosis and appear as cystic masses in the spleen. Aspiration of the lesions may be necessary in the appropriate setting to confirm the diagnosis. Lymphomatous involvement of the spleen can sometimes appear nearly cystic, and its solid nature can be misinterpreted.

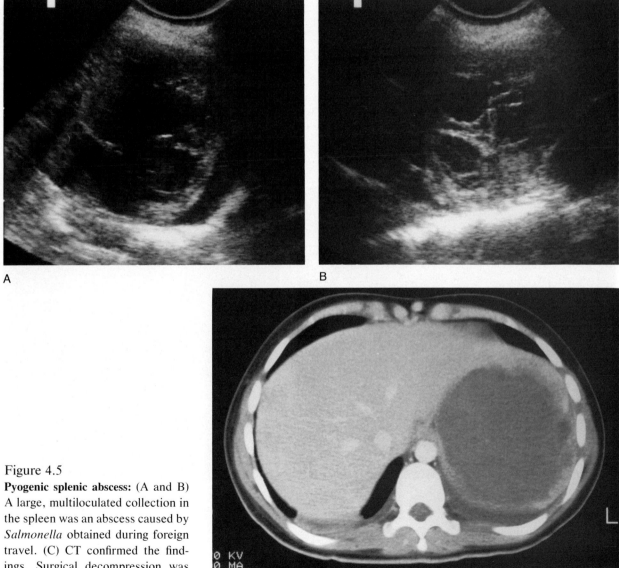

A

B

C

Figure 4.5

Pyogenic splenic abscess: (A and B) A large, multiloculated collection in the spleen was an abscess caused by *Salmonella* obtained during foreign travel. (C) CT confirmed the findings. Surgical decompression was performed.

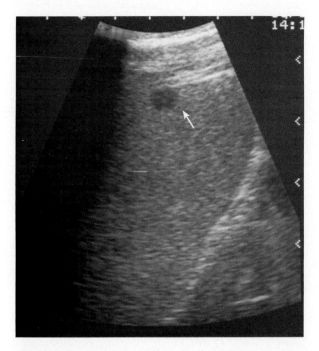

Figure 4.6
Candidiasis: Small, well-defined hypoechoic lesions (*arrow*) were identified in the spleen in this patient with disseminated candidiasis.

Lymphangioma/Hemangioma

Lymphangiomas and cystic hemangiomas are unusual cystic lesions of the spleen that frequently have multiple internal septations. These lesions have endothelial cell linings.

FOCAL, SOLID-APPEARING LESIONS IN THE SPLEEN

> Splenic Infections
> Metastatic Disease
> Lymphoma
> Angiosarcoma
> Posttraumatic Lesions
> Infarction
> Hemangioma/Hamartoma
> Extramedullary Hematopoiesis

Splenic Infections (Figures 4.6–4.7)

Especially in the immunocompromised patient, multiple focal lesions may be the manifestations of hematogenous spread of infection, such as fungal or

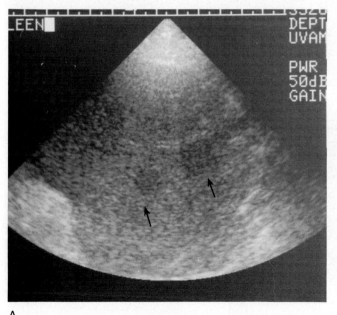

A

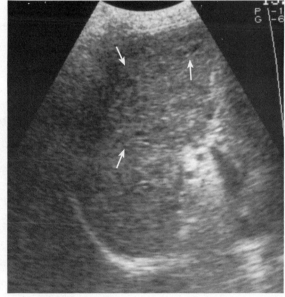

B

Figure 4.7
Tuberculosis: Multiple small, hypoechoic areas in the spleen were present in two different patients with tuberculosis.

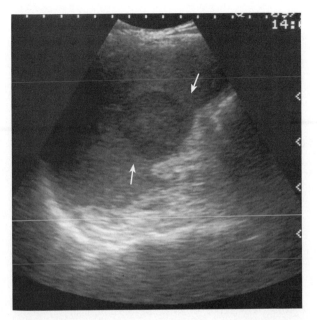

Figure 4.8
Metastatic gastric carcinoma: Invasion of the hilum of the spleen by a locally invasive gastric carcinoma was seen sonographically as a well-defined hypoechoic splenic mass.

bacterial disease. Patients with sepsis or subacute bacterial endocarditis may seed the spleen during episodes of bacteremia, resulting in infective foci in the spleen. Tuberculosis, candidiasis, and pyogenic infection of the spleen may produce similar sonographic findings of hypoechoic lesions or target-type lesions within the spleen. Sampling may be necessary to identify the etiologic agent and initiate therapy.

Metastatic Disease (Figures 4.8–4.11)

Metastatic disease of the spleen has a variably reported incidence from rare to more than 50 percent. Tumors that metastasize to the spleen include lung, breast, prostate, melanoma, colon, stomach, ovary, and pancreas. Metastatic melanoma is probably more common than recognized. Some consider melanoma the most common splenic metastatis.

Metastatic disease of the spleen is usually secondary to hematogenous spread, but direct extension into the spleen from local malignancy can occur. Direct extension into the spleen can occur with tumors from the pancreas, stomach, left kidney, and left colon. Metastases may be solitary or multiple.

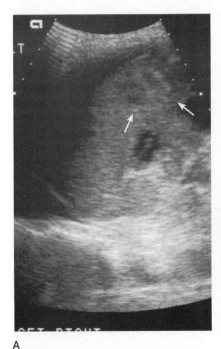

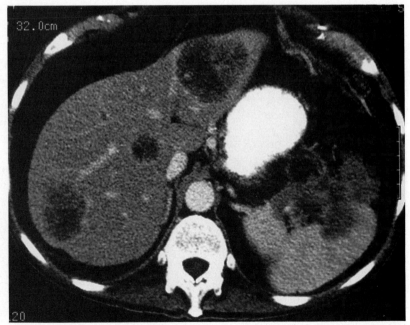

A   B

Figure 4.9
Metastatic pancreatic carcinoma: In this elderly woman with abdominal carcinomatosis, invasion of the spleen by a carcinoma in the tail of the pancreas was (A) obvious on ultrasound and (B) confirmed by CT.

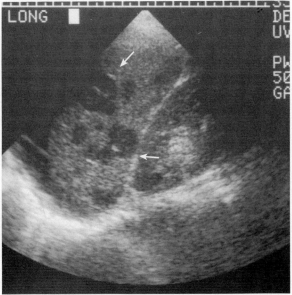

Metastatic involvement may be hyperechoic, hypoechoic, or targetlike on sonography. Fine-needle aspiration of splenic lesions can be performed safely to obtain cytologic confirmation of malignancy.

Lymphoma (Figure 4.12)

Involvement of the spleen with lymphoma is usually part of systemic disease. Primary lymphoma of the spleen is unusual. Besides diffuse lymphomatous infiltration of the spleen, masses—which may be miliary, small and nodular (2–10 cm), or large and solitary—may involve the spleen.

Splenic size may be the only indicator of lymphomatous involvement. It is, however, not a reliable indicator, especially in Hodgkin disease, because one-third of patients with a normal-sized spleen will have splenic involvement at splenectomy and one-third of patients with splenomegaly will not have involvement.

Angiosarcoma

Primary malignant neoplasms of the spleen, such as angiosarcomas, are quite rare. Angiosarcoma of the spleen has a poor prognosis, with life expectancy after diagnosis of only months. Hemoperitoneum sec-

Figure 4.10
Metastatic melanoma: Multiple hypoechoic masses were obvious in this patient 12 years after resection of malignant melanoma. Fine-needle aspiration yielded melanoma.

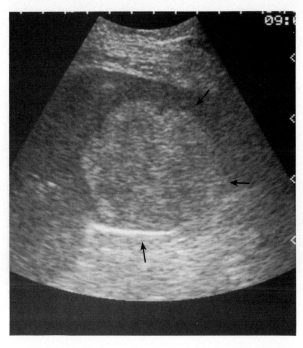

Figure 4.11
Metastatic melanoma: A large, focally hyperchoic mass was present in the spleen in this patient with melanoma.

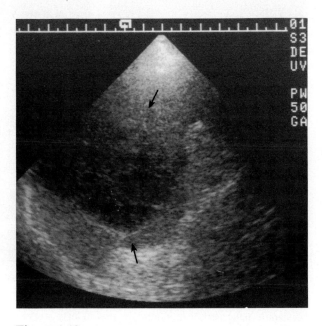

Figure 4.12
Lymphoma: A focal, hypoechoic mass was present in this elderly patient. Aspiration of the mass yielded non-Hodgkin lymphoma.

ondary to splenic rupture may occur. The mass is complex with cystic and solid components. Splenomegaly is usually present.

Posttraumatic Lesions (Figures 4.13–4.14)

Trauma to the spleen may cause subtly abnormal echotexture changes that with time may consolidate to form discrete abnormalities. In the setting of trauma, echotextural abnormalities may indicate splenic injury. Sonography is less sensitive than CT in the acute trauma setting but is quite good in following patients with known splenic injury for signs of change or decompensation. The development of perisplenic fluid collections can be monitored by ultrasound.

Infarction (Figures 4.15–4.17)

Splenic infarction is a common cause of a focal splenic lesion, especially if the sonographic appearance is that of a focal, peripheral, wedge-shaped echotexture abnormality. In the acute stage, splenic infarction may not be demonstrable by sonography. Over time, the infarction becomes more obvious, causing either a focal, wedge-shaped hypoechogenic area or a fibrotic scar.

Peripheral splenic infarction is especially common in patients with splenomegaly. Patients with polycythemia vera with very large spleens and left upper quadrant pain may be suspected of splenic infarction or rupture. In such a setting, the absence of rupture makes infarction likely. Such patients are difficult to manage because splenectomy in a situation of myeloproliferative disorders is often complicated by venous thrombosis or bleeding disorders.

Hemangioma/Hamartoma (Figure 4.18)

Both benign lesions of the spleen, hemangioma and hamartoma, are usually detected incidentally and may have a variable sonographic appearance.

A common cause of solitary solid mass in the spleen, the splenic hemangioma is usually hyperechoic, although it may have cystic spaces within. Multiple hemangiomas are sometimes seen, especially in conditions of hemangiomatosis or lymphangiomatosis.

The splenic hamartoma is a rare lesion that is also usually solitary.

Extramedullary Hematopoiesis

In patients with marrow-packing or replacement disorders, proliferation of hematopoietic tissue within the spleen may occur, resulting in focal hypoechoic masses sonographically.

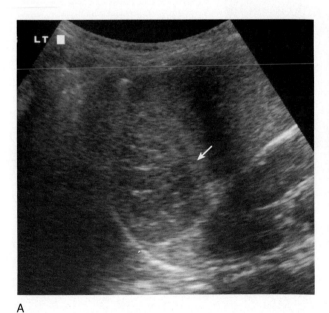

A

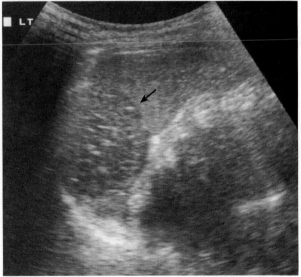

B

Figure 4.13

Posttraumatic lesion: (A and B) This youngster suffered a splenic laceration after a fall from his bicycle. Follow-up sonography revealed extensive hypoechogenicity in the spleen without a defined fluid collection.

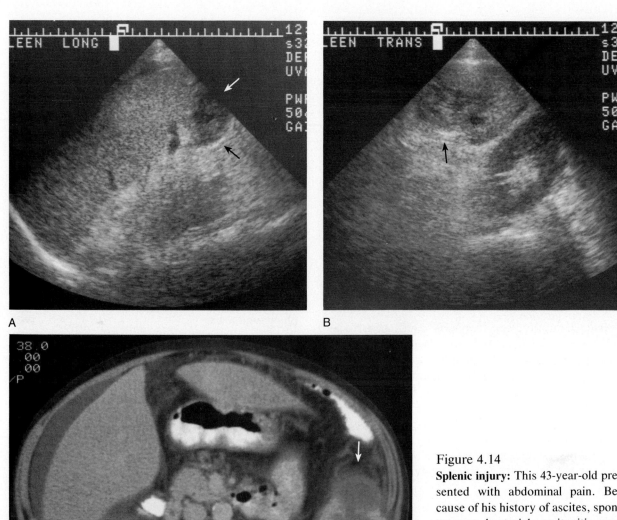

Figure 4.14
Splenic injury: This 43-year-old presented with abdominal pain. Because of his history of ascites, spontaneous bacterial peritonitis was suspected. Aspiration of gross blood at paracentesis led to a search for a source. (A and B) Inhomogeneity of the inferior tip of the spleen (*arrows*) on ultrasound was (C) confirmed by CT. Injury to the spleen was presumed to have occurred during a fall.

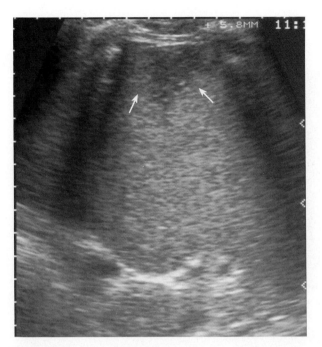

Figure 4.15
Splenic infarction: A wedge-shaped, hypoechoic peripheral lesion was identified in this patient after splenic and splanchnic vein thrombosis related to hypercoagulability.

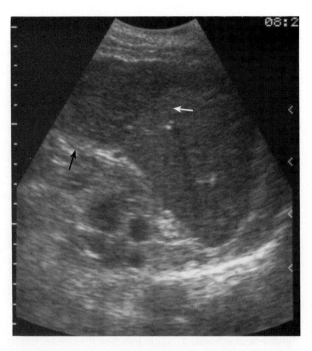

Figure 4.16
Focal splenic infarction: A large wedge of hypoechogenicity was seen in this patient with emboli related to cardiac arrhythmias.

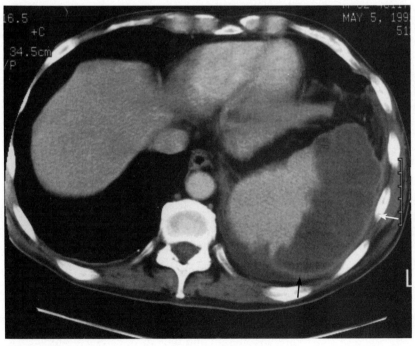

A

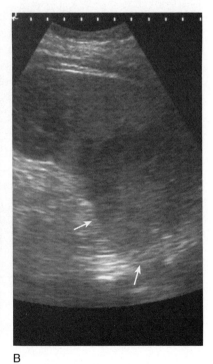

B

Figure 4.17
Splenic infarction: (A) A large area of splenic infarction was present in this patient after splenic vein occlusion related to pancreatitis. (B) Ultrasound showed heterogeneous echogenicity.

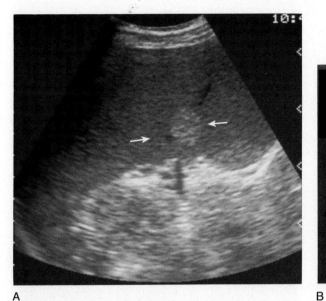

A   B

Figure 4.18
Splenic hemangioma: Focal hemangiomata of the spleen were incidentally identified in two different patients.

Emphasis Points

In the immediate evaluation after trauma, CT is probably the most sensitive way to evaluate for splenic injury. Ultrasound is often useful in the patient with known splenic trauma for follow-up studies, to evaluate the evolution of the injured spleen, and to monitor any perisplenic fluid collection.

In acute splenic infarction, the ultrasound may be remarkably normal, whereas CT shows significant contrast abnormalities.

In patients with focal splenic lesions believed to be secondary to infections or metastatic causes, fine-needle aspiration for diagnosis can be safely undertaken.

CALCIFICATIONS IN THE SPLEEN

Granulomatous Diseases
Old Trauma
Hemangioma
Vascular Calcifications
Sickle Cell Anemia

Granulomatous Diseases (Figure 4.19)

Evidence of granulomatous disease, such as histoplasmosis or tuberculosis, may present as multiple focal calcifications in the spleen. The patient may be asymptomatic despite the sonographic findings. Generally, the findings are incidental. In AIDS patients, extrapulmonary pneumocystis carinii may result in calcific lesions in the spleen in the chronic stage. Deposits of such fungal diseases as candidiasis can calcify in the chronic, treated stage.

Old Trauma (Figure 4.20)

Organizing hematoma or posttraumatic and parasitic cysts of the spleen may develop calcification of the rim of the lesion, obscuring complete ultrasound analysis of the internal architecture of the mass.

Hemangioma

The hemangioma is a common benign splenic tumor that does not usually calcify, but may. Hamartomas are uncommon and may have calcifications.

Vascular Calcifications (Figure 4.21)

Calcifications within the arterioles of the spleen may be noted sonographically. The splenic artery is

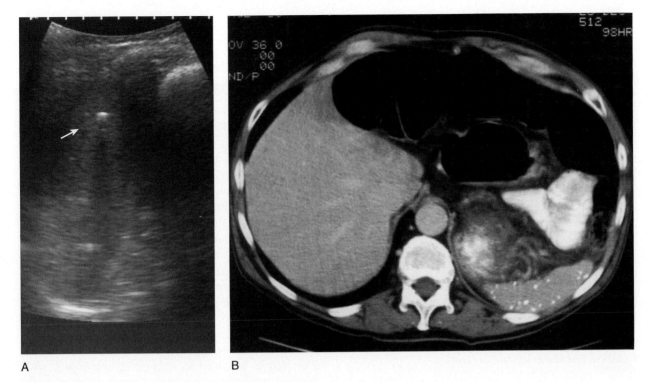

A   B

Figure 4.19

Granulomas: (A and B) Multiple calcified granulomas were seen as brightly echogenic foci with shadowing. Other stigmata of granulomatous disease were calcified hilar nodes and granulomata in the chest.

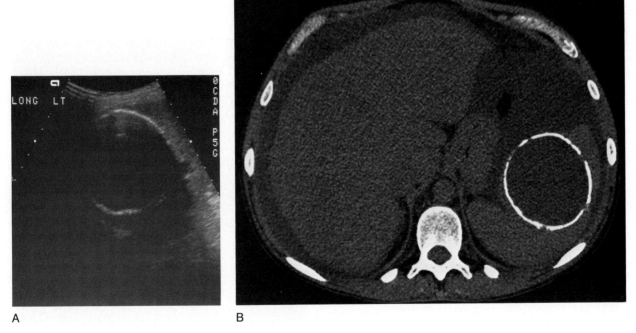

A   B

Figure 4.20

Calcified posttraumatic cyst: (A) A large, calcified cyst of the spleen was present in this woman with a distant history of substantial abdominal trauma. (B) Correlative CT image.

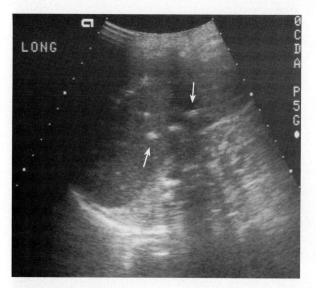

Figure 4.21
Extensive vascular calcifications (*arrows*).

often noted to have calcifications on plain films. Phleboliths in splenic venules may also be seen.

Sickle Cell Anemia

The spleen of a patient with sickle cell disease may calcify as it undergoes autosplenectomy related to recurring episodes of infarction.

PERISPLENIC COLLECTIONS

Subcapsular Hematoma or Perisplenic
    Hematoma
Peripancreatic Fluid Collections and
    Pseudocysts
Subphrenic Abscess
Cystic Neoplasms
    Pancreas
    Ovarian Carcinoma Implants
Splenic Artery Aneurysm

CHILDHOOD

Congenital Duplication Cyst

VARIANTS

The Stomach
Perisplenic Pseudocollection

Subcapsular Hematoma or Perisplenic Hematoma (Figures 4.22–4.23)

Perisplenic collections or subcapsular hematoma may develop after blunt trauma to the left upper quadrant. Injury to the spleen is common, second only to liver injuries in frequency. With relatively acute hematoma formation, the blood products may have an appearance similar to the spleen itself. Recognition of inhomogeneities of the splenic echotexture facilitates the diagnosis of splenic injury and perisplenic hematoma. Subcapsular hematomas assume a crescentic shape with pressure effect on the splenic parenchyma in keeping with the blood under tension in the small subcapsular space. With time, as the blood products of a subcapsular hematoma become liquefied, the subcapsular hematoma will be more cystic. Perisplenic collections, not limited by the subcapsular space, may have a variety of shapes. Perisplenic hematomas suggest splenic injury with blood outside the subcapsular space. Free intraperitoneal hemorrhage may be recognized as well.

In the patient being managed nonoperatively after splenic injury, ultrasound may be used to follow the evolutionary changes of a subcapsular hematoma or perisplenic collection. It is expected that the collections will become more cystic and smaller over time.

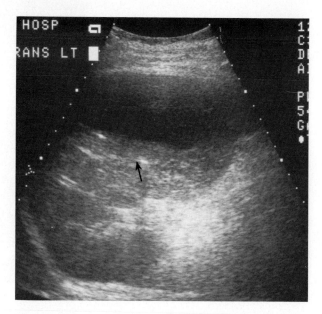

Figure 4.22
Subcapsular hematoma (chronic): This cardiac transplant recipient had a sizable subcapsular hematoma of his spleen that gradually became more cystic over time. Note its scalloping effect on the spleen's edge (*arrow*).

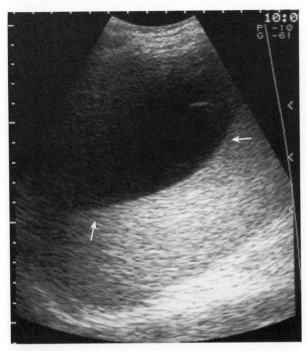

Figure 4.23
Subcapsular hematoma related to trauma: The large, sub-capsular collection in this patient indented the surface of the spleen, compressing the spleen and left kidney. Aspiration of the collection yielded old bloody fluid.

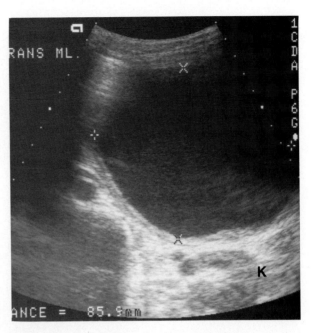

Figure 4.24
Pancreatic pseudocyst: The large cyst filled the left upper quadrant, compressing the left kidney (K).

Secondary infections of posttraumatic splenic fluid collections can occur. Unless air can be recognized within the collection to suggest infection, percutaneous aspiration may be necessary to determine the presence of infection and the etiologic agent.

Peripancreatic Fluid Collections and Pseudocysts (Figure 4.24)

Inflammation of the pancreas may be secondary to a number of causes, including hereditary pancreatitis, biliary calculi, alcohol abuse, and posttraumatic or postsurgical causes. Pancreatic inflammation may be associated with leakage of pancreatic enzymes into adjacent tissues. Necrotic tissue and fluid rich in pancreatic enzymes may be identified sonographically within the peripancreatic tissue. These fluid collections typically develop in peripancreatic areas such as the lesser sac, the left anterior pararenal space, the pericholecystic areas, and the subhepatic space. Because of the proximity of the pancreatic tail and spleen, the spleen is frequently engulfed in severe cases of pancreatitis.

Acute peripancreatic fluid collections are often ill defined and not well circumscribed. With maturation of a pseudocyst, the collection becomes better defined, often with a perceptible wall. Percutaneous drainage procedures are often used to determine whether peripancreatic fluid collections are infected and to eliminate the collection by drainage. Such collections can collect around and impress upon the spleen.

Subphrenic Abscess (Figure 4.25)

Although peripancreatic fluid collections related to pancreatic inflammation are a common cause of fluid collection in the left upper quadrant, other causes exist. Postoperatively, patients may develop collections in the left upper quadrant either because that was the operative site (as after a splenectomy) or because the left upper quadrant is a dependent area in the postoperative patient. Echogenic foci representing air may allow the sonographer to recognize the presence of infection. Percutaneous aspiration or drainage is often effective in such patients. In patients with peptic ulcer disease and perforation of a posterior wall ulcer, fluid collections around the spleen in the left upper quadrant may be seen sonographically.

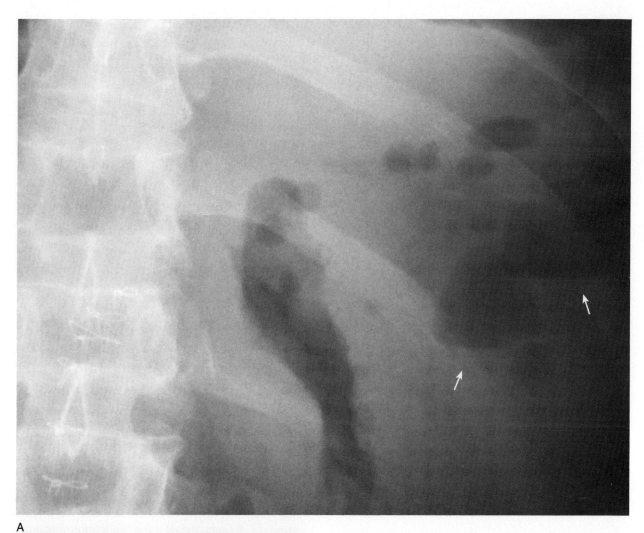

A

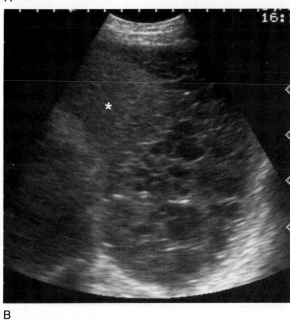

B

Figure 4.25
Subphrenic abscess: (A) Plain film showed air–fluid levels in the left upper quadrant and medial displacement of the stomach. (B) Multiseptated fluid collection engulfing the spleen (*asterisk*) was seen by sonography. Aspiration of the collection yielded grossly purulent material.

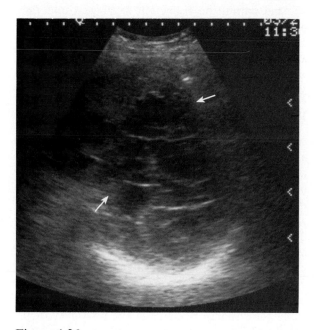

Figure 4.26
Ovarian carcinoma implants: Serosal implants of recurrent ovarian carcinoma (*arrows*) stud the surface of the spleen.

Cystic Neoplasms

Pancreas Cystic neoplasms arising from the pancreas itself or metastatic from the ovary may be discovered in the perisplenic area. Macrocystic, mucin-laden tumors of the pancreas can be in close association with or invade the spleen. These cystic tumors may be misinterpreted as pseudocysts since pseudocysts and fluid collections secondary to pancreatitis are responsible for approximately 80–85 percent of peripancreatic fluid collections. In elderly patients with no etiologic agent or clinical history of pancreatitis, the discovery of a cystic mass of the pancreas must raise the possibility of a cystic neoplasm rather than necessarily being accepted as a pseudocyst.

Ovarian Implants (Figures 4.26 and 4.27) Implants of ovarian epithelial tumors may coat the splenic surface or grow in the lesser sac. Communication with the general peritoneal cavity is present, and the metastatic deposition of cells into the lesser sac is facilitated by malignant ascites, which can enter the recesses of the lesser sac. In a patient with suspected or known ovarian epithelial tumor, cystic or complex masses implanted in the perisplenic area and lesser sac are of concern for recurrent or residual neoplasm.

Splenic Artery Aneurysm

Dilatation of the splenic artery with aneurysm formation may be recognized sonographically as a cystic mass that may be closely associated with the hilum of the spleen. Doppler analysis will allow recognition that the mass is arterial. Curvilinear calcifications may be on the periphery of the mass. The mass will appear cystic by gray-scale imaging unless thrombosis has occurred.

CHILDHOOD

Congenital Duplication Cyst (Figure 4.28)

Usually discovered in children, a congenital duplication cyst of the duodenum or stomach may be discovered as an incidental abdominal mass or secondary to small bowel obstruction. Observation of the mass during ingestion of water will allow assessment regarding luminal communication with the intestinal tract.

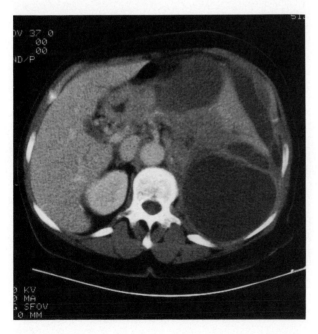

Figure 4.27
Metastatic papillary carcinoma of the ovary: Multiple cystic implants distort the normal contour of the spleen.

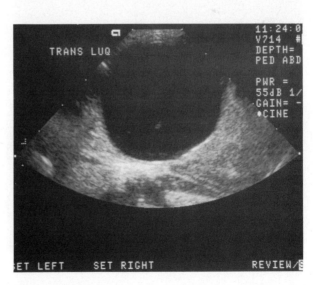

Figure 4.28
Gastric duplication: This large simple cyst, medial to the spleen (S), was detected on prenatal ultrasound. At surgery at 4 weeks of life, a noncommunicating gastric duplication was excised.

VARIANTS

The Stomach (Figure 4.29)

The stomach may be mistaken for a perisplenic collection, as it usually contains quantities of air and fluid, making it appear sonographically similar to an abscess. Having the patient ingest fluid under sonographic visualization will allow the stomach to be distinguished from an infected, air-filled collection. Microbubbles of air introduced during ingestion of water and active motility of the stomach, which can be seen, allow it to be differentiated from an air- and fluid-filled abscess.

Perisplenic Pseudocollection (Figures 4.30–4.31)

In thin patients with a long, narrow left lobe of the liver, sagittal sonographic imaging of the left upper quadrant may lead to the mistaken impression that a perisplenic collection exists. The liver generally is hypoechoic relative to the spleen, and in such patients, the hypoechoic, crescentic-shaped left lobe of the liver will look similar to a subcapsular hematoma unless portal triads and continuity with the rest of the liver are recognized. The left lobe of the liver can cause a so-called pseudocollection around the spleen.

Emphasis Points

The stomach can be easily mistaken for a subphrenic abscess when it is distended with air and fluid. Decompression of the stomach with a nasogastric tube or watching the patient add water to the stomach by drinking will allow the stomach to be differentiated from an abscess.

The perisplenic "collection" that is the left lobe of the liver can look exactly like a subcapsular hematoma of the spleen unless its communication with the rest of the liver and the recognition of portal triads are noted.

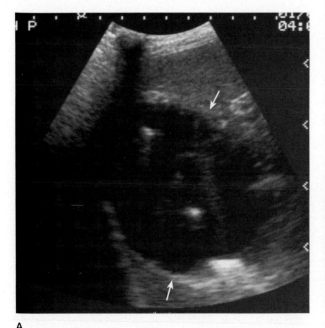

A

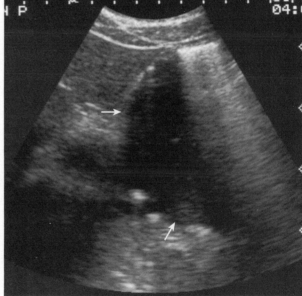

B

Figure 4.29

The stomach: (A and B) The distended gas and fluid-filled stomach can be misinterpreted as a left upper quadrant abscess unless the patient is given water and monitored at realtime.

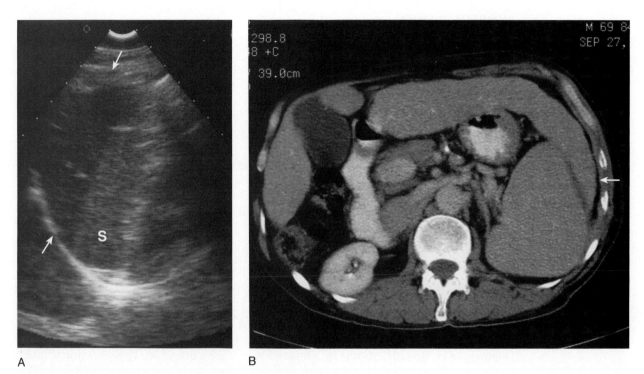

A   B

Figure 4.30
Pseudocollection: (A) In this young woman with a history
of trauma, the hypoechoic "collection" (*arrows*) adjacent
to the spleen (S) was suspected of being a subcapsular
hematoma. Only with close scrutiny was the "collection"
connected to the rest of the liver, since it was the left lobe
of the liver. (B) CT equivalent.

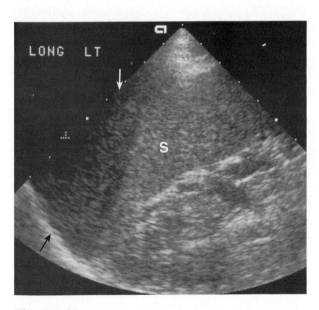

Figure 4.31
Pseudocollection (left lobe of liver): Again, the hypoechoic
"pseudocollection" (*arrows*) was present adjacent to the
spleen (S). Knowledge of this normal variant prevents erroneous judgments.

BIBLIOGRAPHY

Splenomegaly

Frank K, Linhart P, Kortsik C, et al.: Sonographic determination of spleen size: Normal dimensions in adults with a healthy spleen. Ultraschall Med 7(3):134–137, 1986.

Perlmutter GS: Ultrasound measurements of the spleen. In Goldberg B, Kurtz AB (eds): *Atlas of Ultrasound Measurements*. Chicago: Yearbook Medical Publishers, pp. 126–138, 1990.

Rosenberg HK, Markowitz RI, Kolberg H, Park C, Hubbard A, Bellah RD: Normal splenic size in infants and children: Sonographic measurements. AJR 157:119–121, 1991.

Weinberger G, Mitra SK, Yoeli, G: Ultrasound diagnosis of splenic vein thrombosis. J Clin Ultrasound 10:345–346, 1982.

Cystic Lesions of the Spleen

Bhimji SD, Cooperberg PL, Naiman S, et al.: Ultrasound diagnosis of splenic cysts. Radiology 122:787–789, 1977.

Caslowitz PL, Labs JD, Fishman EK, Siegelman SS: The changing spectrum of splenic abscess. Clin Imaging 13:201–207, 1989.

Dachman AH, Ros PR, Murari PJ, Olmsted WW, Lichtenstein JE: Nonparasitic splenic cysts: A report of 52 cases with radiologic-pathologic correlation. AJR 147:537–542, 1986.

Franquet T, Montes M, Lecumberri FJ, et al.: Hydatid disease of the spleen: Imaging findings in nine patients. AJR 154(3):525–528, 1990.

Glancy JJ: Fluid-filled echogenic epidermoid cyst of the spleen. J Clin Ultrasound 7:301–302, 1979.

Goldfinger M, Cohen MM, Steinhardt MI, Rothberg R, Rother I: Sonography and percutaneous aspiration of splenic epidermoid cyst. J Clin Ultrasound 14:147–149, 1986.

Pawar S, Kay CJ, Gonzalez R, Taylor KJW, Rosenfield AT: Sonography of splenic abscess. AJR 138:259–262, 1982.

Propper RA, Weinstein BJ, Skolnick ML, et al.: Ultrasonography of hemorrhagic splenic cysts. J Clin Ultrasound 7:18–20, 1979.

Thurber LA, Cooperberg PL, Clemente JG, et al.: Echogenic fluid: A pitfall in the ultrasonographic diagnosis of cystic lesions. J Clin Ultrasound 7:273–278, 1979.

Focal, Solid-appearing Lesions of the Spleen

Costello P, Kane RA, Oster J, et al.: Focal splenic disease demonstrated by ultrasound and computed tomography. J Can Assoc Radiol 36:22–28, 1985.

Goerg C, Schwerk WB: Splenic infarction: Sonographic patterns, diagnosis, follow-up, and complications. Radiology 174:803–807, 1990.

Goerg C, Schwerk WB, Goerg K: Sonography of focal lesions of the spleen. AJR 156:949–953, 1991.

Hill SC, Reinig JW, Barranger JA, et al.: Gaucher disease: Sonographic appearance of spleen. Radiology 160:631–634, 1986.

Lupien C, Sauerbrei EE: Healing in the traumatized spleen: Sonographic investigation. Radiology 151:181–185, 1984.

Maresca G, Mirk P, De Gaetano AM, et al.: The sonographic patterns in splenic infarct. J Clin Ultrasound 14:23–28, 1986.

Murphy JF, Bernardino ME: Sonographic findings of splenic metastases. JCU 7:195–197, 1979.

Ros PR, Moser RP Jr, Dachman AH, Murari PJ, Olmsted WW: Hemangioma of the spleen: Radiologic pathologic correlation in 10 cases. Radiology 162:73–77, 1987.

Wernecke K, Peters PE, Krüger KG: Ultrasonographic patterns of focal hepatic and splenic lesions in Hodgkin's and non-Hodgkin's lymphoma. Br J Radiol 60:655–660, 1987.

Perisplenic Collections

Asher WM, Parvin S, Virgillo RW, Haber K: Echographic evaluation of splenic injury after blunt trauma. Radiology 118:411–415, 1976.

Crivello MS, Peterson IM, Austin RM: Left lobe of the liver mimicking perisplenic collections. J Clin Ultrasound 14(9):697–701, 1986.

Li DKB, Cooperberg PL, Graham MF, Callen P: Pseudo perisplenic "fluid collections": A clue to normal liver and spleen echogenic texture. J Ultrasound Med 5:(7):397–400, 1986.

Vyborny CJ, Merrill TN, Reda J, et al.: Subacute subcapsular hematoma of the spleen complicating pancreatitis: Successful percutaneous drainage. Radiology 169:161–162, 1988.

PERITONEAL CAVITY

PATTERNS

Ascites
Discordant Quantity of Fluid in the Lesser
   Sac
Echogenic Fluid in the Cul-de-Sac
Right Lower Quadrant Fluid Collection
Omental Thickening
Large Cystic Mass in the Abdomen
Large, Solid-Appearing Mass in the
   Abdomen
Bowel Wall Thickening
Dilated, Fluid-Filled Small Bowel Loops:
   Small Bowel Obstruction versus Ileus

ASCITES

Transudative Causes of Ascites
  Liver Disease
  Congestive Heart Failure
  Portal or Hepatic Vein Thrombosis
  Renal Dysfunction
Exudative Fluid
  Peritoneal Carcinomatosis
  Lymphoma
  Peritoneal Mesothelioma
  Pancreatitis
  Spontaneous Bacterial Peritonitis
  Peritoneal Tuberculosis
  Organ Injury or Rupture
Pelvic Processes

  Ectopic Pregnancy
  Functional Cyst Rupture
  Pelvic Inflammatory Disease
Instillation of Fluid
Cerebrospinal Fluid

CHILDHOOD

Urinary Ascites
Meconium Peritonitis
Chylous Ascites

Free fluid in the peritoneal cavity, ascites, can usually be easily detected by ultrasonography. Only a few milliliters of ascites can be seen if present in the cul-de-sac or right subhepatic space. Ascitic fluid may be transudative or exudative. Free fluid may be serous, bloody, purulent, or chylous. Fluid instilled in the abdomen will appear sonographically similar to fluid from other etiologies.

Ascitic fluid from whatever cause has a pattern of distribution in the abdomen that is influenced by gravity, patient position, origin and volume of fluid, and presence of adhesions. Fluid generated in the upper abdomen generally flows along the mesenteric reflections and pools in the right lower quadrant near the terminal ileum and in the sigmoid mesocolon. The fluid spills over to fill the pelvis, including the paravesical spaces. When the patient is supine, fluid flows up the paracolic gutters from the pelvis. Since the right gutter is deeper than the left and flow is limited on the left side by the phrenicocolic ligament, most fluid moves from the pelvis into the upper abdomen via the right paracolic gutter.

This pattern of fluid distribution is important to realize in imaging patients. This pattern of fluid flow explains how patients with malignant pelvic processes develop upper abdominal disease. The fluid transports malignant cells to the upper abdomen. Recognition of fluid in the subhepatic space must trigger a search for a source, including pelvic processes. Also, the recognition of free fluid in the pelvis may be the only sign of an upper abdominal problem. A small amount of free fluid in the cul-de-sac may be recognized normally in women of reproductive age, usually reflecting the physiologic cycling of the ovaries with cyst formation and rupture.

Transudative Causes of Ascites

Liver Disease (Figure 5.1)   Liver disease is a common cause of abundant free fluid in the peritoneal cavity. There are both local and systemic causes of ascitic fluid formation in patients with hepatocellular dysfunction. The local causes are secondary to portal hypertension and increased flow of hepatic lymph. The systemic causes of ascitic fluid formation are secondary to a decrease in plasma colloid oncotic pressure, hyperaldosteronism, impaired water excretion, and elevated levels of norepinephrine in the plasma.

Free fluid can be identified above and around the liver and spleen, pushing both solid organs medially. Fluid can also be seen in paracolic gutters and in the pelvis. Fluid or air-filled bowel loops may be clustered in the central abdomen, often floating in the ascites. Stigmata of liver disease—such as an irregular, small liver, splenomegaly, venous collaterals, and portal vein enlargement—may be identifiable, allowing the source of the ascites to be recognized. Recognition of a recanalized umbilical

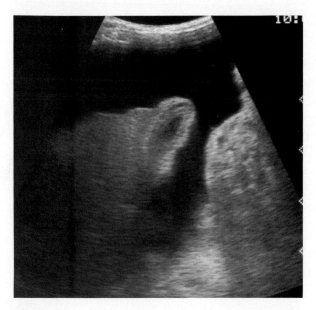

Figure 5.1

Transudative ascites secondary to liver failure: This 56-year-old man being evaluated prior to liver transplantation has abundant ascites anterior to the liver related to liver dysfunction.

collateral is important because it confirms that portal hypertension is present and may be the source of the ascites.

Congestive Heart Failure (Figure 5.2)   Congestive heart failure with associated right-sided congestion may result in ascites. Usually, the vol-

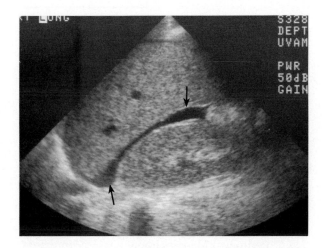

Figure 5.2

Transudative ascites secondary to heart failure: Fluid around the liver, extending into the subhepatic space (Morrison's pouch) (*arrows*), is identified in this patient with ischemic cardiomyopathy. Engorged hepatic veins were also obvious.

ume of ascites is not massive in this condition, although it may be quite large with severe cardiac decompensation. Other stigmata of congestive heart failure seen sonographically include inferior vena caval engorgement with associated distention of the hepatic veins. Hepatomegaly and pleural effusions frequently accompany cardiac decompensation of a severe degree.

Portal or Hepatic Vein Thrombosis Acute thrombosis of the portal and splanchnic veins may result in ascites. Hepatic vein thrombosis of Budd-Chiari syndrome may result in massive ascites and hepatomegaly. Hepatic vein thrombosis may be related to oral contraceptive use, hepatocellular carcinomas or other tumors, veno-occlusive disease after bone marrow transplantation, or congenital stenosis of the IVC. The new onset of ascites warrants Doppler investigation of the portal and hepatic veins and IVC if other causes for ascites are not identified.

Renal Dysfunction Transudative ascites may be seen in situations of renal dysfunction, especially with nephrosis and hypoalbuminemia. The hypervolemic state that accompanies renal failure may also contribute to the presence of ascites.

Exudative Fluid

Peritoneal Carcinomatosis (Figures 5.3–5.4) Peritoneal carcinomatosis is the pattern of tumor spread that is typical of malignant ovarian epithelial neoplasms. In addition to the primary tumor mass in the pelvis, there may be studding of the omental, mesenteric, and peritoneal surfaces with tumor implants. Ascites, often laden with tumor cells, is frequently present. Peritoneal studding and omental thickening are more easily recognized sonographically when ascites is present.

Other carcinomas that may spread in a pattern of peritoneal carcinomatosis include colon, pancreas, stomach, breast, and endometrial carcinomas. Pseudomyxoma peritonei results from the rupture of gelatinous material into the peritoneum, usually after rupture of an ovarian or appendiceal mass. The gelatinous material can fill the recesses of the peritoneal cavity in a pattern similar to ascites with encasement of bowel loops and solid organs.

Lymphoma (Figure 5.5) Lymphoma may be diffusely present in the abdomen with omental, mesenteric, and bowel wall involvement. Ascites may be present in situations of diffuse abdominal disease. Such lymphomatous involvement is usually non-Hodgkin lymphoma. The volume of ascites in patients with lymphoma is not usually as large as with peritoneal carcinomatosis.

Peritoneal Mesothelioma Peritoneal mesothelioma is a rare primary neoplasm of the abdominal surfaces that may have associated ascites. The as-

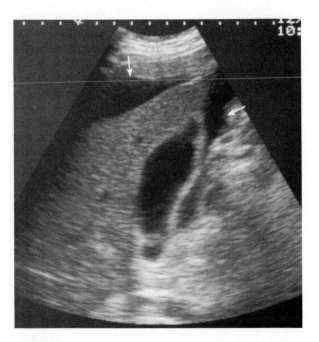

Figure 5.4
Exudative ascites: Malignant ascites surrounds the liver and gallbladder (*arrows*). A large, complex pelvic mass and omental thickening were also present in this patient with ovarian carcinoma.

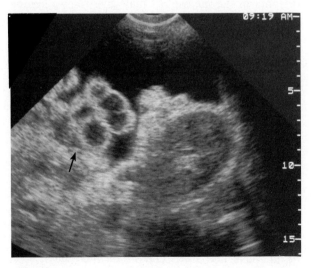

Figure 5.3
Exudative ascites: In a patient with massive malignant ascites related to carcinomatosis from colon carcinoma, bowel loops (*arrow*) are easily visualized.

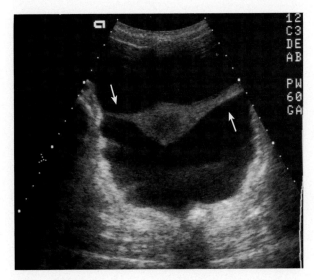

Figure 5.5
Exudative fluid: Pelvic fluid fills the cul-de-sac, delineating the broad ligament (*arrows*) in this patient with abdominal lymphoma.

cites may predominate initially before an obvious mass is seen on imaging studies. Sheetlike peritoneal masses or irregular localized masses may be identified within the ascites. Biopsy is necessary to differentiate this entity from more common metastatic disease to the peritoneal surfaces.

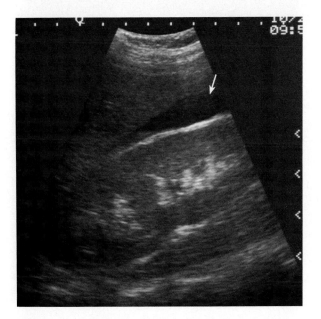

Figure 5.6
Blood: Free fluid in the abdomen (*arrow*) was aspirated under ultrasound guidance and was grossly bloody. Scans through the spleen revealed inhomogeneity consistent with splenic injury, explaining the hemoperitoneum.

Pancreatitis   Generally, the fluid present in the abdomen secondary to pancreatitis is localized in the spaces adjacent to the pancreas. Fluid in the lesser sac, subhepatic spaces, and left anterior pararenal space frequently accompanies acute pancreatitis. Excess fluid may accumulate in the paracolic gutters and pelvis. Fluid collections secondary to pancreatitis may dissect into the pelvis or chest.

Spontaneous Bacterial Peritonitis   Bacterial superinfection of ascites may occur, resulting in abdominal pain, fever, and elevated white count. Features of complication of the fluid may be seen sonographically, including loculations and septations of the fluid with echogenic particulate material within it. Spontaneous bacterial peritonitis often develops in patients with pre-existing ascites, usually related to liver disease. Paracentesis or aspiration of the ascitic fluid will allow bacterial infection to be detected and effectively treated.

Peritoneal Tuberculosis   Tuberculosis affecting the peritoneal surfaces may result in bloody ascites. Usually seen in immunocompromised patients or patients with poor sanitation, peritoneal tuberculosis is often not suggested preoperatively. If tuberculosis is considered in the differential diagnosis, percutaneous aspiration with culture may make operative intervention unnecessary, since tuberculosis can be managed medically.

Organ Injury or Rupture (Figure 5.6)   Patients who rupture solid or hollow organs either related to trauma or as a sequel of disease may have free fluid in the abdomen. Splenic trauma, liver lacerations, or rents in the mesentery may give rise to hemorrage in posttrauma patients. Patients with bowel rupture secondary to inflammatory processes may have complicated ascites. Air within the fluid, seen sonographically as highly echogenic foci, and septations in the ascites suggest that the fluid is complicated.

Pelvic Processes

Ectopic Pregnancy   A ruptured ectopic pregnancy may result in blood in the pelvis and upper abdomen, specifically in the subhepatic space. In a female patient with an acute abdomen and a positive β-HCG, a ruptured ectopic pregnancy may be identified by recognition of a complex or solid adnexal mass and free fluid in the abdomen. Free intraperitoneal fluid is one of the most common findings at ultrasound in women with ectopic pregnancy, reported in 60 percent of cases (range 40–83 percent). Particulate material or echogenic fluid is present with hemoperitoneum and if identified increases the likelihood that ectopic pregnancy is present in appropriate patients. Echogenic fluid carries a very high (92 percent) risk for ectopic pregnancy, and is the only finding in 15 percent of patients with ectopic pregnancy. Echogenic fluid of any amount was equal to large volumes of uncomplicated fluid in predicting ectopic pregnancy in appropriate patients. Recognition of fluid and specifically the echogenic particles in the fluid can be facilitated by transvaginal scanning of the cul-de-sac.

Functional Ovarian Cyst Rupture Rupture of a functional ovarian cyst may result in free abdominal fluid. Acute onset of abdominal pain in a woman of reproductive age with a negative β-HCG assay may be secondary to functional cyst rupture or hemorrhage.

A small amount of fluid in the cul-de-sac may be seen routinely in women with normal ovarian function. The fluid is related to the cycling of the ovary, which yields a dominant cyst each cycle. The cyst ruptures and the fluid is released.

Pelvic Inflammatory Disease Pelvic inflammatory disease (PID) may result in free abdominal fluid. Pelvic inflammatory disease, usually a sexually transmitted ascending infection, causes endometritis, then salpingitis. Weeping of fluid from the fimbriated end of the fallopian tube into the peritoneum may result in cul-de-sac fluid. When the volume of fluid is great enough to travel up the paracolic gutter, the fluid may cause right upper quadrant irritation secondary to inflammation around the liver and right hemidiaphragm. Tenderness generated by pelvic inflammatory fluid in the right upper quadrant is called the Fitz-Hugh-Curtis syndrome.

Instillation of Fluid

Instillation of fluid in the abdomen for either diagnostic or therapeutic purposes (e.g., peritoneal lavage or peritoneal dialysis) may be seen sonographically as free fluid indistinguishable from other types of abdominal fluid. Postoperative patients may have free fluid in the abdomen related to the surgical intervention.

Cerebrospinal Fluid

In children or adults with dilated cerebral ventricles, shunting procedures are often performed to drain the cerebrospinal fluid (CSF) from the dilated ventricles to the abdomen. Fluid that is free in the abdomen will usually be resorbed by the peritoneal surfaces. Small amounts of fluid may be seen normally in patients with CSF shunts to the abdomen. Loculations of fluid around the shunt are clues that the fluid has become complicated, sometimes with infection, and the peritoneal surface is not absorbing completely. Large volumes of fluid may develop, forcing shunt revision.

CHILDHOOD

Urinary Ascites

Urinary ascites is a common cause of ascites seen in utero or in the newborn. Bladder rupture secondary to bladder outlet obstruction results in urinary ascites. Posterior urethral valves can cause severe bladder outlet obstruction and urinary ascites in the newborn, but other forms of bladder outlet obstruction could cause a similar obstructive situation.

In the adult patient, intraperitoneal rupture of the bladder can result in urinary ascites. In these cases the bladder is usually distended at the time of blunt trauma, resulting in a rent in the dome of the bladder, which is covered by the peritoneum. Disruption of the peritoneum results in urine extravasation around loops of bowel in the abdomen. Extraperitoneal bladder rupture does not usually cause free intraperitoneal fluid. Fluid dissects instead into the fascial planes of the extraperitoneal space, including the soft tissues of the scrotum and upper thigh. Extraperitoneal bladder rupture is usually associated with pelvic fractures and trauma at the bladder base.

Meconium Peritonitis (Figure 5.7)

Perforation of obstructed bowel during intrauterine life results in spillage of meconium from the fetal GI tract into the peritoneal cavity. Spillage of meconium results in a chemical peritonitis called meconium peritonitis. Sonographically, ascites and complicated cystic collections, often with calcifications around the rim and scattered calcifications, may be seen. Echogenic particles are commonly seen within the ascites of meconium peritonitis.

The bowel obstruction that leads to meconium peritonitis may be secondary to a vascular accident, causing a bowel atresia, volvulus, or meconium ileus with inspissated meconium in an infant with cystic fibrosis.

Chylous Ascites

In children, chylous ascites is usually secondary to congenital hypoplasia or obstruction of the lymphatic system. In adults, development of chylous ascites is secondary to injury or obstruction of the lymphatics, such as in patients with lymphoma.

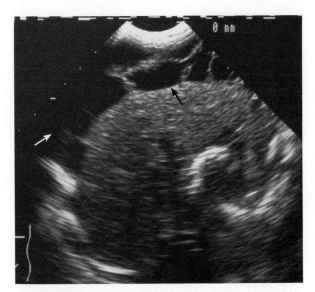

Figure 5.7

Meconium peritonitis: This newborn was noted in utero to have small bowel obstruction. Serial examinations demonstrated small bowel rupture and meconium spillage. Note septated fluid (*arrows*) related to meconium peritonitis.

Emphasis Point

There are many varied reasons for ascites. In middle-aged to elderly men presenting for the first time, the etiology for ascites is often liver disease. Stigmata of liver disease may be obvious sonographically and clinically. In middle-aged to elderly women, ovarian neoplasia is frequently the culprit. Certainly, there are exceptions to these general rules, but screening for pelvic masses, omental cakes, cirrhotic changes in the liver, and venous thrombosis in the upper abdomen will help discover the etiology of ascites. Sometimes ultrasound-guided aspiration of the fluid facilitates discovery of the etiology.

DISCORDANT QUANTITY OF FLUID IN THE LESSER SAC

Acute Pancreatitis
Penetrating Posterior Gastric Ulcer
Recurrent Ovarian Epithelial Malignancy

The lesser sac is the potential space between the back of the stomach and the anterior aspect of the body of the pancreas seen best sonographically on a transverse midline image. Fluid can accumulate in this space.

Acute Pancreatitis (Figure 5.8)

In acute pancreatitis when fluid weeps from the pancreas into the potential space of the lesser sac, fluid can be seen dissecting between the posterior aspect of the stomach and the anterior surface of the pancreas. Fluid in the lesser sac and in continuity with the left anterior pararenal space is very suggestive of inflammation of the pancreas. In the setting of trauma, fluid limited to just these regions suggests pancreatic injury.

Penetrating Posterior Gastric Ulcer

A gastric ulcer located on the posterior wall of the stomach can penetrate the stomach wall. Fluid in the lesser sac would be expected in this situation, whether or not there is associated pancreatitis.

Recurrent Ovarian Epithelial Malignancy (Figure 5.9)

Women with ovarian epithelial malignancy may develop cystic implants in the lesser sac. Recurrent disease may occur in the lesser sac because of the

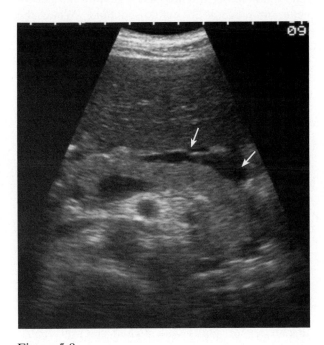

Figure 5.8

Pancreatitis: Slivers of fluid outlined the pancreas in this patient with pancreatitis. Fluid was present in the lesser sac between the back of the stomach and anterior border of the pancreas.

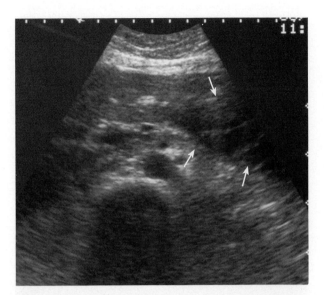

Figure 5.9
Recurrent ovarian carcinoma: Multiseptated implant of ovarian carcinoma was identified in the lesser sac in this patient with epigastric fullness.

difficulty of clearing this recess of malignant cells and ascites.

ECHOGENIC FLUID IN THE CUL-DE-SAC (Figures 5.10–5.12)

Particulate material in cul-de-sac fluid is generally seen in complicated fluid, such as blood, pus, or

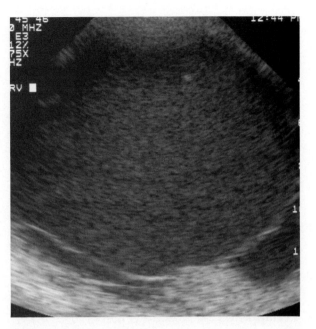

Figure 5.11
Malignant ascites: Echogenic fluid filled the pelvis in this patient with extensive intra-abdominal carcinomatosis from gastric carcinoma.

proteinaceous fluid. Bloody fluid may be present in the cul-de-sac with ectopic pregnancy and traumatic (accidental blunt or surgical) injury to the abdomen, with hepatic or splenic rupture. Purulent fluid may be present with sexually transmitted PID or other causes of abscess in the pelvis, such as appendicitis, diverticulitis, or postoperative infec-

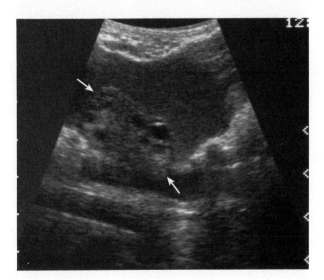

Figure 5.10
Purulent fluid (pelvic inflammatory disease): Echogenic fluid surrounded the ovary (*arrows*) in this patient with severe pelvic inflammatory disease.

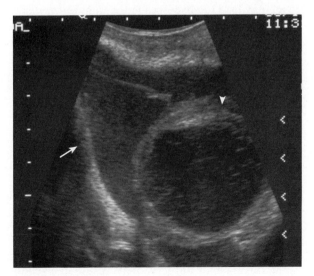

Figure 5.12
Malignant ascites: Echogenic fluid (*arrow*) was present in this patient with diffuse peritoneal mesothelium and functional cyst of the ovary (*arrowhead*) (transvaginal scan).

tions. Proteinaceous fluid includes malignant ascites related to carcinomatosis from a variety of primary sites.

RIGHT LOWER QUADRANT FLUID COLLECTION

    Periappendiceal Abscess
    Other Right Lower Quadrant Abscesses
    Appendiceal Mucocele
    Adnexal Mass
    Atonic Cecum/Neobladder
    Pseudocyst
    Duplication Cysts
    Loculated Ascites

Periappendiceal Abscess (Figures 5.13–5.14)

The recognition of a tender fluid collection in the right lower quadrant may signal the presence of a ruptured appendix with the formation of a periappendiceal abscess. Approximately 15 to 20 percent of patients with appendicitis show evidence of perforation at the time of surgery, and peritoneal abscess formation is a common complication of appendiceal rupture. Percutaneous drainage of periappendiceal abscesses is advocated in some centers to temporize or stabilize appendicitis patients.

Other Right Lower Quadrant Abscesses

Other inflammatory processes, such as Crohn's disease, may lead to abscesses in the right lower quadrant. Percutaneous drainage of abscesses related to Crohn's disease may require lengthy drainage until the nearby diseased bowel has time to heal. Postoperative collections, including hematomas, seromas, and abscesses, may collect in the right lower quadrant.

Appendiceal Mucocele (Figures 5.15–5.16)

Obstruction of the base of the appendix with distention of the appendiceal lumen may lead to a mucocele of the appendix. Often the mucocele is secondary to a slow-growing neoplastic mass of the appendix, a cystadenoma, or cystadenocarcinoma. Rupture of such a neoplasm, either spontaneously or at the time of surgery, may result in pseudomyxoma peritonei, in which gelatinous material fills the peritoneal spaces, compressing bowel and solid viscera.

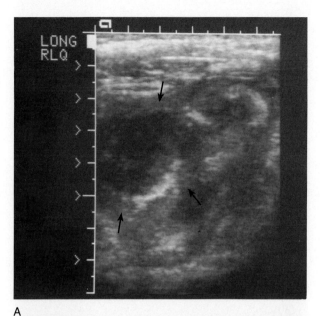

A

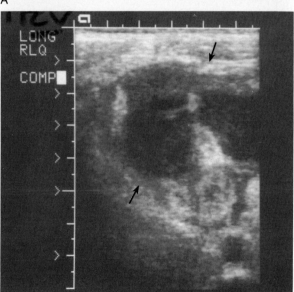

B

Figure 5.13

Periappendiceal abscesses: (A and B) This 45-year-old man with right lower quadrant pain and leukocytosis had a complex cystic collection in the right lower quadrant (*arrows*). At surgery, a walled-off abscess was drained. The appendix had been engulfed and destroyed by the inflammatory process.

A mucocele of the appendix secondary to a cystadenoma or cystadenocarcinoma of the appendix may be an incidental finding of a fluid collection in the right lower quadrant during an abdominal ultrasound or may be identified in the patient presenting acutely who is thought to have appendicitis.

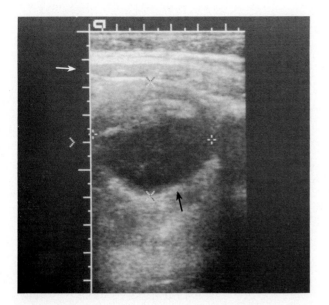

Figure 5.14

Periappendiceal abscess: With an 8-month history of right lower quadrant complaints, this patient was found to have a cystic collection. Percutaneous tube drainage was performed for an actinomyceal abscess. The patient did well with antibiotics and tube drainage and refused surgery.

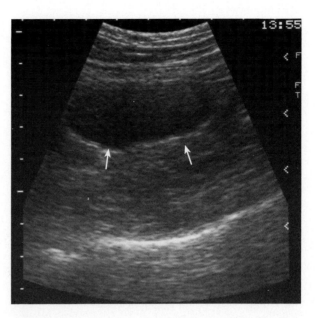

Figure 5.16

Appendiceal cystadenoma: A well-defined cystic mass was identified in this 70-year-old man during renal imaging. Subsequent surgery led to the removal of an appendiceal cystadenoma.

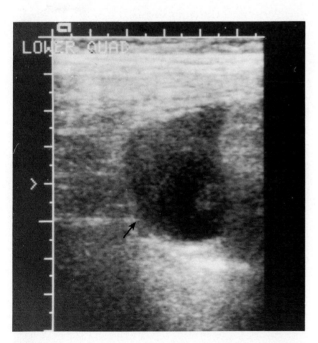

Figure 5.15

Appendiceal mucocele: Presenting with symptoms of appendicitis, this patient was found to have a fluid collection in the right lower quadrant, misinterpreted as a periappendiceal abscess. At surgery, a gelatinous cystadenoma of the appendix was removed.

Adnexal Mass (Figures 5.17–5.18)

In female patients, right lower quadrant adnexal masses, such as functional ovarian cysts, parovarian cysts, and ovarian neoplasms, may cause cystic masses of the right lower quadrant. The uterus and adnexal structures must be carefully studied to identify whether they are involved or are the site of origin of the mass. The mass must be characterized as carefully as possible to narrow the differential diagnosis. Cystic lower abdominal or pelvic masses in female patients are often of ovarian or adnexal origin.

Atonic Cecum/Neobladder (Figure 5.19)

In patients with inflammatory processes, such as appendicitis, it is important that an atonic, fluid-filled cecum not be mistaken for a fluid collection or abscess. The normal cecum is not fluid filled, but with ileus, the cecum may be confused with an abscess, since it may be fluid or air filled and peristalsis may not be visible.

In patients with cystectomy who desire continence, a neobladder is sometimes created using the cecum and right colon. The incorporation of the ileocecal valve facilitates continence. Usually the pa-

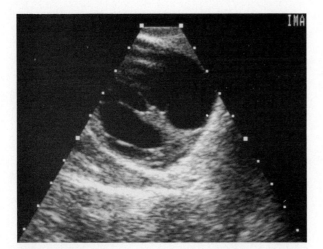

Figure 5.17
Ovarian cyst: A septated functional cyst was palpable in the right lower quadrant (transvaginal scan).

tient can furnish the history of previous surgery and knows that bowel has been used as the reservoir for urine. Such neobladders can be large, unusually-shaped fluid collections which should not be misinterpreted as an abscess if the patient's history is known.

Pseudocyst

Patients with pancreatitis may develop fluid and pseudocysts that dissect into the right lower quad-

rant. Usually, peripancreatic inflammatory fluid predominates in the left anterior pararenal spaces, but especially in pancreatitis affecting the head of the pancreas, fluid can flow down the mesenteric leaves and accumulate in the right lower quadrant. Usually, the patient's clinical presentation will allow the origin of the fluid to be ascertained.

Duplication Cysts

Uncommonly, duplication cysts of the distal small bowel or mesenteric cysts will explain fluid collections in the right lower quadrant.

Loculated Ascites

Loculated ascites may cause a focal fluid collection in the right lower quadrant. Loculations of ascites suggest some complication of the fluid, such as infection or bleeding into the ascites. Malignant ascites may be septated and loculated, leading to a focal collection of fluid.

OMENTAL THICKENING

Peritoneal Carcinomatosis
   Ovarian Carcinomatosis
   Other Carcinomas Resulting in Omental
     Involvement

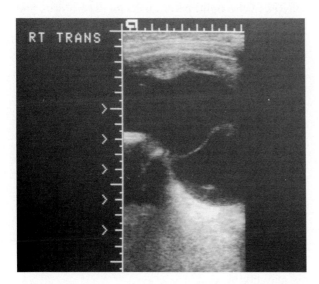

Figure 5.18
Dermoid of the ovary: Multilocular cystic mass of the right ovary proved to be a dermoid in this woman with severe right lower quadrant pain. The mass was thought to be the lead point of adnexal torsion.

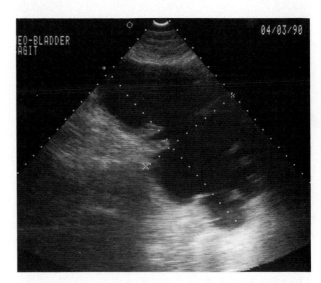

Figure 5.19
Neobladder (Florida Pouch): A large fluid collection identified in the right lower quadrant was the patient's continent diversion created after cystectomy. Haustral markings were identifiable.

Pseudomyxoma Peritonei
Lymphoma
Tuberculous Peritonitis
Peritoneal Mesothelioma
Omental Hematoma

The greater omentum is a fold of the peritoneum that is formed by a merger of the anterior and posterior visceral peritoneum of the stomach. Emanating from the greater curve of the stomach, this sheet of fatty tissue lies anterior to the small bowel, folding on itself and attaching to the transverse colon. The normal omentum is not usually studied or visualized sonographically. Recognition of a thickened or caked omentum anterior to the bowel is very helpful, since it is associated with a fairly short differential possibility list. The thickened omentum or so-called omental cake is best seen with a superficially scanning, near-field optimizing transducer. The presence of ascites facilitates recognition of omental thickening. The abdominal wall structures, peritoneal line, and anterior abdominal contents should be identified when looking for omental abnormalities.

The thickened mantlelike omentum can be readily sampled under ultrasound guidance. Usually, it yields diagnostic cells readily when fine-needle aspiration is performed.

Peritoneal Carcinomatosis

Ovarian Carcinomatosis (Figure 5.20) The omentum is a frequent site of metastatic disease. In women, the most common cause of omental thickening is metastatic disease to the omentum from ovarian carcinoma. Ovarian epithelial tumors spread by direct extension from the primary tumor mass in the ovary to the pelvis, with peritoneal seeding of the mesentery, omentum, diaphragms, and organs of the abdominal cavity. Often there is ascites, which provides a medium of transport for the malignant cells to reach various implantation sites in the abdomen.

Therapy for ovarian carcinoma is founded on surgical removal of as much abdominal and pelvic tumor as possible, followed by chemotherapy. Omentectomy is frequently performed during surgical debulking in these patients.

Other Carcinomas Resulting in Omental Involvement (Figures 5.21–5.22) In men, omental metastases are frequently from neoplasms of the gastrointestinal tract, including colon, pancreas, and stomach. Other primary tumor sites in women and men that can also result in omental metastases include breast, endometrium, and lung. The primary tumor mass may not necessarily be identified sonographically, but reasonably suspicious sites for tumor origin may be speculated. Chest films or imaging with colonoscopy, CT, endoscopy, or contrast studies may confirm the primary tumor site.

In female patients with carcinomatosis related to colonic, pancreatic, or gastric primaries (among others), the pattern of disease may be similar to that of the patient with ovarian carcinomatosis. One significant difference is that patients with ovarian carcinomatosis infrequently have parenchymal lesions in the liver or spleen at the time of diagnosis, since ovarian carcinoma usually spreads by abdominal implantation. The involvement of the liver and spleen in ovarian carcinoma is more often by studding the surfaces of the organs rather than parenchymal involvement. Carcinomatosis secondary to colonic, pancreatic, or gastric carcinomas may have associated hepatic lesions, since the portal vein provides the hematogenous conduit of malignant cells to the liver. Recognition of lesions within the substance of the liver or spleen suggests hematogenous spread and makes ovarian carcinoma less likely, even in the patient with pelvic mass, ascites, and omental thickening. Advanced metastatic disease secondary to a nonovarian primary is often not treated surgically unless a complication requiring surgical intervention develops. It is, therefore, helpful to raise doubt about the diagnosis of ovarian carcinoma in a patient with omental thickening and liver metastases prior to surgery if possible.

Pseudomyxoma Peritonei Pseudomyxoma peritonei is the accumulation of gelatinous material in the abdomen associated with groups of mucinous adenocarcinoma cells. Generally secondary to rupture of a mucinous cystadenocarcinoma of the ovary or appendix, the gelatinous material causes mass effect upon the liver and intra-abdominal organs as well as implants within the omentum. The tumors that cause pseudomyxoma peritonei are often histologically bland-appearing, low-grade adenocarcinoma, so reaccumulation of the material may take months to years after surgical removal.

Sonographically, the material may look like septated ascites, although solid components of the tumor have been documented. Aspiration and evaluation of the gelatinous material will confirm the diagnosis.

Lymphoma (Figure 5.23)

Abdominal involvement with lymphoma, usually non-Hodgkin lymphoma, can result in omental thickening. The hypoechoic solid sheet of omental lymphoma is easiest to recognize if ascites is pres-

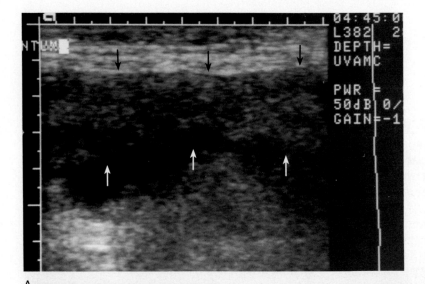

A

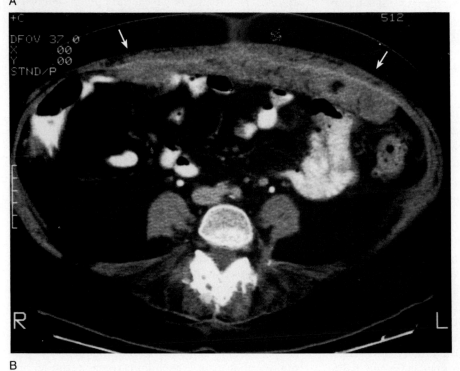

B

Figure 5.20

Ovarian carcinoma: (A) Thickening of the omentum (*arrows*) with displacement of the transverse colon away from the brightly echogenic anterior peritoneal surface was identified in this patient with ascites and pelvic mass. Fine-needle aspiration of the omentum yielded poorly differentiated adenocarcinoma. (B) Similar patient with omental cake (*arrows*) and no ascites.

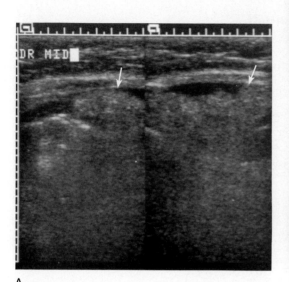

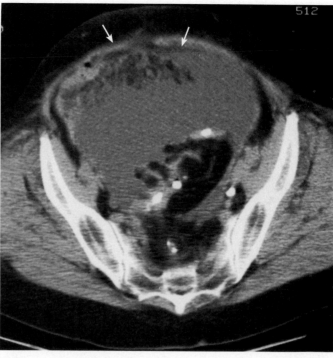

A   B

Figure 5.21

Carcinomatosis from colon primary: This elderly woman with a history of colonic resection for carcinoma presented with abdominal distention. (A) Sonography revealed omental thickening (*arrows*) and ascites. (B) CT confirmed the findings. Biopsy of the omentum was performed.

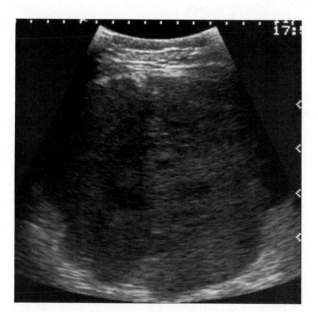

Figure 5.22

Metastatic rhabdomyosarcoma: Huge omental tumor masses were detected in this young man with widespread metastatic rhabdomyosarcoma.

ent. Lymphoma can be differentiated from carcinomatosis when there is relatively prominent lymphadenopathy, bowel wall thickening without obstruction, and lack of a dominant primary mass site associated with the omental thickening. Laparotomy can sometimes be avoided and percutaneous biopsy of the omentum may result in a satisfactory tissue sample, allowing the initiation of therapy.

Tuberculous Peritonitis

Tuberculosis is increasing in incidence, presumably because of severe socioeconomic conditions, homelessness, poverty, and AIDS. Abdominal tuberculosis may be present in as many as one-third of patients with pulmonary tuberculosis. Immunocompromised patients, alcoholics, patients with cirrhosis, and intravenous drug abusers are at higher risk for the development of abdominal tuberculosis.

Abdominal tuberculosis is believed to be due to the swallowing of massive amounts of tuberculosis bacilli in patients with pulmonary tuberculous infection. The intestine is infected, with subsequent involvement of nearby mesenteric lymph nodes. Hematogenous and lymphatic spread as well as direct extension can also result in abdominal involvement.

Three forms of tuberculous peritonitis are recognized: (1) the so-called wet type, which has ascites, often loculated and bloody; (2) a "dry" form, with peritoneal implants and adhesions; and (3) a form in which the omentum is greatly thickened and

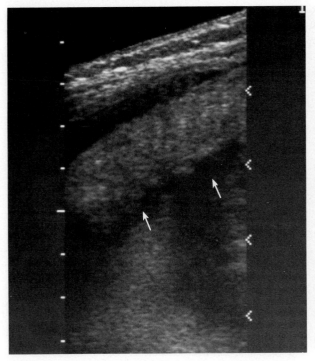

A   B

Figure 5.23

Non-Hodgkin lymphoma: (A and B) A "pancake" of omental thickening (*arrows*), adenopathy, and bowel wall thickening without obstruction were identified in this patient. Percutaneous core biopsies resulted in the recognition of aggressive non-Hodgkin lymphoma. CT confirmed the sonographic findings. The patient was treated with chemotherapy.

often palpable on physical examination. The omental mass may be misinterpreted as neoplastic.

Often the clinical symptoms of abdominal tuberculosis are vague and nonspecific without any pathognomonic laboratory studies. Recognition that omental thickening can accompany tuberculous peritonitis may allow the patient with an unknown diagnosis to avoid invasive procedures, such as exploratory laparotomy, in favor of diagnostic percutaneous procedures.

Peritoneal Mesothelioma (Figure 5.24)

Peritoneal mesothelioma is a rare tumor, most often seen in middle-aged men. It has a very poor prognosis, with death usually occurring within a year of diagnosis.

The tumor spreads along the serosal surfaces of the abdomen, forming sheetlike masses or plaques within the omentum. Patients afflicted with this tumor have vague symptoms and physical

signs, so that the tumor is often advanced at presentation.

Omental Hematoma

Hemorrhage into the omentum may be secondary to trauma or anticoagulation therapy. Omental hematoma may form a large discrete mass or a diffusely thickened omentum. With resolution of the hematoma, the mass effect should lessen, sometimes becoming cystic and septated sonographically.

Sonography may not be able to identify small nodules or mild thickening of the omentum and is not as sensitive as CT for omental disease. With frank "caking" and a careful examination with a high-frequency transducer by the sonographer, this helpful sonographic sign may be recognized.

Emphasis Points

Women with ascites, omental thickening, and pelvic mass frequently have ovarian carcinoma. Recognition of hepatic or splenic parenchymal metastases should raise the possibility of primaries of the stomach, pancreas, or colon since ovarian primaries do not usually have hepatic or splenic parenchymal masses at presentation. Lesions from ovarian

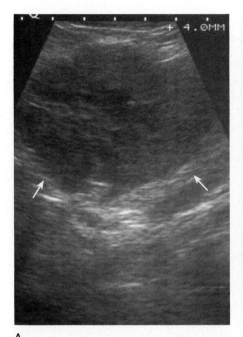

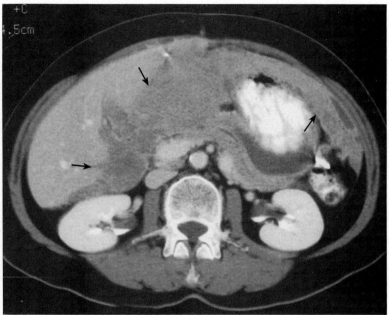

A   B

Figure 5.24

Peritoneal mesothelium: (A) This 55-year-old woman underwent debulking and chemotherapy for peritoneal mesothelium, proven at surgery. Follow-up sonography showed omental thickening that proved to be recurrent mesothelium. (B) Recurrent mesothelium was demonstrated by CT.

epethelial tumors often implant on the surfaces of the liver and spleen rather than in the parenchyma of the organ. This observation is important for determining the therapeutic options for the patient.

Omental biopsies are safe and relatively easy to perform. The omentum readily sheds cells. A transducer that optimizes superficial structures (usually a 5- or 7-MHz linear array) is best to see and biopsy omental thickening.

LARGE CYSTIC MASS IN THE ABDOMEN

Ovarian Neoplasm
Abscess, Postoperative or Other
Parovarian Cysts
Hematoma (Chronic)
Lymphocele
Massive Hydronephrosis
Atonic/Dilated Bowel Filled with Fluid

Neobladders
Pancreatic Pseudocyst
Urinary Bladder

CHILDHOOD

Ovarian Cyst
Enteric Duplication Cysts
Mesenteric/Omental Cysts/Lymphangioma
Fluid Collection Around Ventriculoperitoneal
  Shunt

Ovarian Neoplasm (Figures 5.25–5.26)

The recognition of a large (>10 cm) cystic mass in the mid-abdomen or pelvis of an adult female patient must raise the concern that the ovary is the organ of origin and that the mass is neoplastic. Both benign and malignant ovarian neoplasms may become sizable cystic lesions, extending from the pelvis into the abdomen. Small or young women with large masses may be thought to have an abdominal mass rather than one of pelvic origin because the mass becomes displaced from the pelvis into the more spacious abdomen.

Epithelial tumors of the ovary, including mucinous and serous cystadenomas or cystadenocarcinomas, often have large cystic components, although septations, wall nodules, and calcifications may be seen. When septations, mural nodularity, and solid components are identified by ultrasound, the neoplastic nature of the mass can be suggested.

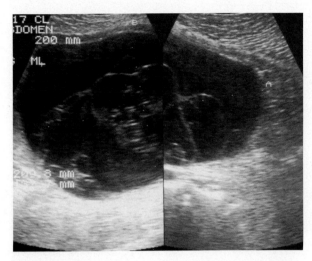

Figure 5.25
Epithelial malignancy (cystadenocarcinoma) of the ovary: This 64-year-old woman noted increasing abdominal girth and bloating. Sonography demonstrated a 20-cm cystic mass with thin septations.

Ascites, omental thickening, or cystic serosal implants seen in the upper abdomen will suggest that the primary mass is neoplastic with metastatic spread. Surgical debulking is often undertaken. Cytologic evaluation of the ascitic fluid or fine-needle aspiration of omental thickening will often confirm the suspected malignancy preoperatively.

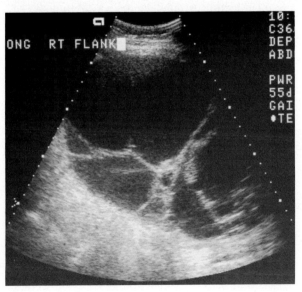

Figure 5.26
Epithelial malignancy of the ovary: A large cystic mass with thin, neoplastic septations was demonstrated in this patient with abdominal fullness.

Abscess, Postoperative or Other (Figures 5.27–5.28)

Large, loculated fluid collections developing in the postoperative patient are often complex, with internal debris and air. The presence of air within the collection is seen sonographically as highly echogenic foci with "ringdown." Large infected fluid collections may develop in the operative bed or may be related to hollow viscous rupture.

Parovarian Cysts (Figure 5.29)

Parovarian cysts, arising from embryonic remnants in the fallopian tube or broad ligament, are often large and may become complicated by hemorrhage or infection. Large parovarian cysts may be the lead point for adnexal torsion. Parovarian cysts are not hormonally responsive, unlike functional cysts of the ovary. Sometimes their origin separate from the ovary can be determined sonographically.

Hematoma (Chronic) (Figure 5.30)

Evolving hematoma, related to blunt or surgical trauma or occurring spontaneously, may develop into a multiseptate cystic mass. Acute hematomas may not be amenable to catheter drainage due to their solid gelatinous nature. As the hematoma evolves into a seroma, however, it will become more cystic and fluid filled and may be drained percutaneously.

Aspiration of an acute hematoma for diagnostic purposes may yield only a small amount of thick bloody material, which can be diluted with sterile saline to form enough material for culture and gram stain purposes.

Lymphocele

Lymphoceles or collections of lymph usually occur after surgical transection of lymphatic channels. In the abdomen, lymphoceles occur most often in the retro- or extraperitoneal spaces and may accompany lymph node dissection for such tumors as testicular, prostatic, cervical, and bladder carcinomas. In organ transplantation, placement of a kidney transplant in the extraperitoneal location may be associated with the disruption of a large number of lymphatic pathways, resulting in the development of a lymphocele around the organ. Usually cystic and often septated, lymphoceles may become quite large and can cause hydronephrosis. Their management is often problematic, as simple aspiration and

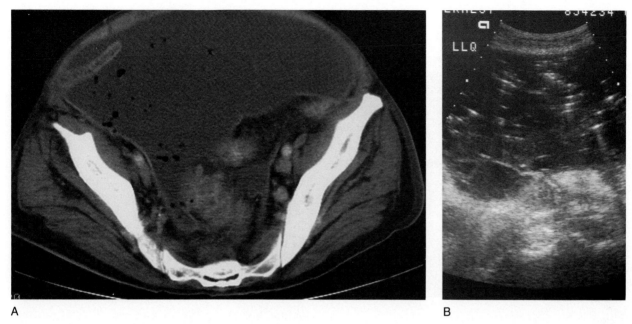

A   B

Figure 5.27

Abscess after diverticular rupture: (A and B) A large fluid collection with echogenic air was identified in the pelvis in this elderly man with diverticulitis. Percutaneous drainage of the abscess provided satisfactory resolution.

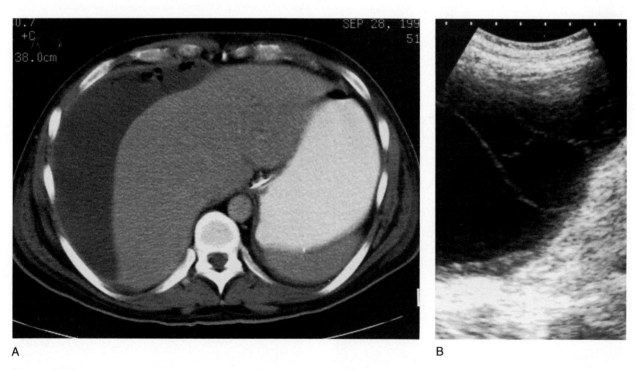

A   B

Figure 5.28

Abscess after colonic perforation: (A and B) This young man with ulcerative colitis suffered colonic perforation complicated by a large abscess in the right flank. Decompression of the abscess was successfully accomplished percutaneously.

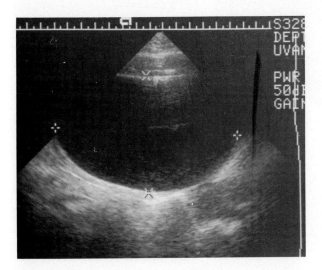

Figure 5.29
Parovarian cysts: This 32-year-old graduate student presented with acute and severe right lower quadrant pain. Ultrasound revealed a very large simple cyst associated with the right adnexa. At surgery, adnexal torsion led by a large parovarian cyst was treated by oophorectomy and salpingectomy.

sometimes catheter drainage may not be sufficient to prevent their reaccumulation.

A lymphocele may be first noted weeks to months after the transplant surgery. Its association with the transplanted organ allows its origin to be suspected.

Massive Hydronephrosis (Figure 5.31)

Dramatic hydronephrosis, often related to a congenital or long-standing ureteropelvic junction (UPJ) obstruction, may give rise to a huge cystic mass in the abdomen. Although congenital, these sizable masses may be detected serendipitously during imaging for other reasons. Recognition of dilated calyces that empty into the central dilated renal pelvis is helpful in explaining the etiology of the cystic mass. Because the kidney can give rise to large cystic masses when hydronephrosis is present, it must be considered and screened as a possible originating site whenever a large cystic mass is identified.

Usually, a massively hydronephrotic kidney is identified in the child or young adult, rather than in the elderly.

Atonic/Dilated Bowel Filled with Fluid

Dilatation of the cecum or other portions of the colon secondary to inflammatory, ischemic, or other causes may result in a large fluid-filled structure that can be misinterpreted as an abnormal fluid collection unless care is taken. Peristalsis may be limited in such a loop of bowel secondary to atony.

Neobladders

Increasingly, the cecum or right colon is being used in continent diversionary procedures for patients

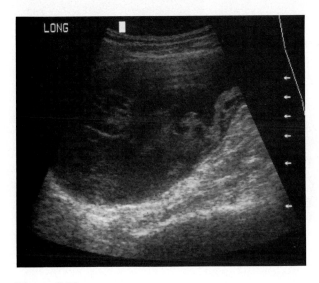

Figure 5.30
Hematoma/Seroma: A large, complex collection was visible in the left flank 2 months after aortic aneurysm rupture in this elderly man. Aspiration yielded bloody, non-infected fluid.

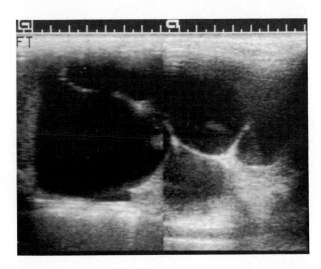

Figure 5.31
Massive hydronephrosis: Massive distention of the collecting system of the left kidney with profound cortical loss led to a large cystic mass in this young patient with chronic UPJ obstruction. This cystic mass was treated by nephrectomy.

who have inadequate bladders or have undergone cystectomy. Utilization of the right colon in such surgery results in a large, irregularly shaped fluid collection, often in the right flank or right upper quadrant. Haustrations are sometimes recognizable. Knowledge of the patient's previous surgery will allow the appropriate conclusions to be made. Decompression of the neobladder with catheter drainage will verify that the bowel-shaped fluid collection is, in fact, a neobladder.

Pancreatic Pseudocyst

Migration of fluid from the pancreas into the pelvis or chest may occur in patients with severe pancreatitis. In such patients, fluid collections with internal septations and debris may be identified in the pancreatic bed or remotely.

Urinary Bladder

A massively distended urinary bladder may be misinterpreted as a large cystic mass of unknown etiology. Recognition that bladder outlet obstruction or neurogenic bladder can cause massive bladder distention will allow the diagnosis to be made. Hydronephrosis may be present in situations of massive bladder distention, which can be a hint of the origin of the large cystic mass in the pelvis. Decompression of the bladder with a catheter will confirm the sonographic impression.

CHILDHOOD

Ovarian Cyst (Figure 5.32)

In the neonate still under maternal hormonal influences, large simple cysts of the ovary may fill the tiny abdomen. The cyst may resolve with time but may be confused with duplication cysts. Torsion of the adnexa may be led by the large mass. Expectant observation may allow the cyst to resolve, making surgery unnecessary.

Enteric Duplication Cysts

Duplication cysts of the small intestine are more common than duplications of the stomach, duodenum, or esophagus. While all enteric duplications contain some epithelium from the alimentary tract, up to 20 percent of duplication cysts may contain ectopic gastric mucosa, so activity may be obvious on technetium 99m pertechnetate studies. The duplication abnormality may come to attention when ulceration, bleeding, or perforation occurs. Most

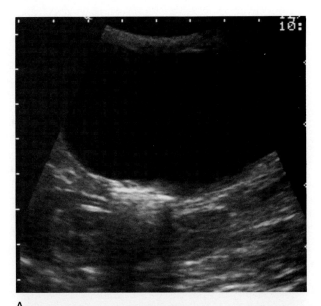

A

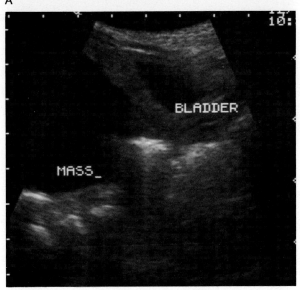

B

Figure 5.32

Large simple ovarian cyst: (A and B) This large, simple cyst had been identified prenatally in this newborn girl and was noted on postnatal imaging to fill the abdomen and interdigitate to the level of the spleen from the lower abdomen. At surgery, the mass was a simple cyst of the left ovary, which was removed.

enteric duplication cysts do not communicate with associated bowel.

Sonographically, duplication cysts have a fairly characteristic ultrasound appearance. The mass is cystic, with a well-defined wall. The mucosa of the mass is highly echogenic with a hypoechoic muscular wall. Hemorrhage or infection of the mass may cause internal echoes or septations. Real-time scanning while the patient ingests fluid will confirm no communication with the contents of the duplication.

Mesenteric/Omental Cysts/Lymphangioma (Figure 5.33)

Often bigger than enteric duplication cysts, mesenteric or omental cysts may appear to fill the abdomen, mimicking ascites. Approximately 25 percent of mesenteric or omental cysts are detected in the first 10 years of life.

Sonographically, the large cystic masses have thin walls and may have internal septations. Hemorrhage into the mass may result in low-level echoes or solid nodules of soft tissue material.

Fluid Collection Around Ventriculoperitoneal Shunt

Children or young adults with ventriculoperitoneal shunts to decompress dilated intracranial ventricles often have a small to moderate amount of free fluid in the abdomen. Loculation of fluid around the tip of the catheter may occur as a complication of the shunting procedure. When loculation occurs secondary to infection, internal debris and septations may develop within the collection. Revision of the shunt may be necessary if loculated collections persist or enlarge.

LARGE SOLID-APPEARING MASS IN THE ABDOMEN

Neoplasms
Hematomas

Large, solid-appearing masses in the abdomen are usually either neoplasms or hematomas. The patient's clinical state usually allows differentiation.

Neoplasms (Figures 5.34–5.37)

Many large (>10 cm), predominantly solid masses in the abdomen are neoplastic. Sarcomas, especially in the retroperitoneum, including malignant fibrous histiocytoma, fibrosarcoma, leiomyosarcoma, and rhabdomyosarcoma, are often large, bulky tumors that may attain great size because of their relatively silent sites of origin and the lack of hormonal activity that would herald their presence. Other retroperitoneal tumors, such as hormonally silent ad-

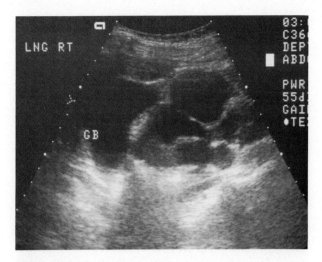

Figure 5.33
Lymphangiogram: A large multiseptate cystic mass was identified in this young patient with a lymphangioma of the mesentery.

renocortical carcinoma, may grow quite large before discovery.

Non-Hodgkin lymphoma involving the abdomen may give rise to large, rapidly growing neoplastic masses that engulf bowel without causing obstruction.

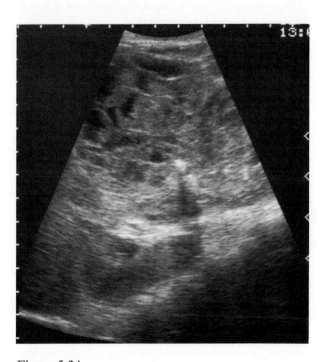

Figure 5.34
Malignant fibrous histiocytoma: A large, heterogeneous tumor filled the left abdomen, displacing bowel.

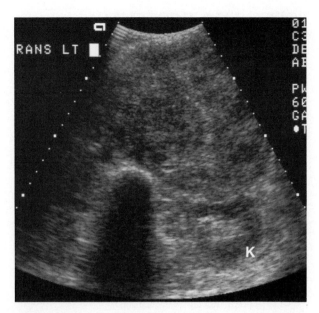

Figure 5.35
Adrenocortical carcinoma: A mass greater than 20 cm was seen displacing the left kidney (K). Surgical decompression found an adrenal primary.

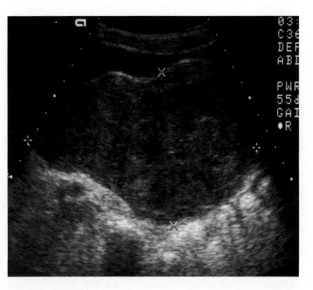

Figure 5.36
Dysgerminoma of the ovary: This solid, fairly homogeneous mass in the lower abdomen in this 10-year-old girl proved to be a dysgerminoma of the ovary.

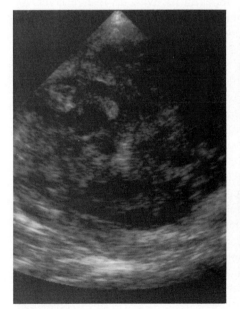

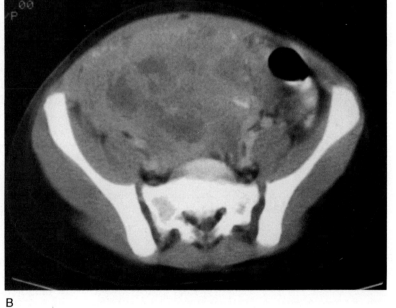

A   B

Figure 5.37
Non-Hodgkin lymphoma in the abdomen: (A) Rapid onset of abdominal distention led to the discovery of a huge, solid mass, encompassing bowel loops without causing obstruction. (B) CT confirmed extensive gastrointestinal compression, and biopsy confirmed aggressive lymphoma.

Percutaneous core biopsy directed either by CT or US will allow the histologic differentiation to be made. Patients with aggressive non-Hodgkin lymphoma can be treated nonsurgically with chemotherapy, whereas most large sarcomas will be treated with multiple modalities, including surgery, chemotherapy, and often radiation therapy.

Uterine leiomyomas or germ cell malignancy of the ovary in young patients may result in large, solid masses that rise into the abdomen from the pelvis.

Hematomas (Figure 5.38)

Large, acute hematomas of the abdomen will result in extensive heterogeneous masses that appear solid sonographically. Usually, the clinical presentation of the patient makes the diagnosis obvious, as frequently a history of trauma, surgery, or anticoagulation therapy and cardiovascular instability suggests that significant blood loss has occurred. Rapid stabilization of the patient is required, with operative intervention in many cases. Percutaneous catheter drainage of large gelatinous hematomas is usually unsuccessful until the collections have become seromatous.

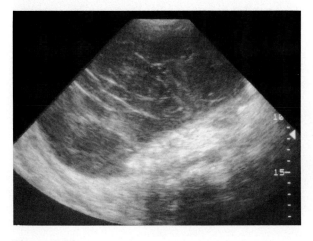

Figure 5.38
Large hematoma: This patient developed severe abdominal pain after liver transplantation. A large, heterogeneous, solid-appearing mass developed acutely in the right flank. Breakdown of the anastomosis of the hepatic artery was repaired during emergency surgery. The large hematoma was evacuated.

BOWEL WALL THICKENING

Inflammatory Conditions
    Appendicitis
    Crohn's Disease
    Infectious Colitis
    Typhlitis
    Diverticulitis
    Pseudomembranous Colitis
Radiation Enteritis
Hemorrhage
Ischemic Colitis
Neoplasia of the Gastrointestinal Tract
    Adenocarcinoma
    Lymphoma/Metastatic Disease

CHILDHOOD

Hypertrophic Pyloric Stenosis
Intussusception

Although sonography may not be the examination of choice for patients with conditions involving the gastrointestinal tract, many with abdominal complaints may first undergo sonography, and abnormal bowel patterns must be recognized.

The normal intestinal tract has a predictable sonographic appearance, with up to five layers of the wall being identifiable, depending upon the patient's size and transducer resolution. In situations of bowel wall thickening, a hypoechoic bowel wall greater than 5 mm may be identified. Bowel wall thickening identified sonographically has been described as having a "pseudokidney" or "target" appearance. The thickened bowel wall causes a hypoechoic rim, with the echogenic mucosa and trapped air seen centrally. The pseudokidney description reflects the similarity to the normal sonographic appearance of the kidney, with the rimming hypoechoic cortex and echogenic central echo complex contributed by sinus fat and nondilated collecting tubules. The target description reflects the highly echogenic central zone, similar to a target pattern. Thickening of the bowel wall seen sonographically is nonspecific and may be secondary to tumor infiltration, edema, inflammatory conditions, or hemorrhage.

Inflammatory Conditions

Appendicitis (Figures 5.39–5.40) Appendicitis is the most common cause of an acute abdomen resulting in operative intervention. Although many patients have a classic clinical course for appendicitis, with periumbilical pain, nausea and vomiting,

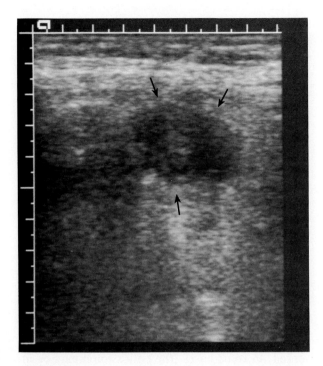

Figure 5.39
Appendicitis: This 42-year-old physician complained of right lower quadrant pain. Graded compression sonography of the right lower quadrant revealed a noncompressible, tender, thickened appendix with a small amount of periappendiceal fluid (*arrows*). An inflamed appendix was removed at surgery.

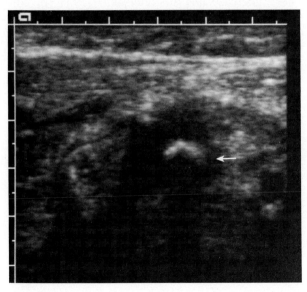

Figure 5.40
Appendicitis: In this 19-year-old being evaluated for a presumed symptomatic ovarian cyst, an appendicolith (*arrow*) and thickened appendix were identified. Plain film confirmed the appendicolith. Appendicitis was present at surgery.

and tenderness that localizes into the right lower quadrant with the development of peritoneal irritation, others may have an atypical presentation. Young women may have a clinical presentation similar to a complicated physiologic ovarian cyst, a ruptured ectopic pregnancy, or inflammatory bowel disease. Ultrasound is valuable in the evaluation of a clinically atypical patient to identify whether or not appendicitis is present. Many times when the clinical presentation is suggestive of appendicitis and an alternate diagnosis exists, the correct alternate diagnosis can be made sonographically.

For the patient with an acute abdomen, a full sonographic evaluation of the abdomen and pelvis is indicated, with careful inspection of the liver, gallbladder, biliary tree, kidneys, pancreas, and pelvis. Graded compression of the right lower quadrant, first described by Puylaert in 1986, should be performed in any patient believed to be a possible candidate for appendicitis.

Graded compression with a superficially focused, high-resolution 5- or 7.5-mHz linear or curvilinear transducer will allow normal gas-filled bowel to be pushed out of the way. Visualization of a thickened (>6-mm-diameter), noncompressible, often tender, blind-ending appendix suggests acute appendicitis. Recognition of a fecalith or appendicolith sonographically can be confirmed by plain film and will usually result in appendectomy—emergently in the symptomatic patient, electively in the asymptomatic patient.

The normal appendix can sometimes be visualized but can usually be differentiated from the inflamed appendix by its size. Usually, the normal appendix will have a luminal diameter less than 6 mm. Visualization of the acutely inflamed appendix is not always possible after appendiceal perforation. Complications of appendiceal perforation, such as periappendiceal abscess formation, free fluid, or, less likely, portal vein septic thrombophlebitis, may be identified during the sonographic examination.

Crohn's Disease (Figure 5.41) Crohn's disease is a chronic, relapsing granulomatous disease of unknown etiology that frequently affects the terminal ileum and cecum but may affect any portion of the gastrointestinal tract from the mouth to the anus. Skip areas of involvement are common. This inflammatory process affects the full thickness of the bowel wall, sometimes with fistula formation. Prominent bowel wall thickening may be obvious sonographically. Conglomerate masses of bowel with regional inflammation and abscess formation may be identifiable. Prominent, thick, inflamed fat may be seen correlating with the so-called creeping

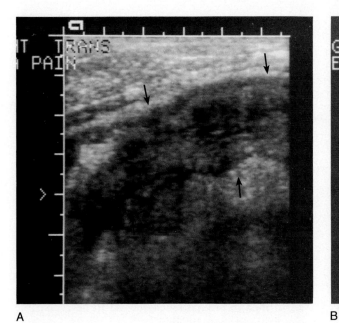

A

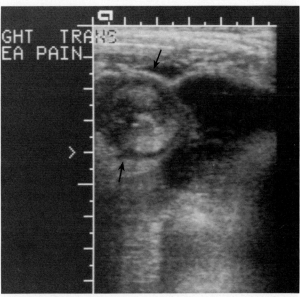

B

Figure 5.41

Crohn's disease: (A and B) This 19-year-old man presented with severe right lower quadrant pain, leukocytosis, and fever. The clinical diagnosis was appendicitis. Sonography showed a long, markedly thickened segment of small bowel (*arrows*) more consistent with inflammatory bowel disease than with appendicitis. At surgery, extensive involvement of the terminal ileum by Crohn's disease was found.

fat present grossly. The thyroidlike appearance of the fat has been described as typical of inflamed mesenteric fat.

Sonography may be useful in the assessment of these patients for recurrent inflammation with bowel wall thickening or abscess formation.

The initial presentation of Crohn's disease may be indistinguishable clinically from that of acute appendicitis. The sonographic recognition of extensive bowel wall thickening in the right lower quadrant, which is too long and too big to be the appendix, will allow the correct diagnosis to be suggested.

Ulcerative colitis, when severe, may be similar to Crohn's disease sonographically and clinically.

Infectious Colitis (Figure 5.42)

Infectious colitis is common in patients with AIDS. Multiple etiologic organisms are possible, but cytomegalovirus and mycobacterium tuberculosis are most common. Other patients with immunosuppression related to chemotherapy or organ transplantation are susceptible to infectious colitis. Pronounced colonic wall thickening is often present, sometimes several times normal. Focal involvement of bowel may be ob-

served. In some cases, the entire colon may be involved and documented by scanning with a relatively superficially scanning (5 MHz) curvilinear or linear array transducer. The distribution of wall thickening can generally be determined by scanning the expected course of the large bowel, noting any thickening of the wall.

Organisms that preferentially involve the right lower quadrant include *Yersinia* and those that cause amebiasis and tuberculosis.

Typhlitis (Figure 5.43)

Immunocompromised, often neutropenic patients may develop sonographic abnormalities in the right lower quadrant, in the ileocecal region. Typhlitis is nonspecific inflammation of the cecum.

Manifest histologically as mucosal ulceration with edema of the bowel wall, typhlitis is common in patients with childhood leukemias, lymphoma, transplant recipients, and AIDS. Organisms implicated include *Pseudomonas, Candida, Cytomegalovirus, Klebsiella, Escherichia coli,* and *Bacillus fragilis.*

Bowel wall thickening in the right lower quadrant with possible extension into the ascending colon is possible. Perforation with abscess formation or air in the bowel wall may be recognized.

Diverticulitis (Figure 5.44)

Diverticulitis of the colon is common, with increasing incidence as the patient ages. Diverticula of the colon are the most common abnormality of the colon in Western countries, reflecting their origin from diets with decreased fecal bulk and roughage.

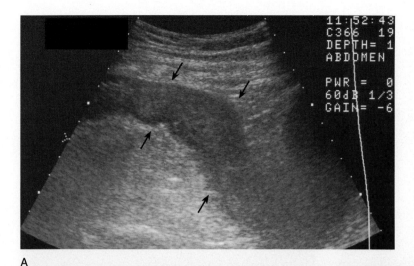

A

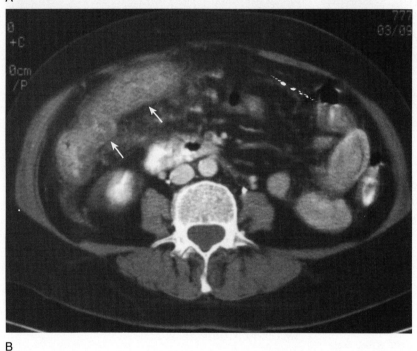

B

Figure 5.42
Cytomegalovirus (CMV) colitis: This cardiac transplant recipient suffered diarrhea. (A) Sonography showed long segment thickening of the colon (*arrows*). (B) CT showed bowel wall thickening. Endoscopic biopsy confirmed CMV colitis.

In 10 to 25 percent of patients with diverticula, inflammation of the diverticula related to inspissated fecal material and perforation of the thin-walled diverticula may result in abdominal pain, fever, and leukocytosis. Sonographic evaluation may be performed in the patient with suspected diverticulitis.

Diverticulitis, which usually involves the sigmoid colon, may be recognized sonographically by bowel wall thickening, inflamed diverticula with trapped air, fecaliths, or pericolonic abscess collections. Sonographic recognition of diverticula is very suggestive of diverticulitis. As common as diverticula are, they are rarely seen if not inflamed. Thickening of the associated mesenteric fat is often related to peridiverticular inflammation. Gas-containing pockets or interloop abscesses may be difficult to differentiate from bowel.

When sonography suggests the diagnosis of diverticulitis, CT scanning may be helpful to assess the extent of disease. Unless abscess or free perforation occurs, medical management of diverticulitis may be adequate. Percutaneous catheter drainage may be helpful in patients who develop abscess.

Pseudomembranous Colitis Frequently seen in hospitalized patients or patients receiving broad-spectrum antibiotics, pseudomembranous colitis is an inflammatory bowel condition characterized by profound watery diarrhea. In most cases, the toxin of *Clostridium difficile* is implicated as the etiologic agent.

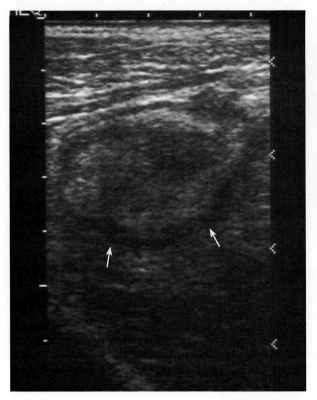

A

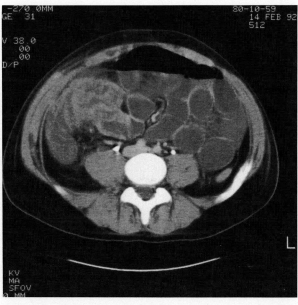

B

Figure 5.43

Typhlitis: This young man underwent bone marrow transplantation for leukemia and was experiencing abdominal pain. CT showed extensive thickening of the cecum and right colon in the right lower quadrant. The patient was treated supportively and the abnormality resolved on subsequent studies.

In many cases, the diagnosis may not be known, and sonographic recognition of long segments of colonic wall thickening in a patient who is receiving or has received antibiotics should lead to further evaluation with *Clostridium difficile* titers and endoscopy. Endoscopically, whitish exudative plaques and ulcerations are characteristic. Inflammation and edema of the colonic wall result in the wall thickening seen readily sonographically. Often the entire colon is involved. The mucosa may be brightly echogenic.

Radiation Enteritis

Radiation therapy for tumors of the abdomen or pelvis may coincidentally affect the regional bowel. Bowel wall thickening secondary to radiation injury with edema and bowel wall hemorrhage may be recognized sonographically. The appearance of the bowel is similar to other inflammatory or neoplastic causes of bowel wall thickening. Knowledge of the history of radiation therapy in the previous weeks to months will suggest the correct diagnosis.

Hemorrhages

Bowel wall hemorrhage secondary to anticoagulation or trauma may be recognized sonographically.

Ischemic Colitis

Ischemic colitis usually affects patients older than 50 years of age. Ischemia to the colon usually involves the territory of the inferior mesenteric artery with involvement of the left colon in 90 percent of patients. The splenic flexure and watershed areas of the sigmoid are affected in up to 80 percent of patients. Because of its blood supply, the rectum is generally spared.

Clinically, the elderly patient will have rectal bleeding, diarrhea, and abdominal pain. Sonographically, bowel wall thickening on the left will be identified secondary to submucosal hemorrhage and edema.

Neoplasia of the Gastrointestinal Tract

Adenocarcinoma (Figures 5.45–5.46)   Adenocarcinoma of the stomach or colon arises from the

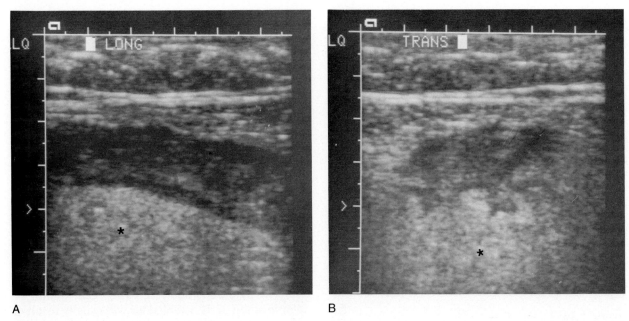

A   B

Figure 5.44
Diverticulitis: In the left lower quadrant, thickened bowel with prominent inflamed fat (*asterisk*) was seen in this patient with diverticulitis. No abscess was present. Diverticula could be identified.

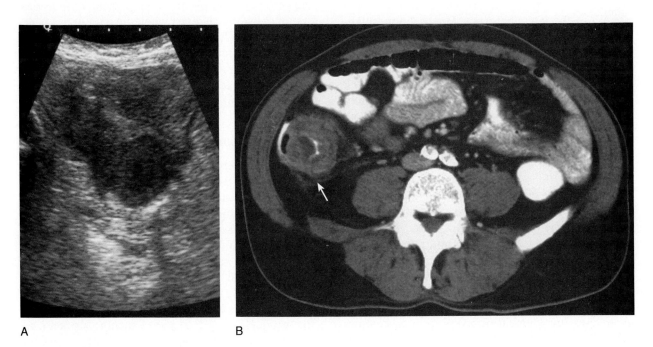

A   B

Figure 5.45
Adenocarcinoma of the cecum: (A) In this elderly woman being evaluated for gallstones, a markedly thickened nontender cecum was discovered. (B) CT confirmed the cecal mass.

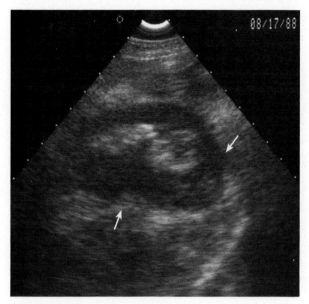

Figure 5.46
Adenocarcinoma of the descending colon: The pseudokidney appearance of thickened bowel in the left lower quadrant was obvious in this patient with anemia, lower abdominal pain, and guaiac-positive stools.

mucosa of the intestinal tract. Mucosal abnormalities and polyps are usually not identified by sonography secondary to the presence of air in the bowel lumen and the lesion's small size. As intestinal neoplasms grow, sonographic recognition may be possible. The colonic wall may be concentrically thickened or thickened in an asymmetric way. A pseudokidney may be recognized and is often asymptomatic. Tenderness of colonic neoplasm may be present if there is superimposed infection or perforation with abscess formation.

Lymphoma/Metastatic Disease (Figures 5.47–5.49)   Non-Hodgkin lymphoma may affect the colon, small bowel, or stomach, infiltrating the submucosa, sometimes having little mucosal abnormality. Wall thickening secondary to lymphomatous involvement may be quite lengthy, extending for many centimeters, a feature differentiating lymphomatous involvement of bowel from carcinomatous infiltration. Even with extensive lymphomatous involvement of the bowel wall, obstruction of the intestine is not necessarily present. Lymphadenopathy and hepatic or splenic involvement may be recognized as well. Submucosal involvement may make the diagnosis difficult to make by endoscopic biopsy. Percutaneous bowel wall biopsy can be safely performed, facilitating diagnosis and medical therapy.

Metastastic disease to the intestinal tract can occur and may have the appearance of focal wall thickening. Malignant melanoma and Kaposi's sarcoma are primaries with a propensity for spread to the gastrointestinal tract. Breast cancer can metastasize to the GI tract, causing linitis plastica of the stomach.

CHILDHOOD

Hypertrophic Pyloric Stenosis (Figure 5.50)

Sonographic evaluation of the thickened pylorus in babies with hypertrophic pyloric stenosis has virtually replaced fluoroscopic studies in most centers. The thickening and elongation of the pyloric channel can be easily identified in most cases using a linear array, superficially focused transducer.

The pylorus is adjacent to the gallbladder, so identification of the gallbladder will usually result in successful visualization of the pylorus. In hypertrophic pyloric stenosis, the thickened hypoechoic wall of the pylorus usually measures greater than 3 mm in thickness, measured in the transverse axis. The pyloric channel is often quite elongated, often measuring more than 14 mm in length. Signs of gastric outlet obstruction are often present with distention of the stomach, even when the patient has been fasting. Peristaltic waves may be visualized sonographically to hit the "wall" of the thickened pylorus, failing to propagate into the duodenum. These infants are treated with electrolyte and fluid support followed by surgery (myotomy).

Intussusception (Figures 5.51–5.52)

Ninety-four percent of patients with intussusception are in the pediatric age group. Intussusception is a common cause of an abdominal emergency in childhood, leading to a small bowel obstruction.

Most intussusceptions occur between the ages of 6 months and 2 years and are idiopathic. Often the patient is recovering from a viral illness with gastrointestinal complaints when intussusception occurs. Usually ileocolic, most intussusceptions are secondary to edema and lymphoid hyperplasia. In the terminal ileum, lead points such as Meckel's diverticulum, polyp, lymphoma, duplication cyst, or inspissated feces are found in only 5 percent of childhood intussusceptions and usually occur in patients older than 2 years of age.

The clinical presentation may be bloody diarrhea, colicky abdominal pain, and bowel obstructive symptoms. Sometimes the clinical picture is less clear, and ultrasound may allow the discovery of an unsuspected intussusception.

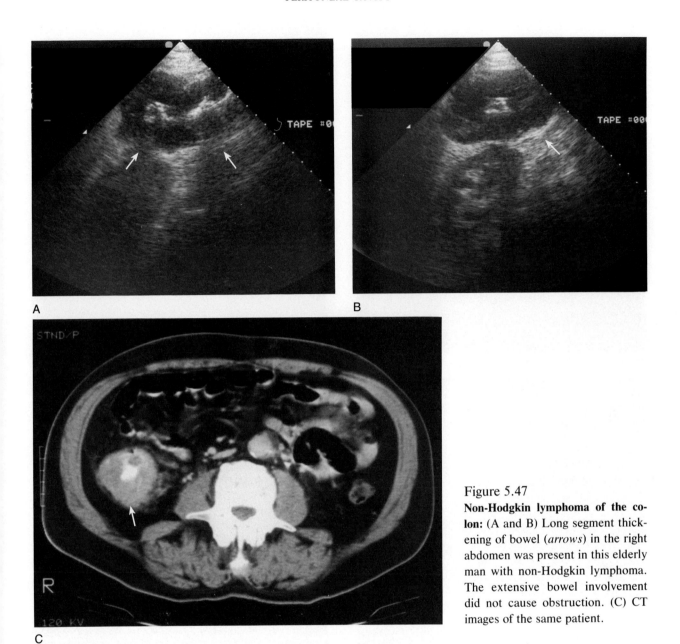

Figure 5.47
Non-Hodgkin lymphoma of the colon: (A and B) Long segment thickening of bowel (*arrows*) in the right abdomen was present in this elderly man with non-Hodgkin lymphoma. The extensive bowel involvement did not cause obstruction. (C) CT images of the same patient.

Sonographically, there is a complex doughnut or pseudokidney appearance. The round appearance on the transverse image can be elongated to show the invagination of one bowel loop into another. The explanation for the sonographic appearance of intussusception has been controversial but is probably related to the rimming hypoechoic, edematous wall of one loop, alternating with the highly echogenic invaginating mucosa.

Reduction of idiopathic intussusception may be performed using hydrostatic or pneumatic pressure under fluoroscopic or ultrasonic guidance.

In the older child or adult patient with intussusception discovered sonographically, a lead point is virtually always present, and therefore surgical decompression of the intussusception is usually necessary to allow diagnosis and surgical therapy for the lead point.

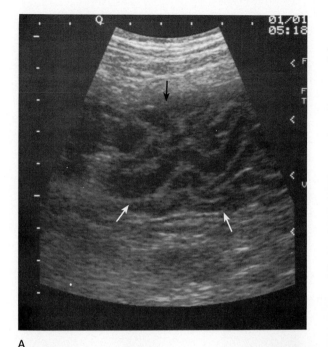

A

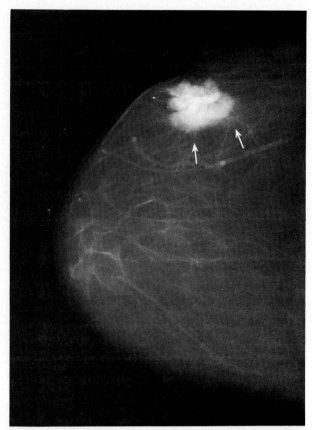

A

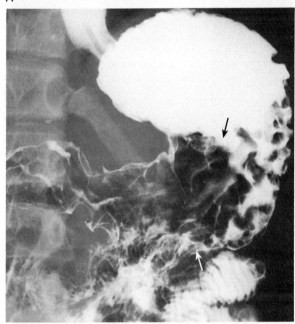

B

Figure 5.48
Non-Hodgkin lymphoma of the stomach: (A) Prominent wall thickening of the stomach is illustrated here. (B) No obstruction was present.

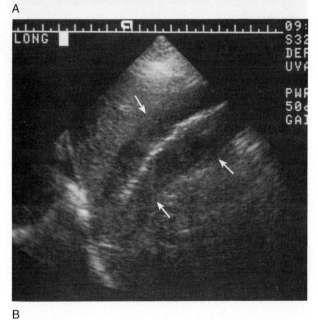

B

Figure 5.49
Metastatic breast carcinoma: This elderly woman with (A) mammographic findings of breast carcinoma (*arrows*) had extensive metastatic involvement of her stomach, seen as wall thickening (B) (*arrows*).

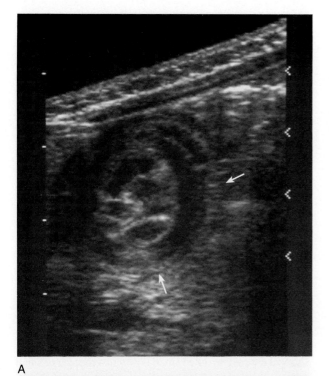

A

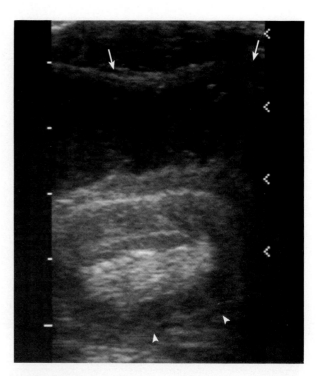

Figure 5.51
Postoperative ileal–ileal intussusception: This 1-year-old was recovering after liver resection when he developed nausea and vomiting. Sonography demonstrated dilated, fluid-filled obstructed small bowel loops (*arrows*) as well as the complex doughnut of an intussusception (*arrowheads*).

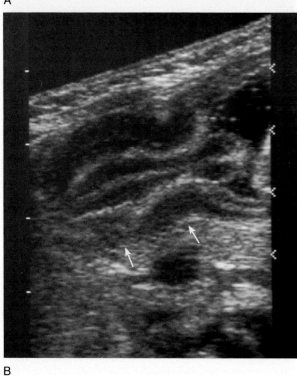

B

Figure 5.50
Hypertrophic pyloric stenosis: (A and B) Dramatic thickening of the pylorus (*arrows*) was identifiable in this 10-week-old with nonbilious projectile vomiting.

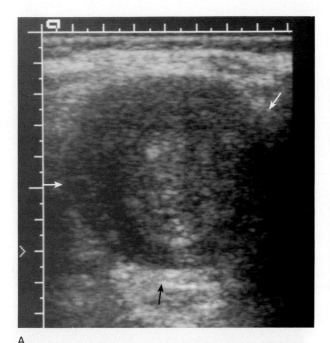

A

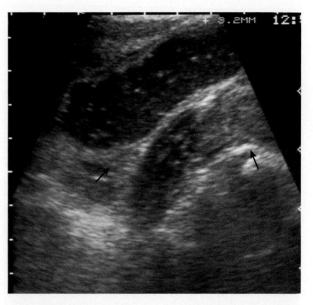

Figure 5.53
Small bowel obstruction secondary to intussusception: This 1-year-old suffered nausea and vomiting. Plain films showed dilated, air-filled small bowel in a pattern of small bowel obstruction. Sonographic evaluation showed multiple loops of fluid-filled small bowel (*arrows*). Other images showed the complex doughnut of intussusception.

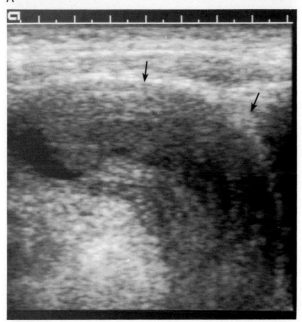

B

Figure 5.52
Intussusception in an adult: This 25-year-old was 5 days postpartum when she presented with abdominal pain. Ultrasound (A and B) showed the typical appearance of intussusception. At surgery, an adenocarcinoma of the cecum was the lead point for the intussusception.

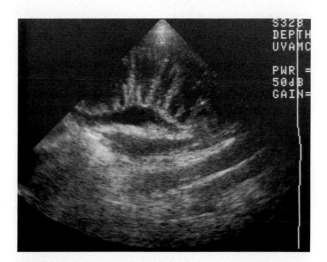

Figure 5.54
Small bowel obstruction secondary to adhesions: This young woman had had multiple abdominal surgeries. Sonography showed evidence of small bowel obstruction. Note the valvulae conniventes, folds which traverse the small bowel lumen.

Emphasis Point

Although the gastrointestinal tract is not the primary "obligation" of the sonographer, recognition of GI abnormalities on ultrasound studies can dramatically advance patient management and care. A screening of all the abdominal contents should be performed with each abdominal or pelvic ultrasound study. This screening should include at least a quick look at areas of the abdomen where no major solid organ is located, such as the left lower quadrant. Recognition of gastrointestinal abnormalities and correlation with the patient's clinical presentation will allow a reasonable list of possibilities to be considered. Additional imaging with CT or contrast studies may be necessary for definitive diagnosis.

DILATED, FLUID-FILLED SMALL BOWEL LOOPS: SMALL BOWEL OBSTRUCTION VERSUS ILEUS (Figures 5.53–5.55)

When the small bowel is filled with fluid, it is readily accessible to evaluation by ultrasound. Small bowel loops dilate and fill with fluid when obstructed mechanically or when an ileus is present. Small bowel loops can be differentiated from colonic segments by the presence of valvulae conniventes, which are thin, closely associated folds of small bowel that can be seen to cross the bowel lumen completely, unlike the haustra of large bowel.

Small bowel loops that are mechanically obstructed, either by adhesions, neoplastic masses, or inflammatory processes, will dilate proximal to the level of obstruction. Obstructed bowel will show active peristalsis against the obstruction. Dilated, fluid-filled hyperperistaltic small bowel will be seen at real time. If hyperperistaltic dilated small bowel is identified, the level of obstruction (e.g., proximal jejunum vs. terminal ileum) should be determined

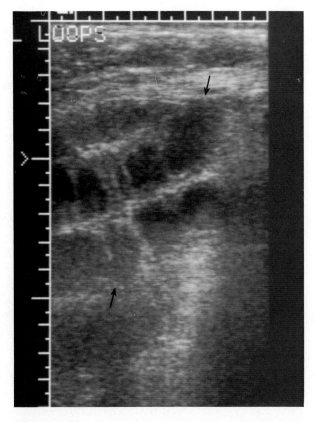

Figure 5.55

Ileus secondary to a ruptured appendix: Multiple atonic loops of small bowel (*arrows*) were present in this patient with peritonitis related to appendicitis rupture.

as well as the possible cause of obstruction. Plain film correlation is helpful. Mass lesions, hernias, and inflammatory disease may be recognized. Adhesions causing small bowel obstruction are not usually seen by ultrasound.

Dilated, fluid-filled small bowel loops that are atonic will be present when the patient has an ileus. Paralytic ileus may be present in the postoperative patient. Medications, metabolic disarray, and intra-abdominal infections may contribute to prolongation of ileus. In the patient with sonographic evidence of ileus, a careful search for intra-abdominal processes must be made.

BIBLIOGRAPHY

Ascites

Brugman SM, Bjelland JJ, Thomasson JE, et al: Sonographic findings with radiographic correlation in meconium peritonitis. J Clin Ultrasound 7:305–306, 1979.
Meyers MA: The spread and localization of acute intraperitoneal effusions. Radiology 95:547–554, 1970.

Newman B, Teele RL: Ascites in the fetus, neonate, and young child: Emphasis on ultrasonographic evaluation. Semin Ultrasound 5:85–101, 1984.
Yeh HC, Wolf BS: Ultrasonography in ascites. Radiology 124:783–790, 1977.

Echogenic Fluid in the Cul-de-sac

Nyberg DA, Hughes MP, Mack LA, Wang KY: Extrauterine findings of ectopic pregnancy on transvaginal US: Importance of echogenic fluid. Radiology 178:823–826, 1991.

Omental Thickening

Epstein BM, Mann JH: CT of abdominal tuberculosis. AJR 139:861–866, 1982.
Goerg C, Schwerk W-B: Peritoneal carcinomatosis with ascites. AJR 156:1185–1187, 1991.
Hamrick-Turner JE, Chiechi MV, Abbitt PL, Ros PR: Neoplastic and inflammatory processes of the peritoneum, omentum, and mesentery: Diagnosis with CT. RadioGraphics 12:1051–1068, 1992.
Seshul MB, Coulam CM: Pseudomyxoma peritonei: Computed tomography and sonography. AJR 136:803–806, 1981.
Wicks JD, Mettler FA, Hilgers RD, Ampuero F: Correlation of ultrasound and pathologic findings in patients with epithelial carcinoma of the ovary. J Clin Ultrasound 12:397–402, 1984.
Wu C-C, Chow K-S, Lu T-N, Huang F-T: Sonographic features of tuberculous omental cakes in peritoneal tuberculosis. J Clin Ultrasound 16:195–198, 1988.
Yeh H-C: Ultrasonography of peritoneal tumors. Radiology 133:419–424, 1979.
Yeh H-C, Chahinian P: Ultrasonography and computed tomography of peritoneal mesothelioma. Radiology 135:705–712, 1980.

Large Cystic Mass in the Abdomen

Amodio J, Abramson S, Berdon W, et al: Postnatal resolution of large ovarian cysts detected in utero. Report of 2 cases. Pediatr Radiol 17:467–469, 1987.
Barr LL, Hayden CK Jr, Stansberry D, et al: Enteric duplication cysts in children: Are their ultrasonographic wall characteristics diagnostic? Pediatr Radiol 20:326–328, 1990.
Filly RA: Ovarian masses . . . What to look for . . . What to do. Ultrasound Categorical Course Syllabus. American Roentgen Ray Society, pp. 11–19, 1993.
Geer LL, Mittelstaedt CA, Staab EV, et al: Mesenteric cyst. Sonographic appearance with CT correlation. Pediatr Radiol 14:102–104, 1984.
Hamrick-Turner JE, Chiechi MV, Abbitt PL, Ros PR: Neoplastic and inflammatory processes of the peritoneum, omentum, and mesentery: Diagnosis with CT. RadioGraphics 12:1051–1068, 1992.
Herrmann UJ Jr, Locher GW, Goldhirsch A: Sonographic patterns of ovarian tumors: Prediction of malignancy. Obstet Gynecol 69:777, 1987.
Lindeque BG, du Toit JP, Muller LM, et al: Ultrasonographic criteria for the conservative management of antenatally diagnosed fetal ovarian cysts. J Reprod Med 33:196–198, 1988.
Ros PR, Olmsted WW, Moser RP Jr, et al.: Mesenteric and omental cysts. Histologic classification with imaging correlation. Radiology 164:327–332, 1987.

Bowel Wall Thickening

Haller JO, Cohen HL: Hypertrophic pyloric stenosis. Diagnosis using US. Radiology 161:335–339, 1986.

Jeffrey RB, Laing FC, Townsend RR: Acute appendicitis: Sonographic criteria based on 250 cases. Radiology 167:327–329, 1988.

Jeffrey RB, Laing FC, Lewis FR: Acute appendicitis: High resolution real-time US findings. Radiology 163:11–14, 1987.

Parienty RA, Lepreux JF, Gruson B: Sonographic and CT features of ileocolic intussusception. AJR 136:608–610, 1981.

Puylaert JBCM: Acute appendicitis. US evaluation using graded compression. Radiology 158:355–360, 1986.

Puylaert JBCM: Graded compression ultrasound in acute disease of the right lower quadrant. Semin Ultrasound CT MR 8(4):385–402, 1987.

Quillin SP, Siegel MJ: Appendicitis in children: Color Doppler sonography. Radiology 184:745–747, 1992.

KIDNEY

PATTERNS

Hydronephrosis
Variants of Obstructed Hydronephrosis
Unilateral Small, Smooth Kidney
Unilateral Small, Scarred Kidney
Unilateral Renal Enlargement Without Focal Mass
Bilateral Renal Enlargement with Increased Echogenicity
Bilateral Small, Echogenic Kidneys
Unilateral Cystic or Complicated Renal Mass
Unilateral Solid-Appearing Hypoechoic Renal Mass
Hyperechoic Renal Mass

Calcified Renal Mass
Bilateral Renal Cysts
Bilateral Solid Renal Masses
Preservation of Reniform Shape with Abnormal Enhancement on CT
Renal Vein Thrombosis
Calcifications in the Renal Collecting System
Cortical Calcifications
Medullary Nephrocalcinosis
Nonshadowing Soft Tissue Material Within Distended Renal Collecting System
Fluid Collections Near the Kidney

HYDRONEPHROSIS

Focal or Segmental Dilatation of Intrarenal
    Calyceal System Within the Kidney
    Obstructive Causes
    Reflux/Postobstructive or Postinfectious
      Dilatation
Focal Dilatation of Intrarenal Calyceal System
    and Pelvis
    Obstruction to the Level of the
      Ureteropelvic Junction
Unilateral Hydronephrosis and Hydroureter
    Dilatation of Renal Collecting System and
      Ureter
Bilateral Hydronephrosis and Hydroureters
    Bladder Outlet Obstruction

    Neurogenic Bladder
    Reflux
    Eagle-Barrett Syndrome
    Megacalyces/Megaureter

Focal or Segmental Dilatation of Intrarenal Calyceal System Within the Kidney (Figure 6.1)

Obstructive Causes   Dilatation of a portion of the intrarenal calyceal system may be secondary to obstructing causes such as neoplasia (often a transitional cell carcinoma), stone material, focal strictures (tuberculosis or postinstrumentation), or sloughed papillary material. A duplication of the collecting system may have an associated ectopic

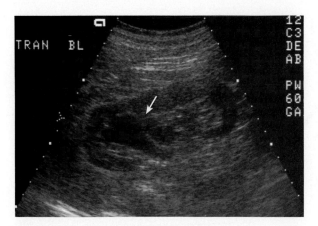

Figure 6.1

Obstructed upper-pole moiety secondary to duplex collecting system and double ureters to the kidney: Focal dilatation of the upper-pole collecting system (*arrow*) is present in this adult with urinary tract infections and a separate ureter to the upper pole. A stone was present in the ureter to the upper pole.

insertion of the duplicated ureter that can lead to focal obstruction.

Reflux/Postobstructive or Postinfectious Dilatation (Figure 6.2)   Focal dilatation of the calyceal system is not necessarily secondary to obstruction, since dilatation from reflux or postobstructive dila-

tation may be seen in a nonobstructed patient. Dilatation without obstruction may be seen in the uncommon situation of megacalyces and megaureters.

Patients with previous obstruction or infection of the kidney may have dilatation of all or a portion of the collecting system with associated cortical loss. The recognition of cortical loss will suggest the chronicity of the finding. Functional studies, such as nuclear medicine imaging or intravenous pyelography (IVP), may be necessary to determine whether the collecting system dilatation is secondary to ongoing obstruction.

Focal Dilatation of Intrarenal Calyceal System and Pelvis

Obstruction to the Level of the Ureteropelvic Junction (Figure 6.3)   The level of the ureteropelvic junction (UPJ) is one of the common sites of blockage to the kidney. Congenital narrowing with functional obstruction at the UPJ may cause mild to severe hydronephrosis, potentially resulting in an end-stage hydronephrotic sac, which in the absence of symptoms may be unrecognized for years. Stones, inflammatory processes, or postoperative strictures as well as tumors may also result in hydronephrotic dilatation of the kidney and renal pelvis. The distal ureter will not be dilated.

In some patients, an extrarenal pelvis may mimic hydronephrosis or UPJ obstruction. The ex-

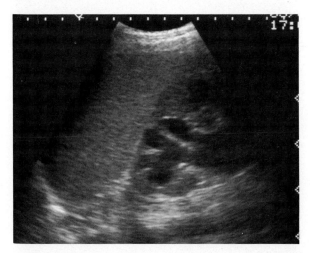

Figure 6.2

Focally dilated calyces in the upper pole secondary to chronic reflux: This young woman was recognized to have cortical loss and focal calyceal dilatation in the upper pole of the right kidney secondary to recurrent episodes of infection and reflux. No obstruction was present. No calyceal dilatation was present in the lower pole.

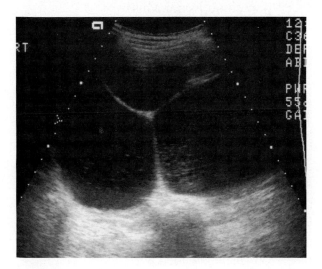

Figure 6.3

Congenital UPJ obstruction: Massive hydronephrosis was coincidentally discovered in this obstetrical patient during routine evaluation. Note complete cortical loss. A hydronephrotic sac is present.

trarenal pelvis may appear distended or flabby be-cause it is outside the supporting renal parenchyma. There should be no dilatation of the intrarenal collecting system or ureter with a simple extrarenal pelvis. The extrarenal pelvis will bulge into the surrounding perinephric fat. Dilatation of the pelvis without infundibular or calyceal dilatation is often considered normal.

Unilateral Hydronephrosis and Hydroureter

Dilatation of Renal Collecting System and Ureter (Figures 6.4–6.10)
Dilatation of the entire renal collecting system and ureter may be secondary to stone, tumor, blood clot, or stricture in the distal ureter causing hydronephrosis and hydroureter. Common sites for stones to lodge leading to obstruction of the ureter are at the ureterovesical junction (UVJ) and where the ureter crosses over the iliac vessels overlying the sacrum. When dilatation of the collecting system and ureter is recognized, a critical evaluation to assess the level of obstruction must be made. The dilated ureter can often be followed sonographically to the point of obstruction. The level of obstruction can often be determined by carefully following the ureter to the site where there is an acute caliber change. Visualization of the distal ureter may be possible through a full bladder. An offending stone or tumor at the UVJ may be seen in some cases. Transitional cell carcinoma is the most common neoplasm of the urothelium of the ureter or bladder.

With acute obstruction, as caused by the passage of a stone, dilatation of the collecting system of the kidney may be very mild or nearly non-existent. A chronically obstructed system may show more severe dilatation and resultant cortical loss over time.

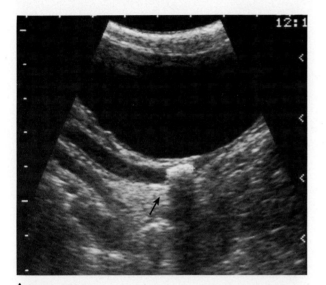

A

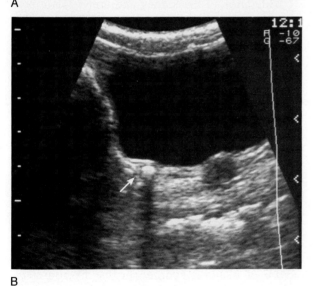

B

Figure 6.4
Distal ureteral stone: This young child had fever and right lower quadrant pain. Appendicitis was suspected. Sonographic evaluation demonstrated mild hydronephrosis. The hydroureter could be followed down to the bladder. At the right UVJ, a 1.5-cm stone (*arrow*) was identified. The stone was extracted cystoscopically.

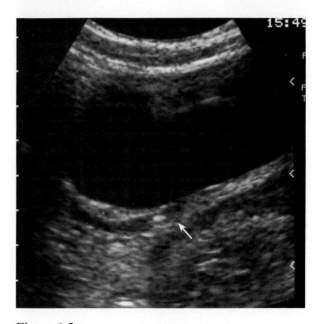

Figure 6.5
Distal ureteral stone: A small stone (*arrow*) was identified within a mildly dilated ureter. The full bladder facilitates visualization of the stone. Sometimes shadowing from the stone is difficult to demonstrate.

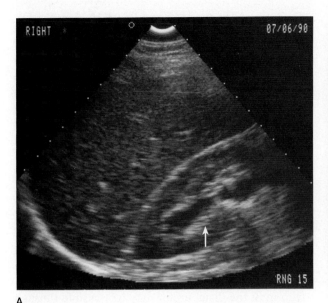

A

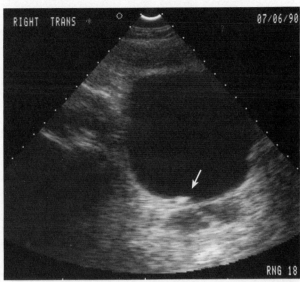

B

Figure 6.6

Distal ureteral stone: (A) Mild hydronephrosis (*arrow*) was secondary to a 5-mm stone at the right UVJ. (B) No significant edema is present at the ureteral orifice. The patient passed the stone without incident.

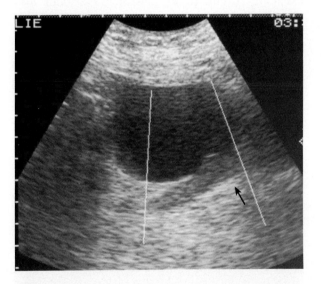

Figure 6.7

Transitional cell carcinoma of the distal ureter with extension into bladder: Distention of the distal ureter by soft tissue (*arrow*) with prolapse of a polypoid mass into the bladder was present in this patient with transitional cell carcinoma of the distal ureter.

In children with hydronephrosis and hydroureter, the possibility of an ectopic insertion of the distal ureter must be considered. Functional studies of the kidney with radionuclides can determine obstruction and the point of obstruction. Cystography may show reflux into an ectopically placed ureter.

Dilatation of the kidney and ureter is not necessarily secondary to obstruction and may be related to reflux.

Bilateral Hydronephrosis and Hydroureters

Bladder Outlet Obstruction (Figures 6.11–6.13)
Recognition of bilateral hydronephrosis, hydroureters, and distention of the bladder suggests that the obstruction is secondary to bladder outlet obstruction such as that produced by benign prostatic hyperplasia, posterior urethral valves, or strictures (benign or malignant) of the urethra.

Neurogenic Bladder (Figure 6.14) Impairment of normal emptying of the bladder secondary to neurologic dysfunction can give the sonographic picture of bilateral hydronephrosis, hydroureters, and a distended bladder. The patient may have a history of spinal trauma or congenital neurologic abnormality such as spinal dysraphism or tethered cord.

Reflux High-grade reflux may give a similar sonographic appearance to bladder outlet obstruction even without obstruction. Reflux may sometimes be actually demonstrated sonographically. Recogni-

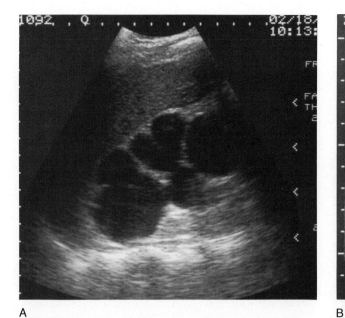

A

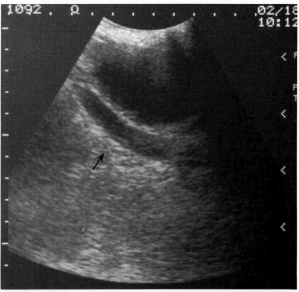

B

Figure 6.8

Reflux: (A and B) Massive right collecting system distention and cortical loss were present in this patient. Hydroureter (*arrow*) could be followed down to the level of the bladder. No obstructing mass or stone was present. Voiding cystography showed high-grade ureterovesical reflux on the right.

tion that reflux is occurring requires a dramatic increase in the collecting system size after the patient voids. Sudden development of hydronephrosis after the bladder is emptied suggests fairly high-grade reflux, which should be confirmed by voiding cystourethrogram (VCUG).

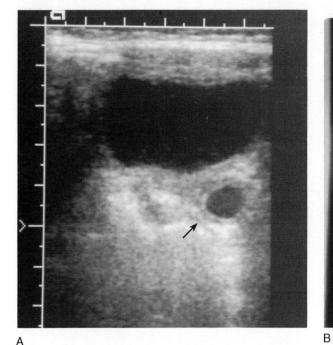

A

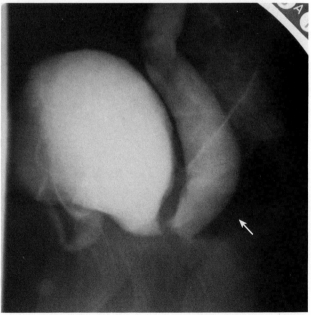

B

Figure 6.9

Ectopic insertion of distal ureter: (A) This 4-year-old was noted to have moderate hydronephrosis and left hydroureter (*arrow*) that could be followed down behind the bladder and worsened when the patient voided. (B) Cystography filled an ectopically placed ureter that freely refluxed (*arrow*).

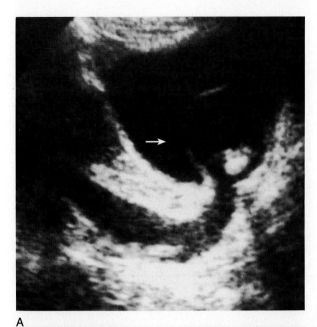

A

Figure 6.10
Ureterocele with stone: (A) Distal ureteral dilatation down to the bladder where a stone is lodged in a ureterocele (*arrow*) was demonstrated and confirmed by (B) contrast study.

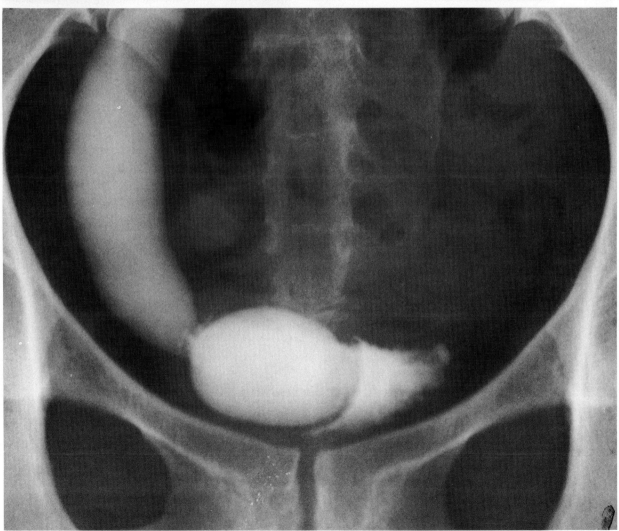

B

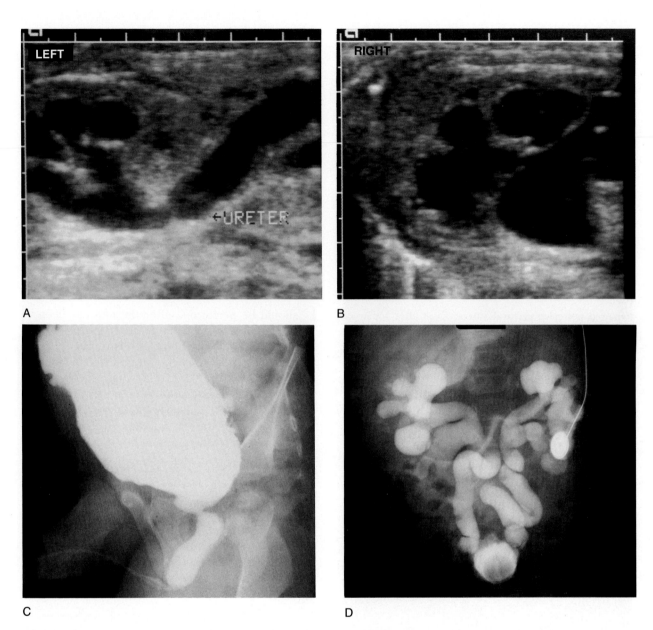

Figure 6.11

Posterior urethral valves: (A and B) Bilateral hydrone-phrosis and tortuous hydroureters were present in this newborn baby boy. Characteristic ballooning of the posterior urethra and urethral valves was identified with voiding cystography (C and D).

latation. Functional studies such as IVP or nuclear medicine imaging are necessary to show that no obstruction is present.

Eagle–Barrett Syndrome   Eagle–Barrett Syndrome, also known as prune belly syndrome, is characterized by bilateral dilatation of the renal collecting systems, hydroureters, absence of the abdominal musculature, and cryptorchidism.

Megacalyces/Megaureter   Megacalyces and mega-ureters are congenital abnormalities rarely seen, but a cause of nonobstructive calyceal and ureteral di-

---

Emphasis Points

The acute passage of a renal stone can be diagnosed by sonography. In a symptomatic patient, a plain film of the abdomen should be performed to look for any obvious renal calculi overlying the kidneys or along the course of the ureter. The abdominal ultrasound

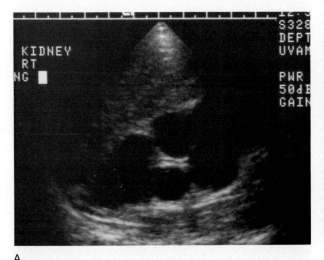

A

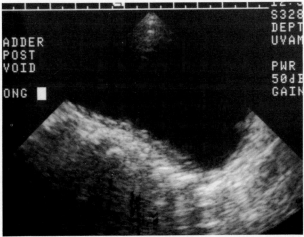

B

Figure 6.12

Repaired posterior urethral valves: Even after repair of posterior urethral valves in this young child, (A) bilateral collecting system dilatation of a severe degree persisted. Hydroureters, as well as trabeculated bladder (B), could be seen sonographically. Renal failure developed despite relief of the urethral obstruction.

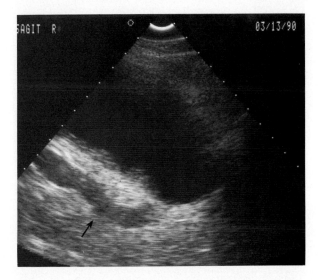

Figure 6.13

Chronic bladder outlet obstruction secondary to benign prostatic hyperplasia: Bilateral hydronephrosis and hydroureters (*arrow*) were identified in this elderly man with urinary retention. The ureters could be followed to a large, trabeculated bladder that appeared chronically obstructed. Indwelling catheter drainage was employed until prostatic resection could be performed.

should be performed after the film has been reviewed, assessing for hydronephrosis, hydroureter, and any point of obstruction. The most common sites the stones would lodge are at the UPJ, UVJ, and where the ureter crosses the iliac vessels. To identify a stone at the UVJ, the bladder should be distended to provide an acoustic window. Transvaginal scanning is another possibility in female patients to facilitate visualization of lower ureteral stones.

Once dilatation of the intrarenal calyceal system is identified, careful scrutiny is necessary to find the level and cause of dilatation. Sonography is not a functional study of the kidneys, and dilatation may be related to obstructive and nonobstructive (i.e., reflux) causes.

Any study of the kidneys should include an evaluation of the bladder, especially if hematuria, hydronephrosis, or stone disease is being considered. Having the patient distend the bladder should be a routine part of evaluation of the renal axis.

VARIANTS OF OBSTRUCTED HYDRONEPHROSIS

Distention with Full Bladder
Parapelvic Renal Cysts
Hypoechoic Medullary Pyramids in the
    Newborn
Distention During Pregnancy
Extrarenal Pelvis

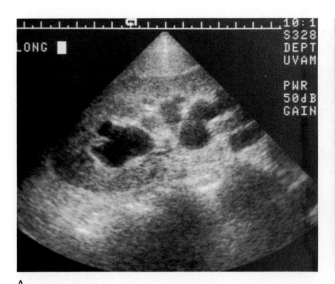

A

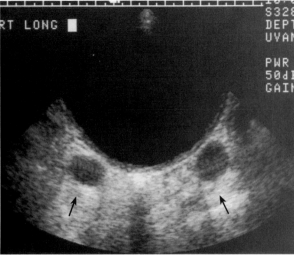

B

Figure 6.14

Neurogenic bladder: (A) Intrarenal calyceal distention, (B) hydroureters (*arrows*) and an overfilled bladder were present in this paralyzed young man after cervical spine injury. The patient needed intermittent catheterization for satisfactory bladder decompression.

Distention with Full Bladder

When a patient has a full bladder and associated distention of the intrarenal calyceal system, the patient should be encouraged to evacuate the bladder so that the presence of collecting system dilatation can be assessed. Often distention of the collecting systems of the kidneys will resolve with emptying of the bladder.

Parapelvic Renal Cysts (Figure 6.15)

Parapelvic cysts may mimic hydronephrosis. The presence of cysts in the renal sinus can be misinterpreted as hydronephrosis. Recognition that the cysts do not interconnect in the same way as a distended renal collecting system and that there is no intrarenal system dilatation will allow diagnosis of parapelvic cysts and avoid misdiagnosis of hydronephrosis. Contrast studies such as IVP or CT are sometimes necessary to confirm this impression. IVP or CT will show spidery calyces surrounded by cysts.

Hypoechoic Medullary Pyramids in the Newborn (Figures 6.16–6.17)

One of the more common situations in which hydronephrosis is misdiagnosed is in the newborn. In such situations, the renal cortical echogenicity is normally slightly elevated, making the medullary pyramid region appear relatively low in echogenicity, mimicking hydronephrosis. Also contributing to the misinterpretation is the lack of sinus fat in the very young patient. Awareness of this situation and recognition that the echo-poor medullary pyramids do not interconnect as one would expect with hydronephrosis will avoid the misdiagnosis of hydronephrosis.

Distention During Pregnancy

During pregnancy, distention of the renal collecting systems and ureters occurs on the right more often than on the left as the pregnancy progresses. The mechanical compression of the ureters by the distended uterus, as well as hormonal effects, contribute to the dilatation of the collecting system. Superimposed obstructive causes may be difficult to identify secondary to the gravid uterus. The collecting system dilatation usually resolves gradually in the weeks after delivery. If there is concern about stone passage or ureteral obstruction in the pregnant patient, careful evaluation of the length of the ureter is required. Visualization of the UVJ by distention of the bladder or transvaginal scanning may be helpful.

Extrarenal Pelvis (Figure 6.18)

The pelvis of the kidney may be located outside the support of the renal parenchyma and may distend. Fullness of an extrarenal pelvis without intrarenal calyceal dilatation should not be mistaken for obstructive hydronephrosis.

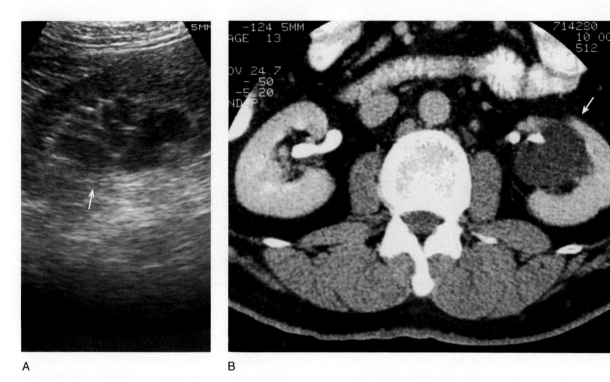

A   B

Figure 6.15
Parapelvic cysts: (A) Cysts clustered in the renal pelvis (*arrows*) can be mistaken for hydronephrosis. (B) CT demonstrated cysts clustered around the renal collecting system.

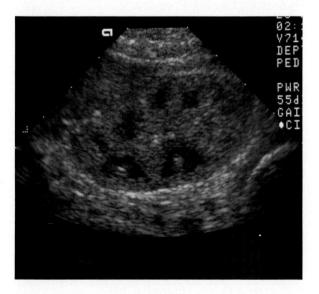

Figure 6.16
Normal newborn kidney: The normal, relatively hyperechoic renal cortex and hypoechoic renal pyramids in a newborn can be misinterpreted as hydronephrosis. Note the lack of interconnection, which would be expected with hydronephrosis.

UNILATERAL SMALL, SMOOTH KIDNEY

Congenital Hypoplasia
Chronic Vascular Compromise
After Partial Nephrectomy
Sequel to Chronic Infection
Postobstructive Atrophy
Sequel to Reflux

Careful measurements of the kidneys are an important part of an ultrasonic evaluation. Recognition of a significant size discrepancy between the two kidneys is a key observation. Generally in children and young adults, the longitudinal dimensions of the kidneys are within 1–1.5 cm of each other. In adults, the left kidney may be up to 1.5 cm longer than the right normally.

In situations in which there is a significant discrepancy in renal size and the smaller kidney is smooth and reniform, this differential listing may be helpful.

Congenital Hypoplasia (Figure 6.19)

Congenital hypoplasia of the kidney represents an unusual entity in which the kidney fails to grow and develop normally. Generally, the hypoplastic kidney stays small, has smooth margins, and often has an identifiable cortex and central sinus. Compensatory hypertrophy of the contralateral kidney may

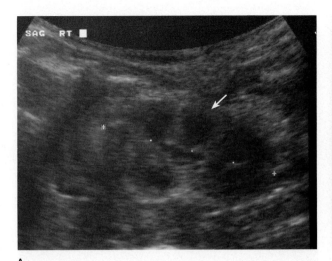

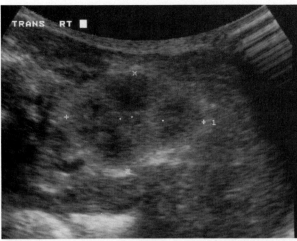

A

B

Figure 6.17

Normal newborn kidney: (A and B) In this newborn with a unilateral multicystic dysplastic kidney, the appearance of the contralateral kidney was very important. Note the relatively echogenic cortex and very hypoechoic medullary pyramids (*arrow*). This is a normal kidney.

be obvious, manifest by increased size and bulkiness of the kidney.

Chronic Vascular Compromise (Figure 6.20)

Vascular compromise, either renal artery occlusion, severe stenosis, or chronic renal vein thrombosis, may result in renal ischemia or infarction and may

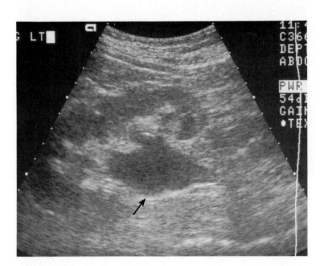

Figure 6.18

Extrarenal pelvis: Note that as the renal pelvis (*arrow*) exits the kidney, it becomes prominent. There is no intrarenal calyceal dilatation.

lead to a small kidney. Renal artery occlusion may result from atherosclerotic disease, blunt or surgical trauma with renal pedicle injury, complications of umbilical artery catheters in neonates, or embolic phenomena. Renal vein occlusion may occur in neonates with dehydration and sepsis. Acutely, the kidney with renal vein thrombosis may be swollen and edematous. The kidney becomes small chronically. Atrophy of the kidney with either arterial or venous compromise may be observed on serial scans, occurring days to weeks after the initial presentation. Radiation therapy can cause a radiation nephritis that results in a smooth, small kidney. For this reason the kidneys are usually not included in the radiation therapy portal if possible.

After Partial Nephrectomy

In patients undergoing partial nephrectomy for whatever cause, the remnant of the operated kidney may be small and smooth.

Sequel to Chronic Infection

Renal infections, such as chronic pyelonephritis or renal tuberculosis, usually leave a kidney scarred and small, but in rare cases the renal outline may be smooth after chronic renal infection.

Postobstructive Atrophy (Figures 6.21–6.22)

Postobstructive atrophy may result in a small, smooth kidney when severe obstruction produces high pressure in the kidney long enough to compromise renal arterial inflow. Even after the obstruction is relieved, the injury to the kidney is evident, because the kidney atrophies and fails to maintain

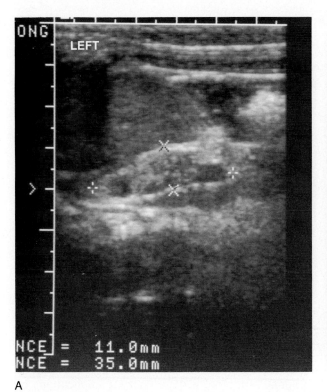

A

B

Figure 6.19
Congenital hypoplasia: This infant with known renal hypoplasia had (A) a small left kidney and (B) a hypertrophied robust right kidney.

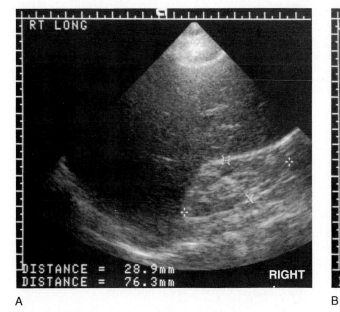

A

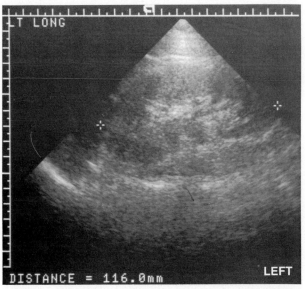

B

Figure 6.20
Right renal artery occlusion: This elderly patient with severe atherosclerosis was found to have a significant size discrepancy between his two kidneys. (A) The right kidney was diminutive, measuring 7.6 cm in length. (B) The left kidney was more robust, measuring 11.6 cm long. Increased cortical echogenicity was present. Right renal artery occlusion was discovered by angiography.

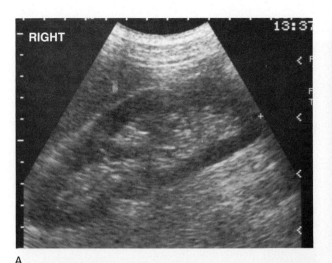

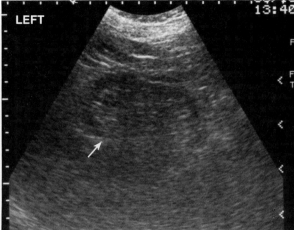

A   B

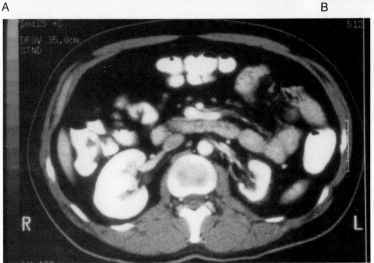

C

Figure 6.21

Postobstructive atrophy: This elderly patient suffered hematuria and was found to have a large bladder mass obstructing the left ureteral orifice causing delayed excretion of the left kidney. After cystectomy, follow-up scans showed the development of a significant size discrepancy between the two kidneys with (A) the right kidney measuring 11.5 cm in length and the left only 7.5 cm. (B) The left kidney had significant cortical thinning and sinus lipomatosis. Even though the obstruction was relieved, the previously obstructed kidney shrank. (C) CT confirmed the size discrepancy.

its previous size and function. The cause of obstruction may have been bladder tumor, benign stricture of the ureter, ectopic ureterocele, or a host of other obstructive etiologies.

Sequel to Reflux

In a minority of young children with reflux, the response of the kidney to high-grade reflux is underdevelopment. Precise measurement of the kidneys in children being evaluated for urinary tract infections and possible reflux is imperative. A significant size discrepancy and recognition of the small, smooth kidney may be the only manifestation of reflux sonographically. Dilatation of the collecting system is not necessarily present on ultrasound. Evaluation for reflux with a voiding cystourethrogram may be necessary to help confirm the diagnosis and dictate medical or surgical management.

Emphasis Point

When a size discrepancy exists between the kidneys, a determination must be made as to which kidney is abnormal, the small, smooth kidney or the large, robust one.

UNILATERAL SMALL, SCARRED KIDNEY

Sequel to Reflux and Infections
Segmental Infarction
After Trauma

When there is an appreciable size discrepancy between the two kidneys and the small kidney has focal scarring with cortical loss, a previous focal in-

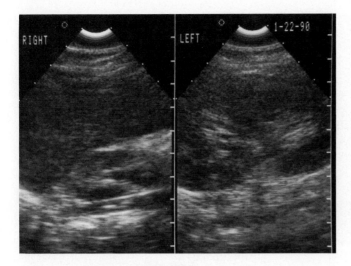

Figure 6.22
Postobstructive atrophy secondary to congenital stricture: This young child was found to have recurrent urinary tract infections secondary to a ureteral stricture at the right UVJ. After repair of the stricture, the right kidney was noted to be significantly smaller than the left.

sult has usually occurred. Associated collecting system dilatation may be present.

Sequel to Reflux and Infections (Figures 6.23–6.25)

Suspected or unrecognized reflux, especially in a young female patient, may result in a small, scarred kidney. Often these patients are aware of recurrent urinary tract infections, confirming that recurrent pyelonephritis may be additive in its effect with reflux in producing a small, scarred kidney. Unusual

infectious agents, such as those that cause tuberculosis, may result in a small, irregular kidney.

At sites of scarring and cortical loss, there may be calyceal blunting with distention of the collecting system.

Voiding cystourethrograms may be done to confirm or exclude ongoing reflux as the etiologic agent of renal loss.

Segmental Infarction

Focal areas of scarring of the kidney may be the sequel of segmental infarction of the kidney, sec-

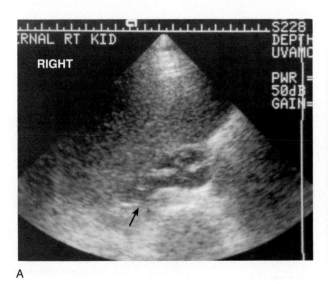

A

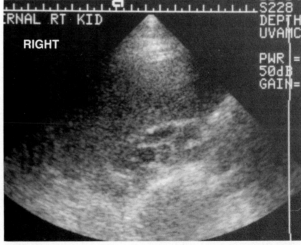

B

Figure 6.23
Chronic reflux: (A and B) This young obstetric patient was noted to have a small, gnarled right kidney with dilatation of the collecting system. Compensatory hypertrophy was present on the left. High-grade reflux was demonstrated on cystogram.

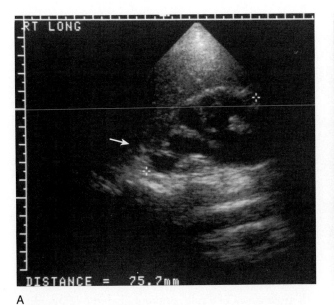

A

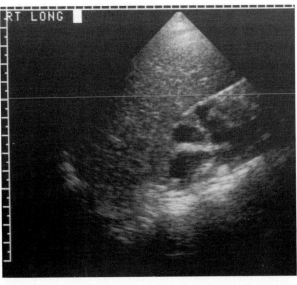

B

Figure 6.24
Sequel to severe pyelonephritis: (A and B) A small, irregularly scarred kidney was noted after episodes of pyelonephritis. The contralateral kidney was robust, without hydronephrosis.

ondary to either arterial or venous occlusion related to a host of causes including embolic events or vasculitis.

After Trauma

Blunt or surgical trauma may result in a small, scarred kidney either related to excision of renal tissue or vascular compromise.

UNILATERAL RENAL ENLARGEMENT WITHOUT FOCAL MASS

Compensatory Hypertrophy
Duplicated Collecting System
Pyelonephritis
Acute Vascular Compromise
    Renal Vein Thrombosis
    Acute Arterial Occlusion
Obstruction
Infiltration of the Kidney by Neoplasia

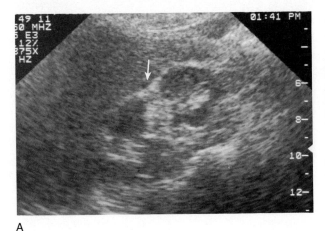

A

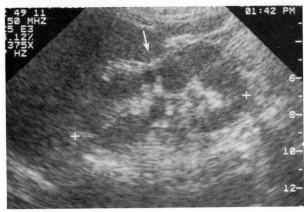

B

Figure 6.25
Sequel to severe pyelonephritis: A scarred kidney was demonstrated in this patient with recurrent urinary tract infections. No collecting system dilatation was present. Arrow marks scars.

When a significant size differential exists between the two kidneys in a patient, sometimes it is difficult to determine which kidney is abnormal. Enlargement of the kidney may be secondary to these differential possibilities.

Compensatory Hyptertrophy (Figures 6.26–6.27)

Compensatory hypertrophy of a kidney develops after functional loss of the contralateral kidney early in life. Hypertrophy may occur in pediatric patients with a multicystic dysplastic kidney on the opposite side or in those who have had surgical removal of a kidney for tumor, after trauma, or after infections or vascular insults. The hypertrophied kidney rapidly increases in bulk and size after loss of renal function on the other side. This phenomenon is most obvious in young patients after renal loss. The recognition in the adult of a single, large, bulky, normal-appearing kidney suggests that the patient never had bilateral kidneys or that there was loss of one kidney in childhood. Usually, dramatic compensatory hypertrophy is not so obvious when there is loss of a kidney in the adult patient.

Duplicated Collecting System (Figure 6.28)

Relative enlargement of a kidney may be observed when there is duplication of the collecting system and failure of complete fusion of the kidney. Although a duplicated collecting system may be difficult to detect sonographically, the presence of a large kidney with two distinct collecting systems separated by a prominent column of cortex (column of Bertin) may suggest the diagnosis. Contrast studies, such as intravenous pyelography, can confirm the diagnosis. The study will show a partial or complete duplication of the collecting system, clarifying whether there are two entirely separate ureters or union of the ureters in the retroperitoneum.

Pyelonephritis (Figure 6.29)

In most cases of acute, uncomplicated pyelonephritis, ultrasonography is normal. With increasing severity of renal involvement with infection, renal sonography may demonstrate a diffusely swollen and enlarged kidney, often with diminished echogenicity. Effacement of the central echo complex with development of focal masslike areas may be seen with severe infection. Swift administration of anti-

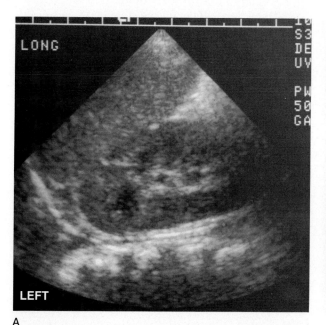

A

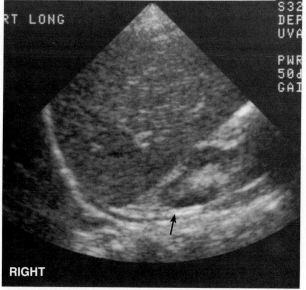

B

Figure 6.26
Compensatory hypertrophy: After suffering right renal vein thrombosis as a neonate, this 8-month-old had a remaining robust left kidney (A) that showed evidence of compensatory hypertrophy manifest by its thick cortex and generous length. (B) The right kidney was quite small.

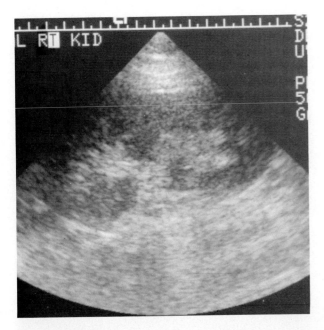

Figure 6.27
Compensatory hypertrophy: With congenital absence of the left kidney, the remaining right kidney is large and has a thick cortex.

biotics may cause the kidney to return to its normal size. In such situations, the patient is generally very symptomatic, with flank tenderness, leukocytes, and fever.

Acute Vascular Compromise

Renal Vein Thrombosis Renal vein thrombosis, unrelated to renal cell carcinoma and tumoral invasion of the renal vein, is most often seen in pediatric patients with dehydration, sepsis, and hemoconcentration. Typically, these pediatric patients have hematuria and may have a palpably enlarged kidney. In the young child, the process may be bilateral but asymmetric and may be associated with adrenal hemorrhage, especially on the left side. This phenomenon is related to the left adrenal vein's origin from the left renal vein. In cases of left renal vein thrombosis, there may be associated hemorrhagic infarction of the left adrenal.

Sonographically, the kidney with renal vein thrombosis is enlarged, with increased echogenicity of the medullary pyramids, presumably secondary to medullary hemorrhage. Doppler flow may be ob-

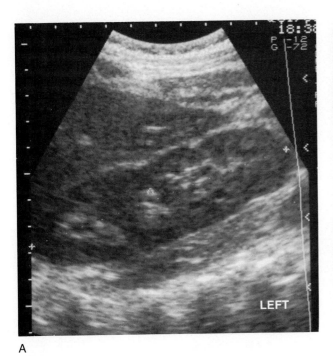

A

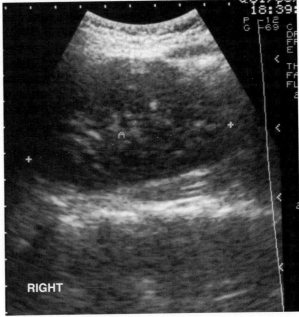

B

Figure 6.28
Duplicated collecting system: The apparent size discrepancy between the two kidneys in this child was related to the duplicated collecting system on the left. (A) The left kidney measured 10.8 cm in length. (B) The right kidney measured 8.2 cm in length. Duplication of the collecting system was confirmed by IVP.

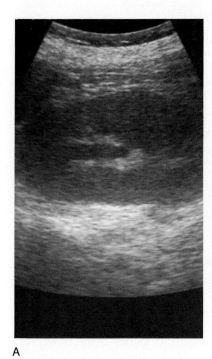
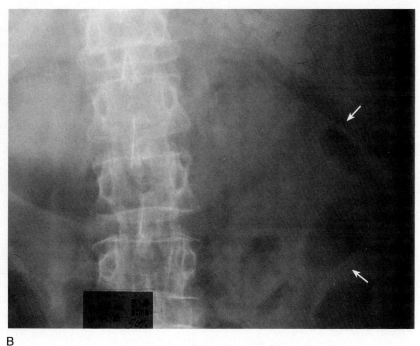

A   B

Figure 6.29

Obstructed, infected kidney: (A) In this patient with tenderness secondary to obstruction and pyelonephritis, the bulky left kidney measured several centimeters larger than the contralateral side. (B) IVP showed poor excretion from the left. Obstruction by a sloughed papilla was relieved by stent placement.

tainable in the main renal vein even when there is extensive thrombosis of the intrarenal venules. High-resistance arterial flow with even reversal of flow in diastole may be recognized in the renal artery of a kidney with renal vein thrombosis. Sometimes a thrombus may be visualized in the renal vein or inferior vena cava.

Acutely, the kidney will be enlarged, but over time the kidney will show the insult of vascular compromise by diminishing in size and failing to grow further.

Acute Arterial Occlusion   It is reported that acute arterial occlusion leads to renal enlargement. In my experience, acute arterial occlusion of the kidney results in a normal-sized to slightly smaller kidney acutely. Over time, the kidney suffering arterial occlusion becomes small and smooth.

Obstruction

Obstruction of the kidney may result in renal enlargement. In most cases, hydronephrosis may be

noted. The etiology of the obstruction may be discovered with careful scrutiny.

Infiltration of the Kidney by Neoplasia

Infiltration of the kidney by neoplasia such as transitional cell carcinoma, metastatic disease, or lymphoma can cause unilateral enlargement of the kidney, often with loss of the normal corticomedullary differentiation. No discrete contour-deforming mass is necessarily present.

BILATERAL RENAL ENLARGEMENT WITH INCREASED ECHOGENICITY

Acute Glomerulonephritis
Multisystem Disorders
Acute Interstitial Nephritis
AIDS Nephropathy
Leukemia
Amyloidosis/Multiple Myeloma
Acute Tubular Necrosis/Rhabdomyolysis with
    Myogloburia
Diabetus Mellitus

CHILDHOOD

Autosomal Recessive Polycystic Kidney
    Disease
Hemolytic–Uremic Syndrome
Renal Vein Thrombosis

The normal adult kidney measures 9 to 12 cm in length, depending upon the size (height and weight) of the patient. The mean renal length is 10.5 cm. Magnification and swelling secondary to contrast administration contribute to renal measurements that are larger on IVP than on sonographic evaluation.

The kidney has a cortical thickness that is normally greater than 1.5 cm. Sonographically, the renal cortex is generally less echogenic than the adjacent hepatic or splenic parenchyma. Most often, when the renal cortex is echogenic, it reflects chronic renal parenchymal disease. Sometimes, the liver parenchyma may be diminished, as in acute hepatitis or leukemic infiltration of the liver. In such a circumstance, the renal cortex may appear to be of similar echogenicity to the liver and be normal. When the cortical echogenicity of the kidney is increased, the severity of renal parenchymal disease correlates with the degree of increased cortical echogenicity.

Enlargement of the kidneys generally correlates with acute toxin, insult, or vascular compromise. Conditions resulting in enlarged, echogenic kidneys are often those in which antigen–antibody complexes and other debris clog the kidney's filtration mechanism. Conditions of cellular infiltration and proliferative disorders may give the same sonographic picture. The small, shrunken kidney is the end stage of many renal insults. The enlarged but echogenic kidney may be afflicted by conditions that have a reversible or treatable component.

Acute Glomerulonephritis (Figure 6.30)

A variety of proliferative or necrotizing disorders affects the kidney only, including acute (poststreptococcal) glomerulonephritis, membrano-proliferative glomerulonephritis, heroin nephropathy, and IgA nephropathy. These conditions can cause an acute decline in renal function and enlarged kidneys with increased cortical echogenicity. The enlargement of the kidneys is consistent with a relatively acute stage of disease and offers hope of improvement in renal function with therapy, since a small end-stage kidney is not present. Renal biopsy will be necessary in most cases to distinguish these entities.

Multisystem Disorders (Figure 6.31)

Polyarteritis nodosa, systemic lupus erythematosus, Wegener's granulomatosis, Goodpasture's syndrome, Schönlein–Henoch syndrome, thrombocytopenia purpura (TTP), and bacterial endocarditis

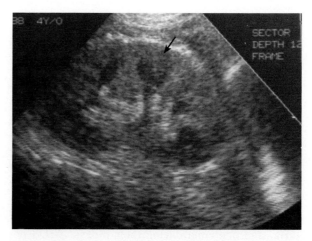

Figure 6.30

Acute glomerulonephritis: This 10-year-old boy presented with anasarca and proteinuria. Sonographic evaluation of the kidneys showed them to be bilaterally enlarged (11.5 cm) and hyperechoic. The medullary pyramids were seen as relatively hypoechoic (*arrow*). Biopsy was performed.

are examples of disorders that affect many different systems, including the kidney.

Multisystem diseases such as these can affect the kidney as part of its vasculitic process. Vasculitides can cause renal dysfunction and yield large, echogenic kidneys sonographically. Renal biopsy may be necessary to differentiate the various types of vasculitides affecting the kidney and to indicate the direction of therapy.

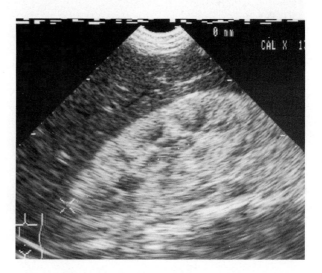

Figure 6.31

Vasculitis: Highly echogenic, enlarged (13 cm) kidneys were present in this patient with acute renal failure. Biopsy of the left kidney was performed under sonographic guidance.

Acute Interstitial Nephritis

Acute interstitial nephritis is an allergic reaction to such drugs as sulfonamides, penicillin and members of the penicillin family, as well as others. The interstitium of the kidney is infiltrated with lymphocytes, plasma cells, polymononucleocytes, and eosinophils. Sonographically, the kidneys are enlarged with smooth, thick parenchyma and have normal to increased echogenicity.

AIDS Nephropathy (Figure 6.32–6.33)

Many AIDS patients will suffer proteinuria, hematuria, and azotemia during their illness. AIDS nephropathy is an irreversible renal failure, with a life expectancy of less than 6 months once azotemia occurs. Its incidence is highest in black men.

Sonographically, the kidneys are enlarged and of increased cortical echogenicity. Histologically, the tubules are dilated and filled with proteinaceous material.

Leukemia (Figure 6.34)

Leukemic infiltration is the most common malignant cause of enlarged, echogenic kidneys. Leukemic involvement of the kidneys is present in 63 percent of autopsies on leukemic patients.

Amyloidosis/Multiple Myeloma (Figure 6.35)

Amyloidosis affects the kidneys in 35 percent of patients with primary amyloidosis but is present in at least 80 percent of patients with secondary amyloidosis. Amyloidosis is the deposition of extracellular proteinaceous material and is associated with rheumatoid arthritis, multiple myeloma, osteomyelitis, and Waldenström's macroglobulinemia.

In the early stages of amyloid involvement of the kidneys, the kidneys are normal to large in size, with increased cortical thickness and cortical echogenicity. A potential complication of amyloid deposition in the kidney is renal vein thrombosis. Hypercoagulability accompanies the amyloid condition and predisposes to renal vein thrombosis.

Multiple myeloma is frequently associated with accumulation of eosinophilic material in the extracellular space, and the kidneys may be affected. The kidneys are initially a normal size or large, becoming small as the condition becomes chronic. Normal to increased cortical echogenicity is seen sonographically.

Acute Tubular Necrosis/Rhabdomyolysis with Myoglobinuria

Acute tubular necrosis (ATN) occurs when there is a marked reduction in renal blood flow because

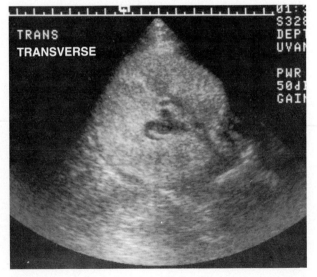

A   B

Figure 6.32

AIDS nephropathy: This 33-year-old woman with AIDS suffered declining renal function. Sonography showed the kidneys to be enlarged and hyperechoic with hypoechoic pyramids.

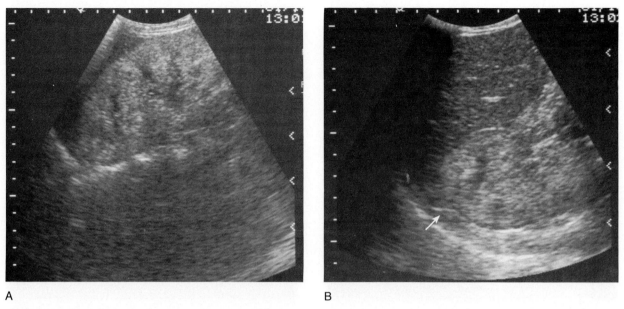

A   B

Figure 6.33
AIDS nephropathy: This 8-year-old with AIDS developed
severe renal insufficiency and eventually renal failure.
Note the highly echogenic, enlarged kidneys.

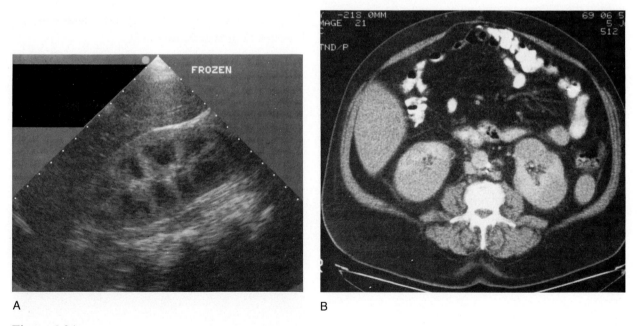

A   B

Figure 6.34
Leukemic infiltration: (A) This child with acute lymphocytic leukemia developed enlarged, hyperechoic kidneys.
Note the prominent pyramids. (B) Poor contrast enhancement was noted on CT.

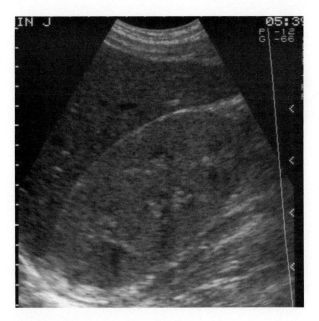

Figure 6.35
Multiple myeloma: Bulky, echogenic kidneys were demonstrated in this patient with acute decompensation related to myeloma.

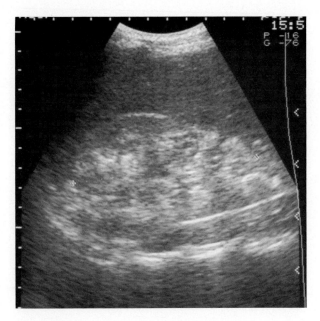

Figure 6.36
Autosomal recessive polycystic kidney disease: This 8-year-old with periportal fibrosis of the liver has bilaterally enlarged, echogenic kidneys.

there is markedly elevated arteriolar resistance within the kidney. Profound ischemia to the kidneys, such as that which accompanies massive trauma or hemorrhage, shock, surgery, or obstetrical catastrophe, can result in ATN. Drugs, including mercury, aminoglycosides, ethylene glycol, and intravenous contrast agents, may cause ATN. ATN is temporary and is usually a reversible cause of renal failure.

On sonographic evaluation, the kidneys are often a normal size or large, secondary to interstitial edema. Most kidneys maintain normal echogenicity, but up to 11 percent show increased cortical echogenicity. Rhabdomyolysis secondary to crush injury, myositis, or ischemic muscle damage can cause myoglobinuria, which can cause renal dysfunction. The sonographic image is of enlarged, echogenic kidneys.

Diabetes Mellitus

Diabetes has been described as a common cause of renal enlargement with or without increased cortical echogenicity. Often the sonographic appearance of patients with diabetes is nearly normal, even in situations of severe renal insufficiency. Renal size and echogenicity are often normal with declining creatinine clearance. As the condition becomes more chronic, renal size may diminish.

CHILDHOOD

Autosomal Recessive Polycystic Kidney Disease (Figures 6.36–6.37)

Autosomal recessive polycystic kidney disease is a spectrum of disease involving renal disease and periportal hepatic fibrosis. The two components of the

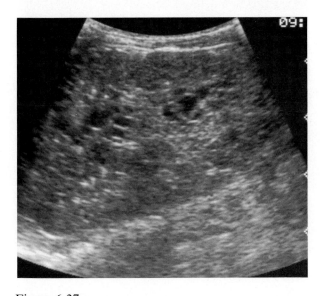

Figure 6.37
Autosomal recessive polycystic kidney disease: Large kidneys with cortical and medullary hyperechogenicity were present in this child. Note that no macrocysts are seen.

disease vary inversely. Young patients with severe renal dysfunction have little hepatic disease. As the child ages, liver disease will predominate, with the development of portal hypertension, portosystemic collaterals, and gastrointestinal hemorrhage. Some consider this juvenile polycystic renal disease.

Sonographically, the kidneys are quite large, often extending into the pelvis of a neonate. Tiny cysts may sometimes be resolved in the cortex or medulla of the kidney. The medullary portion of the kidney is extremely echogenic secondary to the tubular ectasia of the collecting tubules. The sonographic appearance is characteristic.

Hemolytic–Uremic Syndrome (Figures 6.38–6.39)

The most common cause of renal failure leading to dialysis, hemolytic–uremic syndrome usually occurs in children, patients less than 2 years of age. Histologically, there is a microangiopathy that causes endothelial swelling and thrombosis in the renal arterioles.

Clinically, there has often been a recent gastrointestinal illness, and the child develops irritability, bloody diarrhea, and acute renal failure.

The kidneys are of normal or increased size with a hyperechoic cortex. Complete spontaneous recovery occurs in up to 85 percent of patients.

Renal Vein Thrombosis

Although it often affects one kidney more dramatically, renal vein thrombosis can affect both kidneys, resulting in enlargement of both kidneys and increased echogenicity, especially in the medullary pyramids. Renal vein thrombosis often occurs in the large babies of diabetic mothers. Babies predisposed to renal vein thrombosis have hemoconcentration that accompanies diarrhea, vomiting, and dehydration. Usually, hematuria is present, making the clinical suspicion high.

BILATERAL SMALL, ECHOGENIC KIDNEYS

    Chronic Glomerulonephritis
    Atherosclerosis/Nephropathies/Chronic
        Hypertension/Chronic Amyloidosis
    End-Stage Kidneys from Any Cause

The sonographic recognition of bilaterally small, echogenic kidneys usually reflects a long-

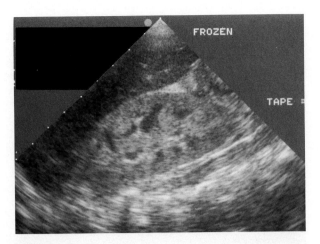

Figure 6.38
Hemolytic uremic syndrome: This youngster developed acute renal failure and bloody diarrhea after a viral illness. The kidneys were bilaterally large and echogenic and signs of fluid overload were present. The patient was supported and recovered renal function eventually.

standing or chronic process rather than an acute event. Such kidneys are often near end state. Renal biopsy to obtain a histologic diagnosis is often not helpful in elucidating the specific cause of the small kidneys.

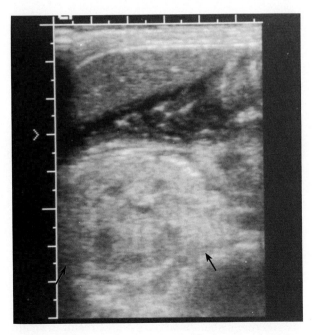

Figure 6.39
Hemolytic uremic syndrome: Renal failure developed after a flulike illness in this pediatric patient. Note the enlarged, extremely echogenic kidneys (*arrows*). Fluid overload was present. Note edematous soft tissues.

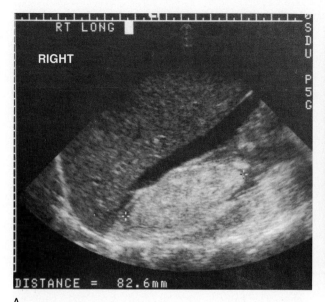

A

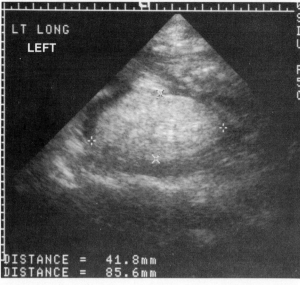

B

Figure 6.40

Chronic glomerulonephritis: This college student presented with acute renal failure with BUN of 112 and a serum creatinine level of 7.3. Signs of fluid overload were present clinically. (A and B) Ultrasound showed the kidneys to be extremely echogenic with no differentiation between the cortex and the medullary portion of the kidney. This appearance reflects chronic renal failure, not acute, reversible disease.

Basically, bilaterally small, smooth kidneys reflect the chronic stage of an insult to the kidneys, either parenchymal or vascular. Function of the kidneys in such a situation is generally declining or severely limited. The discovery of bilaterally small kidneys suggests that there will be little reversible improvement in renal function with medical management.

Chronic Glomerulonephritis (Figure 6.40)

Chronic glomerulonephritis results in bilaterally small, smooth kidneys with increased cortical echogenicity. In young patients, the unexpected finding of bilaterally small, smooth kidneys in the setting of renal dysfunction would especially suggest glomerulonephritis as the underlying etiology. Sonographically, the severity of disease worsens as the cortical and central sinus echogenicities become more similar, making the two regions of the kidney indistinguishable.

Atherosclerosis/Nephropathies/Chronic Hypertension/Chronic Amyloidosis (Figures 6.41–6.42)

Chronic nephropathies of the kidneys causing fibrosis and diminished renal output may result in small, smooth kidneys. The effects of chronic hypertension, severe atherosclerotic cardiovascular disease, and chronic amyloidosis may result in bilaterally small kidneys without collecting system dilatation.

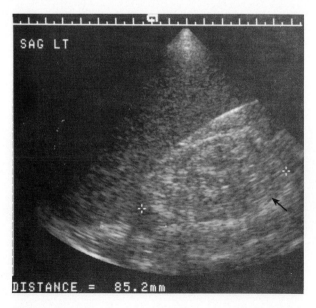

Figure 6.41

Nephrosclerosis: This middle-aged man with a long history of hypertension was studied because of renal failure. The kidneys were symmetrical, both measuring 7.5 cm in length. The cortical echogenicity of the kidney is higher than the echogenicity of the liver.

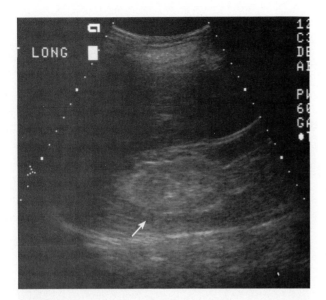

Figure 6.42
Chronic renal failure secondary to hypertension: The native kidneys in this renal transplant recipient are highly echogenic and small. No collecting system dilatation is present.

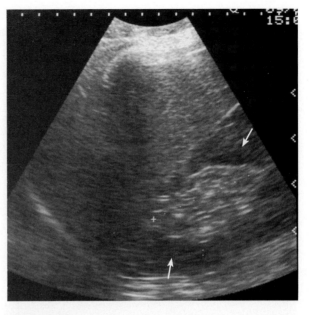

Figure 6.43
End-stage kidneys: Small, echogenic kidneys were barely visible in this chronic dialysis patient. Note the hypoechoic perinephric fat (*arrows*).

End-Stage Kidneys from Any Cause (Figure 6.43)

When small, echogenic end-stage kidneys are discovered, the etiology may never be determined.

Emphasis Point

Some patients present with so-called acute renal failure, arriving with evidence of renal disease of a severe degree of which they were unaware. Sonographic evaluation that identifies two small, echogenic kidneys allows recognition that the patient has had undetected chronic renal insufficiency, perhaps thrown into overt renal failure by a flulike illness or dehydration. In most cases, renal biopsy of end-stage kidneys will not be useful.

UNILATERAL CYSTIC OR COMPLICATED CYSTIC RENAL MASS

Simple Renal Cyst
Complicated Renal Cyst
Focal Hydronephrosis
Hydronephrotic Sac

Calyceal Diverticulum
Renal Neoplasms
Renal Abscess
Hematoma
Arteriovenous Malformation/Splenorenal
    Collateral
Renal Artery Aneurysm
Extrarenal Pelvis

CHILDHOOD

Multicystic Dysplastic Kidney
Wilms' Tumor
Fetal Renal Hamartoma

Simple Renal Cysts (Figure 6.44)

Renal cysts are commonly encountered in adult patients and reportedly are present in more than 50 percent of patients over the age of 50. The renal cyst may arise anywhere in the kidney, including the peripelvic region, and is the most common cause of a mass in the kidney.

Strict sonographic criteria must be adhered to for the diagnosis of a simple renal cyst. Generally, renal cysts are well defined, usually round or oval, with *no* internal echoes, a thin but well-defined back wall, and posterior acoustic enhancement or transmission. Masses that fulfill these criteria do not need further work-up or evaluation.

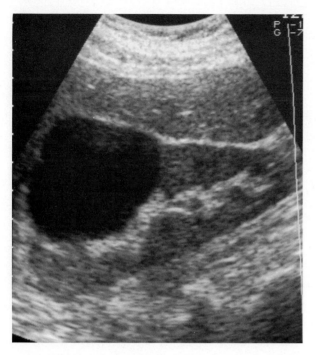

Figure 6.44
Simple renal cyst: A common finding sonographically, this uncomplicated renal cyst had a well-defined wall and no internal echoes.

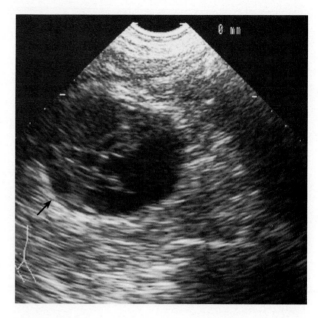

Figure 6.45
Complicated renal cyst: This renal cyst had an extensive soft tissue component after recent hemorrhage (*arrow*). The material resolved on follow-up scanning. In some centers, this mass would have been surgically removed because of its worrisome sonographic appearance.

Complicated Renal Cyst (Figure 6.45)

Renal cysts frequently show features that suggest complications such as hemorrhage or infection. A single, thin (<1 mm) septation, slight lobulation of shape, and low-level internal echoes may be seen in renal cysts after hemorrhage. The more atypical the sonographic appearance of the cyst, with increasing numbers and thickness of septa, irregularity of the cyst walls, large solid components, and irregular calcifications, the more worrisome the lesion is. Further evaluation with CT may be necessary. Unenhanced CT may show high density, non-enhancing mass consistent with a hemorrhagic cyst. In some cases, cyst puncture and surgical enucleation may be necessary to exclude neoplasia. A renal cyst is considered indeterminate in about 6 percent of cases.

Focal Hydronephrosis (Figure 6.46)

Focal areas of dilatation of the pelvis or calyceal system may be secondary to obstructive causes, such as stone, tumor, or benign stricture, or non-obstructive causes, such as after infection with cortical loss and calyceal distention or reflux. Recognition of cortical loss, in association with a scar, a

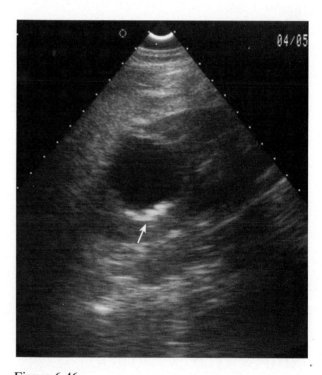

Figure 6.46
Focally obstructed calyx: Stones (*arrow*) caused focal obstruction in this patient. The cystic lesion of the kidney was the dilated, obstructed collecting system, which became secondarily infected.

stone at the base of the cystic lesion, and the shape
of the collecting system will often allow the cystic
structure to be recognized as a focally distended
collecting system. If no obvious cause for the collecting system dilatation is apparent, further work-
up with retrograde pyelograms or contrast opacification may be necessary.

Hydronephrotic Sac (Figures 6.47–6.48)

Sometimes, when the entire kidney or a significant
portion of the kidney becomes an end-stage hydronephrotic sac with profound cortical loss, the kidney may be difficult to recognize. Careful search for
interconnections of the very distended collecting
system and a knowledge of the appearance of severe hydronephrosis will allow the recognition that
the "cysts" in the renal fossa are dilated calyces
rather than cysts. The obstructive and nonobstructive causes for such dilatation must then be ex-
plored.

Calyceal Diverticulum

Usually, a calyceal diverticulum that has a tiny, narrow connection to the collecting system is not identified sonographically, but sometimes large ones can
be seen as cystic structures at ultrasound. If large
and seen at ultrasound, they are generally confused

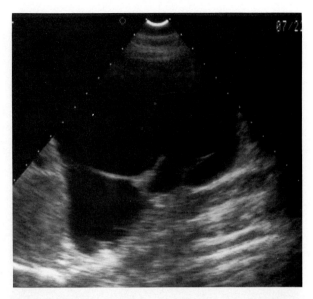

Figure 6.48
Hydronephrosis: A multiseptated cystic mass proved to
be a hydronephrosis sac in this patient with UPJ obstruction.

with a renal cyst or a focally obstructed calyx. Calyceal diverticula are significant because of their
propensity to become infected and because they
produce stasis that contributes to stone formation.

Renal Neoplasms (Figures 6.49–6.50)

Renal cell carcinoma, representing 80 to 85 percent
of primary renal neoplasms, has cystic components
in up to 40 percent of tumors. The cystic components are often secondary to central necrosis and
hemorrhage. Only 1 to 2 percent of renal cell carcinomas are nearly entirely cystic, such as a small
tumor nodule within a cyst.

The uncommon multilocular cystic nephroma,
which has two peaks, one in male children, the
other in adult women, is characteristically a cystic
lesion. The lesion consists of multiple cysts that do
not intercommunicate and are separated by thick
septations. The multilocular nephroma often im-
pinges upon and may distort the central collecting
system or renal pelvis. Generally a benign lesion,
the multiocular cystic nephroma is surgically removed. Two percent have malignant elements.

In nearly all these cystic neoplasms, there are
significant solid components and multiple, thick
septa to make the lesions sonographically suspicious, necessitating further work-up with eventual
surgery for therapy.

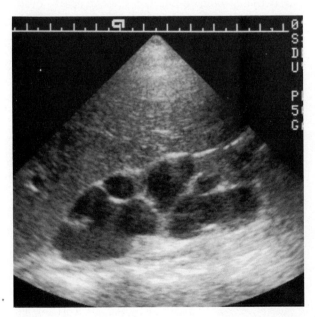

Figure 6.47
Hydronephrosis: End-stage hydronephrosis had the appearance of a multiseptate cystic mass in this patient with
chronic obstruction.

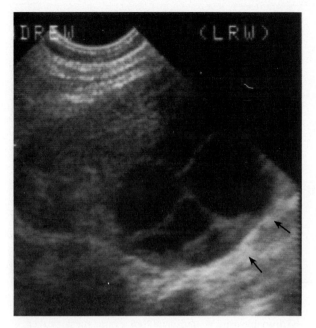

Figure 6.49
Cystic renal cell carcinoma: A multiseptate cystic mass (*arrows*) on the lower pole of the right kidney was resected and was found to be renal cell carcinoma.

Renal Abscess (Figures 6.51–6.52)

Renal abscesses may be secondary to hematogenous dissemination of infection in patients who are septic and immunosuppressed or intravenous drug abusers. Abscesses also arise secondary to severe renal infection, usually ascending from the bladder. Abscesses may be secondary to chronic obstruction by either stone material or stricture. As many as 25 percent of patients with a renal abscess have no organisms present on urinalysis because there is obstruction between the renal abscess and the renal collecting system.

Sonographically, the renal abscess is usually hypoechoic, nearly cystic, with posterior acoustical enhancement often present. Thick walls and septation, low-level echoes, and debris may be noted. Brightly echogenic foci representing microbubbles of air may also be seen.

Generally, the clinical situation of the patient and the rapid change in the imaging features of the abscess, rather than the specific sonographic appearance, will suggest the diagnosis. Diagnostic aspiration and percutaneous catheter drainage may provide definitive therapy.

Hematoma

Ultrasound is not generally the examination of choice in acute blunt trauma to the kidneys, largely because it gives limited information regarding vascular integrity, a feature well studied with contrast-enhanced CT. Ultrasound is frequently used, however, to follow up patients after renal trauma. Intraparenchymal hematomas will appear nearly cystic as they age, often with internal septations and de-

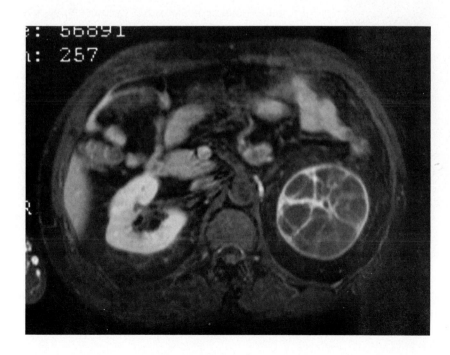

Figure 6.50
Renal cell carcinoma: A large multiseptate mass in the left kidney was obvious in this patient with gross hematuria. Radical nephrectomy was performed.

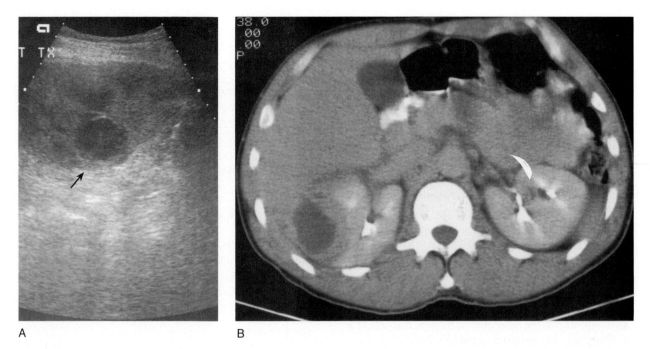

A   B

Figure 6.51
Renal abscess: (A) A hypoechoic, cystic area with low-level echoes developed in this patient with spiking fevers and immunosuppression. Percutaneous catheter placement was used to decompress the fungal abscess. (B) Similar patient prior to drainage.

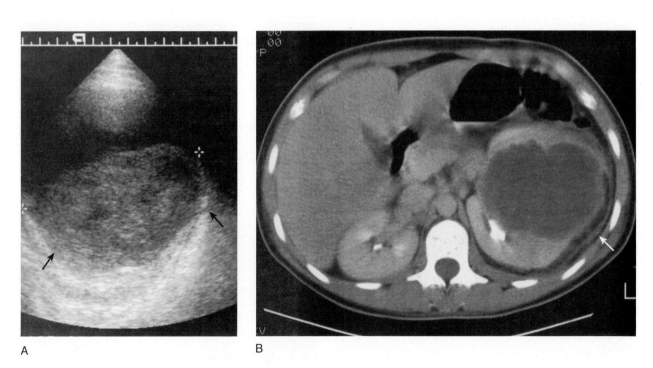

A   B

Figure 6.52
Renal abscess: (A) A large, well-defined mass with fluid and debris (*arrows*) was present in the mid-portion of the left kidney. (B) CT was used for percutaneous decompression of the pyogenic abscess. An obstructing stone was the cause in this patient with medullary sponge kidney.

225

bris. Over time, the hematoma may become smaller and can, in some cases, calcify.

Arteriovenous Malformation/ Splenorenal Collateral

Arteriovenous malformations (AVM) may arise as congenital, posttraumatic, or iatrogenic communications between a renal artery branch and an adjacent renal vein. Characteristically, there is a large renal vein with turbulent, high-velocity flow and arterialization of its waveform.

A renal AVM is often present near the hilum of the kidney but can be identified in the substance of the kidney itself, especially near the zone between the cortex and medulla. Doppler flow analysis will generally allow the vascular nature of the lesion to be clarified. Postbiopsy renal artery pseudoaneurysm can be detected sonographically as well.

In patients with portal hypertension, either a spontaneous or surgically created splenorenal collateral may be misinterpreted as a cyst of the left kidney. Recognition that the "mass" is tubular and extends, usually in a tortuous course, from the splenic hilum to the left renal vein will allow the appropriate diagnosis to be made. Color Doppler or spectral analysis will allow its venous nature to be proven. Other stigmata of portal hypertension may be obvious.

Renal Artery Aneurysm

Generally secondary to atherosclerotic disease, a renal artery aneurysm may be identified, usually in the renal hilum, as a well-circumscribed cystic mass, often with peripheral calcifications. Doppler investigation will delineate its vascular nature, unless the aneurysm is thrombosed.

Extrarenal Pelvis

The renal pelvis frequently extends outside the confines of the renal parenchyma. Distention of the renal pelvis, located outside the supporting parenchyma, may result in a cystic structure that may be misinterpreted as a renal cyst or as hydronephrosis.

CHILDHOOD

Multicystic Dysplastic Kidney (Figure 6.53)

Cystic, dysplastic changes secondary to embryologic obstruction of the kidney is a condition that is most often encountered in the pediatric population. In most cases, the entire kidney is replaced by multiple cysts of variable size with surrounding echogenic tissue. Segmental cystic change of the kidney has been reported as well. The primary entity to be differentiated is hydronephrosis.

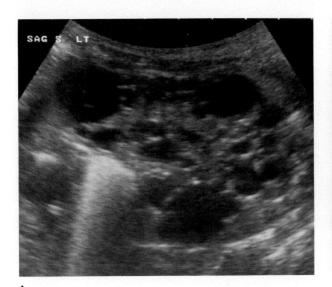

A

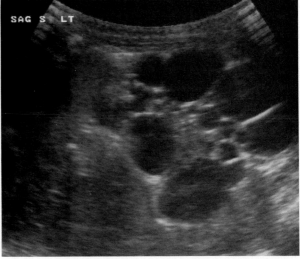

B

Figure 6.53
Multicystic dysplastic kidney: (A and B) Multiple, noninterconnecting cysts and highly echogenic stroma characterize this newborn's left kidney. The right kidney was sonographically normal.

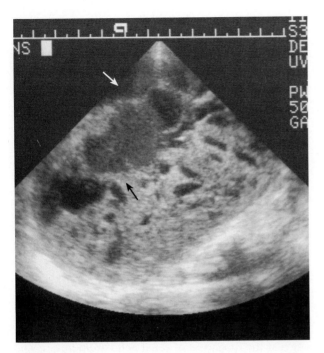

Figure 6.54
Wilms' tumor: Large cystic areas of necrosis (*arrow*) were present in this predominantly solid mass in the left kidney of an 8-year-old.

The natural history of multicystic dysplastic kidney (MCDK) is that the cysts may be identified in utero and may show change in size in utero, suggesting some residual glomerular filtration. At birth, the child may have a large, palpable mass or the MCDK may be undergoing regression. With time, the MCDK will regress and may calcify. Care must be taken to screen the contralateral kidney for abnormalities, since UPJ obstruction, agenesis, and dysplasia may occur in 30–50 percent of contralateral kidneys. An MCDK does not need to be removed unless there is doubt regarding the diagnosis or the large size of the mass causes respiratory or visceral compromise.

Wilms' Tumor (Figure 6.54)

Wilms' tumor in childhood may be a multiloculated cystic mass with thick septations and solid components. In many situations, Wilms' tumor is a homogeneous solid mass without significant cystic components.

Fetal Renal Hamartoma (Figure 6.55)

Fetal renal hamartomas, the most common cause of a solid renal mass in the newborn, are usually solid, but can undergo central necrosis and have large, central cystic spaces if they reach a large size.

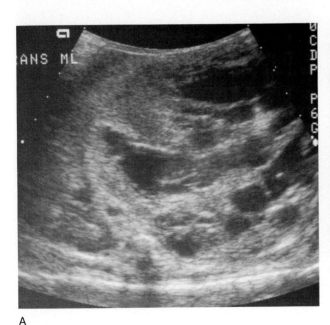

A

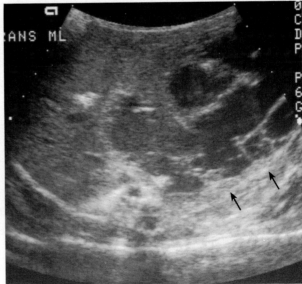

B

Figure 6.55
Fetal renal hamartoma: (A and B) A fetal renal hamartoma is the most common cause of a solid mass in the newborn. This neonate had multiple cystic spaces within the large, hamartomatous mass.

UNILATERAL SOLID-APPEARING HYPOECHOIC RENAL MASS

Malignant Neoplasm
    Renal Cell Carcinoma
    Renal Metastases
    Renal Lymphoma
    Transitional Cell Carcinoma
Benign Neoplasm
    Oncocytoma
    Angiomyolipoma
    Leiomyoma
Inflammatory Mass/Lobar Nephronia
Posttraumatic Hematoma
Column of Bertin/Dromedary Hump
Focal Hypertrophy Near Adjacent Scarring
Hemorrhagic Cyst

CHILDHOOD

Wilms' Tumor
Fetal Renal Hemartoma

When a hypoechoic, solid-appearing renal mass is demonstrated, renal cell carcinoma must be considered and excluded. In situations of renal trauma or severe renal infection, however, hypoechoic renal masses may reflect posttraumatic or inflammatory changes. Normal variants of the kidney such as a column of Bertin or hypertrophy adjacent to focal scarring may give the impression of a hypoechoic renal mass.

Malignant Neoplasm

Renal Cell Carcinoma (Figure 6.56) Renal cell carcinoma is responsible for more than 85 percent of primary renal neoplasms. This tumor is frequently a contour-deforming renal mass that is less echogenic than the normal renal parenchyma. Renal cell carcinoma has a propensity to invade the renal vein and grow toward the right atrium via the IVC. Recognition of a distended, thrombus-filled renal vein in the face of a hypoechoic renal mass should suggest the diagnosis of renal cell carcinoma. Evaluation to screen for retroperitoneal lymphadenopathy and other signs of distant metastatic disease must be attempted.

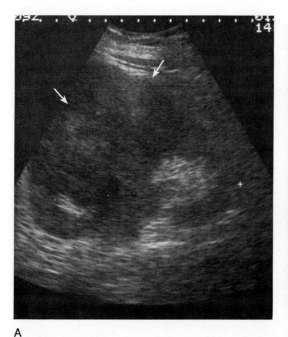
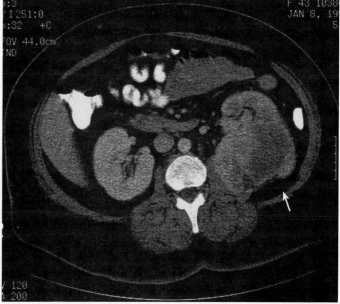

A   B

Figure 6.56
Renal cell carcinoma: (A) A large, hypoechoic renal mass emanated from the midportion of the left kidney in this patient with recurrent hematuria. (B) CT confirmed the extensive nature of the mass. Surgically removed, the renal mass histologically proved to be renal cell carcinoma with sarcomatous elements.

Renal Metastases   Metastatic disease of the kidney is twice as frequent as a primary neoplastic mass. Most metastatic renal masses are small and multiple, but sometimes a solitary lesion can grow to a size that makes it indistinguishable from a primary kidney tumor. Usually, a primary neoplastic site is known and the patient may have evidence of disseminated metastatic disease when renal metastases are identified. The possibility of a second primary tumor must be considered if the patient's original tumor is in remission.

Renal Lymphoma   Involvement of the kidneys is more common with non-Hodgkin lymphoma than with Hodgkin lymphoma. It is most commonly manifest as multiple, bilateral renal masses. A solitary, bulky renal mass occurs in approximately 7 percent of cases of lymphoma and may be indistinguishable from primary renal tumors. Small, multiple tumors may be present in as many as 45 percent of patients.

Sonographically, a solitary deposit of lymphoma appears as a hypoechoic mass relative to the surrounding renal parenchyma. The mass is often homogeneous and of such diminished echogenicity as to appear nearly cystic. Rapid changes in size of the lesion may occur with chemotherapy. Lymphoma has a tendency to involve the perinephric space. Usually, there is evidence of systemic disease when renal lymphoma is identified. Mediastinal, retroperitoneal, or pelvic adenopathy may be present.

Usually clinically silent, renal lymphoma may result in hematuria, flank pain, or mass effect.

Lymphoma of the kidneys, usually part of a systemic process, is often treated with chemotherapy.

Transitional Cell Carcinoma   Transitional cell carcinoma, which is responsible for 5–10 percent of all renal neoplasms, can mimic a renal cell carcinoma when it is extensive. Transitional cell carcinoma infrequently results in a focal, ball-like mass that is indistinguishable from renal cell carcinoma.

Benign Neoplasm

Oncocytoma   The renal oncocytoma, also known as a proximal tubular adenoma, represents 2 to 14 percent of renal tumors. With an average size of approximately 6 cm, the renal oncocytoma is difficult to distinguish from a renal cell carcinoma on imaging studies. The mass occurs most often in middle-aged and elderly patients. Renal oncocytomas are hypoechoic sonographically in more than 50 per-

cent of patients. Local resection or partial nephrectomy would be possible if the benign histology of the mass were known preoperatively.

Angiomyolipoma   Angiomyolipoma, or renal hamartoma, may be indistinguishable from other solid masses of the kidney, especially when there is little fat identifiable in the lesion. The presence of fat in the mass may allow its benign histology to be determined.

Leiomyoma   Leiomyomas of the kidney or other mesenchymal tumors are rare tumors that cannot be differentiated from renal cell carcinoma radiographically, only histologically. Sonographically, they are often hypoechoic, solid masses.

Inflammatory Mass/Lobar Nephronia (Figure 6.57)

Known by many different names, including acute bacterial nephritis, lobar nephronia is a sequel of pyelonephritis often occurring in patients with immunosuppression and chronic obstruction or catheterization. Organisms responsible for the infection include *Escherichia coli*, *Proteus*, and *Klebsiella*.

Sonographically, lobar nephronia is a hypoechoic mass that can efface the normal central sinus fat of the kidney. The clinical circumstances of the patient allow the appropriate diagnosis to be made since the patient will be febrile, with flank pain and septic parameters. Serial imaging is imperative to exclude renal abscess formation. Abscess formation requires drainage. Early and aggressive use of antibiotics may prevent significant renal loss or renal abscess formation.

Posttraumatic Hematoma (Figures 6.58–6.59)

Injury to the kidney may occur after blunt trauma or surgery or may be related to extracorporeal shock wave lithotripsy (ESWL) for renal calculi. Hematoma related to kidney injury can be indistinguishable from other hypoechoic lesions of the kidney. Sonographically, resolution of hematomas may take months, but such lesions should be followed with careful imaging.

Column of Bertin/Dromedary Hump (Figures 6.60–6.61)

A column of Bertin is renal cortex that is present in the mid-kidney, resulting from the fusion of the upper and lower poles of the kidney. It may deform

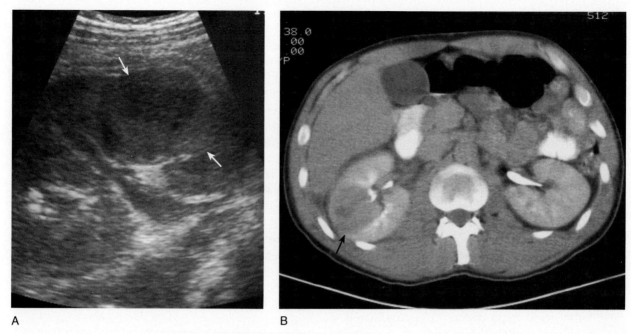

A   B

Figure 6.57
Severe renal infection (lobar nephronia): (A) A hypoechoic mass of the lower pole of the right kidney (*arrows*) effaced the central echo complex in this patient with severe pyelonephritis. (B) CT showed enlargement of the kidney with a heterogeneous contrast enhancement pattern. Follow-up sonography 3 weeks later after aggressive antibiotics showed resolution of the mass and reconstitution of the normal sonographic anatomy of the kidney.

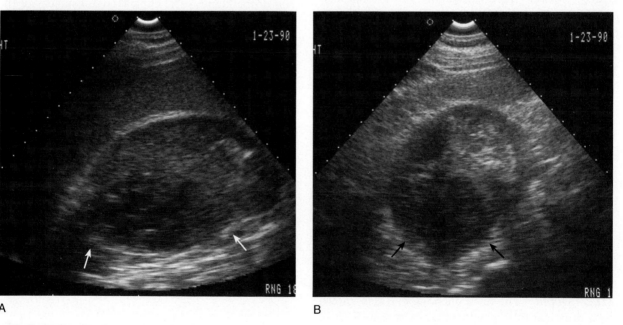

A   B

Figure 6.58
Posttraumatic appearance of the kidney: (A and B) After ESWL for renal calculi, the right kidney was noted to have a large, hypoechoic area of inhomogeneity (*arrows*) that became more cystic and septated on subsequent scans. Significant renal injury had occurred during lithotripsy.

230

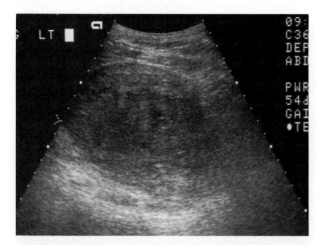

Figure 6.59
Renal injury during surgical revascularization: A large, inhomogeneous mass was seen in this elderly patient with severe left flank pain and hematuria. Renal injury during renal artery revascularization caused a large subcapsular hematoma that compressed the kidney.

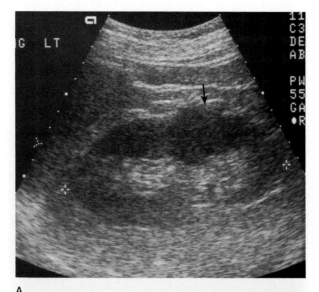

A

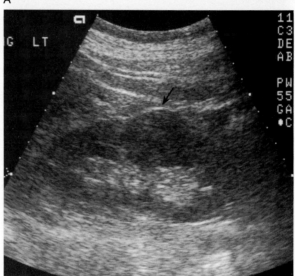

B

Figure 6.61
Dromedary hump: (A and B) A prominent dromedary hump on the left kidney (*arrow*) was proved to be normal renal parenchyma by CT.

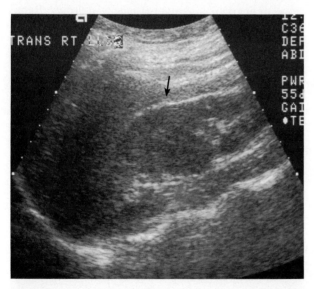

Figure 6.60
Column of Bertin: A prominent, hypoechoic column of Bertin in the mid-kidney (*arrow*) could have been misinterpreted as a renal mass. CT or nuclear medicine imaging can confirm normally functioning parenchyma.

Especially on the left, a dromedary hump, sometimes accentuated by the splenic impression, can be mistaken for a mass and may have to be studied by CT or nuclear medicine.

Focal Hypertrophy Near Adjacent Scarring (Figure 6.62)

In patients with focal cortical loss related to severe previous infection, the nearby normal tissue hypertrophies and can develop a masslike appearance. Recognition of the scarred kidney may suggest the

the central sinus fat. A prominent column of Bertin may be misinterpreted as a renal mass unless its typical midkidney location and lack of lateral contour deformity are noted. Nuclear medicine functional studies of the kidney or CT scanning can confirm that a suspected column of Bertin is normally functioning parenchyma rather than a renal mass.

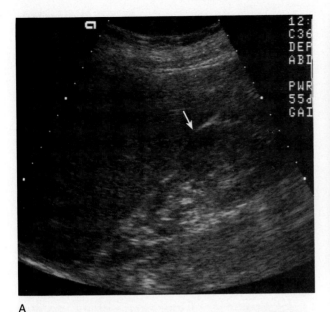

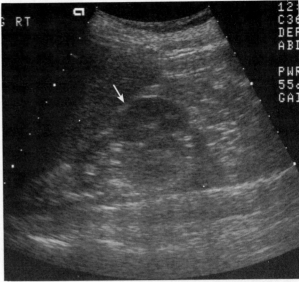

A

B

Figure 6.62

Severely postpyelonephritic kidney with scarring and adjacent hypertrophied parenchyma: (A and B) In this patient with a history of recurrent urinary tract infections, large scars were demonstrated. Nearby normal hypertrophied tissue in the mid-kidney (*arrows*) looked masslike sonographically.

diagnosis, which can be confirmed by nuclear medicine or CT imaging. This pseudotumor needs to be recognized as normal tissue within a scarred pyelonephritic kidney.

Hemorrhagic Cyst (Figure 6.63)

Cysts of the kidney are sometimes complicated by hemorrhage or infection. Sonographically, this results in low-level internal echoes that may make the lesion difficult to distinguish from a solid mass.

CHILDHOOD

Wilms' Tumor (Figures 6.64–6.65)

Wilms' tumor is quite rare in the neonate but is the most common solid renal mass in children aged 1 to 8 years. The peak age for the development of a Wilms' tumor is 2.5 to 3 years of age. Often presenting with a palpable abdominal mass, Wilms' tumor may be associated with hematuria and abdominal pain.

Sonographically, Wilms' tumor is a large, solid mass that arises from the kidney, often compressing

or distorting the residual renal parenchyma. The mass is often homogeneous unless it develops cystic areas of necrosis and hemorrhage as it grows. Renal vein and IVC invasion may be present in as many as 10 percent of patients with Wilms' tumor.

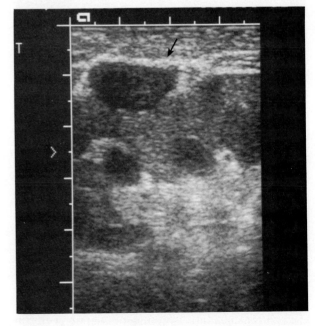

Figure 6.63

Hemorrhagic cyst: This hypoechoic mass was investigated intraoperatively because its etiology could not be clarified. Because it did not fulfill the criteria for a simple cyst, the mass was removed and proved to be a hemorrhagic cyst of the kidney. No tumor was present.

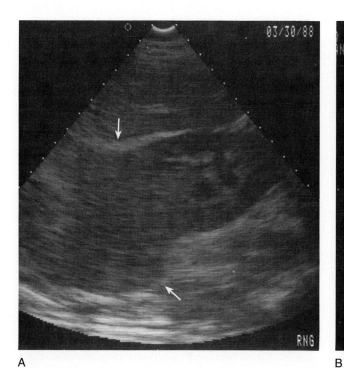

A

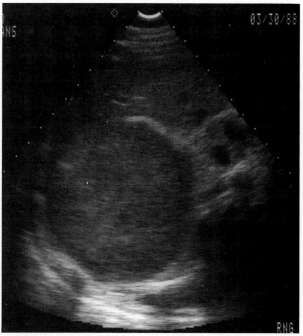

B

Figure 6.64

Wilms' tumor: (A and B) A large, hypoechoic solid mass (*arrows*) emanated from the upper pole of the right kidney in this 8-year-old with an abdominal mass.

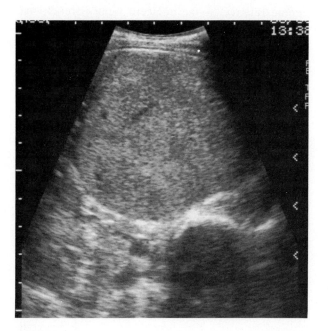

Figure 6.65

Wilms' tumor: A large, homogeneous mass with renal vein involvement was present in this patient with Wilms' tumor.

Fetal Renal Hemartoma

The most common cause of a solid renal mass in the newborn, the fetal renal hemartoma may be quite large. It has a variety of other names, including mesoblastic nephroma, benign congenital Wilms' tumor, or fetal mesenchymal tumor, all reflecting its benign histology and excellent prognosis after resection. The tumor has no malignant potential.

The mesoblastic nephroma may replace most of the kidney and cause a large abdominal mass. The mass is solid and, as it enlarges, it includes areas of cystic necrosis and hemorrhage within.

Emphasis Points

Severe infection of the kidney can result in abnormal enhancement and mass that are especially prominent on CT and can be misinterpreted as a neoplastic mass. Care must be made to consider severe infection in the differential diagnosis when appropriate because with antibiotic therapy the infection may resolve, making radical surgery unnecessary.

Severe trauma to the kidney can also result in hematoma formation that looks masslike. Renal hematomas may resolve with time if surgical intervention is not necessary acutely because of cardiovascular instability or hypertension.

A solid mass of the kidney that is not infectious or posttraumatic is often neoplastic. If extremely echogenic, the mass may contain fat and be a renal hamartoma; if renal vein invasion is present, the mass probably represents a renal cell carcinoma; if evidence of metastatic disease exists elsewhere (e.g., adenopathy, lung, or liver involvement), the kidney can be either a primary or secondary site of involvement. A solid renal mass without fat, renal vein involvement, or distant metastases must be considered an indeterminate, probably neoplastic mass. Such lesions are usually removed surgically.

Beware of normal variants (column of Bertin, dromedary hump, and hypertrophied parenchyma adjacent to scarring) that can mimic malignancies.

HYPERECHOIC RENAL MASS

Neoplasms
    Angiomyolipoma
    Renal Cell Carcinoma
    Metastatic Disease
    Other Tumors
Focal Renal Infarction

VARIANTS

Focal Scarring
Parenchymal Junctional Defect

A mass lesion of the kidney, which is of increased echogenicity relative to the normal renal cortical echogenicity, is often a neoplastic mass.

Neoplasms

Angiomyolipoma (Figures 6.66–6.67) Angiomyolipomas, or renal hamartomas, have variable proportions of fatty tissue, blood vessels, and soft tissue. Depending upon the composition of the angiomyolipoma, the sonographic appearance may vary. Fatty tissue is often highly echogenic, without associated shadowing, suggesting the sonographic diagnosis of fat. CT or MR will confirm the fatty nature of the tumor in such cases.

Although it has been widely held that the CT demonstration of fat within a renal mass confirms that the mass is an angiomyolipoma, two recent reports of renal cell carcinoma with intratumoral fat

and calcifications have shown that fat may be identified in malignant renal masses.

Angiomyolipomas generally occur in two patient populations: (1) the middle-aged or elderly woman and (2) young patients with tuberous sclerosis. In the adult female patient, the most common patient population affected, the lesion is usually solitary and may vary in size from a centimeter to many centimeters. Young patients with tuberous sclerosis will have many bilateral small tumors, which may be difficult to image sonographically.

Angiomyolipomas cause problems when they bleed. Because they are often highly vascular tumors, spontaneous bleeding from the mass may occur, resulting in a catastrophic retroperitoneal hemorrhage. Angiomyolipomas can also become a problem when they do not have visible fatty elements, making the mass indistinguishable from other solid renal masses, and therefore resulting in unnecessary surgical removal. An angiomyolipoma without fat may not be highly echogenic sonographically. Growing renal angiomyolipomas are often removed and angiomyolipomas may be removed when they reach a large size (6 cm or greater). Partial nephrectomy may be attempted if they are obviously benign.

Renal Cell Carcinoma (Figures 6.68–6.69)

Most large renal cell carcinomas are iso- or hypoechoic relative to the adjacent renal parenchyma. Markedly hyperechoic renal cell carcinomas are generally considered unusual, with a cited incidence of less than 5 percent. Recent studies have suggested that hyperechogenicity may be more common with small renal malignancies, with reports that of renal cell carcinomas less than 3 cm in diameter, 77 percent were hyperechoic relative to the rest of the kidney. Nearly a third of the small renal cell carcinomas (32 percent) were markedly hyperechoic, mimicking an angiomyolipoma. Only 2 percent of larger (>3 cm) tumors were so brightly echogenic. Diffuse calcification may contribute to the large mass hyperechogenicity.

Echogenicity characteristics may not allow a definitive sonographic diagnosis to be made, but evidence of renal vein invasion, local adenopathy, or distant metastases will aid in determining the correct diagnosis.

Metastatic Disease

Metastatic disease of the kidney is reported to be four times more common at autopsy than renal cell

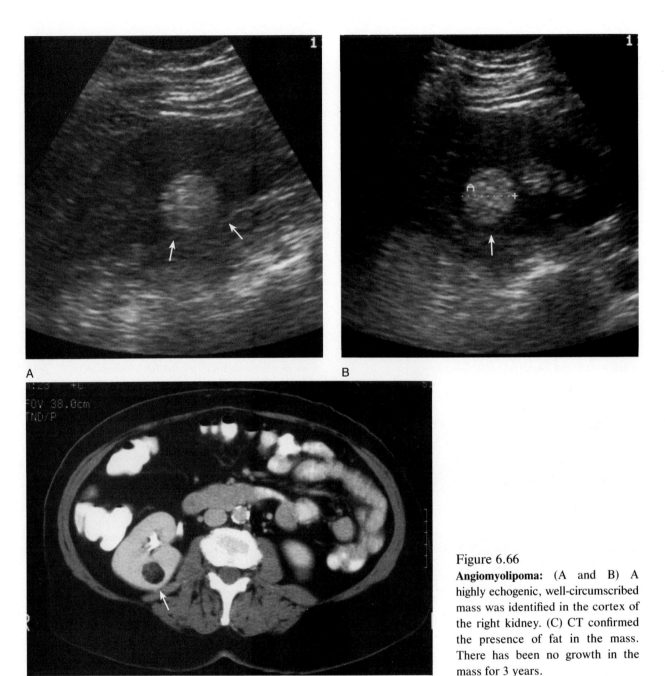

Figure 6.66
Angiomyolipoma: (A and B) A highly echogenic, well-circumscribed mass was identified in the cortex of the right kidney. (C) CT confirmed the presence of fat in the mass. There has been no growth in the mass for 3 years.

carcinoma. Usually small and often bilateral, metastatic masses may be hyperechoic, especially if the primary site is the colon.

Other Tumors (Figures 6.70–6.71)

Other neoplasms, including Wilms' tumor, oncocytoma, lipoma, and liposarcoma of the renal capsule, may be hyperechoic relative to the adjacent parenchyma. Fatty density (-100 to 0 Hounsfield units)

seen on CT may allow some distinctions to be suggested.

Focal Renal Infarction

Although most often hypoechoic and swollen, segmental infarction of the kidney may be seen as a hyperechoic, masslike region in the kidney. Such renal vascular insult occurs with trauma or embolic events. The patient's clinical course and evolving

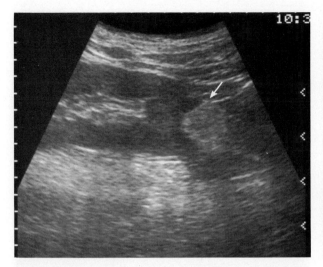

A

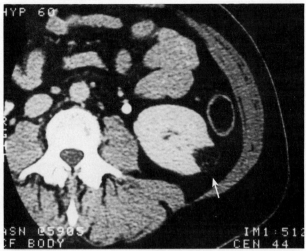

B

Figure 6.67

Angiomyolipoma: (A) A highly echogenic mass (*arrow*) was noted in the lower pole of the left kidney. (B) CT confirmed its fat density.

imaging features may allow differentiation from a neoplastic mass. CT scanning would demonstrate a wedge-like defect in contrast enhancement, with a cortical rim of enhancement.

VARIANTS

Focal Scarring

Focal scarring of the kidney secondary to previous insult may result in a hyperechoic band in the renal cortex. Blunting of the adjacent calyceal system will often accompany scarring and cortical loss.

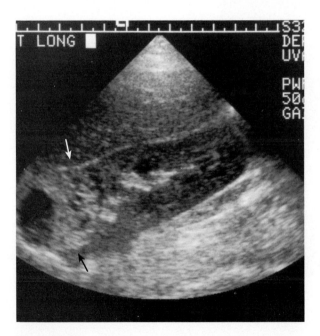

Figure 6.68

Renal cell carcinoma: A well-circumscribed hyperechoic mass was noted in the upper pole of the right kidney. Cystic necrosis was present within the mass. Renal cell carcinoma was removed at surgery.

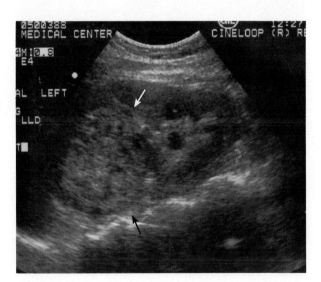

Figure 6.69

Renal cell carcinoma: A large, slightly hyperechoic renal mass was present in this patient and was removed by radical nephrectomy.

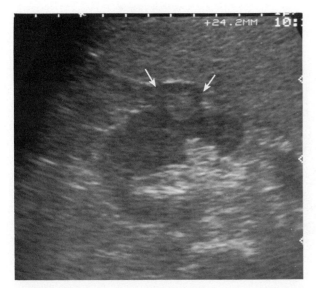

Figure 6.70
Renal oncocytoma: A small, slightly hyperchoic solid mass was detected incidentally during abdominal sonography.

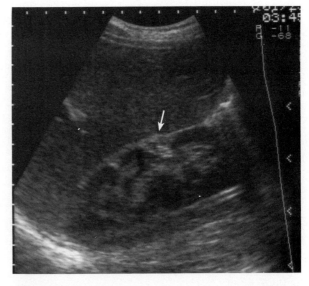

Figure 6.72
Parenchymal junctional defect: An echogenic linear region in the mid-kidney could be misinterpreted as a focal scar of the kidney. Its characteristic location and lack of cortical loss allow it to be correctly recognized.

Parenchymal Junctional Defect (Figure 6.72)

A hyperechoic cortical band frequently misinterpreted as a cortical scar is a parenchymal junctional defect that is the result of fusion of lobules of the kidney. The parenchymal defect is often in the upper third of the kidney and has no associated calyceal abnormality.

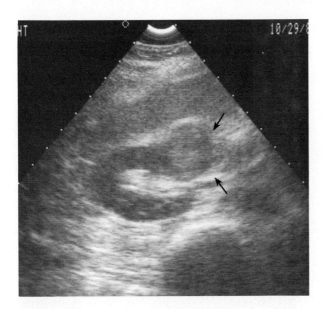

Figure 6.71
Renal oncocytoma: A well-defined mass hyperechoic relative to the rest of the renal parenchyma (*arrows*) was surgically removed by radical nephrectomy. Final pathology was consistent with oncocytoma.

Emphasis Point

Most often, highly echogenic masses in the kidney that contain fat are angiomyolipomas. Recent reports citing intratumoral fat in renal cell carcinomas suggest that, besides the recognition of fat, there are *other* findings, including abnormal soft tissue or suspicious calcifications, that give a clue that the mass needs resection.

CALCIFIED RENAL MASS

Renal Cell Carcinoma
Transitional Cell Carcinoma
Angiomyolipoma
Xanthogranulomatous Pyelonephritis
Infections
    Tuberculosis
    Extrapulmonary Pneumocystis Carinii
    Echinococcal Cyst

Complicated Renal Cyst
Autosomal Dominant Polycystic Kidney
    Disease
Multicystic Dysplastic Kidney
Milk of Calcium in Obstructed System or
    Diverticulum
Renal Artery Aneurysm
Subcapsular Hematoma

CHILDHOOD

Wilms' Tumor

VARIANT

Emphysematous pyelonephritis

Renal Cell Carcinoma (Figures 6.73–6.74)

Renal cell carcinoma has identifiable calcifications in 10 percent of patients. The calcifications are more often central, not in the periphery of the mass, although sometimes the capsule of the mass will calcify.

Transitional Cell Carcinoma (Figure 6.75)

Punctate calcifications may develop in a transitional cell carcinoma. A tumor should be suspected when calcifications are identified within a soft tissue mass. Otherwise, a calcified transitional cell carcinoma can be misinterpreted as a renal stone.

Angiomyolipoma

Renal hamartomas have calcifications in approximately 6 percent of cases.

Xanthogranulomatous Pyelonephritis (Figure 6.76)

Xanthogranulomatous pyelonephritis (XGP) is a rare inflammatory lesion of the kidney whose hallmark is chronic obstruction and nonfunction. More than 70 percent of patients have a large staghorn calculus that has caused obstruction of most of the kidney. Generally, there have been recurring urinary tract infections, usually secondary to infection with *Proteus mirabilis*. The patient is frequently female and diabetic. Clinically, the patient has weight loss, anemia, and a flank mass. The clinical impression may be of advanced neoplastic disease.

Sonographically, XGP is characterized by extensive stone material that casts shadow. An enlarged renal outline and complex renal mass may be recognized sometimes with involvement of the subcutaneous tissues of the flank or the underlying psoas muscle. Focal masslike areas that are abscesses or obstructed calyces can sometimes be distinguished. Radical nephrectomy and antibiotic administration are usually the therapies of choice.

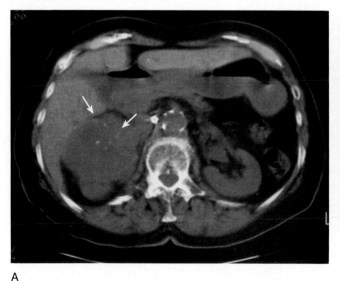

A

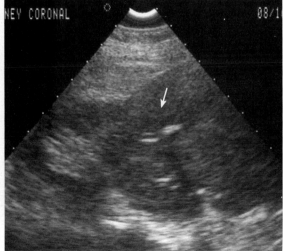

B

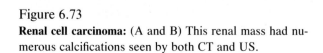

Figure 6.73
Renal cell carcinoma: (A and B) This renal mass had numerous calcifications seen by both CT and US.

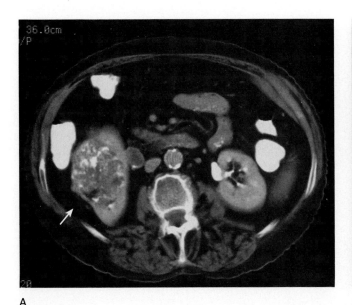

A

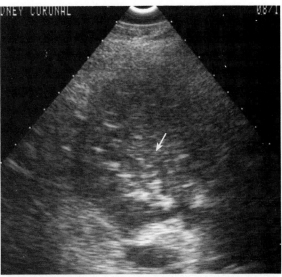

B

Figure 6.74

Renal cell carcinoma: CT showed a calcified renal mass. The mass was difficult to delineate by sonography since it merged with the surrounding echogenic retroperitoneum.

Infections

Infectious etiologies that can result in calcified renal lesions include tuberculosis, extrapulmonary pneumocystis carinii infection, and echinococcal disease.

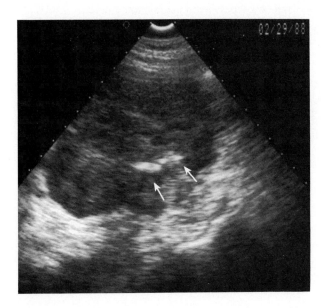

Figure 6.75

Transitional cell carcinoma: Within this infiltrative mass which conforms to the reniform shape of the kidney, echogenic foci (calcifications) were identified.

Tuberculosis Tuberculous infection of the kidney is typically through hematogenous spread in the patient with active pulmonary disease. Tuberculosis may cause the formation of focal, hypoechoic lesions acutely, followed by calcification and autonephrectomy. The resulting "putty kidney" is a densely calcified mass, irreversibly destroyed. Calcifications are seen in 25 to 50 percent of cases.

Sonographically, the calcified kidney casts an amorphous shadow from the renal fossa. Plain x-rays of the kidney show extensive calcific involvement.

Extrapulmonary Pneumocystis Carinii Pulmonary pneumocystis is the most commonly encountered opportunistic infection in AIDS patients, affecting 50–75 percent at some time in their illness. Pneumocystis pneumonia is responsible for high morbidity and mortality. Many AIDS patients are placed on aerosolized pentamidine to protect them prophylactically from pneumocystitis pneumonia. Although it has a protective effect in the lungs, aerosolized pentamidine does not provide high enough blood levels to prevent extrapulmonary pneumocystis.

The liver, spleen, and kidneys may be involved with extrapulmonary pneumocystis. Noncalcified foci may be seen in the initial stages. As the disease progresses, the lesions enlarge and calcify. Other opportunistic infections such as cytomegalovirus or mycobacterial infections may result in multiple calcific cortical foci in the kidneys.

Echinococcal Cyst The kidneys are involved in 3 percent of patients with echinococcal disease. Fifty percent of echinococcal lesions calcify.

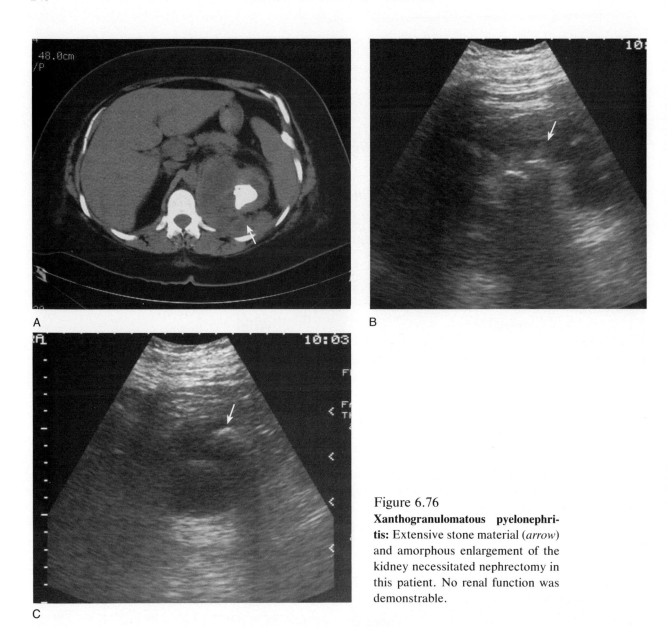

Figure 6.76
Xanthogranulomatous pyelonephritis: Extensive stone material (*arrow*) and amorphous enlargement of the kidney necessitated nephrectomy in this patient. No renal function was demonstrable.

Complicated Renal Cyst

Simple renal cysts, which are very common in patients over the age of 50 years, calcify in approximately 1 percent of cases. Calcifications of the wall of the cyst are usually related to previous hemorrhage or infection.

Autosomal Dominant Polycystic Kidney Disease (Figure 6.77)

Calcifications frequently complicate the numerous cysts of autosomal dominant polycystic kidney disease (ADPCKD).

Multicystic Dysplastic Kidney (Figure 6.78)

The regressed multicystic dysplastic kidney in the adult may calcify diffusely leading to extensive shadowing from the renal fossa.

Milk of Calcium in Obstructed System or Diverticulum

Milk of calcium (calcium in solution) may be identified in calyceal diverticula or within an obstructed calyx. A layer of echogenic material that shadows

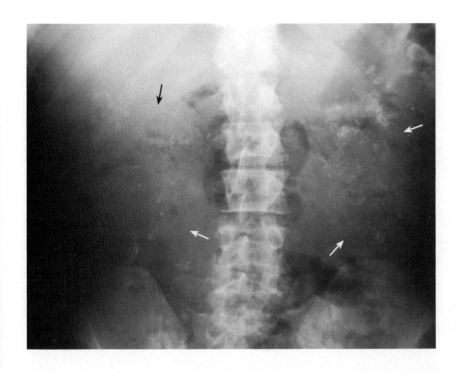

Figure 6.77
Autosomal dominant polycystic kidney disease: Numerous calcifications complicate the cysts of ADPCKD.

may move about within an obstructed system as a patient changes positioning.

Renal Artery Aneurysm

Curvilinear or rim calcification will form on the periphery of a renal artery aneurysm. Usually occurring in the renal hilum, a renal artery aneurysm will

sometimes have arterial flow in the lesion when Doppler analysis is undertaken.

Subcapsular Hematoma (Figures 6.78–6.79)

A subcapsular hematoma secondary to either trauma, underlying renal abnormality (vasculitis or mass), or anticoagulation therapy may calcify.

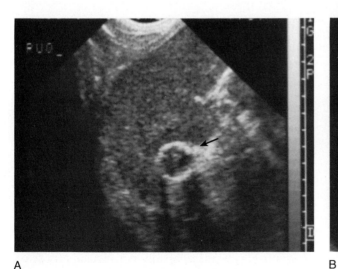

A

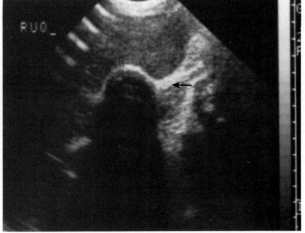

B

Figure 6.78
Multicystic dysplastic kidney: The curvilinear calcification (*arrow*) of this regressed dysplastic kidney was clearly visible as an echogenic mass with pronounced shadowing. Plain films confirmed the findings.

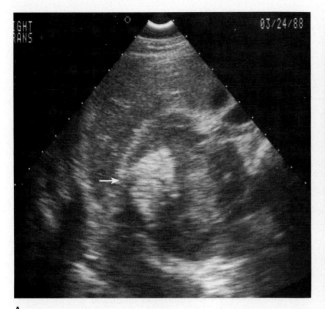

A

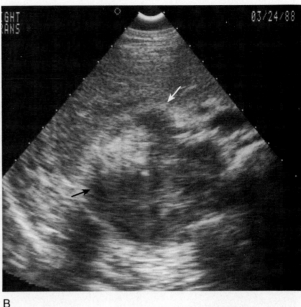

B

Figure 6.79

Calcified hematoma: A subcapsular hematoma with high-level echoes obscured visualization of the right kidney in this patient with a distant history of substantial trauma and renal injury.

CHILDHOOD

Wilms' Tumor

Wilms' tumor has calcifications in approximately 15 percent of patients.

VARIANT

Emphysematous Pyelonephritis

Emphysematous pyelonephritis is a life-threatening infection of the kidney that usually affects diabetic patients. In this situation, air is present within the parenchyma of the kidney. Sonographically, the air may be difficult to differentiate from calcifications. Air is highly echogenic with "shimmering" or "dirty" shadowing, resulting in an amorphous image. Plain films or CT may be helpful in recognizing the diagnosis. Nephrectomy may be necessary for adequate therapy.

BILATERAL RENAL CYSTS

Simple Renal Cysts
Acquired Renal Cystic Disease
Autosomal Dominant Polycystic Kidney
    Disease

Tuberous Sclerosis
Von Hippel–Lindau Disease

VARIANTS

Bilateral Multicystic Dysplastic Kidneys (in
    Utero)
Severe Bilateral Hydronephrosis

Usually unilocular, renal cysts can occur in any portion of the kidney and may be bilateral.

Simple Renal Cysts (Figure 6.80)

Bilateral renal cysts are of variable size, ranging from subcentimeter to many centimeters in size. Simple, bilateral renal cysts should have no impact on renal function. The normal renal parenchyma is often displaced by the presence of the cyst. The volume of functioning renal tissue is not more than expected, although the kidney may be longer than usual, especially if the cyst is incorporated into the dimensions of the kidney.

Acquired Renal Cystic Disease (Figures 6.81–6.82)

Patients in chronic renal failure, especially those on hemodialysis, may develop cysts on their small, failed kidneys. Such acquired renal cysts of uremia or dialysis-related renal cysts are usually multiple, of small size, and on small, echogenic end-stage kidneys. The kidneys may be so echogenic, blending in with the surrounding retroperitoneum, that

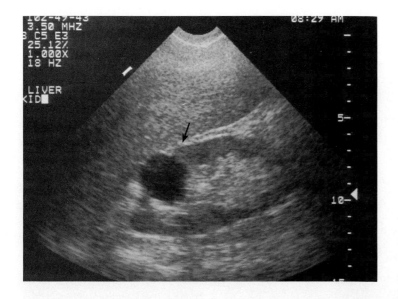

Figure 6.80
Simple renal cysts: Bilateral cysts were present in this patient with normal renal size and function.

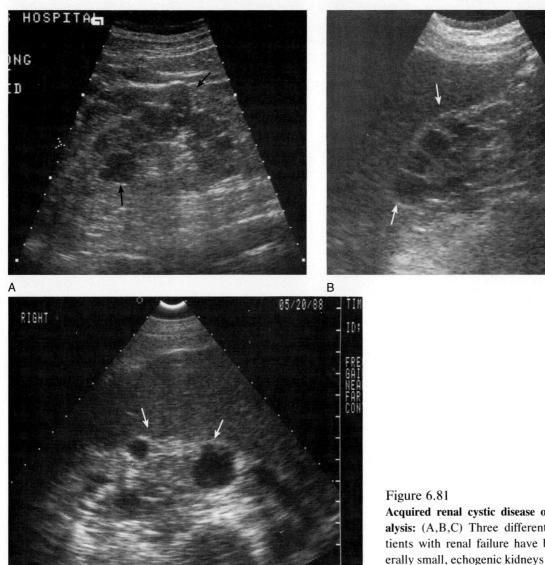

A

B

C

Figure 6.81
Acquired renal cystic disease of dialysis: (A,B,C) Three different patients with renal failure have bilaterally small, echogenic kidneys with cysts (*arrows*) scattered throughout.

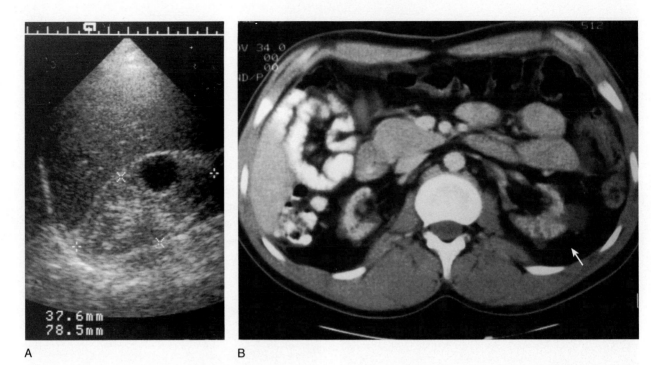

A   B

Figure 6.82
Acquired renal cystic disease of dialysis: (A) Bilaterally small, echogenic kidneys with cysts were seen in this patient who had been on dialysis for 5 years. (B) Note the small size and poor function on CT.

the cysts allow identification of the kidneys, which are otherwise very difficult to visualize. Patients with acquired renal cystic disease related to dialysis can be differentiated from patients with simple bilateral renal cysts by their renal failure and, often, renal size. Patients with autosomal dominant polycystic kidney disease (ADPCKD) are easily differentiated from patients with dialysis-related cystic renal disease because the kidneys of ADPCKD are usually quite large, often extending well into the pelvis of the patient.

Autosomal Dominant Polycystic Kidney Disease (Figures 6.83–6.85)

Autosomal dominant polycystic kidney disease is an inherited renal abnormality that is often not discovered until early or middle adulthood, when hypertension, proteinuria, and hematuria may develop. Renal failure often ensues in middle life, requiring chronic dialysis or transplantation. Associated with ADPCKD is an increased risk of subarachnoid hemorrhage from cerebral aneurysms.

Sonographically, the kidneys of patients with ADPCKD are large with cortical cysts of varying size. The cysts often have associated calcifications and may show evidence of complications, such as hemorrhage or infection. Often there is a strong family history of renal disease in patients with this disorder, but screening of parents, siblings, and children may be necessary if the diagnosis is a new one.

Tuberous Sclerosis (Figure 6.86)

Approximately 10 percent of patients with tuberous sclerosis, also transmitted in an autosomal dominant inheritance pattern, have enlarged kidneys with multiple bilateral renal cysts. Such a presentation may be indistinguishable sonographically from ADPCKD, which can result in an incorrect diagnosis. Recognition of stigmata that accompany tuberous sclerosis, such as mental retardation, seizures, sebaceous abnormalities of the face, and sclerotic bone disease, may allow the differentiation between the two conditions to be made.

Von Hippel–Lindau Disease

Other inherited conditions, mainly von Hippel–Lindau disease, have a propensity for the development of bilateral renal masses, including renal cysts.

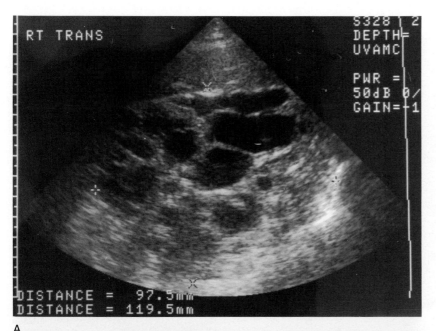

A

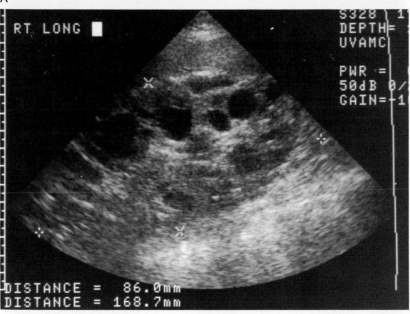

B

Figure 6.83

Autosomal dominant polycystic kidney disease: This 55-year-old with renal failure of 10 years duration had bilaterally large kidneys replaced by cysts of varying sizes. The entire kidneys could not be included because of their size.

VARIANTS

Bilateral Multicystic Dysplastic Kidneys (Figures 6.87–6.88)

Bilateral multicystic dysplastic kidneys may look similar to ADPCK but will not be seen in living pediatric or adult patients. Bilateral multicystic dysplastic kidneys will only be seen in utero as this embryologic developmental problem is incompatible with prolonged extrauterine life. The fetus with bilateral multicystic dysplastic kidneys will be delivered as a stillborn or will die shortly after delivery from pulmonary insufficiency.

In a child with a unilateral multicystic dysplastic kidney, the presence of a nonlethal but obstructive abnormality of the contralateral kidney can result in bilateral cystic renal masses. Ureteropelvic junction (UPJ) obstruction may be a cause of obstruction seen in conjunction with a contralateral multicystic dysplastic kidney. It is imperative that the function of the obstructed but functioning contralateral kidney be maintained, as it is sustaining

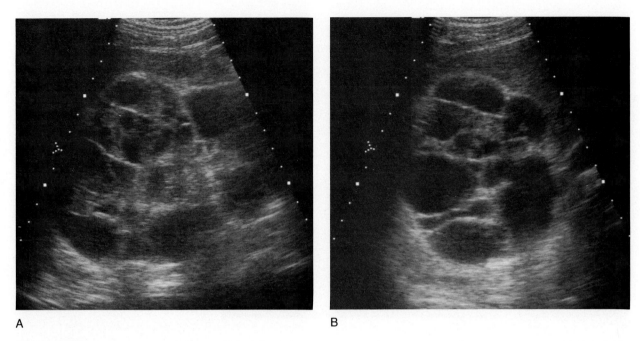

A

B

Figure 6.84
Autosomal dominal polycystic kidneys: (A and B) The kidneys on both sides extended from the upper abdomen into the pelvis. Innumerable cysts, some of which were complicated, replaced the normal cortex.

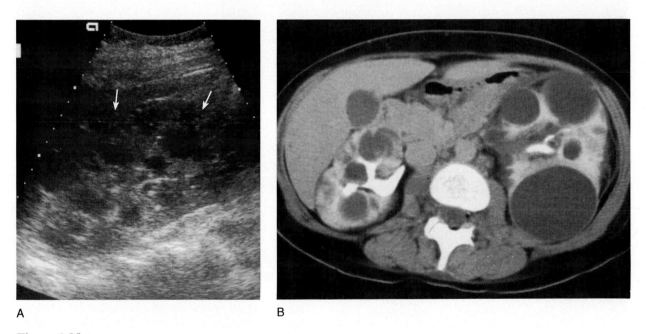

A

B

Figure 6.85
Autosomal dominant polycystic kidneys: (A) In this young patient, the kidneys were enlarged, each measuring at least 18 cm in length with multiple cysts (*arrows*) seen best with a high-frequency transducer. (B) CT confirmed the multiple bilateral cysts.

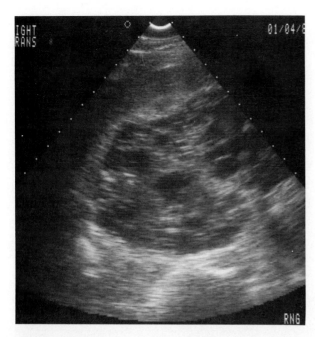

Figure 6.86
Tuberous sclerosis: In this young man with mental retardation, seizures, and a family history of tuberous sclerosis, the sonographic appearance of the kidneys was identical to ADPCKD.

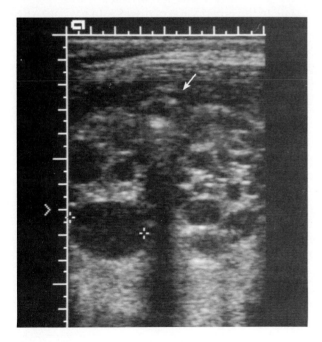

Figure 6.87
Bilateral multiple dysplastic kidneys: Prenatal sonogram showed enlarged multicystic kidneys bilaterally. There was no amniotic fluid and no fluid in the bladder. The infant died at delivery. Arrow is on fetal spine. Note that the renal regions are filled with cysts.

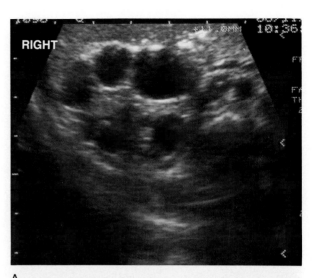

A

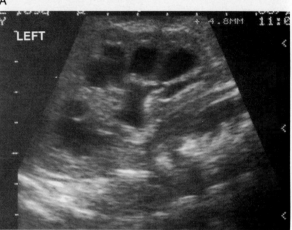

B

Figure 6.88
Right multicystic dysplastic kidney (MCDK) and left UPJ obstruction: (A) Multiple cysts that do not interconnect were seen on the right (MCDK), and (B) moderate hydronephrosis was present on the left in this newborn.

life. In the normal newborn, one must be careful to recognize the normal hypoechoic medullary pyramids and not to misinterpret them as hydronephrotic calyces.

Severe Bilateral Hydronephrosis (Figure 6.89)

Severe bilateral hydronephrosis can sometimes be misinterpreted as bilateral renal cystic disease. Functional studies of the kidneys allowing opacification of the collecting system will permit the distinction to be made.

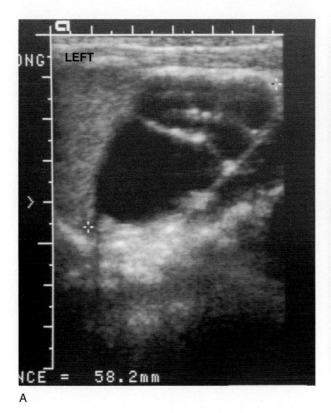

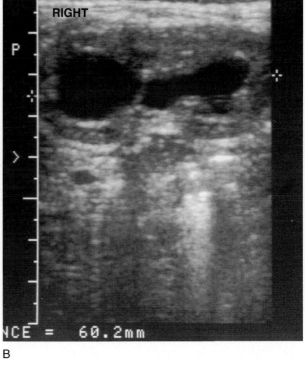

A

B

Figure 6.89
Severe bilateral hydronephrosis: Multiple cystic areas were identifiable on both kidneys in this youngster with severe bilateral hydronephrosis related to posterior urethral values.

volvement of the kidneys is often seen with relapse or late in the progression of disease. In patients with AIDS, lymphoma of the kidneys may be present without significant nodal disease.

BILATERAL SOLID RENAL MASSES

Lymphoma
Bilateral Renal Cell Carcinoma
Metastases

CHILDHOOD

Tuberous Sclerosis
Nephroblastomatosis/Wilms' Tumor

Etiologies for bilateral solid renal masses are usually fairly limited.

Lymphoma (Figures 6.90–6.91)

Lymphoma, usually non-Hodgkin in type, is likely when bilateral hypoechoic renal masses are identified. Multiple bilateral hypoechoic renal masses are the most common way in which lymphoma affects the kidneys, occurring in 45 percent of patients. Usually, the kidneys are not the primary site of involvement with lymphoma, and lymphomatous in-

Bilateral Renal Cell Carcinoma (Figure 6.92)

Bilateral solid renal masses may represent bilateral renal cell carcinoma, especially in the young patient with von Hippel–Lindau disease. Such patients may be considered for partial nephrectomies to maintain renal function, rather than being rendered anephric with bilateral radical nephrectomy. Other stigmata of von Hippel–Lindau disease, such as cerebellar hemangioblastoma or pancreatic cysts, may be seen. Genetic evaluation and typing may be indicated.

Metastases

Metastatic disease of the kidneys is quite commonly seen at autopsy, although infrequently recognized by imaging. CT is more sensitive at identifying metastatic disease of the kidneys than is ultrasound. Primary carcinomas of the lung, breast, and melanoma may spread to the kidney, yielding bilateral solid renal masses.

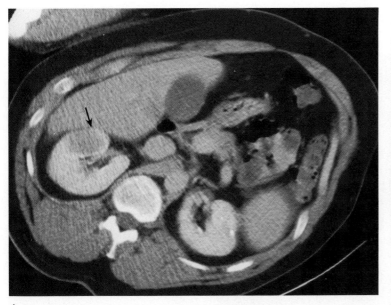

A

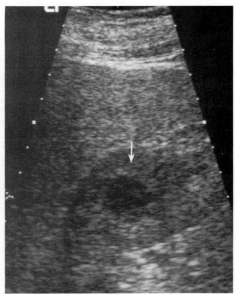

B

Figure 6.90

Non-Hodgkin lymphoma involving kidneys: (A) In this young man with extensive mediastinal adenopathy resulting in tracheal compromise, several low-density masses were identifiable in both kidneys (only one shown here). (B) Ultrasound demonstrated hypoechoic, nearly cystic-appearing lesions bilaterally. Biopsy of the neck masses was consistent with aggressive non-Hodgkin lymphoma. Follow-up scans after chemotherapy showed resolution of the renal masses.

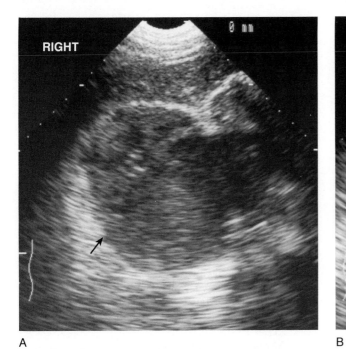

A

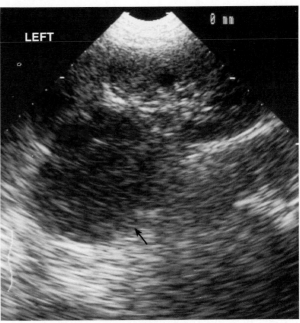

B

Figure 6.91

Non-Hodgkin lymphoma: Large, bilateral hypoechoic renal masses were discovered in this patient with relapsing non-Hodgkin lymphoma. (A) Right. (B) Left.

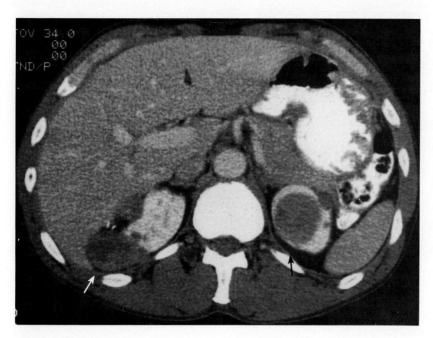

Figure 6.92
Bilateral renal cell carcinoma: Bilateral solid renal masses (*arrows*) were removed in this young woman with hematuria. Both masses were hypoechoic sonographically.

The kidneys may be normal sized to enlarged, with lobulated borders. With diffuse nephroblastomatosis, discrete nodules may be difficult to distinguish. CT will demonstrate the small subcapsular nodules more reliably than sonography.

CHILDHOOD

Tuberous Sclerosis

Tuberous sclerosis, an inherited condition, frequently is associated with renal abnormalities. A common renal finding is recognition of multiple bilateral echogenic renal masses, angiomyolipomas. The relative makeup of the mass of vascular, muscular, and lipomatous elements will determine its sonographic appearance. If fatty elements are present, the mass will be highly echogenic sonographically. Usually, the angiomyolipomas associated with tuberous sclerosis are small and multiple, usually smaller than the solitary angiomyolipomas seen in middle-aged or elderly women.

Nephroblastomatosis/Wilms' Tumor

Nephroblastomatosis is a congenital abnormality in which nests of primitive metanephric blastema are present in both kidneys. Focal masses may be present in a subcapsular position in both kidneys. Thought to be a precursor of Wilms' tumor, nephroblastomatosis is present in 12–33 percent of patients with Wilms' or conditions associated with Wilms'. Bilateral Wilms' tumors have been estimated to occur in 3 to 13 percent of patients.

Emphasis Points

Fine-needle aspiration may be helpful in the patient with bilateral renal masses. The diagnosis of lymphoma generally makes surgery unnecessary since the patient will be treated with chemotherapy. Sometimes, however, patients have other foci of disease that may be more amenable to biopsy.

PRESERVATION OF RENIFORM SHAPE WITH ABNORMAL ENHANCEMENT ON CT

Neoplasms
    Transitional Cell Carcinoma
    Metastatic Disease of the Kidney
    Renal Lymphoma
Renal Infection
Acute Vascular Compromise

Significant abnormality—vascular, neoplastic, or infectious—may be present even when the expected reniform shape of the kidney and relatively normal sonographic echogenicity are maintained.

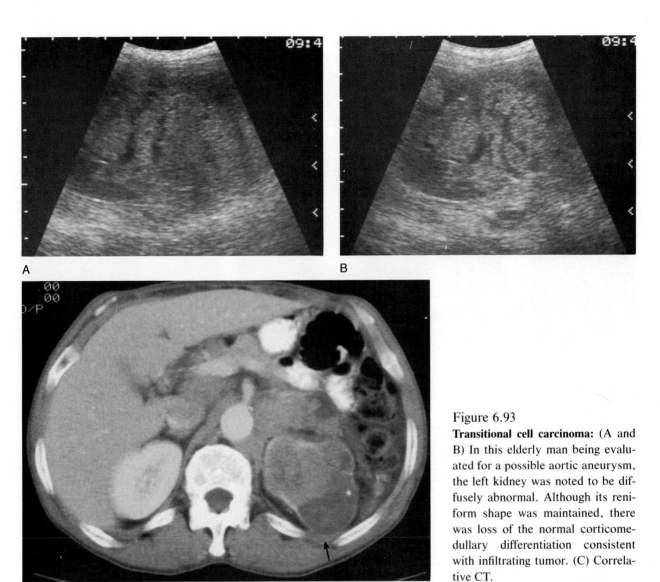

A

B

C

Figure 6.93
Transitional cell carcinoma: (A and B) In this elderly man being evaluated for a possible aortic aneurysm, the left kidney was noted to be diffusely abnormal. Although its reniform shape was maintained, there was loss of the normal corticomedullary differentiation consistent with infiltrating tumor. (C) Correlative CT.

Sometimes normal echogenicity will be lost even though the reniform shape is maintained. CT scanning may show the maintenance of reniform shape, with abnormal contrast enhancement.

Neoplasms

Most renal cell carcinomas affect the kidney by the development of a well-defined, encapsulated mass that causes a contour deformity of the kidney and has some amputation or mass effect on the collecting system. A less commonly encountered pattern of growth for renal neoplasm involves the use of the structure of the kidney as a framework for the proliferation of neoplastic cells. This infiltrative pattern of growth of renal neoplasms enlarges the kidney, preserving its reniform shape. It is different from the more commonly seen focal renal mass. There

may be obliteration of the normal central renal sinus complex.

Transitional Cell Carcinoma (Figures 6.93–6.95) Usually, transitional cell carcinoma is small at the time of discovery, often making the tumor unidentifiable on ultrasound evaluation. When transitional cell carcinoma enlarges, invading adjacent structures and obliterating normal kidney, it infiltrates the normal kidney and destroys the normal corticomedullary differentiation. With extensive transitional cell tumor, the reniform shape of the kidney may be maintained, although normal central collecting system structures are obliterated. The maintenance of renal shape with infiltrative tumor is highly characteristic of a large transitional cell carcinoma.

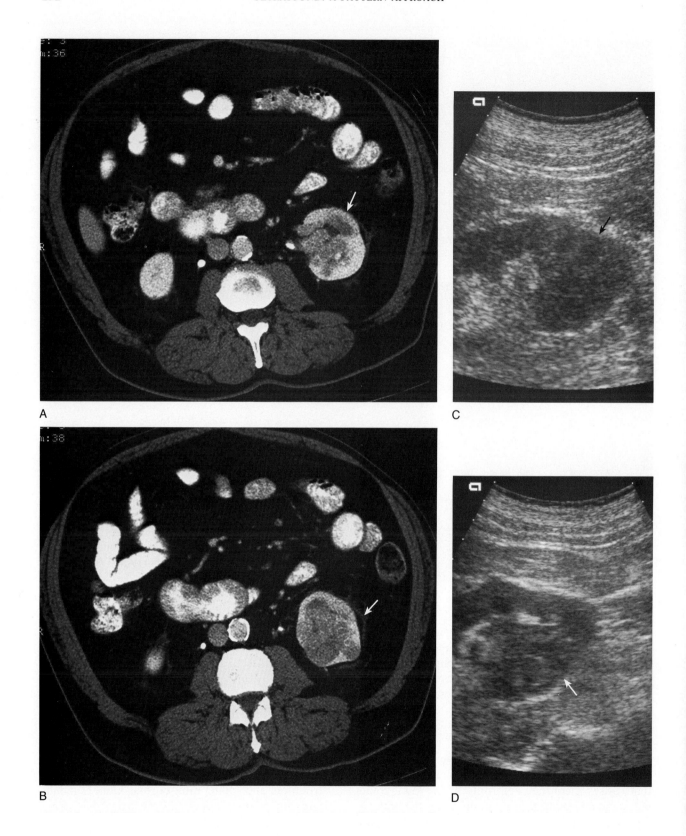

A

B

C

D

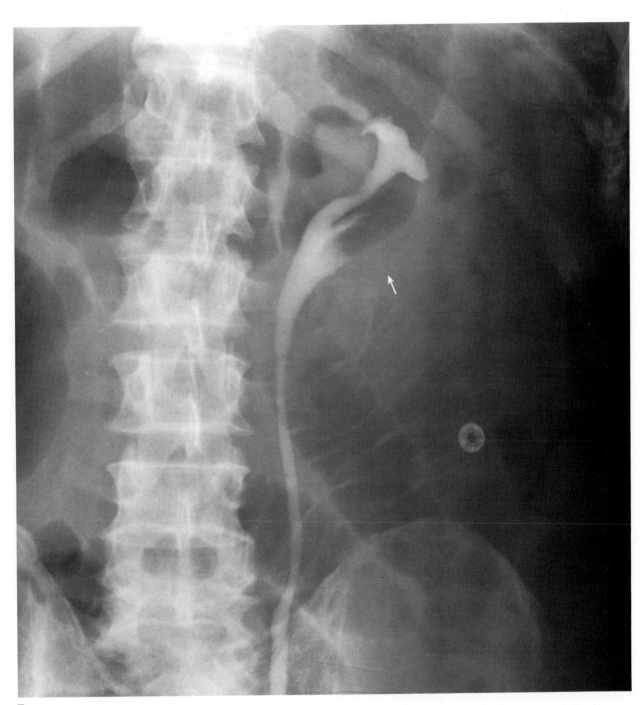

E

Figure 6.94

Transitional cell carcinoma: In this patient with gross hematuria, sonography was interpreted as normal at an outside institution. (A and B) CT showed a mass of the renal pelvis infiltrating the lower pole of the kidney. (C and D) Repeat sonography (with knowledge of the CT results) showed subtle gray-scale abnormalities at the site of the known tumor. The central echo complex in the lower pole of the kidney has been obliterated (*arrows*). (E) Retrograde pyelogram showed no filling of the lower pole.

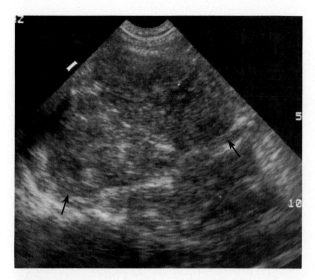

Figure 6.95
Transitional cell carcinoma: Although maintaining its reniform shape, this kidney was diffusely replaced by an extensive transitional cell carcinoma.

A large infiltrating transitional cell carcinoma may have features that make it indistinguishable from renal cell carcinoma, including invasion of the renal vein and local adenopathy. Evidence of distant disease, such as lung or liver lesions, may also be identified in either process.

Metastatic Disease of the Kidney (Figures 6.96–6.97) Metastatic disease of the kidney may originate from carcinoma of the lung, breast, colon, or stomach. Malignant melanoma may infiltrate the kidney or perinephric space. Metastatic disease is often manifest by bilateral foci of disease, often of similar echogenicity to that of the normal noninfiltrated cortex. Because metastatic infiltrative masses may not cause obvious contour-deforming masses, the only abnormality may be related to contrast enhancement on CT. Abnormalities of enhancement will be easily seen by CT and may not be recognized as an echotexture disturbance at sonography. In patients with a history of malignancy, renal metastases greatly outnumber renal cell carcinoma. In most cases, metastatic involvement of the kidneys occurs when there is evidence of widespread metastatic disease elsewhere in the body. Many renal metastases are clinically silent and detected only at autopsy.

Renal Lymphoma Renal lymphoma may diffusely infiltrate the kidney, although multiple, bilateral masses are seen more often.

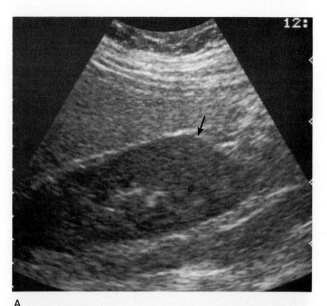

A

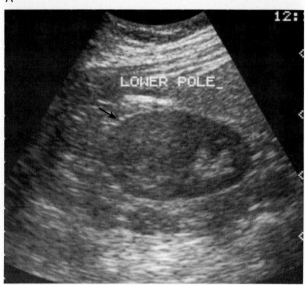

B

Figure 6.96
Metastatic squamous cell carcinoma: In this patient with primary lung carcinoma, CT scan for staging showed multiple renal metastases as hypodense masses. Sonography (A and B) showed subtle sonographic abnormalities in the same areas (*arrows*). Without prior knowledge of the CT findings, the sonographic abnormalities could have been overlooked. The patient had no clinical symptoms of renal metastases.

Although solid renal mass biopsy is not generally performed, in some situations percutaneous biopsy may be necessary and can be performed to differentiate renal cell carcinoma, transitional cell carcinoma, lymphoma, or metastatic disease.

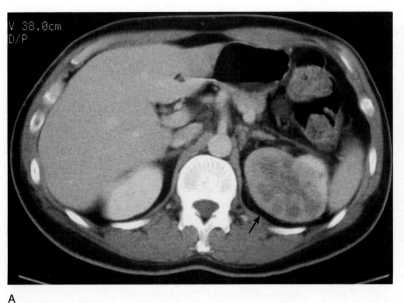

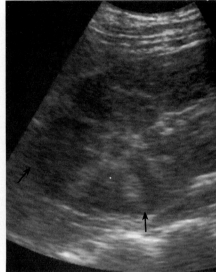

A   B

Figure 6.97

Metastatic germ cell malignancy: (A) This young man with malignant germ cell tumor of the mediastinum developed replacement of the upper pole of the left kidney by metastatic tumor. CT showed enlargement and hypodensity in the upper pole. (B) Subtle enlargement and echogenicity abnormality were identified sonographically.

Renal Infection (Figure 6.98)

Severe infection of the kidney may cause significant edema and infiltration of the kidney with inflammatory cells. Such an infection, variably called bacterial nephritis or lobar nephronia, may cause obliteration of normal corticomedullary differentiation and may, in fact, compress the fat of the central echo complex. Aggressive management of the patient's infection with intravenous antibiotics and hospitalization may prevent renal necrosis, abscess formation, and overwhelming sepsis. The architecture and sonographic appearance of the kidney may return to normal with aggressive therapy. Follow-up imaging to assure that renal abscess formation has not occurred is necessary. With severe infection of the kidney, a marked discrepancy between the nearly normal appearance by ultrasound and the abnormal enhancement at CT may be observed.

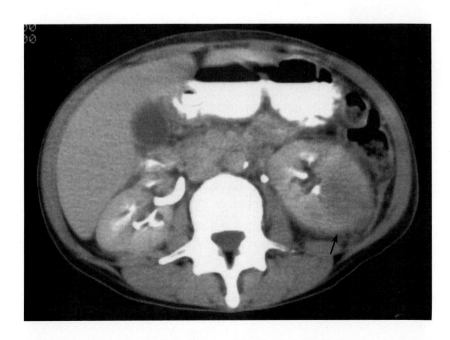

Figure 6.98

Severe pyelonephritis: Although CT showed dramatic enhancement abnormalities interpreted as a renal mass, sonography was nearly normal in this patient with severe pyelonephritis.

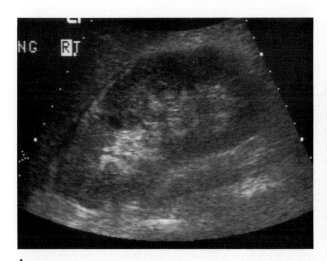

A

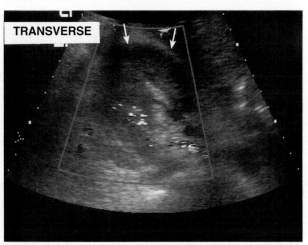

B

Figure 6.99

Acute renal artery avulsion: This young man suffered injury to the renal artery in an automobile accident. CT showed large areas of hypoperfusion to the kidney. (A) The gray-scale images of the kidney were normal. (B [Plate 14]) Color Doppler analysis of the kidney allowed recognition that certain areas of the kidney were not perfused (*arrows*).

Acute Vascular Compromise (Figures 6.99–6.101)

Acute renal artery injury or thrombosis or embolic events may result in a kidney that maintains its reniform shape and relatively normal corticomedullary differentiation. Although swelling may be present acutely, rapid atrophy may be witnessed on subsequent imaging studies. Sometimes the architecture of the compromised kidney is so well maintained that the kidney looks sonographically unremarkable on gray-scale images. Only when Doppler evaluation of the vasculature or CT scanning with contrast is performed will the lack of perfusion be obvious.

In renal vein thrombosis not related to renal neoplasia, the medullary pyramids may become echogenic secondary to venous infarction and hemorrhage.

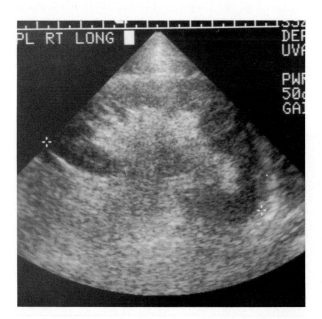

Figure 6.100

Acute renal artery thrombosis: Occlusion of the renal artery was present in this young child after kidney transplantation. Although gray-scale images are normal, no arterial flow was recognizable by either color Doppler or spectral analysis.

Emphasis Points

Infiltration of the kidney by neoplasm is sometimes difficult to identify by ultrasound, especially if there is no contour-deforming mass. If the entire kidney is involved, there will usually be enough echotexture disruption to lead to neoplasm detection. The abnormality will often be more obvious on CT.

Transitional cell carcinoma should be considered when an infiltrative lesion is encountered.

Acute arterial thrombosis may result in normal gray-scale images of the kidney. Attempts

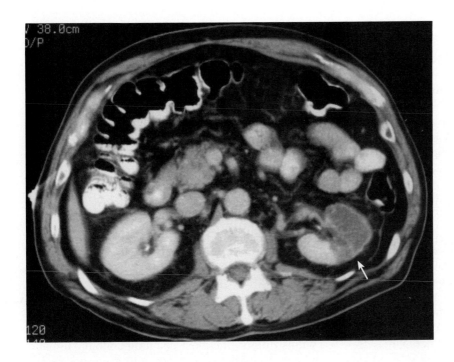

Figure 6.101
Segmental embolic infarction of the kidney: This patient, with intermittent atrial fibrillation, suffered severe left flank pain and hematuria. Although ultrasound images of the left kidney were considered normal, CT showed a large area of infarction of the organ.

at spectral analysis or color flow Doppler may allow the vascular insult to be detected.

Severe pyelonephritis, which is often normal appearing at ultrasound, may have dramatic contrast enhancement abnormalities by CT. The CT appearance may lead to the erroneous diagnosis of a tumor mass. Clinical signs of fever, pain, and sepsis should allow the appropriate conclusions to be made.

RENAL VEIN THROMBOSIS

Renal Cell Carcinoma Invasion

CHILDHOOD

Bland Thrombus
Wilms' Tumor

Renal vein thrombosis is either tumoral thrombus in situations of renal cell carcinoma in the adult and Wilms' tumor in the child or bland thrombus secondary to injury, hypercoaguability, or stasis.

Renal Cell Carcinoma Invasion (Figure 6.102)

Renal cell carcinoma, the most common primary neoplasm of the kidney, has a propensity to invade the renal vein branches of the affected portion of

the kidney. Tumoral invasion of the renal vein has been variably reported in 6 to 24 percent of cases. Tumor can grow into the renal vein, extend into the inferior vena cava, and reach the right atrium. Recognition of the extent of involvement is necessary for appropriate preoperative surgical planning.

Sonographically, a solid or complex renal mass is identifiable with engorgement and distention of the renal vein. The renal vein will be filled with solid

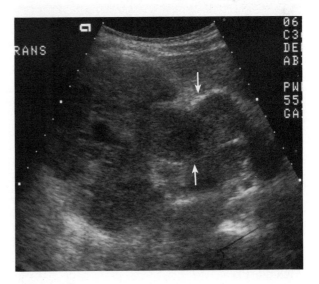

Figure 6.102
Renal cell carcinoma tumor thrombus: A large renal mass arose from the kidney with invasion and engorgement of the renal vein (*arrows*) because of tumor extension.

material. Doppler evaluation of the vein will demonstrate arterial flow within the venous thrombosis consistent with neovascularity. The recognition of renal vein involvement associated with a solid renal mass makes renal cell carcinoma the probable histologic cause.

Adrenocortical carcinoma, a rare neoplasm, may invade the adrenal vein and can sometimes be difficult to differentiate from renal cell carcinoma.

CHILDHOOD

Bland Thrombus (Figure 6.103)

Bland renal vein thrombosis generally occurs in the neonatal period. The infant may be clinically septic and dehydrated. Hematuria is common. Vomiting and diarrhea may predispose to hemoconcentration and renal vein thrombosis.

Renal vein thrombosis in the neonate is frequently manifest by enlargement of the affected kidney and increased echogenicity of the medullary portion of the kidney, with a loss of normal corticomedullary differentiation. The increased echogenicity of the normally hypoechogenic medulla is

related to hemorrhagic infarction secondary to venous thrombosis. The actual thrombus is not necessarily visualized in the main renal vein or IVC even when there is significant thrombosis within the kidney. High-resistance flow in the renal artery with reversal of flow during diastole may be noted by Doppler. Arterial inflow is sometimes so compromised as to be absent.

In the chronic stage of renal vein thrombosis, the kidney may show changes of atrophy with diminishing size, distention of the collecting system, and cortical thinning, all indications of the significant vascular insult.

In adults, renal vein thrombosis may be associated with nephrotic range proteinuria and should be considered whenever an adult is being evaluated for severe proteinuria.

Wilms' Tumor (Figure 6.104)

Wilms' tumor, the most common abdominal malignancy in childhood, extends into the renal vein in approximately 6 percent of cases. The renal vein must be examined sonographically in children with a solid renal mass and the extent of venous involvement determined.

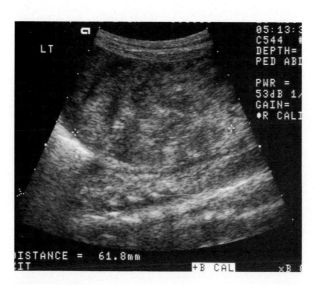

Figure 6.103
Renal vein thrombosis in 2-day-old: The large echogenic right kidney, very asymmetric when compared to the normal left kidney, blends into the surrounding tissues. Gross hematuria was present clinically.

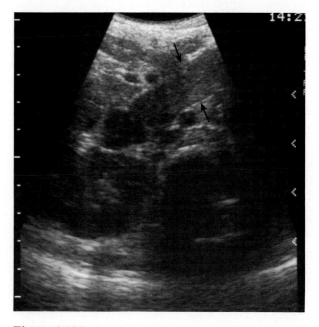

Figure 6.104
Renal vein invasion in a child with Wilms' tumor: A large renal mass was present on the left kidney. The left renal vein was filled with tumor (*arrow*) and tumor extended into the IVC. Note the engorged renal vein anterior to the aorta.

Emphasis Points

The recognition of renal vein invasion in adult patients with renal mass makes the diagnosis of renal cell carcinoma the most likely. Recognition of renal vein invasion is important for surgical planning as well. Children with renal vein thrombosis and renal mass will probably have Wilms' tumor.

In babies with renal vein thrombosis, the actual thrombus may not be identifiable. Enlargement of the kidney and increased echogenicity of the pyramids is present, together with the clinical presentation of hematuria. Unilateral or bilateral renal vein thrombosis, especially on the left, may be associated with adrenal hemorrhage.

CALCIFICATIONS IN THE RENAL COLLECTING SYSTEM

Renal Stones
Stones in Calyceal Diverticula
Calcified Sloughed Papilla
Transitional Cell Carcinoma
Encrusted Stent

VARIANT

Arcuate Artery Calcifications

Calcifications within the collecting system of the kidney are seen as highly echogenic foci that shadow. Higher-frequency transducers may be used to facilitate shadowing from very small calcifications.

Renal Stones (Figures 6.105–6.106)

Approximately 12 percent of the population will have renal calculi by the age of 70. Only approximately 3 percent of these individuals will develop symptoms of acute renal colic during their lifetime. Patients with stones often have metabolic abnormalities predisposing them to stone formation.

Most renal stones have calcium as a component and therefore appear opaque on x-ray. Calcium oxalate is a common radiopaque constituent of stones. Magnesium ammonium phosphate, also known as struvite, is common in staghorn calculi in patients with recurrent urinary tract infections, a result of urea-splitting organisms such as *Proteus*. Stones that are nonradiopaque include uric acid, xanthine, and matrix stones. Cystine stones are usually only mildly radiopaque. All stones are generally seen by sonography to be brightly echogenic with shadowing.

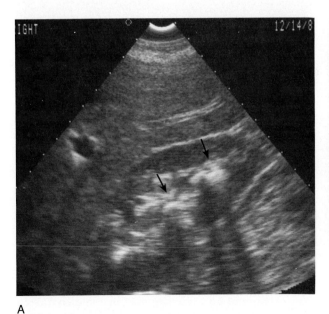

A

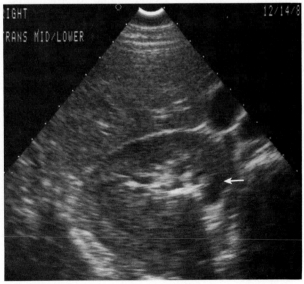

B

Figure 6.105
Multiple renal stones: (A and B) Highly echogenic foci with shadowing (*arrows*) were noted within the renal collecting system in this patient with calcium oxalate stones.

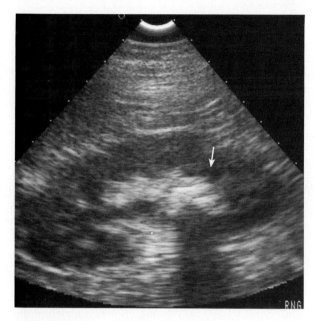

Figure 6.106
Renal stones: Extensive stone material filled the collecting system in the lower pole of the kidney.

Stones in Calyceal Diverticula (Figure 6.107)

Calyceal diverticula usually have a narrow connection to the renal collecting system. Because emptying of a diverticulum may not be complete, stasis of urine occurs, and stones may form within the diverticulum. These stones are similar to other renal calculi except that they are located outside of the expected location of the collecting system.

Calcified Sloughed Papilla (Figure 6.108)

Patients who are at risk for papillary necrosis include those with sickle cell anemia or trait, pyelonephritis, tuberculosis, diabetes, renal vein thrombosis, and analgesia abuse. The sloughed papilla may remain in the collecting system rather than necessarily being passed in the urine. In such a situation, the sloughed papilla may calcify and be indistinguishable from a renal stone.

Transitional Cell Carcinoma

Transitional cell carcinoma is reported to have calcifications in 1–7 percent of affected patients. Calcifications within a mass in the collecting system of the kidney should not be confused with a simple renal calculus.

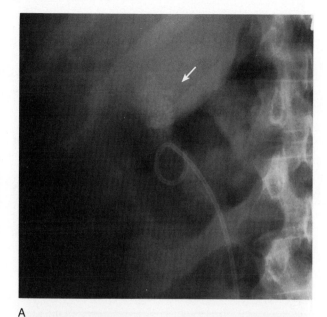

A

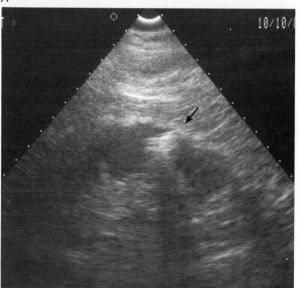

B

Figure 6.107
Stones in calyceal diverticulum: (A) Numerous small stones seen on plain film were located in a diverticulum. (B) Sonography showed the stones in the cortical region of the kidney.

Encrusted Stent

A urinary drainage stent that stays in position for weeks without an exchange may become encrusted with calcium salts and stone material. Plain films will often delineate the degree of stone deposition on the stent. Sonographically, the material will be highly echogenic with posterior shadowing.

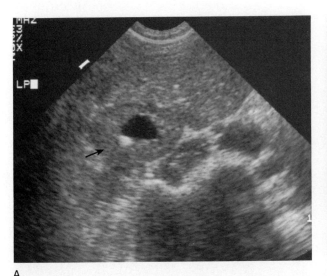

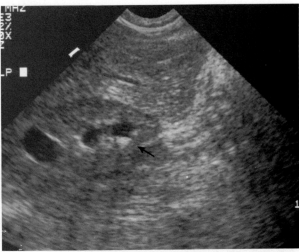

A   B

Figure 6.108

Calcified sloughed papilla: (A and B) This patient with sickle cell anemia had recurrent renal problems and findings of papillary necrosis on urography. A calcified papilla (*arrow*) was indistinguishable from a small renal calculus by imaging. The papilla was passed and evaluated microscopically.

VARIANT

Arcuate Artery Calcifications

Calcifications of the arterial tree to the kidney are commonly seen in the elderly, in the diabetic, and in patients with hypercalcemic states. Generally, arterial calcifications can be differentiated from renal stones because of their typical and expected location at the arcuate artery and their tram track appearance. Doppler analysis can sometimes demonstrate arterial flow at the site of calcification.

CORTICAL CALCIFICATIONS

  Cortical Necrosis
  Chronic Glomerulonephritis/Oxalosis/Alport's
      Syndrome
  Transplant Rejection
  Tuberculosis

Cortical Necrosis (Figure 6.109)

Markedly increased echogenicity of bilaterally small kidneys is seen as the late sequel of cortical necrosis. Cortical necrosis of the kidneys may accompany a variety of conditions causing profound,

prolonged hypotension and resulting in lengthy ischemia to the kidneys. Conditions resulting in prolonged hypotension and renal ischemia may be related to obstetrical catastrophes such as bleeding with placenta previa, anaphylaxis after intravenous contrast administration, snakebites, or other problems related to surgical procedures or trauma.

The calcification of the renal cortex represents a chronic finding after the severe insult to the kidneys. The kidneys are small and poorly functioning. Calcifications of the cortex of the kidney can be seen on CT or plain films.

Chronic Glomerulonephritis/Oxalosis/ Alport's Syndrome (Figures 6.110–6.112)

Small, calcified kidneys may occur with chronic nephrites, such as chronic glomerulonephritis. Oxalosis and Alport's syndrome, inherited conditions affecting renal function, may also result in a similar appearance.

Transplant Rejection

Dense cortical calcification may occur in a transplanted kidney, usually in the setting of chronic transplant rejection.

Tuberculosis

Tuberculous infection of a kidney may result in a diffusely calcified, nonfunctioning kidney. This so-called putty kidney undergoes autonephrectomy.

Cortical calcifications may be recognizable on plain films by the calcified renal shadows.

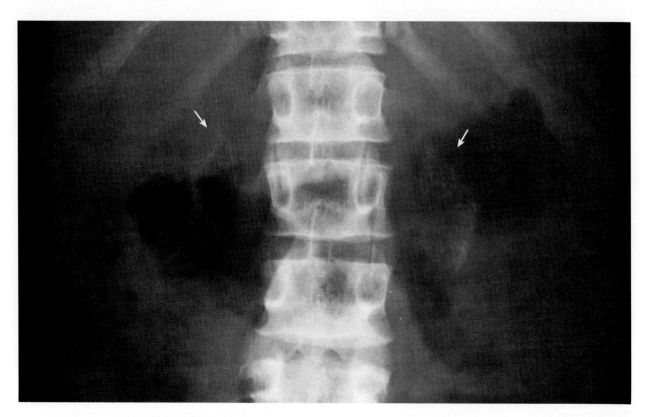

Figure 6.109
Cortical necrosis: Bilateral, small, calcified kidneys are
seen in this patient with renal failure.

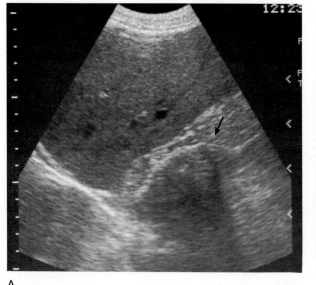

A

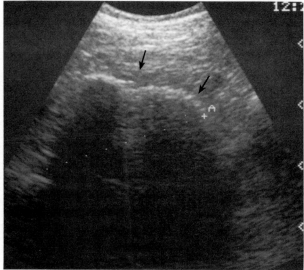

B

Figure 6.110
Chronic glomerulonephritis: (A and B) Small, calcific native kidneys (*arrows*) were obvious in this renal transplant
recipient with a long history of renal failure secondary to
glomerulonephritis. Note the shadowing from the cortex
of the kidney.

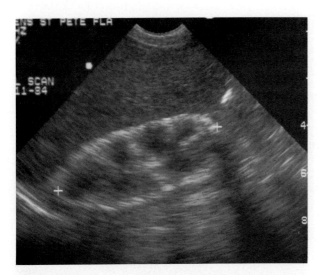

Figure 6.111
Oxalosis: Cortical echogenicity of the kidneys was remarkably high in this child with oxalosis.

MEDULLARY NEPHROCALCINOSIS

Medullary Sponge Kidney
Hypercalcemic States
Distal Renal Tubular Acidosis

Sonographically, medullary nephrocalcinosis is seen as highly echogenic medullary pyramids. This is in contrast to normal patients in whom the medullary pyramids are hypoechoic relative to the renal cortex. The cortical echogenicity of the kidneys re-mains normal, with selective increase in the medullary echogenicity in kidneys with medullary nephrocalcinosis. Acoustic shadowing is not necessarily present behind the echogenic pyramids. The lack of acoustic shadowing suggests that there is not sufficient accumulation of calcification to produce shadowing. The echogenic pyramids are distinct from the renal sinus and separated from each other by columns of cortex.

Medullary nephrocalcinosis detected sonographically is not necessarily detected on plain radiographs but may often be confirmed with unenhanced CT scanning.

Medullary Sponge Kidney (Figure 6.113)

Medullary nephrocalcinosis occurs with medullary sponge kidney, also known as renal tubular ectasia. Medullary sponge kidney is characterized by cystic dilatations of the distal collecting ducts located in the medullary portions of the kidney. These dilated collecting ducts may develop calcifications. Patients with medullary sponge kidney may have no problems with renal function, only symptoms related to stone disease and infections.

Hypercalcemic States

States of hypercalcemia, including hyperparathyroidism, as well as hypervitaminosis D, sarcoidosis, and milk-alkali syndrome, can yield medullary nephrocalcinosis. Hyperparathyroidism is caused by an adenoma, carcinoma, or hyperplasia of the

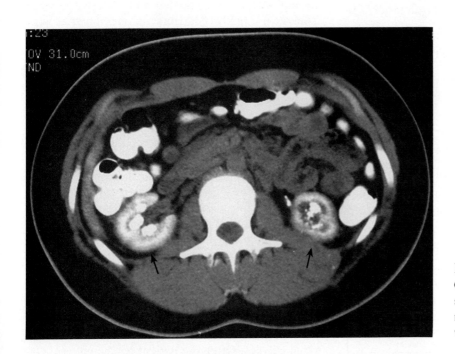

Figure 6.112
Oxalosis: Nonenhanced CT image showed cortical and medullary nephrocalcinosis in this youngster with renal failure.

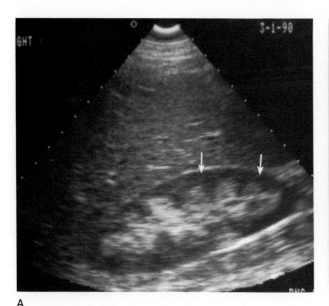

A

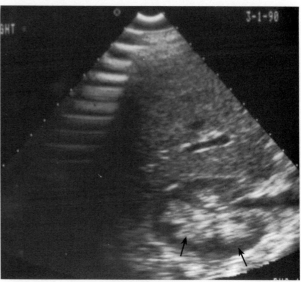

B

Figure 6.113
Medullary sponge kidney: Note the highly echogenic pyramids (*arrows*) in this patient with previous episodes of stone passage.

parathyroid glands. Carcinomas that are metastatic or have an associated paraneoplastic syndrome can cause hypercalcemia and thus medullary nephrocalcinosis. Hypervitaminosis D, sarcoidosis, and milk-alkali syndrome result from increased intestinal absorption of calcium. Other hypercalcemic states may result in medullary nephrocalcinosis too.

Distal Renal Tubular Acidosis (Figure 6.114)

Distal renal tubular acidosis is a defect in the tubule in which the distal nephron is unable to secrete hydrogen ion, so the kidney is unable to make acidic urine. Medullary calcifications form, since the calcium cannot remain soluble in the urine. Passage of stone material is frequent.

Emphasis Points

Nonshadowing medullary nephrocalcinosis can be mistaken for sinus lipomatosis and cortical thinning if the columns of cortex between the prominent pyramids are not recognized.

Medullary nephrocalcinosis is not necessarily seen on plain films even when it is seen sonographically. Unenhanced CT images can verify the fine medullary calcifications.

NONSHADOWING MATERIAL WITHIN DISTENDED RENAL COLLECTING SYSTEM

Transitional Cell Carcinoma
Blood Clot
Infective Debris/Matrix Stone
Sloughed Papilla
Stents and Drainage Tubes

The normal renal collecting system is not distended and is located within the echogenic central sinus of the kidney. When distended, the collecting system should be evaluated and material within it analyzed. Highly echogenic stone material with shadowing is frequently present. Material that does not shadow may also be identified.

Transitional Cell Carcinoma (Figures 6.115–6.116)

The collecting system and pelvis of the kidney, as well as the ureters and bladder, are lined by urothelial transitional cells. The most common tumor of the urothelium is transitional cell carcinoma. The renal collecting system may be distended by neoplasm that arises from the urothelium. Squamous cell carcinoma is less common and is seen in patients with chronic irritation and recurrent inflammation. Arising from the collecting system, small or flat transitional cell carcinomas frequently are not identifiable sonographically. As the tumor grows, it may fill or obstruct the collecting system, appearing as a nonshadowing mass within the pelvis or intrarenal calyces. Often the patient has hematuria. Cy-

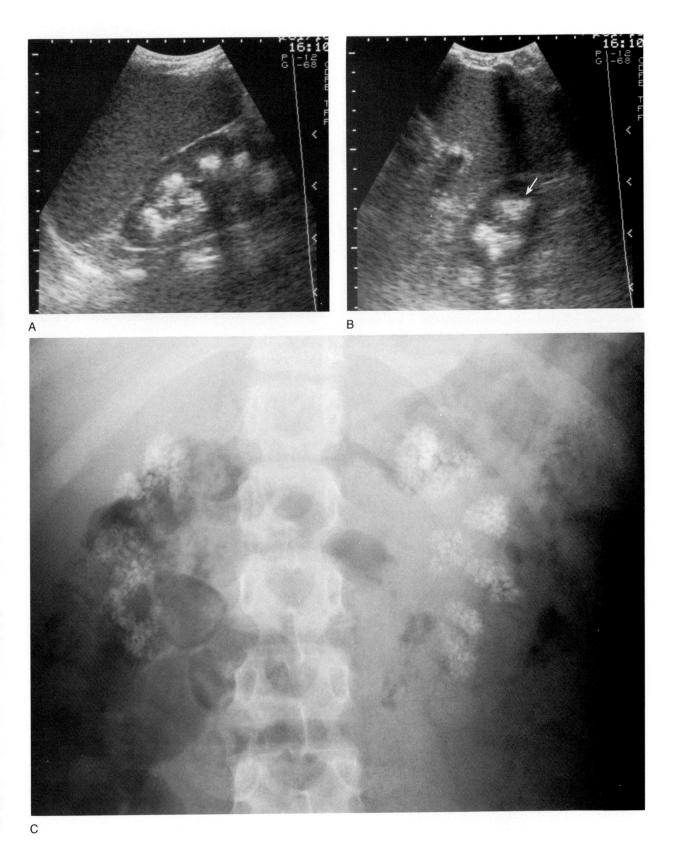

A

B

C

Figure 6.114

Distal renal tubular acidosis: (A and B) Calcifications in
the medullary portions of the kidneys are seen in this patient. (C) Plain films showed numerous medullary calcifications bilaterally.

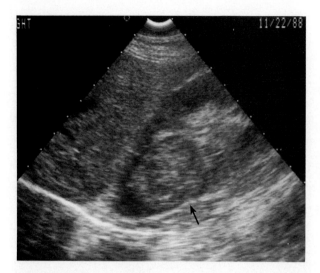

Figure 6.115

Transitional cell carcinoma: This 63-year-old woman presented with gross hematuria. Ultrasound revealed no cortical mass suggestive of renal cell carcinoma. Soft tissue material filled the upper-pole collecting system (*arrow*). At nephrectomy, an extensive transitional cell carcinoma with clot was removed.

tologic evaluation of the urine frequently yields malignant cells.

Blood Clot (Figures 6.117–6.119)

A blood clot within the collecting system can distend the renal calyces and pelvis with soft tissue

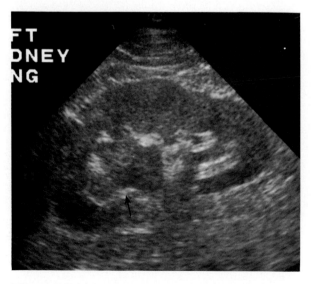

Figure 6.116

Transitional cell carcinoma: Soft tissue material (*arrow*) filled the upper-pole collecting system of the left kidney in this man with urine cytology positive for malignancy.

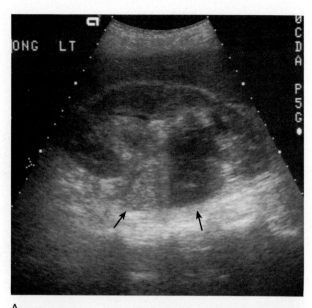

A

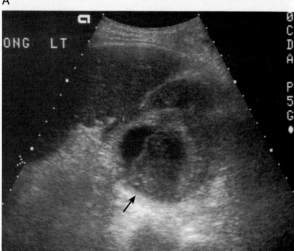

B

Figure 6.117

Blood clot: (A and B) This 55-year-old woman with leukemia and thrombocytopenia developed gross hematuria after instrumentation of the kidney. The renal pelvis was distended and filled with clotted blood (*arrows*).

material indistinguishable from transitional cell carcinoma. A collecting system clot may be secondary to a bleeding renal tumor (usually renal cell or transitional cell carcinoma) or a renal trauma (including biopsy) or may be related to anticoagulation.

Infective Debris/Matrix Stone (Figures 6.120–6.121)

Infective debris may fill the collecting system in a patient with pyonephrosis. Pyogenic debris or fun-

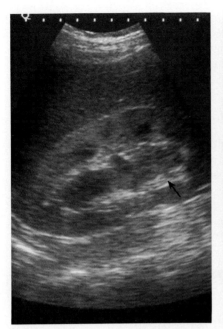
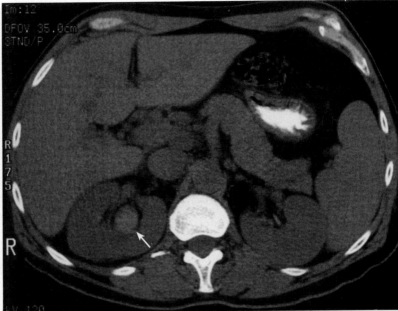

A   B

Figure 6.118

Blood clot: (A) This young man with Factor VIII deficiency developed gross hematuria. Note the distention of the collecting system and soft tissue material within. (B) Nonenhanced CT images showed the high-density hemorrhage within the renal pelvis and ureter. The hemorrhage resolved with Factor VIII replacement therapy.

gus balls can accumulate within an obstructed collecting system. Thick, purulent material may be aspirated from such an obstructed infected system. Relief of the obstruction is the most important therapeutic strategy. This infective material may eventually contribute to stone formation, especially with recurrent infections. At sonography, particulate material with low-level echoes is sometimes identifiable, although obstructed, infected fluid does not necessarily have demonstrable echoes.

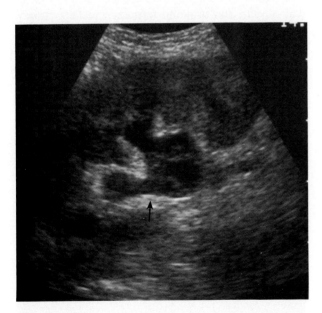

Figure 6.119

Blood clot: One day after biopsy of his transplanted kidney, serum creatinine levels were markedly elevated secondary to obstruction by blood clot within the renal pelvis (*arrow*). No distention of the collecting system had been present prior to the biopsy. After irrigation of the renal pelvis, the serum creatinine returned to normal.

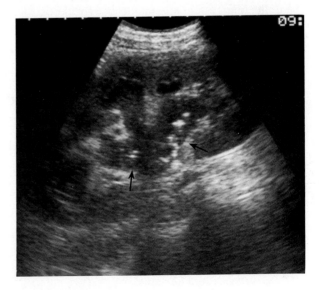

Figure 6.120

Pyonephrosis: Particulate debris and infective material filled the renal pelvis and proximal ureter in this patient with ureteral stones.

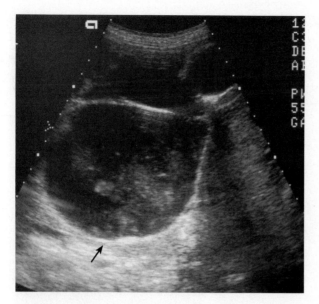

Figure 6.121
Particulate debris: Swirling material (*arrow*) filled the chronically obstructed right kidney in this patient with UPJ obstruction.

Matrix debris, which often forms in situations of infection, does not always cause shadowing.

Sloughed Papilla

Patients who are at risk for papillary necrosis include those with sickle cell anemia and sickle cell trait, recurrent pyelonephritis, diabetes, and renal tuberculosis. The sloughed papilla may be seen in the collecting system and may cause focal obstruction as it moves. Calcification of a sloughed papilla may be indistinguishable from a renal calculus.

Stents and Drainage Tubes

Stents and drainage tubes may be visualized within a dilated collecting system but may have a characteristic appearance with two parallel walls around an open lumen. Shadowing does not usually occur unless the stent becomes encrusted with calcification.

FLUID COLLECTIONS NEAR THE KIDNEY

Peritoneal Fluid (Ascites)
Perinephric Fluid
Subcapsular Collection
Left Anterior Pararenal Space Fluid

Recognizing the pattern of fluid distribution near the kidneys allows the diagnostician to identify the space the fluid occupies and therefore to identify the etiology of the fluid.

Peritoneal Fluid (Ascites) (Figure 6.122)

Fluid in the subhepatic space (Morrison's pouch) is in the peritoneal cavity. Fluid in the peritoneal space may be serous, bloody, chylous, or purulent. Such fluid may be secondary to a host of causes, including liver failure, heart or renal failure, carcinomatosis, and solid or hollow organ rupture.

Perinephric Fluid (Figures 6.123–6.125)

Fluid that is contained by Gerota's fascia will often surround the kidney without distorting it significantly. Fluid within Gerota's fascia is often related to forniceal rupture of an obstructed kidney with extravasation of urine. The fornix is the weakest point of the collecting system and will perforate if under high pressure. The obstructed kidney does not necessarily exhibit hydronephrosis once it has decompressed into the generous perinephric space. Since the perinephric space is large, there is not necessarily significant compression of the kidney by the urinoma. Obstructing lesions that can result in forniceal rupture and urinoma formation include stones,

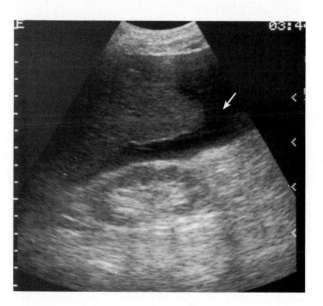

Figure 6.122
Subhepatic ascites: A moderate amount of free peritoneal ascites was present in this patient with cirrhosis. No fluid was within the retroperitoneal space.

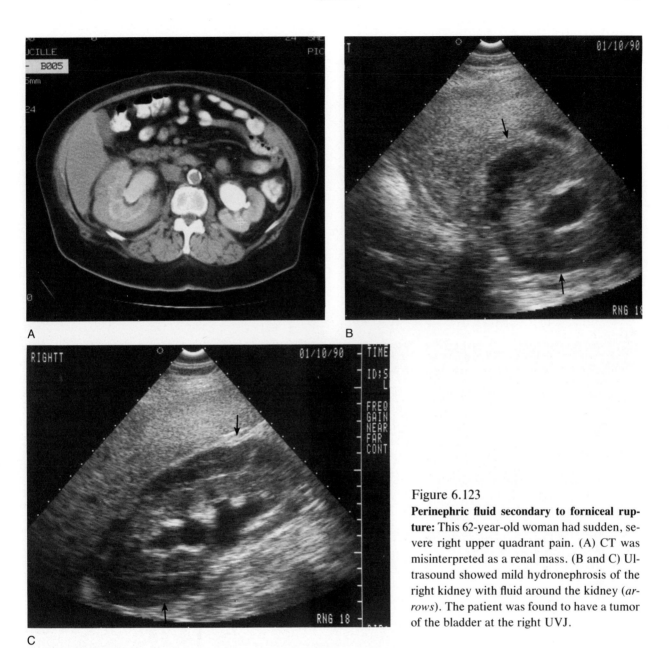

Figure 6.123

Perinephric fluid secondary to forniceal rupture: This 62-year-old woman had sudden, severe right upper quadrant pain. (A) CT was misinterpreted as a renal mass. (B and C) Ultrasound showed mild hydronephrosis of the right kidney with fluid around the kidney (*arrows*). The patient was found to have a tumor of the bladder at the right UVJ.

fibrosis, and ureteral or bladder tumors. In male babies with bladder outlet obstruction secondary to posterior urethral valves, perinephretic fluid collections may be identifiable in utero or in the infant.

Subcapsular Collection (Figures 6.126–6.129)

The hallmark of a subcapsular collection of the kidney is the marked distortion it causes to the kidney's contour. The subcapsular space is a potential space, and fluid or blood must be under high pressure to fill the space and to distort the contour of the solid parenchyma of the kidney. Sub-

capsular collections are usually hematomas, and the causes include trauma (including surgical, blunt, and ESWL) or anticoagulation therapy. In the absence of a satisfactory history of trauma or anticoagulation therapy, an explanation for the development of a spontaneous subcapsular hematoma must be determined. Underlying abnormalities of the kidney, including renal masses such as renal cell carcinoma and angiomyolipoma, may bleed, causing subcapsular hematoma formation. Vasculitis affecting the kidney may result in subcapsular hematoma. Angiographic studies may be necessary to evaluate the vascular tree of the kidney with a spontaneous subcapsular hematoma and no obvious explanation.

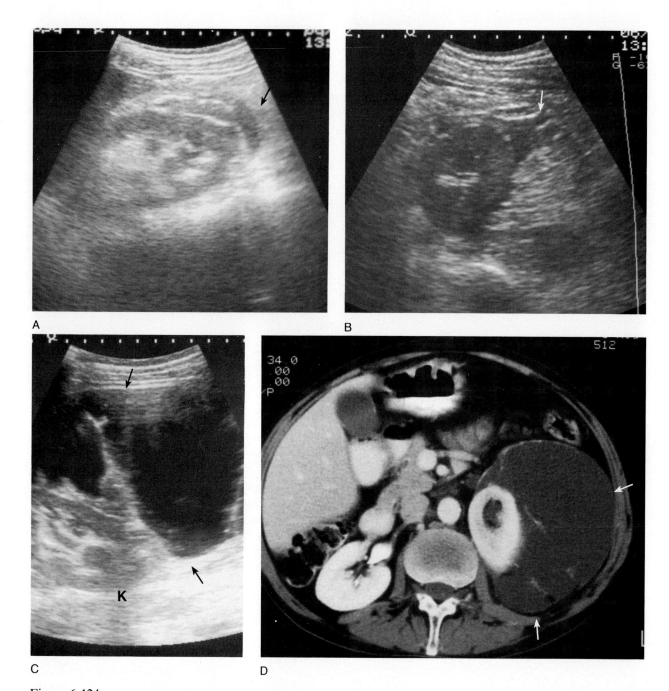

Figure 6.124
Perinephric fluid secondary to forniceal rupture (squamous cell carcinoma of the bladder): (A and B) This elderly man was noted to have a small amount of fluid around the lower pole of the left kidney (*arrow*) and a bladder mass at the left UVJ. (C and D) Follow-up sonography and CT showed enlargement of a septated urinoma (*arrows*) that developed because obstruction of the distal ureter persisted. (K = kidney.)

COLOR PLATES

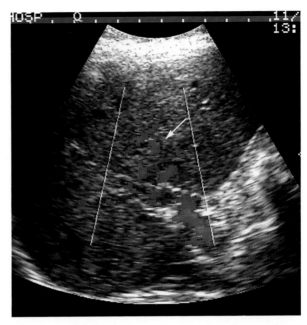

Plate 1. Intrahepatic varices: A color Doppler image. Note the comma-shaped vessels within the hepatic substance. (Figure 1.113C)

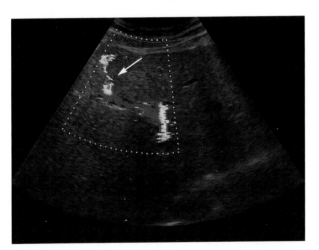

Plate 2. Recanalized paraumbilical vein. Note the expected course from the left portal vein toward the anterior abdominal wall. (Figure 1.114A)

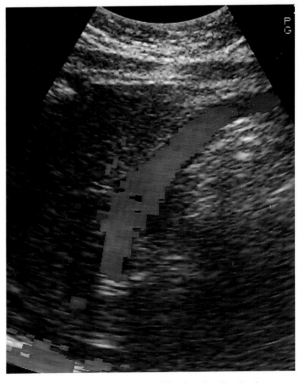

Plate 3. Recanalized paraumbilical vein: Sagittal projection. (Figure 1.114C)

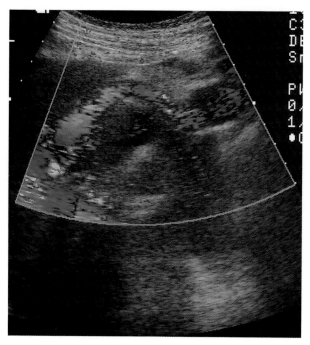

Plate 4. Recanalized paraumbilical vein. (Figure 1.114D)

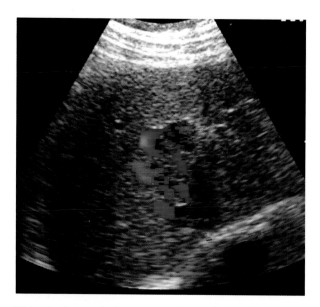

Plate 5. Congenital venous malformation within the liver: Color Doppler image. (Figure 1.115B)

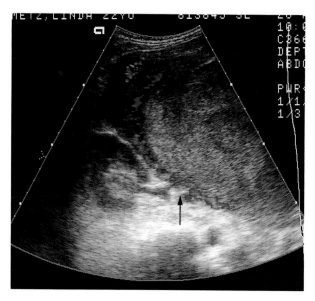

Plate 6. Large draining veins surround this hepatic adenoma. (Figure 1.116)

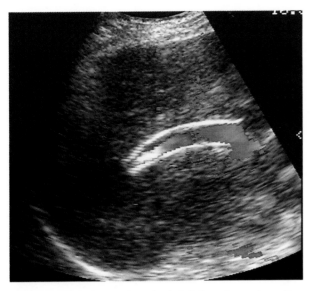

Plate 7. TIPS shunt. Note the brightly echogenic walls of the stent. (Figure 1.117)

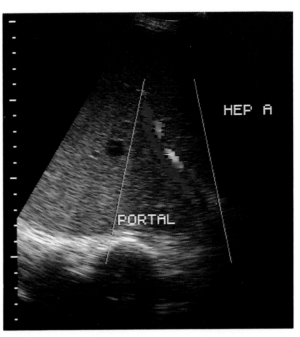

Plate 8. Reversal of flow direction in the portal vein. Note hepatofugal (blue) flow in portal vein and hepatopedal (red) flow in hepatic artery in this patient with severe, acute hepatitis. (Figure 1.118)

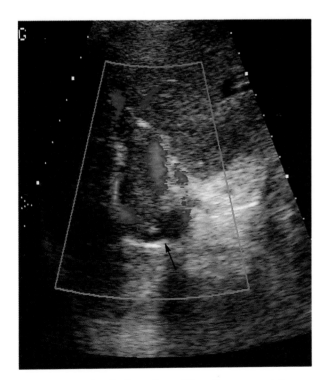

Plate 9. Portal vein thrombus. Note flow around the focal thrombus (*arrow*). (Figure 1.119B)

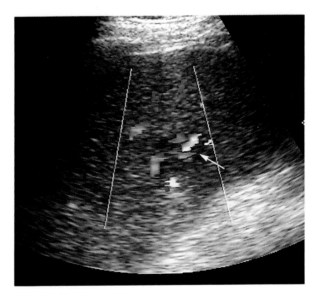

Plate 10. Hepatocellular carcinoma invading the portal vein: Arterial signal was present within the tumor thrombus consistent with neovascularity (*arrow*). (Figure 1.120C)

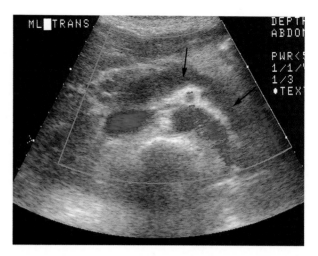

Plate 11. Thrombosis of the splenic vein (*arrow*) extending to portal confluence. (Figure 1.122A)

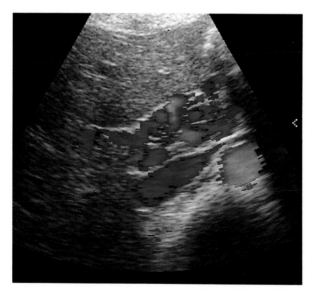

Plate 12. Cavernous transformation of the portal vein. A tangle of collateral vessels is seen in the porta hepatis. (Figure 1.127)

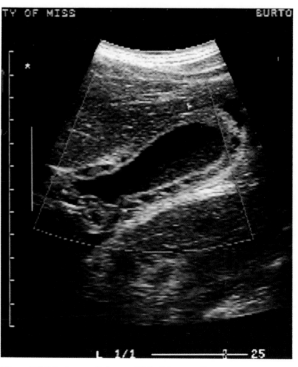

Plate 13. Varices of the gallbladder wall. (Figure 2.12)

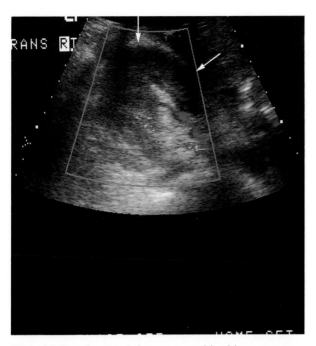

Plate 14. Renal artery injury occurred in this young man suffering blunt trauma (transverse). Note areas of non-perfusion within the kidney (*arrows*). (Figure 6.99B)

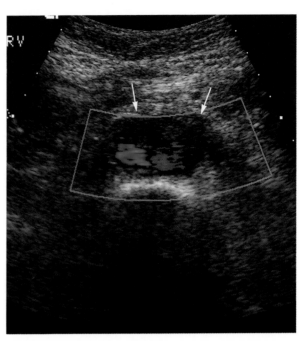

Plate 15. Retroperitoneal fibrosis seen anterior to the aorta and IVC (*arrows*): Color Doppler image. (Figure 8.4C)

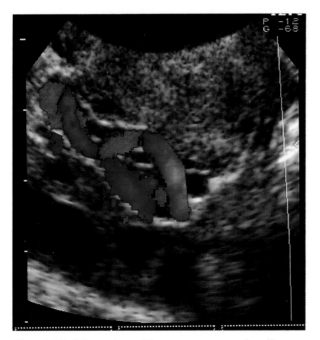

Plate 16. Pelvic varices. Note tortuous vessels adjacent to uterus. (Figure 11.79)

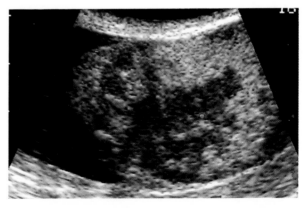

Plate 17. Missed torsion of the testis. No blood flow was detectable. Note the abnormal echogenicity. (Figure 12.20)

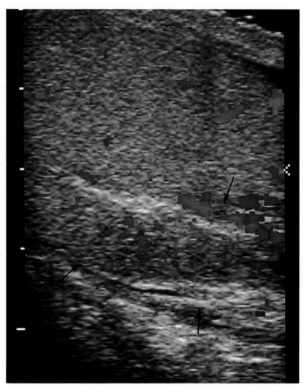

Plate 18. Epididymo-orchitis. Note epididymal enlargement and hyperemia (*arrows*). (Figure 12.31A)

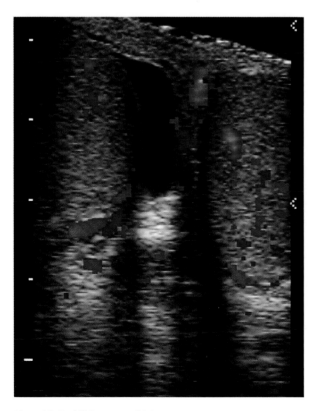

Plate 19. Epididymo-orchitis. Note hyperemia. (Figure 12.31B)

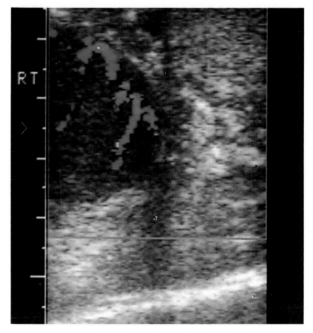

Plate 20. Epididymo-orchitis. Note abnormal echogenicity of orchitis with increased vascular flow. (Figure 12.32A)

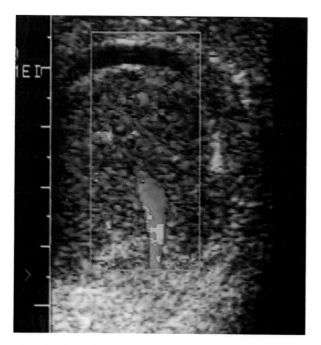

Plate 21. Epididymo-orchitis, Diminished echogenicity of the testis and hypervascularity were present on the affected side. (Figure 12.32B)

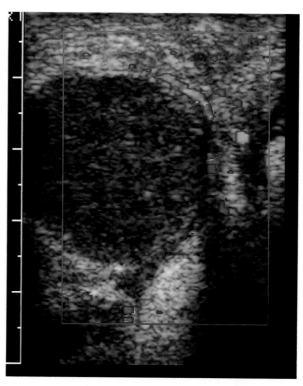

Plate 22. Torsion. No blood flow was detectable within the affected testis, but was noted around the testis. (Figure 12.33A)

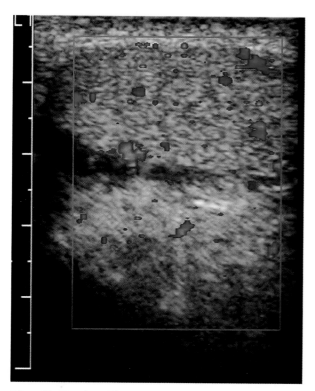

Plate 23. Torsion. The contralateral testis was unaffected, with normal arterial flow and normal ecogenicity. (Figure 12.33B)

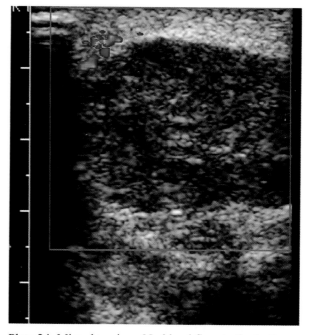

Plate 24. Missed torsion. No blood flow to the testis and abnormal echogenicity were present in this patient after 2 weeks of pain. (Figure 12.34)

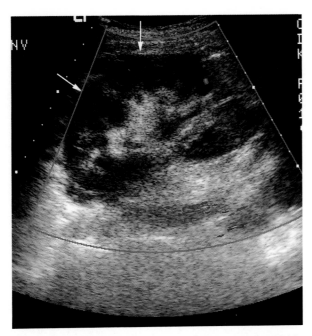

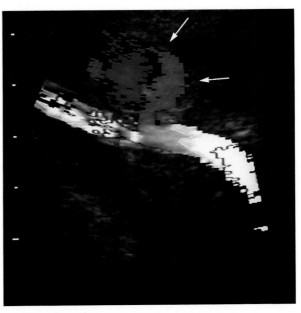

Plate 25. Renal artery thrombosis. This transplanted kidney had two renal arteries. Note evidence of thrombosis of the artery to the upper pole (*arrows*) (Figure 14.8)

Plate 26. Pseudoaneurysm at arterial anastomosis (*arrows*) within the transplanted kidney (Figure 14.11)

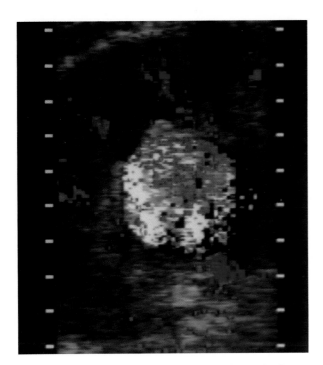

Plate 27. Intrarenal pseudoaneurysm. This resulted from a kidney biopsy. (Figure 14.12)

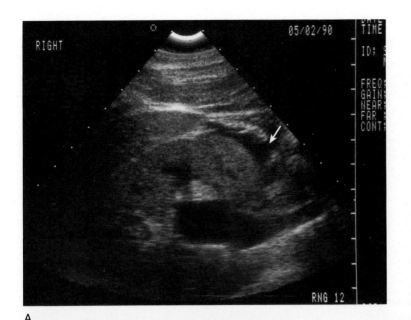

A

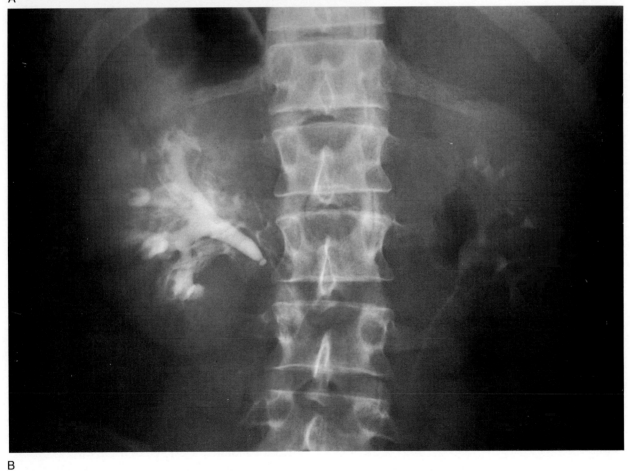

B

Figure 6.125
Sliver of perinephric fluid secondary to renal stone passage:
(A) During an episode of acute renal colic, fluid around
the kidney (*arrow*) suggests forniceal rupture. (B) IVP
equivalent.

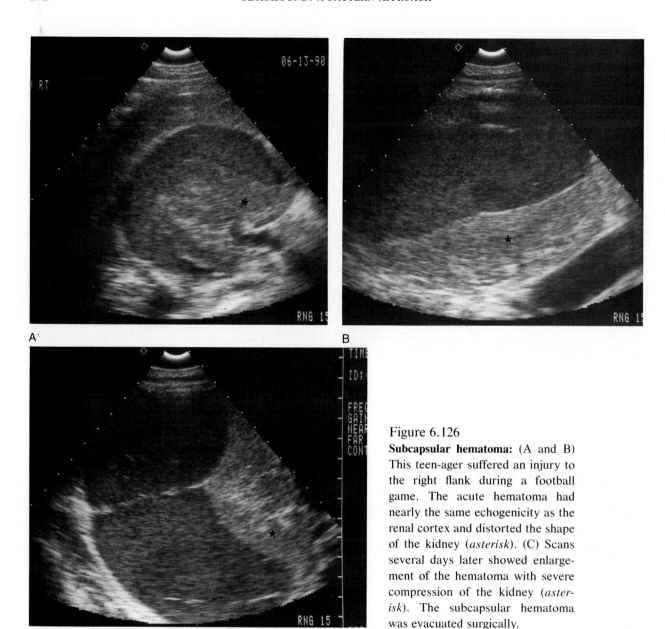

A

B

C

Figure 6.126

Subcapsular hematoma: (A and B) This teen-ager suffered an injury to the right flank during a football game. The acute hematoma had nearly the same echogenicity as the renal cortex and distorted the shape of the kidney (*asterisk*). (C) Scans several days later showed enlargement of the hematoma with severe compression of the kidney (*asterisk*). The subcapsular hematoma was evacuated surgically.

Persistent presence of a subcapsular renal collection can lead to severe hypertension.

Left Anterior Pararenal Space Fluid (Figures 6.130–6.131)

Fluid seen in the left anterior pararenal space is most often identified sonographically when the long axis of the left kidney is studied. The fat within the perinephric space will surround the kidney and be normally preserved. Fluid in the left anterior pararenal space will be separated from the kidney by the fat contained within Gerota's fascia.

Fluid dissecting into the left anterior pararenal space usually is secondary to inflammatory changes of the pancreas or other viscera rather than the kidney. Recognition of left anterior pararenal fluid should spark a search for pancreatic processes, most likely pancreatitis.

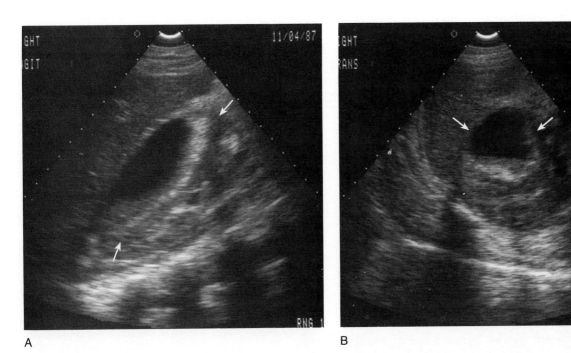

A

B

Figure 6.127
Subcapsular hematoma: (A and B) A subcapsular collection with debris (*arrows*) developed in this patient after ESWL for renal calculi. Note the mass effect upon the kidney.

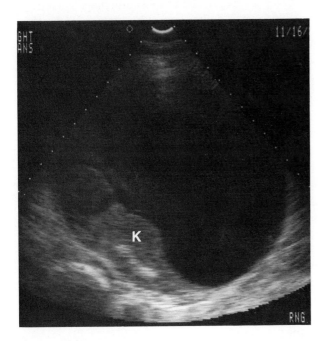

Figure 6.128
Subcapsular hematoma: A large, chronic, subcapsular collection required surgical decompression. The kidney (K) was flattened.

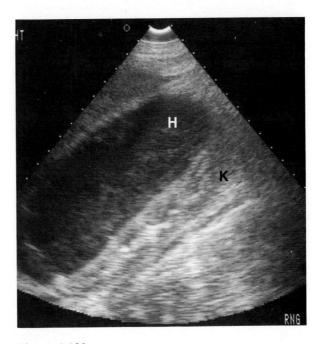

Figure 6.129
Subcapsular hematoma: Anticoagulation therapy was considered responsible for the large, subcapsular hematoma that developed in this woman with chronic atrial fibrillation. (H) Hematoma; (K) Kidney.

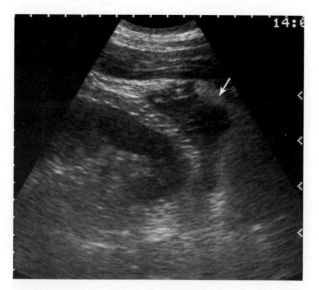

Figure 6.130
Left anterior pararenal space fluid secondary to pancreatitis: Fluid in the left anterior pararenal space, although seen in close proximity to the left kidney, is related to pancreatic inflammation. Note the preservation of the normal perinephric fat.

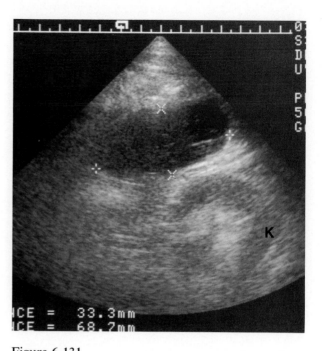

Figure 6.131
Peripancreatic collection: This fluid collection in the left anterior pararenal space was initially believed to be a urinoma but was secondary to pancreatitis. Its location was appropriate for its pancreatic origin. (K = left kidney.)

Emphasis Points

Free fluid in the peritoneal cavity has a host of causes, often unrelated to the kidneys.

A subcapsular collection of the kidney is often hemorrhage, related to trauma or anticoagulation therapy. The subcapsular space is a potential space that can fill with hemorrhage, distorting and compressing the renal contour. Recognition of renal parenchymal distortion by a collection should raise the possibility of a subcapsular hemorrhage.

Once a subcapsular renal hemorrhage is identified, the cause must be determined. If trauma or anticoagulation therapy is not the cause, an underlying renal abnormality, such as a renal cell carcinoma or angiomyolipoma, may be responsible.

Fluid in the left anterior pararenal space is often secondary to pancreatic processes rather than to renal problems.

BIBLIOGRAPHY

Hydronephrosis

Athey PA, Carpenter RJ, Hadlock FP, et al.: Ultrasonic demonstration of ectopic ureterocele. Pediatrics 71:568–571, 1983.

Erwin BC, Carroll BA, Sommer FG: Renal colic: The role of ultrasound in initial evaluation. Radiology 152:147–150, 1984.

Garcia CJ, Taylor KJW, Weiss RM: Congenital megacalyces: Ultrasound appearance. J Ultrasound Med 6:163–165, 1987.

Laing FC, Jeffrey RB, Wing VW: Ultrasound versus excretory urography in evaluating acute flank pain. Radiology 154:613–616, 1985.

Nussbaum AR, Dorst JP, Jeffs RD, et al.: Ectopic ureter and ureterocele: Their varied sonographic manifestations. Radiology 159:227–235, 1986.

Variants of Obstructed Hydronephrosis

Cronan JJ, Amis ES, Yoder IC, et al.: Peripelvic cysts: An imposter of sonographic hydronephrosis. J Ultrasound Med 1:229–236, 1982.

Fried AM, Woodring JH, Thompson DJ: Hydronephrosis of pregnancy: A prospective sequential study of the course of dilatation. J Ultrasound Med 2:255–259, 1983.

Hidalgo H, Dunnick NR, Rosenberg ER, et al.: Parapelvic cysts: Appearance on CT and sonography. AJR 138:667–671, 1982.

Unilateral Small, Scarred Kidney

Kay CJ, Rosenfield AT, Taylor KJW, et al.: Ultrasonic characteristics of chronic atrophic pyelonephritis. AJR 132:47–49, 1979.

Unilateral Renal Enlargement Without Focal Mass

Davidson AJ (ed): *Radiology of the Kidney*. Philadelphia: W. B. Saunders, 1985.

Unilateral Renal Enlargement with Increased Echogenicity

Davidson AJ: A systematic approach to the radiologic diagnosis of parenchymal disease of the kidney, in Davidson AJ (ed): *Radiology of the Kidney*. Philadelphia: W. B. Saunders, 1985, pp. 118–122.

Green D, Carroll BA: Ultrasound of renal failure, in Hricak H (ed): *Clinics in Ultrasound*. New York: Churchill Linvingstone, 1986, vol 18, pp. 55–58.

Hamper UM, Goldblum LE, Hutchins GM, et al.: Renal involvement in AIDS: Sonographic–pathologic correlation. AJR 150:1321–1325, 1988.

Hricak H, Cruz C, Romanski R, et al.: Renal parenchymal disease: Sonographic–histologic correlation. Radiology 144:141–147, 1982.

Kraus RA, Gaisie G, Young LW: Increased renal parenchymal echogenicity: Causes in pediatric patients. RadioGraphics 10:1009–1018, 1990.

Longmaid HE, Rider E, Tymkiw J: Lupus nephritis: New sonographic findings. J Ultrasound Med 6:75–79, 1987.

Platt JF, Rubin JM, Bowerman RA, et al.: The inability to detect kidney disease on the basis of echogenicity. AJR 151:317–319, 1988.

Reuther G, Wanjura D, Bauer H: Acute renal vein thrombosis in renal allografts: Detection with duplex Doppler US. Radiology 170:557–558, 1989.

Schaffer RM, Schwartz GE, Becker JA, et al.: Renal ultrasound in acquired immune deficiency syndrome. Radiology 153:511–513, 1984.

Unilateral Cystic or Complicated Cystic Renal Mass

Avni EF, Thoua Y, Lalmand B, et al.: Multicystic dysplastic kidney: Natural history from in utero diagnosis and postnatal follow-up. J Urol 138:1420–1424, 1987.

Banner MP, Pollack HM, Chatten J, Witzleben C: Multilocular renal cysts: Radiologic–pathologic correlation. AJR 136:239–247, 1981.

Bosniak MA: The current radiological approach to renal cysts. Radiology 158:1–10, 1986.

Feldberg MAM, van Waes PFGM: Multilocular cystic renal cell carcinoma. AJR 138:953–955, 1982.

Grossman H, Rosenberg, ER, Bowie JD, et al.: Sonographic diagnosis of renal cystic disease. AJR 140:81–85, 1983.

Hartman DS, Davis CJ, Sanders RC, Johns TT, Smirniotopoulos J, Goldman SM: The multiloculated renal mass: Considerations and differential features. RadioGraphics 7:29–52, 1987.

Madewell JE, Goldman SM, Davis CJ, Hartman DS, Feigin DS, Lichtenstein JE: Multilocular cystic nephroma: A radiologic–pathologic correlation of 58 patients. Radiology 146:309–321, 1983.

Pedicelli G, Jequier S, Bowen A, et al.: Multicystic dysplastic kidneys: Spontaneous regression demonstrated with ultrasound. Radiology 160:23–26, 1986.

Rosenberg ER, Korobkin M, Foster W, et al.: The significance of septations in a renal cyst. AJR 144:593–595, 1985.

Unilateral Solid-Appearing Hypoechoic Renal Mass

Bosniak MA: The small (less than or equal to 3.0 cm) renal parenchymal tumor: Detection, diagnosis and controversies. Radiology 179:307–317, 1991.

Lafortune M, Constantin A, Breton G, et al.: Sonography of the hypertrophied column of Bertin. AJR 146:53–56, 1986.

Lee JKT, McClennan BL, Melson GL, Stanley RJ: Acute focal bacterial nephritis: Emphasis on gray scale sonography and computed tomography. AJR 135:87–92, 1980.

Levine E, Huntrakoon M, Wetzel LH: Small renal neoplasms: Clinical, pathologic and imaging features. AJR 153:69–73, 1989.

Mahony BS, Jeffrey RB, Laing FC: Septa of Bertin: A sonographic pseudotumor. J Clin Ultrasound 11:317–319, 1983.

Pamilo M, Suramo I, Paivansalo M: Characteristics of hypernephromas as seen with ultrasound and computed tomography. J Clin Ultrasound 11:245–249, 1983.

Hyperechoic Renal Mass

Bret PM, Bretagnolle M, Gaillard D, et al.: Small asymptomatic angiomyolipomas of the kidney. Radiology 154:7–10, 1985.

Curry NS, Schabel SI, Garvin AJ, et al.: Intratumoral fat in a renal oncocytoma mimicking angiomyolipoma. AJR 154:307–308, 1990.

Erwin BC, Carroll BA, Walter JF, et al.: Renal infarction appearing as an echogenic mass. AJR 138:759–761, 1982.

Forman HP, Middleton WD, Melson GL, McClennan BL: Hyperechoic renal cell carcinomas: Increase in detection at US. Radiology 188:431–434, 1993.

Hartman DS, Goldman SM, Friedman AC, Davis CJ, Madewell JE, Sherman JL: Angiomyolipoma: Ultrasonic–pathologic correlation. Radiology 139:451–458, 1981.

Hélénon O, Chrétien Y, Paraf F, Melki P, Denys A, Moreau JF: Renal cell carcinoma containing fat: Demonstration with CT. Radiology 188:429–430, 1993.

Strotzer M, Lehner KB, Becker K: Detection of fat in a renal cell carcinoma mimicking angiomyolipoma. Radiology 188:427–428, 1993.

Zappasodi F, Sanna G, Fiorentini G, et al.: Small hyperechoic nodules of the renal parenchyma. J Clin Ultrasound 13:321–324, 1985.

Bilateral Renal Cysts

Jabour BA, Ralls PW, Tang WW, et al.: Acquired cystic disease of the kidneys: Computed tomography and ultrasonography appraisal in patients on peritoneal and hemodialysis. Invest Radiol 22:728–732, 1987.

Kutcher R, Amodio JB, Rosenblatt R: Uremic renal cystic disease: Value of sonographic screening. Radiology 147:833–835, 1983.

Mindell HJ: Imaging studies for screening native kidneys in long-term dialysis patients. AJR 153:768–769, 1989.

Rosenfield AT, Lipson MH, Wolf B, et al.: Ultrasonography and nephrotomography in the presymptomatic diagnosis of dominantly inherited (adult-onset) polycystic kidney disease. Radiology 135; 423–427, 1980.

Bilateral Solid Renal Masses

Charnsangavej C: Lymphoma of the genitourinary tract. Radiol Clin North Am 28:865–877, 1990.

Chonko AM, Weiss SM, Stein JH, et al.: Renal involvement in tuberous sclerosis. Am J Med 56:124, 1974.

Hartman DS, David CJ Jr, Goldman SM, et al.: Renal lymphoma: Radiologic–pathologic correlation of 21 cases. Radiology 144:759–766, 1982.

Preservation of Reniform Shape with Abnormal Enhancement on CT

Bree RL, Schultz SR, Hayes R: Large infiltrating renal transitional cell carcinomas: CT and ultrasound features. J Comput Assist Tomogr 14:381–385, 1990.

Choyke PL, White EM, Zeman RK, Jaffe MH, Clark LR: Renal metastases: Clinico-pathologic and radiologic correlation. Radiology 162:359–363, 1987.

Hartman DS, Davidson AJ, Davis CJ Jr, Goldman SM: Infiltrative renal lesions: CT–sonographic–pathologic correlation. AJR 150:1061–1064, 1988.

Renal Vein Thrombosis

Braun B, Weilemann LS, Weigand W: Ultrasonographic demonstration of renal vein thrombosis. Radiology 138:157–158, 1981.

Hietala SO, Ekelund L, Ljungberg B: Venous invasion in renal cell carcinoma: A correlative clinical and radiologic study. Urol Radiol 9:210–216, 1988.

Rosenfield AT, Zeman RK, Cronan JJ, Taylor KJW: Ultrasound in experimental and clinical renal vein thrombosis. Radiology 137:735–741, 1980.

Schwerk WB, Schwerk WN, Rodeck G: Venous renal tumor extension: A prospective US evaluation. Radiology 156:491–495, 1985.

Calcifications in the Renal Collecting System

Kane RA, Manco LG: Renal arterial calcification simulating nephrolithiasis on sonography. AJR 140:101–104, 1983.

Middleton WD, Dodds WJ, Lawson TL, et al.: Renal calculi: Sensitivity for detection with ultrasound. Radiology 167:239–244, 1988.

Medullary Nephrocalcinosis

Glazer GM, Callen PW, Filly RA: Medullary nephrocalcinosis: Sonographic evaluation. AJR 138:55–57, 1982.

Patriquin HB, O'Regan S: Medullary sponge kidney in childhood. AJR 145:315–319, 1985.

Nonshadowing Soft Tissue Material Within Distended Renal Collecting System

Goldman SM, Bohlman ME, Gatewood OMB: Neoplasms of the renal collecting system. Semin Roentgenol 22:284–291, 1987.

Grant DC, Dee GJ, Yoder IC, et al.: Sonography in transitional cell carcinoma of the renal pelvis. Urol Radiol 8:1–5, 1986.

Hoffman JC, Schnur MJ, Koenigsburg M: Demonstration of renal papillary necrosis by sonography. Radiology 145:785–787,1982.

Jeffrey RB, Laing FC, Wing VW, et al.: Sensitivity of sonography in pyonephrosis: A re-evaluation. AJR 144:71–73, 1985.

Mulholland SG, Arger PH, Goldberg BB, et al.: Ultrasonic differentiation of renal pelvic filling defects. J Urol 122:14, 1979.

Stuck KJ, Silver TM, Jaffee MH, et al.: Sonographic demonstration of renal fungus balls. Radiology 142:473–474, 1982.

Subramanyam BR, Raghavendra BN, Bosniak MA, et al.: Sonography of pyonephrosis: A prospective study. AJR 140:991–993, 1983.

Fluid Collections Near the Kidney

Belville JS, Morgentaler A, Loughlin KR, et al.: Spontaneous perinephric and subcapsular renal hemorrhage: Evaluation with CT, US, and angiography. Radiology 172:733, 1989.

Boag GS, Nolan RL, Nickel JC: Imaging of giant urinomas. J Med Imaging 2:36–40, 1988.

Kaude JV, Williams JL, Wright PG, et al.: Sonographic evaluation of the kidney following extracorporeal shock wave lithotripsy. J Ultrasound Med 6:299–306, 1987.

Knapp PM, Kulb TB, Lingeman JE, et al.: Extracorporeal shock wave lithotripsy: Induced perirenal hematomas. J Urol 139:700–703, 1988.

Papanicolaou N, Stafford SA, Pfister RC, et al.: Significant renal hemorrhage following extracorporeal shock wave lithotripsy: Imaging and clinical features. Radiology 163:661–664, 1987.

ADRENALS

The adrenals can usually be readily imaged in the normal newborn. On long-axis scans, the adrenal is a caplike structure superior and medial to each kidney. The adrenal has a hypoechoic cortex that surrounds an echogenic stripe, which is the medulla. The two limbs of the adrenal make a triangular shape. The width of a limb is 0.2 to 0.5 cm, and the length of each limb ranges from 0.9 to 3.6 cm. The adrenal may "round up" and fill the renal fossa if the kidney is absent.

The adrenals become more difficult to image as a patient ages. In an adult the normal adrenal is rarely identified. The adrenal is more easily seen sonographically if it is enlarged or has an echotexture abnormality. Specific evaluation of the adrenals is most often performed with CT or MR since they can be more consistently imaged in the adult patient.

UNILATERAL HYPOECHOIC ADRENAL MASS

Adrenal Adenoma
Metastasis to the Adrenal
Lymphomatous Involvement of the Adrenal
Adrenocortical Carcinoma

Pheochromocytoma
Infectious Enlargement of the Adrenal/
    Abscess
Adrenal Cyst
Retroperitoneal Sarcoma
Accessory Spleen

CHILDHOOD

Adrenal Hemorrhage
Neuroblastoma

Adrenal Adenomas (Figures 7.1–7.3)

Nodules of the adrenal gland that measure less than 3 cm are found in 2–9 percent of patients at autopsy. Most such nodules are nonfunctioning cortical adenomas. Small adrenal masses found incidentally by imaging are usually followed with serial imaging unless endocrine studies reveal that the mass is hormonally active or the patient has a primary tumor with a propensity to spread to the adrenal gland. Reports vary as to what size an adrenal mass can attain before being subjected to biopsy. Some researchers suggest a 3-cm maximum diameter, and others allow a 6-cm diameter. In patients with a small adrenal mass and a malignancy with a propensity to spread to the adrenal, such as those with lung

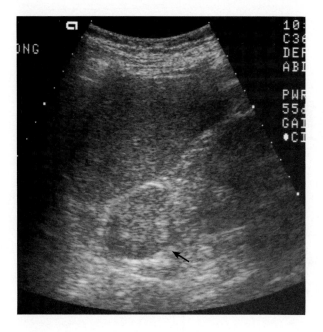

Figure 7.1
Adrenal adenoma: A well-defined 3-cm hypoechoic mass (*arrow*) was identified in the left adrenal region in this patient being evaluated for a possible aortic aneurysm. Laparoscopic removal of the mass proved it to be an adrenal adenoma.

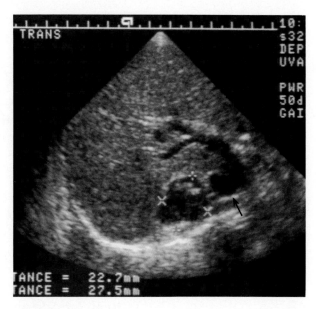

Figure 7.3
Virilizing adrenal adenoma: This child with precocious puberty and virilization was found to have a small, hypoechoic adrenal mass. Note its relationship to the inferior vena cava (*arrow*). A functioning adrenal adenoma was removed surgically. Hormonally active adrenal masses are often detected earlier than hormonally silent ones.

cancer, biopsy will frequently be undertaken to exclude metastatic involvement of the adrenal.

Laboratory evidence that an adrenal mass is functioning, causing Cushing's syndrome or hyperaldosteronism, will result in surgical resection. Adrenal adenomas cause Cushing's in approximately 18 percent of patients and are usually small masses, 2 to 5 cm in diameter.

Metastasis to the Adrenal (Figure 7.4–7.7)

The adrenal is the fourth most common site of metastatic disease after the lungs, liver, and bones. Metastatic disease to the adrenals is most often from a primary carcinoma of the lung. Other primary tumors that may involve the adrenal include melanoma, renal cell, breast, gastric, colonic, and pancreatic carcinomas.

Metastases to the adrenal are often bilateral and mass size is variable, ranging from small (1 cm) to large (10 cm). Needle biopsy may be necessary to exclude metastases in a patient with a known primary tumor.

The sonographic appearance of an adrenal metastasis is that of solid enlargement of the adrenal. With large metastases, central necrosis may be noted.

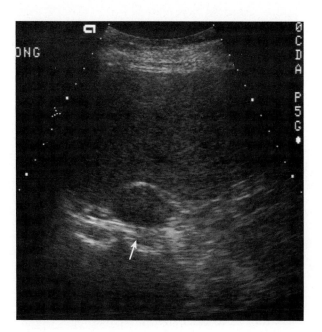

Figure 7.2
Adrenal adenoma: An incidental pickup was an adrenal mass measuring approximately 2.5 cm in its greatest dimension.

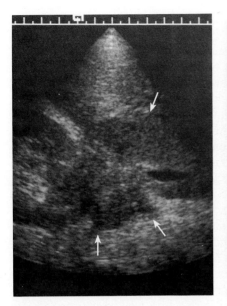
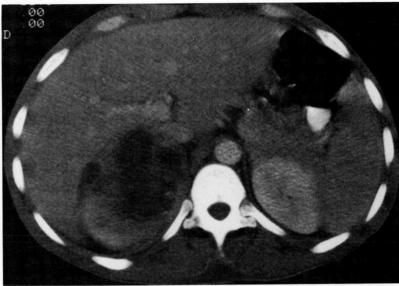

A   B

Figure 7.4

Metastatic lung carcinoma: (A) In this patient with known lung carcinoma, a large, infiltrative right adrenal mass (*arrows*) was present. Note the medial orientation of the mass to the right kidney and the relationship to the liver. (B) Correlative CT images.

Lymphomatous Involvement of the Adrenal

Autopsy studies of patients with non-Hodgkin lymphoma show involvement of the adrenals in 24 percent. Usually, there is associated adenopathy. Sonographically, adrenal involvement with lymphoma may look nearly cystic, as it does when it affects other solid organs, such as the kidneys or liver. There is solid enlargement and the masses are hypoechoic. Often the adrenals are bilaterally involved.

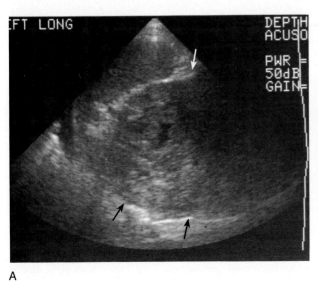
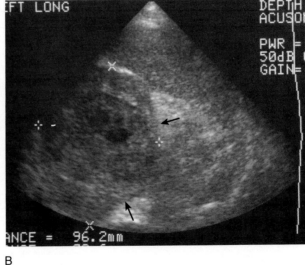

A   B

Figure 7.5

Metastatic adenocarcinoma of the lung: (A and B) A large, heterogeneous adrenal mass was discovered in this man with back pain and a mass seen on chest x-ray.

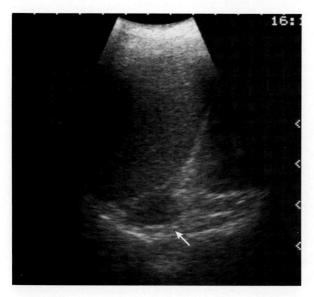

Figure 7.6

Metastatic renal cell carcinoma: This patient, 1 year after radical nephrectomy for renal cell carcinoma on the opposite side, was noted to have a new mass of the left adrenal. Fine-needle aspiration proved it to be metastatic renal cell carcinoma.

Adrenocortical Carcinoma (Figure 7.8)

Primary malignant tumors of the adrenals are rare, accounting for only 0.2 percent of cancer deaths in the United States. Survival of patients with adrenocortical carcinoma depends upon the stage of the tumor at the time of detection. Only about one-half of adrenal carcinomas are hormonally active, so they may become quite large before they are discovered. Hormonally active adrenal carcinomas may be detected when they are small. Hormonal activity is more common in children than in adults.

Symptoms of adrenocortical carcinoma are usually secondary to tumor growth with flank pain, weight loss, and fever. Adults are most commonly affected in the fourth to seventh decades of life, although children may be affected.

The sonographic appearance of an adrenocortical carcinoma is that of a well-circumscribed suprarenal mass that may be quite large (up to 20 cm), having mass effect on the kidney, but generally separate from the kidney. Small masses are often homogeneous, but areas of central necrosis with cystic change are common in large tumors. Calcifications are sometimes seen. Vascular invasion of the adrenal and renal veins can occur as well as IVC involvement.

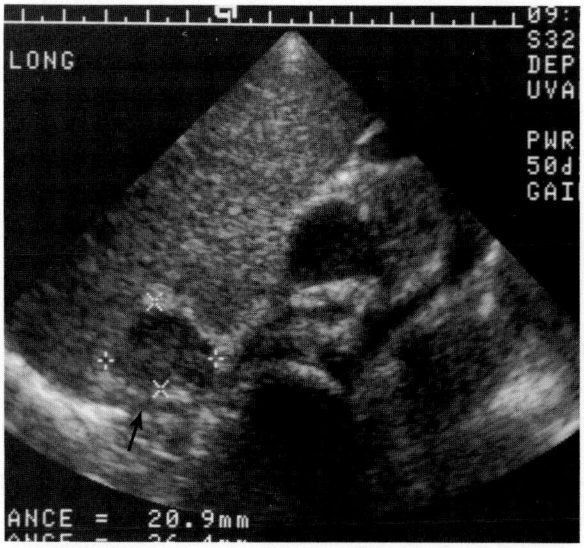

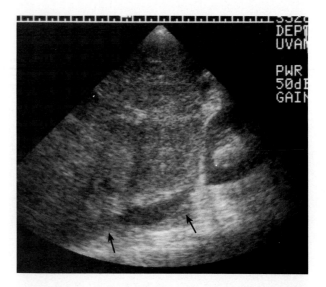

Figure 7.8

Adrenocortical carcinoma: This very large right upper quadrant mass (*arrows*) had a definite cleavage plane between the liver and the right kidney. At surgery, a large adrenocortical carcinoma was removed with some difficulty.

Figure 7.7

Metastatic rhabdomyosarcoma: In this 10-year-old with rhabdomyosarcoma, involvement of the right adrenal was documented by fine-needle aspiration.

Pheochromocytoma (Figure 7.9)

Pheochromocytomas are functioning tumors arising from cells of the sympathetic nervous system. These cells produce catecholamines such as dopamine or norepinephrine. Ninety percent of these tumors arise from the adrenals; 10 percent are extra-adrenal; 10 percent are multiple; 10 percent are malignant.

Clinically, patients may have persistent or paroxysmal hypertension. Tachycardia and hot flashes may accompany the episodes of hypertension.

Because the tumors are hormonally active, they may be quite small when discovered. Pheochromocytomas are prone to internal hemorrhage and necrosis, which may cause a catastrophic event. Biopsy of an adrenal mass without chemical exclusion of a pheochromocytoma should not be

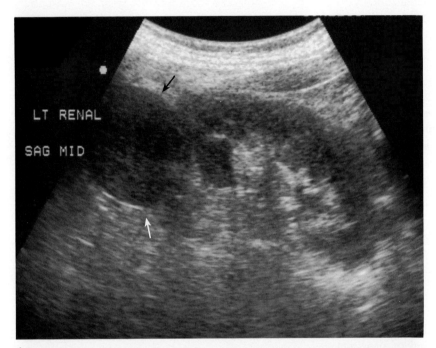

A

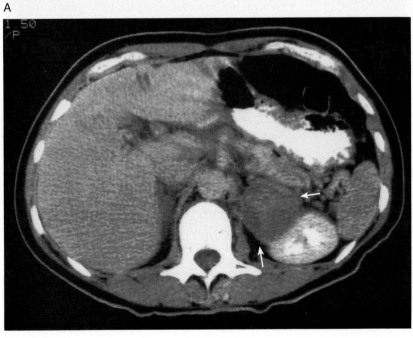

B

Figure 7.9

Pheochromocytoma: (A) In this young woman with severe episodic hypertension, abdominal sonography discovered a solid 4-cm hypoechoic mass superior to the left kidney. (B) CT confirmed an adrenal mass (*arrows*). Chemical studies proved it to be a pheochromocytoma.

performed because puncture of a pheochromocytoma can trigger an explosive hypertensive crisis. The diagnosis is usually made by chemical analysis of urinary metabolites, not by biopsy.

Sonographically, the masses are generally well circumscribed with prominent solid portions. Cystic necrosis is commonly present. Ultrasound is reported to find pheochromocytomas in 89 to 97 percent of cases, with CT having a sensitivity approaching 100 percent. MR is being increasingly used to locate and characterize pheochromocytomas. Nuclear medicine imaging with precursors of norepinephrine is used in some centers.

Infectious Enlargement of the Adrenal/Abscess

Granulomatous diseases such as histoplasmosis or tuberculosis can cause enlargement of the adrenal to several times its normal size. Patients with AIDS may have tuberculosis and fungal and viral infections affecting the adrenal.

Frank abscess of the adrenal is unusual but may occur, appearing sonographically as a necrotic mass. Aspiration of the adrenal mass may be necessary to identify the particular etiologic agent.

Calcifications occur often and persist after the infection has been treated.

Adrenal Cyst

A simple cyst of the adrenal may be a congenital lymphangiomatous cyst or the sequel of previous hemorrhage.

Sonographically, the adrenal cyst will be anechoic with posterior enhancement. Sometimes, associated calcifications will be seen. Adrenal abscess and adrenal lymphoma have the most similar sonographic appearances.

Retroperitoneal Sarcoma

Primary retroperitoneal masses such as liposarcoma, fibrosarcoma, and malignant fibrous histiocytoma may arise in the retroperitoneum and encompass the adrenal.

Accessory Spleen (Figure 7.10)

Especially on the left side, an accessory splenule can mimic an adrenal mass. Careful scanning to show the relationship of the splenule to the spleen and its similar echogenicity will allow the appropriate distinction to be made. Accessory splenules are often present in situations of splenomegaly or after splenic trauma.

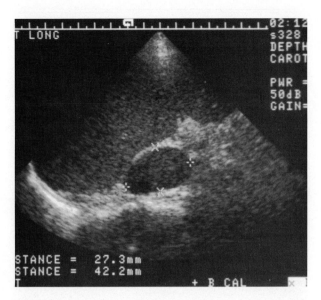

Figure 7.10
Accessory spleen: This well-defined 3-cm splenule was noted adjacent to the spleen in a patient with splenomegaly related to a myeloproliferative disorder. Its position might cause it to be mistaken for an adrenal mass.

CHILDHOOD

Adrenal Hemorrhage (Figures 7.11–7.13)

Hemorrhage into the adrenals occurs most often in the neonatal period because the adrenals are highly vascular and are of proportionately greater size at that time. Traumatic delivery with stress, asphyxia, and septicemia may trigger hemorrhage of the adrenals. In newborns, the triad of abdominal mass, anemia, and hyperbilirubinemia may be present with adrenal hemorrhage. Seventy percent of the time, the hemorrhage is on the right, and bilateral hemorrhage occurs 5 to 10 percent of the time. Adrenal insufficiency may be seen. In the adult patient, trauma and infection, especially with meningococcemia, are the usual causes of adrenal hemorrhage. After liver transplantation, a small percentage of patients may have right adrenal hemorrhage secondary to ligation of the right adrenal vein. Adrenal hemorrhage may occur when there is a preexisting adrenal abnormality such as myelolipoma, metastatic deposit, or congenitally hyperplastic adrenal.

Sonographically, the appearance of an adrenal hemorrhage is related to the age of the hemorrhage. Acutely, an adrenal hemorrhage is a solid-appearing suprarenal mass. Over time, the mass becomes more cystic in appearance, sometimes developing

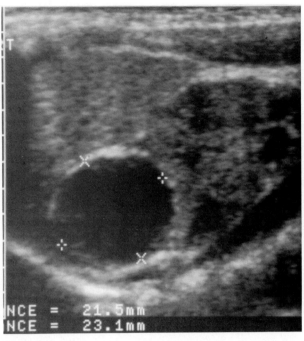

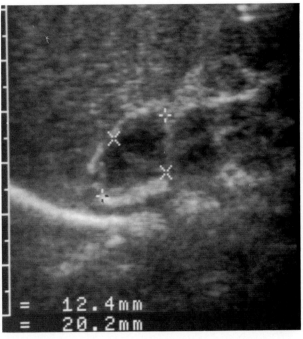

A   B

Figure 7.11

Adrenal hemorrhage: (A) A well-defined cystic mass indenting the upper pole of the kidney was discovered in a newborn who had suffered a traumatic delivery. High serum bilirubin levels and anemia were present. (B) Follow-up imaging 6 weeks after the initial scan showed significant interval decrease in the size of the hemorrhage.

septations. The mass may gradually diminish in size and the adrenal's normal shape may be restored. Dystrophic calcifications may develop over weeks to months as the clot retracts and fibrosis occurs.

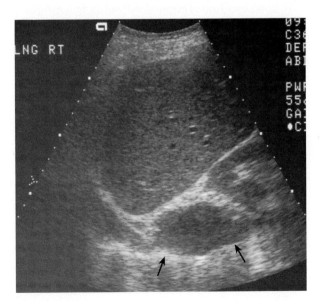

Figure 7.12

Adrenal hemorrhage: A 5-cm hypoechoic mass (*arrows*) was obvious in this patient after liver transplantation. Its hemorrhagic nature was determined on CT images. The adrenal mass resolved on subsequent scans.

Neuroblastoma (Figure 7.14)

The most common adrenal neoplasm in childhood is a tumor of neural origin such as ganglioneuroma, ganglioneuroblastoma, or neuroblastoma.

The sonographic appearance often correlates with the differentiation of the tumor. Ganglioneuromas are well differentiated and homogeneous sonographically. Gangliogneuroblastomas are intermediate in differentiation and thus have more heterogeneity.

Neuroblastoma in childhood often has mass effect on the kidney, displacing it inferiorly or posteriorly. Sonographically, neuroblastomas are often poorly defined, extending out of the adrenal bed and across the midline in many cases. Neuroblastomas, the most undifferentiated of tumors, may show marked heterogeneity of echogenicity, with highly echogenic regions often identifiable. Calcifications may be detected as highly echogenic foci with associated shadowing.

Ultrasound can be quite helpful in determining whether there is additional spread into the abdomen, such as in lymph nodes or the liver. The age

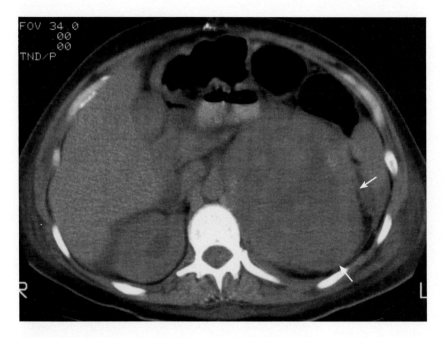

Figure 7.13
Adrenal hemorrhage secondary to metastatic involvement of the adrenal: Acute hemorrhage into the adrenal occurred in this pregnant woman with disseminated, poorly differentiated carcinoma. The mass was acutely enlarged.

of the patient makes the most significant prognostic difference in these patients. In patients younger than 1 year, there is a tendency for spontaneous regression. In patients older than 1 year, the tumor acts more malignantly.

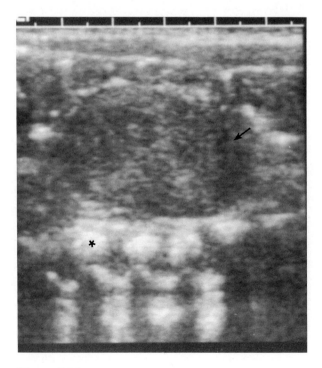

Figure 7.14
Neuroblastoma: A homogeneously solid adrenal mass (*arrow*) proved to be neuroblastoma in this youngster. Note its relationship to the vertebral bodies (*).

Emphasis Points

Usually, to sonographically identify the adrenals in adult patients, adrenal enlargement or an echotexture abnormality such as caused by fat is necessary. CT or MR are usually the imaging modalities chosen to specifically evaluate the adrenals.

A nonfunctioning adrenal adenoma is a common cause of a small adrenal mass. In patients with tumors which metastasize to the adrenals, such as lung carcinoma, the presence of a small adrenal mass may be problematic. The mass may be a nonfunctioning adenoma or a metastatic deposit. Percutaneous biopsy of the mass may be necessary if the patient's clinical management will be altered by the presence of metastatic disease involving the adrenals.

If there is a possibility that an adrenal mass could be a pheochromocytoma, metabolic studies should be performed prior to the performance of a percutaneous biopsy. Such chemical studies can detect the presence of a pheochromocytoma. A biopsy of the mass may, therefore, be unnecessary, thus avoiding the release of life-threatening vasoactive substances.

The larger an adrenal mass, the less likely it represents an adenoma. Most adrenal adenomas are 3 cm or smaller.

In the newborn with an adrenal mass, the differential possibilities are usually adrenal hemorrhage or congenital neuroblastoma. In many cases, the clinical presentation of the child makes the diagnosis clear. Infants with adrenal hemorrhage are often large babies with sepsis, dehydration, or stress. Clinically, there may be anemia and hyperbilirubinemia. Infants with congenital neuroblastoma may have subcutaneous deposits of disease which can be readily biopsied. Observation can be undertaken in both situations with serial ultrasound examinations. In the infant with adrenal hemorrhage, the mass should diminish in size and become more cystic on serial studies. Congenital neuroblastoma usually follows a benign course, so conservative care should not be detrimental to the child.

BILATERAL ADRENAL ENLARGEMENT

    Adrenal Hyperplasia
    Metastatic Disease/Lymphoma

    Granulomatous Diseases
    Adrenal Hemorrhage
    Pheochromocytomas

The most common differential diagnosis list for bilateral adrenal enlargement is adrenal hyperplasia, bilateral metastatic involvement, lymphoma, or involvement with granulomatous diseases such as tuberculosis or histoplasmosis.

Adrenal Hyperplasia (Figures 7.15–7.16)

Adrenal hyperplasia may be a congenital abnormality resulting from an enzymatic deficiency in the production of corticosteroids. Additionally, acquired adrenal hyperplasia may occur in patients with abnormalities of the pituitary adrenal axis, paraneoplastic syndromes, or prolonged, severe stress. On imaging studies, the hyperplastic adrenals are bilaterally enlarged and sometimes nodular, with prominent limbs identifiable.

Metastatic Disease/Lymphoma (Figure 7.17)

Metastatic involvement, as well as lymphomatous involvement, frequently leads to hypoechoic en-

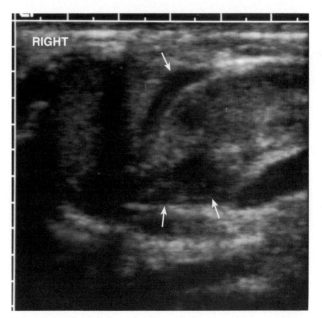

A   B

Figure 7.15
Congenital adrenal hyperplasia: This newborn with ambiguous genitalia was discovered to have congenital adrenal hyperplasia secondary to an enzymatic deficiency. Sonographically, the adrenals were quite large, serpiginous structures in both suprarenal areas (*arrows*).

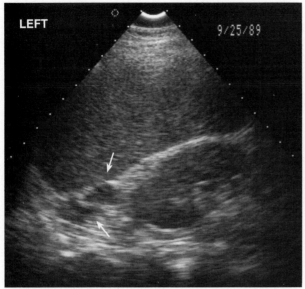

A

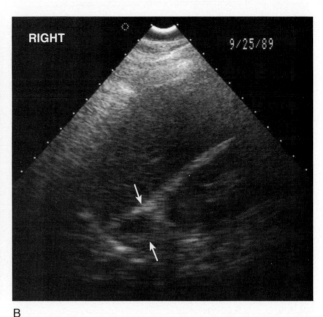

B

Figure 7.16

Congenital adrenal hyperplasia: (A and B) This 25-year-old man with untreated adrenal hyperplasia of several years' duration was being evaluated for infertility. Scans through the adrenal regions showed the adrenals to be enlarged and tubular (*arrows*).

largement of both adrenals. The sonographic appearance is indistinguishable from infectious enlargement.

Granulomatous Diseases

Histoplasmosis or tuberculosis may involve both adrenal glands, resulting in bilateral adrenal enlargement, which may calcify.

Adrenal Hemorrhage

Adrenal hemorrhage is infrequently bilateral, occurring in 5 to 10 percent of patients. Adrenal hemorrhage may accompany septicemia and meningococcemia. Adrenal insufficiency may result.

Pheochromocytomas (Figure 7.18)

Pheochromocytomas are bilateral in approximately 10 percent of patients.

CALCIFICATIONS IN THE ADRENALS

Adrenocortical Carcinoma/
Pheochromocytoma

Hematoma/Adrenal Cysts
Granulomatous Disease
Benign Neoplasms

CHILDHOOD

Neuroblastoma
Wolman's Disease

Adrenocortical Carcinoma/ Pheochromocytoma (Figures 7.19–7.20)

In most cases, adrenocortical carcinoma is a large, solid mass with an inhomogeneous echotexture and calcifications in 25 percent of cases. Vascular invasion of the adrenal and renal vein with extension into the inferior vena cava may be seen.

In childhood, adrenocortical carcinomas are more common than adenomas, which are frequent incidental findings in adults.

Calcifications can be seen in primary tumors, called pheochromocytomas, which arise from the medullary portion of the adrenals.

Hematoma/Adrenal Cysts (Figure 7.21)

Calcifications may develop in an adrenal hemorrhage weeks after the event. A cystic calcified remnant may persist as evidence of previous adrenal hemorrhage.

Approximately 15 percent of adrenal cysts display calcification. Many of these lesions are in fact pseudocysts and are probably the sequel of previous hemorrhage or infection.

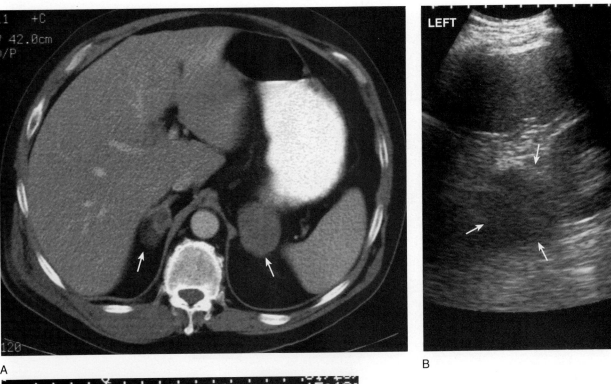

A

B

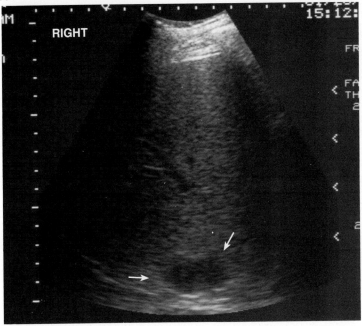

C

Figure 7.17

Metastases to the adrenals: (A) Bilateral adrenal metastases were present in this patient with extensive, disseminated lung carcinoma. (B and C) Sonography could identify both adrenal masses.

Granulomatous Disease (Figure 7.22)

Granulomatous diseases affecting the adrenal glands include tuberculosis and histoplasmosis and may lead to bilateral adrenal enlargement and subsequent calcification. With the HIV epidemic, tuberculosis is increasing, and adrenal involvement by granulomatous processes may be encountered. Neonatal herpes infection may result in a similar sonographic picture. Adrenal insufficiency may result.

Benign Neoplasms

Hemangiomas of the adrenals may result in adrenal enlargement and calcification. Other benign tumors, such as a myelolipoma of the adrenal gland, may have associated calcification. Often, myelolipomas

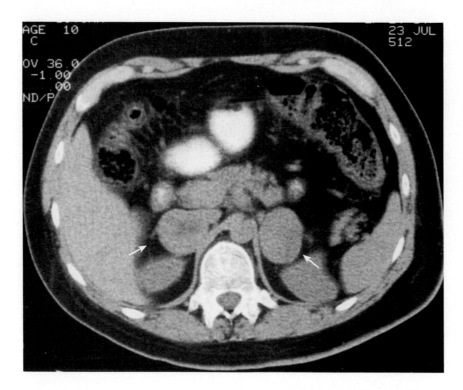

Figure 7.18
Bilateral pheochromocytomas: Bilateral adrenal masses were detected in this patient with multiple endocrinopathies (MEN II). He had previously had thyroid carcinoma.

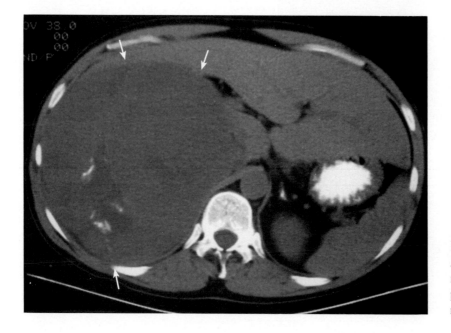

Figure 7.19
Adrenocortical carcinoma: A large mass with calcifications was present in the right upper quadrant.

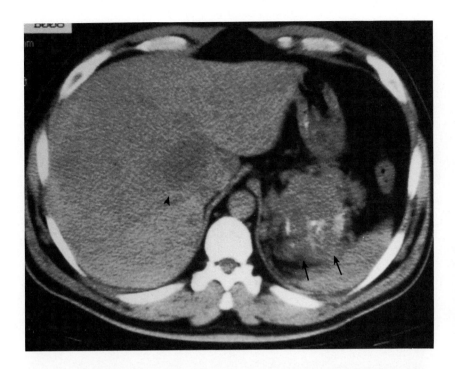

Figure 7.20

Pheochromocytoma: Scattered calcifications were identified in this large adrenal mass (*arrows*). The patient had episodic hypertension and chemical parameters diagnostic for pheochromocytoma. Liver metastases were present at the time of diagnosis *(arrowhead)*.

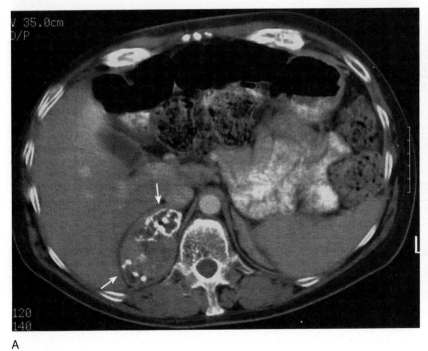

A

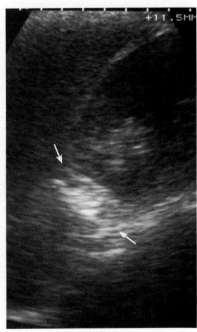

B

Figure 7.21

Calcified adrenal hemorrhage: (A) In this patient with congenital adrenal hyperplasia, there was calcification from previous episodes of hemorrhage, resulting in a calcific mass of the right adrenal. (B) Sonography showed the highly echogenic shadowing mass in the right adrenal fossa. This mass remained stable for years under imaging surveillance.

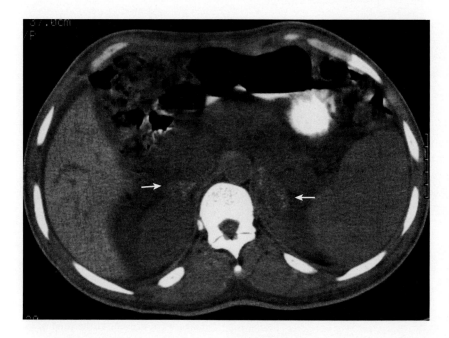

Figure 7.22
Tuberculosis involving the adrenals:
Bilateral adrenal enlargement with
calcifications (*arrows*) was seen in
this patient with tuberculosis.

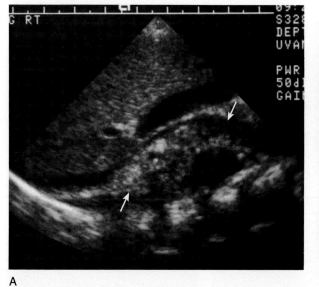

A

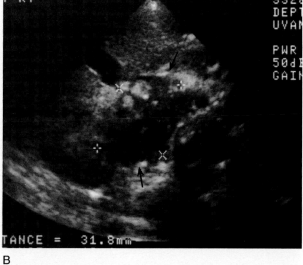

B

Figure 7.23
Neuroblastoma: (A and B) A heterogeneous, calcified
mass was identified in the left suprarenal area. The calcifications are highly echogenic foci, often with shadowing. CT confirmed the adrenal mass.

can be recognized sonographically by their highly echogenic fat content.

CHILDHOOD

Neuroblastoma (Figure 7.23)

Neuroblastomas account for approximately 7 percent of childhood cancers, representing the second most common intra-abdominal tumor. Neuroblastomas are masses of heterogeneous echogeneity with calcifications present in at least 50 percent of cases. Calcifications are seen as highly echogenic foci with shadowing. Poor definition of the margins of the mass and extension across the midline may be identified. In patients with neuroblastoma careful assessment for metastatic adenopathy and bilateral involvement is warranted. Metastatic disease to the liver may be demonstrated in some patients. Bone involvement may be evaluated by nuclear medicine bone scanning.

Wolman's Disease

Wolman's disease is a rare inherited lipidosis that results in calcific enlargement of the adrenals. Mental retardation is frequently seen in affected patients.

FATTY MASS IN THE ADRENAL BED

Myelolipoma of the Adrenal
Angiomyolipoma of the Kidney
Lipoma/Teratoma/Liposarcoma of the
    Retroperitoneum

A highly echogenic lesion without associated shadowing in the suprarenal area is the sonographic appearance of a fatty mass in the adrenal bed.

Myelolipoma of the Adrenal (Figures 7.24–7.25)

The myelolipoma is an uncommon hamartoma of the adrenal gland that contains bone marrow elements. Highly echogenic by ultrasound, the mass may have associated shadowing from dystrophic calcifications within the mass. CT scanning will confirm its fatty density and adrenal origin. Generally, biopsy or surgical removal is unnecessary.

Angiomyolipoma of the Kidney

An exophytic hamartoma of the kidney may appear in a suprarenal position. Such a mass may be highly echogenic and in close association with the kidney. CT again will confirm its fatty density and may suggest its origin from the kidney. If an angiomyolipoma attains a large size, is clinically symptomatic, or is confused at imaging with other renal or adrenal masses, surgical removal may be necessary.

Lipoma/Teratoma/Liposarcoma of the Retroperitoneum

Fatty masses arising in the mesenchymal tissues of the retroperitoneum may be imaged as echogenic masses. A benign lipoma or teratoma may be seen.

Liposarcomas in the retroperitoneum may become quite large. The liposarcoma is the second most common primary retroperitoneal sarcoma, behind the malignant fibrous histiocytoma. The degree of differentiation will determine whether fat is identified. Highly undifferentiated or pleomorphic liposarcomas may have smooth muscle or soft tissue echogenicity rather than the highly echogenic fatty appearance of the well-differentiated liposarcoma. CT scanning will be necessary to assess the full extent of the tumor.

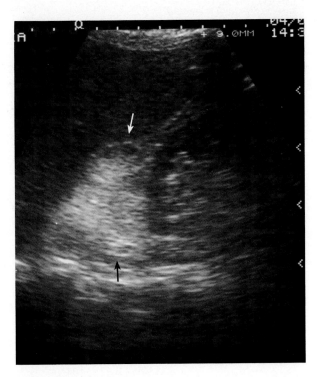

Figure 7.24

Myelolipoma of the right adrenal: A highly echogenic mass in the right suprarenal fossa (*arrows*) was present in this patient with an incidentally discovered fatty adrenal mass.

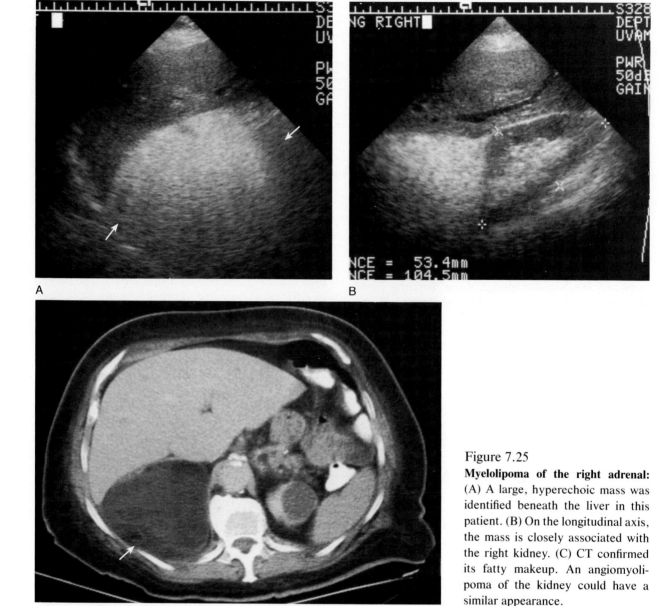

Figure 7.25

Myelolipoma of the right adrenal:
(A) A large, hyperechoic mass was identified beneath the liver in this patient. (B) On the longitudinal axis, the mass is closely associated with the right kidney. (C) CT confirmed its fatty makeup. An angiomyolipoma of the kidney could have a similar appearance.

BIBLIOGRAPHY

Hypoechoic Adrenal Mass

Antoniou A, Spetseropoulos J, Vlahos L, et al.: The sonographic appearance of adrenal involvement in non-Hodgkin lymphoma. J Ultrasound Med 2:235–236, 1983.

Bowerman RA, Silver TM, Jaffe MH, et al.: Sonography of adrenal pheochromocytomas. AJR 137:1227–1231, 1981.

Casola G, Nicolet V, van Sonnenberg E, et al.: Unsuspected pheochromocytoma: Risk of blood-pressure alterations during percutaneous adrenal biopsy. Radiology 159:733–735, 1986.

Cunningham JJ: Ultrasonic findings in "primary" lymphoma of the adrenal area. J Ultrasound Med 2:467–469, 1983.

Davies RP, Lam AH: Adrenocortical neoplasm in children: Ultrasound appearance. J Ultrasound Med 6:325–328, 1987.

Gooding GAW: Ultrasonic spectrum of adrenal masses. Urology 13:211–214, 1979.

Hamper UM, Fishman EK, Hartman DS, et al.: Primary adrenocortical carcinoma: Sonographic evaluation with clinical and pathologic correlation in 26 patients. AJR 148:915–919, 1987.

Hartman DS, Sanders RC: Wilm's tumour versus neuroblastoma. Usefulness of ultrasound in differentiation. J Ultrasound Med 1:117–122, 1982.

Mittelstaedt CA, Volberg FM, Merten DF, Brill PW: The sonographic diagnosis of neonatal adrenal hemorrhage. Radiology 131:453–457, 1979.

Pery M, Kaftori JK, Bar-Maor JA: Sonography for diagnosis and follow-up of neonatal adrenal hemorrhage. J Clin Ultrasound 9:397–401, 1981.

Sarnaik AP, Sanfilippo DJ, Slovis TL: Ultrasound diagnosis of adrenal hemorrhage in meningococcemia. Pediatr Radiol 18:427–428, 1988.

Vicks BS, Perusek M, Johnson J, Tio F: Primary adrenal lymphoma: CT and sonographic appearance. J Clin Ultrasound 15:135–139, 1987.

Wu C: Sonographic spectrum of neonatal adrenal hemorrhage: Report of a case simulating solid tumor. J Clin Ultrasound 17:45–49, 1989.

Bilateral Adrenal Enlargement

Bryan PJ, Caldamone AA, Morrison SC, Yulish BS, Owens R: Ultrasound findings in the adreno-genital syndrome (congenital adrenal hyperplasia). J Ultrasound Med 7:675–679, 1988.

Sivit CJ, Hung W, Taylor GA, et al.: Sonography in neonatal adrenal hyperplasia. AJR 156:141–143, 1991.

Wilson DA, Muchmore HG, Tisdal RG, Fahmy A, Pitha JV: Histoplasmosis of the adrenal glands studied by CT. Radiology 150:779–783, 1984.

Yee ACN, Gopinath N, Ho C-S, Tao L-C: Fine-needle aspiration biopsy of adrenal tuberculosis. J Can Assoc Radiol 37:287–289, 1986.

Adrenal Calcifications

Harrison RB, Francke P Jr: Radiographic exhibit: Radiographic finding in Wolman's disease. Radiology 124:188, 1977.

Kenney PJ, Stanley RJ: Calcified adrenal masses. Urol Radiol 9:9–15, 1987.

Morrison SC, Comisky E, Fletcher BD: Calcification in the adrenal glands associated with herpes simplex infection. Pediatr Radiol 18:240–241, 1988.

David R, Lamki N, Fan S, Singleton EB, et al.: The many faces of neuroblastoma. RadioGraphics 9:859–882, 1989.

Fatty Mass in the Adrenal Bed

Gould JD, Mitty HA, Pertsemlidis D, Szporn AH: Adrenal myelolipoma: Diagnosis by fine-needle aspiration. AJR 148:921–922, 1987.

Hartman DS, Goldman SM, Friedman AC, et al.: Angiomyolipoma: Ultrasonic-pathologic correlation. Radiology 139:451–458, 1981.

Musante F, Derchi LE, Zappasodi F, et al.: Myelolipoma of the adrenal gland: Sonographic and computed tomography features. AJR 151:961–964, 1988.

Richman TS, Taylor KJW, Kremkau FW: Propagation speed artifact in a fatty tumor (myelolipoma): Significance for tissue differential diagnosis. J Ultrasound Med 2:45–47, 1983.

Vick CW, Zeman RK, Mannes E, et al: Adrenal myelolipoma: Computed tomography and ultrasound findings. Urol Radiol 6:7–13, 1984.

RETROPERITONEUM

PATTERNS

Periaortic Soft Tissue
Iliopsoas Muscle Enlargement
Inferior Vena Cava Thrombosis
Inferior Vena Cava Distention

PERIAORTIC SOFT TISSUE

Lymphadenopathy
  Neoplastic Lymphadenopathy
  Infectious Lymphadenopathy
  Reactive Lymphadenopathy
Primary Retroperitoneal Neoplasms
Horseshoe Kidney
Retroperitoneal Fibrosis
Aortic Aneurysm/Grafted Aorta
Retroperitoneal Hemorrhage
Extramedullary Hematopoiesis

VARIANT

Normal Bowel

Ultrasound scanning of the retroperitoneum may be limited if extensive overlying bowel gas is present. Consistent pressure to the central abdomen with the ultrasound transducer will compress the gas-filled bowel out of the way and provide a window for imaging.

In most cases, the aorta and inferior vena cava can be studied. Soft tissue mass may encase or surround the retroperitoneal vessels. Anterior displacement of the vessels off the spine suggests retroperitoneal masses. The following differential diagnoses should be considered.

Lymphadenopathy

Generally, lymph nodes in the retroperitoneum must be 1 cm or greater in size to be identified sonographically. Using CT criteria, many authors consider retroperitoneal lymph nodes abnormally enlarged if the largest short axis of a node is greater than or equal to 1.5 cm. Some authors use 2 cm as the critical dimension for an abnormal retroperitoneal lymph node. Lymph nodes measuring less than 1 cm are considered within normal size limits. Multiple retroperitoneal lymph nodes measuring 1 to 1.5 cm are considered suspicious because of their multiplicity and size. A single retroperitoneal lymph node measuring 1 to 1.5 cm is considered indeterminate. Up to 10 percent of patients with lymphoma will have normal-sized nodes. Enlargement of lymph nodes may occur with neoplastic, infectious, or reactive causes.

Lymphadenopathy may be identified as individually enlarged nodes that must be differentiated from vascular structures or may be seen as confluent, lobulated nodal masses that can encompass or displace normal structures. Generally, lymphadenopathy is hypoechoic relative to the surrounding retroperitoneal fat, and sometimes central necrosis and cystic change can be identified.

Neoplastic Lymphadenopathy (Figures 8.1-8.2)

Neoplastic lymphadenopathy to the retroperitoneum may have a variety of primary sites. The location and pattern of spread of metastatic disease often suggests the primary organ of origin. For example, retroperitoneal lymphadenopathy around the celiac axis and pancreatic bed may be secondary to primary tumors of the region such as the stomach, pancreas, and liver. Retroperitoneal lymphadenopathy at the level of the renal hilum may be secondary to a primary renal mass or be related to a testicular primary in a male patient since the gonadal lymphatic drainage is to the level of the renal hilar vessels.

Lymphoma and leukemia, especially non-Hodgkin lymphoma, frequently involve retroperitoneal lymph node chains. With bulky retroperitoneal lymphadenopathy and no primary tumor visible, non-Hodgkin lymphoma should be suspected.

Infectious Lymphadenopathy

Suppurative lymphadenopathy may be identified in such infectious conditions as tuberculosis or atypical tuberculosis. Central necrosis of involved lymph nodes may be present. Diagnostic aspiration for culture and gram stain can be performed under ultrasound guidance.

Reactive Lymphadenopathy

Noninfectious, nonneoplastic lymphadenopathy can occur in a number of situations. Inflammatory conditions without infection—such as sarcoidosis, inflammatory bowel disease, and hepatitis—can cause hyperplastic lymphadenopathy. AIDs patients can have prominent reactive lymphadenopathy. Generally, hyperplastic nodes are smaller and more numerous than in infectious or neoplastic lymphadenopathy. Aspiration of lymph nodes for cytologic or microbiologic analysis may be necessary to differentiate the possible etiologic agents for the lymphadenopathy. Aspiration may be especially important in AIDS patients, who may have reactive, neoplastic, and infectious etiologies for abnormal lymphadenopathy.

Castleman's disease is a benign condition characterized by prominent lymphadenopathy, which may be diffuse and massive or focal and localized.

Primary Retroperitoneal Neoplasms

Most neoplasms in the retroperitoneum are metastatic, but primary retroperitoneal tumors may be malignant or benign. Benign lesions include lipomas and teratomas. Malignant masses, such as malignant fibrous histiocytoma, liposarcoma, or fibrosarcoma, may arise and become large before discovery. Neoplasms with fatty elements are often hyperechoic at ultrasound. Otherwise, primary neoplasms are generally hypoechoic, with variable heterogeneity of echogenicity. Biopsy either under imaging guidance or as an open surgical procedure may be necessary to define clinical management.

Horseshoe Kidney (Figure 8.3)

A horseshoe kidney is a fusion anomaly of the kidneys in which the lower poles of the two renal moieties are connected anterior to the aorta at the level of a lower lumbar vertebrae, usually the fourth. The renal moieties are generally inferiorly located with medial displacement of the axes of the kidneys. The tissue that connects the lower poles may be functioning renal parenchyma or fibrous connective tissue. The pannus of tissue anterior to the aorta may be recognized as renal tissue, and not misinterpreted as adenopathy or an aortic aneurysm, by recognizing that the tissue joins the lower poles of the kidneys. The abnormal position of the kidneys secondary to the embryologic fusion should serve as an additional clue.

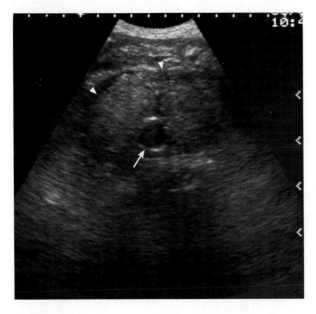

Figure 8.1

Lymphadenopathy secondary to metastatic disease: Extensive echogenic tissue (*arrowheads*) encased the aorta (*arrow*) in this elderly patient with metastatic rectal carcinoma.

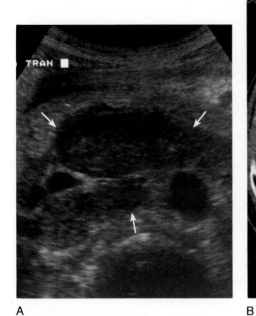

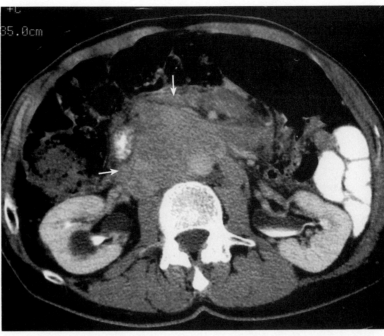

A   B

Figure 8.2
Lymphadenopathy secondary to lymphoma: (A) This 60-year-old patient was believed to have an aortic aneurysm because a pulsatile mass was palpable in his abdomen. Sonography revealed numerous hypoechoic masses surrounding the aorta and inferior vena cava (*arrows*). The presumptive diagnosis was lymphoma, probably non-Hodgkin. (B) CT confirmed the extensive retroperitoneal lymphadenopathy. Non-Hodgkin lymphoma was present at biopsy.

Retroperitoneal Fibrosis (Figure 8.4)

Fibrosis may encase the great vessels of the retroperitoneum as well as encircle the ureters in their course to the bladder. Sonographically, retroperitoneal fibrosis is hypoechoic tissue anterior to and surrounding the aorta and inferior vena cava (IVC). Most often idiopathic, the development of retroperitoneal fibrosis has been linked to certain medications (methysergide), aortic aneurysm leakage, and desmoplastic reaction to malignancy. Surgical biopsy is often necessary to exclude neoplasia and to extricate the ureters from the fibrotic mass.

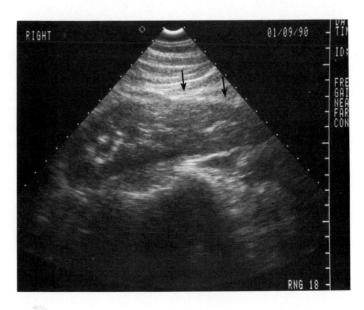

Figure 8.3
Horseshoe kidney: This 50-year-old man underwent ultrasound evaluation to exclude gallstones. Examination of the right kidney revealed it to be low-lying and medially placed. Renal cortex (*arrows*) extended in front of the aorta, over to the lower pole of the left kidney. If the connection between the two renal moities had not been noticed, peri-aortic adenopathy might have been suspected.

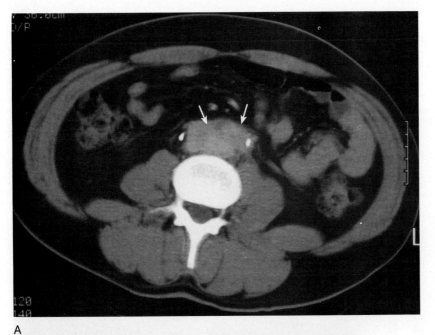

A

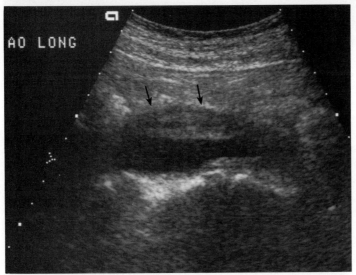

B

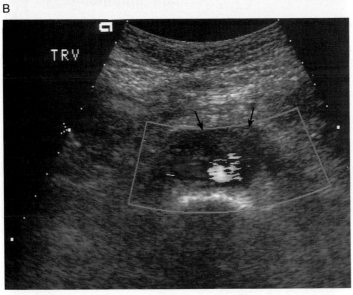

C

Figure 8.4

Retroperitoneal fibrosis: (A) This 40-year-old man developed abdominal discomfort. A CT scan to evaluate the pain showed excessive enhancing soft tissue density anterior to and encasing the aorta and inferior vena cava. (B) A sonographic image in the sagittal plane showed hypoechoic tissue anterior to the aorta (*arrows*). This image is indistinguishable from an aortic aneurysm. (C [Plate 15]) A color Doppler image in the transverse axis showed encasing hypoechoic tissue, anterior to both the IVC and aorta (*arrows*). At surgery, dense fibrotic connective tissue was present. The ureters were rerouted to avoid the development of ureteral obstruction.

300

Aortic Aneurysm/Grafted Aorta
(Figures 8.5-8.8)

Abnormalities related to the aorta itself can lead to the appearance of periaortic soft tissue material. A common abnormality is an aortic aneurysm. Extensive thrombus within the aorta, surrounding a small lumen, can give the impression of periaortic tissue.

Most aortic aneurysms are infrarenal in location and are secondary to atherosclerotic disease. Commonly affected, elderly men may undergo ultrasound examination of the aorta because an abnormality is found on physical examination or for follow-up of an aortic aneurysm documented on other imaging studies.

The ultrasound examination of the aorta can indicate whether the aneurysm involves the renal arteries or not (supra- or infrarenal in location), what the aneurysm's maximal size is, and whether the iliac arteries are involved. Thrombus within the aneurysm may be circumferential or eccentric in location. Usually, thrombus is heterogeneous in echogeneity, but new thrombus may be quite hypoechoic, so that Doppler analysis may be necessary to evaluate the lumen of the aorta. Dissection may occur in a nonaneurysmal aorta, and sonography can identify the intimal flap of a dissected aorta. Blood flow is often present in both lumen in patients with dissection and can be documented by Doppler analysis.

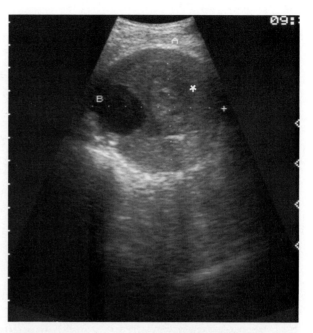

Figure 8.6
Aortic aneurysm: A transverse image of the abdominal aorta showed thrombus (*) filling most of a large infrarenal aortic aneurysm. The luminal size of the vessel was nearly appropriate for a nonaneurysmal vessel.

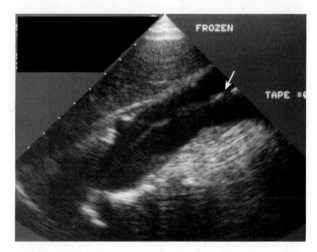

Figure 8.7
Aortic dissection: The linear bright echo or intimal flap within the abdominal aorta was evidence of a chronic dissection of the aorta. The most important information in a patient with dissection is delineation of the proximal extent of the dissection. If the dissection involves the aortic root and ascending aorta in the chest, surgery is usually necessary. If the dissection begins after the takeoff of the left subclavian artery, medical therapy is usually given. Usually CT, MR, or angiography are the modalities used to evaluate the origin and extent of an aortic dissection.

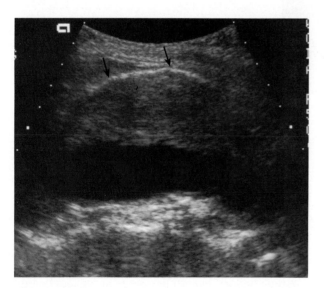

Figure 8.5
Aortic aneurysm: A sagittal image of a large infrarenal aortic aneurysm revealed anterior thrombus filling over one-half of the aneurysm's lumen. This patient underwent elective repair of the aorta.

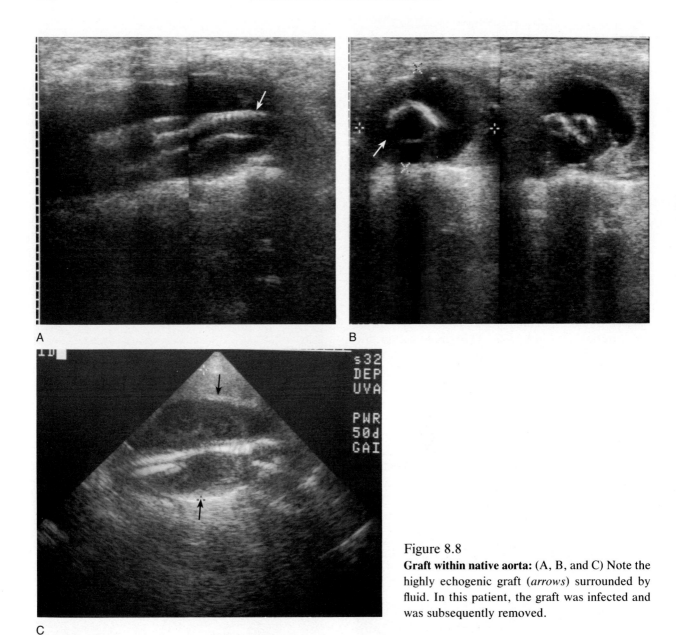

A

B

C

Figure 8.8
Graft within native aorta: (A, B, and C) Note the highly echogenic graft (*arrows*) surrounded by fluid. In this patient, the graft was infected and was subsequently removed.

An aortic aneurysm may be repaired by resection of the aneurysm or by wrapping a prosthetic graft with the native aortic walls. The "wrap-around" appearance of an aortic graft and perigraft seromas or hematomas that form can result in periaortic soft tissue seen sonographically. Although collections around an aortic graft can be seen immediately after surgery, late collections should be investigated. Aspiration of fluid around a graft may be necessary to exclude infection.

Retroperitoneal Hemorrhage

Hemorrhage into the retroperitoneum from either an aortic aneurysm or a postoperative complication may result in a periaortic soft tissue collection. Other causes for retroperitoneal hemorrhage include anticoagulation therapy and trauma. CT is more sensitive in demonstrating the site of origin and extent of hemorrhage than ultrasound.

Extramedullary Hematopoiesis

Extramedullary hematopoiesis is an unusual cause of multilobulated soft tissue masses in the retroperitoneum, arising in situations in which the bone marrow is replaced or inadequate for blood product production. In situations such as beta-thalassemia, additional foci for blood product manufacture become available in the retroperitoneum.

VARIANT

Normal Bowel

Normal gastrointestinal structures in the retroperitoneum such as the duodenum can be misinterpreted as periaortic soft tissue masses unless care is made to watch for peristalsis at realtime.

Emphasis Point

In a young male patient with retroperitoneal adenopathy at the level of the renal hilum, the testis should be considered as a possible site of a primary neoplasm. Testicular neoplasm is the most common neoplasm in young men and has a lymphatic drainage pattern that involves the retroperitoneum initially. Scrotal ultrasound to evaluate for testicular mass should be performed if retroperitoneal lymphadenopathy is discovered.

ILIOPSOAS MUSCLE ENLARGEMENT

Psoas Hematoma
Abscess
    Appendicitis/Crohn's Disease/Postoperative
      Abscess
    Tuberculosis
Metastatic Disease
Primary Neoplasm
Pancreatic Pseudocyst

The hypoechoic iliopsoas muscles are easily seen in most patients, especially in the young and athletic. The healthy psoas may be misinterpreted as a retroperitoneal mass. The central tendon of the psoas is the highly echogenic stripe through the body of the muscle. The iliacus muscle joins the psoas to insert onto the femur, and this muscle compartment is responsible for flexion at the hip.

Psoas Hematoma (Figures 8.9-8.10)

Bleeding into the psoas may occur because of trauma or anticoagulation treatment. Patients on heparin or coumadin or who are deficient in clotting factors may experience pain with flexion of the leg and a drop in hematocrit if they bleed into the muscle. Patients undergoing vascular bypass or vascu-

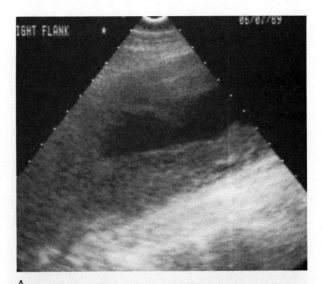

A

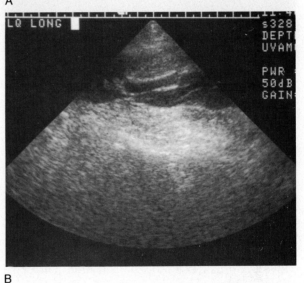

B

Figure 8.9

Psoas hematoma: (A) A large mass developed in the right psoas muscle of this elderly woman receiving anticoagulants. Early scans showed a mass with fluid-debris level. (B) Follow-up ultrasound weeks later showed residual, smaller multiseptate seroma.

lar catheterization procedures are at risk for psoas hematoma formation.

Sonographically, an acute hematoma can cause diffuse enlargement of the psoas with a discrete complex mass identifiable in some cases. If the bleeding is brisk enough, a fluid-debris level, illustrating the hematocrit effect, may develop. Over time, the hematoma should evolve, becoming more cystic and developing septations. The hematoma usually will gradually diminish in size.

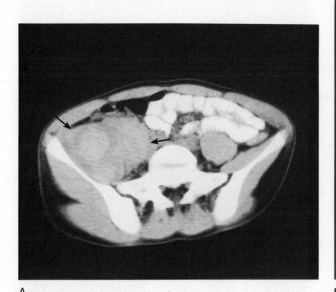

A

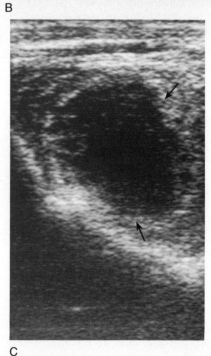

B

Figure 8.10

Iliopsoas hematoma: (A) CT images of large hematoma (*arrows*) in this young man with hemophilia. (B) Ultrasound at the time of acute hemorrhage. (C) Four weeks later.

C

Abscess

Appendicitis/Crohn's Disease/Postoperative Abscess (Figure 8.11)   Inflammatory processes that are in close association with the psoas muscle, including appendicitis or Crohn's disease, may involve the psoas with abscess formation. Duodenal perforation or injury may result in psoas muscle inflammation, since dependent drainage will facilitate involvement of the muscle. Fluid collections in the postoperative patient may be in association with the iliopsoas muscle. Sonographically, a psoas abscess will be a cystic or complex mass, sometimes with highly echogenic foci of air.

Tuberculosis (Figure 8.12)   Tuberculous involvement of the spine may result in destruction of a thoracic or lumbar vertebral body and nearby disc space with extrusion of tuberculous abscess into the psoas muscles.

Clinically, the patient may have chronic back pain, appearing chronically ill with wasting. In most cases, vertebral involvement is related to hematogenous spread in a patient with pulmonary tuberculosis. Percutaneous drainage of the tuberculous abscess in the iliopsoas muscle is possible.

Metastatic Disease

Metastatic disease may arise within or adjacent to the iliopsoas muscle, especially tumors in which the normal lymphatic drainage patterns are in close association with the muscle. In young male patients, metastatic lymphadenopathy from primary testicu-

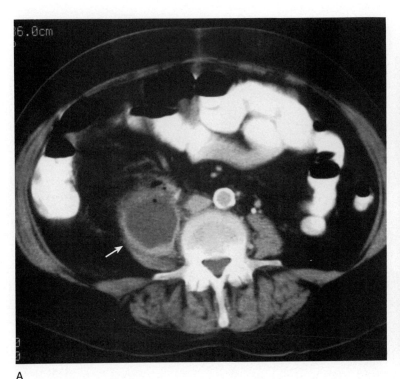

A

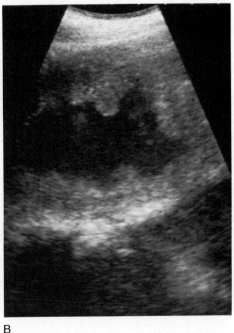

B

Figure 8.11
Psoas abscess: (A) Crohn's disease was the cause of this psoas abscess. (B) Ultrasound provided guidance for tube drainage.

lar tumors may engulf or involve the psoas muscle. Women with cervical carcinoma may develop recurrence in the region of the psoas. Other carcinomas, including breast and lung, may metastasize to the area.

Primary Neoplasm (Figure 8.13)

Sarcomas of the retroperitoneum and lymphoma may arise near and engulf the psoas, leading to global enlargement or multilobular nodal masses. The masses are often quite large at the time of discovery since they arise in a clinically silent area. Biopsy can be performed under sonographic guidance.

Pancreatic Pseudocyst

Peripancreatic collections can easily dissect into the compartment of the psoas in cases of severe pancreatitis.

INFERIOR VENA CAVA THROMBOSIS

Tumor Thrombus
Bland Thrombus

Ultrasound is an important way to evaluate the IVC because flow phenomenon on CT can mimic IVC thrombus. Thrombus within the inferior vena cava (IVC) may be detected sonographically as a solid intracaval mass that may or may not occlude the lumen of the vessel. Occluding thrombus often distends the vein. Color Doppler is helpful in demonstrating flow in the vessel around the clot. Thrombus may be secondary to tumoral invasion or bland thrombosis.

Tumoral Thrombus (Figures 8.14-8.16)

The two most common intra-abdominal tumors that invade and propagate within the IVC, causing tumoral thrombus, are renal cell carcinoma and he-

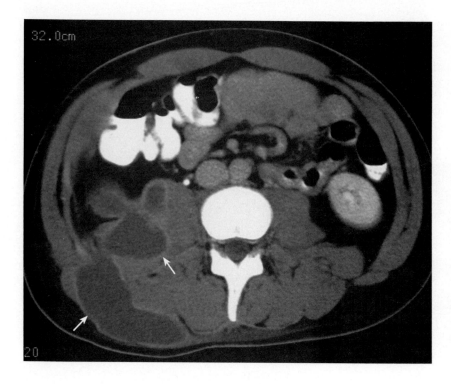

Figure 8.12

Tuberculous psoas abscess: Plain film and CT showed vertebral body destruction and a large psoas collection (*arrows*). Ultrasound was used to place percutaneous drainage tubes.

patocellular carcinoma. These two neoplasms arise within solid organs of the abdomen and have a definite propensity to invade venous structures. Recognition of venous invasion is very helpful in making the correct histologic diagnosis in the setting of a renal or liver tumor. Recognition of the most su-

perior extent of the venous involvement is necessary for surgical planning. Extension of the thrombus into the right atrium may necessitate cardiac bypass at the time of surgery. Wilms' tumor in children, adrenocortical carcinoma, atrial myxoma, and, uncommonly, renal angiomyolipoma can ex-

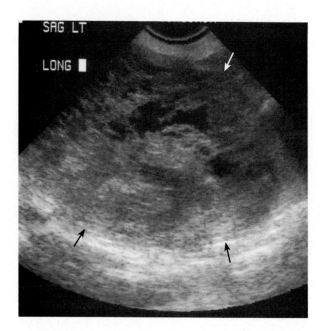

Figure 8.13

Retroperitoneal sarcoma: A large neoplastic mass engulfed the psoas muscle in this patient.

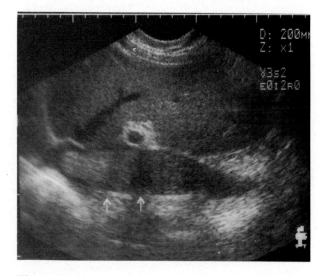

Figure 8.14

Tumoral invasion of the IVC by renal cell carcinoma: In this 76-year-old man with a large, solid left renal mass, the IVC was engorged and filled with solid material. Tumoral thrombus extended up to the level of the right atrium.

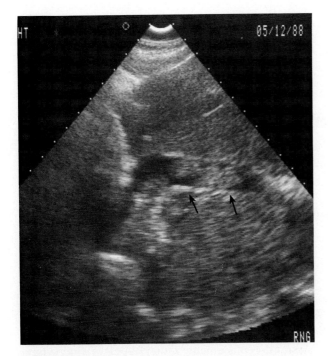

Figure 8.15
Tumoral invasion of the IVC: Renal cell carcinoma grew into the IVC (*arrows*) in this patient.

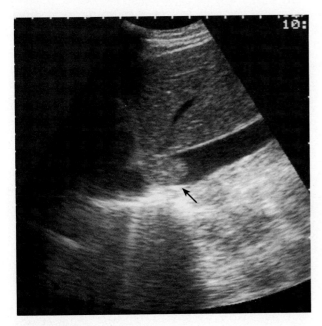

Figure 8.16
Hepatocellular carcinoma in the IVC: This cirrhotic patient developed an acute deterioration of hepatic function. Sonography revealed a large lesion in the right lobe of the liver and obliteration of the right hepatic vein. Extension of hepatocellular carcinoma into the IVC was seen as a focal mass at the level of confluence of the hepatic veins (*arrow*).

tend into the IVC. In these circumstances, a primary mass is identifiable in the organ of origin, such as the kidney or adrenal. The most common primary tumor of the cava itself is the leiomyosarcoma, a rarely encountered mass.

Besides the identification of an engorged soft tissue–filled IVC at sonography, color Doppler or spectral analysis may demonstrate arterial flow within the thrombus, a sign of neovascularity.

Bland Thrombus (Figures 8.17-8.20)

Bland thrombus in the IVC may be secondary to propagation of thrombus from the lower extremity or pelvis. Thrombus may also extend distally from the heart or hepatic veins. Stasis, hypercoagulability, and endothelial injury predispose to venous thrombosis. Hypercoagulable states including pregnancy or myeloproliferative disorders, or compression with stasis by masses or adenopathy may promote the development of inferior vena caval bland thrombus.

Renal vein thrombosis secondary to sepsis and dehydration in the child or related to adult medical renal disorders, such as glomerulonephritis or lupus, may propagate to involve the IVC. Budd–Chiari syndrome and veno-occlusive disorders of the liver result in hepatic vein thrombosis that may secondarily involve the vena cava. Extension of clotting into the cava from the hepatic veins may precipitate massive ascites, liver function abnor-

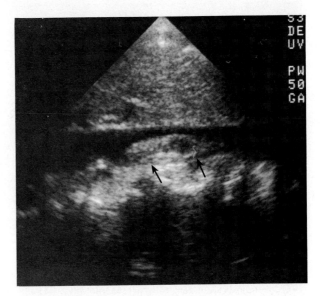

Figure 8.17
Bland thrombus in the IVC: This elderly woman had evidence of deep venous thrombosis of both legs that extended into the IVC (*arrows*).

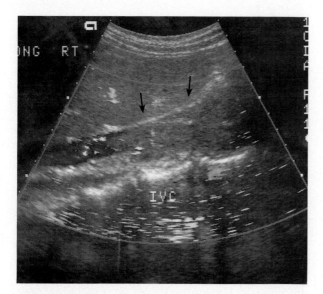

Figure 8.18
IVC thrombosis secondary to compression by metastatic adenopathy: Presenting with severe back pain, this 45-year-old woman was discovered to have metastatic cervical carcinoma and IVC occlusion by thrombus at approximately the level of the renal hilum. Doppler image showed no flow in the midabdominal IVC (*arrows*).

malities, and lower-extremity swelling in patients. Budd–Chiari syndrome is related to hypercoagulability associated with oral contraceptive use, pregnancy, and myeloproliferative disorders as well as hepatocellular carcinoma and congenital stenosis of the IVC. Veno-occlusive disease of the liver may develop as a complication of radiation therapy and chemotherapy associated with bone marrow transplantation.

Ovarian vein thrombosis occurring in the postpartum patient may propagate into the IVC and will be identifiable at the level of the renal hilum where the right gonadal vein enters the cava.

Placement of a filter in the cava to prevent pulmonary emboli in patients with deep venous thrombosis of a lower extremity or pelvis may result in caval thrombus. Placed in patients who cannot tolerate anticoagulants but who need protection from pulmonary emboli, Greenfield filters are associated with caval patency in 95 percent of patients. Only about 5 percent of patients develop caval occlusion after filter placement. Other types of filters have been developed with various thrombogenic potential. Surgical injury to the IVC may also lead to the development of thrombus. The most inferior extent

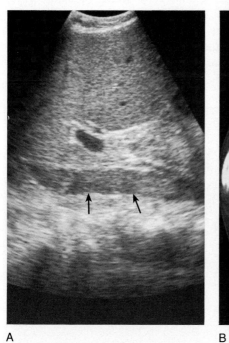

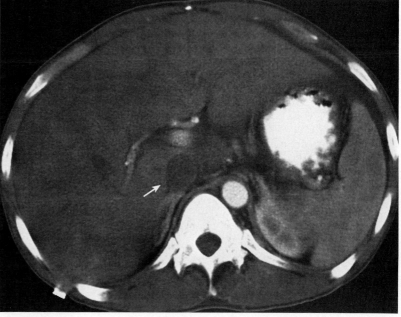

A   B

Figure 8.19
IVC thrombosis secondary to hypercoagulability: (A) This 28-year-old man developed thrombosis of most of the IVC (*arrows*) from the level of the hepatic veins to below the level of the renal veins. The event proved fatal and was believed to be secondary to an inherited hypercoagulable state. (B) CT confirmed the ultrasound findings.

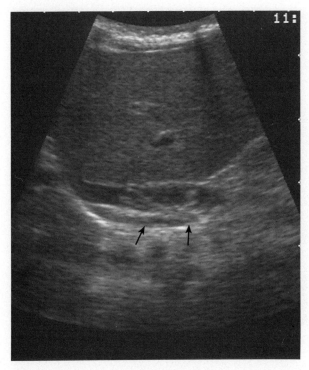

Figure 8.20
Renal vein thrombosis propagating up IVC: In this newborn with renal vein thrombosis related to hemoconcentration, a focal thrombus was identified within the IVC (*arrows*).

of thrombosis in the IVC may be difficult to document by ultrasound secondary to overlying bowel gas.

Emphasis Points

In the abdomen, tumoral invasion of the inferior vena cava is most often secondary to renal cell carcinoma that has involved the renal vein and grown into the cava. Other tumors arising from solid organs and invading venous structures include hepatocellular carcinoma and adrenocortical carcinoma. A mass in the organ of origin is seen sonographically. Primary leiomyosarcoma of the inferior vena cava is unusual.

Bland thrombosis within the inferior vena cava can propagate from thrombosis beginning in the pelvis. Right atrial or hepatic vein thrombosis may involve the vena cava in a retrograde fashion. Hypercoagulable states and injury or compression of the vein can contribute to vena caval thrombus.

Distention and thrombus within the vena cava may be seen sonographically with acute thrombosis.

INFERIOR VENA CAVA DISTENTION

Congestive Heart Failure
Acute Thrombosis of the Inferior Vena Cava
Valsalva Maneuver/Normal Variant

Congestive Heart Failure (Figures 8.21-8.22)

Inferior vena cava (IVC) distention with associated engorgement of the hepatic veins is most frequently seen in situations of right heart failure with passive congestion of the liver and intra-abdominal veins draining toward the heart. Right heart failure is most often secondary to left heart failure. Tricuspid regurgitation will cause prominent vena caval distention. Often the patient with heart failure has other sonographic evidence of congestion, with pleural effusions, a small amount of ascites, and hepatomegaly. The clinical request for the ultrasound examination may be to explain abnormal liver function and hepatomegaly. The ultrasound will show that both are secondary to passive congestion of the liver.

Other volume overload states may also cause caval distention and include pregnancy or renal failure.

Acute Thrombosis of the Inferior Vena Cava

Thrombosis of the IVC with tumor or bland thrombus may distend the lumen, especially acutely. Hypoechoic, nearly cystic-appearing thrombus may be difficult to identify. Color Doppler investigation can help identify such clots. Renal cell carcinoma, hepatocellular carcinoma, and adrenocortical carcinoma are the most common tumors growing into and distending the IVC.

Valsalva Maneuver/Normal Variant

The normal IVC distends and collapses with respiratory variation. In young patients who can perform a rigorous Valsalva maneuver, the cava will distend prominently. The collapsibility of the vessel can be confirmed by continued visualization during respiratory cycling.

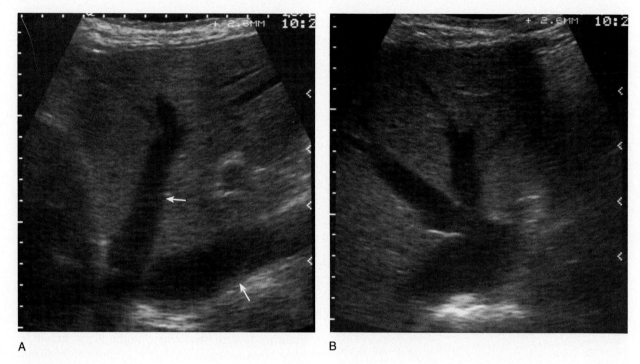

A   B

Figure 8.21
Congestive heart failure: (A and B) This patient with ischemic cardiomyopathy was being evaluated for the possibility of cardiac transplantation. Note the prominent enlargement of the hepatic veins and vena cava.

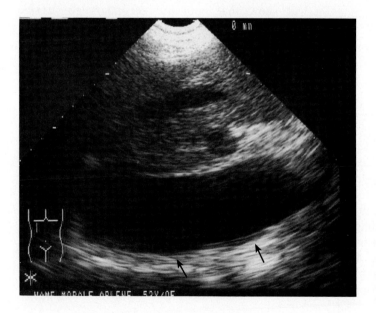

Figure 8.22
Tricuspid regurgitation: Massive caval distention
(*arrows*) was present in this 46-year-old woman
with tricuspid valve insufficiency awaiting surgical repair.

BIBLIOGRAPHY

Periaortic Soft Tissue

Amis ES. Retroperitoneal fibrosis. AJR 157:321–329, 1991.

Bowie JD, Bernstein JR: Retroperitoneal fibrosis: Ultrasound: Findings and case report. J Clin Ultrasound 4:435–437, 1976.

Brascho DL, Durant JR, Green LE: The accuracy of retroperitoneal ultrasonography in Hodgkin's disease and non-Hodgkin's lymphoma. Radiology 125:485–487, 1977.

Fagan CJ, Larrieu AJ, Amparo EG: Retroperitoneal fibrosis: Ultrasound and CT features. AJR 133:239–243, 1979.

Hillman BJ, Haber K: Echographic characteristics of malignant lymph nodes. J Clin Ultrasound. 8:213–215, 1980.

Libson E, Fields S, Strauss S, et al.: Widespread Castleman disease: CT and US findings. Radiology 166:753–755, 1988.

Rochester D, Bowie JD, Kunzmann A, et al.: Ultrasound in the staging of lymphoma. Radiology 124:483–487, 1977.

Sanders RC, Duffy T, McLoughlin MG, Walsh PC: Sonography in the diagnosis of retroperitoneal fibrosis. J Urol 118:944–946, 1977.

Iliopsoas Muscle Enlargement

Graif M, Martinovitz U, Strauss S, et al.: Sonographic localization of hematomas in hemophilic patients with positive iliopsoas sign. AJR 148:121–123, 1987.

Millward SF, Ramsewak W, Fitzsimons P, Frost R, Tam P, Toi A: Percutaneous drainage of iliopsoas abscess in Crohn's disease. Gastrointest Radiol 11:289–290, 1986.

Shirkhoda A, Mauro MA, Staab EV, et al.: Soft-tissue hemorrhage in hemophiliac patients: Computed tomography and ultrasound study. Radiology 147:811–814, 1983.

Inferior Vena Cava Thrombosis

Arenson AM, Graham RT, Shaw P, et al.: Angiomyolipoma of the kidney extending into the inferior vena cava: Sonographic and CT findings. AJR 151:1159, 1988.

Clayman RV Jr, Gonzalez R, Fraley EE: Renal cell cancer invading the inferior vena cava: Clinical review and anatomical approach. J Urol 123:157–163, 1980.

Dal Bianco M, Breda G, Artibani W, et al.: Echography in vena cava invasion from renal tumors. Eur Urol 11:95–99, 1985.

Fong KW, Zalev AH: Sonographic diagnosis of leiomyosarcoma of the inferior vena cava: Correlation with computed tomography and angiography. J Can Assoc Radiol 38:229–231, 1987.

Goiney R: Ultrasound imaging of inferior vena cava thrombosis. J Ultrasound Med 4:387–389, 1985.

Mori H, Maeda H, Fukuda T, et al.: Acute thrombosis of the inferior vena cava and hepatic veins in patients with Budd-Chiari syndrome: CT demonstration. AJR 153:987–991, 1989.

Slovis TL, Philippart AI, Cushing B, et al.: Evaluation of the inferior vena cava by sonography and venography in children with renal and hepatic tumors. Radiology 140:767–772, 1981.

BLADDER

PATTERNS

Focal Bladder Wall Thickening
Diffuse Bladder Wall Thickening
Echogenic Bladder Wall: Calcification
    Versus Air
Perivesicular Cystic Mass

The normal urinary bladder has an echogenic wall that generally measures approximately 3 mm in thickness. The bladder mucosa is not usually separable from the muscular wall. Distention of the bladder lumen with urine allows an accurate assessment of the wall. Every sonographic study of the urinary tract should include a careful examination of the distended bladder for completeness.

The bladder may have a variable shape. In male patients, the seminal vesicles and prostate can be examined through the distended bladder. With bladder distention in a female patient, the uterus and adnexal structures can be examined.

FOCAL BLADDER WALL THICKENING

Neoplasms
Nonneoplastic Masses (Endometriosis)
Cystitis
Blood Clot
Postsurgical Changes
Trabeculae
Benign Prostatic Hyperplasia (BPH)
Ureterocele

CHILDHOOD

Rhabdomyosarcoma

When focal bladder wall thickening is encountered, these differential possibilities should be considered.

Neoplasms (Figures 9.1-9.4)

Bladder tumors make up approximately 3 percent of all neoplasms. Focal bladder tumors often arise from the transitional urothelium. Transitional cell carcinomas make up approximately 90 percent of all malignant tumors of the bladder. Transitional cell carcinomas may be papillary, flat and plaquelike, or polypoid and bulky. Sometimes the tumors are solitary, but they may be multifocal and extensive.

Predisposing risk factors for the development of transitional cell carcinoma include cigarette smoking and chemical exposure in the rubber, oil, and dye industries. The entire transitional urothelium, including the pelvis of the kidney, ureters, and bladder, is exposed and therefore at risk. The incidence of subsequent transitional cell carcinoma in the bladder after a primary upper tract lesion is be-

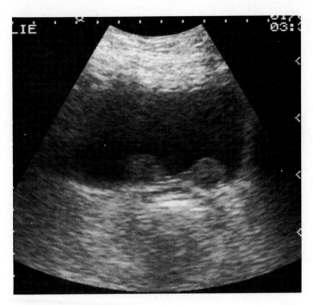

Figure 9.1
Transitional cell carcinoma: Two polypoid bladder masses were identified in a patient with a history of transurethral resection of bladder tumors. Repeat resection was performed. Low-grade transitional cell carcinoma was removed.

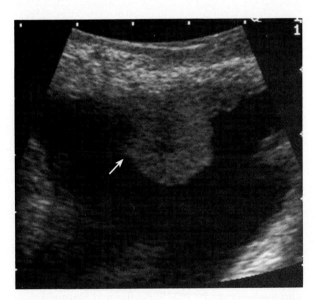

Figure 9.2
Transitional cell carcinoma: Transvaginal scanning in a 60-year-old woman with hematuria revealed a 2-cm polypoid mass in the bladder. This mass was resected and proved to be a low-grade transitional cell carcinoma.

tween 23 and 40 percent. The incidence of developing transitional cell carcinoma in the upper tracts after bladder involvement is lower, at 0 to 6.4 percent. The surface area of the bladder and the relative stasis of urine in the bladder make it the site where most transitional cell neoplasms are found. Once transitional cell tumor has been discovered in the bladder, the upper tracts must be screened for additional lesions. Lesions of the upper tracts may occur at a later time, necessitating continued surveillance after management of the bladder malignancy. The most common clinical presentation of bladder or urothelial neoplasm is hematuria.

Squamous cell carcinoma is a much less commonly seen neoplasm of the bladder, representing 5 percent of bladder tumors. Squamous cell carcinoma is seen in patients with chronic stasis and recurring infection involving the bladder. Patients with long-term indwelling catheters, bladder stones, or parasitic infections, such as schistosomiasis, are at risk to develop squamous cell carcinoma. Such tumors may arise in previously operated bladders or within bladder diverticuli. Squamous cell tumors are often aggressive, resistant to radiation therapy and chemotherapy.

The sonographic appearances of transitional cell carcinoma and that of squamous cell carcinoma are indistinguishable. The bladder needs to be distended to visualize a bladder mass. In most cases, the mass is of homogeneous soft tissue echogenicity, well outlined by extending into the fluid of the bladder lumen. Multifocal masses are frequently seen. Bladder wall calcifications may be present.

An obese patient, incompletely distended bladder, or unusual position of the tumor (on the anterior wall or within a diverticulum) may make the neoplasm difficult to detect.

Mucinous adenocarcinomas are rare tumors that can arise in a urachal remnant. These unusual tumors may lead to mucinous material being extruded in the urine. Usually, these masses arise in the persistent urachus near the dome of the bladder or umbilicus.

Pheochromocytoma occurs rarely in the bladder, giving rise to micturition hypertension.

Metastatic disease to the bladder may be secondary to direct invasion from nearby tumors, such as from the cervix, prostate, or rectum. Hematogenous spread to the bladder from melanoma, leukemia, lymphoma, lung, and breast tumors can be recognized. No specific ultrasound findings allow differentiation of metastatic disease from a primary or benign mass. When a patient with a known primary malignancy has developed a focal bladder wall mass, metastasis should be considered as a diagnostic possibility.

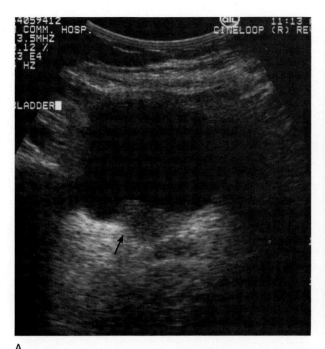

A

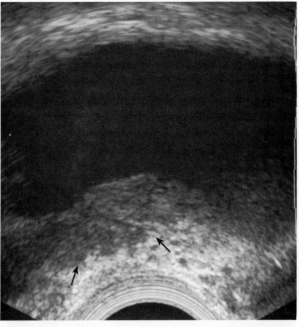

B

Figure 9.3

Transitional cell carcinoma: This elderly woman presented with right upper quadrant pain. Sonographic evaluation showed hydronephrosis of the right kidney (the source of her pain) with fluid around the kidney in the perinephric space. (A) Assessing for the cause of hydronephrosis led to the discovery of a mass (*arrow*) at the right ureterovesicular junction, causing right ureteral obstruction. This patient was treated with cystectomy for the tumor. (B) Transvaginal scan of the same patient.

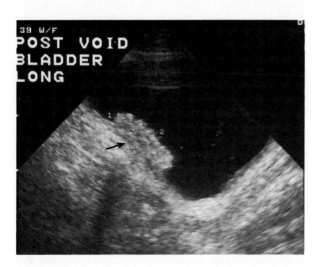

Figure 9.4

Squamous cell carcinoma: Incidental discovery sonographically of a small nodule in the bladder led to a subsequent evaluation. Squamous cell carcinoma was present in the mass.

Benign tumors such as papilloma, leiomyomas, and hemangiomas are infrequently seen sonographically. Neurofibromas may cause a lobulated bladder mass.

Nonneoplastic Masses (Endometriosis)

Endometriosis is a benign, nonneoplastic cause for a mass in the bladder. The urinary bladder may be involved by direct extension from the outside through the bladder wall. Often the patient has had previous surgery and may have symptoms reflecting the involvement of the bladder with endometriosis, such as cyclical suprapubic pain and voiding discomfort. Hematuria may be documented during menstruation.

Cystitis (Figure 9.5)

Inflammation of the bladder usually causes diffuse bladder wall thickening, but sometimes cystitis presents as a focal area of thickening of the bladder wall. Cystoscopic evaluation and biopsy may be necessary to exclude tumor, which would be suggested by imaging studies in focal cystitis. Catheter-induced cystitis may incite focal bladder wall thickening impossible to distinguish sonographically from tumor.

Nearby inflammatory processes, such as Crohn's disease or diverticulitis, may involve the bladder, causing focal thickening and sometimes fistulae.

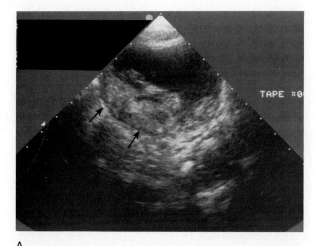

A

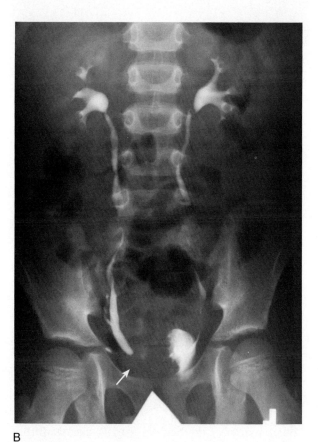

B

Figure 9.5
Herpetic cystitis: This 11-year-old boy had the abrupt onset of terminal dysuria. (A and B) Imaging studies revealed a focal polypoid mass on the right bladder wall. Concern was high for rhabdomyosarcoma, but cytoscopy and fine-needle aspiration could not confirm the suspicion. Finally, surgery was undertaken where focal, bullous involvement with herpes of the bladder was documented.

Blood Clot (Figures 9.6-9.7)

A blood clot secondary to trauma, renal biopsy or tumor, surgery, or hemorrhagic cystitis can cause a focal mass in the bladder. Often, with changes in patient positioning the mobile nature of the blood clot can be determined. An adherent clot can cover underlying bladder wall abnormalities, however.

Postsurgical Changes

Postsurgical edema with focal thickening may mimic a mass of the bladder wall. In patients with bladder tumors who undergo surgical resection or biopsy and have subsequent ultrasounds, edema of the bladder wall can be confused with tumor involvement. Other surgeries that may result in focal bladder wall thickening include bladder wall hematoma after cesarean section, ureteric anastomotic edema after renal transplantation, as well as thickening of the duodenal anastomosis to the bladder after pancreatic transplantation.

Bladders that have been surgically augmented to increase the reservoir effect of the bladder may have very unusual shapes and configurations. Saccular pouches and large capacities may be expected in patients who have had incorporation of bowel

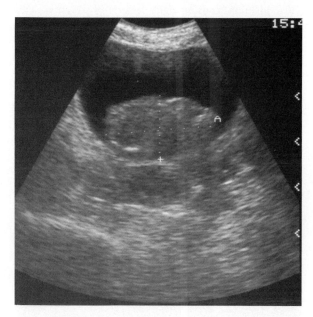

Figure 9.6
Postbiopsy bladder hematoma: This elderly woman had hematuria after renal biopsy for an unexplained climbing creatinine. One day after the biopsy, a focal mass was identified at the bladder base. After irrigation, the mass resolved.

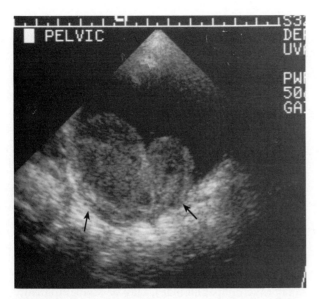

Figure 9.7

Hematoma: Gross hematuria followed this 8-year-old boy's renal transplant biopsy. The clot within the bladder moved about with changes in the child's position (*arrows*). The mass cleared on subsequent scans.

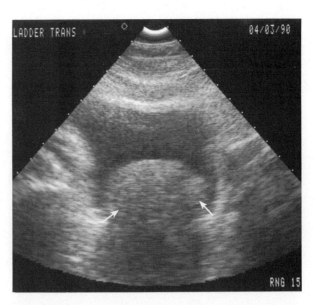

Figure 9.8

Benign prostatic hyperplasia: Dramatic median lobe extension of the prostate into the bladder can be misinterpreted as a bladder mass. The apparent bladder mass in this patient was a large prostate which indented into the bladder base.

into the bladder. Baseline studies to establish the appearance of the postaugmentation bladder are helpful. Postvoiding images to assess stasis should be obtained.

Trabeculae

The trabeculae that develop in the chronically obstructed bladder are usually quite thin and easy to recognize, but sometimes they can be mistaken for a focal bladder mass. The redundant mucosa overlies the often markedly thickened wall.

Benign Prostatic Hyperplasia (BPH) (Figure 9.8)

Enlargement of the median lobe of the prostate in benign hyperplasia can be misinterpreted as a bladder base malignancy unless its relationship and continuity with the prostate are recognized.

Ureterocele (Figure 9.9)

A debris-filled ureterocele of the distal ureter may appear to be a focal bladder wall abnormality. Study of the upper tracts will often show associated hydronephrosis.

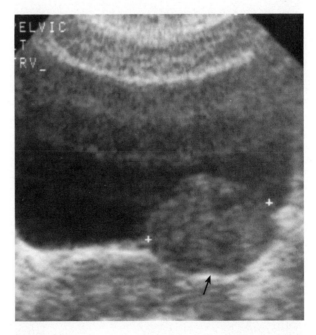

Figure 9.9

Ureterocele: This polypoid mass at the bladder base (*arrow*) proved to be a debris-laden ureterocele of the left ureter. No tumor was present.

CHILDHOOD

Rhabdomyosarcoma (Figure 9.10)

Rhabdomyosarcoma usually affects children younger than 5 years of age with involvement of the trigone of the bladder. The tumor infiltrates the bladder wall and may present as a polypoid mass within the bladder lumen.

Emphasis Point

In women, transvaginal scanning may allow better evaluation of focal bladder wall abnormalities than does transabdominal imaging.

DIFFUSE BLADDER WALL THICKENING

Cystitis
Neoplasm
Bladder Outlet Obstruction
Neurogenic Bladder

Diffuse bladder wall thickening may be secondary to a number of causes. Bladder wall thickening that is diffuse is usually related to infiltration of the wall by inflammatory cells or tumor or muscular hypertrophy secondary to obstruction.

Cystitis (Figure 9.11)

Cystitis with edema or hemorrhage of the bladder wall may be related to infectious agents such as bacteria or viruses. Often seen in women and children, acute cystitis may result in diffuse wall thickening seen sonographically. Parasitic infestation, as with schistosomiasis, will result in similar bladder wall thickening.

Hemorrhagic cystitis, most notable after treatment with chemotherapeutic agents such as Cytoxan (cyclophosphamide), may be sonographically indistinguishable from infectious cystitis. Catheter-induced cystitis is the bladder's response to an indwelling catheter, resulting in bullous edema and small capacity. Radiation cystitis is the bladder's response to radiation therapy and is sonographically identical to other types of cystitis.

Acutely, the bladder wall thickening of cystitis may be secondary to edema and hemorrhage. Over time, resulting fibrosis of the bladder wall may lead

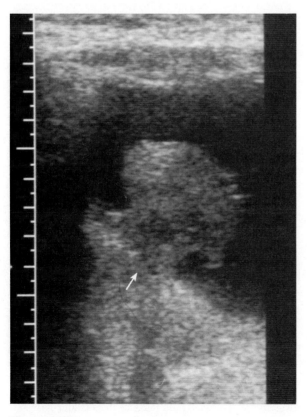

Figure 9.10
Rhabdomyosarcoma: This young girl had a polypoid mass in her bladder.

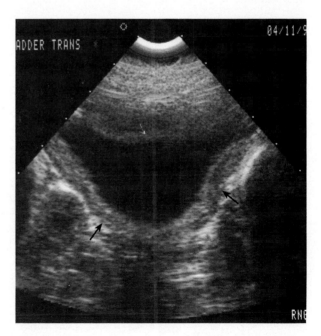

Figure 9.11
Cystitis: This 6-year-old girl complained of dysuria and polyuria. Ultrasound showed no abnormality in either kidney but a diffusely thickened bladder wall (*arrows*) in a small-capacity bladder. The sonographic abnormality and symptoms resolved after therapy for cystitis.

to a permanently thick-walled, small-capacity bladder.

Sonographically, bladder wall thickening related to cystitis is frequently uniform and extensive.

Neoplasm (Figure 9.12)

Although tumors of the bladder often present as polypoid masses projecting into the bladder lumen, transitional cell carcinoma, especially invasive or recurrent, can diffusely infiltrate the bladder wall, resulting in a thick-walled, very rigid, small-capacity bladder. The infiltrating bladder neoplasm is often a high-grade tumor that invades the bladder wall and requires cystectomy, radiation, or systemic chemotherapy, in contrast to the superficial polypoid tumors, which can often be treated by transurethral resection or chemotherapy instillation.

The other, less frequently seen types of bladder cancer, squamous cell or adenocarcinoma, can infiltrate the bladder wall, especially when they are recurrent.

Bladder Outlet Obstruction (Figure 9.13)

Bladder wall thickening related to chronic outlet obstruction may be seen in male children with obstruction secondary to posterior urethral valves or other urethral obstruction. Strictures developing after pelvic trauma or iatrogenic injury or related to sexually transmitted diseases, such as gonorrhea, may result in bladder wall thickening in older patients. In elderly men, a common cause of bladder wall thickening is related to bladder outlet obstruction secondary to benign prostatic hyperplasia (BPH). Prostate carcinoma causing outlet obstruction may be present as well.

Neurogenic Bladder (Figure 9.14)

Neurogenic dysfunction of the bladder secondary to spinal dysraphism, spinal surgery, or trauma may result in a thick-walled, poorly emptying bladder. Often the clinical history will explain the etiology of the bladder dysfunction. Patients who suffer spinal injury or trauma or who were born with spinal dysraphism and have a neurogenic bladder require lifelong surveillance to monitor for changes related to the functional obstruction of the bladder.

Sonographically, the bladder wall is diffusely thickened with large irregular trabeculations. Associated hydronephrosis of the kidneys may be present related to either reflux or obstruction. Large post void residuum may be noted.

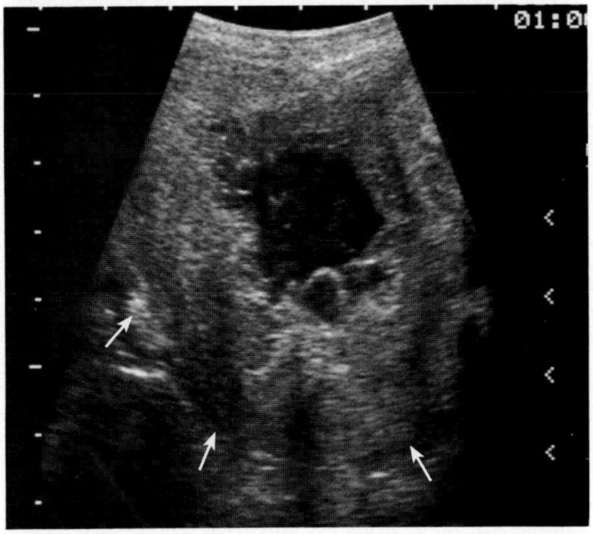

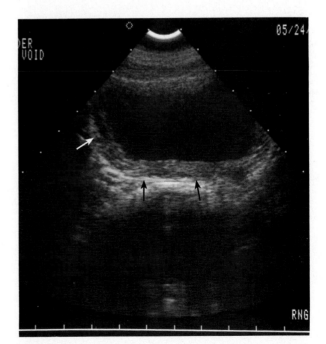

Figure 9.12
Infiltrating adenocarcinoma of the bladder: This transvaginal scan was performed on a 66-year-old woman who presented with gross hematuria. The patient could not tolerate any fluid distention of the bladder. Dramatic bladder wall thickening (*arrows*) with bullous mucosal edema was secondary to extensive, infiltrating adenocarcinoma. Note the small bladder capacity.

Figure 9.13
Ureteral stricture: This young man suffered a gunshot injury to the perineum with a resultant urethral stricture. Diffuse bladder wall thickening (*arrows*) reflected the chronic bladder outlet obstruction.

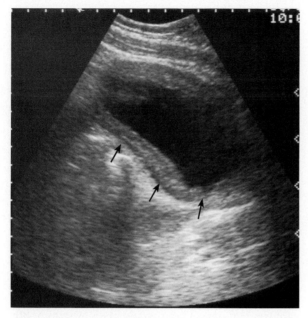

Figure 9.14
Neurogenic bladder: This 35-year-old man with multiple sclerosis had suffered from a neurogenic bladder for months and was studied during an acute exacerbation of his illness. Bladder wall thickening was present (*arrows*).

HIGHLY ECHOGENIC BLADDER WALL: CALCIFICATION VERSUS AIR

    Calcification
        Neoplasm
        Parasitic Infestation
        Postoperative Abnormalities/Radiation
            Therapy
        Infectious Causes of Bladder Calcifications
        Adherent Bladder Stone
    Air
        Emphysematous Cystitis

VARIANT

    Air in the Lumen of the Bladder
    Stone in Ureterovesical Junction

The recognition of a highly echogenic bladder wall, often with associated shadowing at sonography, usually is secondary to the presence of calcification or air within the bladder wall. Causes for bladder wall calcification or air are fairly limited.

Calcification

Neoplasm (Figure 9.15) Histologically many bladder neoplasms have calcifications, but not all

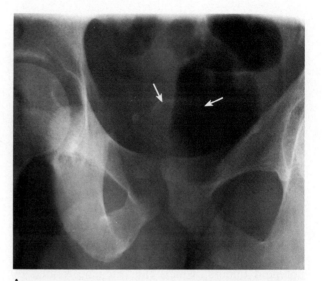

A

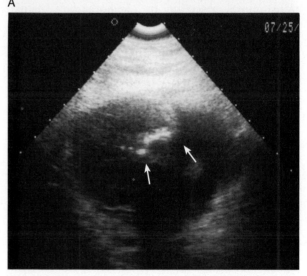

B

Figure 9.15
Calcified transitional cell carcinoma: (A) This elderly man experienced gross hematuria. Plain film showed calcification in the region of the bladder. (B) Ultrasound demonstrated a small-capacity, thick-walled bladder with calcifications (*arrows*).

calcifications can be identified sonographically. Recognition of bladder wall calcification and an associated mass makes identification of a bladder neoplasm likely. Transitional cell carcinoma is most often the cause of a neoplastic calcified bladder mass, as it is by far the most common malignant tumor in the bladder. Other tumors, including squamous cell carcinoma and rarer mesenchymal tumors, can also calcify.

Treated tumors, such as lymphoma, may calcify, especially after radiation therapy.

Parasitic Infestation   Chronic infestation with schistosomiasis may lead to a fibrotic, thick-walled bladder with calcifications. *Schistosoma haematobium* infection is the most common reason, worldwide, for bladder wall calcification. The adult female worm lays her eggs in the submucosa of the bladder. The eggs incite an intense fibrotic reaction that results in calcification around the ova. The calcification is often extensive at the base of the bladder, but may extend to involve the entire bladder. Even with extensive calcification, the capacity and flexibility of the bladder are not necessarily compromised.

The development of squamous cell carcinoma is a recognized phenomenon in the chronically diseased bladder affected by schistosomiasis. Recognition of a soft tissue mass in the calcified bladder of schistosomiasis could herald the development of squamous cell neoplasm.

Postoperative Abnormalities/Radiation Therapy (Figures 9.16-9.18)   Patients who have had surgery involving the bladder, such as ureteral reimplantation for high-grade reflux or ureteric anastomosis to the bladder with kidney transplantation, may have bladder wall irregularities that calcify at the surgical site. The anastomotic area may contain suture material with encrusted material that can break off and act as the nidus for stone formation.

Other foreign bodies can be introduced into the bladder and form a nidus for stone formation. Gen-

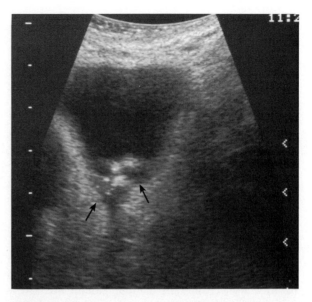

Figure 9.17
Ureteral reimplantation site: This child had experienced severe uretero-vesicular reflux, necessitating reimplantation of the ureter. The surgical site had areas of highly echogenic material (*arrows*), sometimes with shadowing.

erally, calcifications forming around foreign bodies are mobile and can therefore be differentiated from bladder wall abnormalities.

An irradiated bladder may develop wall calcifications. Radiation cystitis may lead to bladder

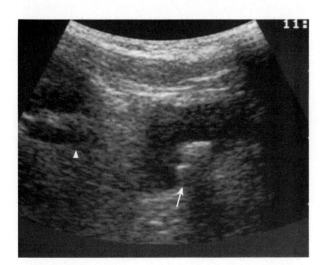

Figure 9.16
Renal transplant ureteral anastomosis: At the site of the ureteral anastomosis to the bladder, highly echogenic foci with shadowing are seen. Normally seen in the operated bladder, the suture sites (*arrow*) may serve as a nidus for calculus development. Note the lower pole of the transplant (*arrowhead*).

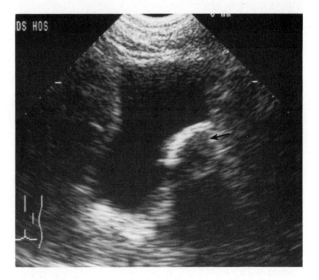

Figure 9.18
Calcification of the bladder wall after radiation therapy: A large, highly echogenic area with shadowing (*arrow*) developed in the bladder of this patient after radiation therapy for lymphomatous involvement of underlying bone. Plain films confirmed the calcification.

wall calcification even if the bladder was not the primary treatment target.

Infectious Causes of Bladder Calcifications
In encrusted cystitis in which precipitation of salts occurs on mucosal erosions, the bladder wall may become echogenic with shadowing secondary to the salt deposition.

Tuberculous involvement of the bladder, usually associated with disease in the upper tracts, is an unusual cause for an irregular, partially calcified bladder wall.

Adherent Bladder Stone (Figure 9.19)
Usually, a bladder calculus is mobile. By changing patient positioning it can be made to move about, and therefore may be differentiated from a calcified bladder wall. Adherent bladder calculi are rarely seen but could be confused with a calcified bladder wall. Bladder stones may develop in patients with chronic urinary stasis and recurrent infections. If present for a prolonged period of time, bladder stones may predispose a patient to bladder neoplasia.

Air

Emphysematous Cystitis (Figure 9.20)
An echogenic bladder wall with posterior "dirty" shadowing and reverberations may be seen sonographically in patients with emphysematous cystitis. Gas in the wall of the bladder results from bacterial fermentation of glucose. Approximately one-half of patients with emphysematous cystitis are diabetics, and the organism causing the cystitis is often *Escherichia coli*. Female patients predominate in this disorder. Plain films or CT can be useful to confirm that the abnormality is bladder wall air and not calcification. In most situations the finding is a relatively incidental one and the patient's clinical status is stable, unlike emphysematous pyelonephritis, which often requires emergent nephrectomy.

VARIANT

Air in the Lumen of the Bladder (Figure 9.21)
Air in the lumen of the bladder from instrumentation or fistulization of the bladder to bowel or vagina may be misinterpreted as a bladder wall abnormality. Changes in the patient's position will allow the air to move about, proving the air is not within the wall of the bladder, but in the lumen.

Stone in Ureterovesical Junction (Figure 9.22)
A renal calculus may lodge at the ureterovesical junction (UVJ) on its way out. Sometimes, patients will be relatively asymptomatic and the stone will be picked up incidentally at sonography. The stone will not move about with changes in position. Its size will determine the chance of successful passage without assistance.

PERIVESICULAR CYSTIC MASS

    Bladder Diverticulum
    Ovarian Cyst or Neoplasm/Ovarian Remnant
    Dilated Distal Ureter
    Peritoneal Inclusion Cyst/Lymphocele
    Parovarian Cyst
    Penile Prosthesis Reservoir
    Seminal Vesicle Cyst
    Free Pelvic Fluid

CHILDHOOD

Urachal Remnant

When a cystic mass is identified in close proximity to the bladder, its origin must be determined. Careful scanning of a distended and then empty bladder, as well as considerations as to the patient's age, sex, and previous surgeries, will help determine the appropriate diagnosis.

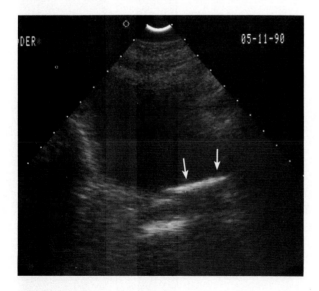

Figure 9.19
Bladder calculi: Extensive bladder stones were present in this young, paralyzed patient with a neurogenic bladder and recurrent urinary tract infections. The stones were seen as a highly echogenic layer of material that caused shadowing (*arrows*).

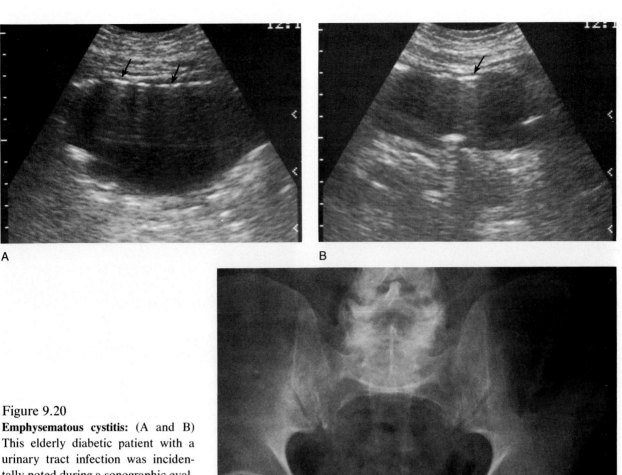

A

B

Figure 9.20

Emphysematous cystitis: (A and B) This elderly diabetic patient with a urinary tract infection was incidentally noted during a sonographic evaluation to have a highly echogenic bladder wall (*arrows*) with reverberations behind it. (C) Plain film of the bladder confirmed air in the wall. The etiologic organism of the infection was *E. coli*.

C

Figure 9.21

Fistula to the bladder from bowel in patient with Crohn's disease: A highly echogenic focus with ringdown artifact was noted in the bladder. Its mobility confirmed that it was within the bladder lumen and not within the wall. In this patient with unexplained recurrent urinary tract infections, the air was secondary to a fistula from the bowel secondary to Crohn's disease.

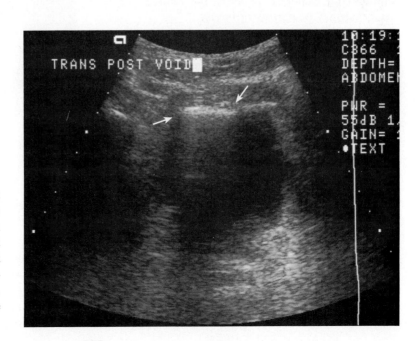

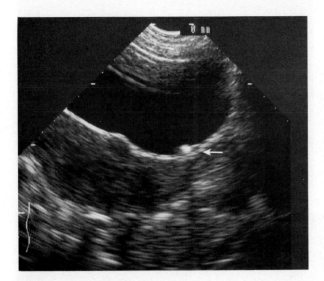

Figure 9.22
Stone at ureterovesical junction: In this patient being evaluated for uterine fibroids, an unsuspected calculus was identified impacted at the left UVJ (*arrow*). It was removed at cystoscopy. Had its position at the left UVJ not been recognized, it could have been mistaken for a focal bladder wall calcification.

Bladder Diverticulum (Figures 9.23-9.25)

Diverticula of the bladder usually develop in patients with chronic bladder outlet obstruction or neurogenic bladder and are secondary to herniation of mucosa through defects in the muscular wall of the bladder. These outpouchings of bladder mucosa do not have the full thickness of the bladder wall for support and usually connect to the bladder via a neck that may be narrow or broad.

Diverticula may be solitary or multiple. They are sites of urinary stasis and may predispose to recurring infections and stone formation. Tumors sometimes develop in bladder diverticula.

Sonographically, a bladder diverticulum is a fluid-filled structure adjacent to the bladder. Visualization of its communication with the bladder lumen will allow its origin to be known. Bladder diverticula may distend with urine when the patient empties the bladder.

Ovarian Cyst or Neoplasm/Ovarian Remnant (Figure 9.26)

Functional ovarian cysts are commonly seen in women of reproductive age and are frequent causes of perivesicular cystic masses in female patients. Cystic pelvic masses in elderly women may be ovarian neoplasia.

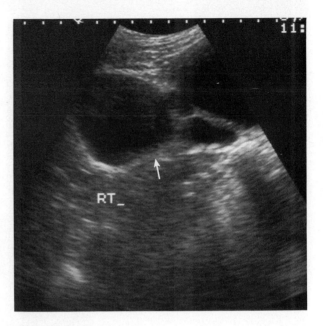

Figure 9.23
Bladder diverticulum: A large diverticulum of the bladder (*arrow*) was present in this elderly man with chronic bladder outlet obstruction. The diverticulum had a small connection to the bladder. On postvoiding films, the diverticulum became larger.

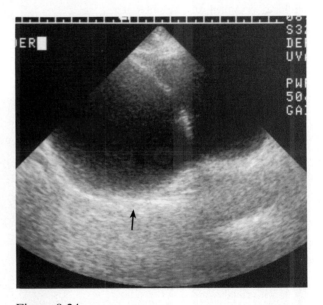

Figure 9.24
Bladder diverticulum: This elderly woman experienced recurrent urinary tract infections. Investigation led to the discovery of a very large bladder diverticulum of nearly the same capacity as the bladder. The diverticulum failed to empty with voiding.

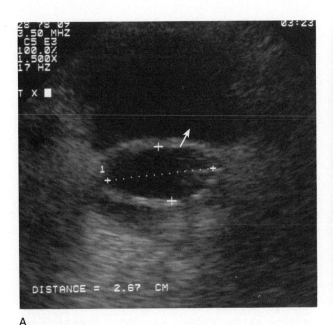

A

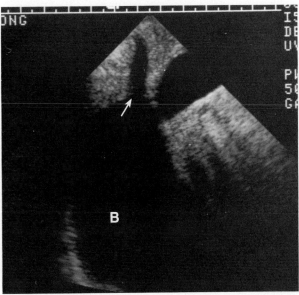

B

Figure 9.25

Bladder diverticulum: (A) A perivesicular cystic mass of unknown origin was identified on transabdominal imaging. (B) Transvaginal scanning clarified its origin from the base of the bladder (B). Note the proximity to the urethra (*arrow*).

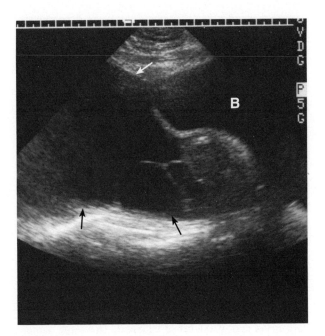

Figure 9.26

Cystadenoma of the ovary: The septations within this large cyst adjacent to the bladder (B) and the advanced age of the patient suggested its neoplastic origin.

It is imperative to identify the ovaries and thus determine whether the cystic mass arises from the ovary. The ovaries are usually identified by the presence of follicles.

(For full discussion of the evaluation of adnexal cystic masses, see related adnexal topics.)

Some patients who report a previous oophorectomy develop recurrent ovarian cysts related to an unrecognized ovarian remnant not removed at the time of surgery. This remnant may also cause functional cysts.

Dilated Distal Ureter (Figure 9.27)

A dilated distal ureter caused by obstruction of the ureter or massive reflux may be interpreted as a perivesicular cystic mass. Recognition of its tubular shape, its insertion into the bladder, and associated hydronephrosis will allow the appropriate diagnosis to be made.

Peritoneal Inclusion Cyst/Lymphocele (Figure 9.28)

In patients who have had previous intra-abdominal surgery, encysted peritoneal fluid may become trapped. Such a postoperative fluid collection is rarely symptomatic but may cause diagnostic concern related to its etiology.

Lymphoceles may develop in patients after lymph node dissections or extraperitoneal surgery such as renal transplantation. Lymphoceles are cys-

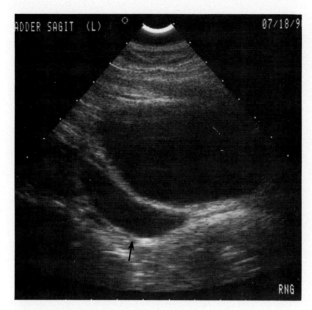

Figure 9.27
Dilated distal ureter secondary to ectopic ureteral insertion: In this child, the cystic perivesicular mass was a dilated ureter.

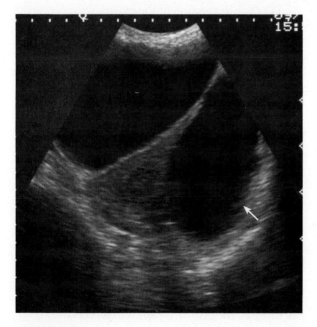

Figure 9.28
Lymphocele: This large cystic mass (*arrow*) developed after lymph node dissection for lymphoma. It was clearly separate from the ovaries and persisted for months.

tic masses of lymph that may be small to quite large, are often septated, and may persist for weeks to months. Sometimes, marsupialization to the intraperitoneal contents is necessary for permanent decompression of the collection.

Parovarian Cyst (Figure 9.29)

Arising from embryologic remnants, paraovarian cysts may be confused with a distended bladder if care is not taken to differentiate the parovarian cyst from the bladder.

Penile Prosthesis Reservoir (Figure 9.30)

In a man with a penile prosthesis for impotence, the reservoir is located in the pelvis, often in close proximity to the bladder. Awareness of the previous surgery and the patient's knowledge of the reservoir's site will allow this cystic mass to be correctly identified.

Seminal Vesicle Cyst

Congenital abnormalities of the seminal vesicles can result in cyst formation behind the bladder.

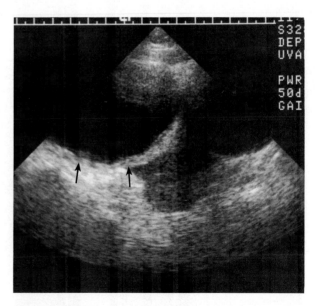

Figure 9.29
Parovarian cyst of the broad ligament: This large, simple cyst in the pelvis (*arrows*) was initially misinterpreted as the bladder. When the bladder was filled, the origin of the mass was determined to be separate from the bladder.

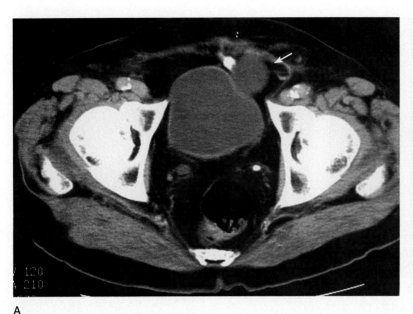
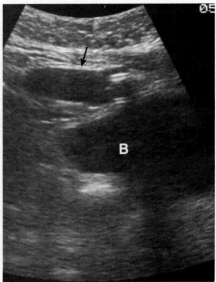

A   B

Figure 9.30

Reservoir for penile prosthesis: (A) This perivesicular cystic mass was originally misinterpreted as a bladder diverticulum on CT (*arrow*). Upon questioning, the patient reported the presence of the penile reservoir. (B) Ultrasound confirmed its cystic and perivesicular nature. (B = Bladder.)

Often asymptomatic, the seminal vesicle cyst may be noted incidentally during imaging or may (less likely) be identified when a patient is evaluated for infertility. Recognition of seminal vesicle cyst or absence should lead to an evaluation of the kidneys, since renal agenesis may be associated on the ipsilateral side.

Free Pelvic Fluid

A small amount of pelvic fluid may be seen behind the bladder and can usually be differentiated from cystic masses because of its free-flowing character. Many possible etiologies for such fluid exist.

CHILDHOOD

Urachal Remnant (Figure 9.31)

The urachus extends from the anterior portion of the bladder to the umbilicus and may remain patent in childhood, leading to a communication between the bladder and umbilicus. When the urachus fails to obliterate, a patent urachus or urachal sinus may lead to chronic drainage from the umbilicus. A urachal diverticulum communicates with the bladder, and a urachal cyst has no communication with either the bladder or anterior abdominal wall.

Sonographically, a urachal abnormality is generally identified with a superficially scanning transducer in the anterior abdominal wall as a cystic mass, which may or may not communicate with the bladder. Debris within the urachal mass often suggests superimposed infection.

Emphasis Point

Scanning the patient with a perivesicular cystic mass may be enhanced by performing the study first with a full bladder and after the bladder is emptied. This allows the relationship of the mass and bladder to be determined, in many cases.

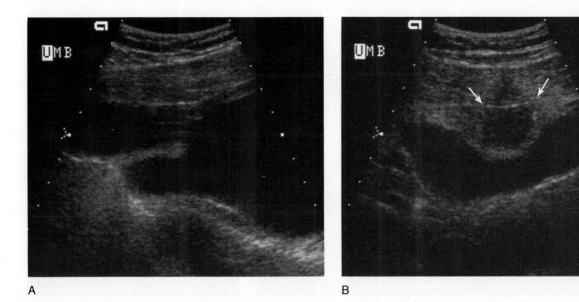

A   B

Figure 9.31

Patent urachus: (A) This 8-year-old girl had recurrent episodes of leakage from her umbilicus. Sonography showed the persistent communication between the dome of the bladder and umbilicus. Surgery was necessary to close the tract. (B) In the axial plane, the patent urachus (*arrows*) was seen anterior to the bladder's dome.

BIBLIOGRAPHY

Focal Bladder Wall Thickening

Abu-Yousef MM, Narayana AS, Brown RC, Franken EA Jr: Urinary bladder tumors studied by cystosonography. Part II: Staging. Radiology 153:227–331, 1984.

Abu-Yousef MM, Narayana AS, Franken EA Jr, Brown RC: Urinary bladder tumors studied by cystosonography. Part I: Detection. Radiology 153:223–226, 1984.

Dershaw DD, Scher HI: Serial transabdominal sonography of bladder cancer. AJR 150:1055–1059, 1988.

Forer LE, Schaffer RM: Transitional cell carcinoma of a simple ureterocele. A specific sonographic appearance. J Ultrasound Med 9:301–303, 1990.

Kumar R, Haque AK, Cohen MS: Endometriosis of the urinary bladder: Demonstration by sonography. J Clin Ultrasound 12:363–365, 1984.

Miller WB Jr, Boal DK, Teele R: Neurofibromatosis of the bladder: Sonographic findings. J Clin Ultrasound 11:460–462, 1983.

Puvaneswary M, Davoren P: Phaeochromocytoma of the bladder: Ultrasound appearance. J Clin Ultrasound 19:111–115, 1991.

Rifkin MD, Kurtz AB, Pasto ME, Goldberg BB: Unusual presentations of cystitis. J Ultrasound Med 2:25–28, 1983.

Yousem DM, Gatewood OMB, Goldman SM, Marshall FF: Synchronous and metachronous transitional cell carcinoma of the urinary tract: Prevalence, incidence, and radiographic detection. Radiology 167:613–618, 1988.

Diffuse Bladder Wall Thickening

Abu-Yousef MM, Narayana AS, Brown RC: Catheter-induced cystitis: Evaluation by cystosonography. Radiology 151:471–473, 1984.

Gooding GAW: Varied sonographic manifestations of cystitis. J Ultrasound Med 5:
    61–63, 1986.
Jaquier S, Rousseau O: Sonographic measurements of the normal bladder wall in chil-
    dren. AJR 149:563–566, 1987.

Echogenic Bladder Wall with Shadowing
(Calcification or Air)

Kauzlaric D, Barmeir E: Sonography of emphysematous cystitis. J Ultrasound Med
    4:319–320, 1985.

Perivesicular Cystic Mass

Bouvier JF, Pascaud E, Mailhes F, et al.: Urachal cyst in the adult: Ultrasound diag-
    nosis. J Clin Ultrasound 12:48–50, 1984.
Boyle G, Rosenberg HK, O'Neill J: An unusual presentation of an infected urachal
    cyst: Review of urachal anomalies. Clin Pediatr 27:130–134, 1988.
Friedman AP, Haller JO, Schulze G, et al.: Sonography of vesical and perivesical ab-
    normalities in children. J Ultrasound Med 2:385–390, 1983.
Haney AF, Trought WS: Parovarian cysts resembling a filled urinary bladder. J Clin
    Ultrasound 6:53–54, 1978.
Hoffer FA, Kozakewich H, Colodny A, Goldstein DP: Peritoneal inclusion cysts:
    Ovarian fluid in peritoneal adhesions. Radiology 169:189–191, 1988.
Siegel MJ: Urinary tract, in Siegel MJ, ed.: *Pediatric Sonography*. New York, Raven
    Press, pp. 302–304, 1991.
Van Sonnenberg E, Wittich GR, Casola G, et al: Lymphoceles: Imaging characteristics
    and percutaneous management. Radiology 161:593–596, 1986.
Williams BD, Fisk JD: Sonographic diagnosis of giant urachal cyst in the adult. AJR
    136:417–418, 1981.

UTERUS, CERVIX, AND VAGINA

PATTERNS

Material Within the Vagina
Cystic Structure in the Cervix
Uterine Enlargement
Thickened Endometrium
Fluid in the Endometrial Cavity: Positive
    β-HCG
Fluid in the Endometrial Cavity: Negative
    β-HCG
Amorphous Material Within the Uterus:
    Positive β-HCG

The uterus can be imaged transabdominally using a distended bladder or transvaginally when the bladder has been emptied. Uterine size and shape will be influenced by the patient's age, parity, and hormonal status. The vagina, cervix, and uterine fundus can be identified sonographically in most patients.

MATERIAL WITHIN THE VAGINA

Air Within the Vagina
Urine
Foreign Body

CHILDHOOD

Hematocolpos

The mucosal stripe of the vagina is usually seen easily during a transabdominal study of the pelvis performed through a distended, fluid-filled bladder. The mucosal surfaces of the two vaginal walls oppose one another, forming an echogenic stripe seen sonographically.

Air Within the Vagina

Highly echogenic foci with ringdown posteriorly may be seen within the vagina when air is present. Air may be present in the vagina after a pelvic examination. Manipulation of the vagina via tampon insertion or sexual intercourse also leads to the presence of air. Rectovaginal fistula formation secondary to neoplastic or inflammatory causes may result in prominent vaginal air.

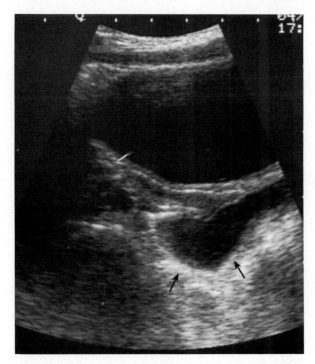

Figure 10.1
Reflux of urine into the vagina: In this young child with recurrent urinary tract infections, reflux of urine into the vaginal fornices (*arrows*) was noted during the ultrasound examination.

Urine (Figure 10.1)

Reflux of urine into the vagina may occur when the patient is supine when emptying the bladder. Fluid may be identified in the vaginal fornices as the urine pools there.

Foreign Body

Foreign material such as packing, tampons, or medication may be placed into the vagina. The composition of the material will determine its sonographic features. Often, highly echogenic foci of air will be trapped with the material.

CHILDHOOD

Hematocolpos (Figure 10.2)

Obstruction of the vaginal outlet is usually identified at the time of the onset of menses. Obstruction of the vagina is usually secondary to either vaginal atresia, imperforate hymen, or high-grade stenosis.

Patients with imperforate hymen generally present at puberty with a history of amenorrhea and recurrent lower abdominal pain and mass. These patients do not usually have the associated congen-

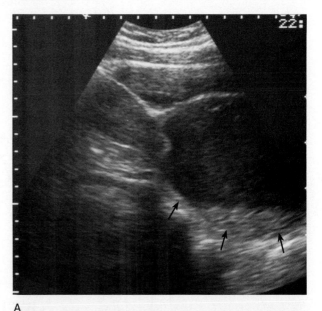

A

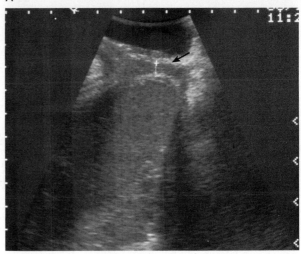

B

Figure 10.2
Hematocolpos: (A) An imperforate hymen led to the distended vagina in this patient (*arrows*). The bloody material was drained after perforation of the obstructing membrane. (B) Transperineal scanning was used to demonstrate the distal obstruction of the vagina. A 4-mm membrane was identified (*arrow*).

ital abnormalities that are seen in patients with vaginal atresia or stenosis. Patients with vaginal atresia frequently have congenital abnormalities, including fusion abnormalities of the uterus, unilateral renal agenesis, congenital heart defects, or imperforate anus.

Sonographically, a mass is present between the bladder and rectum. The vagina and uterus may be markedly distended and filled with old blood and debris. The proteinaceous, bloody fluid causes homogeneous low-level echoes or a fluid-debris level within the distended vagina or uterus. Usually, the vagina contains most of the blood products, but sometimes enough material accumulates to cause distention of the uterus and fallopian tubes. Distention of the oviducts will be seen as tubular structures emanating from either side of the midline uterus.

Perineal scanning with a linear array transducer can help determine the level of vaginal obstruction and direct clinical management. Recognition of a thin membrane (imperforate hymen) will allow different management than the presence of a long segment of vaginal atresia or stenosis, which may require more extensive surgical repair.

CYSTIC STRUCTURE IN THE CERVIX

Nabothian Cyst
Abortion in Progress
Cervical Pregnancy
Postprocedure Fluid
Necrotic Cervical Carcinoma

Nabothian Cyst (Figure 10.3)

Small cysts of the lower uterine segment and/or cervix are frequently seen as incidental findings clinically and sonographically. Often seen in multiparous women, nabothian cysts represent encysted collections of fluid or mucus originating from glands

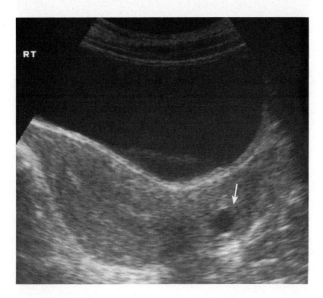

Figure 10.3
Nabothian cyst: A small cyst of the cervix is incidentally identified in this patient. The patient had had two previous pregnancies.

in the lower uterine segment or cervix. These cysts are usually asymptomatic and clinically insignificant. Their sonographic importance is that they must be differentiated from other causes of cysts in the cervix.

Abortion in Progress

An intrauterine gestational sac that is passing out of the uterus may be located in the lower uterine segment or cervix at the time of sonography. Effacement or collapse of the sac and evidence of fetal demise substantiate the diagnosis of abortion in progress. This patient would have a positive pregnancy test and would clinically be expected to have cramping and vaginal spotting with expulsion of gestational tissue. Serial quantitative β-HCG tests should show falling levels.

Cervical Pregnancy (Figure 10.4)

Implantation of a gestational sac in the cervix represents a type of ectopic pregnancy that is rare, but is associated with previous cervical instrumentation, such as curettage. Recognition of cervical implantation is imperative for clinical management. Dilatation and curettage of a cervical pregnancy can be disastrous, resulting in excessive bleeding and sometimes necessitating emergency hysterectomy. Treatment of the patient with a cervical pregnancy by using feticidal agents such as methotrexate results in fetal demise and subsequent expulsion of the ectopic implantation without hysterectomy.

Postprocedure Fluid (Figure 10.5)

Fluid may be identified in the cervix in patients after procedures such as cone biopsies or dilatation and curettage. Such fluid usually drains from the uterus via the vagina.

Necrotic Cervical Carcinoma (Figure 10.6)

Hemorrhage and necrosis in tumors of the cervix or lower uterine segment can cause enlargement and complicated cystic regions of the cervix.

UTERINE ENLARGEMENT

Postpartum State/Multiparity/Hormonal
    Stimulation
Leiomyomatous Involvement/Endometrial
    Carcinoma
Obstructed Uterus

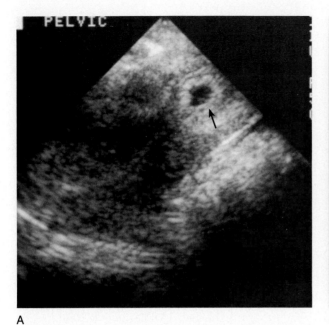

A

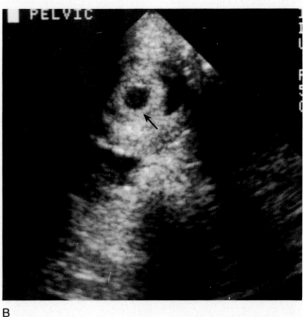

B

Figure 10.4
Cervical pregnancy: (A and B) This patient being treated for infertility underwent an ultrasound evaluation when her pregnancy test became positive. A gestational sac was identified in the cervix (*arrows*). Methotrexate was administered to precipitate fetal demise and successfully terminated the cervical implantation.

The uterus has a variable appearance, depending upon the age and hormonal status of the female patient. In the newborn girl, the uterine size may reflect stimulation by maternal hormones. Generally, within weeks after delivery the uterus involutes and normally remains small until hormonal changes at puberty cause the uterus to again enlarge.

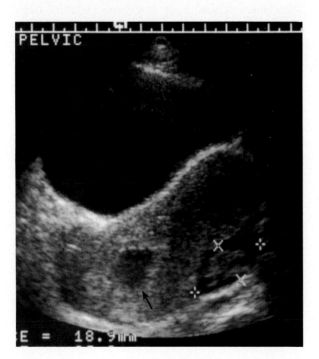

Figure 10.5
Postprocedure fluid: Follow-up scan in this patient 4 days after cone biopsy of the cervix revealed residual fluid in the cervix (*arrow*) and lower uterine segment. The fluid subsequentially drained via the vagina.

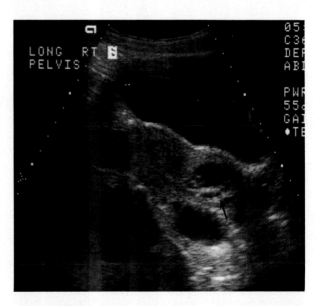

Figure 10.6
Cervical carcinoma with hemorrhage: Enlargement and inhomogeneity of the cervix with central necrosis (*arrow*) were identifiable in this young woman who presented with vaginal bleeding.

Postpartum State/Multiparity/Hormonal Stimulation (Figure 10.7)

The uterus significantly enlarges and develops a thickened endometrium in the pregnant patient. In the postpartum state, the uterus is large and hypoechoic, gradually becoming smaller over weeks. The multiparous uterus is larger than the nulliparous uterus. As a woman enters menopause, the uterus again involutes unless hormonal stimulation is present. Hormonal stimulation such as exogenous estrogenic therapy or tumors with estrogen production such as a granulosal cell tumor may cause uterine enlargement and endometrial thickening.

Leiomyomatous Involvement/Endometrial Carcinoma (Figure 10.8)

Neoplastic involvement of the uterus with endometrial carcinoma can cause enlargement. Clinically, postmenopausal bleeding may be present. The endometrium may be thickened and require histologic evaluation.

Leiomyomatous involvement of the uterus often causes focal contour deformities, but diffuse globular enlargement with leiomyomas can be seen.

Obstructed Uterus

A uterus that is obstructed by cervical carcinoma, a lower uterine segment endometrial carcinoma, or

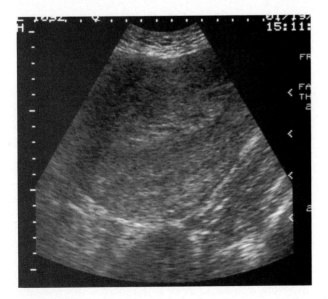

Figure 10.7
Postpartum uterus: One day after routine vaginal delivery, an enlarged uterus and no retained products of conception were demonstrated.

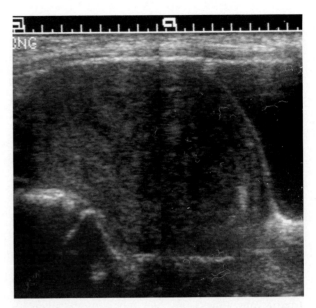

Figure 10.8
Leiomyomatous uterus: Globular enlargement of the uterus without a discrete mass was present in this patient with menorrhagia.

a benign stricture, which may develop after radiation therapy or instrumentation, may become filled with blood, debris, or purulent material. Such a uterus may look large and solid by sonography. CT scans will demonstrate a more cystic-appearing center to the mass and a well-defined wall, the stretched myometrium. Decompression of the uterus may be required.

THICKENED ENDOMETRIUM

Normal Secretory Phase of the Endometrium
Exogenous or Endogenous Hormonal
    Stimulation
Hyperplastic Endometrium/Polyps/
    Endometrial Carcinoma
Endometritis

VARIANT

Material Within the Cavity

The endometrial cavity is identified on pelvic sonography as the echogenic line that marks the two interfaces of opposed endometrium. The sonographic appearance of the endometrium will vary, depending upon the phase of the menstrual cycle. The sonographic measurements of the endometrium should include the hyperechoic opposing layers of the endometrium without including the surrounding hypoechoic halo. The normal endometrium in pa-

tients undergoing menstrual cycling, either spontaneous or induced, will measure 3 to 14 mm, depending on the point in the cycle.

The proliferative phase of the menstrual cycle,
largely under the influence of estrogen, occurs before ovulation. During this portion of the menstrual
cycle, the endometrium measures up to 5 mm in anteroposterior dimension.

After ovulation, the secretory phase of the
cycle is marked by increasing echogenicity of the
endometrium, related to increasing amounts of mucus and glycogen. The endometrium becomes its
thickest, measuring 6 to 14 mm in thickness before
it is shed during menstruation.

Women who are postmenopausal and not receiving estrogen replacement normally have a very
atropic endometrium. Postmenopausal women generally have an endometrial measurement of less
than 8 mm, unless they are receiving estrogen replacement therapy, which causes thickening of the
endometrial lining.

Normal Secretory Phase of the Endometrium

Thickening of the endometrium may be related to
the normal secretory phase of the endometrium.
Measurements as high as 14 mm in thickness may
be expected in normally cycling women.

Exogenous or Endogenous Hormonal Stimulation (Figures 10.9–10.10)

Patients with hormonal stimulation of the uterus
may have uterine enlargement and endometrial
thickening. Examples of patients with hormonal
stimulation include postmenopausal patients receiving estrogen replacement therapy, patients with es-
trogen-producing tumors such as granulosal cell tumors, and patients with early intrauterine or ectopic
pregnancy. In patients with ectopic pregnancy, decidual reaction in the uterus will be seen as prominent endometrial thickening, uterine enlargement,
or fluid within the endometrial cavity.

Hyperplastic Endometrium/Polyps/ Endometrial Carcinoma (Figure 10.11)

Hyperplasia of the endometrium, endometrial polyps, and frank carcinoma of the endometrium may
be found histologically when abnormal thickening
of the endometrium is present, especially in a postmenopausal woman. An endometrial measurement
of greater than 8 mm in a postmenopausal patient
not receiving hormonal replacement is considered
abnormal. An endometrial thickness of 5 mm or less

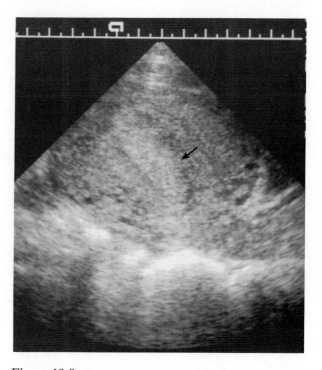

Figure 10.9
Decidual reaction of ectopic pregnancy: Stimulation of the
uterus with thickening of the endometrium (*arrow*) was
present in this young woman with a 15-week extrauterine
pregnancy. The endometrium measured nearly 2 cm in
thickness.

is highly unlikely to be associated with carcinoma.
The risk of endometrial carcinoma rises with increasing thickness of the endometrium in a postmenopausal woman. Usually presenting with postmenopausal vaginal bleeding, hyperplasia of the
endometrium or endometrial carcinoma is generally
detected by endometrial biopsy.

Endometritis

Inflammation of the endometrium either related to
pelvic inflammatory disease or the postpartum state
may lead to thickening of the endometrium and, in
some cases, fluid within the endometrial cavity.

VARIANT

Material Within the Cavity (Figure 10.12)

Retained products of conception, blood, incomplete
abortion, and gestational trophoblastic disease can
appear within the endometrial cavity as echogenic
material and can have the appearance of a thickened endometrium. Generally, the clinical presentation will be that of a woman of reproductive age

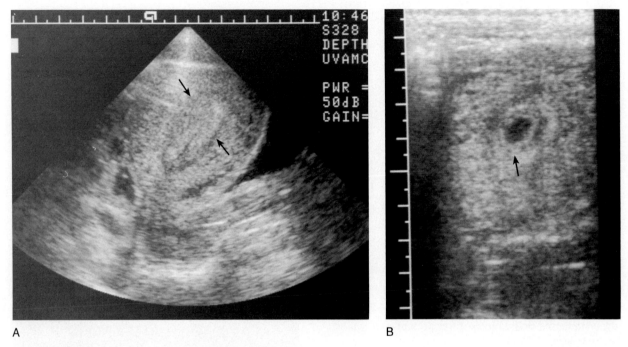

A

B

Figure 10.10

Early intrauterine pregnancy: (A) In this woman with a 6-week intrauterine pregnancy, prominent thickening of the endometrium (*arrows*) is an expected finding. (B) Gestational sac (*arrow*).

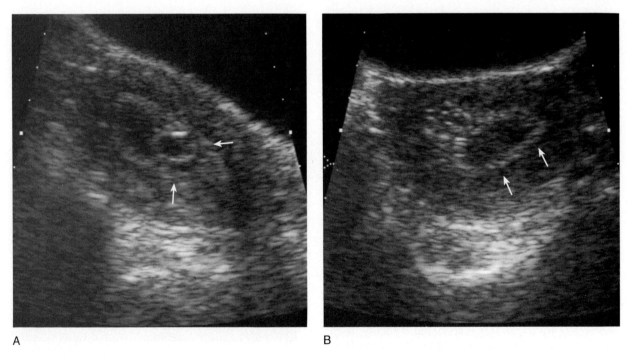

A

B

Figure 10.11

Endometrial hyperplasia: (A and B) Asymmetric thickening of the endometrial lining (*arrows*) was seen in this 59-year-old woman with postmenopausal bleeding.

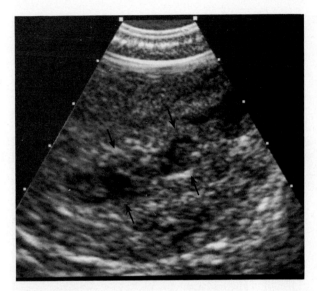

Figure 10.12
Retained products of conception: Residual material within the endometrial cavity (*arrows*) was present after passage of fetal parts.

with a positive β-HCG and bleeding. Dilatation and curettage will clarify the diagnosis.

Uncommonly, an obstructed uterus filled with echogenic material and debris will appear similar to endometrial thickening.

FLUID IN THE ENDOMETRIAL CAVITY: POSITIVE B-HCG

Intrauterine Gestation
Pseudogestation of Ectopic Pregnancy
Anembryonic Pregnancy or Blighted Ovum/
    Missed Abortion

Information important in narrowing the differential possibilities in a patient with fluid in the endometrial cavity is whether or not the patient has a positive pregnancy test.

Intrauterine Gestation (Figures 10.13–10.14)

A normal intrauterine gestational sac can often be seen transabdominally approximately 5 to 6 weeks after the last menstrual period and at approximately 4.5 weeks by transvaginal scanning. Usually, there are sonographic features that allow the intrauterine gestational sac to be differentiated from simple fluid in the endometrial cavity. The normal intrauterine gestational sac may have the so-called double sac sign, which is formed from the decidua capsularis

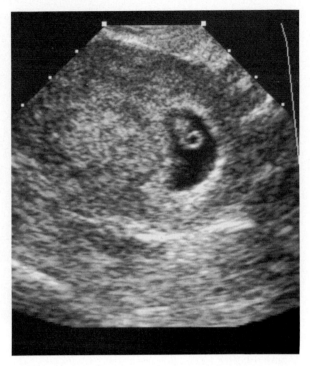

Figure 10.13
Early IUP: An intrauterine pregnancy was demonstrated in this woman with a failed tubal ligation. Note the implantation of the gestational sac in the endometrium.

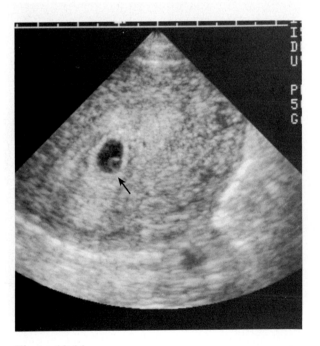

Figure 10.14
Early IUP: Visualization of the yolk sac (*arrow*) of an early intrauterine pregnancy allowed an ectopic pregnancy to be excluded in this case (transvaginal scan).

and decidua parietalis. The gestational sac of a normal intrauterine pregnancy (IUP) will be implanted into the stimulated endometrium and will be eccentric to the endometrial cavity. Using the transabdominal approach, a fetal pole is identifiable in the normal gestational sac when the long axis of the sac is 2.0 cm or greater. Use of the transvaginal probe allows recognition of features of intrauterine pregnancy 7 to 10 days earlier.

Pseudogestation of Ectopic Pregnancy (Figure 10.15)

In patients with ectopic pregnancy, 15 to 20 percent have fluid in the endometrial cavity or a saclike structure that may be called a pseudogestational sac. Such fluid can be misinterpreted as an intrauterine gestational sac if care is not taken. The fluid within the uterine cavity is a response to the hormonal activity of the ectopic trophoblastic tissue. Inability to identify a yolk sac or fetal pole within the uterus, identification of an extrauterine gestational sac or complex adnexal mass, and recognition that the fluid is within the endometrial cavity rather than implanted in the endometrium will allow the pseudogestational sac to be differentiated from the true intrauterine gestational sac.

Anembryonic Pregnancy or Blighted Ovum/ Missed Abortion (Figures 10.16–10.18)

An abnormal intrauterine pregnancy may appear as a large, fluid-filled sac within the endometrial cavity. An anembryonic pregnancy or so-called blighted ovum occurs when no fetal parts develop. Often the pregnant patient presents at approximately 10 weeks' gestation, small for dates, and with spotting. A missed abortion may have a similar sonographic appearance and clinical course. In the latter situation, there has been fetal demise without complete expulsion of fetal parts or trophoblastic tissue. Such abnormal intrauterine pregnancies are treated by evacuating the uterus with suction or dilatation and curettage if spontaneous evacuation does not occur.

FLUID IN THE ENDOMETRIAL CAVITY: NEGATIVE β-HCG

Cervical or Endometrial Carcinoma
Benign Stricture
Vaginal Stenosis or Atresia/Imperforate
    Hymen
Endometritis/Postprocedure Fluid
Hemorrhage

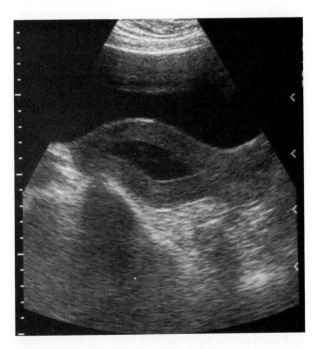

Figure 10.15
Pseudogestational sac of ectopic pregnancy: Fluid within the endometrial cavity was identified in this patient with an ectopic pregnancy in the right adnexa.

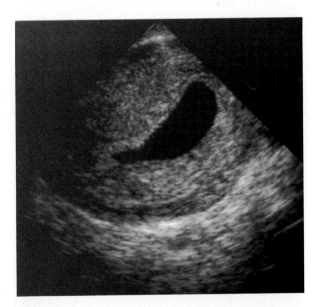

Figure 10.16
Anembryonic pregnancy: This woman presented at 10 weeks' gestation with spotting and a small uterus. Transvaginal scanning showed a fluid collection in the endometrial cavity without a fetal pole or yolk sac. Dilatation and evacuation yielded choriovillous tissue from the endometrial cavity.

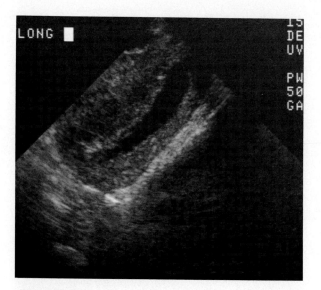

Figure 10.17
Anembryonic pregnancy (blighted ovum): An empty, crenated sac within the uterus was present in this anembryonic pregnancy.

If the patient's pregnancy test is negative, intrauterine pregnancy, normal or abnormal, and ectopic pregnancy can effectively be eliminated as possible explanations for the sonographic findings of fluid in the endometrial cavity.

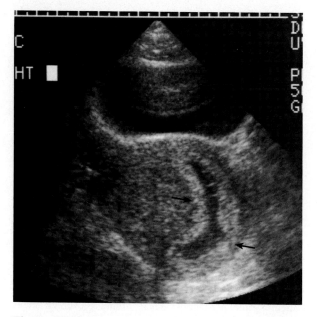

Figure 10.18
Abortion in progress: This young woman had passed fetal parts. Residual fluid and placenta were identifiable sonographically in a retroverted uterus. Dilatation and currettage was necessary.

Cervical or Endometrial Carcinoma (Figure 10.19)

Patients with obstruction of the uterus by carcinoma of the cervix or lower uterine segment can develop a distended fluid-filled uterus. The material within the uterus is often not simple fluid but can be laden with debris. Sonographically, the endometrial cavity may be difficult to delineate and may appear solid rather than fluid-filled. The fluid may become infected and drainage may be necessary to prevent a pyometrium. The presence of fluid in the endometrial cavity in a postmenopausal woman should lead to an evaluation of the uterus, cervix, and adnexa for possible neoplasm.

Benign Stricture

Patients who are treated with radiation therapy for cervical carcinoma or who develop strictures in the cervix or lower uterine segment secondary to previous instrumentation may develop an obstructed uterus even if there is no evidence of active neoplasm.

Vaginal Stenosis or Atresia/Imperforate Hymen (Figure 10.20)

Young girls, generally in the prepubertal years, may show evidence of vaginal stenosis or atresia, resulting in obstruction and distention of the uterus and vagina with retained secretions. The typical history is of the young teenaged girl who has never menstruated and who has monthly cramping and pelvic distention. A palpable pelvic mass may be found on physical examination. Ultrasonography will demonstrate the distended fluid-filled vagina and/or uterus. Sometimes, distended fallopian tubes can also be seen. In such cases, transperineal sonography may be useful to clarify the thickness of the obstructing membrane, which helps in determining what type of surgical correction will be appropriate. Extensive vaginal reconstruction may be necessary in some cases, whereas perforation of the obstructing membrane may be sufficient in other situations.

Endometritis/Postprocedure Fluid

In patients with endometritis, either in the postpartum patient or in the sexually active patient with endometrial infection, fluid may be identified within the uterus. After procedures such as dilatation and curettage, fluid may remain in the uterus. Manipu-

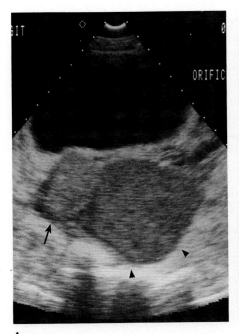
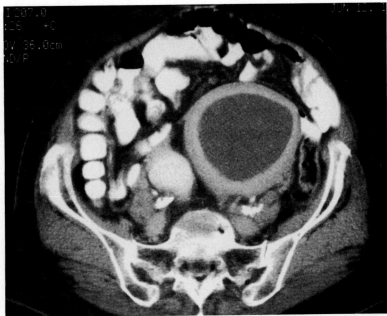

A   B

Figure 10.19

Cervical carcinoma: (A) Squamous cell carcinoma of the cervix was manifest in this patient by a solid cervical mass (*arrow*), causing obstruction of the uterus and a debris-laden cavity that looks solid by ultrasound (*arrowheads*). (B) The CT image confirmed the fluid-filled endometrial cavity with the myometrium recognized as a concentric wall.

lation of the cervix may facilitate drainage of the fluid via the vagina.

Hemorrhage (Figure 10.21)

Withdrawal bleeding after hormonal administration or bleeding from a variety of causes may fill the uterine cavity with echogenic material that can pass out of the vagina.

AMORPHOUS MATERIAL WITHIN THE UTERUS: POSITIVE β-HCG

Retained Products of Conception
Gestational Trophoblastic Disease

In some patients with positive β-HCG values, amorphous soft tissue may be identifiable within the endometrial cavity. Usually, such material is either the residua of an unsuccessful pregnancy (i.e., re-

tained products of conception) or the tissue of gestational trophoblastic disease.

Retained Products of Conception (Figure 10.22)

In situations of incomplete abortion, fetal demise and hydropic degeneration of the placenta, or unsuccessful instrumentation, retained products of conception may be seen within the endometrial cavity. Definable fetal parts may be seen, but it is more likely that amorphous placental remnants and hemorrhage will be present. β-HCG levels are usually positive but may be declining. Dilatation and evacuation (D & E) is used to clear the endometrial cavity.

Gestational Trophoblastic Disease (Figure 10.23)

Gestational trophoblastic disease, including hytadiform mole, invasive mole, or choriocarcinoma, fills the endometrial cavity with amorphous, solid-appearing material. High circulating levels of β-HCG are usually present. Dilatation and evacuation is usually the first therapy, with additional treatment dependent upon histologic examination.

Partial mole is a type of gestational trophoblastic disease in which a fetus may be present along with the amorphous tissue. Partial mole is thought to have no significant malignant potential.

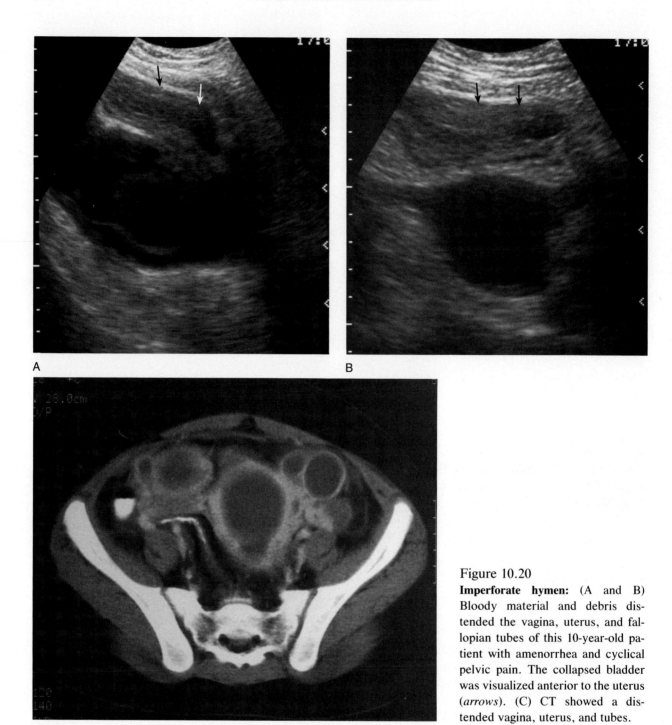

Figure 10.20
Imperforate hymen: (A and B) Bloody material and debris distended the vagina, uterus, and fallopian tubes of this 10-year-old patient with amenorrhea and cyclical pelvic pain. The collapsed bladder was visualized anterior to the uterus (*arrows*). (C) CT showed a distended vagina, uterus, and tubes.

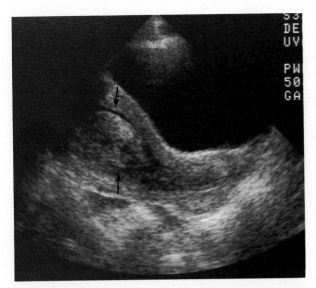

Figure 10.21
Hemorrhage: This young woman had been given long-term, unopposed estrogen for oral contraception and presented with dramatic withdrawal hemorrhage. Ultrasound showed extensive material that was hemorrhage within the endometrial cavity (*arrows*).

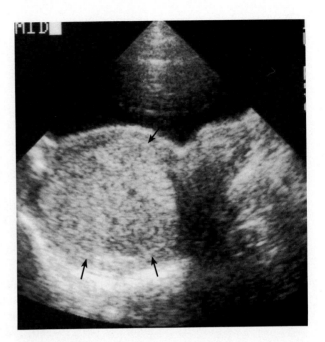

Figure 10.23
Gestational trophoblastic disease: Highly echogenic material distended the uterus and filled the endometrial cavity (*arrows*) in this patient with a markedly elevated β-HCG and vaginal bleeding.

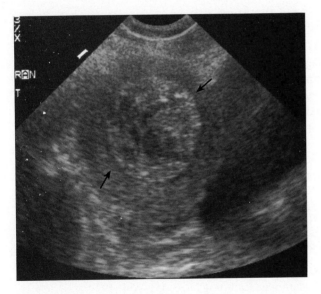

Figure 10.22
Retained products of conception: Highly echogenic material (*arrows*) was present in this patient with retained products after a second-trimester miscarriage. Dilatation and evacuation of the uterus was necessary.

BIBLIOGRAPHY

Material Within the Vagina

Little HK, Crawford, DB, Meister K: Hematocolpos: Diagnosis made by ultrasound. J Clin Ultrasound 6:341–342, 1978.

Sailer JF: Hematometra and hematocolpos: Ultrasound findings. AJR 132:1010–1011, 1979.

Siegel MJ: Female pelvis, in Siegel MJ, ed: *Pediatric Sonography*. New York: Raven Press, pp. 331–334, 1991.

Wilson DA, Stacey TM, Smith EI: Ultrasound diagnosis of hydrocolpos and hydro-metrocolpos. Radiology 128:451–454, 1978.

Cystic Structure in the Cervix

Oyer R, Tarakjian D, Lev-Toaff A, Friedman A, Chatwani A: Treatment of cervical pregnancy with methotrexate. Obstet Gynecol 71:469–471, 1988.

Werber J, Prasadarao PR, Harris VJ: Cervical pregnancy diagnosed by ultrasound. Radiology 149:279–280, 1983.

Yankowitz J, Leake J, Huggins G, Gazaway P, Gates E: Cervical ectopic pregnancy: Review of the literature and report of a case treated by single-dose methotrexate therapy. Obstet Gynecol Surg 45:405–414, 1990.

Thickened Endometrium

Brandt TD, Levy EB, Grant TH, Marut E, Leland J: Endometrial echo and its significance in female infertility. Radiology 157:225–229, 1985.

Fleischer AC, Herbert CM, Hill GA, Kepple DM, Worrell JA: Transvaginal sonography of the endometrium during induced cycles. J Ultrasound Med 10:93–95, 1991.

Fleischer AC, Kalemeris GC, Entman SS: Sonographic depiction of the endometrium during normal cycles. Ultrasound Med Biol 12:271–277, 1986.

Fleischer AC, Kalemeris GC, Machin JE, et al.: Sonographic depiction of normal and abnormal endometrium with histopathologic correlation. J Ultrasound Med 5:445–452, 1986.

Forrest TS, Elyaderani MK, Muilenburg MI, et al.: Cyclic endometrial changes: US assessment with istologic correlation. Radiology 167:233–237, 1988.

Mendelson EB, Bohm-Velez M, Joseph N, Neiman HL: Endometrial abnormalities: Evaluation with transvaginal sonography. AJR 150:139–142, 1988.

Fluid in the Endometrial Cavity: Positive β-HCG

Marks WM, Filly RA, Callen PW, et al.: The decidual cast of ectopic pregnancy: A confusing ultrasonographic appearance. Radiology 133:451–454, 1979.

Nelson P, Bowie JD, Rosenberg ER: Early intrauterine pregnancy or decidual cast: An anatomic-sonographic approach. J Ultrasound Med 2:543–547, 1983.

Nyberg DA, Laing FC, Filly RA, Uri-Simmons M, Jeffrey RB: Ultrasonographic differentiation of the gestational sac of early intrauterine pregnancy from the pseudogestational sac of ectopic pregnancy. Radiology 146:755–759, 1983.

Schaffer RM, Stein K, Shih YH, Goodman JD: The echoic pseudogestational sac of ectopic pregnancy simulating early intrauterine pregnancy. J Ultrasound Med 2:215–218, 1983.

Turetsky DB, Alexander AA, Linden SS: Pseudogestational sac of ectopic pregnancy simulating intrauterine pregnancy with transvaginal sonography. J Clin Ultrasound 19:120–123, 1991.

Fluid in the Endometrial Cavity: Negative β-HCG

Breckenridge JW, Kurtz AB, Ritchie WGM, Macht EL Jr: Postmenopausal uterine fluid collection: Indicator of carcinoma. AJR 139:529–534, 1982.

Laing FC, Filly RA, Marks WM, et al.: Ultrasonic demonstration of endometrial fluid collections unassociated with pregnancy. Radiology 137:471–474, 1980.

McCarthy KA, Hall DA, Kopans DB, Swann CA: Postmenopausal endometrial fluid collections: Always an indicator of malignancy? J Ultrasound Med 5:647–649, 1986.

Scott WW Jr, Rosenshein NB, Siegelman SS, Sanders RC: The obstructed uterus. Radiology 141:767–770, 1981.

C H A P T E R 11

OVARY AND ADNEXA

```
┌─────────────────────────────────────────────┐
│                  PATTERNS                     │
│                                               │
│  Simple Cyst in the Adnexa                   │
│  Complex Adnexal Mass: Negative β-HCG        │
│  Complex Adnexal Mass: Positive β-HCG        │
│  Solid-Appearing Adnexal Mass                │
│  Highly Echogenic Pelvic Mass: Calcification │
│      versus Air versus Fat                   │
│  Bilateral Adnexal Masses                    │
│  "Amorphous" Pelvis                          │
│  Dilated Tubes in the Pelvis                 │
└─────────────────────────────────────────────┘
```

The ovary is a dynamic organ, with a variable appearance depending upon hormonal changes and the phase of the menstrual cycle. Cystic masses of the ovary may be the result of normal physiologic functioning or secondary to neoplastic and infectious causes.

SIMPLE CYST IN THE ADNEXA

Functional Ovarian Cyst
Ovarian Remnant Cyst
Parovarian Cyst
Cystic Ovarian Neoplasm
Peritoneal Inclusion Cyst

To be considered a simple cyst, a mass must have no internal echoes, must have a well-defined wall, and must demonstrate acoustical enhancement.

Functional Ovarian Cyst (Figure 11.1)

The most common cause of a simple cyst in the adnexa is a functional cyst of the ovary. The normally functioning ovary develops a dominant follicle, expels an ovum in a cyclical pattern, with a resulting corpus luteal cyst. Such cysts change during the menstrual cycle and are replaced during subsequent cycles by other cysts. Generally, simple functional cysts are small, usually less than 3 cm, but they are sometimes considerably larger. Follow-up ultrasounds will confirm their resolution.

Ovarian Remnant

Patients who have had the ovaries surgically removed may still have functional ovarian cysts if they have an ovarian remnant. A cyst arising in an ovarian remnant should vary in appearance on se-

347

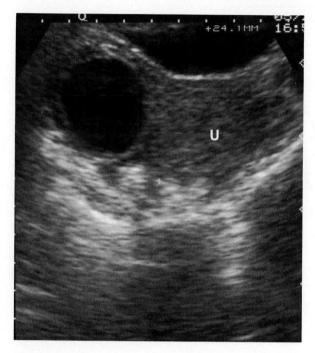

Figure 11.1

Functional cyst of the ovary: A small, simple cyst of the ovary was identified in this asymptomatic patient. The origin of the cyst from the ovary was obvious. The mass resolved in the ensuing weeks. (U = uterus.)

rial ultrasound studies and can be manipulated with hormonal therapy.

Parovarian Cyst (Figure 11.2)

Parovarian cysts arise within the broad ligament and are not hormonally responsive. Parovarian cysts account for approximately 10 percent of adnexal cysts and may be large.

Parovarian cysts may be the leadpoint for adnexal torsion. Large parovarian cysts in the pregnant patient may cause difficulty by preventing normal vaginal delivery.

Cystic Ovarian Neoplasm (Figure 11.3)

Cystic neoplasms of the ovary, such as a cystadenoma, may present as simple cysts. Often, the age of the patient and the failure of the cyst to resolve on subsequent scans will give the clue that the mass is a neoplasm and not a functional ovarian cyst. The absence of septations and solid components suggests that the mass is benign rather than malignant. Cystic neoplasms of the ovary may be quite large.

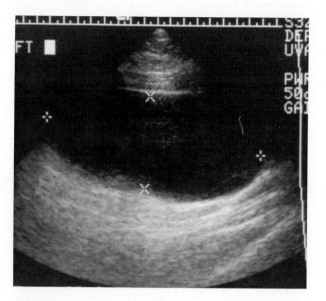

Figure 11.2

Parovarian cyst: A large, simple parovarian cyst was demonstrated in this patient with a palpable mass. The mass did not change on subsequent scans and was surgically removed.

Peritoneal Inclusion Cyst (Figure 11.4)

Patients with a history of extensive pelvic surgery may develop a peritoneal inclusion cyst that is a collection of fluid developing between adherent layers of the peritoneum. Such cysts will not change with hormonal therapy and often reaccumulate if drained.

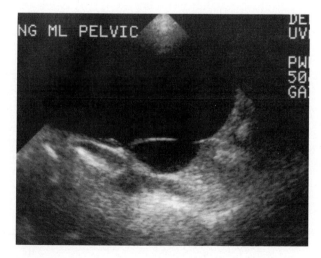

Figure 11.3

Cystadenoma of the ovary: A large, nearly simple cyst was demonstrated during routine scanning of this patient. A single, thin septation was identified at the base of the mass.

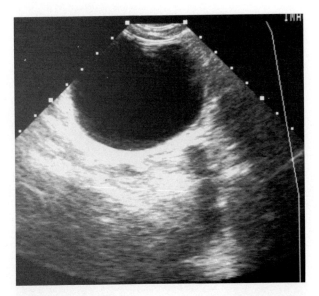

Figure 11.4

Peritoneal inclusion cyst: This cystic collection was present in a 59-year-old woman many years after extensive pelvic surgeries that included removal of both ovaries. Aspiration of the mass yielded negative cytology. The mass reaccumulated after decompression.

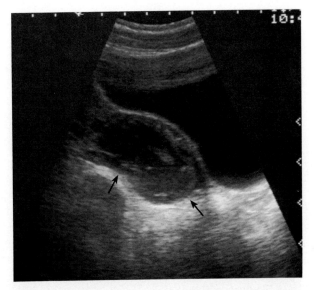

Figure 11.5

Complicated functional ovarian cyst: This 14-year-old developed severe right lower quadrant pain. The clinical impression was of appendicitis. Ultrasound showed a 5.5-cm septated cyst in the right adnexa (*arrows*). At laparoscopy, the dominant cyst was aspirated.

COMPLEX ADNEXAL MASS WITH NEGATIVE β-HCG

Complicated Functional Ovarian Cyst
Endometrioma
Tubo-ovarian Abscess/Hydrosalpinx
Regional Abscess that Engulfs the Adnexa
Primary Ovarian Neoplasm
    Germ Cell Line
    Epithelial Cell Line
    Stromal Cell Line
Metastatic Disease to the Ovaries
Peritoneal Inclusion Cyst
Parovarian Cyst
Hematoma
Complicated Ascites
Miscellaneous
    Iliac Artery Aneurysm
    Collection Around Transplanted Kidney
    Cystic Degeneration of a Uterine
      Leiomyoma

A complex mass is one with cystic components complicated by internal echoes, septations, or thick walls. The complex adnexal mass is one of the most frequently encountered abnormalities of pelvic sonography. Knowledge of the status of the patient's β-HCG, patient age, and clinical presentation (fe-ver, elevated white count, and pain) will allow the best diagnostic possibilities to be given.

Complicated Functional Ovarian Cyst (Figures 11.5–11.9)

Functional ovarian cysts are the most common cause of an adnexal mass in a woman of reproductive age. Every month in which ovulation occurs, a potentially symptomatic corpus luteal cyst develops. Many women have asymptomatic adnexal cysts, too.

Ultrasound allows differentiation of the adnexal mass from the uterus. Cystic components of the adnexal mass, with the presence of increased through transmission even with internal echoes, allow the sonographer to suggest that the organ of origin of the mass is the ovary rather than the uterus. Most uterine masses are solid, and the uterus rarely gives rise to predominantly cystic masses (except for cystic degeneration of a fibroid).

Hemorrhagic functional cysts of the ovary may be quite variable in size, ranging up to 15 cm.

Functional ovarian cysts may hemorrhage, and this hemorrhage leads to a variable sonographic appearance. The variable appearance is related to clot formation and lysis.

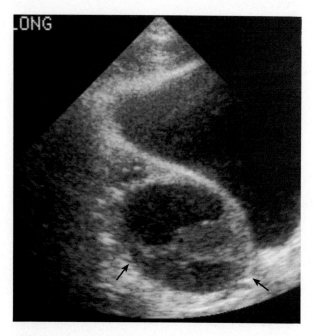

Figure 11.6
Complicated functional ovarian cyst: This 28-year-old woman was noted to have a right adnexal mass. Ultrasound demonstrated a 6-cm complex mass (*arrows*) with a solid component. Serial sonography 2 months later showed resolution of the mass.

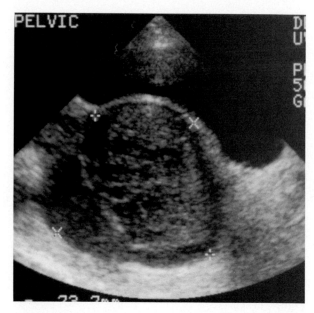

Figure 11.8
Complicated functional ovarian cyst: A 10.5- × 5.5-cm complex mass was surgically removed in this patient with Gardner's syndrome because of the fear of neoplasm. The solid component seen sonographically was clotted blood.

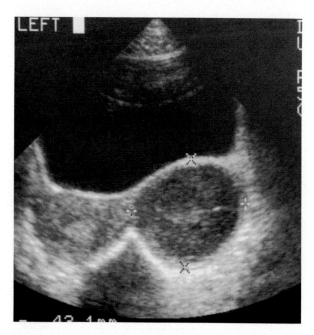

Figure 11.7
Complicated functional ovarian cyst: A well-circumscribed mass with internal echoes was present in the left ovary. This mass resolved without intervention. Note enhancement behind the mass.

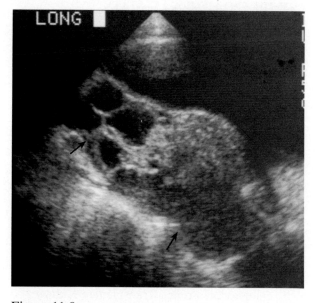

Figure 11.9
Complicated functional ovarian cyst: This young woman had already had surgical removal of an ovary for ovarian cysts when a mass developed in the cul-de-sac. Numerous small cysts were present in the cul-de-sac (*arrows*), surrounding the uterus. To preserve remaining ovarian function, oral contraceptives were given to cause regression of the cysts. This strategy worked, and the cysts resolved.

Acutely, a hemorrhagic cyst may look like a solid mass. Hemorrhagic ovarian cysts may then develop a complex internal echotexture. There may be a reticular pattern with internal echoes and septations. Some patients have a well-defined nodule or mass within the cyst which represents a clot. Usually, hemorrhagic cysts are not anechoic. Thickening of the wall of the mass may be seen, as well as internal septations. Layering hemorrhagic debris and echogenic cul-de-sac fluid are sometimes present. Calcifications do not usually develop in such dynamic masses.

Complete resolution of hemorrhagic cysts may take 1.5–12 weeks.

Approximately 25 percent of women with hemorrhagic functional cysts have a previous history of symptomatic ovarian cyst.

In the patient who is clinically stable and in whom ectopic pregnancy or abscess have been excluded, conservative management with surveillance of the hemorrhagic cyst rather than surgery is warranted. Such an approach may make surgery unnecessary and preserve ovarian tissue. The mass should resolve on subsequent imaging.

Endometrioma (Figures 11.10–11.11)

Endometriosis is a common condition in women of childbearing age in whom there is functioning endometrial tissue outside the uterus. Diffuse endometriosis, in which there are multiple small implants of endometriosis studding the organs of the pelvis and associated ligamentous attachment, may be difficult to see sonographically. The implants are often too small to see. Localized endometriomas are discrete masses, known as chocolate cysts, into which walled-off foci of endometriosis hemorrhage.

Endometriomas are often complicated cystic masses. Endometriomas can be totally anechoic and have septations, scattered internal echoes, or diffuse low-level echoes. These masses typically show good sound transmission. Sometimes an endometrioma is echogenic and solid. Most endometriomas have thin walls, but the walls may be diffusely thickened or of variable thickness.

Endometriosis frequently resembles hemorrhagic functional ovarian cysts sonographically. Both entities contain blood products of varying age. Thick, irregular septations and layering debris can also be seen with tubo-ovarian abscesses or a septated neoplasm of the ovary.

It is estimated that 5 to 20 percent of all women of reproductive age have endometriosis. Endometriosis may result in infertility in 5 to 15 percent of all cases.

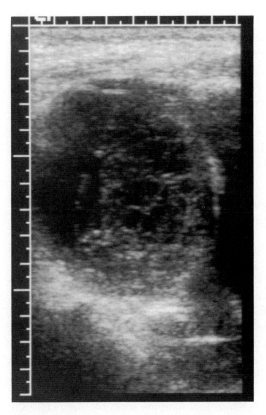

Figure 11.10

Endometriosis: This 39-year-old nurse had cyclic abdominal pain and dyspareunia. The complicated "chocolate cyst" in the pelvis looked sonographically similar to a complicated ovarian cyst.

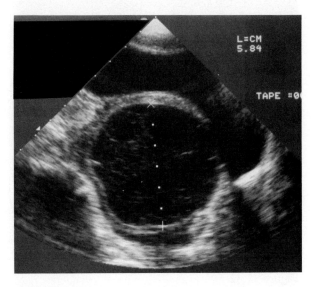

Figure 11.11

Endometrioma: A cystic structure with internal septations and debris was believed to be a functional ovarian cyst. The mass persisted for months. At surgery, a large endometrioma was removed.

Patient age, lack of history of endometriosis, and lack of specific symptoms of endometriosis, such as dyspareunia, dysmenorrhea, or infertility, should not dissuade the sonographer from the diagnosis of endometriosis if the sonographic appearance is appropriate. Endometriomas typically remain relatively constant in size and internal echo characteristics on sequential ultrasound scans, not changing or resolving as one would expect from a complicated functional cyst.

Tubo-ovarian Abscess/Hydrosalpinx (Figures 11.12–11.14)

Tubo-ovarian abscess (TOA) is a serious complication of pelvic inflammatory disease. The most common mode of transmission is via sexual contact and the infection is often polymicrobial. Hematogenous spread and direct extension from local inflammation are less commonly encountered ways in which the reproductive tract becomes infected. Abscesses related to puerperal or postabortion complications may also be seen.

Endometritis and salpingitis occur initially. The spillage of purulent exudate from the tubes into the peritoneal space may result in hypoechoic complex masses with a variable sonographic appearance. Tubo-ovarian abscesses may have septations, inter-

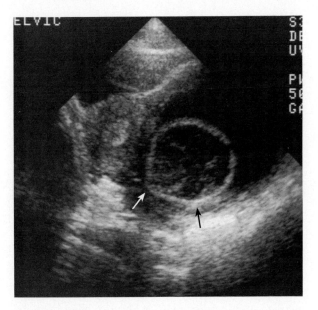

Figure 11.13

Hydrosalpinx: Two months after hospitalization for severe pelvic inflammatory disease, this patient developed a large cystic mass. The obstructed, fimbriated tube end was demonstrated (*arrows*).

nal echoes, irregular margins, and thin walls. Fluid-debris levels are sometimes identified. Sometimes, air may be seen as highly echogenic foci with dirty shadowing. Although such abscesses sometimes look solid, back-wall enhancement of inflammatory masses will give a clue to their cystic character.

Patients with a history of pelvic inflammatory disease have an increased risk of ectopic pregnancy, pain during sexual intercourse, and recurrent menstrual irregularities.

A hydrosalpinx may develop in a patient after an episode of pelvic inflammatory disease. The tubular shape of the mass, often occurring bilaterally and complicated with a debris-fluid level, will suggest its origin.

Regional Abscess that Engulfs the Adnexa (Figure 11.15)

Other abscesses that can engulf the adnexal structures may be related to inflammation of the appendix, diverticula, or Crohn's disease. Interloop postoperative abscesses may gravitate into the pelvis. Fluid collections related to pancreatitis may also be seen ultrasonographically in the pelvis. These collections, like other collections, can vary in appearance. Most often their cystic character can be detected by the recognition of posterior acoustic enhancement. Often the clinical status of the patient

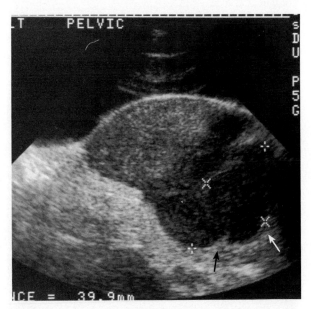

Figure 11.12

Abscess related to pelvic inflammatory disease: A hypoechoic collection (*arrows*) fills the pelvis behind the uterus in this patient with fever, cervical motion tenderness, and leukocytosis. The abscess was drained through the vagina.

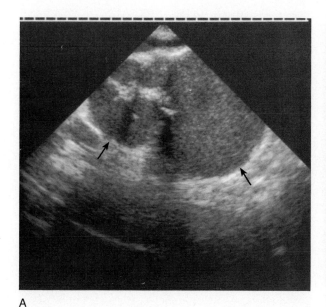

A

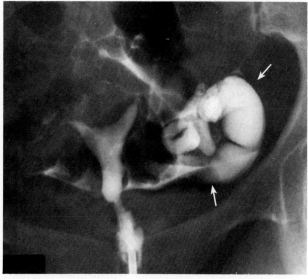

B

Figure 11.14

Hydrosalpinx: (A) This infertility patient had a complicated tubular cystic left adnexal mass with low level echoes. (B) Hysterosalpingography on the same patient showed a sausage-shaped, dilated, obstructed left tube.

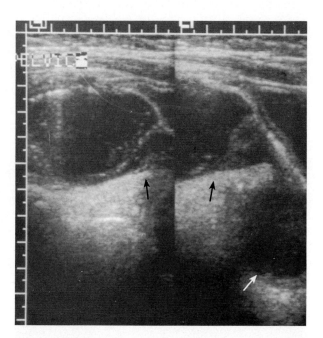

Figure 11.15

Periappendiceal abscess: This 8-year-old girl had suffered flulike symptoms with fever, malaise, abdominal pain, and leukocytosis. After 4 days she improved, but a fluctuant mass was palpable in the cul-de-sac. A multilocular, complex cystic mass (*arrows*) was present behind the prepubertal uterus. A ruptured appendix with periappendiceal abscess was found at surgery.

will allow the infectious nature of the mass to be suspected.

Primary Ovarian Neoplasm

Germ Cell Line Germ cell tumors of the ovary are most common in girls and young women, with the vast majority being the mature teratoma, which is benign. Germ cell tumors constitute 15 to 20 percent of all ovarian tumors.

The mature ovarian teratoma contains tissue from the ectoderm, mesoderm, and endoderm. Squamous epithelium and adipose tissue are common constituents, and teeth and fragments of bone may be found. Teratomas may have a variable ultrasound appearance. Sonographically teratomas may be largely cystic, entirely echogenic masses, but are almost always complex lesions. A dermoid plug or mass arising from the cyst wall may be seen; calcifications, echogenic foci with shadowing, are frequently present, and a fat–fluid level is sometimes identified. Some dermoids are mainly fluid filled. The echogenicity of fat within a dermoid may be variable, appearing highly echogenic (as it does in the normal renal sinus, in perimesenteric fat, or in many angiomyolipomas) or more hypoechoic (as in some lipomas or subcutaneous fat).

Sebum, which is liquid at body temperature, is very hypoechoic and looks cystic when imaged sonographically. The lack of tissue interfaces in sebum probably contributes to its cystic appearance. Fat within the dermoid plug often has associated hair and soft tissue that contribute many interfaces and give rise to a highly echogenic mass sonographically. Fragments of bone or teeth will produce a highly echogenic focus with shadowing. The varying proportions of these constituents result in the highly variable sonographic appearance of teratomas.

Teeth and bone fragments as well as fatty material, which can be difficult to characterize sonographically, may be definitively recognized on plain film or by CT. Such material will define the mass to be of germ cell origin.

Sometimes the sonographic appearance of a teratoma is characteristic, with a dermoid plug, a fat–fluid level, or attenuating fat allowing a specific diagnosis to be made.

If there is confusion as to whether the complex adnexal mass in a young woman or girl represents a hemorrhagic functional cyst or a benign ovarian teratoma, repeat scanning of the patient after several weeks may allow resolution of the complicated functional cyst or confirm the impression of an ovarian teratoma, which will remain unchanged.

Mature teratomas, although benign, are generally surgically removed, since they can grow and can be a leadpoint of adnexal torsion. Mature teratomas can rarely have foci of malignant germ cell elements.

Epithelial Cell Line (Figures 11.16–11.20)

Epithelial tumors of the ovaries may be the source of a complex adnexal mass in the middle-aged to elderly woman.

Ovarian carcinoma is the fourth leading cause of death in American women, and the leading cause of gynecologic death in the United States. The overall 5-year survival for ovarian carcinoma is 30 to 40 percent because the majority of women have advanced disease at presentation. The risk of developing ovarian cancer increases after age 40. In younger women with ovarian carcinoma, the disease has a much more aggressive course.

Approximately 15 percent of ovarian epithelial tumors are considered borderline tumors. These masses often occur in younger women, lack stromal invasion, and are slower growing than their malignant counterparts.

Epithelial tumors of the ovary represent 65 to 75 percent of ovarian neoplasms and 90 percent of ovarian malignancies. The malignant tumors spread primarily within the peritoneal space, with extension to the broad ligament, and have serosal and omental implants. Often there is abundant malignant ascites. Lymphatic involvement may be present in a minority of patients. Hematogenous progression is a late finding.

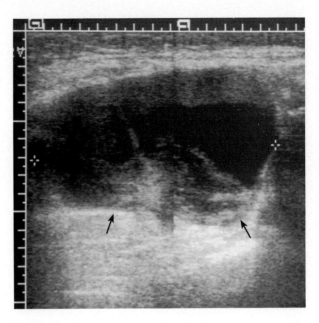

Figure 11.16
Borderline epithelial tumor: A large mass with cystic and solid components in this 60-year-old patient was surgically removed.

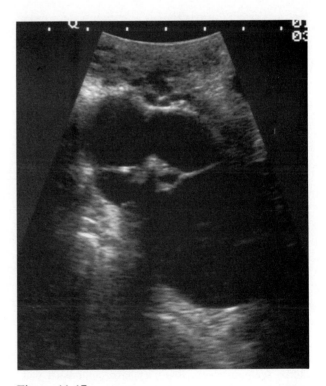

Figure 11.17
Serous cystadenoma of the ovary: A predominantly cystic mass with thin internal septations was incidentally discovered in this patient prior to heart transplantation (transvaginal scan).

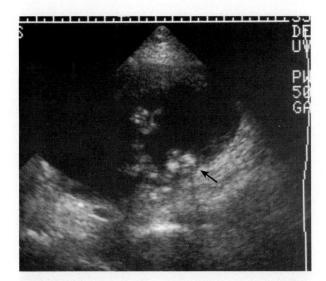

Figure 11.18

Borderline epithelial ovarian tumor: This 54-year-old woman had recurrent bouts of severe left lower quadrant pain, diarrhea, and fever. With antibiotics, the episodes of pain would resolve. During one episode, ultrasound was performed, revealing a cystic mass with thin internal septations and calcifications (*arrow*). At surgery, torsion of a borderline tumor was discovered.

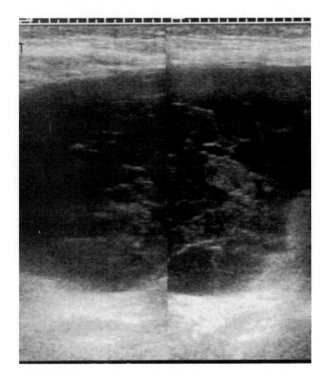

Figure 11.19

Malignant epithelial ovarian tumor: This elderly patient complained of abdominal bloating. A large cystic mass with multiple septations filled the pelvis and lower abdomen.

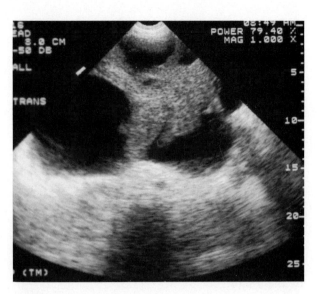

Figure 11.20

Malignant epithelial ovarian tumor: A big mass with cystic and large, solid components was a malignant ovarian primary.

Serous cystadenomas and cystadenocarcinomas, constituting 30 percent of all ovarian tumors, may be quite large and often contain papillary projections arising from internal septations. The tumor walls and septation may be thick or of varying thickness. Nodules of solid tissue may be seen within the cystic masses. The papillary excrescences and septal nodularity allow the recognition sonographically that the mass is neoplastic.

Recent interest in Doppler studies of adnexal masses has suggested that a low resistance spectral waveform is consistent with neovascularity in neoplastic masses. Continuous diastolic flow is expected in such lesions. High resistance arterial waveforms would be expected in benign lesions such as endometriomas.

Mucinous cystadenomas and adenocarcinomas account for 20 percent of ovarian neoplasms. These tumors may be quite large and have multiple septations and low-level echoes within the mass. The majority of giant ovarian neoplasms are of the mucinous type.

Solid nodules and papillary projections are often seen in mucinous cystadenocarcinoma. Pseudomyxoma peritonei with gelatinous material within the abdomen may result when such tumors rupture into the abdominal cavity.

Endometroid carcinoma, representing 15 percent of ovarian carcinomas, histologically resembles endometrial carcinoma. Some ovarian endometroid carcinomas have an associated endometrial carcinoma. The sonographic appearance is often similar to an endometrioma in that it is a hemorrhagic cystic mass. Solid elements can sometimes be seen.

Stromal Cell Line   Stromal tumors of the ovary are rare and can be indistinguishable sonographically from more common ovarian lesions.

Granulosal cell tumors that arise from the stromal elements of the ovary may be hormonally active. They represent 2 percent of ovarian neoplasms and have low malignant potential. Large granulosal cell tumors may be multiloculated and cystic. Ten to fifteen percent of patients with granulosal cell tumors have associated endometrial carcinoma because of the estrogenic milieu produced by the tumor.

Sertoli-Leydig tumors are similar in appearance to granulosal cell tumors. They generally occur in young women and are malignant in 10 to 20 percent of patients. These tumors are rare, representing less than 0.5 percent of ovarian tumors.

Metastatic Disease to the Ovaries (Figures 11.21–11.22)

Usually, metastatic disease to the ovary appears as solid enlargement of both ovaries, but sometimes complex masses with cystic and solid components can be detected. Tumors that spread to the ovaries include primaries of the pancreas, colon, stomach, and breast. In patients with a primary tumor and a complex ovarian mass which does not change on serial imaging, metastatic disease must be considered.

Peritoneal Inclusion Cyst

Peritoneal inclusion cyst is a loculation of peritoneal fluid that is trapped by adhesions. Generally, peritoneal inclusion cysts are seen in patients with a previous history of surgery in the pelvis. These masses may become quite large. Inclusion cysts are frequently confused with cystic neoplasms, parovarian cysts, or pelvic abscesses.

Parovarian Cyst

Parovarian cysts arise from embryonic remnants of mesonephric, tubal, or mesothelial origin. Most parovarian cysts are simple cysts of the adnexa and not the ovary, but they may develop hemorrhage and thus have septations, nodularity, and low-level

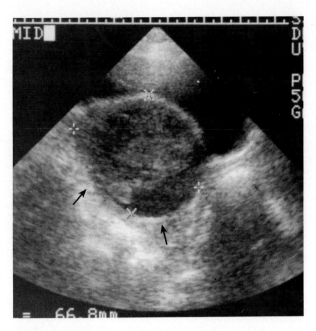

Figure 11.21
Metastatic melanoma: Ovarian involvement with melanoma was present in this woman with recurrent disease several years after removal of the primary skin lesion.

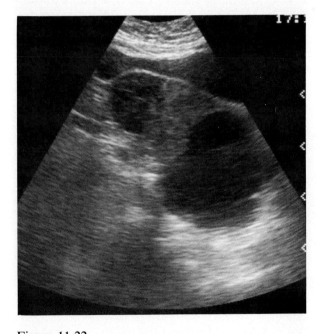

Figure 11.22
Metastatic renal cell carcinoma: This large, complex mass was believed to be a primary ovarian malignancy sonographically. Metastatic renal cell carcinoma was found histologically in this woman 5 years after radical nephrectomy.

echoes. These masses may become quite large, predisposing the adnexa to torsion. They may move up above the uterus and distended bladder and present as an abdominal mass. Their lack of change over time may suggest their etiology.

Hematoma (Figures 11.23–11.24)

Hematomas that accumulate in the pelvis may be secondary to blunt or surgical trauma. The acute hematoma is often echogenic, appearing nearly solid. With time, the hematoma becomes more cystic and septated. Aspiration may be necessary to differentiate it from an abscess.

Complicated Ascites (Figures 11.25–11.26)

Hemorrhagic or infected ascites may be sonographically similar to ovarian epithelial neoplasms, hemorrhagic cysts, endometriomas, or abscess.

Miscellaneous

Iliac Artery Aneurysm   Recognition of Doppler flow in an iliac artery aneurysm will allow it to be differentiated from other complex pelvic masses.

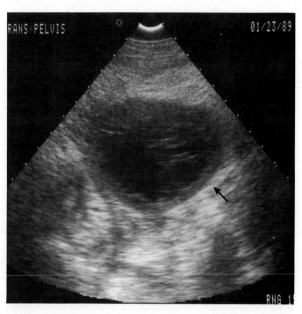

Figure 11.24
Hematoma: One week after hysterectomy, a septated hematoma was evacuated in this patient.

Collection Around Transplanted Kidney   A transplanted kidney is most often placed in the pelvis, in an extraperitoneal location. Urinomas, lymphoceles, and seromas associated with the transplant may form adjacent to the transplanted organ. Knowledge of the transplant and aspiration of the

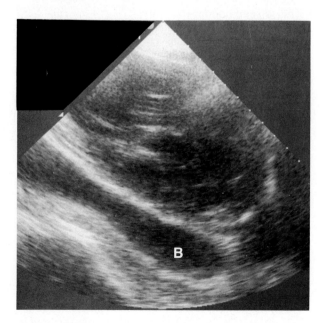

Figure 11.23
Pelvic hematoma: In this young patient with extensive pelvic fractures, a hematoma, a large multiseptate mass, was present anterior to the bladder (B).

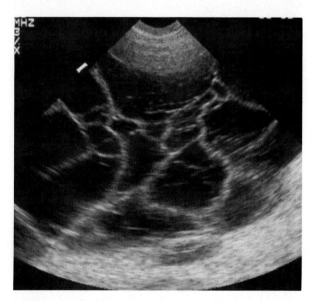

Figure 11.25
Septated ascites: Multiple septations are present in the ascites of an elderly woman with severe heart failure.

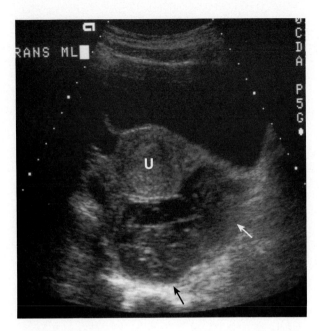

Figure 11.26

Complicated ascites: Hemorrhagic ascites was present in this postoperative patient. The complicated ascites appeared sonographically similar to a complex adnexal mass. (U = uterus.)

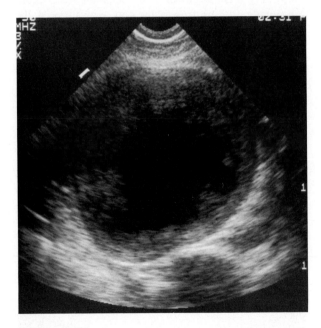

Figure 11.27

Cystic degeneration of a leiomyoma: This young woman suffered severe pain during her pregnancy and was known to have multiple leiomyomas of the uterus. A follow-up scan shows a cystic center to a large leiomyoma.

collection will clarify the source of the complex mass.

Cystic Degeneration of a Uterine Leiomyoma (Figure 11.27)

Rarely, the uterus gives rise to a cystic mass. Degeneration of a leiomyoma during pregnancy may result in a cystic, complex fibroid.

Emphasis Points

Complicated functional ovarian cysts can have a variety of appearances.

Hemorrhagic ovarian cysts are a very common cause of an adnexal mass. In a *clinically stable* patient of reproductive age with a negative β-HCG level and a complicated adnexal mass, allowing the passage of time may result in resolution of the mass without surgery. Ovarian preservation will be encouraged in this way. Obviously, if the patient is clinically unstable or has severe pain, fever, or leukocytosis, operative intervention may be necessary. This must be determined clinically.

Knowledge of the patient's age, β-HCG level, and clinical symptoms usually aids the diagnostic evaluation of the complex adnexal mass seen sonographically.

COMPLEX ADNEXAL MASS WITH POSITIVE β-HCG

    Corpus Luteal Cyst of Pregnancy
    Thecal Lutein Cysts
    Ectopic Pregnancy
    Other Adnexal Masses in Pregnancy
    Germ Cell Malignancy Without Pregnancy

Corpus Luteal Cyst of Pregnancy (Figure 11.28)

In the early intrauterine pregnancy being investigated by sonography, a corpus luteal cyst of the ovary can frequently be identified. This adnexal cyst represents the residuum of the ovulatory event that resulted in the pregnancy. The corpus luteal cyst hormonally maintains the normal pregnancy until approximately the twelfth week of gestation when placental hormone production takes over.

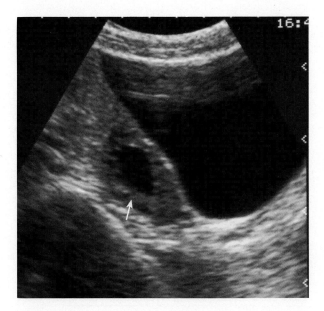

Figure 11.28
Corpus luteal cyst of pregnancy: In this patient with an 8-week intrauterine pregnancy, a simple cyst (*arrow*) of the right ovary was visualized.

The corpus luteal cyst frequently resolves or shows involutionary changes by 15 weeks' gestation.

Generally, a relatively small (3 cm or less), simple cyst, the corpus luteal cyst may be larger and sometimes have internal echoes representing hemorrhage.

In the situation of an early intrauterine pregnancy with a small cyst of the ovary, a corpus luteal cyst is presumed. If the mass is not typical for a corpus luteal cyst because of size and internal echo characteristics, follow-up sonography of the pregnancy and mass is warranted at 15 weeks and beyond. Intervention to remove the mass is not usually performed before 15 weeks because of the possibility that the mass is a corpus luteal cyst maintaining the pregnancy, and the possible teratogenic effects of anesthesia on the fetus in the first trimester. If the mass persists or enlarges during the pregnancy, it does not represent a corpus luteal cyst and may be removed during the pregnancy under tocolytic therapy.

Thecal Lutein Cysts (Figure 11.29)

Thecal lutein cysts develop when there are high circulating levels of human chorionic gonadotropin, (HCG) usually with multiple gestations or gestational trophoblastic disease.

Thirty to fifty percent of patients with gestational trophoblastic disease have thecal lutein cysts

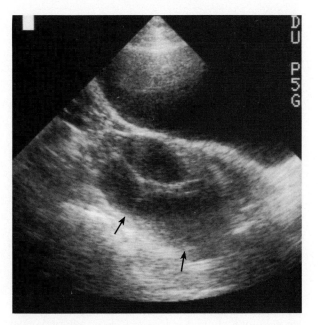

Figure 11.29
Thecal lutein cysts of gestational trophoblastic disease: Bilaterally enlarged, multicystic ovaries were present in this patient with hydatidiform mole. The mole was evacuated by dilatation and curettage. The ovarian cysts (*arrows*) took weeks to involute.

on bilaterally enlarged cystic ovaries. Large, dominant cysts may occur on both ovaries and are secondary to the stimulation of the ovaries by high hormonal levels.

The typical presentation of the patient with gestational trophoblastic disease is that of hyperemesis, with a uterus that is larger than expected for dates, and vaginal bleeding. β-HCG quantities are often higher than expected for presumed gestational age.

Sonographically, the uterus is enlarged and filled with amorphous, solid material. Cystic spaces within the solid material may sometimes be seen. Hydatiform mole, invasive mole, and choriocarcinoma may all have a similar sonographic appearance. Multiple cysts may be identified on both ovaries.

Dilatation and evacuation (D and E) is the usual therapy for gestational trophoblastic disease. Staging for disseminated disease usually includes CT scanning of the chest and abdomen, as well as the head in some cases. Patients with molar pregnancy are followed carefully. β-HCG levels should eventually return to normal after D and E. Often the patient is advised not to become pregnant for 1 year so that the possibility of recurrent disease can be excluded. Thecal lutein cysts may take weeks to resolve despite declining β-HCG levels. Patients with choriocarcinoma are usually treated with chemotherapy.

In partial mole, a fetus may be identified accompanying the more typical molar tissue. The fetus frequently has identifiable structural anomalies, growth retardation, and abnormal chromosomal make-up. Thecal lutein cysts may be identified in this form of gestational trophoblastic disease as well.

Ectopic Pregnancy (Figures 11.30–11.32)

Ectopic pregnancy is a condition with increasing incidence. Maternal mortality is diminishing secondary to earlier diagnosis and improved treatment, but ectopic pregnancy is still an important cause of maternal morbidity and mortality.

Risk factors for the development of ectopic pregnancy include previous ectopic pregnancy, surgery on the fallopian tubes, intrauterine contraceptive device (IUD) use, and previous pelvic inflammatory disease. Infertility is associated with ectopic pregnancy.

Clinically, the presentation of a patient with a ruptured ectopic pregnancy is abdominal pain, adnexal mass, and vaginal bleeding. Increasingly, patients are discovered to have ectopic pregnancy before these symptoms develop.

If a patient with a positive β-HCG has no evidence of intrauterine pregnancy and a complex ad-

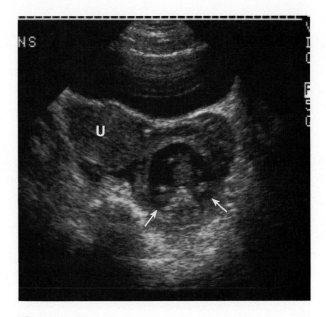

Figure 11.31
Ectopic pregnancy: An extrauterine fetus (*arrows*) was seen in the left adnexa. An extratubal ectopic pregnancy was found at surgery. (U) = uterus.) (Case courtesy of Dr. Cathyrn Powers, Ocala, Florida.)

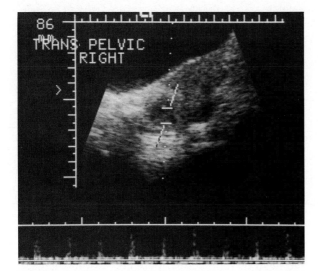

Figure 11.30
Ectopic pregnancy: In this patient with pain, spotting, and a positive β-HCG, fetal cardiac activity was detected within a complex mass of the right adnexa. The uterus was empty.

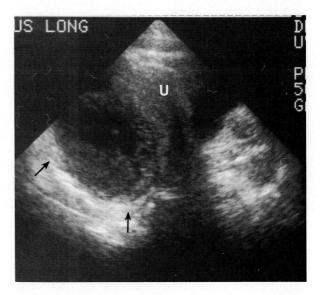

Figure 11.32
Ectopic pregnancy: Complex material (*arrows*) pushed the uterus (U) anteriorly in this patient with a ruptured ectopic pregnancy.

nexal mass (not an ovarian cyst) is visualized, the risk of ectopic pregnancy has been estimated to be 85–90 percent. If large amounts of fluid are present along with the adnexal mass, the likelihood of ectopic pregnancy is nearly 100 percent.

The complex adnexal mass in a patient with a positive β-HCG and no intrauterine pregnancy may contain the extrauterine gestation, recognizable by the fetal pole, yolk sac, or a clearly identifiable fetus. Alternatively, the complex adnexal mass will be a mass of clotted blood and trophoblastic tissue without an identifiable fetus.

Concomitant intra- and extrauterine pregnancies are considered rare, occurring in approximately 1 in 30,000 spontaneous pregnancies. In patients with infertility undergoing reproductive assistance with hormonal stimulation, the frequency of concomitant intra- and extrauterine pregnancy may be as high as 1 in every 6000 to 8000 pregnancies.

Correlation with quantitative β-HCG levels may be helpful when possible ectopic pregnancy is suspected, but it is not always available in the emergency situation. Serial β-HCG levels are also helpful, because β-HCG levels double every 48 hours in normal pregnancies. A less dramatic rise or plateau of β-HCG levels is seen in ectopic pregnancy.

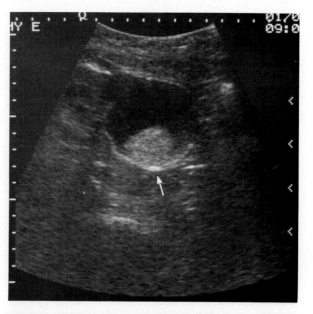

Figure 11.33
Mature teratoma: During routine obstetric ultrasound, a right adnexal mass with a highly echogenic dermoid plug (*arrow*) was identified. The mass was monitored during pregnancy and removed after delivery.

Other Adnexal Masses in Pregnancy (Figure 11.33–11.35

Endometrioma, ovarian neoplasm, parovarian cyst, or abscess may occur in pregnant patients and explain an adnexal mass in a patient with an intrauterine pregnancy. The sonographic features of these masses have been discussed.

A patient with endometrioma may have a history of infertility or cyclic pain prior to pregnancy.

Pregnant patients seldom have acute pelvic inflammatory disease secondary to ascending sexually transmitted disease because of the gravid uterus. Abscesses secondary to a ruptured appendix or inflammatory bowel disease may engulf the adnexa and be interpreted as an adnexal mass. Patients with pelvic abscesses usually have fever, elevated white count, and pain.

In young women of reproductive age, malignant neoplasms of the ovary are unusual. Benign ovarian teratomas may occur in this age group and often may be recognized sonographically by the presence of highly echogenic fat or calcifications. Ovarian masses that may be neoplasms of the ovary can be operated upon after the first trimester of pregnancy with safe maintenance of the pregnancy.

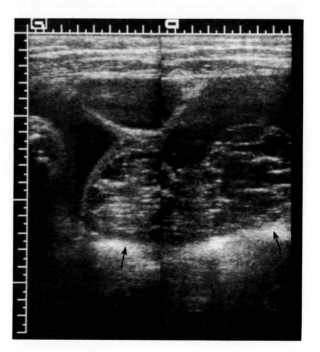

Figure 11.34
Cystadenoma of the ovary: A large, multiseptate mass (*arrows*) filled much of the left pelvis in this young pregnant woman. The mass was removed in the second trimester of pregnancy.

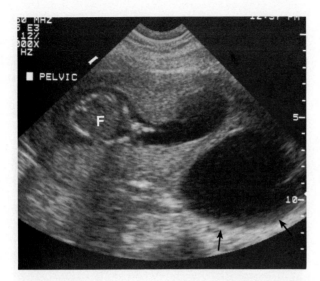

Figure 11.35
Parovarian cyst in pregnancy: A large, simple cyst (*arrows*) was noted during routine obstetric imaging. The mass failed to involute after the first trimester and was surgically removed. A parovarian cyst was proven histologically. (F = fetus.)

Germ Cell Malignancy Without Pregnancy (Figure 11.36)

Infrequently, patients who have no evidence of intra- or extrauterine pregnancy will have positive β-HCG levels and an adnexal mass. Malignant germ cell tumors of the ovary are tumors that may have elevated β-HCG levels. This marker for tumor activity can be followed during therapy. Choriocarcinoma of the ovary frequently has positive β-HCG levels. These are large, solid tumors, sometimes with internal hemorrhage and calcification. The mass may be of such a size as to present in the lower abdomen. Lymphadenopathy may also be obvious.

SOLID-APPEARING ADNEXAL MASS

  Hemorrhagic Functional Cyst
  Endometrioma
  Ectopic Pregnancy
  Tubo-ovarian Abscess
  Ovarian Torsion
  Neoplasm
    Stromal Tumors
    Germ Cell Tumors
    Brenner Tumor
    Malignant Epithelial Tumor
    Metastasis to Ovary/Lymphoma
  Leiomyoma (Pedunculated)
  Pelvic Kidney

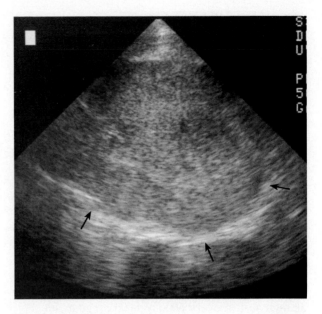

Figure 11.36
Mixed malignant germ cell tumor: A large, solid mass (*arrows*) was present in this young child with a positive serum β-HCG. Multiple para-aortic lymph nodes were involved with tumor. Choriocarcinoma was a predominant element of the mass.

  Hematoma
  Fusion Abnormality of the Uterus

It is unusual for the sonographer to image a completely solid adnexal or ovarian mass, for cystic or complex masses of the ovary are much more frequently seen. Many of the entities that often appear as complicated cystic lesions of the adnexa can also be sonographically solid appearing. Also, solid masses from sources other than the ovary may present in the pelvis and should be considered as a possible "adnexal" mass.

Hemorrhagic Functional Cyst (Figures 11.37–11.40)

Some functional cysts, especially those filled with blood clot, may look as if they are solid, but over time and with rescanning their evolving and changing appearance will allow recognition of the dynamic nature of the mass, making a functional cyst the most likely possibility. In patients who are of reproductive age, a small, solid-appearing adnexal mass is likely to be a hemorrhagic cyst, and it deserves follow-up scanning to make sure it resolves.

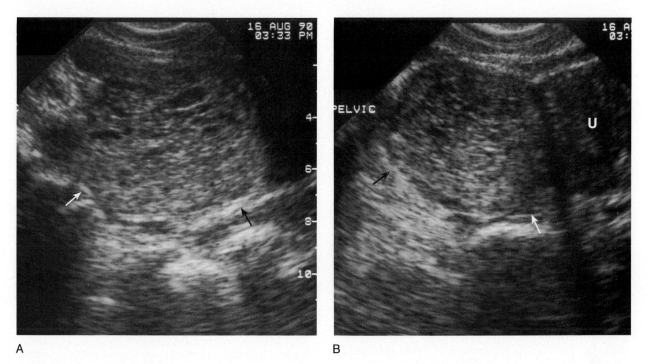

A   B

Figure 11.37
Hemorrhagic ovarian cyst: (A and B) This 26-year-old
woman was incidentally noted to have a homogeneous
solid mass in the right ovary (*arrows*). Surgery was performed, and a complicated functional cyst of the ovary
was removed. (U = uterus.)

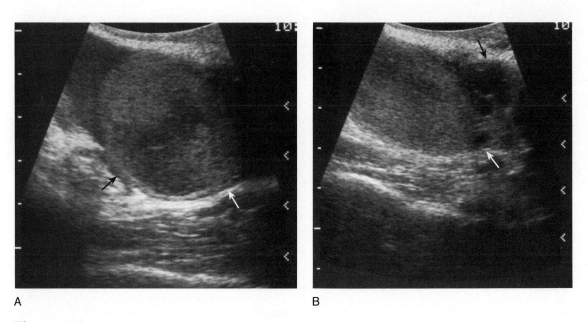

A   B

Figure 11.38
Hemorrhagic ovarian cyst: (A and B) Transvaginal scan of
this 30-year-old woman showed a solid-appearing mass
with an internal matrix. The ovarian origin of the mass was
confirmed, as a group of tiny follicles rim the mass (B–
arrows). Follow-up scanning after two menstrual cycles
showed that the mass had resolved.

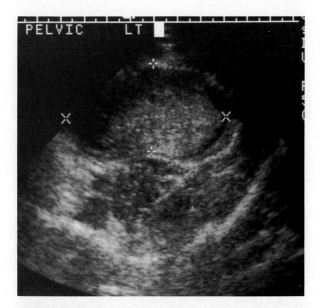

Figure 11.39
Clot-filled ovarian cyst: This 19-year-old, who had previously lost her right ovary because of cysts, now had a large, solid-appearing mass in the left adnexa. Her gynecologist placed her on hormonal therapy to aid cyst regression. Follow-up scanning showed resolution of the mass and a normal-appearing left ovary.

Endometrioma

An endometrioma that is filled with old blood may be mistaken for a solid mass, but the ballotable nature of the mass will sometimes allow its liquid nature to be detected. Some endometriomas are solid, filled with septations, fibrous tissue, and organizing blood products.

Ectopic Pregnancy (Figure 11.41)

An ectopic pregnancy that has resulted in a tube filled with blood or a large hemorrhagic mass in the adnexa or cul-de-sac will be solid appearing at ultrasound. Clinically, the patient will usually have a positive β-HCG assay and abdominal pain. Echogenic free fluid is frequently seen as well.

Tubo-ovarian Abscess (Figure 11.42)

Patients with tubo-ovarian abscess related to either sexually transmitted pelvic inflammatory disease or other causes of pelvic abscess typically have fever, pelvic pain, and elevated white blood cell counts. Debris and solid-appearing infectious material may collect in the pelvis.

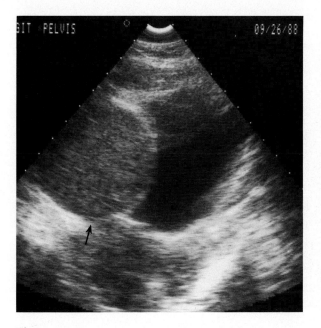

Figure 11.40
Hemorrhagic ovarian cyst: A solid-appearing lesion (*arrow*) was excised and was found to be a hemorrhagic ovarian cyst.

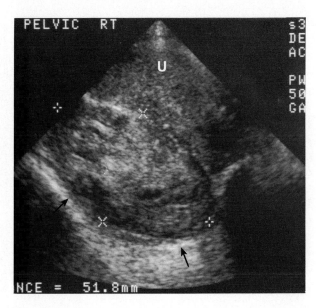

Figure 11.41
Ectopic pregnancy: In this patient with a positive β-HCG, abdominal pain, and a solid-appearing adnexal mass, no intrauterine pregnancy was visible. The solid adnexal material (*arrows*) was blood and trophoblastic tissue from a ruptured ectopic pregnancy. The uterus (U) was bowed anterior to the mass.

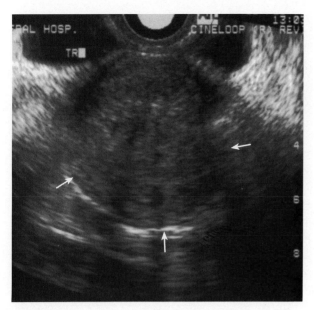

Figure 11.42
Tubo-ovarian abscess: A solid mass in the right adnexa (*arrows*) proved to be a tubo-ovarian abscess at surgery.

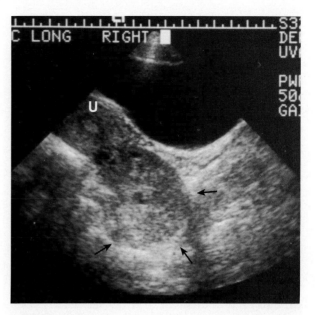

Figure 11.43
Ovarian torsion: In this young woman with severe right lower quadrant pain, a swollen right ovary was identified (*arrows*). At surgery, the engorged ovary could not be salvaged. (U = uterus.)

Ovarian Torsion (Figure 11.43)

Ovarian torsion occurs when the ovary twists on its vascular pedicle, obstructing the egress of blood from the ovary. Usually, the clinical situation is that of an acute abdomen—the patient has severe abdominal pain, vomiting, and fever.

Sonographically, the ovary becomes quite large, up to 28 times normal. It is diffusely edematous and hemorrhagic. In the majority of cases, small, engorged follicles are seen rimming the periphery of the massively distended ovary. A preexisting mass lesion of the ovary such as a functional cyst or neoplasm will predispose a patient to torsion. In young girls, the highly mobile adnexa may undergo torsion even without a mass as a leadpoint. Risk factors predisposing to ovarian torsion include ovarian mass (cyst or neoplasm), hyperstimulation of the ovary, polycystic ovarian syndrome (Stein-Leventhal), and youth.

Neoplasm

Purely solid ovarian neoplasms are usually ovarian stromal tumors, malignant germ cell tumors, malignant epithelial tumors, and metastases.

Stromal Tumors (Figures 11.44–11.45) Masses arising from the stroma of the ovary represent 10 percent of all ovarian neoplasms and 2 percent of all ovarian malignancies. These tumors may be hormonally active, producing estrogen, progesterone, and androgens. Depending on the age of the patient, the abnormal hormone production may result in precocious puberty in a child, hirsutism or virilization, menstrual irregularities, or postmenopausal bleeding. More than 90 percent of stromal tumors of the ovary are thecomas or granulosal cell tumors.

Thecomas account for 2 percent of all ovarian neoplasms. They are almost always benign and usually develop in postmenopausal women. The usual presenting symptom of a thecoma is postmenopausal bleeding. The mass may range in size from 4 to 32 cm. Thecomas are solid and homogeneous in echogenicity. Calcifications may be present.

Fibromas are relatively rare and rarely exhibit hormone production. Meigs' syndrome is present when there is associated ascites and pleural effusions with ovarian fibroma. Meigs' syndrome may be difficult to differentiate from malignant ovarian carcinomatosis. Sonographically the microscopic features of fibromas and thecomas merge; thus it is common to see terms such as fibrothecoma or thecofibroma.

Granulosal cell tumors are also hormonally active and affect postmenopausal women. These tu-

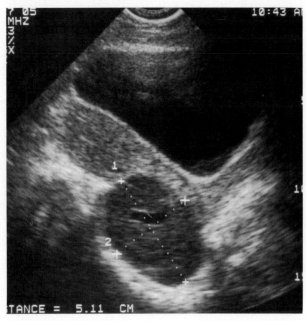

A   B

Figure 11.44

Fibrothecoma: (A and B) This homogeneously hypo-echoic adnexal mass could be mistaken for an exophytic leiomyoma of the uterus (U). Fibrothecoma is an unusual benign mass of the ovary, sometimes associated with as-cites.

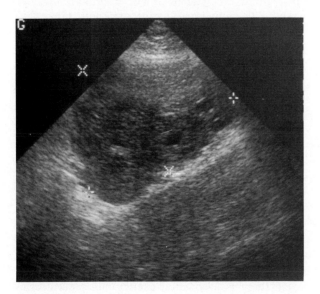

Figure 11.45

Granulosal cell tumor: This elderly woman presented with postmenopausal bleeding. Her uterus was enlarged and inhomogeneous, and endometrial biopsy yielded necrotic tissue. Fine-needle aspiration of a solid left adnexal mass established the diagnosis as granulosal cell tumor, a mass producing an estrogenic environment. Fine-needle aspiration was performed because the patient refused surgery.

mors may cause an estrogenic environment, which predisposes to endometrial carcinoma. These tumors are usually unilateral and solid. Again, the most common presentation for the woman with a granulosal cell tumor is postmenopausal bleeding.

Sertoli-Leydig cell tumors are also stromal tumors, which are often solid.

Germ Cell Tumors (Figures 11.46–11.47) Depending upon the particular make-up of a mature teratoma with varying proportions of liquid fat, bone, teeth, or hair, the mass may have a wide spectrum of sonographic appearances, some of which are bizarre. The "tip of the iceberg" has been used to describe an ovarian teratoma with rapid attenuation of sound secondary to fatty material in the anterior portion of the mass. Tumors with extensive hair, teeth, and fat may look solid sonographically with multiple interfaces.

Dysgerminomas and endodermal sinus tumors, as well as embryonal carcinoma, choriocarcinoma, and immature teratoma, are malignant forms of germ cell tumors representing the minority of all ovarian germ cell tumors. These masses are seen in children and young women and can have markers with positive alpha-fetoprotein or β-HCG assays. The masses may be large and are usually predominantly solid with areas of hemorrhage or necrosis. Typically, these tumors spread not by serosal and omental implantation but through lymphatic and hematogenous channels. Cystic portions of such masses may sometimes be present.

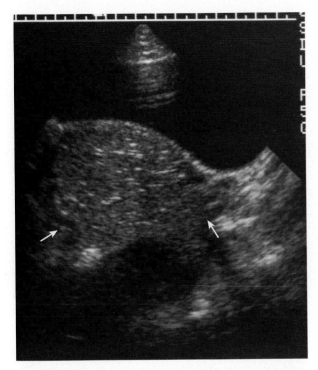

Figure 11.46
Mature teratoma: This homogeneously solid mass (*arrows*) was palpated in a 20-year-old woman. At surgery, a hair-filled mature teratoma was found. The multiple interfaces of the mass are secondary to the hair.

Brenner Tumor The Brenner tumor is a benign, often solid mass that arises from the surface epithelium of the ovary and belongs to the class of epithelial tumors that includes serous and mucinous cystadenomas and cystadenocarcinomas, endometroid carcinoma, and clear cell carcinoma, many of which are predominantly cystic masses.

Brenner tumors may be discovered at all ages from childhood to the elderly and may be of varying size from microscopic to 8 cm. These masses are bilateral in 7 percent of patients.

The masses are solid and firm and resemble fibrothecomas, leiomyomas of the uterus, and metastases to the ovary. The masses may have areas of calcification. Sonographically, the masses are hypoechoic and solid, with some through transmission.

Malignant Epithelial Tumor (Figure 11.48) It is uncommon for the typical malignant epithelial ovarian tumor to be completely solid; more often these masses have large cystic or complex components. Anaplastic or poorly differentiated carcinomas may be made up primarily of large, solid components.

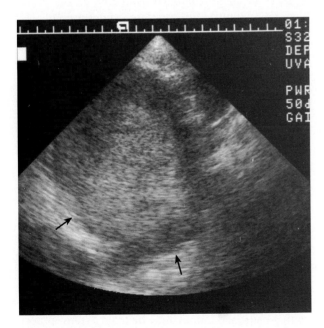

Figure 11.47
Dysgerminoma: Large, solid mass (*arrows*) in an 8-year-old with a trivial history of abdominal trauma. At surgery, the mass was found to be a malignant germ cell tumor.

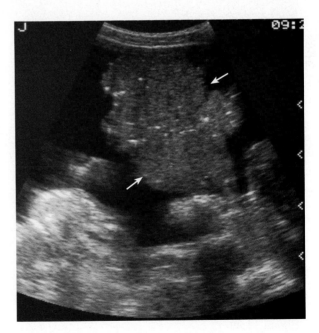

Figure 11.48
Malignant epithelial tumor: An elderly woman with new onset ascites and a predominantly solid adnexal mass (*arrows*) was found to have poorly differentiated adenocarcinoma of the ovary. Debulking surgery followed by chemotherapy was performed.

Metastasis to Ovary/Lymphoma (Figures 11.49–11.50)

Metastases to the ovary represent approximately 10 percent of all adnexal neoplasms. Metastatic disease may originate in primaries of the colon, stomach, pancreas, breast, and lung or may be secondary to melanoma. Endometrial carcinoma may metastasize to the ovary, making it difficult to differentiate from a second endometrioid primary of the ovary. Other primary tumors such as renal cell carcinoma may metastasize to the ovary.

The sonographic appearance of metastatic disease is usually that of solid bilateral masses. Cystic areas of necrosis or hemorrhage may be identifiable.

Lymphoma may develop as a primary process in the ovary, but it is usually part of diffuse disease and is bilateral in 50 percent of cases. Leukemia rarely infiltrates the ovary causing a mass.

Leiomyoma (Pedunculated) (Figures 11.51–11.52)

Leiomyomas of the uterus, also known as fibroids or myomas, are common tumors in the female pel-

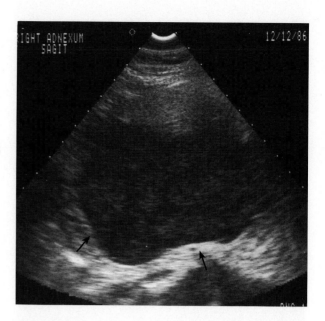

Figure 11.50

Lymphoma of the ovary: A homogeneously hypoechoic, solid mass (*arrows*) was present in this middle-aged woman with non-Hodgkin lymphoma of the ovary. The patient was treated with aggressive chemotherapy after surgery to remove the ovarian mass.

vis that are believed to be present in 25 percent of women older than 35 years. The leiomyoma arises from the smooth muscle of the myometrium. An exophytic or pedunculated leiomyoma of the uterus may be difficult to differentiate from a solid ovarian mass.

Leiomyomas may be hypoechoic, echogenic, or isoechoic, depending upon the composition of smooth muscle, fibrous tissue, and calcification. Homogeneous or quite heterogeneous echogenicity may be demonstrated.

A careful examination to locate the ovary separate from the leiomyoma is most helpful in distinguishing a solid ovarian mass from a leiomyoma.

Pelvic Kidney (Figure 11.53)

Normally, the kidney is located in the upper abdomen at the level of the first three lumbar vertebral bodies. The kidney may be present in the pelvis at the lower lumbar or sacral levels if, during embryologic development, the ureteral bud fails to elongate completely. The blood supply of this ectopically positioned kidney may be from the lower aorta or iliac arteries. An ectopically positioned kidney usually has an unusual axis. Stasis of urine flow may predispose to recurrent infections and stone

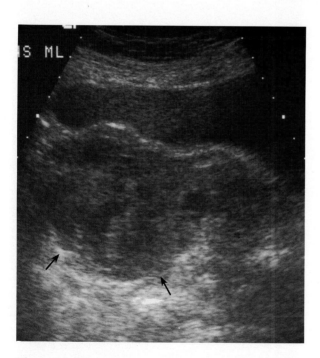

Figure 11.49

Metastatic transitional cell carcinoma: This 60-year-old woman with a history of transitional cell carcinoma of the right ureter presented with a solid adnexal mass (*arrows*) that proved to be involvement of the ovary with recurrent transitional cell carcinoma.

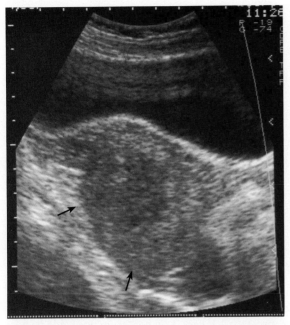

A

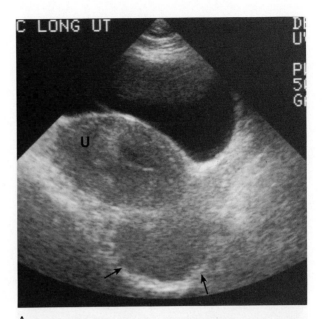

A

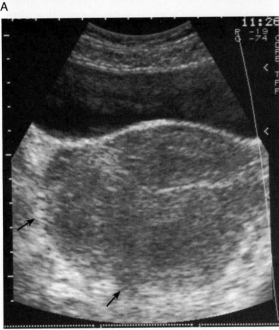

B

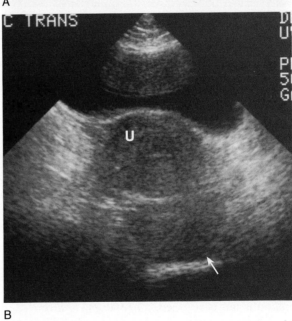

B

Figure 11.51

Leiomyoma of the uterus: (A and B) This 26-year-old presented with acute, severe pelvic pain, dropping hematocrit, and negative β-HCG. A large, solid mass was in intimate association with the uterus (*arrows*). No normal right ovary could be seen. Surgery revealed acute red degeneration of a leiomyoma, a condition unusual in a nonpregnant patient. A leiomyoma had undergone acute hemorrhage.

Figure 11.52

Pedunculated leiomyoma of the uterus: This 35-year-old woman was noted on routine physical examination to have a palpable mass in the cul-de-sac (*arrows*). Ultrasound evaluation demonstrated a mass that appeared to be separate from the uterus (U) but had similar echotexture characteristics. Surgical exploration revealed a pedunculated leiomyoma, easily removed by excision of its stalk.

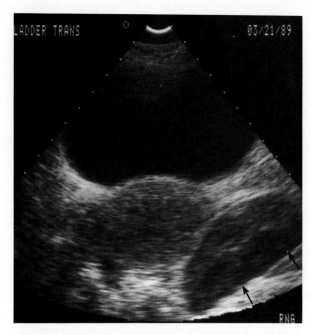

Figure 11.53
Pelvic kidney: A solid, reniform mass (*arrows*) was seen behind the bladder and to the left of the uterus. No kidney was seen in the left renal fossa and the right kidney was unremarkable. Functional studies may be necessary to prove the diagnosis.

formation. Sonographic recognition of the hypo-echoic renal cortex and hyperechoic central renal sinus fat is possible. Absence of a kidney in the ip-silateral renal fossa usually confirms the diagnosis.

Hematomas

Acute hematomas related to blunt or surgical trauma may fill the pelvis with extensive, hetero-geneous solid material. Over time if surgical evac-uation is not performed, a hematoma will retract in size, becoming more cystic and septated. Complete resolution by resorption may take weeks to months.

Fusion Abnormality of the Uterus (Figures 11.54–11.55)

Patients with two uterine horns may be diagnosed as having a solid adnexal mass when one horn is not recognized as part of the uterus. If one horn is ob-structed, it may become filled with debris and old blood, contributing to its solid appearance. In a pregnant patient with two uterine horns, the preg-nancy may develop normally in one horn, but the other horn may enlarge and show decidual reaction in its endometrial cavity. Failure to recognize the

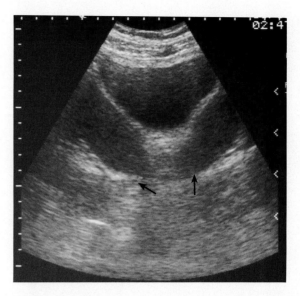

Figure 11.54
Didelphys uteri: Two uterine horns (*arrows*) seen here in transverse axis. If care were not taken, one could be mis-interpreted as a solid adnexal mass. Recognition of the endometrial stripe in both will allow the appropriate di-agnosis to be made. The upper abdomen should be viewed in a patient with uterine fusion abnormalities to confirm that there are no upper urinary tract abnormali-ties, such as agenesis of a kidney or a horseshoe kid-ney.

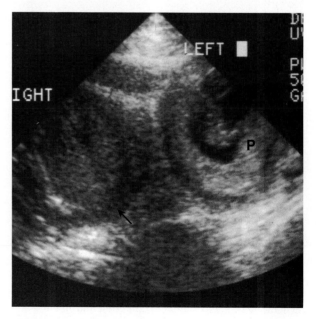

Figure 11.55
Didelphys uteri (pregnancy): A pregnancy (P) was identi-fiable in the left uterine horn. Note the stimulated right horn (*arrow*).

fusion abnormality in a pregnant patient may lead to the erroneous diagnosis of an ectopic pregnancy if the empty horn is seen with an adjacent pregnancy.

Emphasis Points

When a solid pelvic mass is identified, the first task is to decide whether or not it originates from the uterus. Fibroids (leiomyomas) of the uterus are common causes of solid pelvic masses.

Commonly encountered adnexal masses such as hemorrhagic functional cysts can be solid appearing. Follow-up scanning can be offered to the asymptomatic young woman if a hemorrhagic cyst is suspected. Retraction of the clot and resolution of the mass may be seen.

Very large, solid adnexal masses, such as a dysgerminoma of the ovary in a young girl, may be misinterpreted as an enlarged uterus. Care in identifying the small uterus is important. Tumor markers such as alpha fetoprotein and βHCG may be positive and helpful in diagnosing malignant germ cell tumors.

HIGHLY ECHOGENIC PELVIC MASS: CALCIFICATION VERSUS AIR VERSUS FAT

Calcified Pelvic Masses
    Uterine Leiomyomas
    Ovarian Neoplasms
    Pregnancy/Extruded Fetal Parts/Lithopedia
    Iliac Artery Aneurysm
Air-Filled Pelvic Mass
Fat-Containing Pelvic Mass

Highly echogenic pelvic masses contain one of three substances: calcifications, air, or fat. Calcifications are seen by ultrasound as highly echogenic foci with pronounced shadowing, which can often be confirmed by plain films. Air within a pelvic mass usually suggests superimposed infection or a fistulous communication with the bowel. Sonographically, air is brightly echogenic with ringdown seen behind it. Fat that is present in mature germ cell tumors such as the teratoma can have a very distinctive appearance, with echogenic globules or nodules in the mass. The fat does not usually shadow, although there may be associated toothlike calcifications in such masses. The nearby calcifications may cause shadowing.

Calcified Pelvic Masses

If a calcified pelvic mass is suspected, a plain film can be helpful to characterize the calcification.

Uterine Leiomyomas (Figure 11.56) A commonly identified mass in the pelvis, the uterine leiomyoma arises from smooth muscle of the myometrium, may respond to hormonal influences, and may undergo necrosis during pregnancy. Hyalinization, fibrosis, and calcification occur with degeneration of a fibroid. Coarse, popcorn-type calcifications are often identified on plain films. Dense, echogenic foci with broad shadowing are seen sonographically.

Ovarian Neoplasms (Figures 11.57–11.59) Several types of ovarian neoplasms, both benign and malignant, may have associated calcifications. Teratomas, the common benign ovarian tumor of children and young adults, may have teeth and bony parts within the mass. Dense, echogenic foci with shadowing will be seen sonographically. Typically, tooth- or bonelike structures may be seen on plain film.

Malignant germ cell tumors, often large and solid, may have significant calcified elements. These tumors also occur most often in children and young adults. Although the calcification in the benign mature teratoma is usually localized in the mural nodule of the mass, calcifications in malignant germ cell tumors are often scattered throughout the tumor mass. Calcified cartilage and bone are common in malignant masses.

Epithelial tumors of the ovary, including the benign Brenner tumors and the more common malignant cystadenocarcinomas, may show calcifications pathologically in as many as 40 percent of cases. The calcifications may be clustered, psammonatous, and identifiable at various sites in the pelvis and upper abdomen if metastatic implants are present. Sonographically, the calcifications may be difficult to distinguish from air-filled bowel, and plain film or CT correlation may be necessary to recognize the abnormality. CT evaluation without oral gastrointestinal contrast may facilitate recognition of the calcific implants.

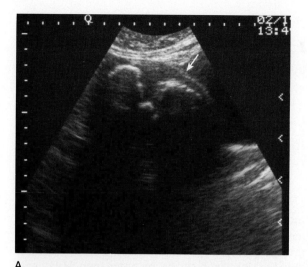

A

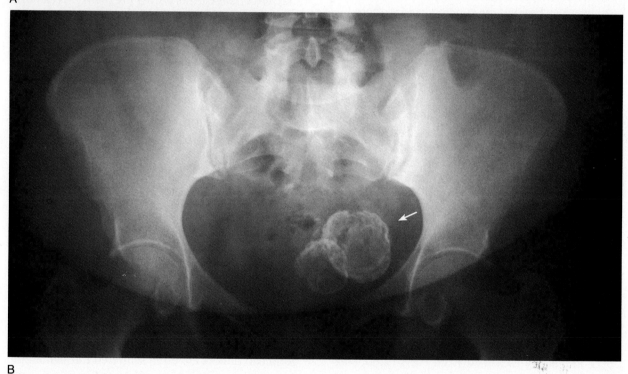

B

Figure 11.56

Calcified uterine leiomyomas: (A) Within the expected location of the uterus, highly echogenic foci (*arrow*) with dense shadowing were seen. (B) Plain film of the pelvis showed the typical coarse calcifications of a leiomyomatous uterus.

Pregnancy/Extruded Fetal Parts/Lithopedia (Figure 11.60) Calcifications related to a normal pregnancy, an advanced ectopic pregnancy, and extruded fetal parts, usually after an unsuccessful instrumentation, can all be identified sonographically. A lithopedion, which is the rarely seen densely cal-

cified remnant of an ectopic pregnancy, may also be encountered.

Iliac Artery Aneurysm (Figure 11.61) The common iliac arteries are usually identifiable by sonography at the point at which they bifurcate from the aorta. Usually 1–1.5 cm or smaller in anteroposterior dimension, the iliac artery is evaluated if an aortic aneurysm exists to determine whether the aneurysm extends into the iliac vessel. The iliac arteries can also be studied using the full-bladder technique since the arteries travel along the lateral pelvis.

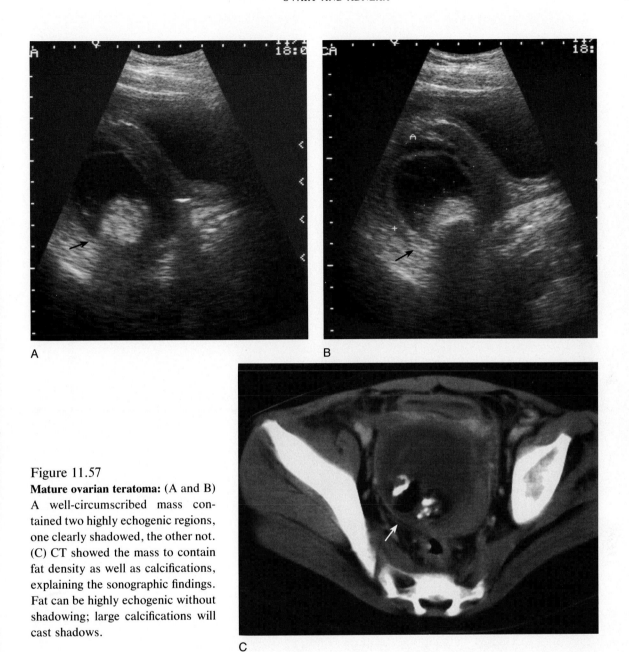

Figure 11.57
Mature ovarian teratoma: (A and B) A well-circumscribed mass contained two highly echogenic regions, one clearly shadowed, the other not. (C) CT showed the mass to contain fat density as well as calcifications, explaining the sonographic findings. Fat can be highly echogenic without shadowing; large calcifications will cast shadows.

Iliac artery aneurysms are usually secondary to atherosclerosis and are less often related to trauma or infection. Often asymptomatic, iliac artery aneurysms may cause hydronephrosis by extrinsic compression of the distal ureter. Calcifications associated with an aneurysm are often rimlike or curvilinear, following the outline of the vessel.

Air-Filled Pelvic Mass
(Figures 11.62–11.64)

Fluid collections containing air are usually infected, representing abscesses from gynecologic causes or regional nongynecologic etiologies. Such collections may be amenable to ultrasound drainage procedures. Air-containing collections may have a fistulous communication with bowel.

Fat-Containing Pelvic Mass
(Figures 11.65–11.68)

A mass that has the characteristic highly echogenic, nonshadowing fat globules can with confidence be called a germ cell tumor, usually a benign mature teratoma. Areas of calcification may be seen separately from the echogenic fat in such masses.

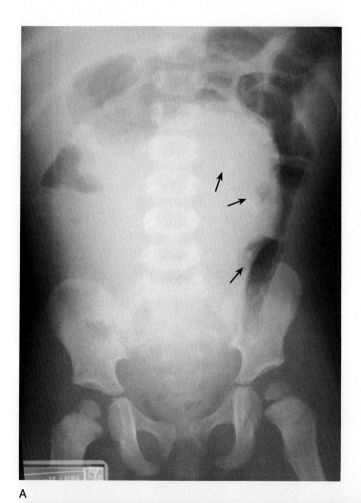

A

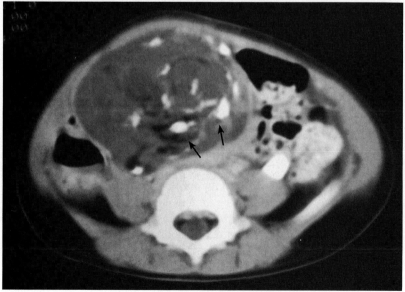

B

Figure 11.58
Malignant germ cell tumor: (A and B) Plain film of the abdomen demonstrated mass effect upon the bowel loops of the central abdomen. Note the calcifications (*arrows*) scattered centrally in the mass. In this 6-year-old girl, the calcifications were within a large teratocarcinoma of the ovary.

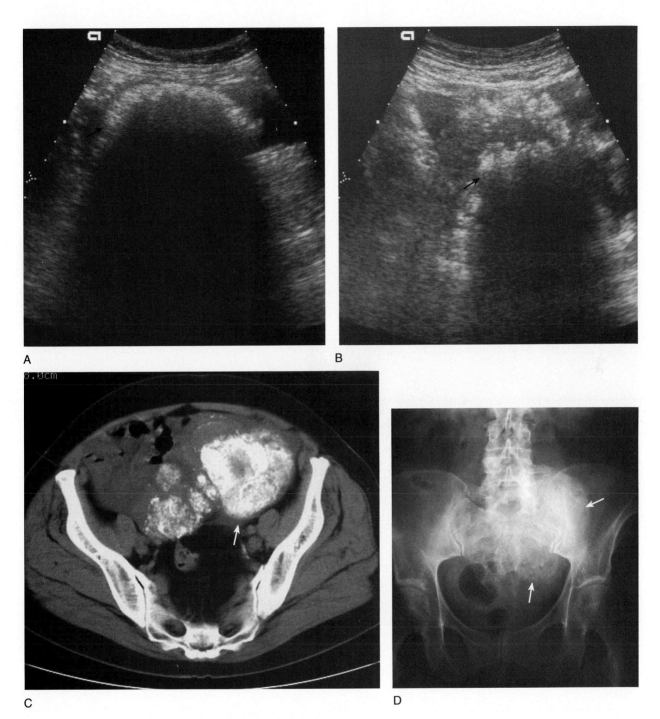

Figure 11.59

Borderline epithelial tumor: (A and B) Ascites and extensive, highly echogenic foci with shadowing (*arrows*) led to the CT confirmation (C) of extensive calcified masses separate from the uterus in the pelvis. These proved to be borderline epithelial neoplasm. (D) Plain film demonstrated the fine, diffuse calcifications.

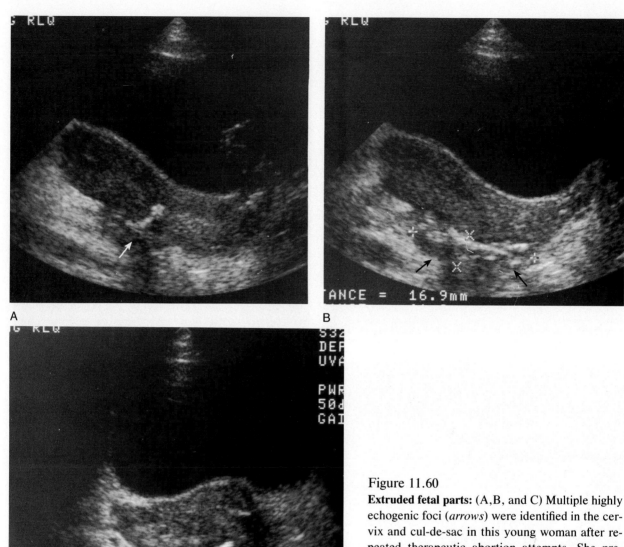

A

B

C

Figure 11.60
Extruded fetal parts: (A,B, and C) Multiple highly echogenic foci (*arrows*) were identified in the cervix and cul-de-sac in this young woman after repeated therapeutic abortion attempts. She presented with fever and exquisite pelvic pain. At surgery, multiple fetal bones that had been pushed through a rent in the lower uterine segment were removed.

Emphasis Points

The highly echogenic fat in an ovarian teratoma is very characteristic and can permit a specific sonographic diagnosis to be suggested.

If calcifications or air is considered possible within a mass seen sonographically, a plain x-ray or CT of the area may help characterize the calcification or air within the mass. Defi-

nition of calcification or air and its characterization may aid in the appropriate diagnosis.

Toothlike calcifications suggest a mature teratoma. More extensive course calcifications scattered through a solid mass suggest a malignant germ cell neoplasm. Psammonatous calcifications suggest an epithelial tumor.

Popcorn-type calcifications of a degenerated leiomyoma are characteristic on plain film.

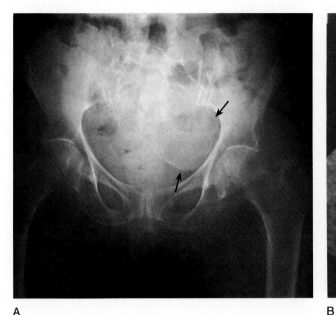

A

B

Figure 11.61

Iliac artery aneurysm: (A) Plain film demonstrated a curvilinear calcification (*arrow*) associated with a pelvic mass. (B) Ultrasound demonstrated a large inhomogeneous mass (*arrows*). The recognition of arterial flow within the mass allowed it to be identified as an iliac artery aneurysm. The left kidney had been chronically obstructed by the aneurysm's compression of the left ureter.

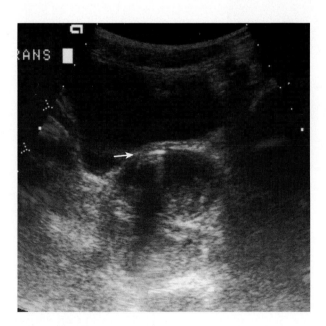

Figure 11.62

Pelvic abscess after appendicitis: A small fluid collection with air (*arrow*) was seen in this patient after surgical removal of an inflamed appendix.

BILATERAL ADNEXAL MASSES

Functional Ovarian Cyst and Other Causes of
    an Adnexal Mass
Neoplasms
    Epithelial Tumors
    Germ Cell Tumors
    Metastatic Disease to the Ovary
Pelvic Inflammatory Disease
Pyosalpinx/Hydrosalpinx
Endometriosis
Polycystic Ovarian (Stein-Leventhal)
    Syndrome
Thecal–Lutein Cysts

Functional Ovarian Cyst and Other Causes of an Adnexal Mass

In a normally cycling female patient, a corpus luteal cyst may be created during each ovulatory cycle of her reproductive life. The corpus luteal cyst or functional cyst of the ovary may persist for weeks, depending on its size and the patient's hormonal status.

The coincidental presence of a contralateral adnexal mass is certainly possible and the etiologies are numerous. Inflammatory processes and tumors (benign or malignant) could result in bilateral adnexal abnormalities.

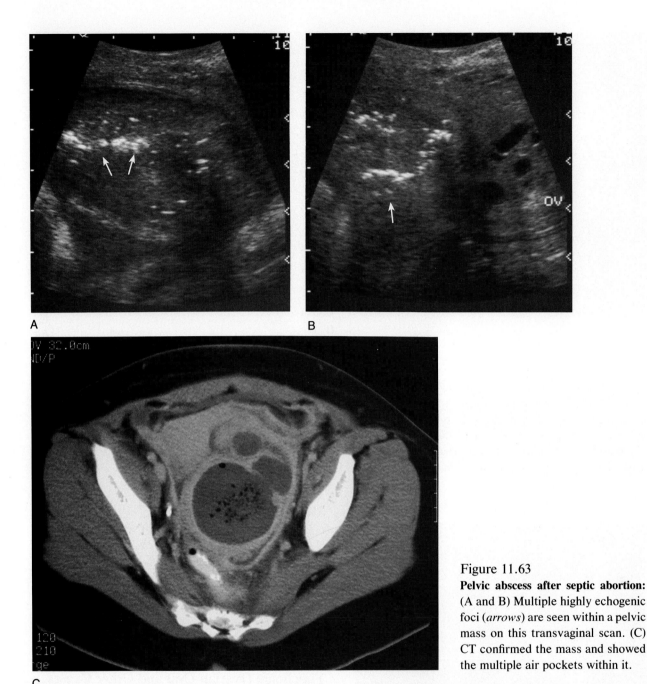

Figure 11.63
Pelvic abscess after septic abortion:
(A and B) Multiple highly echogenic
foci (*arrows*) are seen within a pelvic
mass on this transvaginal scan. (C)
CT confirmed the mass and showed
the multiple air pockets within it.

Neoplasms

Epithelial Tumors   Malignant serous cystadenocarcinoma, the most common malignant primary tumor of the ovary, is bilateral in 30 to 50 percent of
patients. Often, the bilaterality is difficult to detect
sonographically, as there may be a confluence of the
pelvic masses into a conglomerate of neoplastic tissue in the cul-de-sac.

Benign mucinous epithelial tumors are bilateral
in 5 to 10 percent of patients. Brenner tumor, an-

other epithelial tumor, has a 5 percent incidence of
bilaterality.

Germ Cell Tumors (Figure 11.69)   Mature teratomas are bilateral in up to 20 percent of cases.
Many times the characteristic appearance of the teratoma, with extremely echogenic fatty tissue, a dermoid plug, or a fat–fluid level, allows the mass to
be specifically diagnosed sonographically. Small

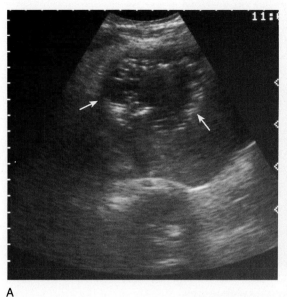 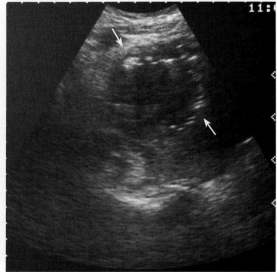

A   B

Figure 11.64
Pelvic abscess after delivery: (A and B) Ultrasound in this febrile, postpartum patient demonstrated ringlike echogenic foci surrounding the pelvis mass (*arrows*); the possibilities included air-containing or calcified mass. CT showed an air-containing collection, which was drained by manipulation of the cervix.

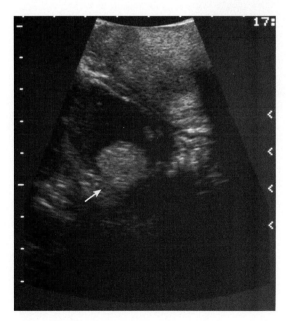

Figure 11.65
Mature teratoma (fat-containing). A highly echogenic mural nodule that did not cast a shadow was indicative of a mature ovarian teratoma.

masses may sometimes be seen, not enlarging the ovary but recognizable by their echogenic appearance.

Metastatic Disease to the Ovary (Figure 11.70)

Metastatic disease to the ovary from breast, stomach, colon, and pancreatic primaries is frequently bilateral. Often solid, metastatic disease to the ovary is frequently associated with ascites and can be hard to differentiate from primary ovarian neoplasm.

Lymphoma, usually part of a diffuse process, bilaterally affects the ovaries in 50 percent of patients.

Pelvic Inflammatory Disease (Figure 11.71)

Severe pelvic inflammatory disease (PID) can cause acute and marked swelling of both adnexal regions. This enlargement sometimes persists after the acute inflammation has subsided.

Pyosalpinx/Hydrosalpinx (Figure 11.72)

Dilatation and obstruction of the fallopian tubes may be the sequel of ascending pelvic inflammatory processes. Often a bilateral process, the pyosalpinx is the infected, pus-laden, dilated tube. Hydrosalpinx suggests previous or chronic infection, without active infection at the time of examination. The dilated tube may have an echogenic wall with nodular excrescences, which are the remnants of the salpingeal folds. Fluid-debris levels can develop in the chronically obstructed structures.

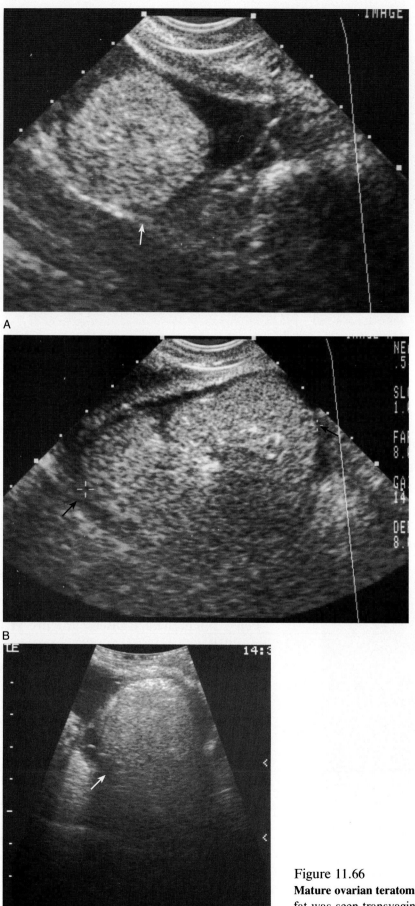

Figure 11.66
Mature ovarian teratoma: (A,B, and C) Highly echogenic fat was seen transvaginally in three patients with teratomas. No shadowing was present.

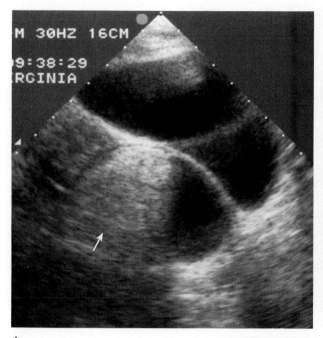

A

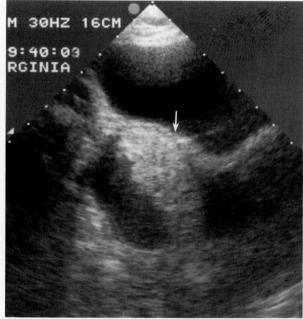

B

Figure 11.67
Mature ovarian teratoma: (A and B) Changes in patient positioning caused movement of the liquid fat-containing material (*arrows*) in this teratoma.

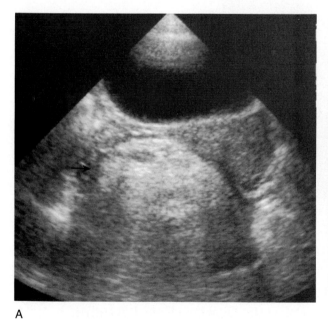

A

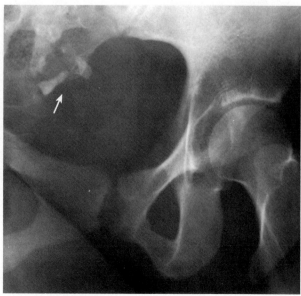

B

Figure 11.68
Mature ovarian teratoma: (A) The highly echogenic fat layer obliterated visualization of the posterior portions of this pelvic mass, known as the "iceberg" effect of an ovarian teratoma. (B) A plain film on the same patient demonstrated teeth, not recognized sonographically.

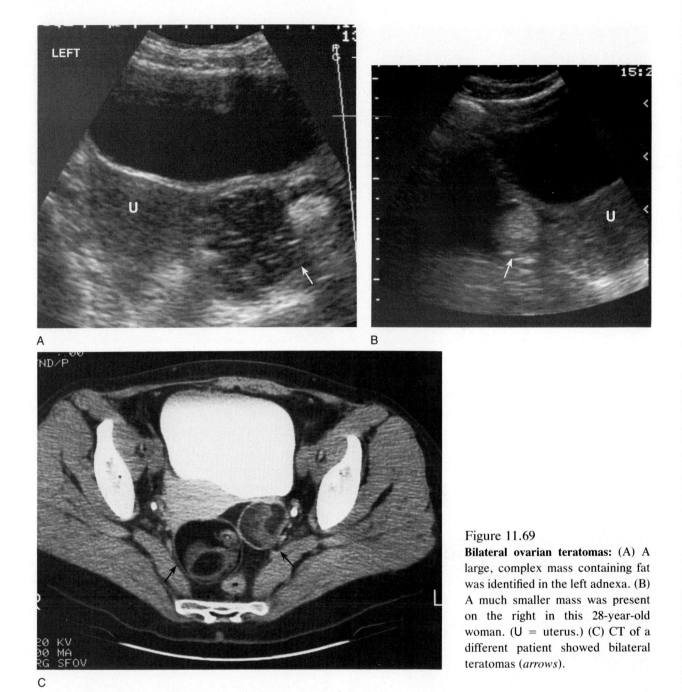

Figure 11.69
Bilateral ovarian teratomas: (A) A large, complex mass containing fat was identified in the left adnexa. (B) A much smaller mass was present on the right in this 28-year-old woman. (U = uterus.) (C) CT of a different patient showed bilateral teratomas (*arrows*).

Endometriosis

Implants of endometriosis may be present in both adnexal areas. Typically, endometriosis does not regress on subsequent menstrual cycles without therapy. Often, too, the patient has symptoms of cyclical pelvic pain, dyspareunia, and infertility.

Polycystic Ovarian (Stein-Leventhal) Syndrome (Figure 11.73)

The polycystic ovarian (PCO) (Stein-Leventhal) syndrome is descriptive of a condition of amenorrhea, anovulation, and infertility in obese, hirsute women. These patients have abnormal follicle-

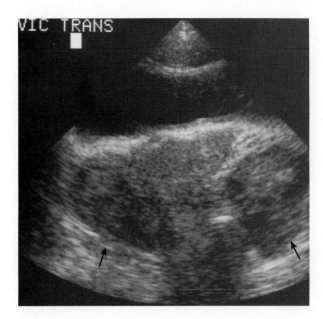

Figure 11.70
Metastatic colon carcinoma of the ovaries: This young woman had a history of a perforated cecal carcinoma. Enlargement and indistinctness of both adnexal areas (*arrows*) indicated metastatic involvement.

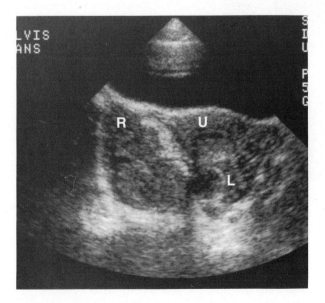

Figure 11.71
Acute pelvic inflammatory disease: Severe inflammation without drainable abscess was present in this young woman with gonococcal infection. Both adnexal regions (R + L) were quite prominent and the uterus (U) was engulfed by the swollen ovaries and tubes.

stimulating hormone (FSH) levels that result in multiple small, immature follicles and anovulation.

Sonographically, the ovaries are often enlarged with multiple tiny follicles. The ovarian volume is frequently greater than 12 cm³. Dominant cysts are unusual with PCO. The enlarged ovaries can be masslike and thus prone to adnexal torsion. As many as 20 percent of patients with hormonal evidence of PCO may have sonographically normal ovaries.

Thecal–Lutein Cysts

Thecal–lutein cysts typically occur in situations of high chorionic gonadotropin levels, which usually occur with multiple gestations or trophoblastic gestational disease. Thirty to 50 percent of patients with molar pregnancy have thecal–lutein cysts, which can be symptomatic with hemorrhage or rupture, or can lead to adnexal torsion.

Sonographically, thecal–lutein cysts are bilateral, large, multiloculated ovarian cysts that may take weeks to months to resolve after the hormonal environment has returned to normal.

"AMORPHOUS" PELVIS

> Pelvic Inflammatory Disease
> Pelvic Abscess from Nongynecologic Causes
> Endometriosis
> Ruptured Ectopic Pregnancy/
>   Hemoperitoneum
> Extensive Pelvic Neoplasm
> Leiomyomatous Uterus

Indistinctness and poor definition of pelvic structures because of encasement by inflammatory, infectious debris, malignant tissue, or endometriosis may be called the "amorphous pelvis." Despite adequate bladder distention and compression with the transducer, the borders of the ovaries and the uterus are difficult to define.

Pelvic Inflammatory Disease (Figure 11.74)

Pelvic inflammatory disease (PID) connotes a sexually transmitted ascending infection of the uterus and fallopian tubes. Although pelvic sonography is frequently normal in PID, a severe episode of PID may lead to an "amorphous pelvis" sonographically. The adnexa may be large, ill defined, and

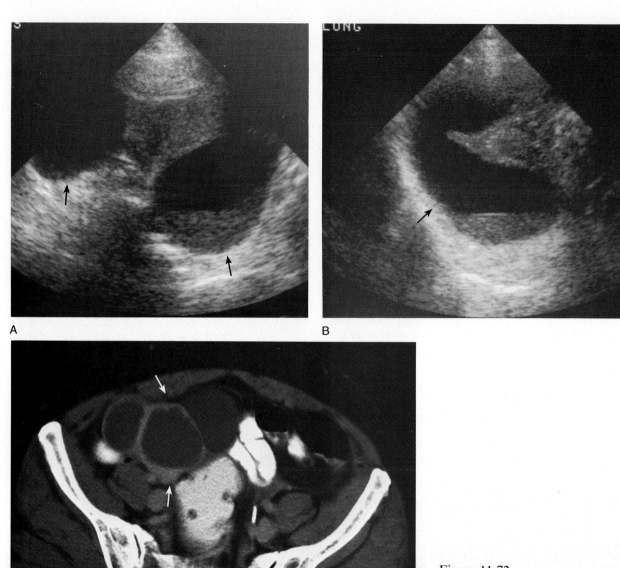

A

B

C

Figure 11.72
Bilateral hydrosalpinx: (A and B) A dilated tubular structure with a long fluid-debris level was present on either side of the uterus (*arrow*) in this infertility patient. (C) A CT of a different patient with hydrosalpinx.

merged with the lateral borders of the uterus. Echogenic fluid may be present in the cul-de-sac.

Pelvic Abscess from Nongynecologic Causes (Figure 11.75)

The pelvis may act as a bowl collecting dependent fluid from processes in the peritoneal cavity. Fluid from inflammatory processes originating in the abdomen may pool in the pelvis. Inflammatory

masses secondary to a ruptured appendix, Crohn's disease, or diverticulitis may gravitate to the pelvis, engulfing the adnexa and uterus in the female patient.

Endometriosis

Generally occurring in the female patient 30 to 45 years of age, endometriosis may lead to a sonographically amorphous pelvis. Numerous small im-

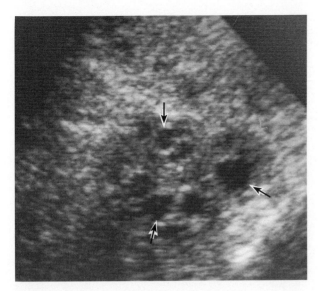

Figure 11.73
Polycystic ovarian syndrome: Bilaterally enlarged ovaries were evaluated in this young hirsute girl with amenorrhea. The right ovary measured 6 × 3 cm on the longitudinal axis. The left ovary was similarly enlarged (transvaginal scan). Note numerous immature follicles.

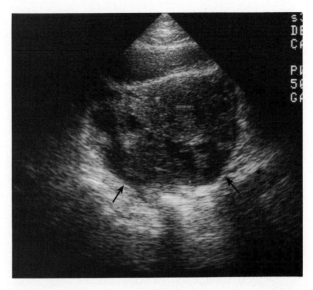

Figure 11.75
Pelvic abscess: This young woman had Crohn's disease, eventually developing an abscess that required drainage. Note the inability to sonographically separate the uterus from the adnexal regions.

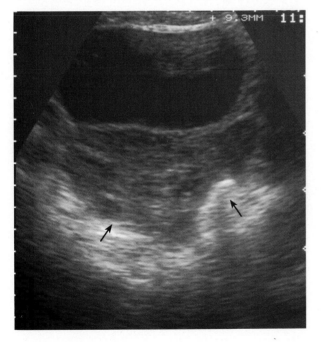

Figure 11.74
Pelvic inflammatory disease: Indistinctness of the adnexa and uterus was present in this patient with cervical motion tenderness, vaginal discharge, and leukocytosis. No discrete abscess was present.

plants of endometriosis and adhesions may make the ovaries difficult to identify specifically. Usually, the clinical history of cyclical discomfort and infertility will suggest the diagnosis.

Ruptured Ectopic Pregnancy/ Hemoperitoneum

Extensive clot and hemorrhage in the pelvis can make visualization of the normal adnexal structures nearly impossible. Rupture of an ectopic pregnancy is a common cause of hemoperitoneum, obscuring pelvic structures in the female patient.

Extensive Pelvic Neoplasm

Bulky pelvic tumor can encompass and obscure visualization of the normal uterus and ovaries. Usually associated with generalized ascites, ovarian neoplasms, either primary to the ovary or metastatic, can fill the pelvis, compressing the uterus. Generally, ovarian primaries have significant cystic components in the tumor mass. Metastatic disease to the ovaries may be sonographically indistinguishable from primary ovarian lesions. The pattern of spread of disease, with intraparenchymal liver lesions, or a pancreatic mass, should suggest that the disease in the pelvis is metastatic to the ovaries rather than arising primarily from the ovaries.

Leiomyomatous Uterus (Figure 11.76)

A large, multilobulated leiomyomatous uterus will give an "amphorous pelvis." The solid nature of the mass will allow the examiner to suggest the uterus as the organ of origin of the mass, rather than the ovary, which generally yields cystic masses. The ovaries are often difficult to identify in cases of such uterine enlargement.

DILATED TUBES IN THE PELVIS

Dilated Fallopian Tubes
Pelvic Varices
Dilated Distal Ureters
Dilated Small Bowel Loops

Recognition of dilated tubular structures in the pelvis must instigate a search for their origins.

Dilated Fallopian Tubes (Figures 11.77–11.78)

The normal oviduct or fallopian tube, which is the conduit between the ovary and uterus for ovulation, usually has a lumen of 1 to 3 mm. If nondilated, the

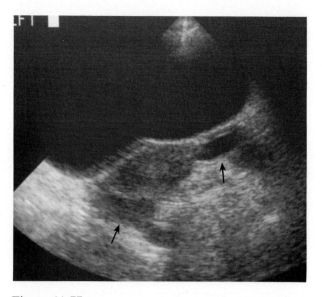

Figure 11.77
Bilateral hydrosalpinx: Small, tubular structures emanating from either side of the uterus (*arrows*) were fluid-filled fallopian tubes in this young woman with a previous history of severe pelvic inflammatory disease. This was confirmed by hysterosalpingography.

fallopian tube is not usually identified sonographically without the introduction of contrast agents.

Obstruction of the fallopian tubes occurs with pelvic inflammatory conditions when there is scarring and adhesion formation. Surgical manipulation

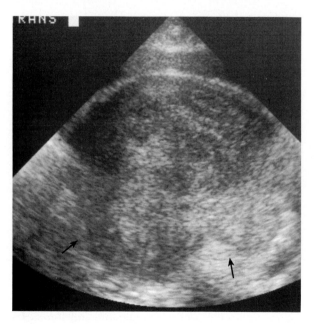

Figure 11.76
Leiomyomatous uterus: A large, multilobulated, inhomogeneous uterus (*arrows*) filled the pelvis. The ovaries were not recognizable.

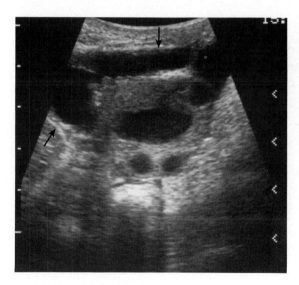

Figure 11.78
Hydrosalpinx: In this patient who has had a vaginal hysterectomy, the dilated fallopian tube (*arrows*) was seen draped over the ovary on transvaginal scanning.

of the oviducts may also cause tubal occlusion and subsequent dilatation.

Sonographically, the dilated oviducts may be seen as paired tubular structures on either side of the uterus. On rare occasions, the dilated tubes can become large adnexal masses. Sometimes a fluid-debris level is identified along the length of the obstructed tube. The obstructed, fimbriated end of the tube will often have the largest dimension. Nodular excrescences may be seen in dilated tubes that are the remnants of the salpingeal folds.

With acute obstruction of the fallopian tubes associated with pelvic inflammatory disease, a pyosalpinx or tube filled with purulent debris may develop. A hydrosalpinx may develop weeks to months after acute infection. Hydrosalpinx is the noninfected, obstructed, fluid-filled tube that is the sequel of previous infection. The tubular shape and its paired configuration will often allow it to be distinguished from other adnexal masses.

Pelvic Varices (Figures 11.79–11.80)

Numerous pelvic veins or varices may develop in patients with venous thrombosis or after pregnancy. Their vascular origin can be confirmed by color

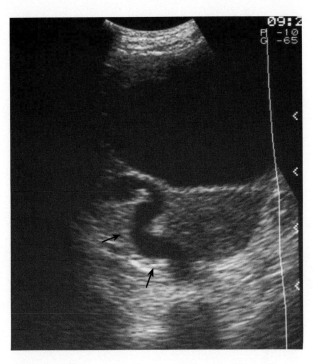

Figure 11.80
Pelvic varices: Multiple venous collaterals were obvious in this young patient with Budd-Chiari syndrome and extensive upper abdominal collaterals as well as pelvic collaterals.

Doppler or spectral analysis. Prominent myometrial veins are often seen in these same patients.

Dilated Distal Ureters (Figures 11.81–11.82)

The normal ureter is not usually seen sonographically except near the renal pelvis unless the ureter is dilated from obstruction or reflux. The nondilated normal ureter is so small as to make it unobservable at ultrasound.

Obstruction of the ureters can be caused by neoplasm, stones, or strictures related to a previous operation. The level of obstruction can often be determined by following the dilated ureter to the point of caliber change. With prolonged obstruction, ureteral dilatation will increase.

To facilitate the sonographic recognition of a ureteral stone or other cause of distal ureteral obstruction, the patient must be scanned from the kidney down the course of the ureter to the bladder. A full bladder will facilitate recognition of the distal ureter. Especially in acute renal colic, the ureter may be only minimally distended, with little associated hydronephrosis. The discovery of a ureteral stone in such a case will require a careful examina-

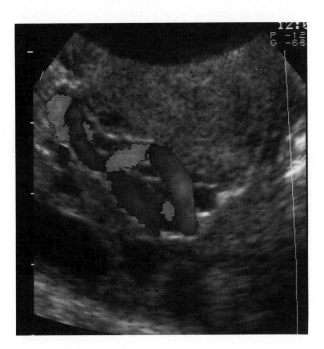

Figure 11.79
Pelvic varices (Plate 16): Numerous venous structures were recognizable in this multiparous patient during routine pelvic scanning.

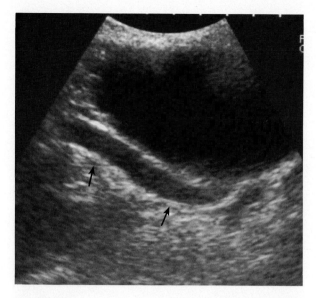

Figure 11.81
Dilated distal ureter: A tubular right distal ureter (*arrows*) was demonstrated in this patient with reflux.

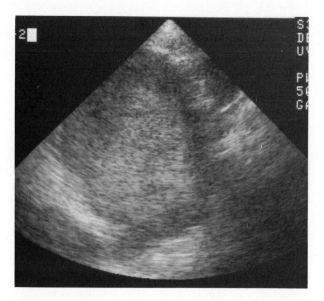

Figure 11.82
Obstructed distal ureter: A dilated right ureter was present in this patient with bladder carcinoma.

tion of the kidney and ureter. A high clinical suspicion and correlation with plain films to check for calcifications will aid in the correct diagnosis.

The ureters may be dilated secondary to reflux. In such a situation, enlargement of the ureter and collecting system may occur with voiding. Cystography may be necessary to document vesico-ureteral reflux.

Dilated Small Bowel Loops

Dilated small bowel loops may be identified in the pelvis. Usually fluid-filled, dilated small bowel is related to either ileus or small bowel obstruction. Watching peristalsis at real-time will often allow small bowel to be recognized. Correlation with plain films may be helpful.

BIBLIOGRAPHY

Simple Cyst in the Adnexa

Alpern MB, Sandler MA, Madrazo BL: Sonographic features of parovarian cysts and their complications. AJR 143:157–160, 1984.

Athey PA, Cooper NB: Sonographic features of parovarian cysts. AJR 144:83–86, 1985.

Hoffer FA, Kozakewich H, Colodny A, Goldstein DP: Peritoneal inclusion cysts: Ovarian fluid in peritoneal adhesions. Radiology 169:189–191, 1988.

Complex Adnexal Mass with Negative β-HCG

Andolf E, Jorgenson C: Cystic lesions in elderly women, diagnosed by ultrasound. Br J Obstet Gynaecol 96:1076–1079, 1989.

Baltarowich OH, Kurtz AB, Pasto ME, Rifkin MD, Needleman L, Goldberg BB: The spectrum of sonographic findings in hemorrhagic ovarian cysts. AJR 148:901–905, 1987.

Coleman BG, Arger PH, Mulhern CB Jr: Endometriosis: Clinical and ultrasonic correlation. AJR 132:747–749, 1979.

Meire HB, Farrant P, Guha T: Distinction of benign from malignant ovarian cysts by ultrasound. Br J Obstet Gynaecol 85:893–899, 1978.

Moyle JW, Rochester D, Sider L, Shrock K, Krause P: Sonography of ovarian tumors: Predictability of tumor type. AJR 141:985–991, 1983.

Reynolds T, Hill MC, Glassman LM: Sonography of hemorrhagic ovarian cysts. J Clin Ultrasound 14:449–453, 1986.

Sandler MA, Karo JJ: The spectrum of ultrasonic findings in endometriosis. Radiology 127:229–231, 1978.

Sheth S, Fishman EK, Buck JL, Hamper UM, Sanders RC: The variable sonographic appearances of ovarian teratomas: Correlation with CT. AJR 151:331–334, 1988.

Sutton CL, McKinney CD, Jones JE, Gay SB: Ovarian masses revisited: Radiologic and pathologic correlation. RadioGraphics 12:853–877, 1992.

Complex Adnexal Mass with Positive β-HCG

Filly RA: Ectopic pregnancy: The role of sonography. Radiology 162:661–668, 1987.

Hess LW, Peaceman A, O'Brien WF, et al.: Adnexal mass occurring with intrauterine pregnancy: Report of fifty-four patients requiring laparotomy for definitive management. Am J Obstet Gynecol 158:1029–1034, 1988.

Mahony BS, Filly RA, Nyberg DA, et al.: Sonographic evaluation of ectopic pregnancy. J Ultrasound Med 4:221–228, 1985.

Montz FJ, Schlaerth JB, Morrow CP: The natural history of theca-lutein cysts. Obstet Gynecol 72:247–251, 1988.

Nyberg DA, Filly RA, Laing FC, Mack LA, et al.: Ectopic pregnancy: Diagnosis by sonography correlated with quantitative hCG levels. J Ultrasound Med 6:145–150, 1987.

Romero R, Kadar N, Castro D, et al.: The value of adnexal sonographic findings in the diagnosis of ectopic pregnancy. Am J Obstet Gynecol 158:52–55, 1988.

Thornton JG, Wells M: Ovarian cysts in pregnancy: Does ultrasound make traditional management inappropriate? Obstet Gynecol 69:717–721, 1987.

Thorsen MK, Lawson TL, Aiman EJ, et al.: Diagnosis of ectopic pregnancy: Endovaginal versus transabdominal sonography. AJR 155:307–310, 1990.

Solid-Appearing Adnexal Masses

Athey PA, Diment DD: The spectrum of sonographic findings in endometriomas. J Ultrasound Med 8:487–491, 1989.

Athey PA, Malone RS: Sonography of ovarian fibromas/thecomas. J Ultrasound Med 6:431–436, 1987.

Athey PA, Seigel MF: Sonographic features of Brenner tumor of the ovary. J Ultrasound Med 6:367–372, 1987.

Eifel P, Hendrickson M, Ross J, et al: Simultaneous presentation of carcinoma involving the ovary and the uterine corpus. Cancer 50:163–170, 1982.

Graif M, Itzchak Y: Sonographic evaluation of ovarian torsion in childhood and adolescence. AJR 150:647–649, 1988.

Graif M, Shalev J, Strauss S, et al: Torsion of the ovary: Sonographic features. AJR 143:1331–1334, 1984.

Guttman PH Jr: In search of the elusive benign cystic ovarian teratoma: Application of the ultrasound "tip of the iceberg" sign. J Clin Ultrasound 5:403–406, 1977.

Moyle JW, Rochester D, Sider L, et al: Sonography of ovarian tumors: Predictability of tumor type. AJR 141:985–991, 1983.

Sandler MA, Karo JJ: The spectrum of ultrasonic findings in endometriosis. Radiology 127:229–231, 1978.

Sheth S, Fishman EK, et al: The variable sonographic appearance of ovarian teratomas: Correlation with CT. AJR 151:331–334, 1988.

Shimizu H, Yamasaki M, Ohama K, et al.: Characteristic ultrasonographic appearance of the Krukenberg tumor. J Clin Ultrasound 18:697–703, 1990.

Sutton CL, McKinney CD, Jones JE, Gay SB: Ovarian masses revisited: Radiologic and pathologic correlation. RadioGraphics 12:853–877, 1992.

Williams AG, Mettler FA, Wicks JD: Cystic and solid ovarian neoplasms. Semin Ultrasound 4:166, 1983.

Highly Echogenic Pelvic Masses: Calcification Versus Air Versus Fat

Brammer HM, Buck JL, Hayes WS, Sheth S, Tavassoli FA: Malignant germ cell tumors of the ovary: Radiologic–pathologic correlation. RadioGraphics 10:715–724, 1990.

Guttman PH Jr: In search of the elusive benign cystic ovarian teratoma: Application of the ultrasound "tip of the iceberg" sign. J Clin Ultrasound 5:403–406, 1977.

Quinn SF, Erickson S, Black WC: Cystic ovarian teratomas: The sonographic appearance of the dermoid plug. Radiology 155:477–478, 1985.

Sheth S, Fishman EK, Buck JL, et al.: The variable sonographic appearances of ovarian teratomas: Correlation with CT. AJR 151:331–334, 1988.

Bilateral Adnexal Masses

Doss NJR, Forney JP, Vellios F, Nalick RH: Covert bilaterality of mature ovarian teratomas. Obstet Gynecol 50:651–653, 1977.

Hann LE, Hall DA, McArdle CR, Seibel M: Polycystic ovarian disease: Sonographic spectrum. Radiology 150:531–534, 1984.

Montz FJ, Schlaerth JB, Morrow CP: The natural history of thecal lutein cysts. Obstet Gynecol 72:247–251, 1988.

Parisi L, Tramonti M, Casciano S, Zurli A, Gazzarrini O: The role of ultrasound in the study of polycystic ovarian disease. J Clin Ultrasound 10:167–172, 1982.

Smith KD, Steinberger E, Perloff WH: Polycystic ovarian disease: A report of 301 patients. Am J Obstet Gynecol 93:994, 1965.

Yeh HC, Futterwert W, Thornton JC: Polycystic ovarian disease: US features in 104 patients. Radiology 163:111–116, 1987.

SCROTUM

PATTERNS

Focal Testicular Mass
Extratesticular Mass
Diffusely Abnormal Testicular Echogenicity
Fluid in the Scrotum
Abnormal Color Flow Patterns Involving the
    Scrotum

The testis is easily scanned in the scrotum, having homogeneous echogenicity when normal. Ultrasound allows precise delineation of testicular and extratesticular abnormalities in the scrotum.

FOCAL TESTICULAR MASS

Primary Testicular Neoplasm
Leukemia and Lymphoma/Metastases
Testicular Abscess
Adrenal Rests
Epididymal Abnormality Mistaken as a
    Testicular Mass
Cystic Dilatation of the Rete Testis

When a scrotal mass is recognized clinically, the primary role of testicular sonography is to determine whether the mass is intra- or extratesticular. Many intratesticular lesions are solid and malignant; many extratesticular masses are cystic and benign.

Primary Testicular Neoplasm (Figures 12.1–12.3)

Testicular carcinoma is the most common primary neoplasm in young men and usually arises from the germ cell line within the testis. Histologically, these tumors are generally separated into seminomatous and nonseminomatous cell types. Seminomas are typically very radiosensitive. Nonseminomatous tumor types include embryonal cell carcinoma, teratocarcinomas, choriocarcinomas, and mixed tumors.

Sonographically, testicular primaries are intratesticular lesions that cause a disruption of the normal homogeneous echogenicity of the testis. The mass may be a well-circumscribed, discrete, homogeneously hypoechoic lesion of the testis, or it may be a complex lesion with cystic areas, calcifications, and a heterogeneous echotexture. The typical seminomatous tumor is a homogeneous, hypoechoic intratesticular lesion. Exceptions to the typical sonographic image of a seminoma are seen and related to the degree of tumoral necrosis, hemorrhage, lymphocytic infiltration, or fibrosis. A nonseminomatous germ cell tumor often has remarkable heterogeneity sonographically.

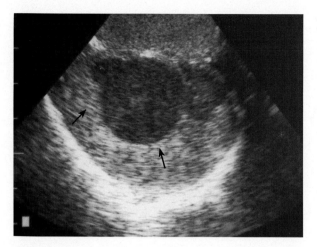

Figure 12.1
Seminoma: A palpable scrotal mass was investigated by ultrasound, which revealed a discrete, homogeneously hypoechoic mass (*arrows*) within the testis. Prompt orchiectomy confirmed the clinical impression of seminoma.

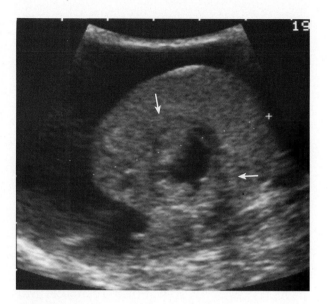

Figure 12.2
Nonseminoma: This 27-year-old man had been treated, without scrotal imaging, for epididymitis. Recurrent discomfort in the scrotum led to sonographic evaluation, which revealed a hydrocele, making testicular palpation difficult, and a heterogeneous mass within the testis (*arrows*). A sonographic look into the retroperitoneum at the level of the renal hilum revealed abnormal lymphadenopathy, which was confirmed by CT. Orchiectomy was performed without delay.

Patients with solid intratesticular masses that are suspected of being neoplastic generally undergo orchiectomy. Percutaneous testicular biopsy is rarely performed and is generally avoided. Staging for the extent of metastatic disease generally includes CT or MR of the retroperitoneum. The lymphatic drainage of the testes generally follows the path of the gonadal vein. On the right, the gonadal vein drains directly into the inferior vena cava at the level of the renal hilum. On the left, the gonadal vein drains into the left renal vein. Metastatic adenopathy in patients with testicular carcinoma is often identified at the level of the renal hilum in the retroperitoneum. Enlarged retroperitoneal lymph nodes can often be recognized sonographically, thus lessening doubt about the nature of a testicular lesion.

Patients with a history of previous scrotal surgery or advanced testicular tumors with invasion of the scrotum skin may have metastatic adenopathy in the inguinal or pelvic lymph node chains. Tumoral invasion of the scrotal skin or previous surgery disrupts the expected pathways of metastatic disease and results in different regional patterns of spread.

Leukemia and Lymphoma/Metastases (Figures 12.4–12.6)

Other neoplastic causes of testicular masses include leukemia and lymphoma. The testis is considered a

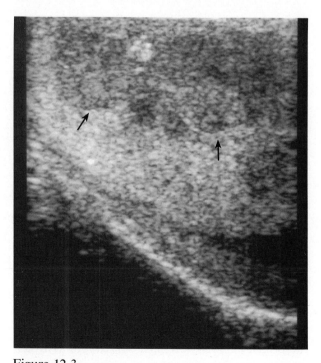

Figure 12.3
Embryonal cell carcinoma: This palpable scrotal mass proved to be a hypoechoic intratesticular mass (*arrows*) with calcification. Micrometastases were present in retroperitoneal lymph nodes.

sanctuary site for leukemia and lymphoma in that it is difficult to attain high chemotherapeutic levels in the testis to eradicate indolent leukemic cells. The testis may harbor leukemic cells and be the site of relapse when painless enlargement of the testis occurs. Diffuse leukemic infiltration of the testis as manifest by diminished echogeneity or focal intra-testicular lesions in a patient with a history of leukemia or lymphoma may herald relapse of the myeloproliferative disorder.

Focal metastatic disease to the testis from other primary neoplasms may occur and is more common in elderly men than primary testicular neoplasia. The sonographic appearance of metastatic disease is similar to that of focal testicular masses that occur in primary testicular tumor.

Testicular Abscess

Frank suppuration and necrosis of the testis is unusual, since the testis is relatively resistant to ab-scess formation, but abscess formation may occur. Epididymal infection is the port of entry to scrotal infection in most instances, and severe, untreated, or recurrent epididymitis may result in testicular abscess. Orchiectomy may be necessary if testicular abscess with necrosis occurs.

Adrenal Rests (Figure 12.7)

In patients with high circulating levels of adreno-corticotropic hormone (ACTH) secondary to long-standing, inadequately treated congenital adrenal hyperplasia or Cushing syndrome, adrenal rests may become identifiable within the testis. These masses are intratesticular, often hypoechoic, with frequent calcification and areas of dense echogenic fibrosis. Such patients may be evaluated for infertility or for a palpable abnormality. The recognition of a testicular mass in a man with the history of inadequately treated congenital adrenal hyperplasia or long-standing Cushing syndrome may make testicular biopsy or orchiectomy unnecessary.

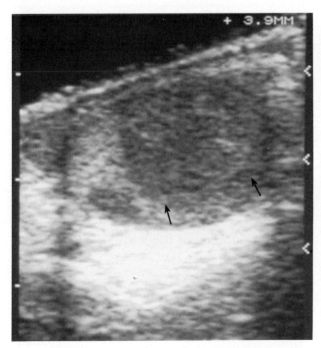

A

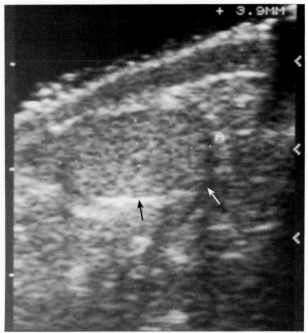

B

Figure 12.4
Leukemic infiltration: (A) This 6-year-old boy with a previous history of acute lymphocytic leukemia noted painless hardening of his right testis. Sonographic evaluation showed a focal hypoechoic mass (*arrows*) consistent with relapse of acute lymphocytic leukemia. Orchiectomy confirmed leukemic infiltration of the testis. (B) Note the small, unaffected left testis (*arrows*).

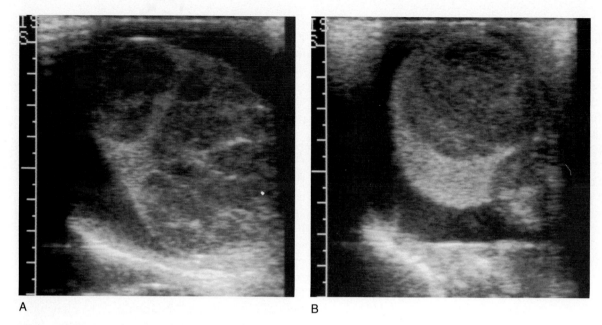

A   B

Figure 12.5

Lymphoma: (A and B) This 76-year-old man developed scrotal swelling and a palpable mass. Sonographically the testis had numerous hypoechoic regions. Non-Hodgkin lymphoma was detected at orchiectomy.

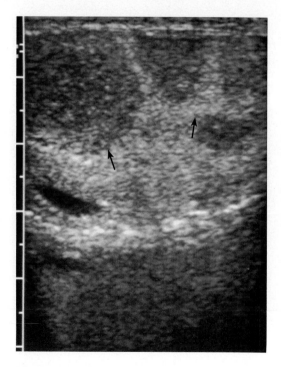

Figure 12.6

Lymphoma: At presentation, multiple bilateral testicular masses (*arrows*) were discovered. Additional imaging led to the discovery of hepatic masses and adenopathy. Biopsy confirmed aggressive non-Hodgkin lymphoma. The patient proved to have AIDS.

Epididymal Abnormality Mistaken as a Testicular Mass

Sometimes when there is an enlargement of the epididymis, either from obstruction or inflammation, and the enlarged epididymis invaginates into the testis, the epididymal abnormality may be misinterpreted as a focal testicular mass. Knowledge that epididymal abnormalities can be mistaken for testicular lesions and careful scrutiny to determine that the lesion involves the epididymis can prevent the erroneous diagnosis of a testicular mass.

Cystic Dilatation of the Rete Testis (Figure 12.8)

The network that connects the seminiferous tubules of the testis to the epididymis is present in the mediastinum of the testis. Cystic dilatation of the rete testis will have the appearance of multiple cysts within the substance of the testis. Recognition of the network of cysts within the mediastinum of the testis will allow one to assure the patient that a testicular neoplasm is not present. Cystic dilatation of the rete testis may be seen after previous surgery or inflammatory processes in the scrotum. Cystic dilatation of the rete testis is rarely palpable as a mass, unless cysts are present in the epididymis as well.

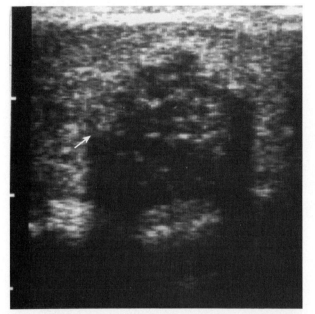

A

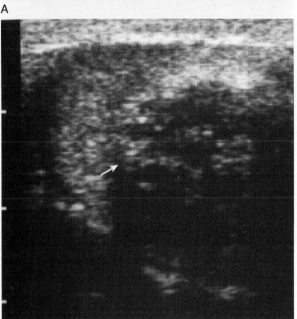

B

Figure 12.7

Adrenal rests in patient with untreated congenital adrenal hyperplasia: This 28-year-old man was being evaluated for infertility. He had a history of congenital adrenal hyperplasia for which he had refused treatment for more than 10 years. Clinically, his testes were hard, with palpable masses. (A and B) Sonographically, dense calcifications and focal hypoechoic masses (*arrows*) were visible. In light of the history of untreated adrenal hyperplasia, the presumptive diagnosis of adrenal rests was made and therapy begun. No significant sonographic change occurred with therapy.

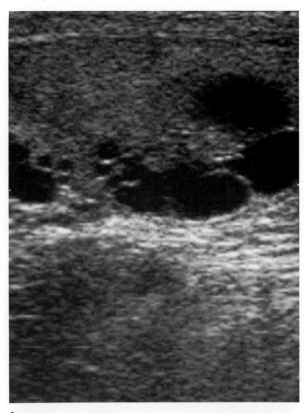

A

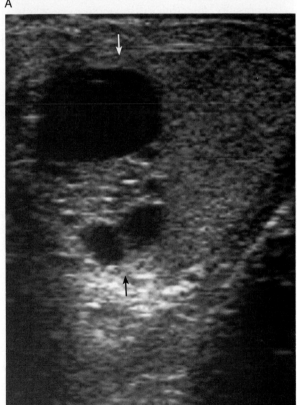

B

Figure 12.8

Cystic dilatation of the rete testis: The recognition of multiple intratesticular cysts can be confusing unless it is realized that the cysts are within the mediastinum testis at the expected site of the rete testis.

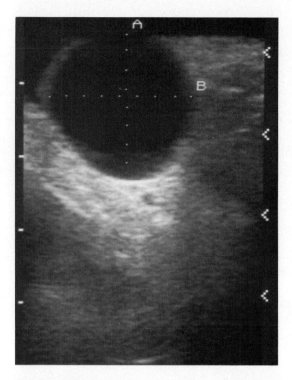

Figure 12.9
Epididymal cyst: A palpable mass in the scrotum proved to be a simple 2-cm epididymal cyst.

EXTRATESTICULAR MASS

Epididymal Cyst/Spermatocele/Sperm
    Granuloma
Epididymitis, Including Granulomatous
    Disease of the Epididymis
Neoplastic Masses Outside the Testis
Hernia

A palpable extratesticular mass often arises from the epididymis. Frequently cystic, many masses of the epididymis are benign.

Epididymal Cyst/Spermatocele/Sperm Granuloma (Figures 12.9–12.10)

An epididymal swelling that is frequently palpated by the patient or doctor, causing concern for a testicular mass, is an epididymal cyst. Ultrasound is important because it very quickly shows the epididymal origin and cystic nature of the mass. Epididymal cysts may develop after epididymitis, after operative intervention, or without an obvious cause. Spermatoceles, containing sperm, look sonographically similar to epididymal cysts. Sperm granulomas may be hypoechoic, firm masses in the epi-

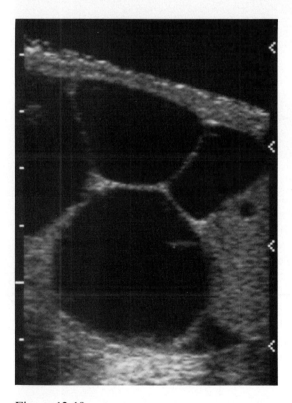

Figure 12.10
Multiple epididymal cysts: Multiple epididymal cysts enlarged the scrotum in this patient.

didymis secondary to a granulomatous reaction to sperm.

Generally, the recognition of their benign epididymal character will make further evaluation unnecessary. Rarely, epididymal cysts or spermatoceles are surgically excised.

Epididymitis, Including Granulomatous Disease of the Epididymis (Figures 12.11–12.12)

Infection of the epididymis can cause dramatic swelling and tenderness. The inflamed epididymis can cause a scrotal mass. Exquisite pain prevents an adequate physical examination and may make sonographic evaluation desirable.

Usually a bacterial infection, epididymitis is often transmitted sexually, although it may complicate a surgical procedure or genitourinary instrumentation.

Sonographically, the epididymis affected by bacterial infection is swollen, so that the entire structure may be easily identified, which is not usually true of the noninflamed epididymis. The swollen epididymis is of the same or less echogenicity as the nearby testis. Chronic epididymitis can result in an echogenic structure. Color flow analysis will show the inflamed epididymis to be hyperemic.

Granulomatous diseases, such as tuberculosis, may affect the epididymis as a chronic infection, causing discomfort and the development of firm swellings in the epididymis. Tuberculosis of the epididymis is generally acquired through a hematogenous mode of transmission and is seen in patients with pulmonary, gastrointestinal, or upper urinary tract involvement with disease. The incidence of tuberculosis is increasing, probably because of poor socioeconomic conditions and the AIDS epidemic.

Sonographically, epididymal involvement with tuberculosis may result in hypoechoic masses of the epididymis, which are palpable as firm, often non-

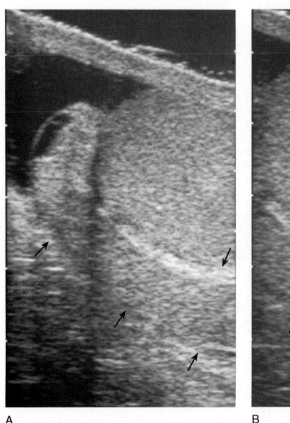

A

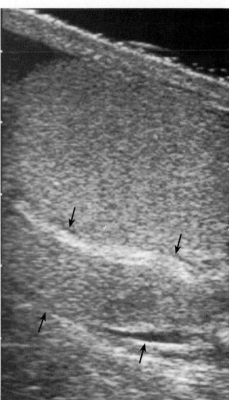

B

Figure 12.11

Acute epididymitis: Dramatic swelling of the entire epididymis (*arrows*) was present in this patient with epididymitis. Severe pain made definitive palpation impossible, although a scrotal mass was suspected.

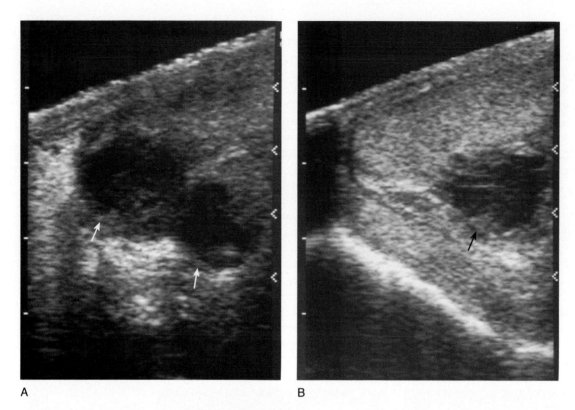

A   B

Figure 12.12

Tuberculous epididymitis: (A and B) Firm hypoechoic nodules (*arrows*) were present in this patient with pulmonary, epididymal, and prostatic tuberculosis.

tender swellings. Abnormal chest film findings will frequently accompany the epididymal abnormalities.

Neoplastic Masses Outside the Testis (Figure 12.13)

Primary neoplasms arising outside the testis are unusual but may include a mature lipoma of the spermatic cord or a malignant tumor, such as a malignant liposarcoma or fibrous histiocytoma, arising from the mesenchymal elements in the scrotum. In childhood, the most common malignant mass of the spermatic cord is a rhabdomyosarcoma. A lipoma will be a very echogenic mass sonographically. CT can confirm its fatty nature. Any growth, change in consistency, or pain related to such a mass may herald its conversion to a sarcoma.

Sarcomatous masses of the scrotum often require multimodal therapy with wide excision of the primary mass, followed by radiation therapy and chemotherapy.

Metastatic disease may sometimes involve the epididymis and include lung and prostate carcino-

mas. Such lesions would be small, hypoechoic masses sonographically.

Hernia (Figures 12.14–12.15)

Herniation of bowel or fat into the scrotum may be recognized sonographically as highly echogenic fat or fluid-filled bowel loops. Sometimes fluid surrounds the hernia; sometimes the hernia sac can be identified. Recognition of a hernia should prompt an evaluation of the abdominal contents by ultrasound or plain film to assess for bowel obstruction. Tender, strangulated bowel may need immediate surgical decompression.

DIFFUSELY ABNORMAL TESTICULAR ECHOGENICITY

Testicular Neoplasm
Testicular Torsion
Testicular Atrophy
Testicular Trauma
Severe Orchitis

The testis is normally very homogeneous, easily scanned with a superficially focused high-frequency transducer. Any abnormality of its echogenicity can be easily recognized. When the

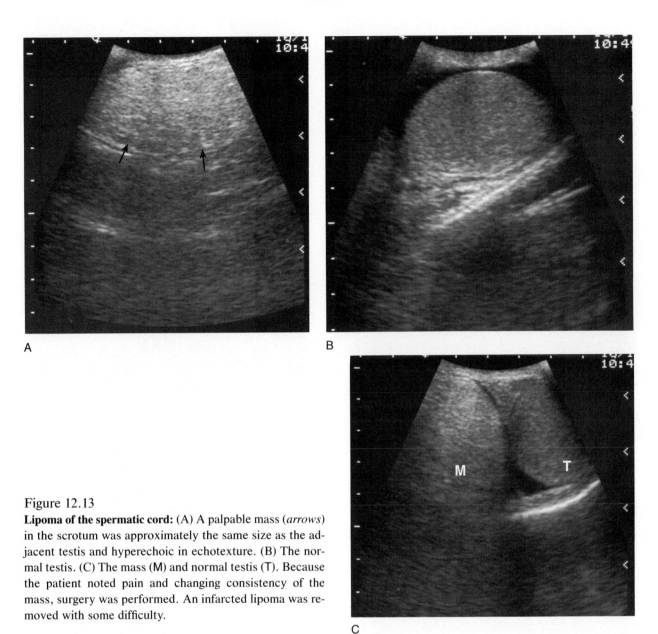

Figure 12.13

Lipoma of the spermatic cord: (A) A palpable mass (*arrows*) in the scrotum was approximately the same size as the adjacent testis and hyperechoic in echotexture. (B) The normal testis. (C) The mass (M) and normal testis (T). Because the patient noted pain and changing consistency of the mass, surgery was performed. An infarcted lipoma was removed with some difficulty.

echogenicity of the testis is diffusely abnormal, it reflects a global insult, usually vascular, infectious, or neoplastic.

Testicular Neoplasm (Figures 12.16–12.18)

When testicular neoplasm completely replaces the testis, it is imperative that the examiner use the other normal testis for comparison of the expected homogeneous testicular echogenicity. Tumors replacing the testis often have areas of heterogeneity with cystic regions and hyperechogenicity. Non-seminomatous tumors usually have fairly striking heterogeneity, although seminoma, which is usually homogeneous, may have central necrosis when it

becomes quite large. Besides seminomatous tumors, leukemic infiltration or lymphoma in the testis can be homogeneously infiltrative, replacing the normal tissue. Infiltrative neoplasms usually enlarge the testis and, with extensive involvement, are palpable as firm masses.

Testicular Torsion (Figures 12.19–12.20)

Compromise of testicular blood flow by twisting of the spermatic cord results in severe scrotal pain. Usually, the differential considerations in patients with severe scrotal pain are testicular torsion or severe epididymo-orchitis. These two conditions can

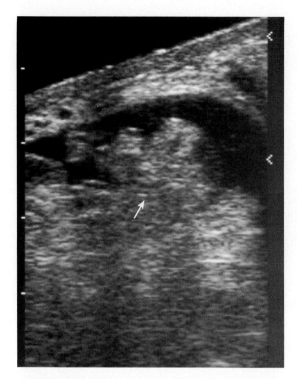

Figure 12.14
Hernia: Omental fat (*arrow*) herniated into the scrotum in this patient.

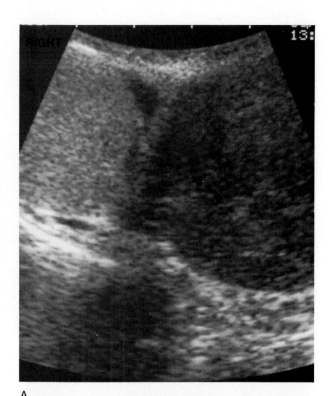

A

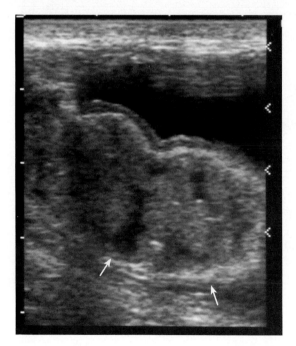

Figure 12.15
Hernia: Dilated bowel loops (*arrows*) with surrounding fluid were detected in this patient with scrotal swelling. Surgery was performed for bowel obstruction.

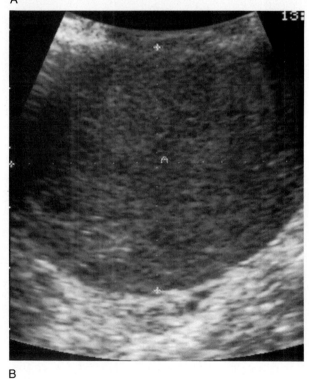

B

Figure 12.16
Seminoma: (A and B) This young man had noted testicular enlargement for several months. Ultrasound showed complete replacement of the left testis by tumor. The left testis was diffusely homogeneous, hypoechoic, and enlarged, filled with seminoma at surgery.

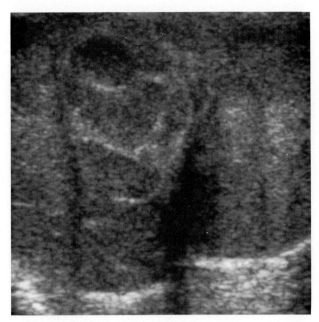

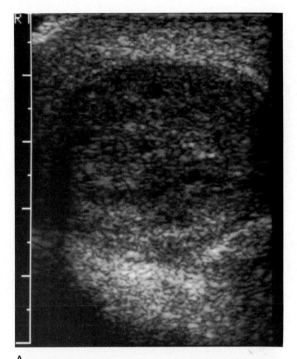

A

Figure 12.17
Seminoma: This young man with multiple pulmonary nodules and retroperitoneal adenopathy was investigated for the possibility of a testicular primary. The right testis was enlarged and replaced by tumor.

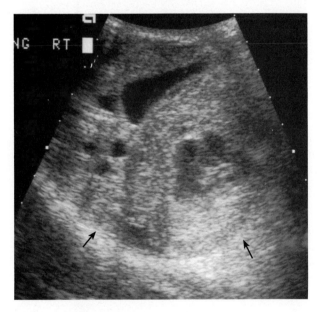

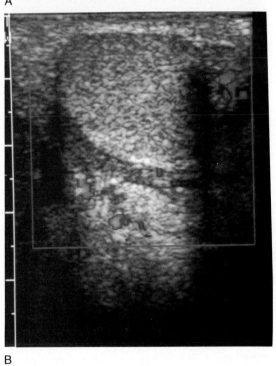

B

Figure 12.18
Nonseminomatous tumor: A 45-year-old executive noted scrotal swelling while playing golf. The initial clinical impression was testicular trauma and hematoma formation. Sonography showed a diffusely heterogeneous mass with cystic spaces and hypervascularity and no normal testis. Immediate orchiectomy revealed nonseminomatous tumor with elements of malignant teratoma.

Figure 12.19
Subacute torsion: (A) Diffuse enlargement and hypoechogeneity of the right testis was seen in this patient with testicular pain for 24 hours. Testicular torsion was diagnosed by sonography secondary to the absence of testicular blood flow. The testis could not be salvaged at surgery. (B) The normal left testis.

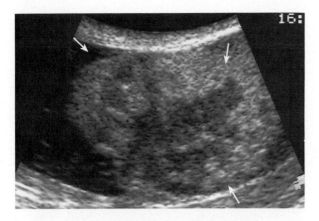

Figure 12.20
Missed torsion (Plate 17): This 27-year-old man cited a 10-day history of testicular pain. No testicular blood flow was detectable by Doppler. Diffuse heterogeneity of testicular echogenicity (*arrows*) correlated with testicular necrosis found at surgery.

complaints of pain may diminish as infarction of the testis occurs. Sometimes, a hydrocele, skin thickening, and hematoma may form in the scrotal sac.

Color flow Doppler of missed torsion will show hyperemia around the infarcting testis but no flow within the testis itself.

Testicular Atrophy (Figure 12.21)

A chronically missed torsion will result in testicular atrophy. Atrophy can occur within weeks if surgery is not performed. The size of the atrophied testis will gradually diminish, and the testis will have a heterogeneous, usually hypoechoic echogenicity. The atrophied testis that results from testicular torsion may have a similar echogenicity to the chronically cryptorchid testis that is small and atrophied with heterogeneous echogenicity.

be differentiated by nuclear medicine imaging or ultrasound with color flow Doppler. In situations of testicular torsion, the testis itself will have absent blood flow; with epididymo-orchitis, the scrotal contents are usually hyperemic.

Whether or not the testis can be salvaged in situations of testicular torsion will depend upon the length of time the blood supply has been compromised before repair. The shorter the length of time before torsion repair, the greater the likelihood of testicular salvage. The sonographic appearance of the torsed testis will depend upon the duration of vascular compromise.

In acute testicular torsion, symptoms have been present for fewer than 24 hours. For the first 4–6 hours, the testis will appear normal on gray-scale imaging. Color flow Doppler will show absent blood flow. Normal blood flow to the testis is low, so it is important to have sensitive Doppler settings to look for low flow, using the contralateral asymptomatic testis as a control.

After the first 4–6 hours of vascular compromise, the involved testis develops more sonographic abnormalities on gray-scale imaging. The testis may become enlarged and hypoechoic. Because the epididymal blood flow is also compromised, the epididymis may become enlarged and inhomogeneous too. With subacute torsion, testicular necrosis and hemorrhage cause the sonographic appearance to be heterogeneous. When the testicular blood supply remains compromised, the sonographic appearance will become more and more abnormal. The patient's

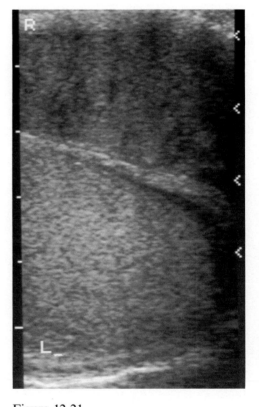

Figure 12.21
Testicular atrophy: The chronically cryptorchid or atrophied testis will have an abnormal echotexture relative to the normal contralateral side. Often smaller than the normal testis, an atrophied testis may be diffusely hypoechoic and heterogeneous or have wedge-shaped hypoechogenic bands along the orientation of the seminiferous tubules. (R = atrophied right testis. L = normal left.)

Testicular Trauma (Figure 12.22)

Extensive injury and fracture of the testis may result in a diffusely abnormal echogenicity of the testis. The testis is relatively protected by its mobility and the dense protective covering of the tunica. To effect major testicular trauma, the testis must be rendered relatively immobile and must sustain substantial force.

The most severe injury of the testis is the stellate fracture, resulting in a shattered testis. Surgical repair in such a case is often unsuccessful and orchiectomy may be necessary. In cases of less severe trauma and small rents in the tunica, the extruded seminiferous tubules of the testis can be removed and the tunica can be repaired. Unless an extensive stellate fracture exists, surgical salvage is possible in 90 percent of cases if surgery is undertaken within 72 hours. After 72 hours, the success of testicular salvage drops to 55 percent. If the testicular injury has been severe, orchiectomy will be required.

Severe Orchitis

Heterogeneity of testicular echogenicity will occur when severe infection is present. Serial imaging of the patient with severe epididymo-orchitis is war-

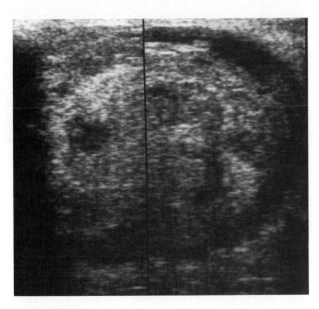

Figure 12.22
Testicular trauma: A crush injury to the testis resulted in tunical rupture and a stellate fracture of the testis. Sonographically, the testis was heterogeneous in echogenicity with inhomogeneity throughout the substance of the testis. A surgical attempt to save the testis was unsuccessful and orchiectomy had to be performed.

ranted to assure that abscess formation within the testis does not occur that would necessitate orchiectomy.

Emphasis Points

Complete replacement of a testis by tumor can be misinterpreted as a hematoma. A nonseminomatous tumor will be heterogeneous in echogenicity with cystic spaces and calcifications. The patient may give a trivial history of trauma, so the incorrect diagnosis of hematoma could be made. Recognizing that no normal testicular tissue is identifiable because it has been replaced by neoplasm will facilitate the correct diagnosis. Blood markers of alpha-fetoprotein and β-HCG will often be positive in nonseminomatous tumors. Recognition of arterial flow within the mass will convince the examiner that the mass is not a hematoma.

Examination of the upper abdomen for metastatic disease at the level of the renal hilum will be helpful in the patient with diffusely abnormal echogenicity of the testis. Recognition of retroperitoneal adenopathy will confirm the impression of testicular tumor.

Patients with testicular torsion may give a trivial history of trauma, usually related to sporting events. The use of color Doppler is very helpful in diagnosing torsion early enough to salvage the testis. Using the other nonaffected testis as a control, the examiner can determine whether vascular flow is intact on the symptomatic side.

FLUID IN THE SCROTUM

Hydrocele
Extratesticular Hematoma
Fluid in Fascial Planes of Scrotum
("Onion Skin" Appearance)
Cellulitis
Anasarca
Extravasation of fluid in the fascial planes

Hydrocele (Figures 12.23–12.27)

A small amount of fluid may be normally present in the scrotal sac and can be seen on sonographic eval-

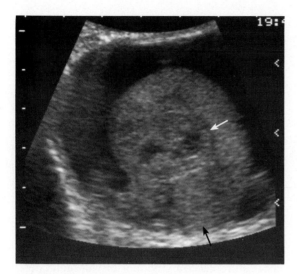

Figure 12.23
Hydrocele in patient with nonseminomatous tumor: A moderate amount of scrotal fluid was present in this patient with scrotal pain. The presence of fluid made the testicular mass (*arrows*) difficult to palpate.

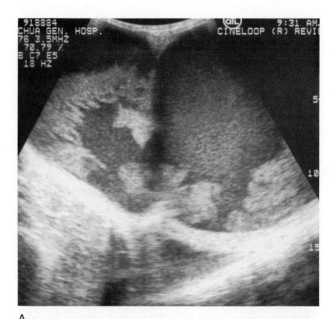

A

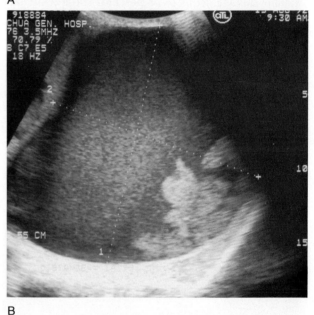

B

Figure 12.25
Complicated hydroceles: (A and B) Homogeneous low-level echoes were present in bilateral gelatinous hydroceles that were surgically decompressed.

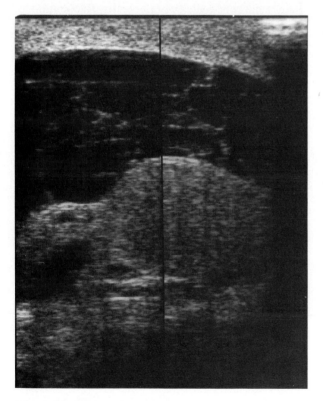

Figure 12.24
Multiseptate hydrocele in patient with epididymitis: Multiple septations were identified in the hydrocele of this patient with chronic epididymitis.

uations. Large volumes of fluid in the scrotal sac may lead to patient complaints of scrotal heaviness. Large hydroceles can make accurate palpation of the testis difficult. Hydroceles may develop in situations of scrotal infection and sometimes will be septated and complicated. Hydroceles may develop in patients with testicular torsion and neoplasm. A persistently patent processus vaginalis that unites the scrotal sac to the peritoneal cavity will allow

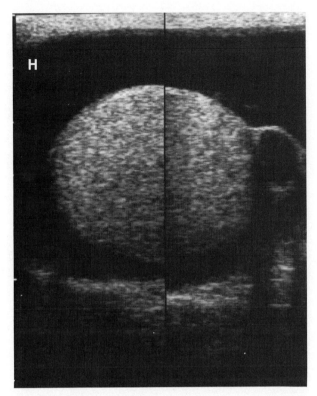

Figure 12.26
Hydrocele in patient with ascites secondary to liver disease:
The development of a hydrocele (H) in this patient with
liver disease coincided with the onset of ascites. A patent
processus vaginalis allowed the communication between
the abdomen and scrotum.

fluid to accumulate in the scrotum in situations of
ascites, dialysate infusion, or meconium peritonitis
in newborns. The recognition of a significant hydrocele must also prompt an evaluation for ascites in
the abdomen.

Extratesticular Hematoma (Figures 12.28–12.29)

Hematoma outside the testis may develop in situations of scrotal or testicular trauma. Trauma may
include a blow to the scrotum or surgery. Scrotal
hematomas may be well-circumscribed masses or
may diffusely infiltrate the scrotal skin, causing skin
thickening. Initially echogenic and solid-appearing,
masslike hematomas will evolve with the development of cystic spaces, septations, and diminishing
size. Scrotal hematomas may be quite dramatic
clinically, causing marked scrotal enlargement and
discoloration.

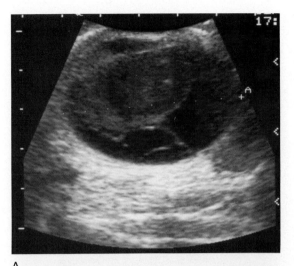

A

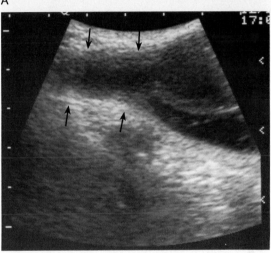

B

Figure 12.27
Infected hydrocele: This premature infant suffered an
acute abdomen secondary to the development of necrotizing enterocolitis. Several weeks later a swollen scrotum was noted. Surgical decompression of the scrotum
led to the discovery of a (A) coagulum of debris and infective material. (B) Presence of a patent processus vaginalis (*arrows*) allowed intraperitoneal material to enter
the scrotum.

Fluid in the Fascial Planes of the Scrotum ("Onion Skin" Appearance)

Cellulitis   Thickening of the skin of the scrotum
can be secondary to infiltration of the skin by inflammatory cells and cellulitis. The skin will be tender, thickened, and red. Sonographically, thickening of the skin with alternating layers of hypo- and
hyperechogenicity is seen.

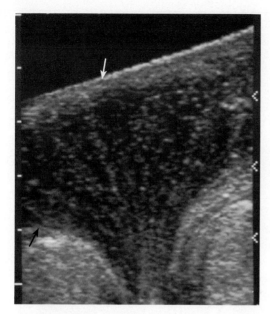

Figure 12.28
Scrotal hematoma: Acute scrotal swelling and pain developed in this man with diffuse bleeding into the scrotal skin after trauma. Note thickening of the scrotal skin (*arrows*) caused by dissecting blood.

Anasarca Skin thickening with alternating layers of hypoechogenicity will be identified sonographically in patients with edema of the scrotal skin. Scrotal skin edema may be secondary to a host of etiologies, including liver disease and hypoproteinemia, congestive heart failure, and renal failure.

Extravasation of Fluid in the Fascial Planes (Figure 12.30) Dissection of fluid through the fascial layers of the scrotum may occur whenever fluid is present in the extraperitoneal space and can gravitate into the scrotal spaces. Extraperitoneal bladder rupture, usually associated with pelvic fractures, may result in urine and blood dissecting into the scrotum. Ureteral disruption in patients with extraperitoneal renal transplants may result in fluid (urine) in the scrotal layers. Other extraperitoneal processes may give rise to dissection of fluid into the scrotum, resulting in the so-called onion skin seen sonographically.

ABNORMAL COLOR FLOW PATTERNS INVOLVING THE SCROTUM

Epididymitis
Testicular Torsion
Varicocele

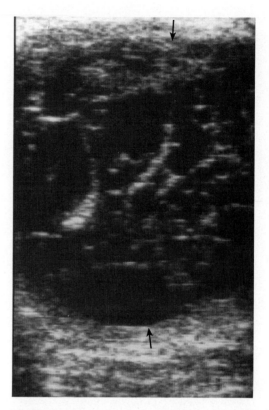

Figure 12.29
Scrotal hematoma: A focal multiseptate hematoma (*arrows*) was present in this postoperative patient.

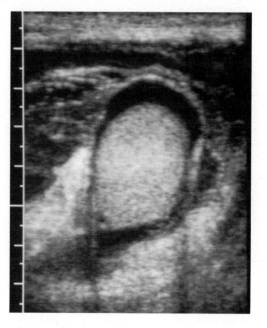

Figure 12.30
"Onion skin" appearance of urine in fascial planes of scrotum: Disruption of the distant ureter occurred in this patient 7 days after renal transplantation into the right iliac fossa. Extravasating urine collected in the scrotum.

Normal blood flow to the uninflamed testis is quite low, and to detect it, a sensitive spectral analysis or color flow system is necessary.

Color flow Doppler evaluation of the scrotum adds important additional information to the routine gray-scale evaluation of the testis. Color Doppler evaluation is particularly helpful in the analysis of the acute scrotum. In the patient with an acutely painful scrotum, the two major diagnostic possibilities are epididymitis and acute testicular torsion. Epididymitis is usually treated medically with antibiotics. Testicular torsion, acute ischemia of the testis, is usually treated with emergency surgery to relieve the vascular compromise. The correct differentiation of these two conditions is imperative.

Epididymitis (Figures 12.31–12.32)

Epididymitis presents as an acute, severely tender scrotum. Sonographically, the epididymis may be

swollen and hypoechoic relative to the testis. Color Doppler analysis will show hypervascularity to the epididymis and normal or hypervascular flow to the testis. If no focal abscess or drainable collection complicates the epididymal infection, antibiotics will be given. Recognition of a scrotal abscess will often result in surgical decompression.

Testicular Torsion (Figures 12.33–12.34)

Vascular compromise of the testis occurs when there is twisting of the spermatic cord, resulting in occlusion of the arterial supply to the testis. Patients with torsion often are children or young men, although men of all ages may be affected. Sometimes there is a trivial history of trauma, such as during a sporting event, at which time the pain begins. When testicular torsion is acute, gray-scale imaging of the testis may be normal, but color Dop-

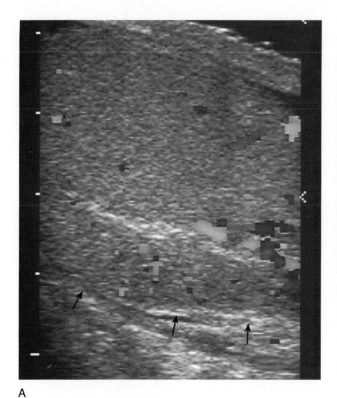

A

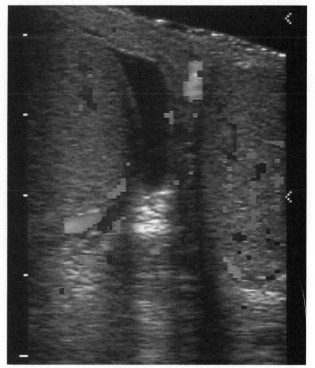

B

Figure 12.31

Epididymo-orchitis (Plates 18 and 19): This young man presented with exquisite scrotal pain. Color Doppler confirmed blood flow to the testis and showed marked hyperemia of the epididymis and testis. Note epididymal enlargement (*arrows*). The patient was treated with antibiotics.

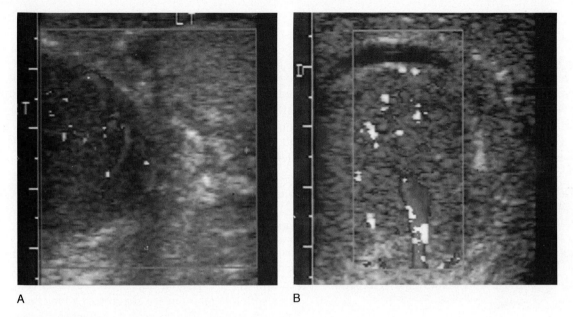

A   B

Figure 12.32
Epididymo-orchitis (Plates 20 and 21): Diffusely diminished echogenicity of the testis was noted on the symptomatic right side in this patient. Prominent hypervascularity was present within the epididymis and testis on that same side. Antibiotics and supportive therapy were employed in this patient.

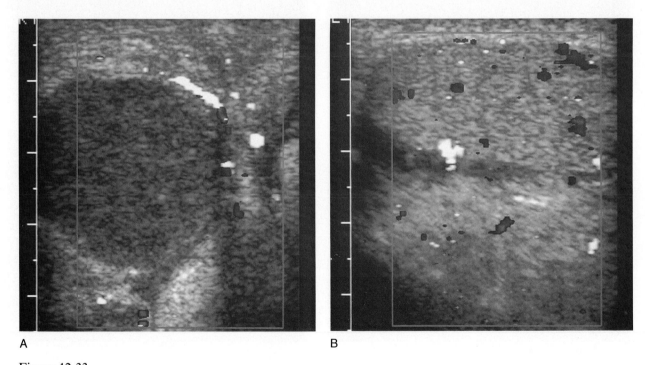

A   B

Figure 12.33
Torsion (Plates 22 and 23): This teenaged male complained of 2 days of scrotal pain. (A) The affected side was diffusely hypoechoic relative to the asymptomatic side. No arterial flow was detectable within the substance of the affected testis, but was present surrounding the testis. (B) Arterial flow was identifiable on the unaffected side. At surgery, salvage of the infarcted testis was not possible.

408

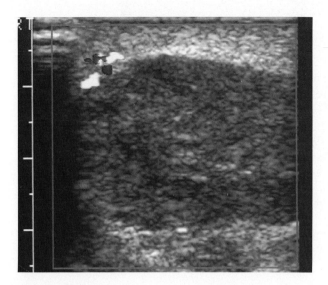

Figure 12.34

Missed torsion (Plate 24): This young man gave a 2-week history of severe scrotal pain. He told of a previous episode involving the opposite side several years before with severe scrotal pain and swelling that gradually diminished over time, leaving a residual testis that was very small. Sonographically, the acutely tender testis had abnormal echogenicity and no vascular flow. On the opposite side, a small, atrophied testis was present.

pler analysis will show no arterial flow to the affected testis.

The longer the testis suffers ischemia, the more abnormal the gray-scale imaging of the testis will become. By color flow, hypervascularity may be identified surrounding the testis in the situation of missed torsion. Missed torsion occurs when the testis has suffered irreparable damage because of lengthy ischemia. This vascular pattern correlates with the "doughnut" pattern seen on nuclear medicine imaging of missed testicular torsion. Despite the hypervascularity surrounding the testis, no significant arterial flow will be recognized within the testis itself.

Varicocele

Abnormal prominence of the veins of the spermatic cord may cause scrotal discomfort, although not usually an acute scrotum. Although an excess of veins in the plexus of the spermatic cord may be idiopathic and unrelated to other processes, an investigation of the retroperitoneum is indicated to exclude adenopathy or a mass when a varicocele is identified. Thrombosis of the renal veins or inferior vena cava by tumor thrombus may cause the fairly sudden appearance of a scrotal varicocele and should be excluded by imaging.

Maneuvers that can be performed to evaluate a varicocele include Valsalva maneuvers to enlarge the veins, compression by the transducer, or use of very low flow settings by Doppler.

Emphasis Points

The two major differential considerations for the acute scrotum—epididymitis or testicular torsion—can usually be reliably and rapidly differentiated using ultrasound, especially using color Doppler. Appropriate differentiation will determine whether surgical or medical therapy should be used.

The examiner must be aware that normal testicular arterial flow can be difficult to detect, so sensitive Doppler settings are necessary. The unaffected testis serves as a very valuable control for the symptomatic side and should be used in such a way. Spectral analysis can complement color Doppler to assure arterial flow is present.

Color Doppler studies of the acute scrotum can be as reliable as nuclear medicine imaging for detection of acute testicular torsion.

BIBLIOGRAPHY

Focal Testicular Mass

Grantham JG, Charboneau JW, James EM, Kirschling RJ, Kvols LK, Sequra JW, Wold LE: Testicular neoplasms: 29 tumors studied by high-resolution US. Radiology 157:775–780, 1985.
Krone KD, Carroll BA: Scrotal ultrasound. Radiol Clin North Am 23:121–139, 1985.
Rifkin MD: Scrotal ultrasound. Urol Radiol 9:119–126, 1987.
Seidenwurm D, Smathers RL, Kan P, Hoffman A: Intratesticular adrenal rests diagnosed by ultrasound. Radiology 155:479–481, 1985.

Extratesticular Mass

Gooding GAW: Sonography of the spermatic cord. AJR 151:721–724, 1988.

Haller J, Tscholakoff D, Gundry C, Wittich G, Mostbeck G, Gritzmann N: Sonography of unusual extratesticular lesions. Urol Radiol 11:190–193, 1989.

Mevorach RA, Lerner RM, Dvoretsky PM, et al: Testicular abscess: diagnosis by ultrasonography. J Urol 136:1213–1216, 1986.

Moudy PC, Makhija JS: Ultrasonic demonstration of a non-palpable testicular tumor. J Clin Ultrasound 11:54–55, 1983.

Phillips G, Kumari-Subaiya S, Sawitsky A: Ultrasonic evaluation of the scrotum in lymphoproliferative disease. J Ultrasound Med 6:169–175, 1987.

Ramanathan K, Yaghoobian J, Pinck RL: Sperm granuloma. J Clin Ultrasound 14:155–156, 1986.

Subramanyam BR, Balthazar EJ, Raghavendra BN, et al: Sonographic diagnosis of scrotal hernia AJR 139:535–538, 1982.

Tepperman BS, Gospodarowicz M, Bush RS, et al.: Non-Hodgkin lymphoma of the testis. Radiology 142:203–208, 1982.

Diffusely Abnormal Testicular Echogenicity

Jeffrey RB, Laing FC, Hricak H, et al.: Sonography of testicular trauma. AJR 141:993–995, 1983.

Lupetin AR, King W, Rich PJ, et al.: The traumatized scrotum: Ultrasound evaluation. Radiology 148:203–207, 1983.

Abnormal Color Flow Patterns Involving the Scrotum

Burks DD, Markey BJ, Burkhard TK, Balsara ZN, Haluszka MM, Canning DA: Suspected testicular torsion and ischemia: Evaluation with color Doppler sonography. Radiology 175:815–821, 1990.

Chen DCP, Holder LE, Kaplan GN: Correlation of radionuclide imaging and diagnostic ultrasound in scrotal diseases. J Nucl Med 27:1774–1781, 1986.

Lerner RM, Mevorach RA, Hulbert WC, Rabinowitz R: Color Doppler US in the evaluation of acute scrotal disease. Radiology 176:355–358, 1990.

Middleton WD, Melson GL: Testicular ischemia: Color Doppler sonographic findings in five patients. AJR 152:1237–1239, 1989.

Middleton WD, Siegel BA, Melson GL, Yates CK, Andriole GL: Acute scrotal disorders: Prospective comparison of color Doppler US and testicular scintigraphy. Radiology 177:177–181, 1990.

Middleton WD, Thorne DA, Melson GL: Color Doppler ultrasound of the normal testis. AJR 152:293–297, 1989.

Wolverson MK, Houttuin E, Heiberg E, et al.: High-resolution real-time sonography of scrotal varicocele. AJR 141:775–779, 1983.

C H A P T E R   13

SOFT TISSUES

PATTERNS
Anterior Abdominal Wall Mass
Groin Masses
Swellings Around the Knee

Ultrasound can be used to evaluate a mass present in the superficial structures of the anterior abdominal wall, groin, or knee.

ANTERIOR ABDOMINAL WALL MASS

Mesenchymal Neoplasm
   Lipoma
   Desmoid Tumor/Sarcoma
Metastatic Disease
Rectus Sheath Hematoma/Seroma/Abscess
Hernias
   Incisional hernia
   Umbilical or ventral hernia
   Spigelian hernia
Endometriosis

CHILDHOOD

Urachal Cyst

Abnormalities within the anterior abdominal wall are usually palpable, since they are so close to the skin surface. After an abdominal wall mass is discovered on physical examination, the mass may be evaluated sonographically. Relatively high-frequency (5–7 MHz), superficially focused (linear array or curvilinear) transducers are needed to evaluate such lesions best.

Mesenchymal Neoplasm

Lipoma (Figure 13.1) Masses arising from the mesenchymal elements of the anterior abdominal wall may be encountered and include benign lesions, such as a lipoma. Lipomas, made of mature fat, are often soft, pliable masses that the patient may have noticed for years. If the mass grows larger, hardens, or causes discomfort because of its location, evaluation and removal may be warranted.

The typical lipoma in the anterior abdominal wall is often of similar echogenicity to the surrounding subcutaneous fat. Lipomas are not necessarily highly echogenic. The mass is often well defined and encapsulated. Fat density (-100 to 0 Hounsfield units) can be confirmed by CT scanning.

Desmoid Tumor (Figures 13.2–13.3) Exuberant fibrosis may develop in the anterior abdominal wall after trauma or surgery, resulting in desmoid formation. Such a growth is frequently found in the abdominal wall near surgical incision sites. Aggressive fibromatosis and fibrosarcoma are masses of fibrotic tissue that would require biopsy to differentiate, since the imaging features can be very similar

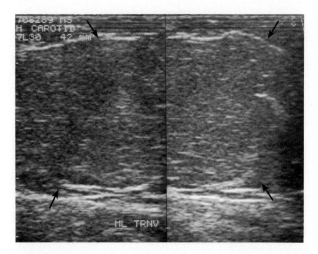

Figure 13.1
Lipoma: The patient had noted a soft, mobile anterior wall mass for years (*arrows*). Notice its well-defined margins and homogeneous echogenicity. CT confirmed its fat density.

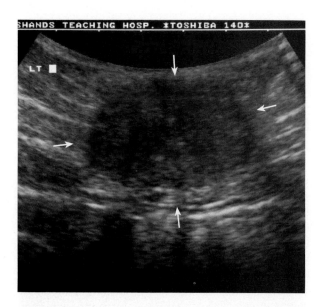

Figure 13.2
Desmoid: This young woman had noted a hard mass beneath an incision site in her anterior abdominal wall. Biopsy of this homogeneously hypoechoic mass (*arrows*) was extremely difficult, because the cutting needle would not penetrate the dense mass. Histologic evaluation showed the tumor to consist of dense, benign connective tissue.

to the desmoid. Often surgically removed, the desmoid may recur after excision.

Metastatic Disease (Figures 13.4–13.5)

Metastatic deposits to the anterior abdominal wall may occur frequently in patients with disseminated malignant melanoma. Other primary tumors, such as those of the colon, breast, and lung, may also yield subcutaneous metastases, although such lesions are less common.

Rectus Sheath Hematoma/Seroma/Abscess (Figures 13.6–13.8)

Hemorrhage into the muscles of the anterior abdominal wall may occur spontaneously or secondary to trauma. Anticoagulant therapy is the most frequent explanation for spontaneous rectus sheath hemorrhage. Surgery, trauma, or vigorous contraction of the rectus muscle may result in intramuscular hemorrhage. Hemophiliac patients may suffer from acute muscular bleeding.

Usually, the patient has pain, and a palpable mass develops when there is significant rectus sheath hemorrhage. Sonographically, a heterogeneous mass causing expansion of the transverse abdominis muscle is seen. Often, if the bleeding is brisk enough, a hematocrit level with fluid and sediment is identifiable. If it is not evacuated, the chronic rectus sheath hematoma will become smaller, cystic, and septated over time.

A seroma may be present in patients after surgery involving the abdominal wall. Percutaneous drainage procedures can decompress these fluid collections. Infected collections may complicate surgical procedures, often near incision sites. An abscess may occur secondary to fistulization from intra-abdominal processes through the fascia into the abdominal wall.

Hernias

Incisional Hernia   Abdominal fat and bowel may herniate through a defect in the fascia at a surgical incision site. In most cases, the hernia develops within the first year after abdominal surgery. This complication of abdominal surgery is believed to occur after approximately 5 percent of abdominal operations. Sometimes asymptomatic, the incisional hernia may be detected incidentally during an abdominal ultrasound or when a palpable anterior abdominal wall abnormality is investigated.

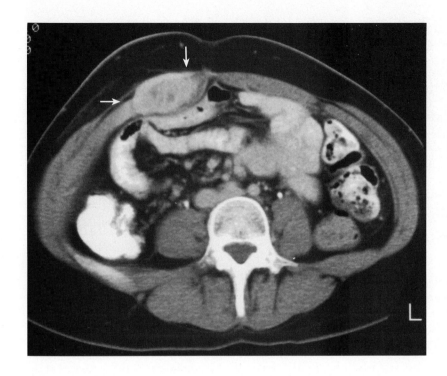

Figure 13.3
Desmoid: CT shows prominent enhancement of the fibrotic mass (*arrows*).

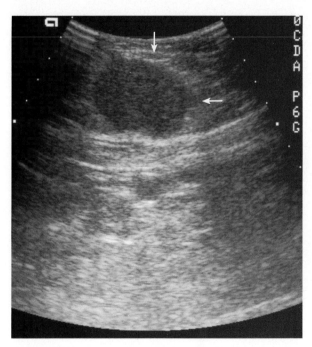

Figure 13.4
Metastatic disease to the anterior abdominal wall—melanoma: A subcutaneous implant of malignant melanoma is identifiable as a homogeneously hypoechoic mass (*arrows*).

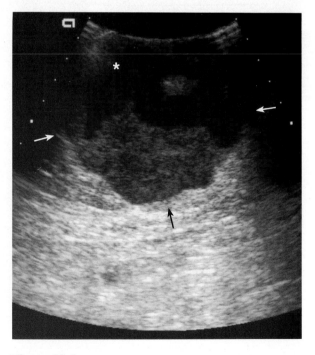

Figure 13.5
Metastatic disease—lung primary: In this patient with a history of squamous cell carcinoma of the lung, a metastasis to the anterior abdominal wall drained spontaneously. Note the large cystic component (*) of the mass secondary to tumor necrosis.

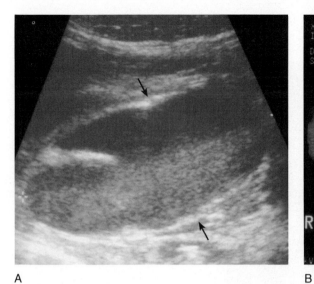
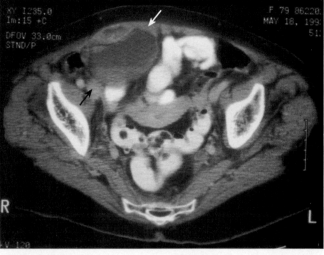

A   B

Figure 13.6
Rectus sheath hematoma: (A) This elderly patient, on anticoagulation therapy for atrial fibrillation, developed severe right lower quadrant pain and a mass in the rectus sheath identified by ultrasound. (B) CT showed a hematocrit level and confirmed the origin of the hematoma in the rectus sheath.

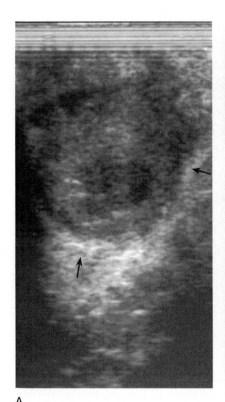
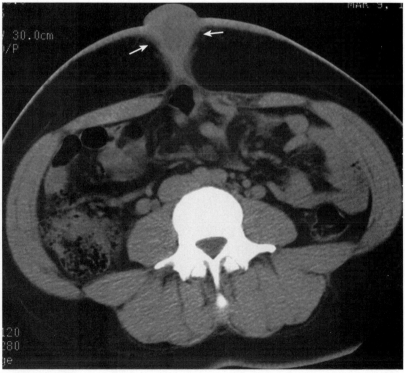

A   B

Figure 13.7
Anterior abdominal wall abscess: This young woman, who was receiving steroid injections to diminish scar formation, developed severe pain. (A) An ultrasound showed a small collection beneath the umbilicus. (B) CT confirmed the mass (*arrows*), demonstrating no herniating bowel. Aspiration of the mass yielded purulent material.

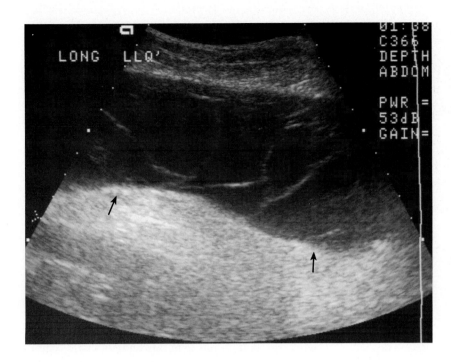

Figure 13.8
Seroma: A large, multiseptate fluid collection (*arrows*) was present in this patient after ventral hernia repair. Percutaneous catheter placement was necessary for its resolution.

Umbilical or Ventral Hernia (Figure 13.9) Defects in the midline of the abdomen and subsequent herniation often occur in obese, elderly patients with weakness of the abdominal wall related to previous surgery, pregnancy, or trauma. Ultrasound scanning with a high-frequency (5–7 MHz) transducer will allow recognition of the fascial defect in the anterior abdominal wall and often will demonstrate bowel or fat herniating through the defect. Reducible hernias may be observed to move in and out of the defect or may need provocative maneuvers to elicit. Valsalva maneuvers and changes in patient positioning to the sitting or upright stance may be necessary to demonstrate the herniation. Incarcerated or strangulated bowel will not be reducible.

The type of tissue within the hernia can often be determined by sonography. Echogenic fat can be seen if omentum is within the hernia. Fluid-filled bowel with valvulae conniventes may be identified if small bowel is obstructed while trapped in the hernia. Nonobstructed bowel may also be seen within such a hernia. Patients with ascites may develop fluid within the hernia.

Spigelian Hernia (Figure 13.10) The spigelian hernia is a spontaneous herniation that occurs just lateral to the rectus sheath, usually in the lower quadrant. Usually, patients have pain at the orifice of the hernia.

Endometriosis (Figure 13.11)

Women with endometriosis may develop implants of endometriosis in the anterior abdominal wall, usually in or related to an incisional site. Endometriosis may yield small nodules or large masses with low-level echoes, cystic components, or fluid-debris levels. Often the patient gives a history of infertility, cyclic pelvic pain, and dyspareunia. The anterior abdominal wall mass may exhibit the same cyclic pain features. Fine-needle aspiration can confirm the diagnosis of endometriosis.

CHILDHOOD

Urachal Cyst

Urachal abnormalities include a patent urachus, which is a persistent communication of the dome of the bladder to the umbilical region. Young patients complaining of umbilical discharge need evaluation for continuity between the bladder and umbilical region. Such embryologic remnants can become secondarily infected. Rarely, adenocarcinoma can arise within the urachal remnant.

Sonographically, the continuity between the bladder and umbilical region can be demonstrated if there is a patent urachus. Debris and a fluid level may be illustrated within this persistent channel.

Other urachal abnormalities are urachal cysts that fail to communicate with either the bladder or umbilicus but that may be a cause of an umbilical-

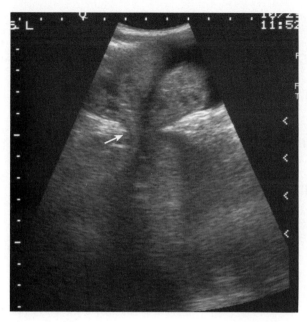

Figure 13.9
Umbilical hernia: This cirrhotic patient with massive ascites was noted to have an umbilical hernia filled with ascites and bowel. Note the fascial defect (*arrow*) and the herniating bowel loops.

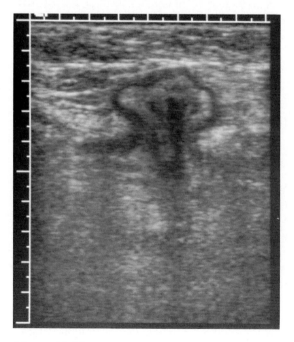

Figure 13.10
Spigelian hernia: A reducible loop of bowel was identifiable in this patient with a palpable abdominal mass in the right lower quadrant.

region mass, and urachal diverticulum, which communicates with the dome of the bladder but not the umbilicus.

GROIN MASSES

> Lymphadenopathy
> Pseudoaneurysm/Aneurysm
> Hematoma/Seroma
> Undescended Testis
> Primary Neoplasia
> Hernia

Masses felt in the groin are frequently subject to ultrasound interrogation.

Lymphadenopathy (Figure 13.12)

Enlarged lymph nodes in the groin may develop when the patient has generalized neoplastic lymphadenopathy, such as with lymphoma. Tumors that drain to the groin because the inguinal nodes are regional lymph nodes include mesenchymal tumors of the leg, squamous cell carcinomas of the vulva or penis and lower third of the vagina, as well as anal carcinoma. Necrotic centers to the nodes may develop in rapidly growing tumors or if they are of squamous cell histology.

Infectious or reactive lymphadenopathy may develop in a variety of infectious conditions. Lymph nodes involved with lymphadenitis may be indistinguishable sonographically from neoplastic nodes. Aspiration and culture will usually allow the offending agent to be appropriately identified and treated.

Pseudoaneurysm/Aneurysm (Figure 13.13)

A pseudoaneurysm is a contained rupture of a vessel. Usually secondary to an iatrogenic cause, a pseudoaneurysm occurs when the hemorrhage from a bleeding artery is contained by the fascial layers around the vessel. Usually, a pseudoaneurysm develops after a catheterization or surgical procedure on a vessel. Multiple cannulations of a small artery and inadequate postprocedure compression contribute to the formation of a pseudoaneurysm.

Sonographically, a pseudoaneurysm is a cystic mass that communicates with an arterial structure. Color Doppler will frequently allow the identification of the narrow neck that connects the vessel to the pseudoaneurysm. During systole, flow jets into the mass. During diastole, there is at first reversal of flow, then swirling within the mass. Color flow

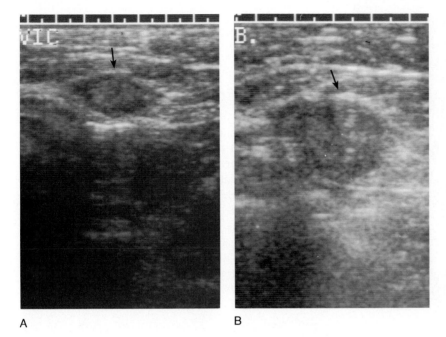

A   B

Figure 13.11
Endometriosis: This young woman noted cyclic pain in a nodule of the anterior abdominal wall. Serial sonograms months apart (A and B) showed interval growth. Endometriosis was suggested by fine-needle aspiration and confirmed by surgical excision of the mass.

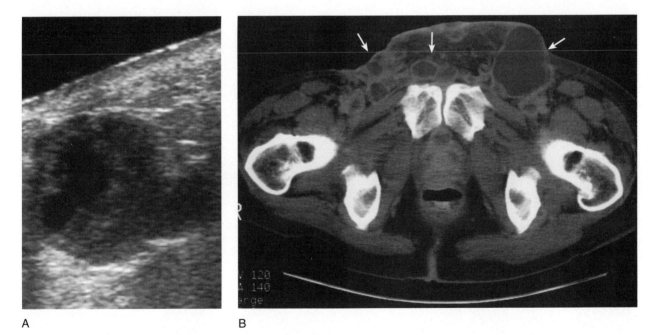

A   B

Figure 13.12
Metastatic lymphadenopathy: (A) Multiple necrotic lymph nodes were obvious in the groin in this patient with squamous cell carcinoma of the penis. (B) Correlative CT images in the same patient shows low-density centers (*arrows*) to the nodes consistent with squamous cell histology.

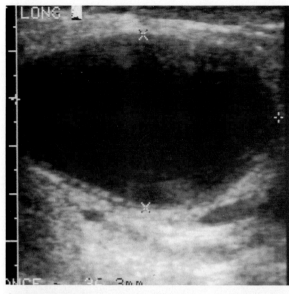

A

Figure 13.13

Pseudoaneurysm: A pseudoaneurysm of the femoral vessel after cardiac catheterization may be related to a low puncture site, multiple catheter exchanges, anticoagulation therapy after catheterization, and incomplete compression of the vessel after catheter removal. (A) A large cystic collection was identified at the groin anterior to the vessels. (B) High-velocity jet illustrated by spectral analysis (∗ = vessels).

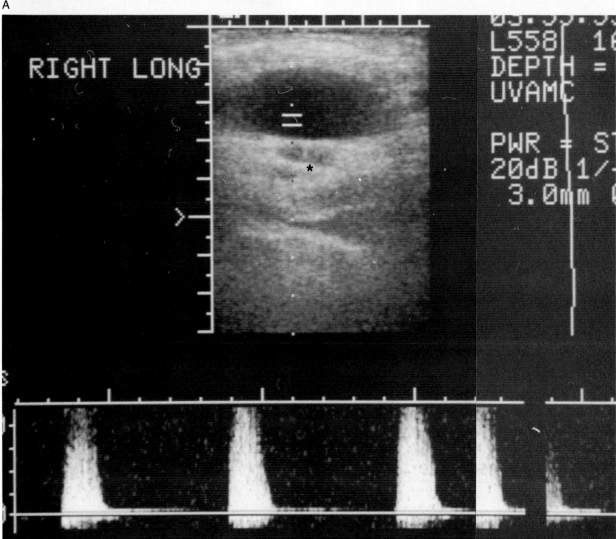

B

Doppler or spectral analysis allows differentiation from a hematoma.

Sometimes ultrasound-guided compression at the neck can be used to cause a pseudoaneurysm to thrombose. Surgical correction may be necessary for an enlarging pseudoaneurysm.

Aneurysms of the femoral artery may cause a palpable groin mass but are usually easy to distinguish from a pseudoaneurysm by imaging. An aneurysm involves dilatation of all the layers of the involved vessel.

Hematoma/Seroma (Figure 13.14)

Frequently, in the postcatheterization patient, a palpable groin mass at the site of catheter insertion will lead to an ultrasound evaluation. The two most likely possibilities for such a mass are a pseudoaneurysm of the vessel or a hematoma. A pseudoaneurysm often requires repair of the vessel; a hematoma will be absorbed and eventually resolve.

A hematoma is a solid-appearing mass outside the vessel. It may be well defined and encapsulated or more diffuse, with blood dissecting through the fascial layers of the thigh. Recognition of the common femoral artery and vein and confirmation that there is no arterial inflow into the hematoma will allow the differentiation between a pseudoaneurysm and hematoma to be made.

A seroma represents the residuum of a hematoma related either to a surgical procedure or to catheterization. Seromas are usually cystic with septations.

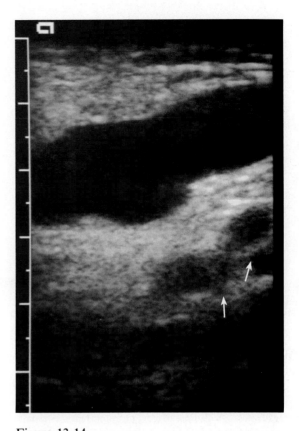

Figure 13.14

Seroma: Often indistinguishable clinically from a pseudoaneurysm, a seroma may cause a palpable groin mass in a patient after catheterization or regional surgery. Note a simple fluid collection, anterior to the groin vessels (*arrows*). No arterial flow is present in the collection. Resolution of the seroma generally occurs spontaneously unless the lesion is quite large.

Undescended Testis (Figure 13.15)

Incomplete testicular descent is very common in premature male infants, occurring in nearly one-third of those less than 2500 grams in weight. Only 3 to 4 percent of term infants have evidence of incomplete testicular descent. Testicular descent continues for weeks after birth, so that fewer than 1 percent of infants are cryptorchid at 12 months of age.

Arrest of the descent of the testis can occur anywhere from the site of origin of the organ near the kidneys in the retroperitoneum to the scrotum. Most undescended testes are located in the inguinal canal or near the inguinal ring. In most cases, the undescended testis is repaired before the child undergoes puberty.

Ultrasound is the examination of choice for locating an undescended testis, since most will be located in the inguinal canal. A testis higher in the

pelvis or in the retroperitoneum may be difficult to identify sonographically, and CT or MR may be necessary to identify the testis.

The two risks for the prolonged undescended testis include infertility and an increased incidence of malignancy. The chronically cryptorchid testis will undergo atrophy, losing its spermatogenetic potential. Seminoma is the tumor most likely to arise within an undescended testis.

Sonographically, the undescended testis is a small, hypoechoic mass in the inguinal canal that may be indistinguishable from a small lymph node. Often the cryptorchid testis is cigar shaped, reflecting its chronic position in the inguinal canal. Heterogeneity of its echogencity is common, reflecting testicular atrophy. Valsalva maneuvers to move the testis into the scrotal sac may be useful, showing the mobility of the testis.

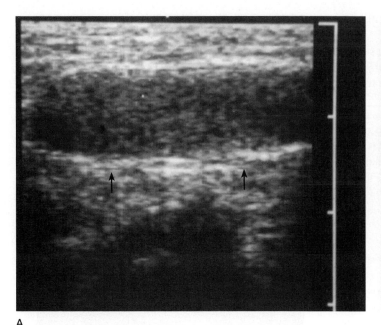
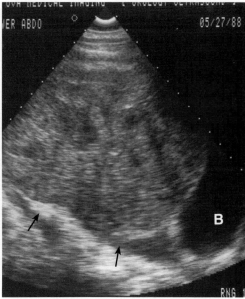

A   B

Figure 13.15

Undescended testis: (A) When the testis is not palpable in the scrotum, it is often discovered sonographically in the inguinal canal. Note the cigar shape of the undescended testis (*arrows*). A chronically cryptorchid testis is small, with hypoechogenicity related to testicular atrophy. (B) In another patient with undescended testis, a large seminoma (*arrows*) was seen in the pelvis. (B = bladder.)

Primary Neoplasia (Figure 13.16)

Besides enlarged neoplastic lymphadenopathy of the groin, neoplasms arising from the mesenchymal elements of the lower abdominal wall and upper thigh may be the cause of a groin mass. Generally solid lesions, sarcomas—including malignant fibrous histiocytoma, liposarcoma, fibrosarcoma, and rhabdomyosarcoma—may have cystic necrosis when they outstrip their central blood supply. Biopsy can be easily performed for tissue histology.

Hernia

Physical examination is usually more sensitive in identifying inguinal hernias than ultrasound, but ultrasound can be used when a hernia is present to distinguish what is within the hernia sac, specifically whether or not bowel is present or obstructed. Omental fat seen as highly echogenic material, peristalsis of bowel loops, or fixed nonperistalsing strangulated loops may be visualized.

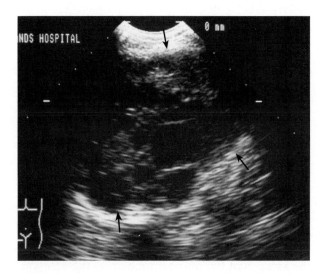

Figure 13.16

Malignant fibrous histiocytoma: Primary malignancies of the extremities uncommonly present as groin masses. In this case, a multiseptate mass with solid components (*arrows*) was a large, malignant sarcoma of the thigh. The clinical suspicion was of a hematoma because of recent vascular surgery.

SWELLINGS AROUND THE KNEE

Baker's Cyst
Joint Effusion
Deep Venous Thrombosis
Popliteal Artery Aneurysm
Primary Neoplasms

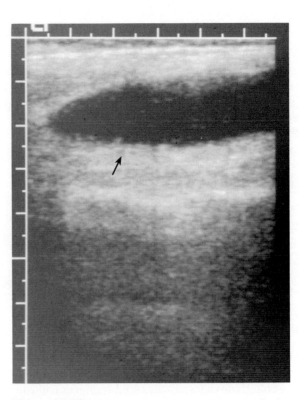

Figure 13.17
Baker's cyst: In this patient with rheumatoid arthritis suspected of having deep venous thrombosis, a Baker's cyst was identified dissecting into the posterior calf.

Baker's Cyst (Figure 13.17)

The patient with a symptomatic Baker's cyst clinically has leg swelling and pain. Sometimes it is impossible to differentiate a ruptured Baker's cyst clinically from deep venous thrombosis involving the lower leg, since the clinical symptoms are so similar.

A Baker's cyst is a cystic collection, often with internal septations and debris, that may dissect from the posterior and medial portion of the knee into the calf. Visualization of the communication of the cyst with the joint space is usually possible. Usually, a joint effusion is also present in the suprapatellar bursa. Plain films of the knee frequently show degenerative or arthritic changes, since it is the deranged mechanics of the knee that predisposes to a Baker's cyst.

Joint Effusion (Figure 13.18)

When a knee effusion is present, fluid anterior to the femur is easily recognizable by ultrasound by scanning just superior to the patella.

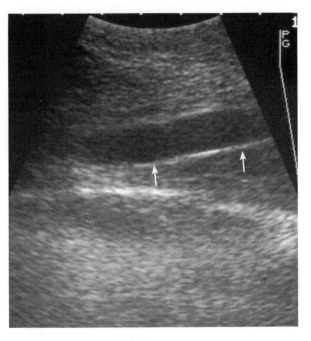

Figure 13.18
Joint effusion: In this patient with a swollen knee, fluid was present in the suprapatellar bursa.

Deep Venous Thrombosis

Venous thrombosis originating in the calf and propagating into the popliteal fossa can be recognized sonographically as a noncompressible, thrombus-filled vein. When scanning the popliteal fossa, the knee should not be overextended, as that can flatten the vein, making it invisible. Slight flexion of the knee facilitates venous evaluation.

Popliteal Artery Aneurysm (Figure 13.19)

Aneurysmal dilatation of the popliteal artery can accompany atherosclerotic disease elsewhere. A popliteal artery aneurysm can be a source of emboli to the feet, if present. The maximal dimensions of an aneurysm and its internal characteristics (i.e., plaque, thrombus) can be noted sonographically.

Primary Neoplasms

Mesenchymal masses arising from the soft tissues around the knee can be evaluated by ultrasound, if present. Synovial sarcomas and malignant fibrous histiocytomas are only two tumors which can develop in this region. Usually solid, such masses may have heterogenicity and central necrosis as they enlarge.

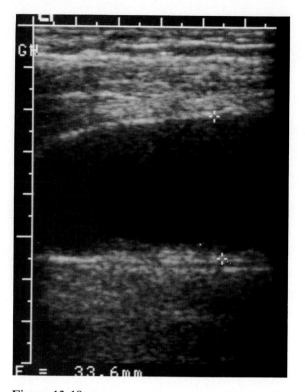

Figure 13.19

Popliteal artery aneurysm: This patient with an aortic aneurysm also had popliteal artery dilatation, seen here. Color Doppler confirmed arterial flow within the vessel's lumen.

BIBLIOGRAPHY

Anterior Abdominal Wall Mass

Brasfield RD, Das Gupta TK: Desmoid tumors of the anterior abdominal wall. Surgery 65:241–246, 1969.

Engel JM, Deitch EE: Sonography of the anterior abdominal wall. AJR 137:73–77, 1981.

Fried AM, Meeker WR: Incarcerated Spigelian hernia: Ultrasonic differential diagnosis. AJR 133:107–110, 1979.

Kaftori JK, Rosenberger A, Pollack S, Fish JH: Rectus sheath hematoma: Ultrasonographic diagnosis. AJR 128:283–285, 1977.

Lee PWR, Bark M, Macfie J, Pratt D: The ultrasound diagnosis of rectus sheath haematoma. Br J Surg 64:633–634, 1977.

Mantello MT, Haller JO, Marquis JR: Sonography of abdominal desmoid tumors in adolescents. J Ultrasound Med 8:467–470, 1989.

Spangen L: Ultrasound as a diagnostic aid in ventral abdominal hernia. J Clin Ultrasound 3:211–213, 1975.

Tromans A, Campbell N, Sykes P: Rectus sheath haematoma: Diagnosis by ultrasound. Br J Surg 68:518–519, 1981.

Groin Masses

Abu-Yousef MM, Wiese JA, Shamma AR: Case report. The "to-and-fro" sign: Duplex Doppler evidence of femoral artery pseudoaneurysm. AJR 150:632–634, 1988.

Madrazo BL, Klugo RC, Parks JA, et al: Ultrasonographic demonstration of undescended testes. Radiology 133:181–183, 1979.

Mitchell DG, Needleman L, Bezzi M, et al: Femoral artery pseudoaneurysm: Diagnosis with conventional duplex and color Doppler US. Radiology 165:687–690, 1987.

Rapoport S, Sniderman KW, Morse SS, et al: Pseudoaneurysm: A complication of faulty technique in femoral arterial puncture. Radiology 154:529–530, 1985.

Weiss RM, Carter AR, Rosenfield AT: High resolution realtime sonography in the localization of undescended testis. J Urol 135:936–938, 1986.

RENAL TRANSPLANTS

PATTERNS

Peritransplant Fluid Collections
Renal Transplant Vascular Complications
Renal Transplant Collecting System Dilatation

With increasing use of renal transplantation to manage patients with renal failure, ultrasound is being used to monitor the allograft and associated complications.

PERITRANSPLANT FLUID COLLECTIONS

Hematoma/Seroma/Abscess
Urinoma
Lymphocele
Ovarian Cyst
Bladder Diverticulum

In most large adolescent and adult patients receiving a renal transplant, the kidney is placed in the extraperitoneal space of one of the two iliac fossae. Unless communications are created between the peritoneal and extraperitoneal spaces, fluid accumulating around the kidney will remain contained in the extraperitoneal space. Fluid can therefore track up into the retroperitoneal space to the region of the native kidneys or can dissect into the scrotum or upper thigh. Renal transplants in pediatric patients will usually be placed in an intraperitoneal location since renal donor size often precludes placement of the kidney into the small, extraperitoneal space of the iliac fossa. Fluid around the pediatric intraperitoneal transplant may freely flow around bowel loops.

Hematoma/Seroma/Abscess (Figures 14.1–14.2)

Hematomas may occur in the immediate postoperative period. A hematoma may be an inhomogeneously echogenic mass and can appear nearly solid sonographically. Disruption of one of the vascular anastomoses or hematoma after percutaneous biopsy may require operative intervention.

As a hematoma ages, it becomes more fluid filled. An incisional or perinephric seroma may be identified as a cystic, sometimes septated collection, usually in close proximity to the transplanted organ. In this immunosuppressed group of patients, aspiration of the fluid collection may be necessary to exclude infection.

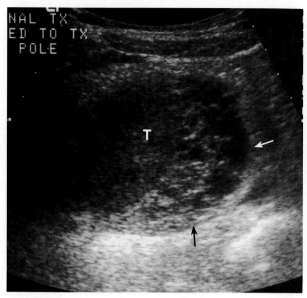

A

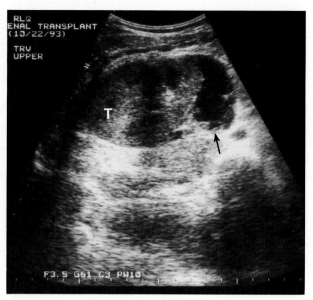

B

Figure 14.1
Hematoma: (A) After mild trauma in an automobile accident, a complex peritransplant collection (*arrows*) was noted. (B) With time, the localized hematoma became more serous. (T = transplant.)

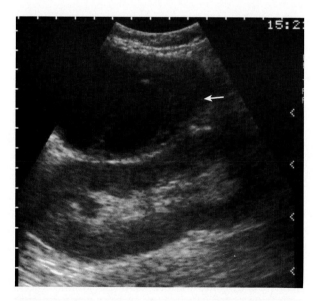

Figure 14.2
Seroma: A lenticular fluid collection was noted beneath the surgical incision. Aspiration of the fluid yielded thin, serosanguinous fluid.

Urinoma (Figures 14.3–14.4)

Ischemia of the distal end of the donor ureter may result in anastomotic breakdown and urinary extravasation, usually into the extraperitoneal space in the adult patient. Often a result of overzealous harvesting of the donor ureter, the blood supply to the transplanted ureter is compromised, resulting in urine leak and urinoma formation. This frequently occurs at day 7–10 after transplantation, a time when ischemic necrosis of the ureter becomes most pronounced. With urinary extravasation, a well-defined fluid collection may collect near the leaking distal ureter. A well-defined mass does not necessarily develop, however, and fluid may dissect through the fascial planes of the extraperitoneal space. Fluid dissection into the scrotum, down the inner thigh, and into the retroperitoneum may originate from the disrupted ureteric anastomosis.

Often the history for ureteric disruption is typical. The recuperating transplant recipient is about a week out from transplant surgery, moving about some, when he feels a "pop" and notices that urine output has diminished in the ensuing hours. Pain often accompanies the extravasation of urine into the extraperitoneal space.

Sonographically, ureteric anastomotic leak may be subtle. If a well-defined fluid collection develops, the collection can easily be aspirated to rule out a urinoma. Often, however, the fluid will dissect through the fascial planes, not causing a discrete collection. Recognition of fluid dissecting through the planes and awareness of the typical time course and history will allow the appropriate diagnosis to

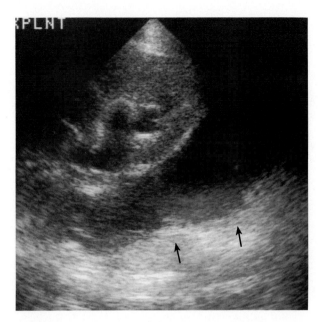

Figure 14.3
Urinoma: Seven days after transplantation, severe pain developed in the transplant bed and the patient's urine output diminished. Fluid was obvious beneath the kidney (*arrows*). The fluid had high creatinine levels consistent with urine. A ureteral anastomotic disruption was present and repaired.

be made. Functional studies (e.g., nuclear medicine) to assess for extravasation may be necessary.

Operative reanastomosis is necessary in most cases, but sometimes stenting procedures will provide a mechanism for a partial leak to heal.

Lymphocele (Figures 14.5–14.7)

Since the transplanted kidney is placed in a pocket in the extraperitoneal tissue of the iliac fossa, some dissection and division of lymphatic channels occurs to allow proper placement of the transplant. A collection of lymph will accumulate around or adjacent to the transplant if significant disruption of lymphatic channels has occurred. Lymphoceles may take some time to accumulate and may be seen sonographically on routine follow-up studies. Usually nonobstructing, a lymphocele may be discovered when the serum creatinine level rises secondary to obstruction from the mass.

Sonographically, lymphoceles are cystic masses, varying in size from a few to many centimeters, often with internal septations. Diagnostic aspiration may be necessary to differentiate a lymphocele from other peritransplant fluid collections and to exclude superimposed infection.

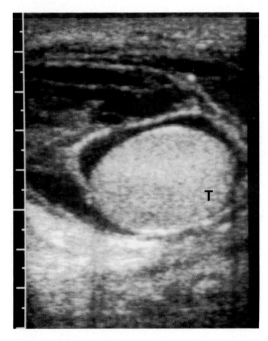

Figure 14.4
Urine leakage: In this male patient with ureteral anastomotic leak of a transplanted kidney, urine dissected into the scrotum, causing scrotal swelling and fluid. (T = testis.)

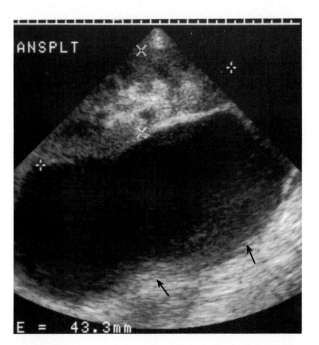

Figure 14.5
Lymphocele: A large, simple fluid collection (*arrows*) developed beneath the undersurface of the transplanted kidney 4 months after transplantation. The volume of the collection caused mass effect on the kidney.

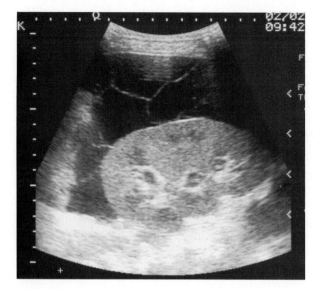

Figure 14.6
Lymphocele: A large, multiseptate lymphocele developed in this patient in the weeks after transplantation.

Management of large lymphoceles may be problematic. Simple aspiration of a lymphocele will usually be followed by reaccumulation of the collection. Long-term catheter drainage has been successful in some cases, but the fear of infection from the percutaneously placed catheter often causes concern. Marsupialization of the lymphocele to the peritoneal space will result in decompression of the lymphocele with absorption of lymphatic fluid by the peritoneal surface.

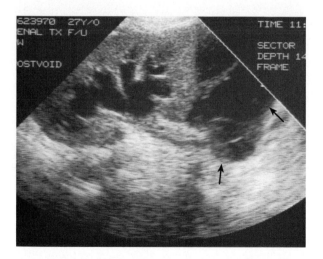

Figure 14.7
Lymphocele: Mild hydronephrosis was caused by this lymphocele (*arrows*) and was relieved by lymphocele decompression.

Ovarian Cyst

In female transplant recipients, large cysts or cystic masses of the ovary can be mistaken for a perinephric collection. Sometimes transvaginal imaging will allow the ovarian origin of the mass to be distinguished.

Bladder Diverticulum

The presence of a bladder diverticulum is usually known from preoperative evaluation of the bladder.

Emphasis Points

The length of time after transplantation and the clinical course sometimes will help to differentiate the specific cause of a perinephric collection.

Aspiration to screen for infectious agents as well as to obtain chemistries on the fluid may be necessary for definitive diagnosis. Elevated creatinine levels in the collection that far exceed the serum creatinine may be present in a urinoma.

RENAL TRANSPLANT VASCULAR COMPLICATIONS

Increasing Vascular Resistance Within the Transplant
Renal Artery Thrombosis
Renal Vein Thrombosis
Pseudoaneurysm/Arteriovenous Malformation
Renal Artery or Venous Stenosis

Surveillance of the vasculature of a transplanted kidney is the province of the sonographic examiner. Declining renal function, as manifest by diminished urine output and climbing creatinine, may be related to abnormalities in the renal artery or vein. Vascular complications happen in approximately 12 percent of renal transplants and include thrombosis or stenosis of the renal artery or vein, pseudoaneurysms, and arteriovenous fistulas.

Increasing Vascular Resistance Within the Transplant

Diminished diastolic flow in the renal artery suggests heightening of vascular resistance within the graft. Often secondary to rejection, the high resistance pattern of renal artery flow may be secondary to other causes of high vascular resistance, and biopsy of the allograft may be necessary to distinguish them and to dictate therapy.

Renal Artery Thrombosis (Figures 14.8–14.9)

Thrombosis of the renal artery can result in allograft loss and is generally considered an emergency requiring immediate repair. Renal artery thrombosis of a transplant most often occurs in the perioperative period, probably secondary to endothelial damage at the anastomotic site. Clinically, the patient with renal artery thrombosis to the transplanted kidney will have anuria. Patients believed to have acute tubular necrosis (ATN) secondary to long ischemic times during transplantation, especially recipients of cadaveric organs, may have little urine output, so renal artery thrombosis may not be suspected.

Sonographically, the transplanted kidney with no arterial flow may look nearly normal on grayscale imaging. No hydronephrosis would be expected. No arterial flow will be detectable by spectral analysis or color imaging. If infarction of the kidney occurs secondary to unsuspected renal artery thrombosis, signs of infarction may be identified by increasing heterogenicity of the renal cortex.

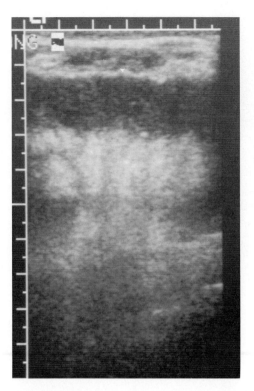

Figure 14.9
Renal artery occlusion secondary to organ torsion: This 18-month-old with prune-belly syndrome (Eagle-Barrett) received a kidney from his mother 4 months prior to the development of an acute abdomen. The kidney surgically placed in the peritoneal cavity in the right lower quadrant was located in the left lower quadrant at the time of the study and had no arterial inflow. Emergent surgery showed the kidney to be twisted on its pedicle, preventing arterial inflow. The patient's lax abdominal musculature was believed to contribute to the event. Transplant nephrectomy was eventually necessary.

Renal Vein Thrombosis (Figure 14.10)

Renal vein thrombosis may lead to transplant dysfunction. A complication that usually occurs in the perioperative period, renal vein thrombosis may also be secondary to propagation of clot into the kidney from thrombus beginning in the deep veins of the lower extremity or pelvis weeks or months after transplant surgery.

Sonographically, the transplanted kidney may be enlarged and edematous, with hyperechoic medullary pyramids. Renal artery flow may be present, but in a high-resistance pattern with little or reversed diastolic flow. Sometimes renal arterial flow may not be obtainable secondary to prolonged high pressure impeding arterial inflow.

Sometimes anticoagulation therapy may be sufficient if the thrombus is limited; in other situations,

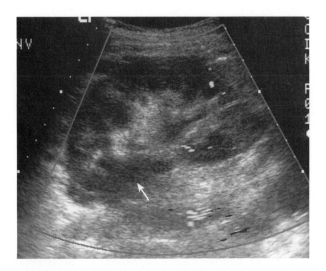

Figure 14.8
Renal artery thrombosis (Plate 25): This patient, 4 days after kidney transplantation and with declining urine output, had no arterial flow to the upper pole of the kidney (*arrow*). Arterial flow was present in the lower pole. Discussion with the surgeon led to the information that two renal arteries had supplied the transplanted organ. The artery to the upper pole was thrombosed.

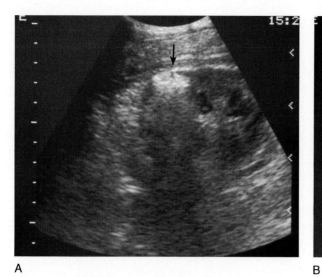

A   B

Figure 14.10

Renal vein thrombosis: (A and B) Air (*arrow*) was identifiable within the allograft in this patient 3 days after renal transplantation. Renal infarction and necrosis was found at surgery. Transplant nephrectomy was performed.

thrombolysis or thrombectomy will be necessary. If renal vein thrombosis is extensive, transplant nephrectomy may be necessary.

Pseudoaneurysm/Arteriovenous Malformation (Figures 14.11–14.12)

A pseudoaneurysm may develop at the arterial anastomosis or may complicate a percutaneous biopsy procedure. A pseudoaneurysm is a cystic collection that will contain an arterial jet at its connection to the artery. Color Doppler may allow recognition of the neck of the pseudoaneurysm and the jet of blood into it.

An arteriovenous fistula is a communication between the renal artery and vein, usually after a biopsy procedure. Arterialization of venous flow and high output flow characterizes such a lesion. Color Doppler is usually helpful in identifying arteriovenous fistulas. Patients with large, functioning dialysis shunts or florid congestive heart failure may have hyperdynamic venous return, which should not be mistaken for a renal transplant arteriovenous fistula.

Renal Artery or Venous Stenosis

Stenosis of the renal artery at the anastomosis may develop months to years after transplantation and can be a cause of climbing creatinine or worsening hypertension. Changes in renal size reflect profound stenosis. Anastomotic vascular stenosis may be recognized by evaluating Doppler waveform changes. Sometimes the anastomotic stricture can be seen by gray scale. More often, characteristic Doppler waveform changes of marked velocity increase at the stenosis and marked turbulence just distal to the stenosis will signal significant stenosis. Angioplasty procedures can be performed in such situations.

RENAL TRANSPLANT COLLECTING SYSTEM DILATATION

Stricture at Ureteral Anastomosis with
    Obstruction
Reflux

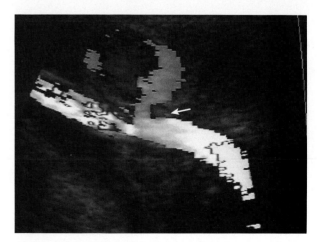

Figure 14.11

Pseudoaneurysm at arterial anastomosis (Plate 26): Turbulent flow within the pseudoaneurysm was easily identified by color Doppler. The pseudoaneurysm neck (*arrow*) was easily seen as well.

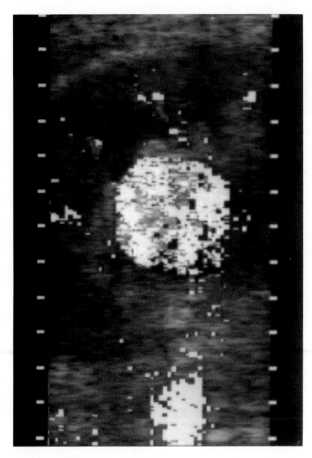

Figure 14.12

Intrarenal pseudoaneurysm (Plate 27): Three weeks after renal transplant biopsy, a large cystic lesion was identified within the lower pole at the site of biopsy. Color Doppler confirmed communication with the arterial tree.

Stricture at Ureteral Anastomosis with Obstruction (Figure 14.13)

Mild fullness of the collecting system of a renal transplant may be present postoperatively related to atony of the system and not necessarily secondary to obstruction. With persistent or worsening calyceal or ureteral dilatation, one must exclude obstruction of the transplanted organ. Sonographic identification of the cause and level of obstruction may be possible. Nuclear medicine studies may be helpful to quantitate the severity of obstruction. Such extrinsic masses as urinomas or lymphoceles can cause obstruction. The ureteral anastomosis is the expected site of obstruction secondary to scarring and fibrosis. In some situations, dilatation and stenting of the stricture are sufficient; in other cases, reimplantation of the ureter is necessary.

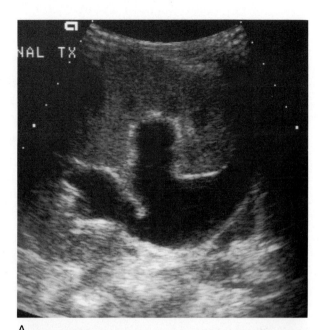

A

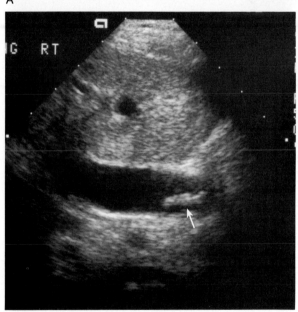

B

Figure 14.13

Moderate hydronephrosis secondary to suture debris in the ureter: (A and B) Debris with suture material as its nidus caused obstruction in this renal transplant recipient (*arrow*).

Reflux

Reflux of urine into the transplanted ureter may cause ureteral dilatation and lead eventually to renal dysfunction. Although dramatic changes in collecting system and ureteral size may be identified at real-time, a cystogram will be necessary to plan effective management of the problem.

BIBLIOGRAPHY

Peritransplant Fluid Collections

Silver TM, Campbell D, Wicks JD, Loiber MI, Surace P, Turcotte J: Peritransplant fluid collections. Radiology 138:145–151, 1981.

Renal Transplant Vascular Complications

Pozniak MA, Dodd GD, Kelcz F: Ultrasonographic evaluation of renal transplantation. Radiol Clin North Am 30:1053–1066, 1992.

Snider JF, Hunter DW, Moradian GP, Castaneda-Zuñiga WR, Letourneau JG: Transplant renal artery stenosis: Evaluation with duplex sonography. Radiology 172:1027–1030, 1989.

Taylor KJW, Morse SS, Rigsby CM, Bia M, Schiff M: Vascular complications in renal allografts: Detection with duplex Doppler ultrasound. Radiology 162:3138, 1987.

BREAST

Breast sonography is used in most imaging centers in conjunction with mammography to determine whether a mass detected on physical examination or mammography is solid or cystic. Initial hopes that breast sonography alone would be an adequate screening test for breast cancer were dashed when (1) it became clear that sonography could not detect malignant microcalcifications, the only sign of cancer in some patients; (2) sonography could not histologically differentiate malignant solid masses from benign solid ones; and (3) it was difficult to identify small deep lesions in large, fatty breasts.

Ideally, the mammogram should be available to the sonographer when a breast ultrasound is performed. By correlating the ultrasound with the mammogram, the sonographer can be assured that any masses seen mammographically have been explained sonographically. The sonographer is at a tremendous disadvantage if the mammogram is not available for review at the time of the breast ultrasound study.

Breast ultrasound is most often performed with a hand-held small-parts transducer, which is similar to the transducer suited to testicular and thyroid studies. A linear array or curvilinear 5–7.5-MHz transducer with a water path is the transducer of choice. This transducer may be attached to a small portable ultrasound machine used only for breast imaging, or simply be one of an array of transducers that are part of the general sonographic equipment. Some breast-imaging centers have dedicated, automated breast ultrasound machines that perform tomographic sonography of the breast. When equipped with high-frequency transducers, automated units can provide diagnostic information similar to that provided by the hand-held transducer. Automated machines usually require more time and space than hand-held units which are limitations to their daily use.

Breast ultrasound is necessary for the well-defined mass seen mammographically that does not have a characteristically benign appearance. The intramammary lymph node with a recognizable fatty hilum does not need sonographic evaluation if all the features of a small, low-density mass with a fatty hilum are recognized mammographically. A breast hamartoma with soft tissue and fatty components can be recognized mammographically, making ultrasound and diagnostic biopsy unnecessary. Other masses that have a mammographically typical appearance that makes ultrasound evaluation unnecessary include lipoma, calcified oil cyst, galactocele, calcified degenerated fibroadenoma, and skin lesions. Ultrasound is also useful for the palpable mass hidden by dense tissue on the mammogram.

The obviously malignant-appearing lesion seen

433

mammographically does not need evaluation with ultrasound. The high-density spiculated mass with malignant-appearing calcifications needs biopsy, not ultrasound.

The worst features of a breast mass must be the ones determining the course of further work-up. The well-defined mass needs ultrasound to determine whether it is cystic or solid; the high-density, ill-defined mass needs biopsy unless there is a history of trauma or surgery to explain the appearance.

WELL-DEFINED BREAST MASS

Cystic Breast Mass
    Simple Breast Cysts
    Complicated Cysts
    Breast Hematoma/Seroma
    Breast Abscess

Cystic Breast Mass

Simple Breast Cysts (Figures 15.1–15.2)
Breast cysts are part of the spectrum of fibrocystic breast disease that reflects the breast's response to its hormonal environment. Fibrocystic changes in the breast include cysts, fibrosis, and adenosis. Cysts are most common in women 35 to 55 years of age and can be stimulated by exogenous hormonal administration such as that given to many postmenopausal women. Breast cysts may be symptomatic, as tender, palpable masses, or may be incidentally detected during breast imaging.

Mammographically, the breast cyst is an oval or round, well-defined, medium-density mass that is oriented toward the nipple and that sometimes has a halo. The size of the mass may range from less than a centimeter to many centimeters.

The breast sonographer must have strict criteria for the diagnosis of a simple breast cyst. The simple breast cyst is usually well defined, having *no*

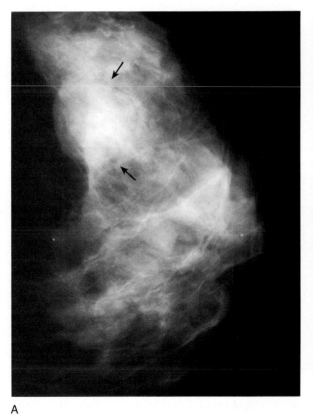

A

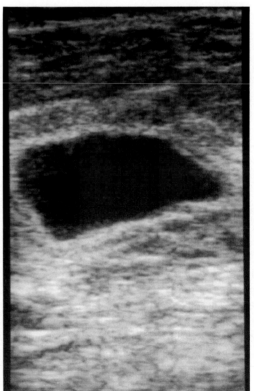

B

Figure 15.1
Breast cyst: (A) In this 60-year-old woman receiving estrogen replacement therapy, a 3-cm, fairly well-defined mass (*arrows*) was identified mammographically. (B) Sonography demonstrated a simple cyst.

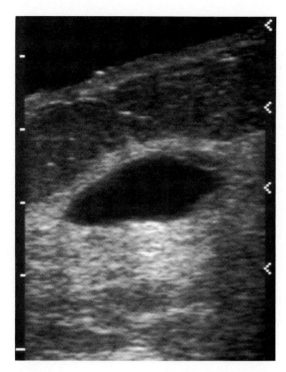

Figure 15.2
Breast cyst: This woman with a recent mammogram had noted the new onset of a palpable lesion in the right breast. Ultrasound showed it to be a cyst. Note acoustical enhancement posterior to the mass.

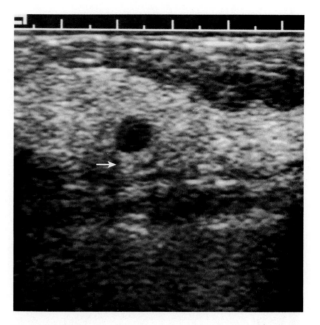

Figure 15.3
Complicated breast cyst: This 40-year-old woman had developed a small, well-defined nodule in the upper outer quadrant since her previous mammogram. Ultrasound showed a hypoechoic lesion with low-level internal echoes. Posterior acoustical enhancement was prominent (*arrow*). Percutaneous aspiration proved the mass to be a hemorrhagic cyst.

internal echoes, with posterior acoustic enhancement. Accurate diagnosis of breast cysts requires appropriate instrumentation and technique. Recognition that a mass is a simple cyst makes further evaluation or biopsy unnecessary. The patient with a symptomatic breast cyst may request aspiration for comfort.

Complicated Cysts (Figure 15.3)   A breast cyst that has had some internal hemorrhage may no longer fulfill the sonographic features of a simple cyst. Internal echoes, septations, and nodules of clotted blood can be disturbing to the examiner. Diffuse low-level echoes may cause the cystic mass to be misinterpreted as solid. Aspiration of the complicated cyst under sonographic or mammographic guidance may be accompanied by instillation of air into the mass so that the walls can be evaluated mammographically. Cytologic evaluation of cyst fluid is necessary only when the fluid is bloody. For small (<1 cm) complicated cystic lesions, follow-up ultrasound may show that the lesion has disappeared, making further evaluation or work-up unnecessary.

Breast Hematoma/Seroma (Figure 15.4)   A hematoma of the breast may develop after trauma to the breast. The most common cause of a breast hematoma is surgery on the breast, but blunt trauma, such as hitting the steering wheel in a motor vehicle accident, may result in accumulation of blood in the breast. Patients receiving anticoagulation therapy may have spontaneous hemorrhage in the breast with trivial or no trauma.

Breast hematomas may result in diffuse skin thickening and increased density of the breast parenchyma mammographically. This appearance reflects the dissection of blood through the breast tissue. Sometimes breast hematomas are discrete masses, often with heterogeneous echogenicity. With time the uncomplicated breast hematoma becomes a seroma, appearing more cystic, often septated sonographically. A hematoma may take weeks to resolve.

Breast Abscess (Figure 15.5)   Infections of the breast generally occur in the postpartum period in lactating women or in the woman who has had trauma or surgery to the breast. The spontaneous

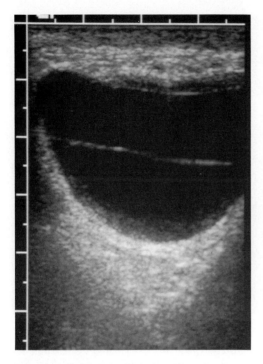

Figure 15.4
Seroma: A multilocular seroma was present in this patient after breast surgery.

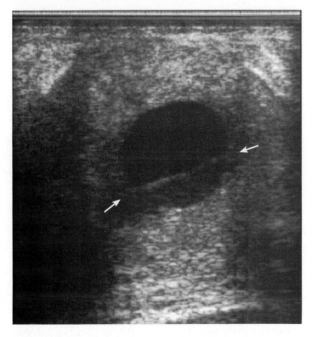

Figure 15.5
Abscess: This young girl had exquisite pain and tenderness and was not able to tolerate mammographic compression or even an adequate physical examination. Ultrasound showed a cystic lesion with a fluid-debris level (*arrows*). Grossly purulent material was drained at surgery.

development of a breast abscess in a woman who does not have any predisposing risk factors must raise some doubt of the diagnosis of infection. Inflammatory breast carcinoma can be indistinguishable from mastitis and breast abscess clinically.

Sonographically, a breast abscess may be a hypoechoic or complicated cystic mass with internal debris, fluid-debris levels, septations, and sometimes air. Aspiration and drainage can be performed under sonographic guidance. Ultrasound offers a good way to study these patients, who often cannot tolerate the compression necessary for mammography. Ultrasound may allow the identification of focal drainable collections that cannot be recognized on clinical examination.

Solid-Appearing Breast Mass

Fibroadenoma
Breast Abscess
Carcinoma
    Infiltrating Ductal
    Mucinous
    Medullary
    Other Neoplasms
    Metastatic Disease

VARIANT

Rib

Fibroadenoma (Figure 15.6) The fibroadenoma is the most common benign neoplasm of the breast. Its natural history is that it appears in girls or young women and may grow with hormonal stimulation and pregnancy. In the postmenopausal woman, the fibroadenoma undergoes involution and hyalination. Fibroadenomas may develop coarse, popcorn-type calcifications that can be identified mammographically as characteristic.

Sonographically, the fibroadenoma that has not developed associated macrocalcifications will appear as a solid, well-defined breast mass. The mass may be of homogeneously low-level echoes or of heterogeneous echogenicity secondary to fibrosis within the mass. Some homogeneous fibroadenomas have posterior acoustical enhancement.

The sonographic features of a well-defined solid breast mass are not specific for a fibroadenoma, and biopsy may be necessary to distinguish this benign solid mass from a malignant solid mass.

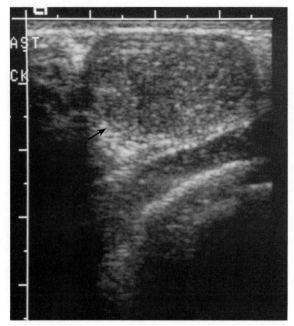

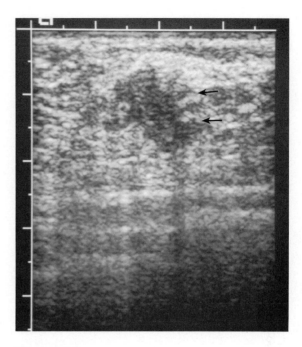

Figure 15.6

Fibroadenoma: This 19-year-old with a palpable breast mass had extremely dense breast mammographically. No calcifications were present. Sonographic evaluation showed the mass (*arrow*) to be solid, measuring 3 cm. A fibroadenoma was removed at surgery.

Breast Abscess   A breast abscess may be solid-appearing to sonographic evaluation. If the diagnosis of breast abscess is considered, aspiration may be necessary to differentiate it from a solid hypoechoic carcinoma.

Carcinoma

Infiltrating Ductal Carcinoma (Figures 15.7–15.10)

The most common invasive breast carcinoma is infiltrating ductal carcinoma, representing at least 75 percent of breast carcinoma. In most women, the tumor is a firm, spiculated, poorly circumscribed mass that may invade the skin, fascia, or muscle. About 6 percent of infiltrating ductal carcinomas are well-defined masses, indistinguishable sonographically from other causes of well-defined solid breast masses. The well-defined mass seen mammographically needs ultrasound evaluation to ascertain its cystic or solid character. Small solid nodules, less than 8 mm in greatest dimension, are sometimes followed on serial mammograms to assess for growth or resolution rather than being subjected to immediate biopsy. Further evaluation with biopsy is necessary to determine the histology of solid masses, especially when they are larger than 8 mm in diameter or have developed since a prior mammogram.

Figure 15.7

Infiltrating ductal carcinoma: This 38-year-old pregnant woman had noted the development of a palpable breast mass. Initial mammogram showed clustered microcalcifications in the area of palpable abnormality and extremely dense breasts, in keeping with the patient's pregnancy. Ultrasound of the palpable abnormality showed a solid mass with shadowing calcifications (*arrows*). Biopsy confirmed the presence of a carcinoma of the breast.

Mucinous Carcinoma

An unusual tumor found most often in postmenopausal women, mucinous carcinoma is usually well circumscribed with currant jelly–like material within it. Microscopically, these masses are made up of a few cells floating in a sea of mucin. If they are less than 3 cm, pure mucinous carcinomas have a 2–4 percent incidence of nodal metastases, and thus an excellent prognosis. Sonographically, these masses are well-defined solid lesions.

Medullary Carcinoma

Particularly common in Japanese women and women younger than 50 years of age, medullary carcinoma represents 2.5 percent of invasive breast cancers. It is frequently a well-circumscribed mass that may be indistinguishable from a fibroadenoma. Medullary carcinoma is thought to be a slow-growing lesion with a better prognosis than the typical invasive breast cancer. Sonographically, medullary carcinoma is usually a well-defined, homogeneously solid lesion.

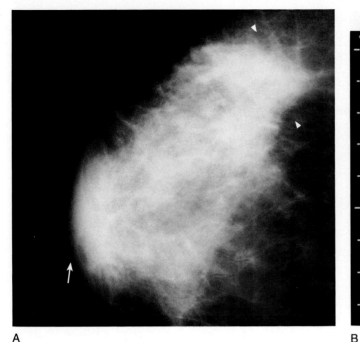

A   B

Figure 15.8

Infiltrating ductal carcinoma: (A) This young woman with a history of trivial trauma to the breast developed breast pain and swelling. Treatment with antibiotics was not helpful. A mammogram showed a high-density mass (*arrowheads*) with thickening of the skin (*arrow*) and architectural distortion. Differential possibilities were breast abscess or inflammatory breast carcinoma. (B) Sonography showed a hypoechoic solid-appearing mass. Biopsy confirmed an aggressive infiltrating ductal carcinoma.

Other Neoplasms

Other forms of invasive breast carcinoma are encountered and include invasive lobular carcinoma, tubular, papillary, and carcinoid tumors. These may present as well-circumscribed masses. Of all well-circumscribed primary breast cancers, infiltrating ductal carcinoma is the most common.

Adenoid cystic carcinoma, cystosarcoma phylloides, and angiosarcoma are unusual tumors of the breast that also may be well circumscribed and solid sonographically. The breast is a modified sweat gland, explaining the origin of the adenoid cystic carcinoma.

Cystosarcoma phylloides of the breast is rare. Approximately 80 percent of such lesions are benign, but because the lesion has projections into the breast, it may recur locally. Sonographically, this

mass may be indistinguishable from a large fibro-adenoma.

Metastatic Disease (Figure 15.11)

Metastatic disease to the breast from melanoma, lung, the other breast, lymphoma, and sarcoma can present as a well-defined solid nodule. Usually, the primary tumor is known. Multiple nodules and diffuse skin infiltration are less commonly encountered manifestations of metastatic disease to the breast.

VARIANT

Rib (Figure 15.12)

To the unfamiliar, the cross section of a rib can be misinterpreted as a breast mass. Scanning in various planes through a rib will usually allow it to be recognized.

Emphasis Points

Well-defined masses seen mammographically need ultrasound to distinguish whether they are solid or cystic. Simple cysts may need no further work-up. Solid masses may be either benign or malignant. Complicated cysts may need aspiration to prove their benign nature.

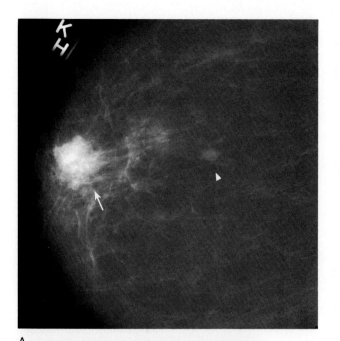

A

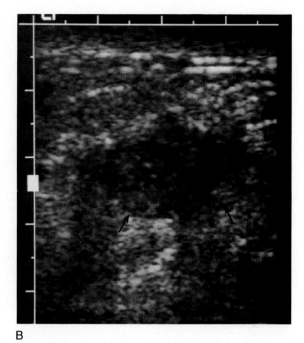

B

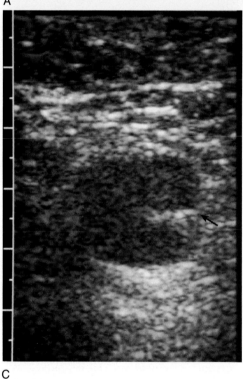

C

Figure 15.9

Infiltrating ductal carcinoma: (A) This 63-year-old who presented for screening mammography had a fairly well-defined high-density mass behind the nipple (*arrow*) with a second suspicious focus in the mid-breast (*arrowhead*). (B) Ultrasound demonstrated a well-defined solid mass and (C) enlarged lymph nodes in the axilla. Note echogenic hila of node (*arrow*). Histologically, multicentric breast carcinoma with positive lymph nodes was present.

If a mass seen mammographically is not identified sonographically, one must conclude that the mass is solid rather than that the mass does not exist.

Although mucinous and medullary carcinomas are typically well-defined solid breast cancers, infiltrating ductal carcinoma is the most common primary neoplasm of the breast that presents as a well-defined solid mass, because it is so much more common than the more unusual cell types.

A well-defined solid mass may be a benign fibroadenoma, but it may also be a malignant mass. Fine-needle aspiration, core biopsy, or excisional biopsy can distinguish malignant from benign masses.

Breast abscess and inflammatory breast carcinoma may have identical clinical and mammographic findings. Quick use of aspiration biopsy may expedite appropriate patient care.

Small (< 8 mm) solid or solid-appearing breast nodules are sometimes followed on serial mammograms and ultrasounds to assess for resolution or interval growth rather than immediate biopsy. If growth occurs, biopsy will be recommended.

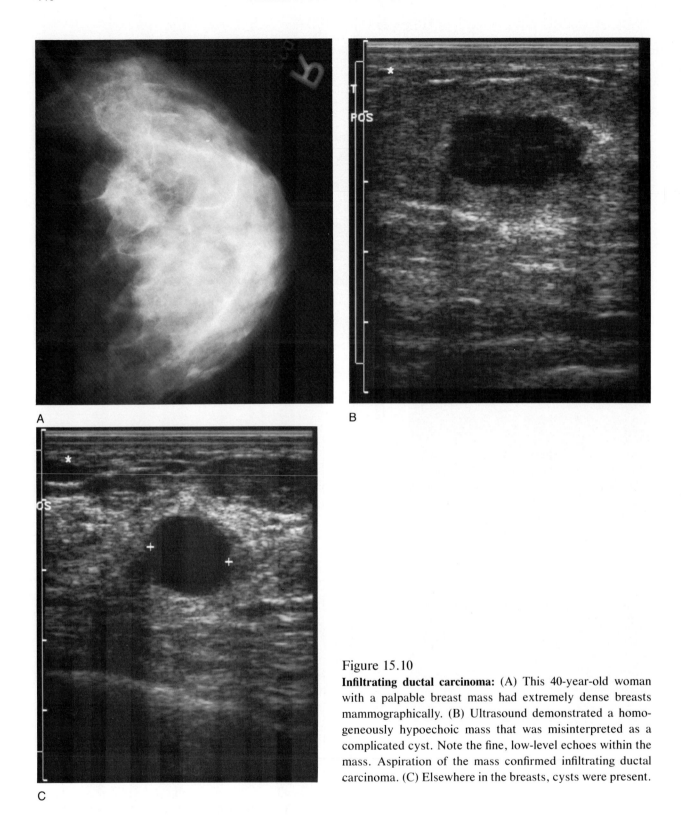

A

B

C

Figure 15.10

Infiltrating ductal carcinoma: (A) This 40-year-old woman with a palpable breast mass had extremely dense breasts mammographically. (B) Ultrasound demonstrated a homogeneously hypoechoic mass that was misinterpreted as a complicated cyst. Note the fine, low-level echoes within the mass. Aspiration of the mass confirmed infiltrating ductal carcinoma. (C) Elsewhere in the breasts, cysts were present.

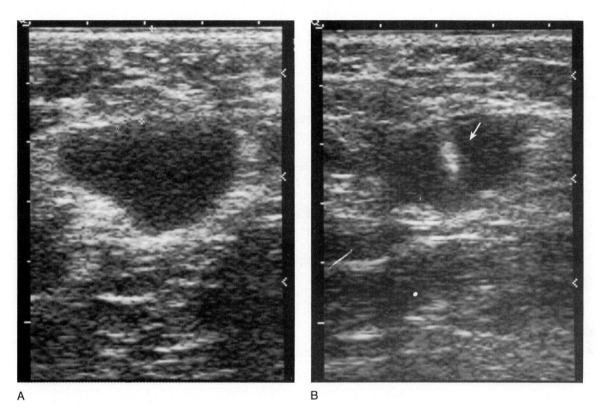

A   B

Figure 15.11
Non-Hodgkin lymphoma: (A) This middle-aged woman
with generalized adenopathy and a palpable breast mass
underwent sonographic evaluation that showed a well-
defined homogeneous hypoechoic mass. (B) Core biopsy
of the mass diagnosed a B-cell lymphoma. The echogenic
needle tip can be seen within the mass (*arrow*).

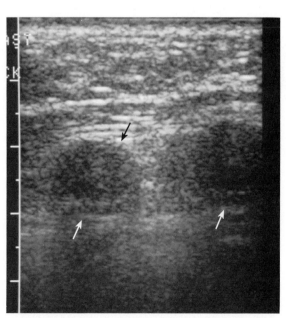

Figure 15.12
Rib: Cross section of a normal rib. The rib could be
interpreted as a breast mass by the uninitiated.

C

BIBLIOGRAPHY

Well-Defined Breast Mass

Adler DD: Ultrasound of benign breast conditions. Semin Ultrasound CT, MR 10:106–118, 1989.

Bassett LW, Kimme-Smith C: Breast sonography. AJR 156:449–455, 1991.

Feig SA: The role of ultrasound in a breast imaging center. Semin Ultrasound, CT, MR 10:90–105, 1989.

Harper AP, Kelly-Fry E, Noe JS, et al: Ultrasound in the evaluation of solid breast masses. Radiology 146:731–736, 1983.

Hilton SV, Leopold GR, Olson KL, Wilson SA: Real-time breast sonography: application in 300 consecutive patients. AJR 147:479–486, 1986.

Jackson VP: The role of US in breast imaging. Radiology 177:305–311, 1990.

Jackson VP, Rothschild PA, Kreipke DL, et al: The spectrum of sonographic findings of fibroadenoma of the breast. Invest Radiol 21:31–40, 1986.

Sickles EA, Filly RA, Callen PW: Benign breast lesions: Ultrasound detection and diagnosis. Radiology 151:467–470, 1984.

Venta LA, Didiak CM, Salomon CG, Hisak ME: Sonographic evaluation of the breast. RadioGraphics 14:29–50, 1994.

NECK

PATTERNS

Cystic Neck Mass Outside the Thyroid
Solid Neck Mass Outside the Thyroid
Solid Thyroid Nodule
Cystic Thyroid Nodule
Diffuse Thyroid Enlargement and
   Inhomogeneity

Sonography is an appropriate first test for the palpable neck mass. In many cases, ultrasound will allow the origin of the mass to be determined, specifically whether or not the mass has arisen from the thyroid. Masses originating outside the thyroid include cervical lymphadenopathy, thyroglossal duct cyst, and cystic hygroma.

CYSTIC NECK MASS OUTSIDE THE THYROID

Necrotic Lymphadenopathy
Aneurysm
Seroma

CHILDHOOD

Lymphadenitis
Thyroglossal Duct Cyst
Cystic Hygroma
Branchial Cleft Cyst

Sonography can not only help determine the organ of origin of a neck mass, but can clarify its internal characteristics. Cystic neck masses may be simple and fluid-filled or have septations and debris.

Necrotic Lymphadenopathy

Enlargement of a single or multiple lymph nodes may be the cause of a palpable neck mass that is outside the thyroid gland.

Lymphadenopathy often will be secondary to neoplastic disease or will have a reactive or suppurative etiology. Rapidly growing, necrotic nodes will appear cystic. Aspiration of a lymph node filled with squamous cell carcinoma yields necrotic material that can be misinterpreted as purulent, infected material until microscopic analysis is undertaken. Neoplastic lymphadenopathy may be secondary to a regional (head and neck) or more distant primary.

Aneurysm (Figure 16.1)

Tortuosity or dilatation of the subclavian or carotid artery can result in a prominent mass of the neck. Usually, the pulsatile nature of the mass with obvious Doppler flow allows its arterial origin to be confirmed.

Seroma

A cystic, multiseptate collection may develop in the neck at a site of previous surgery or trauma. Usu-

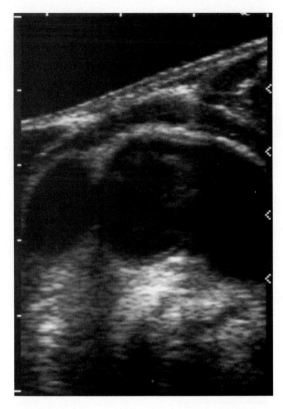

Figure 16.1

Ectasia of the subclavian artery: An obviously pulsatile mass in the right neck proved to be a tortuous subclavian artery. Arterial flow was present by Doppler.

ally the clinical history facilitates recognition of the cause of the extrathyroidal cystic seroma.

CHILDHOOD
Lymphadenitis

Lymph nodes that are enlarged and reactive or frankly suppurative secondary to regional infection may become tender and can be indistinguishable from neoplastic lymphadenopathy. If the patient clinically has pain, fever, and signs of infection, antibiotics may be given to treat the symptomatically enlarged lymph nodes, making lymph node aspiration unnecessary. Lymph node drainage may be necessary if abscess formation occurs or if the diagnosis is uncertain.

Lymphadenitis in children is fairly common and usually reflects regional infection, such as sore throat or ear infections, although systemic disease, such as cat scratch fever, chronic granulomatous disease of childhood, tuberculosis, and AIDS lymphadenopathy, can result in palpable nodes.

Sonographically, the lymphadenopathy of infection is similar to enlarged neoplastic nodes. Hypoechoic multilobulated nodal masses may be identified. Areas of suppuration will be nearly cystic, although debris and internal echoes would be expected in necrotic infected nodes. Gram stain and culture, as well as fungal or tuberculous cultures, may be necessary to determine the offending agent in lymphadenitis.

Thyroglossal Duct Cyst (Figure 16.2)

A thyroglossal duct cyst is the embryologic remnant resulting from the descent of the thyroid gland from the base of the tongue to its final position in the neck. The thyroglossal duct cyst is usually a midline cystic mass that is in continuity with the thyroid gland at the isthmus. The midline location is critical in allowing the thyroglossal duct to be recognized. This mass may be tender and is usually easily palpable. Inflammation and hemorrhage into the mass frequently complicate the structure and result in low-level echoes, internal debris, and septations seen sonographically.

Cystic Hygroma (Figure 16.3)

A cystic hygroma or lymphangioma may present in the pediatric patient with neck or facial swelling. The sonographic appearance of a cystic hygroma is

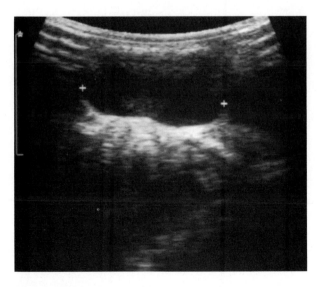

Figure 16.2

Thyroglossal duct cyst: This young child presented with a midline neck mass that was intermittently tender. The midline cystic mass extended to the thyroid isthmus.

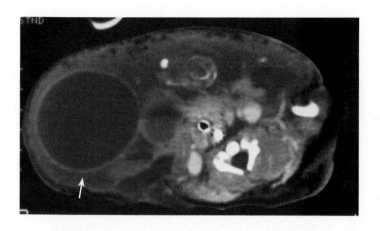

Figure 16.3
Cystic hygroma: A multiloculated cystic mass was present in this newborn with a chromosomal abnormality. The infant died shortly after delivery.

that of a multiseptate mass with cystic components as well as solid areas.

Cystic hygromas detected in the fetus can be associated with chromosomal or syndromal abnormalities and often predict a grave prognosis for the affected fetus. In the pediatric patient, the cystic hygroma is more of a cosmetic problem. Although the mass may be removed surgically, cystic hygromas frequently recur. Imaging of the mediastinum is warranted in the child with a cystic hygroma of the neck to determine whether or not the mass extends into the chest. A nonmalignant lesion, the cystic hygroma has multiple interstices that can extend into the tissue planes of the neck and chest.

Branchial Cleft Cyst

Persistance of the embryonic branchial clefts may result in the development of a cystic or complicated cystic lesion from the tonsillar region to the supraclavicular area. Most arise from remnants of the second branchial cleft and are located in the neck anterior to the sternocleidomastoid muscle. The location of the mass in the upper and lateral neck may allow the branchial cleft cyst to be distinguished from other neck masses.

Solid lesions arising in the soft tissues of the neck unrelated to the thyroid may also be evaluated by sonography.

SOLID NECK MASS OUTSIDE THE THYROID

Lymphadenopathy
Parathyroid Enlargement
Hematoma
Venous Thrombosis

Lymphadenopathy (Figures 16.4–16.7)

Lymphadenopathy related to infections or neoplastic disease is often solid. Neoplastic lymphadenopathy may be secondary to a local primary tumor with regional lymph node involvement. In the young woman, lymphadenopathy in the neck may be secondary to an unsuspected thyroid carcinoma,

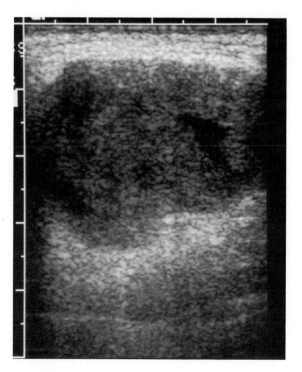

Figure 16.4
Metastatic squamous cell carcinoma: A large, palpable mass in the neck was evaluated by ultrasound and found to be a solid, featureless mass. Aspiration yielded squamous cell carcinoma presumed metastatic from the upper airway.

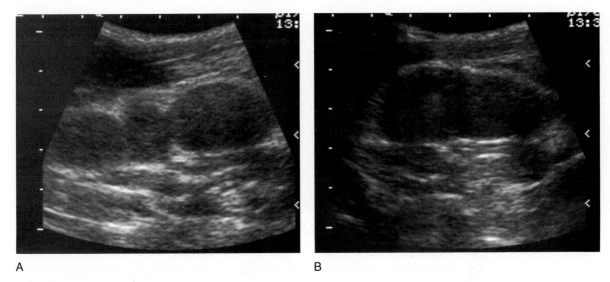

A   B

Figure 16.5
Lymphadenopathy secondary to Hodgkin disease: A chain
of enlarged lymph nodes was visualized in the lateral neck
in this 22-year-old man. Chest films showed superior mediastinal adenopathy. Excisional biopsy revealed Hodgkin disease.

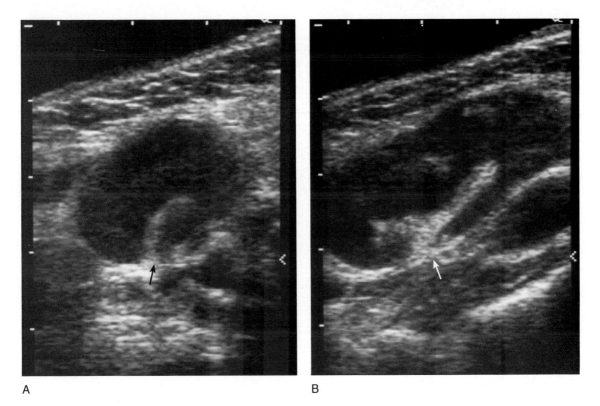

A   B

Figure 16.6
Lymphadenopathy secondary to Hodgkin disease: This 18-
year-old pregnant woman had noted a painless neck mass
for 3 weeks. Large, hypoechoic lymph nodes with identifiable fatty hila (*arrows*) were seen. Biopsy confirmed
Hodgkin disease.

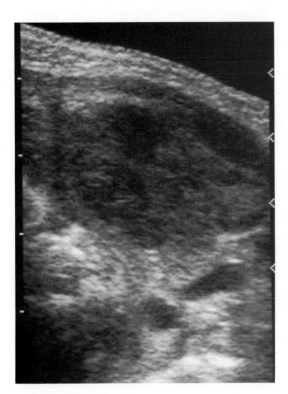

Figure 16.7
Lymphadenitis: This 4-year-old developed neck pain and a palpable mass. This mass resolved with antibiotic therapy.

whereas in the older man with a history of smoking, squamous cell carcinoma arising in the mouth, throat, or sinuses may have regional lymph node involvement in the neck. More distant primary sites, such as the lung, stomach, cervix, breast, and testis, can result in lymphadenopathy in the neck.

Diffuse involvement of multiple lymph nodes is likely in a generalized process such as lymphoma. The young adult with enlargement of multiple lymph nodes in the neck may have either Hodgkin or non-Hodgkin lymphoma. Lymph node biopsy can clarify the diagnosis. A significant volume of tissue is necessary at the time of biopsy for the marker studies necessary to diagnose lymphoma. Chest x-ray or CT scanning will be employed to assess whether the disease has extended into the chest. Once the diagnosis has been made, staging will include imaging of the chest, abdomen, and pelvis.

Sonographically, the lymphadenopathy of neoplastic disease appears as a single or multilobulated mass in the neck. Enlarged neoplastic nodes frequently have a chainlike appearance.

Sometimes the fatty hilum of lymph nodes can be identified as an echogenic center. This confirms that the mass identified is of lymphoid origin.

Parathyroid Enlargement (Figures 16.8–16.9)

Purposeful investigation of the parathyroid glands is usually undertaken when the patient has chemical evidence of hyperparathyroidism with elevated serum calcium levels and inappropriately elevated parathormone levels.

Evaluation of the parathyroid glands requires a high-frequency transducer (7.5–10 MHz), although in patients with a short, thick neck, a 5-MHz transducer may be necessary. The patient's neck should be hyperextended. This can be facilitated by placing a support between the scapulae. Most patients have four parathyroid glands, two located near the superior poles of the thyroid and the others located near the inferior aspect of the thyroid. The normal parathyroid gland is small, measuring approximately 5 × 3 × 1 mm.

Most parathyroid adenomas are homogeneously hypoechoic relative to the thyroid and oval when identified sonographically. The homogeneous nature of the lesion is secondary to the uniformity and hypercellular nature of the adenoma. Calcifications and areas of cystic necrosis are unusual.

Involvement of multiple parathyroid glands may be secondary to hyperplasia or multiple adenomas. Hyperplasia is more common than multiple

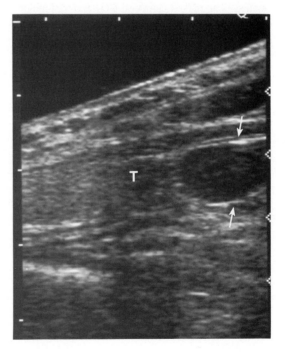

Figure 16.8
Parathyroid adenoma: In this patient with clinical hyperparathyroidism, a 16-mm adenoma (*arrows*) was identified at the lower pole of the left lobe of the thyroid (T). The adenoma is well-circumscribed and homogeneously hypoechoic.

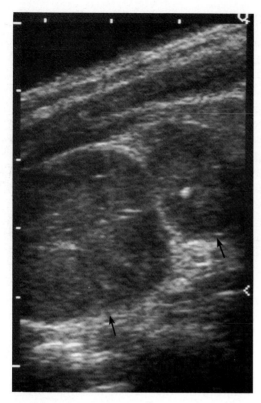

Figure 16.9

Parathyroid adenomas: A large, palpable parathyroid adenoma was demonstrated sonographically with a nearby smaller mass. The masses (*arrows*) were well defined and homogeneous in echogenicity. The patient had symptoms of hyperparathyroidism.

adenomas. Patients with multiple endocrine neoplasia I (MEN I) have multiple gland enlargement in more than 90 percent of cases secondary to parathyroid hyperplasia.

Primary hyperparathyroidism is rarely caused by parathyroid carcinoma. Usually larger and more heterogeneous sonographically than an adenoma, parathyroid carcinoma is most often associated with a very high serum calcium level. The tumor may be invasive and metastatic.

The presence of multinodular or diffuse thyroid enlargement may make identification of the parathyroids difficult. To the novice, the esophagus can be mistaken for a parathyroid gland. Having the patient swallow will usually allow the esophagus to be recognized, since air or fluid will usually be seen within its lumen.

Hematoma

Acute hematoma of the sternocleidomastoid muscle may be related to trauma, blunt or surgical, or an-

ticoagulation therapy. Often clinically tender, the hematoma does not necessarily result in a discrete mass sonographically, since the hemorrhage can infiltrate the muscle planes. The muscle may be acutely enlarged with hemorrhage. Cystic regions may develop as the hematoma ages.

In babies after difficult or forceps delivery, fibromatosis collis may present either as diffuse enlargement of the sternocleidomastoid muscle or as a well-defined mass within the muscle. The condition usually regresses within months with conservative therapy.

Venous Thrombosis (Figure 16.10)

Acute thrombosis of the jugular or subclavian veins may cause a palpable neck swelling. Thrombosis is often secondary to the presence of a central venous access line that acts as a foreign body and possible initiating site for thrombus. Other causes of neck and upper-extremity venous thrombosis include hypercoagulable states and central compressive lesions that may restrict venous drainage, such as a lung carcinoma, causing superior vena caval obstruction.

Examination of the venous structures of the neck is easily performed using a 7.5-MHz transducer. The normal jugular vein is often smaller on the left than on the right and shows changes in size with respiratory variation. The vessel is freely compressible normally and, in fact, may be completely coapted with minimal pressure on the neck. The subclavian vein behind the clavicle and to the axilla should be examined. Since compression of the subclavian vein is generally not possible because of its position behind the clavicle, reliance on gray-scale imaging, color flow Doppler, respiratory cycle collapsibility, and spectral analysis is necessary to assess whether a thrombus is present.

The acutely thrombosed jugular vein will be engorged, filled with material, and noncompressible. The clot itself may be hypoechoic, nearly cystic in appearance, or echogenic, depending upon the proportions of its constituents.

SOLID THYROID NODULE

Colloid Nodule
Follicular Adenoma
Thyroid Carcinoma
    Papillary Carcinoma
    Follicular Carcinoma
    Medullary Carcinoma

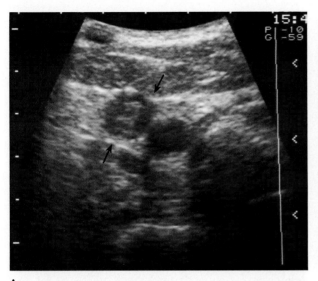

A

B

Figure 16.10

Septic thrombosis of the jugular vein: (A and B) This patient presented with neck pain and swelling and was difficult to evaluate. Ultrasound demonstrated a thrombosed, noncompressible jugular vein (*arrows*). Superimposed infection was suspected.

Anaplastic Carcinoma
Lymphoma
Intrathyroidal Parathyroid Adenoma

Thyroid masses may be adenoma, carcinoma, or cysts. Sonography allows the thyroid mass to be characterized as either a solid or cystic lesion and can discern whether the mass is solitary or one of multiple lesions.

The thyroid is a frequent site for nodules, and most of the time the nodule has a benign etiology. Studies have shown that 4 to 7 percent of patients have palpable thyroid nodules, with women being more often affected than men. Radiation exposure increases the incidence of thyroid nodularity by 20–30 percent.

Incidentally detected, nonpalpable thyroid nodules can be problematic. Ultrasound studies have revealed that approximately 35 to 41 percent of patients have sonographically identifiable thyroid nodules without clinical evidence of disease. Autopsy studies in patients with clinically normal thyroid glands revealed that 49.5 percent had visible nodules.

Only a small minority of patients with thyroid nodules have thyroid carcinoma, since the annual incidence of detected thyroid carcinoma is five per 100,000 persons. Since 90 percent of thyroid carcinoma is papillary carcinoma, which has an excellent prognosis, work-up of the nonpalpable, incidentally detected thyroid nodule is probably impractical beyond routine neck palpation or serial ultrasound studies to assess for growth.

Colloid Nodule (Figures 16.11–16.12)

Most palpable benign thyroid nodules are adenomatous or colloid nodules. Rather than neoplastic masses, colloid nodules are secondary to hyperplasia and involution of the stimulated thyroid tissue. Many colloid nodules are hypoechoic. In fact, most hypoechoic thyroid nodules are benign because most are colloid nodules. Hyperechoic thyroid masses are also often adenomatous. Coarse, peripheral calcifications, when present, are a fairly reliable sign of benignity. A well-defined halo around a thyroid nodule is more commonly seen with benign lesions than with malignant ones, but this is not a specific sign that a mass is benign. Foci of hemorrhage and necrosis are common, resulting in a mass with cystic components. In fact, the recognition of cystic components in a thyroid nodule often suggests its benign origin.

Follicular Adenoma (Figures 16.13–16.16)

Follicular adenoma is a benign thyroid neoplasm indistinguishable sonographically from some malignant thyroid masses, specifically follicular carcinoma. The follicular adenoma is often a well-defined, encapsulated, solid mass of the thyroid.

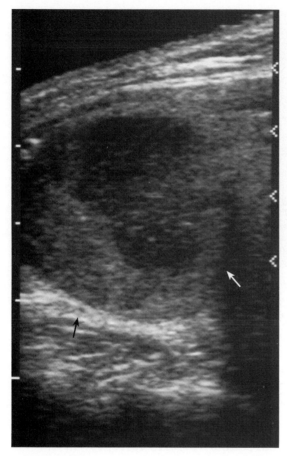

Figure 16.11
Colloid nodule: A well-defined 3 × 2-cm hypoechoic mass was the only focal abnormality in an otherwise homogeneous thyroid gland. Aspiration of the nodule yielded abundant colloid material and macrophages.

Thyroid Carcinoma

The type of thyroid cancer will often explain its pattern of spread and sonographic appearance.

Follicular cells, the most numerous cell type of the thyroid, are the cells of origin for 90 percent of thyroid carcinoma. Both papillary and follicular thyroid carcinoma arise from follicular cells. Some tumors are mixed with papillary and follicular elements.

Papillary Carcinoma (Figures 16.17–16.18)   Papillary carcinoma is especially prevalent in young patients, especially women. Papillary carcinoma, the most common of all thyroid carcinomas, may be multifocal and nonencapsulated. The tumor typically invades lymphatics and metastasizes to local lymph nodes. Cervical lymphadenopathy may be the presenting complaint in a patient without a palpable thyroid abnormality.

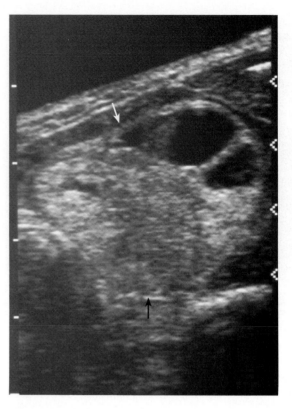

Figure 16.12
Colloid nodule: This palpable mass was of heterogeneous echogenicity with cystic components. This mass was the only abnormality of the gland. It was surgically excised.

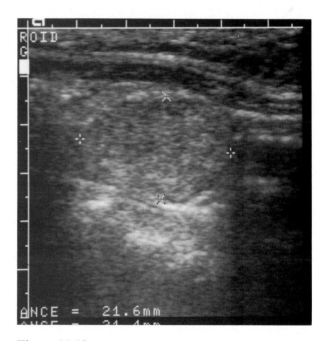

Figure 16.13
Follicular adenoma: A well-defined, nearly isoechoic mass was palpable in the right lobe of the thyroid. Surgical excision was performed.

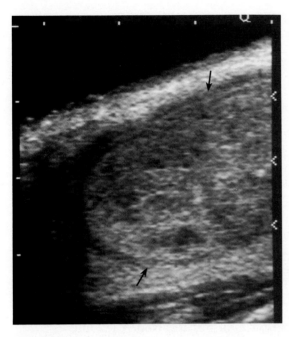

Figure 16.14

Adenoma: A well-defined solitary thyroid mass was aspirated. Abundant follicular cells were present in the aspirate. At surgery, the follicular adenoma shelled out easily.

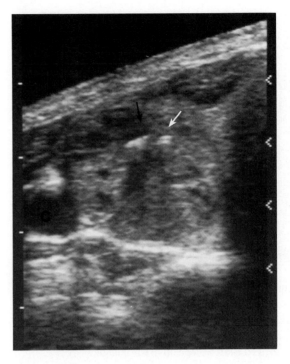

Figure 16.16

Adenoma: Calcifications (*arrows*) and heterogeneous echogenicity characterize this thyroid nodule (C = carotid.).

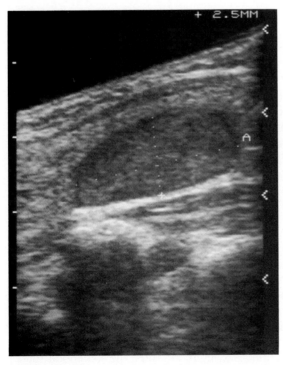

Figure 16.15

Adenoma: A well-defined hypoechoic mass proved to be a benign adenoma.

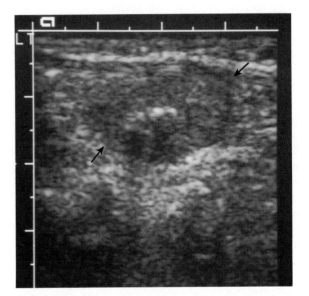

Figure 16.17

Papillary thyroid carcinoma: This 54-year-old woman had noted a neck abnormality for almost 1 year and underwent a thyroid ultrasound, which showed a solitary thyroid nodule and a single small extra-thyroid mass. Aspiration of the thyroid mass confirmed papillary carcinoma (*arrows*). Metastases to lymph nodes were present at surgery.

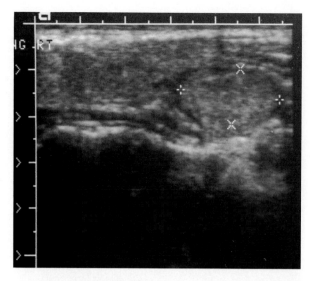

Figure 16.18
Mixed follicular and papillary carcinoma: This young woman with a previous history of neck irradiation had a 1.5-cm nodule off the lower pole of the right lobe of the thyroid. Excision was positive for malignancy.

Lymph node metastases at the time of presentation do not adversely affect the long-term prognosis of the patient. Papillary carcinoma does act more aggressively in the older patient. Radiation to the thyroid is clearly a risk factor in the development of papillary carcinoma.

Sonographically, papillary carcinomas of the thyroid are often hypoechoic solid masses, sometimes with cystic components. Often papillary carcinomas may be indistinguishable from benign nodules of the thyroid. Fine, psammonatous calcifications may be present in papillary tumors.

Follicular Carcinoma   Follicular carcinoma is a well-differentiated carcinoma that is frequently encapsulated and indistinguishable sonographically from the benign follicular adenoma. Microscopically, invasion into veins and metastases to bone or lung are more common than invasion into regional lymph nodes. Again, older patients have a worse prognosis. Radiation has a less important role in the etiology of follicular carcinoma than papillary tumors. Follicular carcinomas arise more frequently in iodine-deficient areas and may be related to elevated levels of thyroid stimulating hormone (TSH).

Medullary Carcinoma   Medullary carcinomas arise from the parafollicular cells of the thyroid and represent only about 5–10 percent of all thyroid malignancies. Often genetically mediated, medullary carcinoma is associated with the multiple endocri-

nopathy syndrome (MEN II). Involvement of regional lymph nodes is common.

Sonographically, medullary carcinomas may have brightly echogenic foci within a solid mass, which may have associated shadowing. Fibrosis and calcification cause these findings.

Anaplastic Carcinoma   Anaplastic thyroid carcinoma is a very aggressive, usually lethal carcinoma of the elderly that presents with a rapidly enlarging mass. Often inoperable at presentation, anaplastic carcinoma invades nearby structures.

Lymphoma   Lymphoma of the thyroid usually affects the elderly patient. Thyroiditis that has chronically plagued the gland may be a factor leading to the development of lymphoma.

Intrathyroidal Parathyroid Adenoma

Parathyroid adenomas within the substance of the thyroid gland are unusual but may be the cause of a failed neck exploration for hyperparathyroidism. Sonographically, the parathyroid located within the thyroid lobe is generally hypoechoic relative to the surrounding thyroid parenchyma, making it indistinguishable from other causes of thyroid nodules.

Emphasis Points

Small, nonpalpable solid nodules of the thyroid are often picked up as incidental findings during sonographic evaluations. Such small lesions have a low likelihood of malignancy in most patients, and performing serial sonograms to assure stability is probably the most prudent course of action.

A solitary, solid thyroid nodule that is palpable or of appreciable size may warrant further evaluation. In our hands, fine-needle aspiration of dominant thyroid nodules has been very helpful in diagnosing neoplasm or determining that the mass is a colloid or adenomatous nodule. A nodule which has been identified by nuclear medicine imaging to be hyperfunctioning does not need aspiration for cytologic evaluation, since the likelihood for neoplasm is quite low, and it is likely an adenoma.

CYSTIC THYROID NODULE

Colloid Nodule
Papillary Carcinoma
Necrotic Anaplastic Carcinoma
Suppurative Thyroiditis
Epithelial Cyst

Colloid Nodule (Figures 16.19–16.20)

Hemorrhage into a colloid nodule is common, and cystic components of a thyroid mass often reflect its benign character.

Papillary Carcinoma

Papillary carcinoma may have cystic components within the solid tumor.

Necrotic Anaplastic Carcinoma

Rapidly growing neoplasms, such as anaplastic carcinoma, may have necrotic areas within a large, solid mass.

Suppurative Thyroiditis

Rarely, bacterial thyroiditis will result in frank abscess formation, seen as a complicated cystic mass by ultrasound.

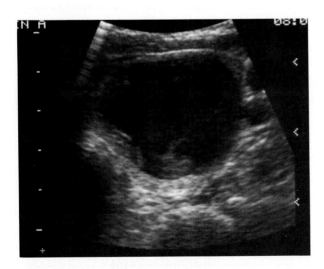

Figure 16.19
Hemorrhagic colloid nodule: A palpable thyroid nodule was evaluated by ultrasound in this 46-year-old man. The cystic mass was well-defined, with homogeneous low-level echoes and soft tissue nodularity along the posterior wall. Aspiration of the mass yielded hemorrhagic fluid containing colloid.

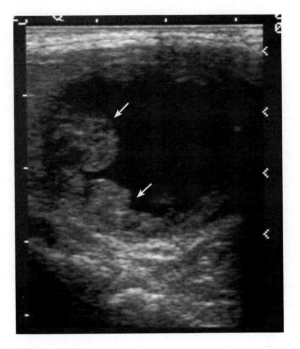

Figure 16.20
Hemorrhagic colloid nodule: In this 17-year-old, a palpable thyroid nodule was predominantly cystic, with nodular excrescences (*arrows*) along its wall. The mass was surgically decompressed.

Epithelial Cyst

The pure epithelial cyst of the thyroid is rare. True epithelial-lined cysts account for about 1 percent of benign thyroid masses. Its appearance is similar to that of any other cyst.

DIFFUSE THYROID ENLARGEMENT AND INHOMOGENEITY

Multinodular or Adenomatous Goiter
Chronic Thyroiditis
Graves' Disease
Anaplastic Carcinoma/Lymphoma

Diffuse thyroid disease usually results in enlargement of the gland with the development of an inhomogeneous echotexture at ultrasound.

Multinodular or Adenomatous Goiter (Figures 16.21–16.22)

The multinodular goiter may appear sonographically as a diffusely enlarged thyroid gland with thickening of the thyroid isthmus and heterogeneous echotexture. On the other hand, the multi-

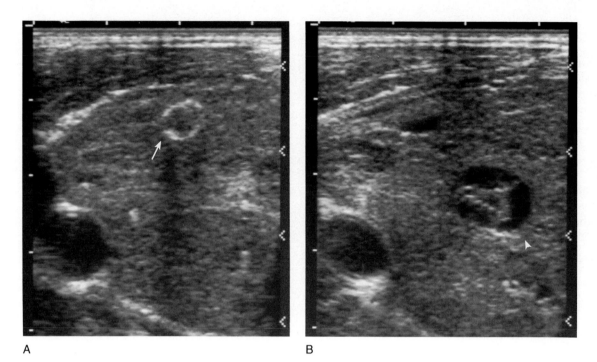

A   B

Figure 16.21

Multinodular goiter: (A and B) Diffuse thyroid enlargement led to sonographic evaluation, which showed global
enlargement with areas of hyperechoic nodularity, egg-
shell calcification (*arrow*), and complicated cysts (*arrowhead*).

nodular goiter may have multiple discrete masses,
either hypo- or hyperechoic, which are separated by
normal-appearing thyroid parenchyma.

Clinically, patients with goiter often have
asymptomatic neck swelling. Such patients are
most often chemically euthyroid but may be hy-
pothyroid.

Chronic Thyroiditis (Figure 16.23)

Several types of thyroiditis exist, including chronic
lymphocytic (Hashimoto's) thyroiditis, acute suppurative thyroiditis, and granulomatous thyroiditis
(de Quervain's disease). In all cases, sonographically the thyroid is diffusely enlarged, with abnormal echogenicity.

Chronic lymphocytic thyroiditis is a condition
of young and middle-aged women resulting in hy-
pothyroidism. Patients with chronic lymphocytic
thyroiditis appear to be at increased risk for the development of thyroid lymphoma.

Acute suppurative thyroiditis is caused by a
bacterial infection. Ultrasound is useful in the detection of drainable abscess collections.

Granulomatous thyroiditis, probably secondary to viral infection, has no specific sonographic
features.

Invasive thyroiditis, seen in patients with retroperitoneal fibrosis and sclerosing cholangitis, may
extend to nearby vascular structures and can be indistinguishable from extensive neoplasm of the thyroid.

Graves' Disease

Graves' disease usually results in florid hyperthy-
roidism and is seen as a diffusely enlarged, markedly hypervascular gland. The use of color Doppler evaluation in patients with Graves' may show
dramatic hypervascularity called the "thyroid inferno."

Anaplastic Carcinoma/Lymphoma

Diffuse replacement of the thyroid by tumor may
occur with these two neoplasms. The sonographic
picture is one of diffuse enlargement of the gland
with heterogeneous echogenicity.

Emphasis Point

Ultrasound is useful in differentiating diffuse
thyroid enlargement from a dominant mass of
the thyroid. Diffuse enlargement is often secondary to changes of a goiter, whereas a solitary, dominant mass has a more likely possibility of malignancy.

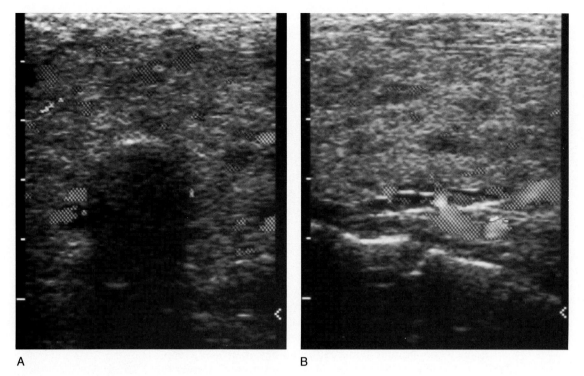

A   B

Figure 16.22
Multinodular goiter: (A and B) Diffuse and persistent thyroid enlargement prompted thyroid study in this case. Diffuse enlargement and inhomogeneity with thickening of the thyroid isthmus were consistent with goiter.

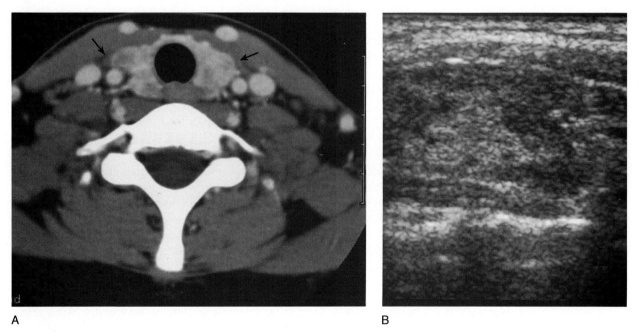

A   B

Figure 16.23
Hashimoto's thyroiditis: (A) CT of the neck for unrelated reasons led to the discovery of a heterogeneously enhancing thyroid (*arrows*). (B) Ultrasound showed the thyroid to be heterogeneous in echogenicity without significant enlargement of the gland. Fine-needle aspiration was consistent with Hashimoto's thyroiditis.

BIBLIOGRAPHY

Cystic Neck Mass Outside the Thyroid

Badami JP, Athey PA: Sonography in the diagnosis of bronchial cysts. AJR 137:1245–1248, 1981.

Friedman AP, Haller JO, Goodman JD, Nagar H: Sonography evaluation of noninflammatory neck masses in children. Radiology 147:693–697, 1983.

Sheth S, Nussbaum AR, Hutchins GM, Sanders RC: Cystic hygromas in children. Sonographic–pathologic correlation. Radiology 162:821–824, 1987.

Solid Neck Mass Outside the Thyroid

Albertyn LE, Alcock MK: Diagnosis of internal jugular vein thrombosis. Radiology 162:505–508, 1987.

Daly BD, Coffey SL, Behan M: Ultrasonographic appearance of parathyroid carcinoma. Br J Radiol 62:1017–1019, 1989.

Edmonson GR, Charboneau JW, James EM, et al.: Parathyroid carcinoma: High frequency sonographic features. Radiology 161:65–67, 1986.

Graif M, Itzchak Y, Strauss S, et al.: Parathyroid sonography: Diagnostic accuracy related to shape, location and texture of the gland. Br J Radiol 60:439–443, 1987.

Marchel G, Oyen R, Verschakelen J, et al.: Sonographic appearance of normal lymph nodes. J Ultrasound Med 4:417–419, 1985.

Reading CC, Charboneau JW, James EM, et al.: High-resolution parathyroid sonography. AJR 139:539–546, 1982.

Simeone JF, Mueller PR, Ferrucci JT, Jr. et al.: High-resolution real-time sonography of the parathyroid. Radiology 141:745–751, 1981.

Wing V, Scheible W: Sonography of jugular vein thrombosis. AJR 140:333–336, 1983.

Solid Thyroid Nodule

James EM, Charboneau JW: High-frequency (10 MHz) thyroid ultrasonography. Semin Ultrasound, CT, MR 6:294–309, 1985.

Katz JF, Kane RA, Reyes J, et al.: Thyroid nodules: Sonographic–pathologic correlation. Radiology 151:741–745, 1984.

Rojeski MT, Gharib H: Nodular thyroid disease: Evaluation and management. N Engl J Med 313:428–436, 1985.

Scheible W, Leopold GR, Woo VL, et al.: High-resolution realtime ultrasonography of thyroid nodules. Radiology 133:413–417, 1979.

Simeone JF, Daniels GH, Mueller PR, et al.: High-resolution real-time sonography of the thyroid. Radiology 145:431–435, 1982.

Solbiati L, Volterrani L, Rizzatto G, et al.: The thyroid gland with low uptake lesions: Evaluation by ultrasound. Radiology 155:187–191, 1985.

Cystic Thyroid Nodule

Hammer M, Wortsman J, Folse R: Cancer in cystic lesions of the thyroid. Arch Surg 117:1020–1023, 1982.

Diffuse Thyroid Disease

Hayashi N, Tamaki N, Konishi J, et al.: Sonography of Hashimoto's thyroiditis. J Clin Ultrasound 14:123–126, 1986.

Ralls PW, Mayekawa DS, Lee KP, et al.: Color-flow Doppler sonography in Graves' disease: "Thyroid inferno." AJR 150:781–784, 1988.

CHEST

PATTERNS
Simple Pleural Effusion
Complicated Pleural Effusion
Pneumonitis/Consolidation
Neoplastic Mass

In the normal patient, the air-filled lungs prevent much useful information from being gleaned during an ultrasonic evaluation of the chest. If fluid collects in the pleural space and consolidation or mass develops in the lung parenchyma adjacent to the pleural surface, a window for ultrasound may be provided.

SIMPLE PLEURAL EFFUSION (FIGURES 17.1–17.2)

Ultrasound can be used to localize a pleural effusion that develops in the chest. Pleural effusions may develop in patients with cardiac dysfunction, fluid overload, pneumonitis, or after trauma.

An uncomplicated pleural effusion will be identified as fluid that flows freely with changes in patient position. Ultrasound can be used to localize the largest pocket of fluid to optimize thoracentesis procedures.

COMPLICATED PLEURAL EFFUSION (FIGURE 17.3)

Septations and loculations may be seen in pleural fluid collections that are complicated by infection.

Sometimes thickening of the wall of the fluid collection is noticeable. Empyemas need large-tube drainage, which can often be placed under ultrasound guidance. Thickening of the pleural surface which can accompany infection or hemorrhage may need decortication. Fibrotic or neoplastic thickening of the pleural surface may be amenable to biopsy to exclude neoplasm.

PNEUMONITIS/CONSOLIDATION (FIGURES 17.4–17.5)

Review of the patient's chest film will certainly be helpful when a chest abnormality is being evaluated by ultrasound. A consolidated lung will appear solid by ultrasound, frequently having trapped air within the consolidation, which is seen as brightly echogenic foci with ringdown posteriorly. An associated pleural effusion will sometimes accompany the consolidation.

NEOPLASTIC MASS (FIGURES 17.6–17.7)

Neoplastic masses which are not surrounded by aerated lung, but abut the pleural surface may be identified, localized, and sometimes even biopsied

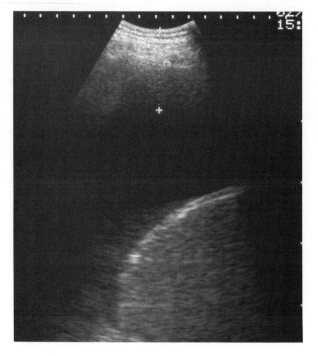

under sonographic guidance. Review of the patient's plain film or chest CT, if available, can be very helpful in deciding where to perform a biopsy or aspiration. The use of ultrasound guidance for biopsy of such lesions provides a fast safe approach, since the biopsy can be monitored at realtime.

Emphasis Point

Some interventional procedures in the chest can be easily performed using ultrasound guidance. Appropriate ultrasound-guided procedures include thoracentesis, chest tube placement for empyema, and biopsy of pleural-based masses. Review of a plain film or chest CT prior to the procedure is often very helpful.

Figure 17.1
Pleural effusion: A large amount of fluid was noted above the diaphragm in this patient undergoing abdominal sonography. The pleural effusion was secondary to congestive heart failure.

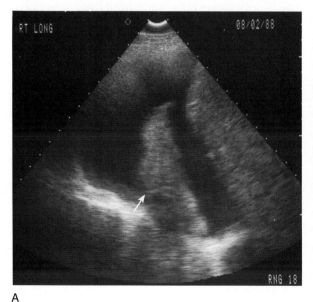

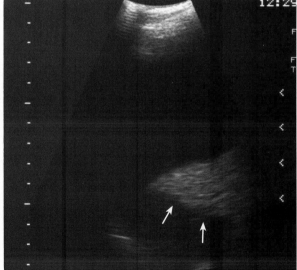

A   B

Figure 17.2
Pleural effusion with atelectasis at the lung base: (A) Prior to thoracentesis, this large pleural effusion was localized. Volume loss of the lower lobe (*arrow*) was present. (B) Note the triangular-shaped collapsed lower lobe (*arrows*) in a different patient.

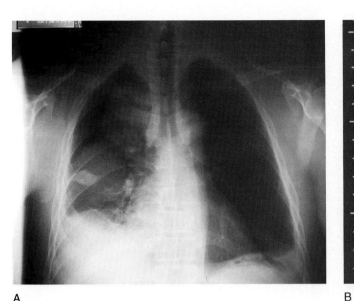

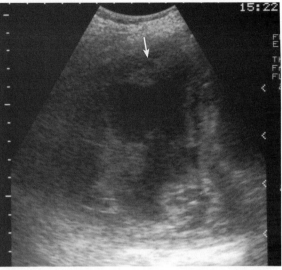

A

B

Figure 17.3

Empyema: (A) This young man presented with fever and a large loculated pleural effusion. (B) Complicated fluid was seen on ultrasound with associated pleural thickening (*arrow*). Large-bore catheter drainage was necessary for decompression. CT confirmed the loculated nature of the fluid.

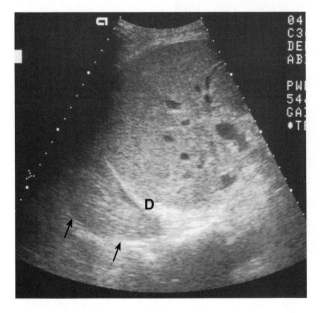

Figure 17.4

Consolidation: Pneumonia at the right lung base (*arrows*) was recognized in this patient and confirmed by chest film. (D = diaphragm.)

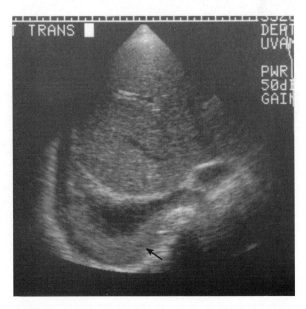

Figure 17.5

Atelectasis: Volume loss at the right base (*arrow*) and pleural fluid were demonstrated sonographically.

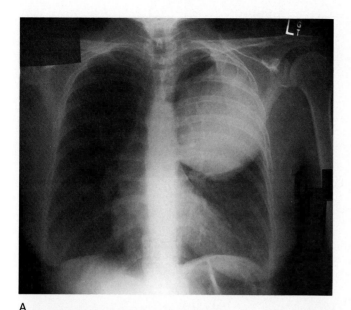

A

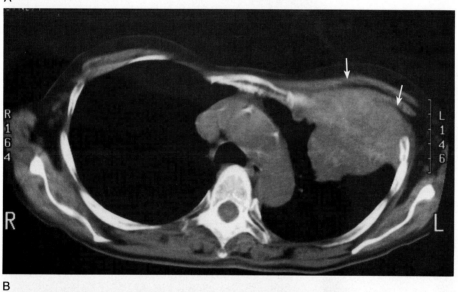

B

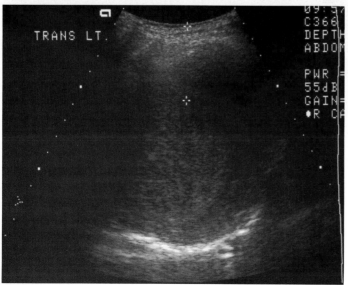

C

Figure 17.6
Squamous cell carcinoma of the lung: (A) Chest film of this patient with hemoptysis and a history of heavy smoking showed a large mass in the left upper lobe. (B) CT showed the involvement of the chest wall by the mass (*arrows*). (C) Ultrasound was used to biopsy the mass rapidly. No complications occurred.

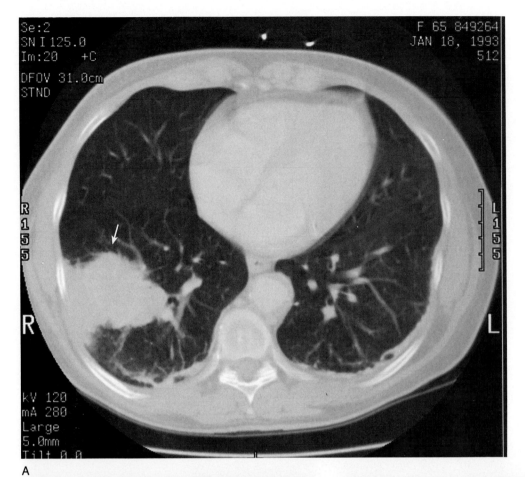

A

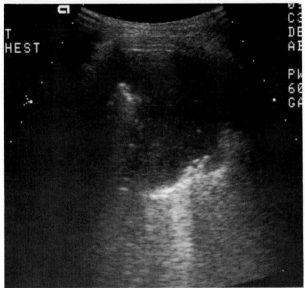

B

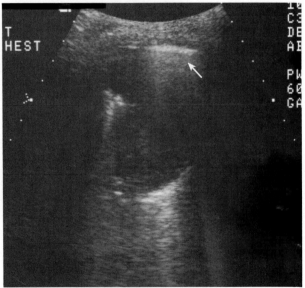

C

Figure 17.7

Non-small-cell lung carcinoma: (A) This patient presented with a seizure. Plain film showed a large pleural-based chest mass that was evaluated by CT. (B) Sonographically, the mass was hypoechoic. (C) After biopsy, evidence of a small pneumothorax was recognized sonographically by the appearance of highly echogenic air anterior to the mass (*arrow*). This was confirmed by chest film.

461

INDEX

Page references in *italic* indicate illustrations.

ISBN 0-07-000031-X

90000>

9 780070 000315